# The Memorial Book of Serock (Serock, Poland)

**Translation of:** *Sefer Serotsk*

Original Hebrew and Yiddish Book

Edited by: Mordechai Gelbart

Published in Tel Aviv, by Former Residents of Serock in Israel, 1971

**Published by JewishGen**

An Affiliate of the Museum of Jewish Heritage - A Living Memorial to the Holocaust
New York

The Memorial Book of Serock (Serock, Poland)
Translation of: *Sefer Serotsk*

Copyright © 2014 by JewishGen, Inc.
All rights reserved.
First Printing: December 2014, Kislev 5775
Second Printing: March 2019, Adar II 5779

Translation Project Coordinator: Howard B. Orenstein
Layout: Alan Roth
Image Editor: Howard B. Orenstein
Cover Design: Rachel Kolokoff Hopper
Publicity: Sandra Hirschhorn
Yiddish and Hebrew Consultant: Josef Rosin
Indexing: Moshe Kutten

**This book may not be reproduced, in whole or in part, including illustrations in any form (beyond that copying permitted by Sections 107 and 108 of the U.S. Copyright Law and except by reviewers for public press), without written permission from the publisher.**

Published by JewishGen, Inc.
An Affiliate of the Museum of Jewish Heritage
A Living Memorial to the Holocaust
36 Battery Place, New York, NY 10280

"JewishGen, Inc. is not responsible for inaccuracies or omissions in the original work and makes no representations regarding the accuracy of this translation. Digital images of the original book's contents can be seen online at the New York Public Library Web site."

The mission of the JewishGen organization is to produce a translation of the original work and we cannot verify the accuracy of statements or alter facts cited.

Printed in the United States of America by Lightning Source, Inc.

Library of Congress Control Number (LCCN): 2014958367
ISBN: 978-1-939561-28-2 (hard cover: 586 pages, alk. paper)

Front cover image from the original Yizkor book
Back cover from the collection of Dr. Slawomir Jakubczak
Cover background photograph by Rachel Kolokoff Hopper of the railroad car at the Auschwitz-Birkenau Memorial

## JewishGen and the Yizkor-Books-in-Print Project

This book has been published by the **Yizkor-Books-in-Print Project,** as part of the **Yizkor Book Project** of **JewishGen, Inc.**

**JewishGen, Inc.** is a non-profit organization founded in 1987 as a resource for Jewish genealogy. Its website [www.jewishgen.org] serves as an international clearinghouse and resource center to assist individuals who are researching the history of their Jewish families and the places where they lived. JewishGen provides databases, facilitates discussion groups, and coordinates projects relating to Jewish genealogy and the history of the Jewish people. In 2003, JewishGen became an affiliate of the **Museum of Jewish Heritage - A Living Memorial to the Holocaust** in New York.

The **JewishGen Yizkor Book Project** was organized to make more widely known the existence of Yizkor (Memorial) Books written by survivors and former residents of various Jewish communities throughout the world. Later, volunteers connected to the different destroyed communities began cooperating to have these books translated from the original language—usually Hebrew or Yiddish—into English, thus enabling a wider audience to have access to the valuable information contained within them. As each chapter of these books was translated, it was posted on the JewishGen website and made available to the general public.

The **Yizkor-Books-in-Print Project** began in 2011 as an initiative to print and publish Yizkor Books that had been fully translated, so that hard copies would be available for purchase by the descendants of these communities and also by scholars, universities, synagogues, libraries, and museums.

These Yizkor books have been produced almost entirely through the volunteer effort of researchers from around the world, assisted by donations from private individuals. The books are printed and sold at near cost, so as to make them as affordable as possible. Our goal is to make this important genre of Jewish literature and history available in English in book form, so that people can have the personal histories of their ancestral towns on their bookshelves for themselves and for their children and grandchildren.

A list of all published translated Yizkor Books can be found at:
http://www.jewishgen.org/Yizkor/ybip.html

*Lance Ackerfeld, Yizkor Book Project Manager*

*Joel Alpert, Yizkor-Book-in-Print Project Coordinator*

This book is presented by the
Yizkor Books in Print Project
Project Coordinator: Joel Alpert

Part of the
Yizkor Books Project of JewishGen, Inc.
Project Manager: Lance Ackerfeld

These books have been produced solely through volunteer effort of individuals from around the world. The books are printed and sold at near cost, so as to make them as affordable as possible.

Our goal is to make this history and important genre of Jewish literature available in English in book form so that people can have the near-personal histories of their ancestral towns on their bookshelves for themselves and for their children and grandchildren.

Any donations to the Yizkor Books Project are appreciated.

Please send donations to:
Yizkor Book Project
JewishGen
36 Battery Place
New York, NY 10280

JewishGen, Inc. is an affiliate of the
Museum of Jewish Heritage
A Living Memorial to the Holocaust

Title Page of Original Yizkor Book

# ספר סֵרוֹצק

העורך:
מרדכי גלברט

המערכת:
ברוך קצנלנבוגן – חנוך ורדי – שלמה סטרדינר

הוצא ע"י ארגון יוצאי סרוצק בישראל
תל-אביב, תשל"א — 1971

Translation of the Title Page of Original Yiddish Book

# Book of Serock

**Editor:**
**Mordechai Gelbert**

**Editorial Committee:**
**Baruch Katzenelenbogen – Hanoch Vardi - Shlomo Sterdyner**

**Former Residents of Serock in Israel**

**Tel Aviv ---1971**

**Memorial Candle**

**To the Jews of Serock
Who Were Murdered by the Hands of the Nazis**

## Acknowledgements

Several people need to be recognized for their efforts in completing this English translation of "Sefer Serock," the Yizkor Book for Serock, Poland. Each added something unique and in toto, you see the result before you. When I took on the role of coordinator, only a few chapters had been translated; it seemed like a gargantuan task to get this 700-plus-page tome transformed into a version that would be accessible to an English language audience. But, along came Lance Ackerfeld, the JewishGen Yizkor Book coordinator, who offered to provide the services of Pamela Russ (of Montreal, Canada), a translator extraordinaire, who went far beyond the call of duty to translate practically all of the Yiddish appearing in this memorial book. Although fewer words herein were written in Hebrew, the major portion of such translation was ably performed by Ruth Kilner (Israel), and to a lesser extent, Sara Mages. Lance also arranged for the online layout of the translations, which ultimately determined the style for this printed edition.

Many thanks to Dr. Slawomir Jakubczak of Poland, who allowed the use of the photo from his personal collection for the back cover.

Finally, I would like to acknowledge the assistance, financial and otherwise, of Israel Mida (Toronto, Canada), a generous soul who shares an abiding interest in our ancestral town of Serock (his father's shtetl) and the roles our forebears played there. If it were not for his interest and support, this project would be languishing.

Howard Orenstein
Sefer Serock Translation Coordinator

**Map of Poland showing location of Serock**

## Geopolitical Information:

Located at 52°31' North Latitude, 21°04' East Longitude
19 mi North of Warszawa

Alternate names for the town are: Serock [Polish], Serotzk [Yiddish, Russian], Serotsk, Sierck, Sierock, Srotsk

| Period | Town | District | Province | Country |
|---|---|---|---|---|
| Before WWI (c. 1900): | Serock | Pułtusk | Warszawa | Russian Empire |
| Between the wars (c. 1930): | Serock | Pułtusk | Warszawa | Poland |
| After WWII (c. 1950): | Serock | | | Poland |
| Today (c. 2000): | Serock | | | Poland |

## Nearby Jewish Communities:

Radzymin 8 miles SE
Jabłonna 12 miles SSW
Nasielsk 12 miles WNW
Wołomin 14 miles SE
Pułtusk 14 miles N
Marki 14 miles SSE
Nowy Dwór Mazowiecki 16 miles WSW
Praga 17 miles S
Tłuszcz 18 miles ESE
Wyszków 18 miles ENE
Warszawa 19 miles S
Rembertów 19 miles SSE
Zakroczym 19 miles WSW
Okuniew 20 miles SSE
Nowe Miasto 20 miles WNW
Kamieńczyk 21 miles ENE
Brańszczyk 24 miles ENE
Jadów 24 miles E
Maków Mazowiecki 24 miles N
Falenica 25 miles SSE
Kuchary Żydowskie 26 miles WNW
Pruszków 26 miles SSW
Leszno 26 miles SW
Sochocin 28 miles WNW
Łopianka 28 miles E
Długosiodło 28 miles NE
Otwock 28 miles SSE
Poręba-Kocęby 29 miles ENE
Dobre 29 miles ESE
Poręba Średnia 29 miles ENE
Błonie 29 miles SW
Różan 29 miles NNE
Płońsk 30 miles WNW
Jeziorna Królewska 30 miles S
Piaseczno 30 miles S

# History of the Town of, and the Jewish Presence, in Serock, Poland*

## Compiled by Howard Orenstein

Almost 1,000 years ago, the town of Serock (pronounced Serotsk) developed into a major riverside marketplace, thanks to its location on the trade route along the Bug River. Initially, the people of Serock were farmers, fishermen, and rafters who transported goods on the Narew and Bug Rivers. The central market expanded by early 15th century and there were scales, a bathhouse and a cloth cutting place in town.

A century later, Serock was a heavily populated and wealthy town in the region called Mazovia. There were ten slaughterhouses and two water mills. In 1564 there were 56 craftsmen, who were exempted from rent and 30 fishermen in the town. At that time 264 houses could be found in Serock; local law courts and land tribunals were held in town.

During the Polish-Swedish War (1655 – 1660), however, the town was destroyed. In the second half of the 17th century and in the subsequent century, Serock was a poor and depopulated town. In 1662 only 66 people lived in Serock. In 1797 there were 77 houses. Because the town's location was strategically important to the defense of Warsaw, in 1794, 1809 and 1831, Serock was within the range of battles for the capital. The establishment of a farming tools factory in 1845 and of other companies in the subsequent years contributed to the development of the town. Fairs that took place four times a year and a weekly market were important factors that influenced local economy.

Before the outbreak of World War II, there were a few industrial factories and around many workshops in Serock. Currently, the town is a local center of trade, production and administration.

Jews came to Serock in the 1400s and from the outset they belonged to the neighboring Nasielsk kehilla (congregation). In 1781, the seven Jewish families who lived in town earned their living by leasing taverns and distilleries. At the time of the Duchy of Warsaw (1807-1815), the fortification industry, which involved many workers and engineers, contributed to the flood of Jewish tradesmen and lessees of taverns. Others earned their living by providing supplies to the French army stationed in Mazovia. In 1830, out of 69 craftsmen living in Serock, 16 were Jewish (23%). These mainly included tailors (Szlama Zendlowicz, Lewek Kotek, Chaim Krawiec, Szulim Szusmacher, Abraham Szmulowicz, Judka Zelkowicz), bakers (Lewek Piekarz, Herszek Leyzerowicz, Lejbka Leyzerowicz, Zelek Cukier), groats (cereal grains) makers (Szlamowicz, Icek Boruchowicz, Josek Wielka Broda), a hat-maker (Abraham Peysakowicz), a butcher (Mordka Rzeźnikier) and a tanner (Moszek Nasielski). There were no

Jews among the Serock shoemakers, potters, millers, blacksmiths and fishermen. Some merchants dealt in the distribution of tobacco., and in 1830, these included Josek Kronenberg and Chaim Cukier.

Jews living in Serock were also involved in industry. Chaim Tykociner, for example, ran a paving company. He won a tender for paving the market area (Rynek, in Polish) as well as the following streets in Serock: Zakroczymska, Nasielska and Farna. In 1841 a famous businessman, Mojżesz Kohn (Maurycy Koniar), became a shareholder in the Serock foundry.

In 1911 Janek Nowomiński from Pułtusk established a big lumber mill in Serock; it employed six workers. Some Serock Jews started to produce harnesses and parts for mills. The Serock Jews made their first attempts to break away from the Nasielsk kehilla in the beginning of the 19th century. They appointed their own rabbi. In 1816 this post was held by the 40-year old Abraham Jankielowicz from Konstantynów Nowy. In the 1820s Jews from Popówo, across the Narew River, were incorporated into the Jewish community in Serock.

In the second half of the 19th century Hasidim started to play a more important role in the life of the local community. The Serock rabbi, Chenoch Zandel Grodziński, who in the 1870s settled in Pułtusk, opposed them. Rabbi Josef Lewinstein became his successor; he enjoyed considerable respect. He set up the famous yeshiva in Serock. Jakow Heinrich Zimmerman, who later became rabbi in London, graduated from that school. Josef Lewinstein was the rabbi of Serock for 50 years.

Despite the new, different tendencies and political trends, most of the Serock Jews were traditionalists. This was reflected among other things, by the results of the 1931 elections to the Jewish kehilla board. Agudas Israel received six seats in the community board, Hassidim – one, while the Craftsmen Block – also one seat.

In 1924, Rabbi Josef Lewinstein was succeeded by Rabbi Itzchak Morgenstern. In the second half of the 1930s, there were some anti-Semitic riots in Serock. Towards the end of 1939, after Serock had been captured by the Nazis, local Jews started to be brutally expelled from town.

On 10 September 1939, Jews from Serock were ordered to turn up in the marketplace. Women and children were sent home. Men were taken to the synagogue. On the way there, some of them were killed. They were kept in the building for five days. Then, men under 18 and over 45 were set free. Others - around 150 people - were sent to Pułtusk or Ciechanów. Before the final displacement in 1939, a tribute payment of 15,000 zloties was imposed on Jews. After it had been paid, a few days later, another one was imposed, amounting to 1000 zloties; and towards the end of the month—yet another one, estimated at 5,000 zloties.

2,078 Jews staying in Serock were displaced on 5 and 8 December 1939. All of them were transported through Nasielsk, Ostrołęka, etc., to Biała Podlaska. Some of them were placed in other towns, e.g., Jabłonna, Kock, Łomazy, Łuków, Marki – Pustelnik, Międzyrzec Podlaski, Radzymin, Węgrów and Warsaw. The local synagogue was destroyed and a town bath house was set up there. The cemetery was also ruined. There was also a camp in Serock. Jewish people were kept in there for some time before the displacement. The camp played various roles. It was established in October 1939. At first, Polish people stayed there; then, before the displacement, Jews. The camp was located in the synagogue located at 11 Listopada Street. It was dissolved in May 1944.

*The main source of this brief historical summary is the Museum of the History of Polish Jews, located in Warsaw.

## Notes to the Reader:

The original Yizkor book contains many duplicated articles, one in Hebrew, one in Yiddish. Only one is included in the translation, so often the reader will see the pages numbers cited for both articles.

Within the text the reader will note "{34}" standing ahead of a paragraph. This indicates that the material translated below was on page 34 of the original book. However, when a paragraph was split between two pages in the original book, the marker is placed in this book after the end of the paragraph for ease of reading.

Also please note that all references within the text of the book to page numbers, refer to the page numbers of the original Yizkor Book.

# Family Notes

# "Sefer Serock" ("Sefer Serotsk") [1] [2] [3]

## Table of Content of this Translation

### Translated by Howard Orenstein

## Our Old Home

*First pages*

## History of the Town

| | | |
|---|---|---|
| Jews in Old-Time Serock | Dr. Yakov Goldberg | 16 |
| Jews in Serock from the End of the 19th Century Until the Outbreak of World War II | Khanokh Vardi | 25 |

## Religious Life

| | | |
|---|---|---|
| The Serocker Rabbi Yosef Lewinstein, ZT"L | Reb[4] Yakov Henekh Cymerman, Z"L[5] | 54 |
| The Serocker Magid Rabbi Aharon Katzenelenbogen, ZT"L | Reb Yakov Henekh Cymerman, Z"L | 59 |

## Community Life

| | | |
|---|---|---|
| Community Life | Khaim Kopec/Kopetch | 73 |
| The Economy Life (Work and rest in the Shtetl) | Moishe Kanarek | 86 |
| Serock city of my youth (H) | Aharon Czesner/Tz'esner | 91 |
| Memories of our childhood-years | Sh. Rozental | 96 |
| The Shtetl until WW II | Yakov Brukhanski | 102 |
| Serocker Jews | Yehudah Mendzelewski | 104 |
| Military conscription in Poland between the Two World Wars | Yehudah Mendzelewski | 107 |
| Our former hometown | Elimelekh Hershfinger | 109 |
| My Town (*Shtetl*) | Yisroel Markewicz | 110 |
| Figures from my childhood | Kalman Koligowski/Kuligowski | 113 |
| The Serock Self-Education League And Her Activities | Shmuel Brukhanski | 115 |
| The Beginning of the Modern Cultural-Social Activity | Yosef Feynboim | 117 |
| Jewish Serock | Zwi Apelboim | 119 |
| Serock - A Long Time Ago | Refoel Fridman | 120 |
| The first buds of Hebrew education in Serock (H) | Shlomo Rabinowicz/Rabinowitz | 125 |
| The Modern *Kheder* (Jewish School) | Melekh Mendzelewski | 128 |
| Our Town … | Yosel Grosbard, Z"L | 130 |

## Destruction

| | | |
|---|---|---|
| The Destruction of Serock | Moishe Gudes/Godes | 132 |
| In years of terror (H) | Khava Konkl-Kanarek | 159 |
| Help Under All Conditions (H) | Itkah Miedownik | 163 |
| The inquisition in *shul* | Tzvi Kleinman, Z"L | 175 |
| From Jablonna to Treblinka | Shlomo Sterdiner | 179 |
| The destruction of Serock | Hillel Friedman | 189 |
| Wandering (H) | Miriam Krikah-Kanarek | 195 |
| Experiences During the Second World War | Abraham Spilka, Z"L | 203 |
| War experiences | Rivkah Mendzelewski | 218 |
| At the time of destruction (H) | Arieh Jagoda/Yagoda | 225 |
| In the First Days… | Alter Grinboim | 231 |
| In the Sway of Destruction (H) | Feiga Kanarek–Magid | 237 |
| The Destruction of Serock | Yehudah Mendzelewski | 248 |
| Escape from Death | Nekhemiah Grinboim | 249 |
| Escaped from Nazi hell | Abraham Khaim Pzykorski/Pshikorski | 250 |
| German Inquisition | Brokheh Hadas Pzykorski/Pshikorski | 255 |
| My childhood years | Arieh Mendzelewski | 257 |
| From the Holocaust- to Israel | Pinkhas Kaluszki/Kaluski | 263 |
| From Nazielsk to Biala-Podlask | Tzvi Kleinman | 267 |
| The Road of Pain | Yehoshua Bobek/Babek | 272 |
| The Evacuation of Serock | | 273 |
| From Auschwitz Prisoner # 24667 | Rakhel Brandt | 277 |
| War experiences | Leah Komelgorn-Blumberg | 288 |
| Yekhiel Rosenberg, may his blood be avenged | Shlomo Sterdyner | 291 |

## Serock After The Holocaust

| | | |
|---|---|---|
| I Am Looking for My Brothers and Sisters | Khanokh Vardi | 295 |
| The Jewish Serock | Sh. L. Shnayderman | 332 |

## Images and Pictures /Sights from the town

| | | |
|---|---|---|
| Reb Yaakov Khenokh Cymerman/Tzymerman, Z"L | Rabbi Yosef Katzenelenbogen | 340 |
| Reb Menakhem Brukhanski | Shmuel B. | 342 |
| Our neighbor Reb Mendel Frenkl, A"H | Yakov Brukhanski | 345 |
| Mendl Bobek/Babek, Z"L | Melekh Hershfinger | 348 |
| My brother- the poet Yosel Grosbard | Yehoshua Grosbard | 350 |
| A greeting to you Berglson from Shtetl | Yosel Grosbard | 355 |
| My brother Shepsl Brukhanski, HY"D | Yakov Brukhanski | 357 |
| Yakov (Yantche) Kuzhinksi, Z"L | Yosef Fajnboim | 359 |
| Neta Grabiya, Z"L (H) | Hanna Brauda | 362 |
| Images from Pages 540 to 553 | | 365 |
| Khannuka in the Big Shul | Yakov Mendzelewski | 378 |

## Serocker Landsmanschafts in Israel and in the World

| | | |
|---|---|---|
| Organization of the emigrants from Serock in the State of Israel (H) | Khanokh Vardi | 380 |
| Aliyah from Serock to Israel | Khanokh Vardi | 380 |

*[Page 735]*

| | | |
|---|---|---|
| Serocker Countrymen in America | Nakhman Feinboim | 392 |
| Serocker Countrymen in Argentina | Shlomo Ashenmill | 400 |

## Liberated by fire

| | | |
|---|---|---|
| Yehudah Ben Zev, Z"L (H) | | 407 |
| Tzvika Rosenberg, of blessed memory (H) | Hanoch Vardi | 415 |
| In Memory (H) | A. Turban | 418 |

## List of Martyrs

## In Memory of the Missing Ones

## Necrology          470

| | | |
|---|---|---|
| Calendar of events (H) | Khanokh Vardi | 550 |
| I am Leaving You, Serock, my Town (H) | Yechiel Meir Vardimon | 554 |
| Index | | 557 |

**Footnotes**

1. Many thanks to Frida Grapa Cielak (Mexico City, Mexico) for her help with the Yiddish translations and transliterations.
2. Among the Jews of Serock, the name of their *'shtetl'* was written in Yiddish as: "Serotsk," but the contemporary spelling is used here.
3. Most of the articles were written in Yiddish, but for those written in Hebrew, an (H) is added.
4. Reb = Mr.
5. Abbreviations:
    - **Z"L** = Zikhroyne Levrokhe = his/her memory shall be blessed
    - **ZT"L** = Zeykher Tsadik Levrokhe = may the memory of the righteous be blessed
    - **HY"D** = Hashem Yinkom Damo = May Hashem avenge his/her blood
    - **A"H** = Alav Hashalom = may peace be upon him/her

# "Sefer Serock" ("Sefer Serotsk") [1] [2] [3]

## Table of Contents of the Original Yizkor Book

### Translated by Howard Orenstein

## Our Old Home

*First pages*

## History of the Town

| | | |
|---|---|---|
| Jews in ancient Serock | Dr. Yakov Goldberg | 21 |
| Jews in Old-Time Serock | Dr. Yakov Goldberg | 30 |
| Jewish Serock (H) | Khanokh Vardi | 43 |
| Jews in Serock from the End of the 19th Century Until the Outbreak of WWII | Khanokh Vardi | 65 |

## Religious Life

| | | |
|---|---|---|
| The Serocker Rabbi Yosef Lewinstein, ZT"L | Reb[4] Yakov Henekh Cymerman, Z"L[5] | 99 |
| The Serocker Magid Rabbi Aharon Katzenelenbogen, ZT"L | Reb Yakov Henekh Cymerman, Z"L | 105 |

## Community Life

| | | |
|---|---|---|
| Community Life | Khaim Kopec/Kopetch | 123 |
| The Economy Life (Work and rest in the Shtetl) | Moishe Kanarek | 139 |
| Serock city of my youth (H) | Aharon Czesner/Tz'esner | 146 |
| Memories of our childhood-years | Sh. Rozental | 150 |
| The Shtetl until WW II | Yakov Brukhanski | 157 |
| Serocker Jews | Yehudah Mendzelewski | 159 |
| Military conscription in Poland between the Two World Wars | Yehudah Mendzelewski | 162 |
| Our former hometown | Elimelekh Hershfinger | 165 |
| My Town (*Shtetl*) | Yisroel Markewicz | 168 |
| Figures from my childhood | Kalman Koligowski/Kuligowski | 170 |
| The Serock Self-Education League And Her Activities | Shmuel Brukhanski | 172 |
| The Beginning of the Modern Cultural-Social Activity | Yosef Feynboim | 175 |
| Jewish Serock | Zwi Apelboim | 177 |
| Serock - A Long Time Ago | Refoel Fridman | 178 |
| The first buds of Hebrew education in Serock (H) | Shlomo Rabinowicz/Rabinowitz | 184 |
| The Modern *Kheder* (Jewish School) | Melekh Mendzelewski | 187 |
| Our Town … | Yosel Grosbard, Z"L | 190 |

## Destruction

| | | |
|---|---|---|
| The Destruction of Serock | Moishe Gudes/Godes | 197 |
| In years of terror (H) | Khava Konkl-Kanarek | 231 |
| Help Under All Conditions (H) | Itkah Miedownik | 236 |
| The inquisition in *shul* | Tzvi Kleinman, Z"L | *247 |
| From Jablonna to Treblinka | Shlomo Sterdiner | 252 |
| The destruction of Serock | Hillel Friedman | 266 |
| Wandering (H) | Miriam Krikah-Kanarek | 274 |
| Experiences During the Second World War | Abraham Spilka, Z"L | 282 |
| War experiences | Rivkah Mendzelewski | 304 |
| At the time of destruction (H) | Arieh Jagoda/Yagoda | 313 |
| In the First Days… | Alter Grinboim | 319 |
| In the Sway of Destruction (H) | Feiga Kanarek–Magid | 327 |
| The Destruction of Serock | Yehudah Mendzelewski | 338 |
| Escape from Death | Nekhemiah Grinboim | 340 |
| Escaped from Nazi hell | Abraham Khaim Pzykorski/Pshikorski | 342 |
| German Inquisition | Brokheh Hadas Pzykorski/Pshikorski | 349 |
| My childhood years | Arieh Mendzelewski | 352 |
| From the Holocaust- to Israel | Pinkhas Kaluszki/Kaluski | 360 |
| From Nazielsk to Biala-Podlask | Tzvi Kleinman | 366 |
| The Road of Pain | Yehoshua Bobek/Babek | 372 |
| The Evacuation of Serock | | 375 |
| Prisoner of Auschwitz No. 24667 (H) | Rakhel Brandt | 380 |
| From Auschwitz Prisoner # 24667 | Rakhel Brandt | 391 |
| War experiences | Leah Komelgorn-Blumberg | 406 |
| Yekhiel Rosenberg, may his blood be avenged | Shlomo Sterdyner | 411 |

## Serock After The Holocaust

| | | |
|---|---|---|
| I ask for my brother (H) | Khanokh Vardi | 417 |
| I Am Looking for My Brothers and Sisters | Khanokh Vardi | 449 |
| The Jewish Serock | Sh. L. Shnayderman | 500 |

## Images and Pictures /Sights from the town

| | | |
|---|---|---|
| Reb Yaakov Khenokh Cymerman/Tzymerman, Z"L | Rabbi Yosef Katzenelenbogen | 513 |
| Reb Menakhem Brukhanski | Shmuel B. | 516 |
| Our neighbor Reb Mendel Frenkl, A"H | Yakov Brukhanski | 519 |
| Mendl Bobek/Babek, Z"L | Melekh Hershfinger | 523 |
| My brother- the poet Yosel Grosbard | Yehoshua Grosbard | 526 |
| A greeting to you Berglson from Shtetl | Yosel Grosbard | 531 |
| My brother Shepsl Brukhanski, HY"D | Yakov Brukhanski | 533 |
| Yakov (Yantche) Kuzhinksi, Z"L | Yosef Fajnboim | 535 |
| Neta Grabiya, Z"L (H) | Hanna Brauda | 538 |
| Khannuka in the Big Shul | Yakov Mendzelewski | 554 |

## Serocker Landsmanschafts in Israel and in the World

| | | |
|---|---|---|
| Organization of the emigrants from Serock in the State of Israel (H) | Khanokh Vardi | 559 |
| Aliyah from Serock to Israel | Khanokh Vardi | 566 |
| Serocker Countrymen in America | Nakhman Feinboim | 577 |
| Serocker Countrymen in Argentina | Shlomo Ashenmill | 586 |

## Liberated by fire

| | | |
|---|---|---|
| Yehudah Ben Zev, Z"L (H) | | 597 |
| Tzvika Rosenberg, of blessed memory (H) | Hanoch Vardi | 604 |
| In Memory (H) | A. Turban | 607 |

## List of Martyrs

## In Memory of the Missing Ones

## Necrology

| | | |
|---|---|---|
| Calendar of events (H) | Khanokh Vardi | 725 |
| I am Leaving You, Serock, my Town (H) | Yechiel Meir Vardimon | 730 |

\*see page 372

[Page 736]

**Footnotes**

1. Many thanks to Frida Grapa Cielak (Mexico City, Mexico) for her help with the Yiddish translations and transliterations.
2. Among the Jews of Serock, the name of their 'shtetl' was written in Yiddish as: "Serotsk," but the contemporary spelling is used here.
3. Most of the articles were written in Yiddish, but for those written in Hebrew, an (H) is added.
4. Reb = Mr.
5. Abbreviations:
   - **Z"L** = Zikhroyne Levrokhe = his/her memory shall be blessed
   - **ZT"L** = Zeykher Tsadik Levrokhe = may the memory of the righteous be blessed
   - **HY"D** = Hashem Yinkom Damo = May Hashem avenge his/her blood
   - **A"H** = Alav Hashalom = may peace be upon him/her

[Unnumbered page 2]

לְמַעַן יֵדְעוּ, דּוֹר אַחֲרוֹן – בָּנִים יִוָּלֵדוּ; יָקֻמוּ, וִיסַפְּרוּ לִבְנֵיהֶם
(תהילים ע"ח ו)

That the generation to come might know them,
even the children that should be born;
who should arise and tell them to their children

(Psalm 78)

*[Unnumbered page 3]*

# Sefer Serock

Editor:
Mordechai Gelbert

Editorial Board
Baruch Katzenellenbogen – Hanoch Vardi – Shlomo Stardiner

Published by Former residents of Serock in Israel Tel Aviv, 1971

*[Unnumbered page 4]*

(Blank page)

*[Unnumbered page 5]*

*[Unnumbered page 6]*

# Yizkor

**May G-d remember the pure and holy souls of our Brethren in Israel, the residents of the town of Serock: men and women, elderly and infants, martyrs and heroes of the holocaust, who were murdered, strangled, burned, and buried alive for the sanctification of G-d's name.**
**May the memory of their sacrifice and their brave deeds never leave us, and may their souls be bound up in the bonds of everlasting life, together with the souls of the holy ones and the brave ones of the Nation of Israel forever and ever.**

*[Unnumbered page 7*

# Book Editorial Board

From Left: Mordechai Gelbert, Editor, Baruch Katzenellenbogen, Chairperson, Hanoch Vardi, Initiator of the book and Editorial Consultant, Shlomo Stardiner, Secretary and Treasurer.

# Book Committee Members

From left to right:
Row 1: **Yisrael Markovitz, Bunim Fogelman, Chava Fogelman, Artist Yehoshua Grossbard, Rav Yosef Katzenellenbogen**
Row 2: **Yechiel Mair Vardiman Werschevsky, Yaakov Mendolevsky, Rivka Mendolevsky, Yehuda Mendolevsky, Mela Yoskovitz Rosenberg**
Row 3: **Malka Rosenberg, Rafael Friedman, Baruch Gorman, Yosef Penivsky**

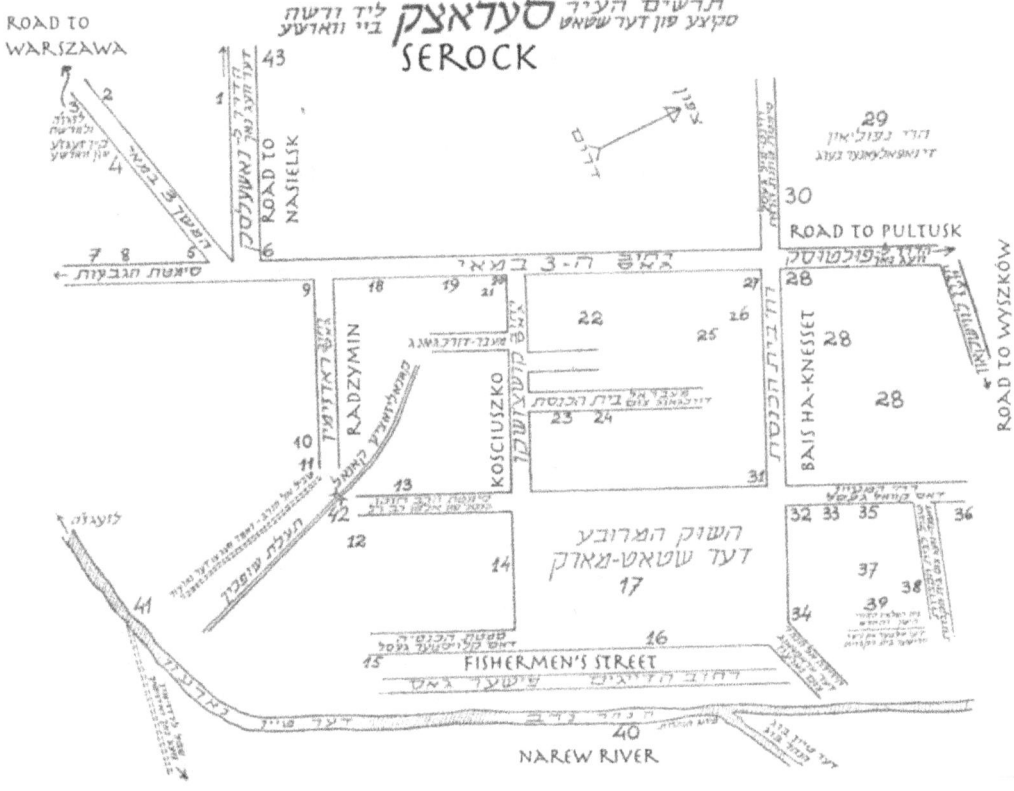

**Legend**
1. Mill of Moshe Rozenberg
2. Mill of Beryl Itshkovitsh and Motel Viernik
3. The Catholic Cemetery
4. The New Town Council House
5. ---- no entry -----
6. The House of Milshtein
7. The House of Abraham Yaakov Pniyevsky
8. The House of Village Doctor Tyk
9. The Pharmacy of Cybulski
10. The House of Sokolovsky
11. The House of The Family Bukhenek
12. The Town Mikveh
13. The House of the Old Rabbi
14. Club of the League
15. The Catholic Church
16. The House of the Last Town Rabbi: The Rav Morgenshtern
17. The Well in the Market-place
18. The Old Council House
19. Meeting Place of the Zionist Federation and Mizrachi
20. The House of Yaakov Rozenberg
21. Cellar where 70 Jews of Serock perished during the first bombardment
22. The Big Gerer Hassidim Shtibl
23. Club of Jewish Orchestra
24. Club of "Hashomer Hatzeir"
25. The Kehilah (Jewish Community) -House
26. The Large Town Shul
27. The Forge (i.e., blacksmith's) of Aba-Leib Freidman
28. Goretsky's Vegetable-Garden
29. Napoleon's Hill
30. The Theater Zol "Yotshenko"
31. The House of Rav Menachem Koshemacher
32. The Store of Aaron Paskowicz
33. The Residence of the Magid (i.e., preacher)
34. The House of Hillel Katsev (butcher) and Yitzhak Myer Apelboym
35. Cheder "Yesoidey HaToiro" (name given to schools network of Agudas Yisroel in Poland)
36. The Spring
37. The Hot Well
38. The Big Sawmill
39. The New and Old Cemetery
40. The Island in the Narew River
41. The Crossing Point of Yehoshua Przeworznik
42. A Small Wooden Bridge
43. The Last Road (at the time of the extermination, December 5,1939)

[Unnumbered page 11 - Hebrew] [Unnumbered page 13 - Yiddish]

## To All the Former Residents of Serock
(On Publication of this Book)

Following the shocking holocaust that annihilated thousands of Jewish communities in Europe, including our very own Serock, we felt – we, the former residents of Serock in Israel – a righteous obligation to publish a "*Yizkor* book" to serve as a memorial and a *Ner Tamid* for the Jewish lives filled with life and creativity that made noise in our town for the pure and holy souls of parents, brothers, sisters, friends and acquaintances, against whom the hand of the Grim Reaper was raised, and who perished in the ghettoes, extermination camps, gas chambers and incinerators, amongst whom are many who have no survivors or refugees.

This was not an easy undertaking. Not many refugees remained from the Serock community, and the few who survived had scattered all around the globe, and we had to travel to them to collect and organize the material. Nor was it simple to raise the financial means to publish the book, and only after an enormous effort by a small handful of people who devoted themselves to this huge task with great determination, and with the help of the emigrants of Serock, living all around the globe, this book has been published, and with the excitement of one fulfilling a sacred duty – we deliver it to you.

In this book, there are chapters on Jewish Serock before its destruction, chapters about the people who lived there, chapters about the atrocities of its annihilation, about the distressing and agonizing paths of the few survivors and their fights for their lives and freedom, and information about the activities of the former residents of Serock in Israel and the Diaspora. There is also a list in the book of our dear ones that perished in the holocaust, and obituaries written by family and friends.

It is possible that the book is incomplete, and that there are many areas of life missing, and many people who have not been mentioned, but please do not hold us responsible; these omissions were unintentional. The book was written by refugees that remained from Jewish Serock, and if we were unable to find someone to write about a particular area, or if someone was not metioned, then, unfortunately, they will have no mention in this book, and only the one that remembers the forgotten ones will remember them for good…

*[Unnumbered page 12 - Hebrew] [Unnumbered page 14 - Yiddish]*

We will accept and receive this book with love and understanding, because it is ours. Within its pages the stories of our parents and our families are told, as are tales about the place we lived and spent time in our youth, where we hoped and we dreamed about a better world.

We will make it a practice to read chapters from this book on memorial days for the community of Serock.

We will bring this book into our homes, and tell its stories to our children, who will never know the town, or the people and the events mentioned within, so they too will know who and how their ancestors were, and all about their aspirations and how they fought for their Jewish and human lives!

And even with the new generation, who have grown up in the state of Israel, and do not know what exile and diaspora is, we will tell them about their full heritage, and the bravery and glory of those that paved the path to redemption.

May this book be a memorial for the Jewish Serock that has been destroyed and is no more, and it should be bound up in the bonds of life of the people of Israel forever and ever!

**Baruch Katzenellenbogen**
**Chairperson of the Organization for the**
**Former Residents of Serock in Israel**

*[Unnumbered page 15]*

Upon the conclusion of Sefer Serock, we feel proudly obligated to thank all the former residents of our city, currently in Israel, Europe, North America and Argentina, with whose full and wholehearted cooperation and financial aid, we were able to publish this book.

Special thanks must be offered to the eminent President of the State of Israel:

### Mr. Zalman Shazar

for his generous financial contribution for the publication of this book.

We must also recognize our dear and unforgettable friends who have passed on:

**Shlomo Merla** of blessed memory (Israel) and **Calman Weinkrantz** of blessed memory (Canada), who were amongst the founding members of our organization and our business.

Our late and unforgettable friends, Shlomo Merla of blessed memory (Israel) and Calman Weinkrantz of blessed memory (Canada), who were amongst the founding members of our organization and our business.

**Organization of the Former Residents of Serock in Israel**

[Page 21 - Hebrew] [Page 30 - Yiddish]

# Jews in Old-Time Serock
### Dr. Yakov Goldberg (Jerusalem)
### Translated by Pamela Russ

When the Jews settled in Serock in the 18th century, the town had already existed for a long time. Because of the opportune situations that the merging of the rivers Narew and Bug presented, there was already a settlement there in the early Middle Ages, and in the 12th century, there was already a princely fortress built there. In the first half of the 15th century, in this area, there was an intense surge of establishing settlements, and a buildup of manual labor and business, which resulted in the establishment of a row of new cities that in turn established a population group that occupied itself with manual labor and business. From the new towns that rose up in the 15th century in Mazowsze (Mazovia), 75% of them were concentrated in the area southeast and north of the Vistula River. Serock belongs to the northern group that surrounded Zakroczym, Nowe Miasto, Makow, and Janow. When in 1417 Serock received its civic rights, it was already, from an economic standpoint, a developed settlement. The neighboring town of Nasielsk, was given civil rights even earlier, that is in the year 1386, and the neighboring town of Pultusk – one of the oldest cities in Poland, had the civic privileges in 1257.

In approximately the first 150 years of the existence of the city of Serock, it established the fundamental properties of an urbanized settlement, introducing with that the necessary manpower potential of all sorts of professions of that population.

The greatest rise in Serock coincides with the period of prosperity for the Polish feudal states during the Renaissance era, that is in the 16th and beginning of the 17th centuries. In 1564, there were 264 houses in Serock in which there were approximately 2,000 residents. According to the standards of those times, this was no small number. What is relevant of the population number, is that Serock was almost always behind the parallel, upcoming city of Zakroczym, where, in the same year, there were already 371 houses. For the benefit of Serock, as fact has it, there were already 57 different types of manual laborers; that means, there was no small percent of competent residents. The great communication artery that went from Mazowsze for the length of the river Bug all the way to Russia, and went through Pomjakhovek, Serock, Wiskow, Brok, Nowy Kaweczyn, and Bransk, was opportune for the local development of business and manual labor. Here went the transports of materials, and contact with many other merchants, making it easy to market the articles that were produced by Serocker laborers.

*[Page 31]*

During the blossoming of the Renaissance, Serock was the center of manufacturing products. There was a factory for manufacturing there that was used by the local weavers who had to be paid to use it. The money from these payments was designated for the expenses of taking care of the city's fortification walls. Aside from the laborers and weavers, there already existed in 16th century Serock a significant professional group of fishermen who also lived there in the later centuries. In 1564 they totaled 30 people. In other small cities, a part of the population occupied itself with agriculture, particularly when the city made available large areas of land. In 1417, city privileges awarded Serock approximately 900 hectares of land, which later came under the ownership of several residents.

For half of the 17th century, Serock underwent an economic crisis which later became more accentuated because of the destructions of war. In the fifties of that same century, even though they didn't keep accurate statistical facts about the losses, it is known fact that in the year 1660, approximately 88% of the city's land remained fallow because there was no one there to work the soil. This indicates the great destruction and emigration from the city. The rebuilding of the city came about very slowly, and it never really came back to the original position that it held in the 16th century but in this detail Serock was not an exception because most of the similar cities found themselves in a depressed situation at that time and the process of long years of rebuilding did not return them back to the level they existed in during the Renaissance era. Also, later on, Serock divided the lots from the largest portion of the Polish state settlements that were always being destroyed through wars and internal strife in the first half of the 18th century. Without looking at the trials of building up the city or of the generally favorable circumstances that governed the second half of the 18th century, Serock acquired a different economic profile than it had earlier. In the 16th and beginning of the 17th centuries, the number of residents declined. In 1777, there were 57 houses, meaning 21.5% of the total number of houses built in 1564. And in 1797, the number of houses rose to 77. But this present number that was given does not bring with it a description of all the changes that took place, because in the 18th century, the small town manner of building Serock brought with it a village-like character, and without any memory of the houses of the 16th and beginning of the 17th centuries.

*[Page 32]*

The most important changes were related to the structure of the professions of the residents, and with that, the regular functional maintenance of the town. Serock established her significance as a point on the international trade route, since because of the general depressed state of business in the country, even business lost its former position. The number of manual laborers that lived there declined to a minimum, and the weavers disappeared completely. Some of them left the town or died out in wars or epidemics, giving rise to a pause in maintaining the continuity of the traditional professions of the local residents. The basis of the economic existence became agriculture, and in the economic life of the town, the production of whiskey and beer grew, with which the residents became busy, but the main source was the distillery and the tavern that belonged to the landowner's court. There, they also sold processed alcoholic drinks, such that it was one of the smaller domains, outside of agriculture, that was able to provide an opportunity for livelihood in the town. Generally, it was known that with the leases of the bars, distilleries, and breweries, the Jews occupied themselves in earlier Poland. Similarly, here the earliest residents occupied themselves with the same thing. Jews arrived here in the first half of the 18th century, but first news of them came only in the year 1765.

[Page 33]

Jews lived in Serock and in the suburbs, where the office of the bailiff was located. As was understood, the first families lived in the tavern belonging to the bailiff, for which they did not need consent from the local residents, nor from the magistrate. The bailiff's office set the salary for the bailiff who headed his own committee and passed judicial rulings. In many cities, the landowners took over the offices of the bailiff, such that the members themselves of this office no longer busied themselves with other municipal offices. In Serock, which in 1432 was already a majestic town, the bailiff's office was already in landowners' hands. This was a property that occupied approximately 60 hectares of land. In the bailiff's grounds, there was a tavern that was covered with shingles. The tavern consisted of two rooms and a cellar, and nearby, a horse's stall. This was the type of thing that was called a "passing through" inn that served a purpose similar to a hotel. You can well imagine the tight quarters there, because in those two rooms there was the family of the tavern, the tavern itself, and also place to sleep for the travelers who were passing through. According to the official information, in the year 1765, there were 8 people sleeping in the tavern, other than those family members who were being hidden for tax reasons.

At that time, the tavern was under the lease of Melekh Abramowicz. He lived there with his wife Zirl, their son Mordekhai and his wife Nekha, and their daughter Pesha. Mordekhai did a lot of work there, which was tied up to the running of the inn – work that in other inns was taken up by the servants. In the inn lived Yossel, the brother-in-law of Melekh Abramowicz, with his wife and son whose name was also Mordekhai.

[Page 34]

In Serock, there were two other Jewish families: Itzik Shmulewicz, the lessee of the distillery and the brewery, with his wife Rokhel and his two sons, Leibish and Berek, and a daughter Freide. With them lived the bachelor Yakob, the brother of Itzik Shmulewicz. The second Jewish family was the innkeeper Yisroel and his wife Rokhel and daughter Yite. Other than those noted two Jewish families, there was also the teacher of Jewish children,

Shmuel Abramowicz. Interesting to note that most of the teachers in the small towns and villages were unmarried individuals. By the lessee, Itzik Shmulewicz, lived the teacher Shmuel Abramowicz, who, because of his profession, was called the "Inspector."

The Jews' tavern were cordoned off by wires because of the competition with the local priest who also ran a tavern. The innkeepers did not have a large income because of the weakened development of the city. In 1765, the city's administration stated that the city had no date of establishment, and was dragging its feet behind the other cities. Because of that, in the year 1781, there were already no Jewish families there of those who had lived there in 1765. The first to leave was Melekh Abramowicz, and after him, there was already no one who wanted lease the bailiff's inn. So, it remained empty, and in the journals describing the businesses of the bailiff in the year 1773, it is written that "the inn and the horse's stall will not have any fulfillment."

In 1781, there were 7 Jewish families in Serock, from which 2 earned a living collecting the alcohol tax ([from] the distillery). The lessee of the distillery and the brewery at that time was an elderly man who lived there with his wife, son and daughter-in-law, and a hired Jewish worker. The 5 other families did manual labor and had small businesses.

This is what small community life looked like in the town of Serock in the 18th century that really had representative characteristics of the other small towns in Poland of that time. In the year 1765, the Jews of Serock were primarily involved in tenant leasing and running taverns. This is exactly how all the other settlements looked, inhabited by only several Jewish families.

*[Page 35]*

However, in the period of a few years, the situation changed. In 1781, the fathers of the 5 families tried to do something different. The little courtyard that ran a poor life in a poor town put itself under great stress to retain a teacher for the children. In 1765, there were already 10 men there that enabled the men to pray with a quorum.

Nonetheless, in the 18th century, the Jews in Serock were still in numbers too small to establish their own organized community. And because of that, they belonged to the community in Nasielsk, which was managed with the Jewish population of 11 villages and 4 towns from southeast Mazowsze (Nasielsk, Serock, Zakroczym, and Nowe Miasto). Nasielsk was in those times a large Jewish settlement. In the year 1765, there were about 420 Jews living there. Of the Jewish towns that belonged to the community of Nasielsk, Serock was the largest, because in Zakroczym there were only 12 and in Nowe Miasto there were 18. An independent Jewish community was established in Serock in the 20s of the 19th century.

After the third division of Poland – that is in 1795, Serock belonged to the Prussian government, and from the year 1806, it belonged to the Polish duchy established at that time. Around the time of that duchy, there were certain changes set up in the internal relations of the town that suffered terribly on account of Napoleon's battle campaign. On Napoleon's orders, in the year 1810 they started to build military fortifications between the rivers Bug and Narew that were to serve as strategic points according to Napoleon's military plans. Serock was also included in these plans, and the result of this was that it caused a real revitalization in the town, and led to favorable services for the business activity of the Serocker Jews. These accompanying circumstances were written up by a Serocker Jew, Tuvia Levin, who in later years was at the head of the community over there, and we read in his letter to the authorities of the Warsaw duchy, that it was then "a city that is strengthening itself, in which soldiers and workers are busy in the trenches and are also masters in the factories. Everything in large numbers."

[Page 36]

In spite of this, the economic revitalization, which took place because of such reasons, had a transitional character, when in fact it lasted only two years, during the building of the fortress. Tuvia Levin wrote in 1812: "The work with the fortress in the town of Serock had stopped, and the soldiers, manual laborers and workers moved over to the Modlin fortress." Because of the construction of the fortress, the residents of Serock also suffered certain damages, because some of their fields, meadows, and gardens were taken away on account of the situation. During Napoleon's brief stay in Serock in the year 1810, the local residents submitted a request in which they asked that he improve the damages by decreasing the taxes. They resubmitted this request in 1812, but the general way of things did not permit this situation to be resolved.

During the time of the construction of the fortress, a military garrison was stationed there. As one can see in Levin's drawings, a group of people came to Serock with stable and varying incomes, and with that increased the volume in the local taverns and the production of whisky and beer. Whisky was also produced through the state's residents, but they had to pay taxes on that. The administration of that time had not yet established a business statute for annulling those taxes, and the tax law applied primarily to the Jews. In 1811, the lessee in Serock was the noted Tuvia Levin, and the intention was that in order to increase his profits from the alcohol tax collection, he would also be able to earn money from the tenant's taxes. The growth in volume also gave rise to the increase in the tax quotas. Levin, who in 1811 was the lessee for three years, had to pay 2,860 zlotys, while his predecessor in 1810 had to pay only 2,400 zlotys. Because he had taken the workers over to Modlin, Levin was not able to keep up the conditions of the leasing agreement, because in the new difficult situation, the income from the whiskey and beer production suddenly decreased.

[Page 37]

The building of the fortress on Serock also created job potential for the Jews who worked in the wood business. For that type of business, Serock was a convenient spot because it was between two rivers that carried transport, enabling the wood to be moved. At the beginning of 1807, Elijahu Meyer organized the river transports and executed the job in large volume. So much so, that by the year 1820, he owed the city hall the significant amount of 250 zlotys in taxes for transporting across the Narew. For sailing across the waters, it was primarily Serocker residents whose business this was, and they were already doing this for a while, so that by the year 1870, there were already 17 qualified raftsmen there.

From the year 1815, Serock belonged to the Polish kingdom. Over the next years, this town had the opportunity to develop itself a little. The Jewish population increased, and the internal business structure changed. Out of the 16 professions with which the population of Serock occupied itself in the first half of the 19th century, the Jews were only involved with 7. In those times, the Jews worked as potters, smiths, millers, raftsmen, fishermen, carpenters, locksmiths, and shoemakers. The majority of the Jews were in the tailoring business, which in the 18th century was already a widespread profession. In neighboring Nasielsk, in the beginning of the 18th century, there was already a Jewish tailor's guild that grouped together the handworkers of the garments line at the request of the Nasielsk community at that time. In Serock, the majority of the bakers were Jewish, who were also in the commodity business.

[Page 38]

Some of the Serocker residents earned their living from producing and selling beer and whiskey. In 1873, there were 23 residents of Serock that were in this business, of which 15 were Jews, and amongst those were bakers and merchants. The income from the alcohol tax collection significantly complemented their house expenses. Just as in earlier years, the lessee of the alcohol tax collection was also in the hands of the local Jews. According to the written journals, one could only lease through an auction, so that the one who put forth the largest sum was the one who got it, and he himself had to be content with only a small percent. This happened in the following way: The magistrate presented the issues and terms of the forthcoming auction, and they also presented this information in the town synagogues, and the informants had to sign a document confirming that they had informed the Jews about this. The auctions had a certain characteristic course, and the Jews played a prominent role in this. In one of these auctions, in the year 1819, there was one such participating Jew, the innkeeper Eliezer Hersh, who heroically rivaled three landowners. There was only a small difference in the sums they put forward, because the landowner Ignazi Dmokhovski offered 23 zlotys, and the noted Jew 24 zlotys.

**The professional structure of the population in Serock in the year 1830**

| Profession | # Jews | # Non-Jews | Total |
|---|---|---|---|
| Baker | 4 | 1 | 5 |
| Butcher | 1 | 6 | 5 |
| Stone mason | 3 | 1 | 4 |
| Miller |  | 3 | 3 |
| Fisherman |  | 12 | 12 |
| Tailor | 6 | 2 | 8 |
| Shoemaker |  | 4 | 4 |
| Tanner | 1 |  | 1 |
| Milliner | 1 |  | 5 |
| Locksmith |  | 1 | 1 |
| Blacksmith |  | 2 | 2 |
| Tinsmith |  | 4 | 4 |
| Carpenter |  | 1 | 1 |
| Potter |  | 3 | 3 |
| Raftsman |  | 17 | 17 |
| Storekeeper | 12 |  | 12 |
| Total | 28 (33%) | 57 (67%) | 85 |

*[Page 39]*

In the later years, at these auctions, there was serious competition amongst the Jews because being a lessee for the alcohol tax was one of the few opportunities for some easier earnings. In the year 1847, the lessee in Serock incidentally became Hersh Igelberg. Against him, stepped up Pesach Mjodovnik who wrote a letter about this to the commission of internal affairs in Warsaw, in which one reads: "As a stable resident of Serock at the time of being informed about the auction to collect the income from the alcohol tax, and not being at home at that time, but being on my way home, it was made known to me that the Jew Hersh Igelberg received the above mentioned lease for 330 silver rubles. I declare the sum of 375 silver rubles, with the request that the esteemed government commission should grant that between me and him there should be a repeated competition auction, or that they should organize with me directly a signed contract." This was not the only attempt to take away the lessee's right from Igelberg. At the same time, another Serocker Jew, Berek Rosental, offered 400 rubles for the same thing, which is even more than Mjodovnik. Nonetheless, Igelberg remained as lessee, even though he was always attacked for this by the Jews. The behavior of Mjodovnik and Rosental indicate that the interactions amongst the Jews in Serock in the half of the 19th century already did not have the character of the small settlements with the small number of families, because only there did the togetherness support good neighborly behavior. On that account, there were already several Jewish societies in Serock which naturally, came to rivalry and competition for more lucrative income sources.

[Page 40]

The Serocker Jews struggled in many ways to lease the alcohol profits, even those who did not spend the necessary capital. Part of this last group, was the noted Tuvia Levin, who in 1811, was not able to put in the required capital. The vice-prefect of the Pultusk Commons later determined that not only was it difficult for Levin to put forward the funds, but he was so poor that in times of money losses, he would not even be able to cover that. It is worth remembering that in the year 1820, Levin – together with another lessee – Eliezer Hersh, were the forerunners of the town's community.

In 1822, Eliezer Cohen was the collector for the alcohol tax, but because he did not possess his own money, he had to pass on the job to sub-collectors. The go between was Moshe Goldberg from Makow, bringing in the collector Pesach Kupchik. The last one always gave over the collecting to other Jews. In this fashion, there was always a standing row of sub-collectors, who did not dispense the necessary money and had to give the collection to other Jews. Only by always giving over the collection to other colleagues, did they have the opportunity to earn small sums of money. Applying this method [of earning money] was also tied in to the general life situation of the Jewish population of Serock at that time, where the economic conditions allowed only for singular professions and for small businesses, because it was only individuals themselves who took business initiative in other areas.

However, even in these conditions, over the years, occasionally, more Jews bought established estates. It is worthwhile noting that in this area, there were no limitations imposed on the Jewish population in Serock, as was done in the larger, more developed settlements. Because of that, in the first years of the 19th century, some of the Serocker Jews lived in their own homes. Understandably, these were not large, city houses, but small, wooden houses. In the year 1809, Chaim Itzkowicz bought one such house from Jan Polakowicz. And according to the official documents, this was a building: "From 2 houses – an alcove with a chamber, a barn with a feeder (for animals and not pigs) in the town of Serock, on the *rebitve*.(?) The new owners were obliged to pay 12 zlotys a year, and for the building, he paid the large sum of 4,360. That means, twice the amount that it cost for the payment of the annual leasing of the alcohol tax in Serock.

*[Page 41]*

In the second half of the 19th century, a large portion of the Jews had their own established estates. And in the year 1864, there were already 197 Jewish families there – 50 families, 25.4% living in their own wooden houses, because at that time, there was only one brick house. The ratios for this amongst the non-Jews in Serock presented differently: 65% of the non-Jews lived in their own houses, but they were mainly land workers, bath owners, and had businesses of buildings and apartments. A small number of Jews, primarily innkeepers, took up gardening, and in the year 1825, 8 Jews had their own gardens.

The business structure in Serock of the 19th century created a business basis for only a limited number of residents. The administration of the Polish monarchy and the occupying powers did nothing to industrialize the town. So, Serock remained a small settlement that had groups of manual laborers, small businesses, and land workers, a part of whom also took on other types of work.

**Growth in Population in Houses in Serock**

| Year | Population | # houses | Avg. residents per house |
|---|---|---|---|
| **1827** | 1008 | 100 | 11 |
| **1862** | 1979 | 140 | 14 |
| **1864** | 2116 | 142 | 15 |
| **1885 (approx)** | 2500 | 200 | 12+ |

*[Page 42]*

Already in 1864, there were 197 Jewish families living in Serock. In general, there were 1164 Jews, who comprised 55% of the general population. This indicates the level of development in the Jewish population in early Serock. A group of a few families who settled there in the first half of the 18th century, and who supported itself by managing an inn, a distillery, or a brewery, in the fifties of the 19th century, was transformed into a large circle, spreading out in their professions and fortunes, constituting the majority of the residents of the town.

## Sources:

Archiwum Skarbu Koronneo, oddzial LVI, Nr. 22, k. 42-44.
Zakroczymskie Grodszkie Relacje, Nr.67, k. 376-377, 274, 277.
Zakroczymskie Grodzkie Relacje, Nr. 76, k. 278, 816-874 v.
Konisja Rzadowa Spraw Wewnetrznych I Duchownych, Nr. 4673, 4674, 4675, 4676, 4678, 4680.

*[Page 43 - Hebrew] [Page 65 - Yiddish]*

# Jews in Serock from the End of the 19th Century Until the Outbreak of World War II

### By Khanokh Vardi, Ramat Gan
### Translated by Pamela Russ

## Forward

Until the year 1856, Serock belonged to the district of Plotsk, and after that to the district (duchy or state system "*vojvudstvo*") of Warsaw, of the Pultusk circle.

By the end of the 19th century, in the year 1897 - according to the statistics, the numbers of the Serock population were as follows:

| General numbers: | Jews: | Poles: |
|---|---|---|
| 3,916 souls | 2,054 (52.5%) | (47.5%) 1862 |

("*Yevreiskaya Encyklopedia*" in Russian, Volume 14, page 174)

## Chapter One
## From the Beginning of the 20th Century Until the Outbreak of WWI in the Year 1914

The general life of the Jewish community is saturated with its traditional ways: the center of life was the *Beis HaMedrash*, education was exclusively in *kheder* and in *yeshivos* (religious schools), and the principal leader was - the city's *Rav* (rabbinic leader).

Economic life was in ruins, partly because of little capacity to earn wages, and life was discreetly supported through charity.

Events that occurred in the outside world and in the general Jewish world, such as wars, revolutions, strikes, unrests, the Zionist and socialist awakenings, etc., reached the town in only pale resonances. From time to time, a Zionist speaker would come to town, and they would listen thirstily to his speech. From mouth to ear, they would talk about a familiar person that spread forbidden invitations to the farmers in the surrounding areas, and how the gendarmes (police) would be looking for him in all corners.

*[Page 66]*

After the revolution in 1905, the Czarist Russian powers strengthened the attacks against the Jews even in the places - such as Serock - where until now they had not felt it.

Several Jewish revolutionaries - Ahare'le the revolutionary and others - ran away to North America, and some, through many different means, came to Israel.

In the year 1912, anti-Semitism worsened at the hands of the Poles, because on account of the Jewish voices, a representative of the Polish socialists, Jagiello[1], was elected to the Duma (Russian representative assembly), and the representative of the *Endekes* (Polish Nationalist and Anti-Semitic Party), Jan Kucharzewski, suffered a total loss.

The Polish anti-Semites declared an economic boycott against the Jews, from which the Jews in the small towns suffered in particular, and among these small towns was Serock.

In the situation of a half-dormant society and an economic standstill, and in the voice of sharp national conflict and poisonous anti-Semitic propaganda, along with unknown expectations for the future, WWI erupted in August 1914, for which the Jews in all parts of Poland were unprepared.

# Chapter Two
# From the Outbreak of WWI until the Establishment of the State of Poland on November 17, 1918

Soon after the beginning of the war, the oppression of the Serock Jews began. The representatives of the community were immediately arrested and after a long time, they had to pay a high fine. All males fifteen years and older were forced to dig security ditches and to protect the telephone and telegraph lines from the insurgents.

Every minute, the Cossacks broke into Jewish homes "searching for arms," but in fact they stole everything they possibly could, and paid with violence and curses.

As the final retreat by the Russians, the city of Serock was bombed by the Germans, and a large portion of the houses was ruined

*[Page 67]*

The Jews were hiding in the cellars. But during the final moments of the retreat, the Cossacks even attacked those in the cellars, searched for arms, and stole anything worthwhile.

In one cellar, the brave and daring Khaim-Isser, may his memory be blessed, physically stood up to the Cossacks, and in this uneven contest, died from a revolver shot.

The last bomb fell in a courtyard and killed fourteen Jews, among them the well known rich man Khaim Hillel Ubogi, of blessed memory.

In the spring of 1915, the town was taken over by the Germans, and this was received by the Jews with mixed feelings.

The war and the German invasion caused fundamental changes to Jewish life: the social dormancy disappeared, the traditional walls were broken, and many barriers fell away, and the earlier community leaders began to fall away from the arena.

The German occupants blocked up the wells of earning a livelihood, and all means were cut off through the many prohibitions. In order to survive, many Jews were forced to smuggle foodstuffs from the villages into the towns, and from here to Warsaw.

New life flowed into the town, and the bearers of this new life were the youth that was looking for a way out of this difficult situation. The youth, as the parents, remained completely unemployed.

Zionist, Zionist-socialists, and Communist organizations sprouted, along with cultural organizations, etc. The *Beis Hamedrash* began to empty out.

In the time of the German invasion, several families immigrated to America.

By the end of the German invasion, anti-Semitism increased within the Polish population, such that on the day that the establishment of an interim Polish Republic was proclaimed (November 11, 1918), for all the Jews - and in particular the Jews in the small towns, that became a day of unrest and fear.

A few days after the establishment of the Polish Republic, the military of General Haller made a pogrom on the Jews of Lemberg. As a protest against the pogrom, the leaders of the Polish Jewry decided to proclaim December 1, 1918, as a day of general mourning.

*[Page 68]*

The Jewish youth in Serock, that concentrated itself around Zionist organizations and the "Progress" library, organized the protest day in the large *shul* in the city, in which the Ark (where the Torah scrolls are kept) was draped in black. All Jewish stores closed at a designated time, and the masses marched to the designated place. The large *shul* was packed tight and the youth and their pickets were found in all corners of the town in order to offset any chance of anti-Semitic activity.

The Polish security organizations knew of all this and tried to convince the storekeepers to remain open, but they were not successful.

The day of protest against the Lemberg pogrom was well organized and ended without incident, thanks to the brazen youth that had thrown off their sleepiness and were now searching for some relief of their needs.

# Chapter Three
# Jewish Institutions between the Two World Wars 1914-1939

## A. The Zionist Movement:

By the end of the year 1916, two Zionist organizations had been established:

"**Kadima**" for men, and at the head was Aharon Krongold, Zvi Kleinman, of blessed memory, and others.

"**Bnos Tziyon**" for women, and at the head were the Krongold sisters of blessed memory, Esther Leah Shljakhtus and Devora Granjewicz. The abovementioned organizations, which evoked a great opposition amongst the religious elders, did not remain in existence for long because the majority of their members left the town.

After the establishment of the new Polish state, in 1919, through the members Shmuel Dunner (now in the U.S.), Zvi Kleinman, of blessed memory, Borukh Krystal, of blessed memory, and Yehoshua-Dovid Babek, of blessed memory, there was established in the house of Reb Yakov Rosenberg, of blessed memory, on May Third Street, the *Algemeine Tzionistishe* (General Zionist) organization where those who had left the *Beis HaMedrash* got together. In this organization there was an active library in three languages:

Yiddish, Hebrew, and Polish. In the 1930s, the head of this library was Yekhiel Meyer Werdiman (Warshawski) - today living in Israel, and after him, there was Dr. Inwentarz, of blessed memory, and Aharon Chesner (today in Israel). The last chairman was Khaim Aharon Faskowicz, of blessed memory.

In the lap of the organization, all the Zionist and Zionist socialist youth organizations were organized, along with societies for mutual help and labor unions.

*[Page 69]*

44. *"Hashomer Hatzair"* was established in the late 1920s by the Warsaw *"shomeres"* ("guard") Lonka Goldman (today a pediatrician in Hedera, Israel) and Yekhezkel Friedman, of blessed memory. Two hundred children from all the working classes belonged to *Hashomer Hatzair*, boys and girls aged eleven to seventeen. The *Hashomer Hatzair* strengthened the youth, new songs were sung in every corner, and the flows of people leaving the town brought important changes for the young children. Khanokh Werdi (Warshawski) was the leader of this group until his *Aliyah* to Israel in the year 1934, and after him, until the outbreak of WWII, the leadership was held by: Elkhonon Rosenberg, Yehuda Kronenberg (both now in Israel), and Grinboim, of blessed memory.
45. *Histadrut Hekhalutz* founded in the mid 1920s, and at her head was Raphael Freedman (today in Israel).
46. *Hanoar Hatzioni* founded at the end of the 1920s by Avrohom Rosenberg of blessed memory, and at her head was Shakhna Freedman, of blessed memory.
47. *Beitar* was founded at the beginning of the 1930s by Yosef Pnjewski (today in Israel) in the mill of Berl Itzkowicz, of blessed memory, and Motl Melnik, of blessed memory, and they took in hundreds of children from all the working classes. In the final years, until the outbreak of WWII, Avrohom Shpilke the teacher, of blessed memory, was at her head.
48.

*[Page 70]*

1. *Histadrut Hamizrachi* was founded in the 1920s by Yeshayohu Hofman, of blessed memory, and Moishe Fogelman, of blessed memory, in the house of the abovementioned Reb Yakov Rosenberg, of blessed memory. The members here were *Beis Hamedrash* learners, religious craftsmen, and also those who had distanced themselves from the Khassidic little *stiebelech* (small synagogues). The place of the *Histadrut Hamizrachi* also served as a modern *kheder* under the direction of Reb Yehuda Leyb Gutkowski, of blessed memory, and also served as a place for a *minyan* (quorum) for prayer.

Within the framework of this organization, the following religious Zionist youth organizations were established:

1. ***Hashomer Hadati*** to which the children of the *Mizrachi* group belonged. At the head of this organization until its end was Borukh Levinson, of blessed memory.
2. ***Hekhalutz Hamizrachi*** to which religious young men belonged, candidates for making Aliyah to Israel. At the head of this organization, until his move to Israel in 1933, was Borukh Gurman, and after him Yehuda Salyarzh, of blessed memory.
3. **Kibbutz *Hakhshara*** from *Hekhalutz Hamizrachi*. At the beginning of the 1930s, a commune called *Hakhshara* was established from *Hekhalutz Hamizrachi*. It was located in a house in a courtyard opposite the city's large *shul*. There were dozens of boys and girls there that worked at various jobs in town such as in the flour mills, the grain mills, wood chopping, and in various jobs in the home. The organizer and patron of this *Kibbutz Hakhshara* was the abovementioned Borukh Gurman.

## Agudas Yisroel

*Agudas Yisroel* was founded in 1919 by Reb Yitzkhok Swarc, of blessed memory, Reb Khaim Rosenberg, of blessed memory, Reb Yitzkhok Meyer Kuperboim, of blessed memory, and Reb Dovid Warshawski, of blessed memory. Membership consisted of the Ger and Radzymin *khassidim*, with the majority being teachers and religious business people.

Until the mid 1920s, the Agudah was the only ruling voice in the lives of the community, but after that she had to step down and share her influence with the new, rising power in the city - the Zionist movement, and all her offshoots, and the camp of the extreme left that gathered around the "Yiddish People's Education League." Within the framework of the *Agudah*, the following organizations were established:

*[Page 71]*

**Tzeirei Agudas Yisroel** to which the young students in the *Beis Hamedrash* belonged, along with a few of the young boys from the *Agudah* groups. At the beginning, the journalist and writer Nute Berliner of blessed memory was at her head, along with Shloime Marcus, of blessed memory. The last chairman was Meyer Salyarzh, of blessed memory.

*Poalei Agudas Yisroel* to which religious workers belonged, *Khassidic* children, and at the head of the organization until his *Aliyah* to Israel in 1932, was Gershon Prag.

### The "Progress" Library:

The "Progress" library was established at the end of the year 1915 (at the time of the German invasion) by Shmerl Anshmill (he died in Argentina), Esther Leah Shlyakhtus, of blessed memory, and Aharon Krongold, of blessed memory. The first building of the library was on the Warsaw highway, a little outside of the city.

The youth that was thirsty for knowledge thronged to the library, and the demands for reading material was enormous. Friday nights there were recitations and "*Kestel-oventn*" [evenings with a variety of speakers and writers presenting their ideas, designed for people with little education], and also collective singing. The staunchly religious parents put forth a strong opposition to the library, but none of these battles made the slightest difference because the youth was its protector. The library also had an active drama circle.

At approximately this time, the library settled into a large place, in a house in the city's marketplace, and there it evolved, for many years, into a center for the enthusiastic youth.

In the time of the Polish-Russian war (1920), the library's main hall was confiscated for military needs. After the war, the Polish powers did not want to renew the library's permit, and the fruitful activity of the cultural institution was brutally destroyed.

[Page 72]

## D. The Professional Union for Unskilled Laborers:

The union was founded by Communist circles at the beginning of the year 1922 in the house of Baile Merker (today in Argentina), on May Third Street. The union was the gathering place for both the working youth that worked in the city as tailors, shoemakers, carpenters, stitchers, and also for those working in Warsaw who would come home every Shabbos. At the union's location there was an active, large library. In the year 1925, two members of the union were arrested - Hershel Mendzelewski, of blessed memory, and Simkha Esterowicz (today in Paris), during the distribution of illegal Communist notices during a market day among the farmers wagons.

After the arrest, the power organizations shut down the Professional Union.

## E. Jewish People's Education League:

The circles that participated in the now closed Professional Union for Unskilled Laborers, received a new permit in a very short time to open a club by the name of "The Jewish People's Education League."

The one responsible for developing the regulations was the Polish Parliament deputy of the Jewish People's Party, Noakh Prilutski, of blessed memory.

At the head of the "League" at the beginning were Khaim Kopetch (today in Argentina), Yosel Feinboim (today in the US), and Shloime Ostrowski, of blessed memory.

The League evolved into multi-pronged activities, such as: a multilingual library (Yiddish, Polish, etc.), readings, self-education circles, a drama circle (under the leadership of Shloime Ostrowski, of blessed memory), and a football team.

Around the League, there gathered a large number of the Jewish working and general youth of the extreme left orientation.

In the later years, at the head of the League, until its demise at the hands of the Polish powers in 1937, were: Avrohom Gutkowski, of blessed memory, Hersh Zaltsman, of blessed memory, Avrohom Jaszombek, of blessed memory (one of the best actors in the drama circle), and Bunim Fogelman (today in Israel).

*[Page 73]*

## F. The Wind Orchestra:

In the year 1926, a wind orchestra was established by the master carpenter, Hershel Borenshtayn, of blessed memory, who was also the director. The conductor himself played in a military wind orchestra in the Czar's times, and he himself was a passionate music lover. All the performances were held in the director's (carpenter's) workshop. There, there were all types of musical instruments as well. Practically all the musicians were carpenters. The orchestra participated in all open, general, and Jewish events, and brought some joy and cheer into the gray and difficult lives.

## G. The Handworkers' Union:

In 1926, the union was established by the tinsmith Reb Meyer Pshikorski, of blessed memory, and the tailor Reb Aharon Leyb Grinboim, of blessed memory. The union's business was to acquire raw materials for reduced prices and represent the handworkers in their tax evaluation in front of the finance office in the Jewish community.

## H. Financial Institutions:

**The People's Bank (*Bank Ludovi*):** The Polish-Russian war in 1920 impoverished the Jews in Serock. Many of those who occupied themselves with work, merchants and vendors in the villages, were forced to borrow capital with low interest just to keep going. The People's Bank filled this need. The initiator and organizer of this was the young man Avrohom Maimon (today in Israel) - a recent newcomer to Serock. In the beginning, he collected from those closest to him a few hundred zlotys, and distributed them, according to the traditional ways, to the needy workers, small businessmen, etc., as a donation without interest, but with set amounts for paying back. It is worth noting that Avrohom had the hard work, such as: collecting the money, calculating the pledges and doing the bookkeeping - and he did it all voluntarily, without any recognition.

*[Page 74]*

Meanwhile, the needs grew. The financial help that had existed until now was not appropriate for the new situation, and so there was the need to find a way to extend these services.

To the fruitful activities of Avrohom Maimon, there was also Reb Yeshayahu Hofman, of blessed memory. Both of these men, by the end of 1922, moved to the "Union of the Jewish Cooperative Businesses" in Warsaw with a request to help them and permit them to establish an offshoot of the Union in Serock. The directors of the Union, the revered Dr. Khaim Shoshkes, of blessed memory, M. Shmoish, of blessed memory, and Dr. Alexander Birkenheim, of blessed memory, were very positively inclined to these requests, and also put forth to the "Joint" head office to decide about the accreditation of the new Serock offshoot.

By the end of 1923, and with the strong organizations, the regulations for the Serock People's Bank were established as an offshoot of the Union in Warsaw. A Jewish resident offered half a room without rent to the deposition of the People's Bank, and the new work began from the onset of the new laws.

The Joint organization put up a credit of 10,000 zlotys towards this new department, and the Serock Jews brought in as a one time contribution a few thousand zlotys that immediately enabled the increase of dispensed funds. The bank began working according to the laws, taking a certain percent, and the profit grew, and they began depositing funds in this department as well.

In a short time, the number of members grew to 500. Because of this extension, there was now a special location in the market, just opposite the grain mill of Reb Menakhem Novogrodski, of blessed memory. Avrohom Maimon was officially elected as bookkeeper and secretary, and Yehuda Zimerman, of blessed memory, as treasurer.

The first general meeting of all People's Bank members took place at the end of 1924, in the large Gerer *khassidic shul*.

*[Page 75]*

The financial status of the bank at that time was:

| | |
|---|---|
| **Capital Activity** | 10,000 zlotys |
| **Income from Joint** | 20,000 zlotys |
| **Deposits** | 100,000 zlotys |

In the General Annual Assembly meeting, all the members participated, and in the first election, the following were elected: Reb Yitzkhok Swarc, of blessed memory; Reb Yeshayohu Hofman, of blessed memory; Reb Khaim Rosenberg, of blessed memory; Reb Yitzkhok Meyer Kuperboim, of blessed memory; Reb Dovid Warshawski, of blessed memory (they replaced the merchants); and Reb Meyer Pshikorski, of blessed memory (representatives of the Handworkers Union). Aside from the election, there was a council of nine people elected as a revisions committee.

The responsibilities of the elected were: deciding on grants and budgets, and remaining alert as to how to receive distributions from the Joint and from other charitable institutions.

The People's Bank was transformed into an economical place of the first class, and the main advisory and influential aspects came from the people of the *Agudas Yisroel*, representatives of the merchants.

The Handworkers' Union, at whose head were Reb Aron Leyb Grinboim, of blessed memory, Reb Yosef Oryl, of blessed memory, and Reb Yehoshua Dovid Babek, of blessed memory, with all its strength, in about one year's time, together with other opponents from the acting committee, tried to increase its influence, but it was never successful.

In the General Assembly meetings that took place in the final years, which because of the large number of members took place in the city's large theater hall "Yuchenko," representatives of the "Union" in Warsaw participated and always took active participation in the ongoing proceedings and set the way for future activities.

And because the Handworkers' Union and other opponents from the bank's acting committee were not successful in extending their influence, they established their own bank, a "mutual bank" (*Bank Udzhalove* [the Interest Bank]), that was run by Reb Gershon Prag (today in Israel), Reb Yakov Dovid Milshtayn (also known as the "*Moyreh Hoyra'ah*" [the rabbi who decides matters of rabbinical law]), and Reb Shloime Krimkowicz, of blessed memory (the son of Reb Meyer Ailmakher, of blessed memory), but after a short time, the competing bank closed down.

[Page 76]

In the year 1929, in all the Jewish cooperative banks, among which was the Serock affiliate, a difficult and lengthy crisis erupted.

The large Polish anti-Semitic party (*Endekes*) strengthened their economic discrimination against all the Jews, and in particular against the small shopkeepers, by opening cooperatives for the consumers and by picketing in front of the Jewish stores. The picketers did not allow the Polish farmers to make their purchases by the Jewish merchants nor to make any orders by the Jewish craftsmen.

This paralyzed Jewish business and Jewish work, and the clients from the Jewish cooperative bank were unable to pay off their debts on time. The bank began to suffer from losses of the capital turnover against their debtors, and because of that, according to the regulations, the bank had to stiffen measures against the debtors. The bank also lost the members' trust because the bank could not pay off in the designated time the deposits that were being reclaimed.

After that, there were the occasional rises and falls, the Union intervened, and Joint helped, but the bank could already not save itself completely from the fierce anti-Semitic scourge.

At the end of 1929, Avrohom Maimon left the bank, because the central bank moved him out as a controller of land measuring (surveyor). His replacement as secretary and main bookkeeper was elected, Yehuda Cymerman, of blessed memory.

In the last bank election, the following were elected: Reb Dovid Warshawski, of blessed memory, Reb Yitzkhok Meyer Kuperboim, of blessed memory, Reb Yitzkhok Meyer Solyarzh, of blessed memory, and Reb Meyer Pshikorski, of blessed memory.

The bank administrator was Reb Avrom Broin, of blessed memory.

**The Community Charity Fund (*gemillas khasodim* fund):** The fund was established in the year 1926 and her first elected president was the active Reb Yekhiel Rosenberg, of blessed memory, who was devoted to his post until he moved to Jablonna Legionowa.

[Page 77]

The mandate of the fund was: distribute small loans from 50 to 200 zlotys without interest to small business men, villagers, handworkers, etc., and also to ensure from time to time allotted sums of money to the needy that had lost every source of income.

The fund's capital was collected from membership and from Joint subsidies.

In the last election, the following were voted in: Yehoshua Dovid Babek, of blessed memory, Moyshe Fogelman, of blessed memory, Alter Zakharek, of blessed memory, and Yosef Oryl, of blessed memory (all representatives from the Handworker's Union).

The last secretary was Elimelekh Pjenik, of blessed memory.

**Societies for Mutual Aid:**

Women's Union The Women's Union was established in 1926 by the woman Khana Uldak, of blessed memory, the daughter of the old *geldsher* (person with some money in his pocket for quick assistance?), Reb Yisroel Juskowicz, of blessed memory. The responsibilities of the Women's Union were: mutual help, social gatherings, donating charity discreetly, and giving courses in baking and cosmetics. In the management of the Union were - other than the woman Uldak, of blessed memory, this was a place (like a drop-in center) for women who were suffering, and for women with family conflicts. In the management were - aside from the woman Uldak, of blessed memory, the social activists and devoted women - Fraydel Warshawski, of blessed memory, and Khaya Nowogrodski, of blessed memory.

**The committee for overnight help** No one knows when this group was established. It existed from the first day that the community existed. The members were ordinary, kind people with a compassionate heart. The responsibilities of the group were: to stay overnight with those who were very sick; to give free medical help (such as doctors, prescriptions, etc.) to the poor, and to lend medical instruments against a pledge (i.e., promise to be returned) to anyone that needed. In the services that were provided to fill the need for open socialized medical help - such as medical insurance, hospitalization, available pharmaceuticals - the members of this organization filled that need and their work had an ethical, community service delivery of the highest caliber. This strong and invaluable assistance was provided by the "overnight assistance" group on a voluntary basis, not gaining in any way any personal profit.

*[Page 78]*

**The group to help brides prepare for marriage (Hakhnosas Kalah).** This is an age old institution in which only its members change from time to time; an institution that is run single-handedly, without election, without bookkeeping, where only the devotion of those committed who work discreetly give life to all the activities. The responsibilities of the "*Hakhnosas Kalah*" institution were: discreet help for poor Jewish "daughters" to help them build their homes (nests). Lastly, the heavy burden was carried by the remarkable, simple Jew, the smith Reb Avrohom-Yekel Pnjewski, of blessed memory, whose heart was filled with compassion. In his role, Reb Avrohom-Yekel, of blessed memory, spoke very little. As he crossed over the threshold of a house, his mouth clearly but quietly said: "*hakhnosas kalah*," and he stretched out his right hand. A heart touches a heart - and everyone gave him according to their means.

# Chapter Four
# The Jewish Community and Her Activities

The Jewish community presented itself as a corporate (legal) body in harmony with the special law that was established in the Polish *Sejm* (lower house of parliament), and her mandate was: to satisfy the religious needs of the Jewish community. Each Jew was obliged to pay an annual community tax. The Polish *Sejm* worried about not giving this institution just any status of nationalist autonomy.

The community institutions were:

The Rabbinate; b) the ritual slaughter; c) the synagogues; d) religious education; e) the burial society; f) the cemeteries; g) the *mikva* (ritual baths); h) the charity organizations.

**The Rabbinate** The first city rabbi of the Serock community was Rav Yosef Lewinshtayn, of blessed memory, author of the famous bibliographic work "Dor ve'dor... ... ve'dorshov" (generations, and generations, and his generations), one of the greatest in his generation in Polish Jewry in the last eras in Torah and in *khasidic* knowledge.

[Page 79]

Rav Lewinshtayn, of blessed memory held his position of city rabbi of Serock for about 55 years, from 1870-1924.

He died in his old age, on a Wednesday, 26 days in the month of Nissan, 1924. He was 84 years old.

The second and last city rabbi was Rav Yisroel-Yitzkhok Morgenshtern, of blessed memory, son of the Wyszkow city rabbi, a great intellect and *khasid*. Rav Yisroel-Yitzkhok Morgenshtern, of blessed memory, held his position of city rabbi of Serock from 1924 until the destruction of the community.

**The ritual slaughter** The community took care of the *kashrus* of the meat (making sure the meat was kosher), and was also responsible for sanitation responsibilities of the Jewish section in the general slaughter-house. The ritual slaughterers (*shokhtim*) and butchers of that time were:

*Shokhtim*: Reb Eliyahu Stelang, of blessed memory; Reb Refoel Lewinson, of blessed memory, Reb Menakhem Mendel Frenkel, of blessed memory; and Reb Khaim Shloime, of blessed memory.

Butchers: Reb Menakhem Mendel Markowicz, of blessed memory; Reb Gimpel and Reb Moyshe Zilbershtayn, of blessed memory; Reb Khaim Nosson Winogura, of blessed memory; and Reb Avrohom Pshikorski, of blessed memory (he died in Israel).

The income from the slaughter payments was divided up evenly for the city magistrate and the Jewish community.

**The synagogues** At the beginning of the 20th century, a large synagogue was built from wood with the initiative of Reb Dovid Rosenberg, of blessed memory, the president of the community at that time. One section of the synagogue served as the *Beis Hamedrash*, where they studied and prayed every day. In the large *Beis Hamedrash*, every evening after *minkha* (evening prayers), the working Jews would sit at a long table and on one side they would listen to a study of *Ein Yaakov*, delivered by Reb Berish Solyarzh, of blessed memory (he was called "Berish the speaker"), and on the other side of the table, there was a study of the Talmud delivered by the intellectual, Reb Yitzkhok Blakhman, of blessed memory.

*[Page 80]*

The smith Reb Avrohom-Yakov Pnjewski, of blessed memory, a remarkable Jew and individual, took care of the large bookcase of religious books (*seforim*) and the large *Beis Hamedrash*.

Also, the *khasidic shteibelekh* (small *shuls*) of the Gerer and Radzimin *khasidim*, served as places of prayer and of studying Torah.

The place of prayer (*minyan*) in the house of Rav Lewinshtayn, of blessed memory, continued to exist even after his passing, until the destruction, thanks to the devotion of the esteemed Jew, the tinsmith Reb Meyer Pshikorski, of blessed memory.

## Religious Education
## Private schools (under the supervision of the community)

Children aged five to six began their learning with the teacher Reb Avrohom Leib, of blessed memory, a short man with a shining face. His school was on Kosciuszko Street. Almost all of the young children learned the Alef Beis with him over the last thirty years, along with how to pray, and the beginnings of Torah studies (*khumash*). They studied with him about a year or two and then they moved on to the school with the teacher Reb Khaim Yoine Sempf, of blessed memory.

For many years, the school of Reb Khaim Yoine Sempf, of blessed memory, was located in large cellar area that was also the living quarters for his large family, on Kosciuszko Street in Kuzhnicki's house. Around a large table, there sat up to forty boys who studied *khumash* and started to learn the Talmud (*gemara*) with the *Rashi* commentary only [author of comprehensive commentary on the entire *Tanakh* and Talmud]. Reb Khaim Yoine Sempf, of blessed memory, was a short man with a heavy white beard, an enthusiastic *khasid* of the Gerer Rebbe, and a master of dreams. His students liked him very much because of his wondrous stories which he would tell during the break time between one subject and the next. Studies began very early in the morning and continued until seven or eight in the evening, with a lunch break. The dear mothers would bring breakfast to the school.

The children studied in this school for two or three years and after that they went over to another school at a higher level - they were now ten or eleven years old - and studied with Reb Shimon Sempf, of blessed memory. Reb Yosef Soljarzh, of blessed memory (called Yosef the speaker) and Reb Yisroel Zelig, of blessed memory. There they learned the Torah portion of the week with Rashi commentary (*parshas hashevua*), Talmud with commentaries and super-commentaries (*gemara* with *tosefos* and *meforshim*), and also *shulkahn arukh* (book of laws for conducting daily life).

[Page 81]

Here they learned for two or three years, until the students reached the level where they could study independently. Some progressed in their studies by attending *yeshivos* that were close by or far away.

In the school of Reb Dovid Itzik, of blessed memory, and Reb Efraim Sandler, of blessed memory, the children who studied there were mainly those whose parents who decided to have their children work and become apprentices at a young age with different workers, etc. In these schools, they learned the *Alef Beis*, prayers, Jewish law, up until the point where they knew a portion of *khumash* and could read the portion themselves.

**Yesoidei Hatorah school (a communal institution under the supervision of the community itself)** In order to avoid a conflict with the Polish government law that required each child without exception, from religious to nationalist, except those who attended private or community schools established by the Polish education ministry, to attend a public government people's school, where for the Jewish children there were only two hours per week of religious classes - and all of it in the Polish language - the *Agudas Yisroel* in Serock established a school called "*Yesoidei Hatorah*" whose regulations and program were defined by the Polish education ministry. The school was established at the beginning of the 1920s, and was located in an especially beautiful building with a pretty garden around it on the street that ran from the market to the wells (*zdroi* [health]). The furnishings there were like those in a modern school. There were ten grades in the school, and only for two hours per week did the teacher Khaim Jurkowicz (today in the U.S.), director of the public government people's school (*powszechna*) for Jewish children in Serock - teach the higher grades the following subjects: Polish, math, geography, and history (all in the Polish language).

[Page 82]

In this school there were also some of the teachers from the abovementioned private schools.

The first director of this school was a *khasidic* Jew from Warsaw, Reb Shloime Gavriel, of blessed memory, a good organizer, an understanding person, and someone beloved by the students.

At the head of the management were: Reb Yitzkhok Swarc, of blessed memory, Reb Dovid Warshawski, of blessed memory, Reb Yakov Moyshe Zlotogurski, of blessed memory, and Reb Nute Berliner, of blessed memory.

(In all of the abovementioned religious educational institutions the parents themselves paid the tuition.)

**Elementary school** Many attempts were made by Reb Kalman Winekrantz, of blessed memory, to organize an elementary school in Serock and to set it on strong grounds. All efforts were in vain, and after a short time, the school was closed because it was impossible to assemble even the most minimal number of maintenance days (where there would be food) for the *yeshiva* boys.

***Talmud Torah*** The *Talmud Torah* school was at the cost to the community and was located in a room opposite the big *shul*. In this school, there were orphans, those children of the very poor, and those who did not fit in to the other schools. The last *Talmud Torah* teacher was Reb Yitzkhok Meyer, of blessed memory.

**Private modern school (partially under the supervision of the community)**

In the room of the *Mizrakhi* organization in the house of Reb Yakov Rosenberg, of blessed memory, Reb Yehuda Leyb Gutkowski, of blessed memory, a longtime teacher in the Lithuanian *yeshivos* and a great scholar of Hebrew, ran a proper school in which there were thirty children, particularly from the *Mizrakhi* followers. There were two classes in this school: a beginner's class, ages six to eight, proceeding to the next level, ages nine to twelve. Other than the traditional religious studies the following were also studied: Hebrew and Hebrew grammar, math, geography, a bit of history, and the Polish language.

[Page 83]

Reb Zwi Hersh Efraim Boguslawski, of blessed memory, an enlightened Lithuanian *yeshiva boy*, ran a proper school in his private house on Kosciuszko Street. There were twenty students with him, children from craftsmen. The primary studies were: Torah studies, Hebrew (language and grammar), Talmud, and the Polish language.

Reb Yitzkhok Meyer Apelboim, of blessed memory, a former Ger *khasid* "*tishzitzer*" [someone who participated at the Rebbe's gatherings] and a great scholar, ran a proper school in his house on the market street (in the house of Hilel Katzav, of blessed memory). In this school, there were boys and girls together. Other than the traditional religious studies, they also learned Torah studies, Hebrew (language and grammar), and the new Hebrew literature. This school was closed in 1929.

Reb Eliyahu Aron Rosental, of blessed memory, a great scholar, and a deeply religious man and an enlightened man, tried to set up a school with a few classes, where they would study religious studies as well as secular studies according to a detailed, thought out plan. The original achievements of the school were the music and song lectures. Because of financial difficulties, the school closed down.

**The Burial Society (*Khevra Kadisha*)** The members of the burial society were individuals with an internal sense of obligation to fulfill the final will of the person, the one that had died. The entire work, from busying oneself with the body until the actual burial, was done voluntarily. At the head of this organization for many years (until the destruction) was Reb Menakhem Kronenberg, of blessed memory, who always used his free time for holy work and for good things for the community. This organization was under the supervision of the community. But its daily tasks were based on an independent set of activities and regulations. On the group's day, the seventh day of Adar, there was a general meeting and a special meal, and at the end they would elect a new *gabay* (the person who helped run the *shul*).

*[Page 84]*

**The cemeteries** The old and new cemeteries were located three kilometers outside of the city, on the road to Pultusk (past the large sawmill) and in the glow of the clear river Narew. The area belonged to the community, but the administration belonged in the hands of the Burial Society. In the cemeteries, the bones of our dearest ancestors from approximately 150 years ago were buried. At the time when the community was destroyed (December 1939), the German vandals destroyed the graves and used the tombstones to build highways. The cemetery was dug up, and they planted grass there, and shepherds tended to their flocks there. The cemetery is erased, without any trace at all.

**The bathhouse (*mikveh*)** The bathhouse was located on a side road, not far from the elder Rav's house, may his memory be blessed, in a large stone building. In those times of non-sanitary activities in the town, the bathhouse protected the Jews from many illnesses and diseases. The bath attendant, who was hired for the baths by the community, received a designated payment from each visitor. Among the Jewish children in the town, there were many frightening tales about the attendants, and so they were afraid to go there at night.

**Charity** The principle of "everyone being responsible for the other" has always been the foundation and the driving force of the activities of the Jewish communities for all generations.

**Food for the poor (*ma'os khitin*)** Before each Passover, with the community's initiative, there was a special project called *ma'os khitin*, and with the monies collected they would purchase products for Passover (such as matzo, meat, potatoes, etc.) and they would distribute these to the needy.

*[Page 85]*

Those active with this *mitzvah* were: Reb Yekhiel Winekrantz, of blessed memory, and Reb Yosef Dorn, of blessed memory (the last president of the community).

**Discreet charity (*matan be'seiser*)** From time to time there were special activities for the good of the Jews who had become poor suddenly, and who had been left with nothing. Those active in this *mitzvah* were: Reb Yosef Jagoda, of blessed memory, and Reb Yisroel Isser Hiller, of blessed memory.

**Winter project** Shortly after the holiday of *Sukos*, the winter activities for the needy went into action. Using the collected funds, they bought coal and wood for heating and potatoes, and distributed them amongst the needy. Those active in this *mitzvah* were: Reb Moyshe Granjewicz, of blessed memory, and Reb Moyshe Rosenberg, of blessed memory.

# Chapter Five
# The Last Community Election

There had been no election for many years, and in those times, at the head of the community were: Reb Aron Yoel Granjewicz, of blessed memory, Reb Feivel Rosenberg, of blessed memory, and after him his son Reb Dovid Rosenberg, of blessed memory. This last one held his office for many years as head of the community until 1928.

In 1931, the community held elections in which 90% of the people voted.

The following heads were elected:

1. Yosef Dorn, of blessed memory, represented the butchers
2. Aron Leyb Grinboim, of blessed memory, Handworkers' Union
3. Moyshe Botshan, of blessed memory, Handworkers' Union
4. Menakhem Kronenberg, of blessed memory, Burial Society
5. Yosef Jagoda, of blessed memory
6. Yakov Moyshe Zlotogurski, of blessed memory, *Agudas Yisroel*
7. Eliezer Oryl, of blessed memory, private list

As the leader of the community, Reb Yosef Dorn, of blessed memory, was elected, and as treasurer - Reb Aron Leyb Grinboim, of blessed memory.

As the community secretary, from 1929 until the end of 1935, Khaim Ber (now in Israel) held the office, and after him, M. Borenshtayn, of blessed memory, assumed the office.

*[Page 86]*

(2) On the 20th of Elul, 5696, or September 7, 1936, the last elections in the Serock community were held.

The results of the election, in which there were only three candidate lists, gave rise to a significant change in the social makeup of those elected. They are as follows:

Name of the list:

*Gemillas khassodim* fund (money for the poor), to which the Handworkers and Butchers Unions belonged:
Reb Aron Leyb Grinboim, of blessed memory
Reb Yehoshua Dovid Babek, of blessed memory
Reb Yosef Dorn, of blessed memory

The *Khevra Kadisha* (Burial Society)
Reb Menakhem Kronenberg, of blessed memory
Reb Yosef Jagoda, of blessed memory
Reb Motel Melnik, of blessed memory
Reb Yakov Moyshe Zlotogurski, of blessed memory

Zionist organizations.
Reb Zwi Kleinman, of blessed memory
As the head of the community, Reb Yosef Dorn, of blessed memory, was elected again.

*[Page 87]*

(3) Numbers about income sources, expenditures, budget, community tax payments, number of families - of the Jewish community of Serock.

## In the years 1932-1939

Income sources:
community tax
money for *shkhita* (ritual slaughter)
bathhouse attendant from the baths
donations and gifts
Obligatory expenses:

A. Monthly expense for:

49. the city rabbi
50. the rabbi's *shamash* (assistant)
51. secretary for the community
52. the *shokhtim* (ritual slaughterers)
53. the *shamash* of the *shul* (takes care of the synagogue)
54. the caretaker of the cemeteries

B. Other expenses:

Renovations for:

2. the *shul*
3. the bathhouse
4. the cemeteries
5. subsidies for the needy
6. unforeseeable expenses

The community properties:

4. the large city *shul*
5. the community house
6. the *mikve*
7. the cemeteries

Average annual budget: 300,000 - 350,000 zlotys
Number of Jewish families: 600-640
Number of community tax payers: 450 heads of households

[Page 88]

*Lag be'Omer* outing of school children in Serock with their teacher Reb Shimon Sempf

[Page 89]

# Chapter Six
# The Secular Education

Until the end of World War One, almost all of the Jewish children were raised in religious schools (*kheder*) and *yeshivos*, and only very few studied in schools in town or in other cities. At the beginning of the 1920s, in accordance with the special laws of the Polish government, public schools (*powszechna*) for the Jews were opened, whose program was identical to the program of the Polish children, but with the addition of several weekly classes about the Jewish religion. The official language of all the connected schools was Polish. Such a school was opened for the Jewish children at the beginning of the 1920s, and the teacher and director was Khaim Jurkewicz from Pultusk (today in the U.S.). It was obligatory to attend the abovementioned school, except for those children who studied in private or community schools accredited by the

Education Department. In the beginning, this school was completely Jewish (both students and teachers), but when it was built up by the beginning of the 1930s - this large, new school building on the road to Pultusk - according to a ruling by the Polish Education Department, it had to merge with the existing school for Polish children. The director of this united school was the Pole Jan Sokalnicki. The hope with this ruling for the merge was to extinguish even the most minimal Jewish "color" in the general state school. In the end, there were several hundred Jewish boys and girls in the school. This peculiarity shook up the Jewish cultural phenomenon.

The Hebrew People's School. Close to the establishment of the new Polish Republic in 1918, a few Zionist parents established a modern Hebrew People's school - under the supervision of the teacher Halperin (today in the U.S.).

*[Page 90]*

**The Jewish ("*powszechna*") school**

**Male and female students in the Jewish("*powszechna*") school with the teacher Ring**

*[Page 91]*

The school was free, and the boys went with their heads uncovered. This phenomenon created strong anger in the religious circles.

The school existed for only two years, and then it closed because the director Halperin left for America.

# Chapter Seven
# Society's Last Struggles

In the fall of 1938, there were elections in the whole of Poland for all municipal institutions. The Jews of Serock, despite their depressed state and oppression by the Polish powers, elected two councilmen into the city council.

All the Zionist organizations in Serock took active participation in the elections of the 21st Zionist Congress, which took place in the month of July, 1939 (several weeks before the outbreak of WWII), and the results were as follows:

| | | |
|---|---|---|
| List #1 | - the general Zionist organizations | - 38 votes |
| List #2 | - *"Eit Livnot"* | - 11 votes |
| List #3 | - *Mizrakhi* | - 10 votes |
| List #4 | - Block for workers in Israel | - 34 votes |
| List #5 | - *Hanoar Hazioni* | - 20 votes |

("*Haynt*," issue 170 from July 25, 1939)

[Page 92]

# Chapter Eight
# Tables of Statistics

## Table I

### The Professional Make-Up of the Jews in Serock before the Outbreak of World War II (1939)

| Consecutive Numbers | Professions | Numbers of Oldest in Family |
|---|---|---|
| 1 | storekeepers | 200 |
| 2 | restaurateurs | 4 |
| 3 - TRANSPORT: | passenger transports | 5 |
|  | cargo (merchandise) drivers | 25 |
| 4 | orchard managers (lessees) | 20 |
| 5 | glaziers | 5 |
| 6 | watchmakers | 4 |
| 7 | bakers (bakeries) | 7 |
| 8 | tailors (workshops) | 6 |
| 9 | carpenters (workshops) | 6 |
| 10 | shoemakers (workshops) | 18 |
| 11 | shoe stitchers (workshops) | 4 |
| 12 | package carriers | 12 |
| 13 | knitter (workshops of scrap, sweaters) | 3 |
| 14 | tinsmiths (workshops) | 5 |
| 15 | rope makers | 3 |
| 16 | smiths (workshops) | 4 |
| 17 | grain merchants | 20 |
| 18 | village peddlers | 9 |
| 19 | fishermen and merchants | 2 |
| 20 | fish traders | 5 |
| 21 | wood merchants | 2 |
| 22 | water carriers (drinking water from the wells) | 5 |
| 23 | seamstresses | 10 |
| 24 - MILL OWNERS: | flour | 2 |
|  | kasha | 1 |
| 25 | meat markets (butchers, animal merchants | 8 |
| 27 | feather pluckers | 10 |
| 26 | *kishke* makers | 2 |

| 28 | milk merchants | 4 |
| 29 | oil pressers | 2 |
| 30 | hairdresser | 4 |
| 31- **OFFICIALS:** | bookkeepers | 4 |
|  | secretaries, treasurers | 3 |
|  | teachers | 2 |
| 32 - **RELIGIOUS POSITIONS:** | rabbi | 1 |
|  | *Shokhet* (Kosher slaughterer) | 4 |
|  | *menakrim* * | 3 |
|  | *mohel* ** | 1 |
|  | *shamesh* | 2 |
|  | religious teachers | 15 |
|  | *khazen* (cantor) | 1 |
| 33 | doctor's assistant | 2 |
| 34 | medical doctor | 1 |
| 35 | midwife | 1 |
| 36 | dentist | 1 |
| 37 | lawyer | 1 |
|  | TOTAL: | 459 |

\* *Menaker*: the person who removes forbidden fat and veins from meat
\*\* *Mohel*: the person who performs the circumcisions

| Year | General Population | Number of Jews | % of Jews |
|---|---|---|---|
| 1808 | 1,277 | 270 | (1) 21.1 |
| 1827 | 985 | 375 | (1) 38.1 |
| 1856 | 1,602 | 901 | (2) 56.2 |
| 1857 | 1,637 | 920 | (1) 56.2 |
| 1884 | 2,536 | 1,821 | (3) 71.8 |
| 1897 | 3,916 | 2,054 | (2) 52.4 |
| 1908 | 4,352 | 2,290 | (4) 52.6 |
| 1921 | 4,694 | 2,295 | (5) 48.9 |
| 1931 | 5,413 | 2,641 | (6) 48.8 |
| 1939 |  | 3,150 | (7) * |

## Sources for Table #2

1. **Bohdan Wasiutyński**: Ludność Żydowska w Polsce w wiekach XIX—XX; Studjum statystyczne, Warszawa 1930.

2. Еврейская Энциклопедия, vol. XIV; col. 174.

3. A. **Eisenbach**: Ludność Żydowska w Królestwie Polskim w XIX w. Biuletyn Żydowskiego Instytutu Historycznego, Warszawa, Styczeń-Marzec 1959, Nr. 29, Str. 72—112.

4. **Dr. Jacob Segal**: Internationale Konfessionsstatistik; Berlin, Bureau für Statistik der Juden in Deutschland, 1914; aus Manuskript gedruckt.

5. Spis Miejscowości Rzeczypospolitej Polski (Skorowidz).

6. Czasopismo — Życie Gospodarcze, Nr. 24, 19.XII.1956.

7. הערכה מעוטרת — ספירת האוכלוסיה לפי הזכרון.

## Summary

The economic situation of the Jews in Serock at the beginning of the 1920s - after the distress of WWI, the German invasion, the establishment of new Polish republic, the Russo-Polish war - was completely upset, the means of earning a living were stopped up, and poverty was spread into all corners.

In those times, American Jewry came to help the community. "Joint" opened a soup kitchen, distributed clothing, handworkers received raw materials, loans were given without interest, and for the children there were special food products.

This invaluable help actually only slowed the process of the community losing their footing, and even this help could not fulfill all the needs.

In those years, emigration of the Jews in Serock began in large numbers as they left for the U.S. and Argentina, and in smaller groups, also to France, England, and Israel.

The inner political organizations, and all its facets, with the responsibilities of the newly established Polish republic and its aggressive anti-Semitism, strengthened the Jews of Serock and their will for independence against discrimination, and also resulted in a change in leadership in the community.

The Jews in Serock searched for opportunities to live, not only in the countries overseas, but also in countries around them. At the end of the 1920s, and in the beginning of the 1930s, many families settled in the nearby city of Jablonna Legionowo, 15 kilometers south of Serock, with the hope to be able to earn a living there.

This new city was called a division of the Serock community.

The population:

The Jewish population did not grow in the years 1908-1921, because the First World War and the German invasion, and times even until after the Russo-Polish war resulted in a large number of deaths, a diminished size, and many leaving the city.

*[Page 95]*

In the years 1921-1931, many emigrated overseas or moved to other places nearby.

The number of Jewish souls grew only by 350, even with a decrease in the number of deaths and an increase in size (see Table #2), and in proportion to the Polish population, there was no increase.

In the year 1939, there were approximately 3150 Jews, 620-640 families (see Table #2). Among the young adults and the youth, there was little income and high unemployment.

From among the 640 eldest in the families [primary supporters], only 459 had a source of income (71%), and 181 families were without income (see Table #1). The situation among those youths of working age and those youths who would be occupied with business was even more difficult.

The Jewish youth of working age were about 650, and those among them that were working were about 120-150 (23%). (See comment 13 of Table #1.)

In addition to the difficult economical situation, anti-Semitism was boiling in the streets.

A small number of youths, despite the shut doors, went to Israel illegally.

In a situation where there was no way out, the Jewish youth passed the time with dancing and all sorts of recreation.

The Nazi shadow spread over Poland. In the last few months prior to the war, some of the Polish population drew closer to the Jews. On April 25, 1939, the Jewish community of Serock received an official invitation to participate in promoting the national loan for the security of the country.

The Serock Jews, along with all of Polish Jewry, were isolated in their heroic struggle against the steel wall of hatred and indifference.

No one could have imagined the magnitude of the approaching disaster.

## Translator's Footnotes

55.  Eugeniusz Jagiello was a Polish socialist politician, elected deputy to the Fourth Duma from the city of Warsaw. The elections to the Warsaw electoral college had been won by Jewish parties, who mustered 46 electoral votes while the non-Jewish bloc gathered 34. However the Jewish bloc decided to elect a Polish Duma member in an attempt not to inflame anti-Semitic feelings towards the Jewish community. Initially the Jewish bloc had approached Kucharzewski, but he declined the nomination. Thus the Jewish bloc had turned to Jagiello, electing him as the deputy from Warsaw. Once in the Duma, the Bolsheviks strongly objected to his admission to the Social-Democratic group because he was elected with the support of the bourgeoisie and the electoral bloc consisting of the Polish Socialist Party - Left and the Bund. Under the pressure of Bolshevik deputies his rights in the group were restricted: on all internal Party matters he had a voice but no vote. (Wikipedia: Eugeniusz Jagiello)

[Page 99]

# Religious Life

## The Serocker Rav, the Rabbi and Genius, Rav Yosef Levinshtayn, May his memory be blessed

**Harav Yakov Henokh Cymerman, of blessed memory**
**Translated by Pamela Russ**

I remember him with his long white beard and sidecurls, with his patriarchal appearance and his enormous kindness.

His origins are from famous ancestry:

He was born in the year 1840 (Hebrew year 5600). His father, Rav Abish, of blessed memory, was one of the great scholars, a great-grandson of the genius Rav Avrahom Abish, of blessed memory, chief of the Jewish court of Frankfurt Am Main, and the renowned genius of the Talmudic book "Pnei Yehoshua," of blessed memory.

When he was 17, Rav Levinshtayn married the daughter of Rav Itche Nissels of Prague, a Warker khassid [follower of the Warker Rabbi and his teachings], and a great scholar. He also received his rabbinic ordination from the great rabbi of Lublin, the great rabbi and genius Rav Yehoshua Heshel Ashkenazi, of blessed memory.

One year later, he assumed the position of judge in the religious court in the town of Karczew [unsure of this], and a short while after that, in the town of Zaklikow in Lublin. When he started to become famous as a great genius, he was taken on with great reverence as the rabbi and chief of the Jewish court of Serock, at the approximate age of 30.

He was beloved by everyone in the city: the khassidim, the scholars, the misnagdim [those who opposed the khassidim], and those who were "enlightened" because he was a great genius with a sharp mind, a historical and good person. At the beginning he was a *misnagid*, but he became a khassid with the goal of elevating the levels of joy and hope for the Jews.

When the Warker Rebbe, Rebbe Yizkhok, of blessed memory, died, the significant Warker khassidim turned to the Serocker Rav, and wanted to acknowledge his as their Rabbi, but he responded to them with a smile, saying "Be happy that I myself am a khassid."

I had the great merit of being the Rav's student, many times sitting at his side during his Jewish court cases, and was awed by his wisdom and humor.

Here are two flowers ["gems"] from those times:

[Page 100]

44. Reb Levi Yitzkhok the butcher came to see him, and said: "Rebbe, I would like you to call Avrom Yankel Koval to a court case." When asked what this was about, he replied: "Avrom Yankel is spreading bad rumors about me." The Rav asked him if he himself had heard these rumors. "No," he said, "Hershel the tailor told me." "If that's the case," said the Rav, "then you have to call Hershel the tailor to court, because you heard it from him. You don't really know if this information about Avrom Yankel is true." Levi Yitzkhok asked the Rav to send for Hershel. The Rav asked that he not call him, "because he is an impudent fellow and may say this again." Levi Yitzkhok left with that with which he came.

45. In the time of the conflict about Reb Eliyahu the shokhet [ritual slaughterer], someone tattled to the governor in Warsaw that the Rav is getting too old, that he doesn't know what he is doing and asked the governor to order that they select a new Rav (the Rav himself was already a senior). Just at that time, the governor had to be in Serock. When he arrived, the Rav and his guardians went to the administrative offices to greet him. The Rav did not know any Russian, so he took his son-in-law, Shulem Yakov, as interpreter. The governor welcomed him warmly, and told him right away that he had received a letter saying that the Rav is no longer of clear mind. The Rav calmly responded, "The person who wrote this was clearly angry that I still understand too much and lead the community with a strong hand. If I were not of clear mind, the author would be content and not have written anything." The governor was very impressed with the answer and shook his hand warmly.

Serock had two ritual slaughterers: Reb Refoel Levinson and Reb Chaim Shloime, both learned khassidim – the first a Gerer khassid, the second an Alexanderer khassid. Both were not only khassidim, but people of action. Wherever there was someone sick, or someone who was needy, they were the first to help with whatever was at all possible. Once there was a rumor about one of them, saying that his hands shook, and about the other that his vision was becoming weaker, and because of that, they needed other slaughterers. The Rav turned it around and revealed that this was The Serocker Magid, the Rav, Reb Aron Katzenelenbogen, of blessed memory On Rosh Hashana, I ate with my family at my parents' home. After prayers, leaving the Ger shtiebel, we went to the elderly Rav to wish him a "le'shono toive" (a good year); that's what my father did for many years. Leaving the Rav's home, my father said to me: "You have to go up to the Rebbe and say le'shono toive." I was very surprised and I said to him: "But you're not going either!" He said to me: "There's no question about me not going, I don't know him and he doesn't know me, but you were there today, and so he may be very disturbed that you left, and you have to be respectful to him – after all, he is a descendent of holy people!"

[Page 101]

כתב-יד פון סעראצקער רב זצ"ל, אין וועלכן ער דערמאנט די דורכגעמאכטע שווערע צייט און די הילף וואס ער האט באקומען פון סעראצקער מגיד זצ"ל. גענומען פון דער „מגילת יוחסין" פון מגיד זצ"ל, וואס דער רב זצ"ל האט געשריבן) דער טעקסט פון דער פאטא-קאפיע לייענט זיך:

לעת זקנתי כבדו עלי איברי וקשה עלי הכתיבה. אמנם זכרתי ימי קדם ימי עניי אשר בני העיר רחקו מעלי אף לחם לאכול ובגד ללבוש הייתי חסר. והרב המגיד שליט"א הוא פותח יד ומשביע לכל הפושטים ידיהם אליו ואף אוהב מרחוק. הן בכבוד יו"ט. ומתנגד בצדקותיו וביחוסו והוא מזרע רבינו פנחס מקארץ שסבינא דמלכא ומטרונתא. אהבה דוחקת הבשר כאלו הנני נער גם שפר שכר טרחתי ששה מילאן. כאלו לא הכרתי טובתו. בשמחה בלי עצב. ב' תזריע בכל קודש פ"ך.

סעראצק הק' יוסף במהר"א ז"ל מלובלין.

**Translation of letter:**

This is handwritten by the Serocker Rebbe, of blessed memory, in which he remembers the terribly difficult experiences and the help he received from the Magid [the learned individual who traveled from town to town teaching and lecturing] of Serock. Taken from the "Genealogy List" from the Magid, of blessed memory, which the Rav himself wrote. The text of the photocopy reads as follows:

"In the time of my old age, my body has become heavy and it has become hard for me to write. In truth, I remember the early days that were poor and the people in the city were distant from me. Even food and clothing for me were scarce. And the Rav, the Magid, opened his hand and gave sustenance to those who put out their hands, even loving those who were distanced. Yes, this was in honor of Yom Tov (the holidays), as we derived pleasure from his righteousness and his ancestry. His origins are from our Rabbi Pinkhas of Koretz, who was a friend and a companion of the king. **Love can force the flesh** *as if I were a young man,* **and the reward for my efforts are six Milan,** *as though I did not acknowledge his goodness.*

With joy and no sadness,
Parshas Tazria
With all that is holy, 1904

Serock, the Holy Rav Yosef the son of our great Rav Avrahom, of blessed memory Lublin

**Translator's note:**

The last three lines of this letter pose some challenges in their interpretation. Without a larger context or an original document, there is little context to assist in a closer analysis of the text. Therefore, interpretations abound. The translator provides several possibilities for the three lines; one can only guess. These are possible interpretations:

The expression "love can force the flesh" is often used in Jewish texts, originally from the Talmud, meaning that the spiritual overrides / presses / takes over the material. One possible translation could be: The love of G-d and work of G-d makes me ignore the physical pain, as if I am a boy, and my salary is six milan [likely the name of a particular currency], as if I am not rewarded without the salary.

This is another possible interpretation: I acted like a young man swept by love for this man [the Magid], accepting a wage of six coins for labor I had done for him, ungrateful and unable to recognize the generosity and goodness shown to me by this noble man.

Thank you to the following translators for their assistance:
   Orit Lavi
   Yael Lajmer Liber
   Dr. Perets Mett
            Vered Schussman-Dayan

**The Serocker Rav, the Rabbi and Genius,**
Reb Yosef Levinshtayn, of blessed memory

Hana Shayer

# The Serocker Magid, the Rav, Reb Aron Katzenelenbogen, of blessed memory

**The Serocker Magid, the Rav,
Reb Aron Katzenelenbogen, of blessed memory**

So, too bad. If your father says go, then you go. So I went. There were a few hundred Jews there. This was the first time I had seen such a sight. Everyone was still wearing their prayer shawls (taleisim [plural of talis]), because there, on Rosh Hashana night they would wear their prayer shawls[2] for the evening prayers. When I approached the Rebbe and said "le'shono toive," he answered me with a great smile, in Hebrew, and said: "I am inviting you to my tish (table)."[3] I said nothing and left, almost angry.

When I returned home, I tell my father everything that happened, and declare that I will definitely not go to the Rebbe's tish. My father immediately replies: "No, my child, you will really have to go." I was silent. As we were waiting to wash our hands for the meal, my father said to me: "Don't forget, remember to have in mind[4] that you will say the blessing after the meal at the Rebbe's."

[Page 108]

**Torah writings from the Serock Magid, of blessed memory, in the year 1912;
recorded by Reb Eliyohu Shokhet, may his blood be avenged.
Content: Commentaries and exegesis about Torah verses in Book of Genesis (Bereishis)**

[Page 109]

**Reb Eliyahu Shokhet,
may his blood be avenged**

A crowd from the Ger shtiebel came to our house. We finished our meal. Before saying the blessings after the meal, my father said: "Yakov Henokh has to go to the Rebbe's tish, and if any one of you wishes to accompany him, he'll feel that much more comfortable." Sure enough, there were some young men who came with me.

As I appeared at the doorstep, Elya immediately called loudly to me to come to the table. I was seated in the first seat next to the Rebbe, and the Rebbe immediately asked me to sing "Ve'ye'esoyu kol le'avdekho" (taken from the afternoon prayers of Rosh Hashana). It was a table of food, song, and intellectual Torah. After the blessings at the end of the meal, the Rebbe stood up and said to me: "Yakov Henokh, I am asking you to lead the morning prayers (shakharis). Gut Yom Tov! (Happy holiday)," and he left to his room. The crowds came right at me: "Mazel tov to you, the leader of the prayers!" The Rebbe himself used to lead the afternoon prayers. I said to them: "There's nothing to talk about. Let your Rebbe know that he shouldn't rely on me, because I won't lead the prayers."

There was one khasid, Moishe Hirsh Srebro (Mendel Litman's son-in-law), he lived in Pultusk, a fiery khasid of the Serock Rebbe, who said: "You should know that on Rosh Hashana at night, after the tish, no one can disturb the Rebbe.[5] If I disturb him, I am risking my life for you, but I'll go knock at his door."

I said nothing. Soon, the Rebbe's door opens, and the Rebbe appears. The bais medrash becomes silent. The Rebbe calls me over and says: "Why does one not wish to lead the prayers? Because one is not yet thirty years old? The people want what I want, and in the merit of my parents I ask that Yakov Henokh should lead the prayers. I assure Yakov Henokh a better year than the last one." And not waiting for a response, he shut the door.

They celebrated until 3AM with drink, song, and dance, and of course, I did lead the prayers. I have to confess, since then, I remained a baal tefilla (one who leads the prayers), but to pray as I did on that day of Rosh Hashana, I never had the merit to do again, and in that year, the Rebbe's blessings were fulfilled perfectly. From that time on, I remained an indescribable follower.

I'm not really a believer of miracles, but I'll just comment on a few things that I and others noticed.

The Rebbe brought in all the young boys from the city's bais medrash, and from the Ger shtiebel (there were no other types of khasidic shtiebelekh [plural] in Serock at the time) to his bais medrash, and there they learned beautifully. The Rebbe, as usual, was dressed very elegantly with an ironed collar, stiff cuffs, polished shoes and boots, and silk clothing. This gave the young boys "permission" to dress better, and some even did so. Because of that, there were some parents who did not permit their children to go there. In the end, all the boys from the Rebbe's bais medrash remained God-fearing, religious Jews, and it was those others who actually became Communists. Once, the Rebbe went to the bais medrash and found the door locked. He knocked until someone opened the door. When he entered, he asked: "Why is the door locked? What have you done?" With great trepidation, they answered and confessed that they were playing chess. So, the Rebbe said: "From now on, you should take one hour each day – but no more than that – to play chess with an open door." He dealt with the boys as a father to his children.

A lot of money was given to him, but if it weren't for these few Jews who took care of the Rebbe's home and the guests, the Rebbe's wife and children would have suffered difficulties. Not only did he give the needy much money, but he gave them household items, clothing, and even his own clothing. It's important to remember the two Rosenbergs: Yitzkhok and Yeshiye, two wealthy Jews, who assumed the responsibility of sustaining the Rebbe's home.

[Page 112]

Later, when there was a change, he became the Magid instead of the Rebbe, but I had already left Serock and was living in Danzig. The Magid came to Danzig with the intention of spending that summer in a cottage in Sopot (near Danzig). He came to have a look and he was not pleased. Meanwhile, he was my guest for a week. At that time, there was a khasidic Jew, Yitzkhok Segal, who was sick in the hospital. I said to the Magid: "If I knew that they would let us see him, we would go visit him in the hospital." The Rebbe said: "Let's go." I took an open automobile, and because the Rebbe himself wasn't well, I asked the driver to drive slowly. On the entire route, the crowd grew on either side of the vehicle. I overheard as the non-Jews were saying to each other: "The holy Rabbi is going." No one said a word in the hospital. Everywhere we went, the guards were welcoming and opened the doors obligingly. The only one who did ask a question, was the sick person: "The doctors say that they have to operate." The Magid quickly responded: "You'll go to Berlin, and there you'll hear what they say." The following day, he actually discharged himself from the hospital, went to Berlin, and there became healthy again.

A small characteristic of the Magid: At the Sabbath tish, behind the Magid, the smart young men would stand, and on long benches against the wall would sit the poor people who would go collecting alms for themselves from door to door. The Rebbe took better care of them than of his khasidim. Once, at his tish, he did not distribute his shirayim[6] to his khasidim, but gave them all to the poor who were there. Elya Khasid leaned over to the Magid and said something quietly to him. I heard the reply: "If I give everyone a small piece, what will each person have? These poor Jews will eat the food, and all the khasidim will have a share in this merit."

*[Page 113]*

**The tent (term used for religious gravesite) of the Magid of Serock, of blessed memory, in the Warsaw cemetery**

*[Page 111]*

# Khasidim

The khasidic life in Serock does not lend itself to much to division. The majority of the town were khasidim. The only ones who had a *shtiebel* (small house of prayer) were the Ger khasidim. For a certain time, the Radzimyn khasidim also had a *shtiebel*. In the small town synagogue, the first *minyan* (quorum) prayed according to the religious style of the Ashkenazi Jews;[7] the other quorums (*minyanim*) would pray according to *Nusakh Sefard*.[8] On the Shabbath there were two quorums: the first was the early group that prayed *Nusakh Ashkenaz,* and was not a large group. In the second group, that prayed *Nusach Sephard,* there was a crowded and packed synagogue.

If we had to divide the town, we would be able to do so only according to status. There were few rich people, with the majority being middle class and poor. But the poor were also respectable. On the Sabbath, for example, one couldn't see any poverty.

There were only a few wealthy people. Just very few had the merit of being wealthy-khasidic, such as, for example, Reb Leib Leviner, of blessed memory. They called him "Leibel from down there," because he lived "down there" near the Narew. He was a humble man, a man of character, a scholar, a fiery Ger khasid, and a wealthy (prominent) man. He had a very good heart, helped everyone with their needs, and his house was open to every Jew. His children followed in his footsteps.

There were three distant relatives of his in the Rosenberg family: 1) Reb Feivel was an old khasid of Kotzk, a great man to his brethren. For many years, until his passing, he was the first *gabbai* (manager of the affairs of the synagogue). He built the synagogue and the ritual baths. During his time, the town was known in the world. He left three sons: Dovid, who became the *gabbai* after Reb Faivel's passing; Shmulik and Moishe, who ran the mill; and two sons-in law, Yeshayohu Melnik and Moishe Fishman. All the children were prominent businessmen in the town. 2) Zanwill Rosenberg was considered the town's rich man. He was already a modern man, but a very devout Jew. He was very active, a great philanthropist, ran a rich home, and left behind three sons: Yeshayohu, Khone, and Yankel, and two sons-in-law, Avrohom and Eliezer Merker. The sons-in-law were brothers, sons of the Otwocker Rebbe, both Talmudic scholars. 3) Moishe Rosenberg, not a wealthy man, but a man who ran a khasidic house (with the lifestyles and traditions), and a man who was a khasid of the Otwocker Rebbe, and he left three sons: Yitzkhok, who became a rich man during the time of the Magid (as was mentioned earlier); Khaim, a fine Torah scholar and khasid, and Yekhiel, a prominent Jewish businessman; and one son-in-law Asher, who was Yosef Beker's son.

*[Page 114]*

There were learned, wealthy, and pious young men, and there were those who had "days" (it was the custom of the community to assume the responsibility [select a "day"] of providing meals for the yeshiva boys at no cost), who sat and studied and were busy with charitable, community issues, and learned Talmud with young boys in the Gerer *shtiebel*: these were Avremel, son-in-law of Yisroel Yitzkhok, and also the father-in-law, a pious man known by the name Yisroel Yitzkhok Arzikhover; Yakov Dovid Milshtayn, who was a real scholarly teacher (he was Itche Meier Jekel's son-in-law); Dovid Warsawski (Mendel Kristal's son-in-law). In town, he was called Dovid Jores, which was his mother-in-law's name; and Itche Swarc who was Moishe Pienik's son-in-law; Khaim Elezer, Yitzkhok Aron's son, and Itzel Janishe's son-in-law, and so on.

I remember the time when Serock still had a few Kotzker *khasidim*. Of Binyomin Kristal, I only remember his funeral. He was a Kotzker khasid, a Talmudic scholar, the rich man of the town. Another person, Moishe Yosel (the father-in-law of Leibel Leviner) and Meier Moishe (Mendel Wiernik's first father-in-law; later Mendel Wiernik married Yore Kristal, the widow of Mendel Kristal). Mendel Kristal was a man of total virtue from his father Binyomin who was a Talmudic scholar, a Ger khasid, and a wealthy man.

My grandfather, of blessed memory, Reb Yosef Eliezer Shokhet (the ritual slaughterer) was a young man who during his years of "days" (learning Talmud and being supported by the community) was with his pious, wealthy father-in-law in Serock, and was a sharp young man, and went to the Alexander Rebbe with the intention of staying there a few weeks, as he normally did. As he entered to greet the Rebbe, the Rebbe said to him that he should go to Radzymin to Moishe Avrohom, and study how to be a *shokhet* (Moishe Avrohom was the *shokhet* in Radzymin and also a khasid of the Alexander Rebbe), and said he should immediately leave Alexander and go to Radzymin by "ox" (there were no trains on this route yet) and they had to pass through Serock and wait there for about two hours until a wagon would come by and go to Radzymin. He went, and stood on the highway and waited. Meanwhile, his father-in-law came out and told him to come into his house. He responded: "The Rebbe told me to go to Radzymin, so I don't have the right to go into other places."

As he entered Radzymin and came to Moishe Avrohom's house, Moishe Avrohom says to him:

*[Page 115]*

"Yosef Eliezer! I just received a postcard from the Rebbe this moment!" He immediately took out his knife and began teaching him what to do. Only in about a half hour did he invite him to sit down and have something to eat.

Since the Rebbe told him about teaching Yosef Eliezer, they could say or do nothing else first.

After two months of being in Radzymin, Moishe Avrohom says to him that now he already knows how to be a *shokhet*. When Yosef Eliezer asked for a certificate to prove that he now has the knowledge, Moishe Avrohom says to him: "The Rebbe wrote only about teaching, not about a certificate," and then told him to go back to the Rebbe and say that "Moishe Avrohom says that now Yosef Eliezer knows."

He immediately went back to Alexander, and passing through Serock, again the same story happened as before. He came before the Rebbe and told him what Moishe Avrohom told him to say, no more and no less. The Rebbe said nothing. On the Sabbath, the Rebbe gave him much honor, and the congregation was very puzzled. After the Sabbath, the Rebbe summoned him. As Yosef Eliezer entered, the Rebbe said to him: "Go home and become a *shokhet* in Serock." And he immediately took his leave. He didn't understand the whole thing, but if the Rebbe says go, you go. This time, as he came to Serock, he went directly home because the Rebbe had told him to do so. Once he was in the house, he already heard the news that two weeks earlier, one of the *shokhtim* (plural) had suddenly died. The following morning, Yosef Eliezer went to see the Rav and told him the entire story, from beginning to end, exactly as it happened. The Rav did not say a single word, but took an ordinary piece of paper and his goose quill (the Rav, of blessed memory, used a goose quill all his life), and immediately wrote that he takes on Yosef Eliezer as the primary *shokhet* in Serock and will accompany him at night to the first slaughter.

The slaughterhouse was two *viorst* (one *viorst* is 2/3 of a mile) outside the city, in the village of Wierbice. The Rav says, he doesn't even have any knives yet. He tells him to go back home, eat something, and come right back. When Yosef Eliezer comes back, the Rav gives him a package and says, "Here are the knives and the rocks [to sharpen the knives]," and he will have to pay as much as the widow of the *shokhet* decides, because there was no price yet established with her. He went right away, and set the knives in order. That night, the Rav went with the grandfather to the slaughterhouse and all the khasidim in the town joined them. In the Alexander *shtiebel*, after the slaughtering, there was a festive meal. The Rav and many of the wealthy townspeople were also there, and Yosef Eliezer became the *shokhet* for the town of Serock. A week later, he went to see the Rav and reminded him that he did not yet have a certificate, and he asked for a "receipt" (that's what the certificate of a *shokhet* was called). The Rav responded: "The (Alexander) Rebbe sent you to us to be a *shokhet*, but he did not send you here for a certificate."

[Page 116]

A year later, the Alexander Rebbe, of blessed memory, went to Pultusk for a wedding and passed through Serock where he spent the night. There was a great festive meal held, and everyone in the city was present. After the meal, the Rebbe said that he would like my grandfather to slaughter a chicken that he would be able to take with him. They brought two white chickens right away and my grandfather showed him the knife. He took the knife, gave one look at it, and gave it directly back and said to proceed with the slaughter. The Rebbe covered the blood, asked for paper, and wrapped the chickens himself, not allowing anyone to help, and at that very moment, he declared loudly: "All you Jews should know that it is a *mitzvah* to eat from this young man's slaughtered animals." In the morning, the Rebbe left for Pultusk. The entire city escorted him until a good distance out of town – all the Jewish wagon drivers: Zelde's Yekele and Itche Berl and their wagons, Khantze's Feivel Moishe (Henokh Faskowicz' father-in-law) who was a pious Jew and had a horse and wagon and used to travel to Warsaw for merchandise; Moishe Didak and Moishe Margolias also rode out with their smaller wagons and drove the crowd from Serock to Pultusk free of charge.

My grandfather became greatly respected in the town. The khasidic Jews held him as if he were a half chosen Rebbe, and the rest of the people actually were afraid of him.

The other *shokhet* was Nakhman Shokhet, a khasid from Pilew, also a great Talmudic scholar, and also greatly respected in the town. Nakhman Shokhet had great respect for my grandfather.

Two years later, the Alexander Rebbe passed on. At that time, a delegation from Pultusk arrived to my grandfather, proposing that he become the primary *shokhet* in Pultusk, which would mean double the salary and honor. My grandfather received the delegation very respectfully, made a festive meal for them, and afterwards said to them that he cannot go with them because the Rebbe, of blessed memory, had told him to "go home and become the *shokhet* in Serock." Since the Rebbe is no longer alive, no one can change that, and "I remain a *shokhet* in Serock." Years later, my grandfather was already over fifty years old, the terrible disease of cholera was spreading around. People died like flies. Whoever was caught by the disease, died within a few hours, or at most a few days, God have mercy on us. Nakhman Shokhet caught the disease, and died on the second day, may we be spared. My grandfather came back from the funeral and summoned the *gabbai'im* (plural of *gabbai*, managers of the synagogue), and told them to hire another two *shokhtim* (plural of *shokhet*) because he too is no longer a *shokhet*. Immediately after that, he went directly to bed and became ill. The doctor came and said it was nothing, but my grandfather summoned all the children and told each of them things, including that none of them should become a *shokhet*. He died on the third day. The town went into black mourning. Until after the thirty day mourning period, there was no mention of getting a new *shokhet*. After that, they took on Refoel and Khaim Shlomo.

*[Page 117]*

From my grandfather's children, in Serock lived a son-in-law (my father, of blessed memory) and a son who became a famous circumciser (*mohel*). Both of these men were called Itche Meier.

## Religious Jews

The majority of the Jews in Serock were religious. In the town, a non-religious Jew was someone who already allowed himself to trim his beard a little, but almost not even one Jew ever missed a day in the place of study (*bais medrash*) for prayers. One can say that the "ignoramus" type did not exist there because of the groups that studied in the *bais medrash* between the afternoon services (*minkha*) and night services (*maariv*); they studied *Khayei Odom* (famous book on Jewish law), *Ein Yakov* (commentary on the Talmud), the *Talmud,* and Psalms. Every simple Jew loved and respected the Torah. Ordinary Jews gave up the last bits of food in their mouths to be able to pay large sums of mone to prominent teachers for education fees so that their children should become knowledgeable Torah Jews.

*[Page 118]*

There was one Jew named Avrohom Yekel Koval. One of his sons, Yehoshua, was a brilliant scholar, and he married someone from Pultusk. In Serock at that time they used to send the sons away to other towns to study in *yeshivas* (religious Torah institutions for boys). There were many young men who were provided for in those towns ("*kestkinder*") and there were many scholars as well. They would study with the younger boys. The youths who would come into the places of study (*bais medrash*), would immediately begin to study the Talmud and its commentaries because before that, they did not leave their *kheder* (children's religious school) for any higher studies. Even the butchers were Torah Jews. For example, Moishe Kozak-Wineberg. The whole family was called Kozak because their father, the old Yosel Kozak, was a Cantonist. As a child, he was captured and sent somewhere deep into Russia where he served for 25 years, and he still came home as a Jew. He raised a generation of children who were devout Jews: Moishe, a scholar, was one of them, and he had two sons – Yitzkhok Meier and Motele, both exceptional scholars. There were many sorts like this.

There was a Jew Yekel Shneider who was asked by the Rav, of blessed memory, to make the Rav's casket and tombstone from the table that Yekel used for cutting and sewing his clothing (that's how holy Yekel was). About Yekel, the Rav guaranteed, that not even one stitch was sewn without him reciting Psalms, and he never had even the smallest piece of leftover material. There was no Sabbath or other Jewish holiday (*Yom Tov*) without a guest.

There was also a Mendel Bobek, an exceptional Jew. Until after his wedding, he was a simple person. He hired a teacher for himself, Reb Shlomo Pesakh Melamed, this was Refoel Shokhet's father, a renowned teacher and a pious Jew. Mendel began his studies as if here were a young boy, studying *khumash, rashi, Talmud* (Torah and commentaries). He maintained this teacher until he was able to recite all six books of *mishnayos* (Talmud). Mendel Bobek was my book of ethics. I lived with him on the opposite wall. Early in the morning, still lying in bed, I already heard Mendel learning, so it chased me out of bed. He had one daughter, so he took a true Torah scholar from Nacielsk as a son-in-law, and provided for him for several years with great respect. His reverence for a Torah scholar was something to behold.

*[Page 119]*

There was a Jew, Yisroel Yitzkhok Stoler. He had a son who was scholar who studied Torah with me at the Rav's. There was Moishe, Dvoira Jerel's, a baker, who had two sons: one Refoel, a genius, and Moishe, also a great Torah scholar.

Many Serock Jews raised their children as workers. Every ordinary Jew kept his children in religious school for young children (*kheder*) then in higher learning (*Talmud Torah*), and after that they started learning a trade. Many had children who were Torah scholars. It's important to remember one particular Jew who lived in the same court as my parents, may their memories be blessed. His name was Hersh Meier Kozak (his real name was Wineberg), he was a son of Yosel Kozak. He earned his living as a water porter on a wagon with two wheels and a big barrel hammered on, and a horse that no doubt other than Mondays and Thursdays (as was the tradition), also fasted on the other designated fast days. This Jew's earnings were at best, three rubles a week – this was the time when Poland was under Russia. His son – Avrohom Noson, learned with Yisroel Zelig Melamed, and Meier Kozak paid one ruble and 20 kopeks per week as fees, and whatever was left was used for living.

My mother, of blessed memory, came home one day, and cried bitterly, and when my father, of blessed memory, became frightened and asked: "What happened?" She answered with even more outcry, that she was in the courtyard and overheard Aunt Bina say to her husband that he should go wash his hands and go eat, and then she excused herself that she had only one small piece of bread, but had a few potatoes in the house, and she had prepared it with a little fried onions (for flavor). So the husband asks her whether Avrohom Noson had already eaten. No, she said, because he's not yet home from school. He answered that she should give him (the husband) only two potatoes and leave the rest for their son Avrohom Noson because he needs energy to study.

At this point, she burst into another cry and said to my father: "This is the kind of poverty we have here in this court and we know nothing. What's the good of us sitting and learning if this can happen right next door in the same court!"

Their son, Arohom Noson, actually did become a Talmudic scholar. In 1910 he was called up to military service. He left for London and became a "machine man," that is somewhat of a tailor. Avrohom Noson, in his 53 years in London, never yet missed a day without studying a page of *gemara* (Talmud), or of praying with the quorum, and remained truly a pious Jew.

*[Page 120]*

# Teachers

All the teachers were Torah Jews, even the teachers of young children. These teachers of young children were Avrohom Leib and Yehoshua Merle, who taught how to pray, to read, and the beginnings of *khumash* (Torah studies). For the older children, who were already studying *khumash* and the commentary *Rashi*, and a page of Talmud without commentaries, there were the teachers Khaim Yoine, Yosef Shmijes, Dovid Itziks, and Efraim Sandler, of blessed memory.

The most prominent teachers were Yisroel Zelig, Yosef Mendels, Yakov Hirsh, and so on. Their style was that of a *yeshiva*: Yosef Mendels taught limitless amounts of Talmud with commentaries every two weeks. Once a boy completed Yosef Mendels' *heder*, he continued with Yisroel Zelig or Yakov Hirsh. There, the boys would learn in greater detail with all the commentaries. The boys would study in these classes until age 14 or 15.

After that, when the boys could study Talmud independently, along with all the commentaries (*tosefos and poskim*), they would go into the Ger *shtiebel* and study with the other boys and young men.

## Translator's Footnotes

1. A Magid is a traditional Jewish religious "itinerant preacher," a talented and skilled narrator of Torah and religious stories.

2. A prayer shawl (talis) is generally worn only for morning prayers.

3. A Rebbe's tish (table) is a mass gathering of the Rebbe's followers, where food, lengthy Torah discourses, singing, and dancing take place at a large table. These events normally take place on Sabbaths, festivals, or commemorative days, and can last many hours, long into the night.

4. Before eating bread, one washes the hands and recites certain blessings, with the intention of having the meal in one place. If one is to leave the place where he has eaten, when washing for bread he needs "to have in mind" that he will recite the blessings after the meal in another place.

5. That was the time when a Rebbe would prepare himself mentally and spiritually to be able to pray unhindered for his congregation (and Jews everywhere) for the New Year.

6. These are foods from which the Rebbe has eaten, which were distributed to those present. It was considered a great honor to partake of these foods, as they had been originally served to and touched by the Rebbe himself.

7. *Nusakh Ashkenaz* -- this is a style of religious service conducted by Ashkenazi Jews originating from Central and Western Europe.

8. *Nusakh Sefard* -- the name for one of the various forms of the Jewish prayer book that merged Ashkenazi customs with kabbalistic customs and content; this "style" of prayer is commonly used among khasidim.

[Page 123]

# Community Life

## Community Life
**by Chaim Kopetch (Buenos Aires)**
**Translated by Pamela Russ**

On the right bank of the river, where the Bug and the Narew meet and pour into the Wis³oka (Vistula) River, all of them merge and empty into the Baltic Sea. There, on the high, mountainous shore, was spread out our little town of Serock – short houses, rarely with two levels, and with a four-cornered market. From each corner, in every direction, there were inhabited and uninhabited little streets, and a highway with little houses and shops on either side that come from somewhere and go off into somewhere... As you enter the town, there is a non-Jewish cemetery, and as you leave the town there is a Jewish cemetery. Depends from which direction you arrive. So, in the area of the water, there are cemeteries, broad, plowed fields, and blooming orchards, where for generations Jews and non-Jews have lived and died.

A long, long time ago, before the time of highways and trains, the old folks used to say that our little town played an important role in the communications for the country. It was a common transit point for boats, ships, and rafts that came through the Bug and Narew rivers with lumber, wheat, and many other types of materials for the European markets. This was their last stop before going onto the Vistula and then moving directly into Danzig. Here, the materials were examined and inventoried, rated and measured, sold and resold, calculated for profits and losses. Because of this, there were always guests in our town: merchants, brokers, measurers, appraisers, and experts.

This was a long time ago, a long time ago. The 20th century found our town fallen – a shrunken place, a poor place, with an impression of no today and no tomorrow. The stormy and angry events of wars, pogroms, strikes, and revolutions, were also riled up in the still-standing and half-asleep state of life in the town's settlement.

[Page 124]

For those of us who were children in those times, there remain undefined and unclear memories of the events and happenings of the things we lived through, but at that time, they were beyond our strength to understand and withstand. Now, shreds and indistinct memories are coming up that were protected during those stormy times: the Russo-Japanese War, strikes, the Kishinev pogroms, Borukh Shulman's attempted assassination of the Warsaw governor. The songs about the events and heroes carried from the Warsaw courtyards to our town and were sung there. We also had our own heroes. Areh'le the revolutionary had to flee to America, then committed suicide for political reasons; a young woman poisoned herself; a pharmacist's son shot himself; and other incidents – some maybe of lesser importance, like personal arguments about *shokhtim* or just regular arguments.

The outbreak of World War One, with its horror and ……destruction, also did its portion in loosening the restraints that for years contained the hovering youth energy.

**From right to left:** Khaim Vaynkrantz, Khaim Kapetch, Yantshe Kuzhinski, Schmerl Aschenmill, Yakov Borenshtayn

[Page 125]

Some of the youths looked around in their new conditions, and saw that they were naked as Adam, without any preparation for daily life and its problems. So, they threw themselves into their books with all their youthful fire, and with everything they had, in order to find something that would give them substance as support and response to a lot of questions that life presented to them.

That's when the "Progress" library was born. A private library also existed before that distributed books as payback for bail. Mottel Tzukerman, a dry-goods merchant, who tried to improve his downtrodden lot and his earnings, thought of this idea for a livelihood. This library was only for use by select individuals, for the better class of youths who had better material opportunities and who were also under the influence of the nearby big city of Warsaw. But it did not reach the large masses of the youth.

The new library "Progress" was established as a community library, and early on sought out the reader who felt that it was "his" library with which he was a partner. Therefore, he sought her out to help her evolve. Hard to remember exactly when the library was established and all the names of the founders. It was probably in the beginning of 1915, and among the founders were: Schmerl Aschenmill, Esther Leah Schlyakhtus, Aron Korngold. I found the library behind the city, on the Warsaw highway, amongst the non-Jews (there were no Jews living there) in one room, with the requisite political books, a few chairs, and a table.

The youth met every Friday night and Shabbos during the day, sat around the table, read something from a book or sang all types of Yiddish songs that were timely then, sang it all with the crowd, with heart and feeling, and most importantly, with the fire of youth. The older generation struggled at home against the new way of the youth, against reading that which was "*treif*" (not kosher or acceptable), etc. One Friday night, it happened that a father came to the library and slapped his daughter for having the *chutzpa* to be sitting there and singing songs. This had the reverse effect on the youth, and with love they surrounded her and helped the library grow.

[Page 126]

The second period begins with the moving from the small room behind the city to the marketplace at Glovackin's into two rooms. The rooms were large – one was for the library and the other was a reading room. This gave the library more importance and helped spread the culture for the youth. The institution also began helping with the community kitchen that used to distribute lunches to the poor and hungry people and helped ration the American products that arrived. At approximately that time, there was an effort made to establish two Zionist organizations: for women it was called "*Bnos Tzion*" (daughters of Zion), headed by Esther Leah Schlyakhtus, her sister Krongold, and Dvoira Granyewicz; for the men it was called "*Kadimah*" (Forward!), with Aron Krongold, Tzvi Kleinman, and so on. Neither organization really had long life in the lives of the young masses. There was also an attempt to move the library "Progress" to the Party center, but that never really happened.

**Founders of the county newspaper "*Unzer Vort*"**

*[Page 127]*

The activities of the library were concentrated around distributing books to the homes, conducting discussions on timely themes, question / answer evenings, a drama circle, and they even tried to establish evening courses and other similar institutions. One of the other initiatives was to bring in writers for lectures. The first writer and speaker that was brought in was the well known staff writer of *Der Moment* newspaper, Hillel Zeitlin. Also, they elected to put up opposition to the circles for the very religious. But after Zeitlin's visit to the elderly Rav Yosef Levinshtayn, where they discussed Torah, the youth was appeased and things worked out well.

The second speaker that the library invited to speak was Yosef Heftman, also a staff member at *Der Moment* (under the pseudonym 'Emanuel'). His visit was also a great coup, both in terms of morale and materialism. And here I would like to tell a small anecdote: When we were saying our good-byes to him, we asked him, Heftman, to leave us with a valuable final word. After much back and forth, at the last minute, he said: "From today forward, let's write Serock with a '*yud*' (so that it would become 'Syerock'), that would give it the initials for:

סעראסק יוגנט עמאנציפירט רופט אלעמען צו קולטור

*Meaning: The Emancipated Youth of Serock Invites Everyone for Culture (Cultural Events)*

Our guest was escorted out with cheers, enthusiastically looking forward to future presentations.

There was a great event that happened in our town when our very first acting troupe presented from our own drama circle. This happened approximately at the end of the seventeenth year. From mid-summer, the drama group was already preparing and rehearsing to present an entire piece. When everything was already prepared, the most important things was still missing – an appropriate room (hall) for the performance. After a long search, the location of a government school became available during the days of Sukkos. The teacher there was Khaim Jurkewicz. The teacher's first warning was that he would leave the key on Erev Sukkos before leaving the building, when he would no longer have to fear an inspection. They had to remove the school chairs to put in a stage, put out benches for the audience, get decorations, a curtain, and other things that were relevant to the event.

Soon the whole activity was mobilized. Yakov Aryeh Stolyer……quickly brought boards from his warehouse, and his carpenters – familiar with this type of work – became busy right away. Opening was scheduled for *motzei yom tov*, at the end of Sukkos. And, even though all this was at the border where the Jews lived, the news that there was going to be a performance spread like a spark that falls on dry hay. On the second day of Sukkos during the services in the big *shul*, the usually quiet and elderly Rav asked Lozer Shamash to announce a ban on the theater. The troupe decided to send a delegation to the Rav requesting that he remove the ban.

[Page 128]

**ن memory of the election day gathering for the YFLB
The elected and the participants
…30th, 1929**

The select people in the delegation were: the author of the script and Schmerl Aschenmill. After much arguing with the Rav, he agreed to remove the ban in order that peace reign in the town, but only if he would be coerced to do so by government powers.

In the end, he sent Lozer Shamash, and during *Mincha* reneged on the ban. But Lozer Shamash prepared a new surprise for us. He went up to the podium and announced: He is making this announcement in the name of the Rav, that the ban should remain in effect, but because the Rav was forced to remove it, it will be removed. The fate for the performance was already sealed. The performance actually took place, but before a room of empty benches. The audience comprised mainly those who were involved in the theater.

[Page 129]

That's what it was like, and so it was with other happenings. That's how the young town lived its life and filled its time until November 1918 when the Austro-German army left occupied Poland and was replaced by the Polish independent rule.

In the month of November, when the new Polish rule began to take its first steps, a new chapter opened in the community life of the Jewish youth in the Polish towns. If until now the struggle was to bring in worldliness and culture into their own settings, a new front now opened with the establishment of an independent Poland: a fight for the rights of Jewish citizens to live and exist independently – culturally, economically, and politically.

The youth in our town was more or less prepared for the struggle at that time. It was the end of November, beginning December, when a general day of mourning was declared protesting the first pogrom that the newly organized Polish army had organized on their first entry into the city of Lemberg.

In just a few hours, the youth organized and mobilized themselves, preparing themselves for all types of eventualities. The big *shuls* and their arks were decorated with black and white crդpe paper that was brought in for this cause especially from Warsaw. In the entranceway to the *shul* from the street, there stood two big flags made of black and white crդpe, and the youth wore colored armbands on their sleeves and flowers in their lapels. The entranceway was guarded as were several surrounding streets. Other groups of youths went to different parts of the city saying that the Jews should shut down their businesses and gather at the central place in the *shul*, and some would stay in the streets to protect against the reactions from the Polish anti-Semitic population.

*[Page 130]*

**A Youth Group**

**Seated in the first row from right to left:** Yosef Faynboim, Gavriel Gal, Shlomo Ostrovski, Faivel Barab, Pyenik
**Second row:** Temeh Shtelang, Khave Shtelang
The picture and the frame are from Volf Gerwer, of blessed memory

Probably, the concentration of people, and the closing of the businesses in the middle of a Wednesday afternoon, along with the organized presence of the youth in the streets had the desired effect. The non-Jewish........ element, began to consider what was going on and went to the police. The unsettled police appeared in the streets, and soon reserve reinforcements arrived. There was also an attempt by the officials to frighten the storeowners into opening their shops and businesses, but the power of the youth and the general voice of protest that ruled the area quashed all attempts for counteractions. The day of protest actually passed calmly, but the youth left an incredible effect, and the "profit" of this should be calculated as part of the youth library, "Progress."

In those times, the "Progress" library, with her multi-faceted activities, were feeling tight in the two rooms they occupied at Glovacki's. The library also needed a room with a stage for the activities of the drama circle, where they would also be able to have elections and other events. They found such a place neighboring Vallash – an entire floor was rented. According to an agreement with the landlord, some walls were removed, and a large room with a stage was designed, another room for the library, and so on.

[Page 131]

With love and devotion, the committed boys and girls threw themselves into the work and gave all their free time to build furniture, paint the walls, wash, sweep, polish, and decorate their own place.

While painting the walls and the stage, the young shoemaker – Khaim Mintz -- came to the foreground as a talented painter and artist, and for the acting, Leibel Blumberg presented as a fine comedian with talented ideas. All of these have vanished into the past.

Meanwhile, the new standing Polish regime began to form its huge army to get Poland back to her glory that once was in Central Europe, and realize Pilsudski's wild mania to establish a Poland "from wherever possible, to wherever possible." The youth, aged 20-26, were drafted into the army. Even though this absorbed many young people, the activities of the library were not disturbed. First, when the Bolshevik army marched to the gates of Poland, the library was requisitioned as quarters for the military. The books were thrown into the streets as useless items and the furniture destroyed. Some of the young people came to the town and tried to save some of the things. At that time, Schmerl Aschenmill, Melekh Pyenik, Mottel Vyernik, and Yisroel Kohn were arrested and sent away to Dom-Pulaski, Krakow, where there was a concentration camp for political criminals. On top of that, other than Schmerl Aschenmill, no one had any connection – not even remotely – to community life in the town, not cultural nor political.

Two weeks later, when the Polish army took back our town, the writer of a series (then serving in the military in a town nearby) got himself home, and finding the destruction, went along with Baila Pyenik from house to house for two days, and wherever possible, collected funds in order to be able to reopen the library. But the police and administrative powers did not permit the library to open again.

[Page 132]

In February 1922, when I returned home from military service, I found a new Jewish institution had opened under the name "Professional Union for Unskilled Laborers," with the main office in Warsaw and was a product of the right-wing *Poalei-Zion* party (movement of Marxist Zionist workers). To us in the town, this name was lost, because this was one of the legitimate means of opening a youth library. The Professional Union was located on the highway near Baila Merker, and that was the central meeting place of the working youth – both for those that worked in town as tailors, shoemakers, spat makers, and carpenters, and for those that worked all week in Warsaw in all sorts of businesses and then came home for *Shabbos*.

In the town, the union was feeling a shortage, and thought it should consider those youth that were not working as well as those who were better off. A union of this sort was established at a meeting at the home of teacher Khaim Yurkewicz. This was the Zionist group "*Kadima*" wth Tzvi Kleinman as chairman. They used a room in the home of the fisherman Makhlewski on Radziminski Street, an area generally of only non-Jewish fishermen.

At that time, there were also activities of a particular division whose goal was the fight against extravagance (or overindulgent behaviors) amongst the youth. These activities received a vociferous reaction from the progressive circles of the youth, lots of arguing and fighting, and as a result of that, and for other economic reasons, a portion of these youths left for Argentina.

The activities of the youth, organized in the Professional Union, began to expand and deepen. Every week, there were literary discussions, question / answer evenings, literary debates, and conferences with lecturers from Warsaw. Because the residence that the union had became too small, a new place was rented on the Warsaw highway at Shmuelke Rosenberg's that was in a large place with two large rooms and a stage for small theaters and other activities.

[Page 133]

At that time, the Polish reactionaries began to gain strength and put greater pressure on the almost completely right-wing Jewish population, and placed the burden of the economic crisis on their poor, weak shoulders. This strengthened the yearning for emigration, particularly amongst the youth that had no opportunities or prospects to fulfill their aspirations. But the countries to which they would go were restricted, and the means to reach them – few.

The management of the Prof. Union made an agreement with the representatives of "ICA" in Warsaw (Jewish Colonization Association) that promised it would donate $15 to each person who wanted to go to Argentina, and would arrive there with their certification. Then began a greater emigration from our town to Argentina, with the discount and ship's boarding pass as the basis for the agreement to leave. Not everyone was able to settle into their new home, and some had to come back; but the majority stayed and planted the roots, forming the kernels of the Serocker Jewish community in Argentina.

The Prof. Union, that was in fact a youth's institution, occupied themselves primarily with cultural and social rights activities, and developed much importance amongst the entire population of the town.

The multi-faceted activities always extended the field of action. It was like that when the town separated from the registered municipality and received status as an independent city. They had to elect 24 councilmen, a mayor, aldermen, and magistrates. It was the Prof. Union that cemented the unity of the Jewish population. Since the membership comprised almost all of those younger than the voting age, and some even younger than that, but included those who had the right to be elected according to the election rules, it happened that the author of the series was elected councilman. Not having completed his full term, he was later discharged because he had meddled too much in the town's issues.

*[Page 134]*

The Prof. Union was not really professional in the exact sense...... of the word. For everyone it was the nerve center for the town's cultural life, and as such, was completely apolitical. The Union's infiltration into other disciplines of life belonged totally to the local character and was affected by the circumstances. Any type of person was able to be a member – anyone that wanted, regardless of orientation or direction. But the youth, a distinct number of the population that takes on and feels the current problems as their own, worked through these problems amongst each other. Their energy and vitality pushed these problems out, finding ways for a resolution. The youth also noticed the wrongdoings and injustices that she found en route in her life. So, the youth is reacting to everything and her voice can be heard everywhere; in fact, sometimes too hasty and irrational, but always truthful and committed. This youth, that experienced World War I, Poland's liberation and mania to become a superpower while suppressing her minorities, also had problems of its own regarding life-situations, and therefore became ready to take up the slogans that that era produced. That's how it happened, that internally, everything was dealt with in the youth institution that was relevant to that time. In that fashion, they had both support and opposition, but in general, they were a united body under the name of Professional Union of Unskilled Workers.

Because of that, it is no wonder that this happened on January 25, 1925, that was designated as the next election date for the Prof. Union – a day that vanished into eternity, just as the library. This is what happened: January 25 fell on a freezing Friday. On market day, two young members of the Prof. Union and the Communist Party (Hershel Mendzelewski and Simkha Esterowicz) were strolling around the market, touching the merchandise in the wagons (the merchandise was brought by the peasants). They bought nothing but certainly left something behind. In each wagon that they had touched, they left a propaganda leaflet from the Communist Party. They kept doing that until one peasant accused them and grabbed Mendzelewski's hand; Esterowicz managed to run away. The peasant handed Mendzelewski over to the police who spread out over the city to find the fugitive and anyone else who needed to be caught. When the police went into Yontshe Kuzhnicki's house, they found him in a minute, as he prepared to throw a package of papers into the fiery oven.

[Page 135]

The Friday and Shabbos after that, were two black, cloudy days in the community life of the city's youth.

The regular evening strolls, particularly on the Shabbos days, were completely paralyzed. If they did meet, the discussion was only about what was happening in the police stations, how they were holding the two arrested people, judged and severely punished. On Monday, the two arrested ones were taken to the prison in Pultusk. And the consequence was that the Prof. Union was shut down.

However, life didn't stop. The youth did not want to give in to the administration's will, and they took up their own struggle to forge their own path.

Soon, another permit was given to open a new institution under the name "Jewish People's Education League" that was administered under the deputyship of Noakh Prilutcki and his People's Party.

The cultural events were renewed with more zeal and diligence. A lodging was rented right in the center of the marketplace, and a library and reading room were once again established. Discussions were reopened, with literary lectures and guest speakers from Warsaw. Get-togethers on Shabbos and Yom Tov days in a warm and homey atmosphere became a set thing in the city, and almost an obligation for every young person.

At that time, there was also the establishment of a wind orchestra under the direction of the shoemaker Hershel Borenshtayn (Shustak), who, in the Czar's times, played in the people's orchestra. He probably had his skill, got the orchestra on its feet, and they blew and jingled not too badly. It goes without say that the initiative for this came from the People's Education League. And in general, the activities of the wind orchestra bore fruit and gave a glow and life to the youth element in the town.

[Page 136]

There were also other initiatives, both before and after, but they left little influence and had a brief life. That's how it was with the "Shomer Hatzair" (a Socialist Zionist Youth [Guard] movement), that was established and directed by the "guard" Leonke Goldman. The same thing happened with the football club that even went to play a match with the Wyszkower football team. But none of these teams took root. One of the main reasons for this was the emigration of the youth.

For many years, there was a dream of an organized youth unit for the cultural activities for their own, their near ones, the town's youth – a unit that would understand the town's youth, to show and help them deepen their acquired knowledge. A sort of division and strangeness opened towards those who used to come from Warsaw, the large city, and plead for a "culture" donation in a rehearsed speech. They were hungry for intimacy and warmth between teacher and student, lecturer, and audience. This very concept, along with its provincialism andnaivete, was at that particular moment ripe for its time and acquired more supporters also among some of the Pultusker youth, amongst whom was the poet Simkha Dan, some of the teachers of the schools, and other authorities such as the director of the Polish-Jewish Gymnasium, Dr. Lipman. It was decided to try to assemble the representatives of the institutions that had libraries and partake in cultural events without a distinct direction, but [to join with those] whose problems were basically the same. They tried to create a united committee.

From there, they sent out invitations to all the institutions in Pultusk. Serock, Nasielsk, Wyszkow, Rozan, and Krasnosielc. That means, from the Pultusker to the Makowier counties. The only response came from the Leftists of the *Poalei Tzion* in Pultusk, Serock, and the YFBL *(yiddisher folks bildung liege)* of Nasielsk, the Bundist library in Krasnosielc, and the other library there; Makow took a wait-and-see position and said they would send observers; and Wyszkow and Rozan didn't respond at all.

[Page 137]

At the end of the winter of 1926, the meeting took place in Pultusk, and lasted for a Shabbos and a Sunday. Right from the start, the meeting didn't go smoothly, and the first obstacle already met with failure. This is what happened: In order to receive a permit, the police required a list of the participants. On that list was the name of the writer of the series and Yosef Feynboim. They were both classified as staunch Communists. The conference did receive the permit, but the political representative of the police, a former spy, came to the meetings in "all his glory," to take notes for himself. The identified Pultuskers and their organizers, when they saw the great "honor" that was bestowed upon them with the presence of such a distinguished "personality," wanted to withdraw unnoticed. It took a lot of energy to hold them back, but the program had to be changed. Not all the speakers were now willing to speak. And, after all that, what resulted was that a committee to publish a local newspaper would be set up for cultural issues that would be the forerunner for a larger conference.

The first issue of the newspaper was issued under the name "*Unzer Vort*," in which the Serocker participated with materials and administration. The newspaper did not have much funding to succeed, and all the plans ran dry.

From Wronki, where Yonche Kuzhnicki and Hershel Mendzelewski were sent for two and a half years, sad news began to arrive. After experiencing much hunger, Mendzelewski became terribly weakened, and one evening had a stroke that went on all night without any medical attention. His friends in the cell saved him from certain death. It became urgent to mobilize anyone who was able to do anything in order to remove him from there and rush him into freedom [and help]. After many and persistent interventions from the appropriate legal rights organizations for appeals, and visiting important personalities and the head prosecutor Kyernik, the sentence was put on hold for one year. After one year, he was imprisoned again, in the Mokotower prison (in the hospital unit).

Meanwhile, one of our healthiest and most talented friends became sick, Volf Gerwer, secretary of the YFBL, no one could have imagined Gerwer as ever being sick. It soon became urgent to operate on him. He was operated on twice in the Jewish hospital. The second operation did not help him. He died, as far as I know, on September 27, 1927 (Rosh Hashana). I immediately notified our friends by telephone, and everyone gathered at the YFBL, had a meeting, conferred, and decided to go to Warsaw and give our friend his last respects.

[Page 138]

After long negotiations with the administration of the undertakers in the Jewish division, with the active intervention of the *gabbai* of the synagogue Leo Finkelshtayn, we managed to get a burial plot in the cemetery in Warsaw. Because of that, the funeral took place late at night, and even here, the escorts of the deceased showed piety and love. A few neighborhoods before the cemetery, the casket was removed from the wagon, and in rows, they carried him, with a group at the head, heading into the cemetery. The burial took place late, by the light of lanterns.

April 27, 1928, a second loss upset the town. On that day, the town's active youth escorted the activist and role model Yonche Kuzhnicki to his final resting place. Up until the final minute of his tragic life, he actively maintained his position; always ready to help, although everyone knew from before that his lot was set because of his illness; nonetheless, his death unsettled everyone and they found it difficult. He, too, was escorted by the youth with great respect, as he warranted. Both of these men were given appropriate tombstones. Notwithstanding these terrible losses, the community's cultural life in the town did not cease.

[Page 139]

# The Economy Life
## (Work and Rest in the Town)
### Moshe Kanarek (Azur, [Israel])

**Translated by Pamela Russ**

How did the Jews occupy themselves in Serock, and from what did they eke out some earnings?

### The Carriers

Why was it necessarily they, the elderly Jews, who had to labor in this type of work? In general, no one complained about any type of work. The carriers worked very hard, in order to sustain their families. They carried heavy bolts of material on their shoulders, and dried themselves from sweat with their already wet scarf. When they worked in the streets, they wore torn clothing: an old jacket, a pair of torn trousers, old worn-out boots, and even the hat on his head was half torn, because while carrying the sack of wheat on his shoulders, the body was hunched over, and the burden rested on his head and tore his hat. They used to work in the streets, in the cold, rain, and heat – dirty, harried, and always tired. After unloading a shipment of flour, their clothing used to be white as snow – or black, after unloading a shipment of coal. And yet, the carriers were happy that they had work, did not have many demands in life, were happy with the daily work whenever they had that, although that was not always, because there were also critical times because of unemployment.

### Shoemakers

In this profession, in Serock, scores of Jews occupied themselves. The shoemakers divided themselves into several groups, according to their quality. There were shoemakers who occupied themselves only with fixing......old shoes, because they were unable to make new shoes. Also, the majority of their fathers, by whom they learned the trade, were also unable to make new shoes. Often, the work had to be done on time because there wasn't a second pair of shoes with which to change.

[Page 140]

As soon as one entered the shoemaker's place, on the side of the window was a small, low table with the necessary work tools. Around the table – a few old wooden forms; near the table was a shoemaker's bench with three legs, and on the seat were a few rags. This was the "earnings" corner. On the other side of the room – a stove with four flames for cooking, a table, three or more beds, an old bureau and old fashioned pictures, mainly of deceased parents or other relatives.

Life looked different for the shoemakers who were "professionals" (experts). They lived in better conditions, worked with their own materials, made new shoes, and earned a better living. The work place was already in a separate area, in somewhat of an alcove. A small kitchen – and from the kitchen, a door to a more or less furnished room. The workplace itself looked like a small shop.

There were also Jews who had shoe stores.

## Tailors

The needle trade in Serock held a respected position. A large portion of Jews took on the profession of tailoring. The tailor of the cheaper materials had to work very hard until he completed his daily earnings. They used to work 15 to 16 hours per day. Their work consisted only of stitching on the machine. They also didn't live in the best of means. The home based tailors who did better quality manufacturing, also worked hard. There were also "made to order" tailors, who worked according to specific measurements. With the made to measure work, there was a lot to iron. The apprentice became very upset many times before he was allowed even to heat up the iron, and the presser also sweated plenty while ironing collars and lapels from the overcoats or jackets. In tailoring the wife or grown child were also able to help (with sewing) by putting protections on seams and taking out the basting (stitches), etc.

[Page 141]

## Fruit Traders (Lessees of Fruit Orchards)

There were Jews who rented orchards from non-Jews while the fruit was being taken down and their contracts ended. At the beginning of the summer, these lessees used to drive out to the villages with their families to the rented orchards, and spend the entire summer there. Often, they would stay over until after Rosh Hashanah and Yom Kippur. These fruit traders would borrow a Torah scroll, hire someone to lead the prayers, and have a quorum on the spot. The work in the orchard supported the entire family. When the fruit began to ripen, they had to protect it from thieves or ordinary harm from those who threw stones at the trees. The children used to gather the fallen apples and pears (called "spuds").

Ripe fruit were taken off the trees, packed in boxes with straw, and put into a cellar for the winter. It's understood that even during the winter there had to be some control over the fruit, to make sure there were no rotten ones. Before Passover, the fruit traders took their merchandise to Warsaw, and after their sales, made a total calculation.

## Carpenters

The Serocker carpenters made beautiful furniture. For example, Yosl Mendzelevski (Mendzelewski) made beautiful furniture and sent it to Warsaw. There were also construction carpenters who built windows and doors for houses. They often also used to take on work in the village.

## Blacksmiths (Smiths)

They did ironworks on wagons, putting tires on the wheels, and blacksmithing for the horses. The season for blacksmithing for the horses was winter when the roads were slippery. The blacksmiths were big men with strong muscles from using heavy hammers to forge the iron. I remember even today the clang of the hammer on the anvil as I was going to school, and the boys used to run and look into the smithy of Reb Abba Leib Koval.

[Page 142]

## Butchers

Most of the butchers had wagons with horses. They would ride to the fairs to buy animals (cattle), slaughter them, clean them (according to the laws of kashrut), de-bone them, cut, chop, and sell the meat. It was difficult and unclean work. One had also to rise up early in the morning, be en route carrying a side of meat on his back.

## Grain Merchants

They would go the market and buy up the wheat, corn, oats, barley, and later sell them with set earnings.

## Village Travelers and Store Owners

These Jews used to travel to the surrounding villages buying all kinds of things from the non-Jewish residents, and from that they earned a living. There were small groceries, or other small stores. Many Jews had manufacturing places. The earnings from manufacturing were not too bad, because the non-Jewish villagers provided lots of business. There were stores of iron, lumber warehouses, and so on. Two large mills were also Jewish owned.

## Shabbos (Sabbath) and Yom Tov (Holidays)

After the hard bustle of the whole week, the restfulness of Shabbos came to the town. Friday afternoon, everything would become quiet. The street prepared itself for Shabbos. Soon, Reb Lazar the beadle, may his memory be blessed, would go into the street, and belt out his beautiful melody that still rings in my ears, and say, "Jews, it's time to light the candles." When it was only beginning to get dark, the Jews would go to the synagogue to pray – each one, beautiful, clean, dressed well – Jewish hats, long coats, with the feel of Shabbos and Yom Tov.

[Page 143]

In Poland there were Jews, famous for being persecuted, but they kept up the traditions nonetheless.

The traditions in Serock – as in all other Jewish settlements in Poland – were strictly followed, starting with making the dishes kosher, getting rid of all the leavened food for Passover, conducting a beautiful seder, buying greenery for the holiday of Shavuot in order to beautify the house, baking cheese cakes, and generally following all the holidays throughout the year. Particularly memorable is Yom Kippur, the mood in the house before Kol Nidre [prayer for Yom Kippur evening], when our parents would bless us and wish that we have only good health and that nothing bad befall us. The big synagogue is filled with congregants, hundreds of candles are lit, and a holy silence reigns.

## The Zionist Youth in Serock

In Serock, there was a well developed youth. In conjunction with the fact that in Poland great anti-Semitism ruled, some of us saw that in Poland there was no great future. The goal for a great number of youth in Poland was (to move to) the Land of Israel. The Zionist organizations had a great effect. In Serock, there was a center (nest) for the Beitar movement, which totaled about

200 youths. The director of the center was Avraham Shpilke (Spilka). He was a young man, soaked in Torah and wisdom. There was also Shomer Hatzair, with a fine group of youth. Hashomer Haleumi, an organization of religious youth, and Hekhalutz Hamizrakhi.

The youth would come to these organizations and there would immerse themselves in the Yiddish-Zionist ideology. There were meetings, readings, discussions. They learned about Jewish and Zionist history.

There were several youths who left their homes, and went on "Hakhshara," a preparation for a certain type of people to do farm work. After two years of Hakhshara, this youth was ready for Aliyah [moving, Heb. "rising up"] to the Land of Israel. There was a certain number of certificates distributed. There were also youths from Serock who left to Israel.

Each organization had a library where one received books to read, and a wall-newspaper where one could write articles. The youth in Serock knew that he was part of a large camp that should and must bring an end to the exile.

[Page 144]

On Lag b'Omer [holiday marking 33rd day from second day of Passover], there was a tradition that all the youth in the city went on an excursion a few kilometers outside the city. At 5 a.m., they all assembled in a large place, dressed in their uniforms, and each bearing the flag of their own organization. Each group had its own flag. Nicely and appropriately dressed, we stood at the head, with a Jewish orchestra and with song, and we left for the entire day. When we arrived at the place, we set up camp, and spent the entire day with games and contests.

What an exceptional impression it made when approximately 1000 youths arrived back in the town. Really, like an army. People and uniforms. With song, everyone marched proudly in rhythmic step. Each one of us felt like a fighter for our own home.

In Serock, there was also a football team and orchestra. We learned to swim, took part in many sport activities, etc. There was also a drama circle that produced many different plays, with the direction of Avrohom Yezumbeck, Sabina Tik, Aharon Tz'esner (Czesner), etc.

## A Stroll Through the Serocker Marketplace and the Surrounding Area

At the beginning of the marketplace, (there was) a yard with a few families. Hillel Katzav, Tuvia Barnshtayn (Barnstein), Avrohom Vellner, Yisroel Barnshtayn (Barnstein). More: Khatzkel Mendzelevski and his family, Yaakov Aryeh Temess, Khaim Rosenberg, and Itche Meir the Mohel (circumciser). At the end, Brakha Malka's daughter had a grocer. Opposite that was the family Novogrodski (the kasha maker), the Pupaver baker Hershel Grossman, the spats stitcher and the leader of the prayers. At the other end, there was the family Leviner, Baila Shmeunz with her good shutters, Brakha Malka and her crockery store, Menakhem Kronenberg, a fine Jewish man and his family, Itche Meir Solyarzh, Yankel Yonish, Meir Pshikorski (the tinsmith), Borukh Yosef and his dairy store, and the family Shpilke. At the edge near the main road, the grocery of Leviner, in the basement Kalina's bakery, and a storehouse for wood. Opposite that, was the family Kaluski, the family Varshavski (Warszawski), past the bakery was Veinshtok (Weinstock), the poor barber. There was a monopoly, a liquor store, that was in Jewish hands, with family Kuperboim. Farther at the end was the coal warehouse of a religious family, Yaakov Dovid Millshtayn (Millstein). His son, Yehuda Millshtayn (Millstein), with his partisan history (is now in Israel). On "the other side," as it was called, was the large mill of Moshe Rosenberg, the cabinets of Khana Margolis, and near them the Faskovitzes (Faskowiczs). At the end of that, on the other side, lived my grandmother, Khaim Kiva's Esther Rokhel, with the grandchildren Shmuel Shimon Shifman, and his sister Khana Yitl.

[Page 145]

On the second side, beyond the non-Jewish cemetery, was the beautiful house of the Granyevitzes (Graniewiczs). Farther down, the new house, that Hoffman built, and Vishnyevitz's (Wisniewcz's) butcher shop. At the end, was a soda shop. I remember from there Khavale, the cousin of Pinyevski (Pniewski), and the rats, the parents of Yosef Pinyevski (Masha was my sister's friend), and Yankel Stelmakh's family with the name Konkol. Farther, the familiar yard of Yankel Rosenberg. It was homey there. That was the location of the Hashomer Hatzair and Hashomer HaLeumi organizations. The shoe and tailoring store of Itche Shvartz (Schwartz). The businesses: Leibel Liss, Yaakov Zlotogorski, Moshe and Pesakh Shneider, Shimon Mendzelevski, Yosl the cabinetmaker, Khaim Mintz. In the market: Yaakov Aryeh the cabinetmaker, Roiza the laundress, Rabbi Morgenshtern (Morgenstern), Motl the butcher and his sons, and Faige's Mala Baila. Jewish fishermen lived by the Narov (Narew) River: the Kanareks, Khaim the fisherman, Alter the fisherman, Yankel the fisherman, Hershel the fisherman, Yekhiel the fisherman. There also lived a family Khaim Melnik, and Baila Leah Linker.

[Page 146]

## Serock City of My Youth
**Aharon Czesner/Tz'esner (Haifa)**
**Translated by Sara Mages**

A typical Jewish town located in the heart of Poland where Jews lived for many generations. Most of the Jews were Hassidim and men of action who loved the "Jewish community" and devoted their hearts and souls to the Torah and tradition. Among them were scholars who studied the Torah day and night, and were ready at all times to give their lives on the sanctification of God's name.

There were few affluent rich Jews. The Jews of the middle class were engaged, as in most of the towns in Poland, in lumber, grain and livestock trading. Many were shopkeepers and craftsmen who worked between twelve to fourteen hours a day to find bread and clothing for their families. The rest were the poor whose livelihood came from the "fair" – the regular weekly market day. There were quite a few craftsmen who didn't have the means to build a workshop to support their family members – they wandered around the villages with their few tools every day of the week, and return on Friday afternoon to bring the meager income needed to support their families. They were called "village peddlers." There were also two mechanical flour mills – one belonged to R' Moshe Rosenberg and the other to my father-in-law, R' Brill Itzcowicz, May they rest in peace. They employed many Jews and supported them with dignity.

The city of Serock is located between the Polish capital Warsaw and the district city of Putusk[3] besides to two beautiful rivers, the Narew and the Bug. The city's residents were proud of the beautiful landscapes and the rivers, and pointed to the "water line" which passed in the middle and separates the two rivers that united not far from the city, as if each one keeps its own independence. They saw it as the symbol of both nations – the Jews and the Poles – who lived together in the city of Serock, keeping their own independence and culture. The wooded green hills that adorned the city infused a special charm and served as a place for trips and recreation for the Jewish youth who wer healthy and developed in body and spirit, and like all teenagers - was inclined to romance.

Over the years, the influence of city of Warsaw increased. The Polish government wanted to spread its culture among the national minorities, and accelerate their assimilation within the Polish people.

The children and youth who studied in the Polish schools, and the adults who read Polish newspapers and books, knew, of course, about the Polish national heroes, its kings, poets and authors – but the heroes of ancient Israel and Jewish figures from the national revival period were strangers to them. They didn't know about Herzl the founder of Political Zionism, and didn't hear about Ahad Ha'am [Asher Zvi Hirsch Ginsberg]. They didn't see the "Auto-Emancipation" of Leon [Yehudah Leib] Pinsker, and didn't read the poems of Bialik and Tchernichovsky - also Brenner and Borochov were strangers to most of the youth and adults.

[Page 147]

But, there was a core of *"Hahalutz Hale'umi"* [national pioneers] in the city who didn't come to terms with the current situation - he knew that this wasn't the way and was anxious for the fate of the Jewish youth and the future of Jewish children.

Meanwhile, the ground began to "burn" right under our feet. The Polish anti-Semitism, which was passive during the first years of Poland's revival and was mostly satisfied with the distribution of newspaper articles and books – became aggressive and endangered the lives of the Jews, their economy and spirit. Over time, stores and workshops were founded by anti-Semitic Poles who placed gangs of hooligans at the entrances of Jewish shops and workshops. They incited them by force and deprived them of their livelihood. Matters reached came to attacks on Jews in public gardens, in the universities, and also on Jewish children who were studying in the state's elementary and high schools. We, the youth group of *"Hahalutz Hale'umi"* aspired to bring the Jewish children and precious youth closer to the source of our origin, to instill in them a national pride, to teach them the values of Jewish culture and saved them from assimilation and idleness in the presence of the arrogant Poles. We aspired to educate the Jewish youth in the spirit of national revival, train them for immigration to Israel and for productive life in the Diaspora and in Israel. In meetings and gatherings, at parties and conversations with individuals, we managed to conquer a large portion of our good youth. We planted in them a belief in their future in Israel, the aspiration for Israel, and we wanted them to walk straight and not to be afraid from the anti-Semites and the hooligans.

**A group of Zionist activities**
**From right to left:**
**Standing:** Yehiel Jonisz, Aharon Paskowicz, Yehiel Meir Warszawski-Weridman, Yehoshua David Bobek
**Sitting:** Bluma Rosenberg-Markus, Chaya Jonisz-Godes, Dr. Chaim Inwentarz, Chana Feinbaum-Paskoricz, the visitor Dr. Lipman, Bila Buber.
**Sitting:** Sara Wolinski, Leah Warszawski, Tova Wierniky

*[Page 148]*

Members of "Hanoar Hatzioni" [Zionist Youth] excited the hearts and devoted themselves to "Keren HaKayemet LeYisrael" [The National Fund], "Keren Hayesod" [United Israel Appeal], "Hakhshara" [pioneer training] kibbutzim, and the distribution of Jewish culture among the assimilated. Unfortunately, many of them perished during the days of the Holocaust and didn't realize their aspirations. And these are some of my dear friends whose memory will always stay with me. I will always see them alive before my eyes each time I think about them - and it is impossible not to think about them – and they are: Avraham Rosenberg, Aharon Paskowicz, Yehezkel Friedman, Simcha Friedman, Meir Muszkatenblit, Leah Warszawska, Henia Rosenberg, the other young women who collaborated with us, and the dear gentle souls who were plucked at the prime of their lives: Regina Rosenberg, Mania Barab, Regina Kuperbaum, Ester Kuperbaum, Nechama Katz – the fine group which was affectionately called - the "package"; and, May they live long: Genya Lewiner and my wife Rachel Itzcowicz who were rewarded to fulfill their dream and aspiration. They immigrated to Israel to build and be built.

I'm happy when I see the activists from our association who were rewarded to fulfill their oath and realize the dream of their youth in our country, and they are- the brothers Hanoch and Yehiel Meir Warszawski. Hanoch (who changed his surname to Vardi), enlisted in the "Haganah" and the Jewish Brigade to rescue the survivors and avenge our enemies. Yehiel Meir (who changed his surname to Vardimon), a cultural Zionist since his youth who was rewarded to realize his pioneering aspiration and settled as a farmer in Kfar Vitkin. I will also mention our friend Eliezer Hasman, a veteran Zionist who underwent pioneer training, immigrated to Israel and was rewarded to establish a family there and live the life of toil and respect.

**The Zionist Youth Flower Day for "*Keren HaKayemet LeYisrael*"**

**From right to left:** Bracha Pienik, Rivka Kuligowski, Eliezer Erenbaum, Rivka Rosenberg, Yisrael Pienik, Hana Charmilaz, Shmuel-Shalom Borenstein, Yente Szpilka.
**Sitting:** Yosef Tykolski, Yehiel Meir Warszawski-Vardimon, Yitzchak Friedman.
**Sitting:** Meir Kronenberg, Yosef Sterdiner

[Page 149]

Many of the youth that followed us went to *"Hakhshara"* kibbutzim, and didn't submit to their wealthy parents who urged them to emigrate to America and Australia. They immigrated to Israel, joined the camp of builders and fighters and together with thousands others, who were loyal to the ideology of their youth, laid the foundations for Israel's independence and the State of Israel. I see before my eyes the emotional sights when we accompanied our friends who immigrated to Israel. The warm hand shakes, the eyes shining from tears, and the stormy Hora [Israeli folk dance] in our city's train station. And I will never forget our beloved friends who stayed behind and weren't rewarded to realize their aspiration and dream. Their names will be remembered for eternity!

I was in Serock for eight years during my beautiful and vibrant youth. I was influenced by the city's beautiful scenery and the splendor of its nature. I convinced my girlfriend to leave her rich parents - the home of Brill Itzcowicz – who was respected by the people. She followed me and joined the circle of activists, at first she became a pioneer and then my wife. We immigrated together to Israel and built our home at the foot of Mount Carmel.

I'm asking for forgiveness from my friends that I didn't mention because of lack of space.

With sacred emotion I bring up the memory of my wife's family: the father Brill Itzcowicz, the mother Biltza, May they rest in peace; my wife's brother, Meir, a member of *"Hanoar Hatzioni"* who stubbornly refused to obey the Germans and didn't want to be a Kapo and beat the workers. He suffered severe beatings but stood the test of a martyr. When he was transferred in a closed railway car along with thousands of other tortured Jews, he jumped off the moving train and was shot and killed. The uncle Moshe Silberstein, his wife Shifra, and their only daughter Alti'le who were killed by the hands of impure villains. May their memory be blessed!

[Page 150]

## Memories of Our Childhood Years
**Sh. Rozental (Tel Aviv)**
**Translated by Pamela Russ**

It was in the 1920s. I remember the day well, it was a Friday. The door was thrown open and Dube'le, our neighbor, stood there wringing her hands and called out to my mother: "Dvoire, my crown! Dvoire, my life! The town is burning! It's a fire, a terrible tragedy has befallen us!" Motel the *shamash* arrived from the marketplace, exhausted, carrying the fish in his red kerchief. In his hoarse voice, he hurriedly told us the entire story, saying that some young *shkutzim* (non-Jewish troublemakers): the oil maker's son, the grain merchant's son, and another lunatic, decided to throw *treife* (non-kosher) leaflets into the wagons in the marketplace. The police noticed this going on, and with their whips, they invited all those troublemakers to really partake in this spectacle. The entire road of the marketplace and the surrounding area was covered with blood. The oil maker's son suffered most – the tall foreman packed him into his garret, both of his hands loaded with the "golden material".

After the neighbor left our house, I asked my mother what had happened. I received the answer that one cannot run away from *kheder* (school) and whoever does so will be caught by the police. That summer my mother brought me to the *kheder*, to Avrohom Leyb the teacher. The Rebbe sat me at a long table where two rows of boys were seated. A wooden stick stood in one corner where the Rebbe would "send" those who committed a misdemeanor, after twisting their ears. Every day, the Rebbetzen Tchortel (the Rebbe's wife) would put a bowl of hot water onto the Rebbe's table, and then bring thin, old pieces of bread. The Rebbe ate and learned with us. Every Friday we would be free after learning for half a day.

Once my mother gave me a small, white sack and asked me to take it to my father at the mill. There I saw what looked like a circus of wagons, going in and going out, weighing, and pouring out grains. The first one to notice me there was the boss himself, Moishe Rozenberg. He looked at me quickly with two kind eyes, and called out: "Eliyahu Aron! Your son is here!" My father had no time for me, so Moishe Rozenberg came over to me, pinched my cheek, asked me about my *kheder*, took me by the hand, and led me into the mill. I came back to my mother with great effort, all sweaty and white from the scattered flour because the sack was old and weak. That's how every Friday I was a comfortable visitor to Moishe Rozenberg's mill. The boss's wife would be upset with her youngest son Khono (today in Israel) because he didn't want to go to *kheder,* and because he was covered in tar from bathing in the water vapor near the mill. And here comes Khono'le with a piece of dry, rye bread in his mouth. My father would always mention this to us at home and complain that he is a bigger spender [was more generous] than his boss. We were careful with our monies all the years, but not for ourselves. Some fine people already sensed this, came to my father "by chance" with a serious face, did some sort of business from which my father always came away a "shaved one,"and with that he was even well beaten up. That reckoning day, for which my father was always afraid, and he wondered how he would ever be free of his boss, finally came. One frosty Shabbos at dawn in the year 1926 the mill burned down, and with the smoke his job disappeared as well.


[Page 151]

I came to the *kheder* to Yehuda Leyb the teacher. His wife and my father were sister and brother. I did not have any special privileges with my uncle. Not only once did I receive a smack. But I did have a little bit of good fortune in that my father did test me on the portion of the *khumash* (*sedra*) only once a week – Thursday afternoons. I had to review well until that time. My uncle Yehuda Leyb, of blessed memory, was a *kohein*. He had a sharp eye, saw everything, and woe to the one that tried to whisper or help out his friend. My current Rebbe always suffered from heartburn. Summers and winters he would drink soda and eat farina with milk. Whichever of the students would make trouble, would receive – other than smacks – also a load of curses with rich, but soft whippings. This didn't mean that he wasn't beloved by the whole family and everyone was proud of his fables and stories. Because of her small stature, my aunt was called Sheine Rukhe'le

She would never sleep, but would nap sitting up, as a hen *lehavdil* (to differentiate) at night. At night she would strip the tallow and make soap from it, and then late at night she would go by wagon to the neighboring towns to sell it.

[Page 152]

With my other uncle, Dovid Berl, my mother's brother, we were not as friendly because of his wife, Aunt Miriam, who was very stern. Whatever she said, you had to agree, otherwise she would become angry. She had a nature to give examples and descriptions: "this thing," and "that thing" – words from the intelligent one. In the family she had the name "Santa Maria." My father's brother, Dovid Berl, was the opposite of my father, he was a man strongly in this world. He trimmed his beard into a Van Dyke, and his clothes shone on him. His black patent leather boots lit up the cobblestones, and he had a majestic walk, with an adorned stick in his hand. In this house, no one would dishonor the father's chair (by sitting on it), and every *Shabbos* or *Yom Tov* after the meal, it would be very quiet because the father was sleeping. My uncles prayed with my father in the same place, the *Mizrachi shtiebel*, in Yekel Rozenberg's house, where his partner Yekhiel Rozenberg set the tone. Yekhiel Rozenberg, temperamental by nature, loved festive occasions, feasts with many people. He loved when the community celebrated on an ordinary *Shabbos*, let alone on a *Yom Tov*. For Hershel Grossman the spat maker's reciting the prayer of "*omar rab elozor*" or an "*ovinu malkeinu*" he would pledge a keg of beer, a *shtof* (one tenth of a vedro [A Russian liquid measure, equal to 3.249 gallons of a U.S. standard measure]) of whiskey or wine, and others would follow his example but in a lesser manner. The tall Tzalke was the waiter and brought beer, wine, and so on. The *gabbai* Khaim Hersh, the painter, was always in a good mood. There were plenty of *baalei tefilos* (those who led the prayers): Alter the grain producer, Yehoshua Hofman the glazier, and my father Dovid Berl, who prayed loudly in the Sirota style [Gershon Sirota was a famous cantor in Europe, 1874-1943]. My uncle Yehuda Leyb was responsible for the "*Linat Hazedek*" (medical assistance society) that the entire town used for a tabernacle/dwelling place, for hot water bottles, cupping, and so on.

[Page 153]

There was a Jewish "doctor" who practiced for many years in Serock, his name was Yisroel Shmuel. He was a shoemaker by profession, and he would stitch up shoes until late into the night in order to be able to earn his lowly livelihood. If someone would fall ill in town, he would quickly remove his shoemaker apron, and as quick as an arrow leaves its bow, he would run to the patient. Yisroel Shmuel would treat by cupping, alcohol compresses, massages, guinea pigs[1], leeches, and all kinds of herbs. He would never take any payment for this, would throw back the few coins, and would become angry at anyone who tried to give him anything. Even the non-Jews would wake him up in the middle of the night to take care of their sick ones.

Other than shoemakers, tailors, fishers, blacksmiths, orchard lessees, and teachers, the Jews in town had a strength behind them – the Didaks. These were three brothers with sons and daughters. All of them were blessed by God with physical strength, and so with that they would protect the lives and honor of all the Jews in the entire town. The oldest one, Shia Didak, was then in his fifties – tall, broad-shouldered, an absolute giant. He worked with horses, and not once did he end up in an argument with the Polaks at a fair. He would win all the arguments simply because of his strength – basically, as they grabbed a swingletree from the wagons, he would beat them on the right and left. He had a slow gait. All his life, he and his son would carry heavy sacks. Yankel Didak's sons were the wagon drivers. Exceptionally thin, but the entire town would tremble before them. The third brother, Moishe Didak, and his sons, were breakers of bones. By nature, they were pretty calm as long as you didn't step on their skin, and they would fight until "wet," that means that with knives and daggers they would show respect for parents [meaning, they would really show what they could do]. Aside from that, they had great respect and would go through fire for their enlightened small-town sister of whom the entire family was very proud, who was active in the Peretz Library that was in the marketplace next door to the shoemaker Shtajnski. Here, all the workers' sons, those who "were caught up in the issue" (of the enlightenment) would gather. But, even those sons of the wealthier families would come – those such as Volf Gerwer, the Kapecz brothers, Yancze Kuznicki, Yosel Fajnboim, Feivel Borob, and so on.

This youth was lively and dynamic. Almost every week there was a reading on a political or literary theme.in the Peretz Library, there was also a drama circle that would perform in City Hall on the Pultusk main road. The lively, spirited person there was Shloime, Baila Shim'es (Ostrowski), a strongly built and always happy person. With sacrifice and talent, he would play a main part in the theater; he loved football. During the entire match, like a little boy, he would chase the ball with the players, and work himself hard, hands and feet, and shout "Pass it to him! Go get him!" Many times it happened innocently that people would get a shove in the side or a kick in the leg. Matches with teams from other cities began with parades through the entire town with a band at its head, where all the different layers of the Jewish population were represented.

[Page 154]

The soul of the orchestra was Hershel the carpenter. He gathered in his house all the youth who played the wind instruments as a livelihood. In the evenings after work, he taught them to play until he was proud of them. Not waiting for the Polaks and for their Polish holiday of November 11, he appeared in the streets of Serock at the head of a Jewish orchestra. The Polaks clenched their teeth out of envy and humiliation, but it didn't help. When they played the Polish anthem "*Jeszcze Polska*," they removed the hats from their heads. In that way, they unwillingly gave respect to the Jews (*Zhides*) and their orchestra.

[Page 155]

As was mentioned, the *Mizrachi shul* was located in Yekel Rozenberg's house. All the Jewish Zionist organizations were there: *Hashomer Haleumi*, *Beitar*, and *Hashomer Hatzair*, where it was always humming with youth in scouts', colorful clothes. The exercises in the Napoleon mountains, at the foot of the Narew, the Hora dances and singing deafened the Warsaw road. Children of the people yearned for Zion but didn't live to see it: Zishe Zukor, Shakhne Fridman, Khaskele Fridman, Yehoshua Hofman. Everyone carried a deep faith in his heart and was tolerant. When the Peretz Library organized a

"Flower Day," the Zionists also participated, and even came to their readings. From time to time, they would organize debates in town. I remember one day, the first to go to the podium was the Rav and he called the people to repent (*teshuva*), and the second person was Khanokh Warsawski (today in Israel), and he told everyone to leave the exile and return to Zion (Israel). The last to step forward was Khaim Kapecz. He always spoke like a philosopher. We said at that time that his Rebbe was Bakunin [Mikhael Bakunin, famous Russian revolutionary]. Understandably, he called for everyone to remain and to fight for a "better tomorrow."

I was ten years old and I was privileged to have my father as my teacher. This was not the first school where my father taught. As I remember, my father taught in a school and in a kindergarten in 1922 in the house of Hendzhe then in Yankel Zadik's house on the mountain, and in the old Rav's house. The students called my father "Moreh." My father was fair with the students, never lifting a hand to them. The rascals would not always use this behavior properly. Boys would also learn to write Yiddish, Polish, Hebrew, and to do bookkeeping. Aside from all these shortcomings that my father had his whole life, which they would tease him about, and that all his businesses went up in smoke, my father defined himself as an enlightened person in those times. Later his students became the backbone of the entire socialist life. When they would meet their former "*Moreh*," they would treat him the greatest respect.

[Page 156]

When my father received the news that I too was "caught up in the issue," he took me for a walk behind the town, told me to rethink all this, and advised me to learn what would give me Paradise in my lifetime. I was deaf to his truthful words, unfortunately.

One Friday, Jancze Kuznicki and his friends were arrested. After a few years in prison, he was freed, but he coughed up blood. He looked at his friends benevolently, as if they would have said: "Yeah, personally I've done my time for the 'holy cause,' now it's your turn to pull the wagon." In the middle of one Thursday night, his soul left him. The funeral was the following day. A tombstone was placed on his grave where a tree was etched with the familiar cut off branches as a symbol of his being cut off early from this earth.

**Translator's Footnote**

7. Guinea pigs (yam khazerlech): Folk doctors [in the Andes] employ the black guinea pig to determine the cause of illness—pressed against an ailing body. The animal reportedly squeals when it finds the source of disease. http://polymer.chph.ras.ru/asavin/swinki/gvp.pdf Return

**Youth stay outdoors**

[Page 157]

# The Shtetl until World War II
### Yakov Brukhanski (New York)
### Translated by Pamela Russ

At the foot of a mountain range called "Napoleon Mountains," right beneath, flowed the Narew River, where in the center it joined and flowed together with the larger Bug River. Above that, the town of Serock spread itself out comfortably. With the glow of the water, it [Serock] appeared as if it were the landscape of a master painter. Once, when we came out of there after a summer swim, through the mountains, the first thing that greeted you was the warm, homey, four-cornered built-up marketplace, and from there to the town's center – the Kosciuszki and May Third streets that were inhabited by more than 95% Jewish residents, approximately 600 families. The town was about 800 years old, and was always a Jewish settlement that drew its earnings from small businesses, such with basic needs, workers, shoemakers, tailors, carpenters, wagon drivers, and others who lived off the Jewish townspeople and the Polish city and village population.

There were almost no large factories in the town of Serock. Because there was no railroad line, larger industry was unable to develop. The nearest train was 7 kilometers behind the town near Port Zegrze. For the same reason, many of the young adults left to Warsaw to find work, or to the closer town, Legionowo. By far, most of them stayed at home in Serock where they found businesses.

The children received their basic schooling primarily in Cheder [a traditional Jewish school], and also in the more modern Agudah or public cheder, and with the private Hebrew teachers or religious teachers. For the last 10 years before World War II, more Jewish children started to study in the new Polish Povshechner school [Polish public school]. A large part of the intellectual spirit of the youth was taken over by the Zionist organizations and other cultural organizations, and also the People's Education League with a large library, sports club, and drama circle. Altogether, this resulted in an intelligent, well-known group of youth, with a good name in the area.

[Page 158]

For a large part of sport and entertainment, the young people used the river and the so-called Napoleon Hills; starting with the cheder children's Lag b'Omer celebration with fireworks, to the "Shomer" groups [These are the Leftist groups, such as the Shomer Hatzair, etc.] and "Bais" groups [These are the more Right groups, such as Bais Yaakov, etc.], gymnastic exercises and drills, to secret gatherings and meetings. In a span of many generations, have these mountains absorbed much joy, love, and fantasy from these spirited Jewish Serocker youth.

The Warsaw highway or May Third Street was always the most beloved place for the strollers on Shabbos and Yom Tov [holidays]. The density of numbers grew when guests arrived from the big towns for Yom Tov so that they could cozy up to their homes in the small towns that always drew them and tied them with thousands of strings.

With the arrival of a new Catholic priest to Serock, a new Nationalist Democratic [known as the ND Party] anti-Semitic party was established, that quickly became settled in. As in the other Polish cities, the plague spread quickly and gave rise to many hooligan ambushes and boycotts of Jewish stores, in order that the perpetrators become beloved to their Nazi neighbors who were first to demonstrate how this is done. Thanks to the well-prepared town's Jewish self-defense of the youth and the strong hand of the butchers and wagon drivers, heroism was demonstrated on several occasions as they gave back strong beatings to the village peasants who instigated fights.

[Page 159]

# Serocker Jews
### Yehuda Mendzelewski (Bat Yam)
### Translated by Pamela Russ

We see you lonely, poor, and honorable Jews. We see you handsome and proud Jews. We see you God-fearing Jews all going with your *taleisim* (prayer shawls) at dawn to pay back a debt to the Master of the Universe of whatever debts you always owed him. We see you sitting in the study halls (*beis hamedrash*) learning until after midnight.

We also see your dear children going out of their schools (*kheder*) and on the way reviewing the verses from the Torah that they did not complete in school. We also see you - happy, rejoicing children - as you leave school, jumping and dancing. We also see you, children, playfully pushing each other - some with a round ball, some with a football, in winter on the ice with snowballs in your hands. We see you also grown boys and girls, fiery idealists and a struggling youth.

**A youth group**
First on the left in the second row from the bottom is Shloime Ostrowski

*[Page 160]*

**A youth group**
**From right to left, first row, standing:** Chava Blumberg, Hershel Rosenfeld, Feige Kopetch, Avrohom Jazombek, Feige Bresler, Avrohom Gutkowski
**Second row, sitting:** Feivel Borow, Chava Stelang, Hershel Zalcman, Gutman Kalina, Liba Khaimowicz
**Third row, sitting:** Laya Zalcman and Dvoire Kreda

We see all the groups, helping institutions, all kinds of unions, Zionist organizations from all directions, the famous Jewish orchestra, culture corners, and drama circles.

A small town, this Serock, with so much energy, so much intellectual strength and idealism to the point of self-sacrifice - Yakov Kuznicki, Hershel Mendzelewski, and others. Who didn't know Shloime Ostrowski? How much energy! How much strength! And how much enthusiasm! And with how much motivation did he organize the Yiddish drama circle in Serock. All performances produced by him were presented with great success. The Serock drama circle was comprised of tens of members. Shloime Ostrowski, with his sharp eye, knew everyone individually. When he needed a good-hearted mother, he found her in Feige Bresler, and when he needed a Yeshiva boy (*bokhur*) he got to know one through Avrohom Jazombek. The same was with Moishe Bresler, Feivel Borow, Rele Gladek, Volf Gerwer, Hersh Zalcman, Rochel Grinberg, and may he live and be well, Shmuel Brukhanski, and others. That's how everyone gave their tireless assistance to the Serock drama circle, turning it into one of the best in the entire area.

[Page 161]

**The Football Team**

There was no work center for people to be able to exist financially in Serock. The majority of the youth went to look for work in the large city of Warsaw, but no one stayed there for a long time. They were all homesick. The magical town drew them with her beautiful, delightful, natural landscape, also the early morning *Shabbos* flights into the beautiful forests and the enchanting, secretive, artistic mountains helped one completely forget about his existence. It was never a late hour (too late), an inner quiet song poured over you from the silent murmuring and flowing of the Narew River. Life in the town was free and carefree, and the belief was that here the sky was clearer, more beautiful, and everyone trusted and believed that there would be a glorious future, but what came was the destruction.

[Page 162]

## Military conscription in Poland between the Two World Wars

**Yehuda Mendzelewski (Bat Yam)**
**Translated by Pamela Russ**

When the time came to present yourself to the military commission, the Serock youth, both Polish and Jewish, had to go to the main city of Pultusk on that day. It always came out at the end of spring. A day before the conscription, the Polish conscripts (*prizivnikes*), fired up by the NKVD (the People's Commissariat for Internal Affairs [the government's secret police organization]), went into the Jewish shops and demanded compensation (money), or they would do terrible damage that night. The owners of the shops, knowing what was waiting for them, paid themselves out, giving the demanded monies to the hooligans. Woe to those who tried to negotiate the monies. The damage done at night to those was much greater. The hooligans used the money they collected to get drunk. After such a night of drinking, they became completely wild, breaking and destroying whatever got in their way. Those who had paid themselves off earlier in the day, suffered less damage. The hooligans kept a list to keep tabs on this.

The conscripts for the army called themselves *losownikes* (note: "Losovnikes" were a group of conscripts already picked by lottery waiting to be called up for mobilization). The Jewish *losownikes* kept themselves separate and also did not use the free transportation (*podvoda*) from city hall, but put together their few pennies (*groshen*) and got a wagon driver to drive them to the military commission in Pultusk, 21 kilometers from Serock. The wagon driver was Leibele Zuker (Yankele Zeldes), a very bold and strong young man, and one who could give you a real blow if ever necessary. Leibele Zuker was often found on the road, and often found himself up against the Polaks, one against many. But no one dared put a hand on him, knowing this was not going to end well.

[Page 163]

But this time, in 1933, bloodshed was incited by the Polaks as to why Jews are also involved in the holy undertaking of the Polish military - and they vowed to teach the Jews (*zhides*) a lesson. Our driver, sensing that the return trip would not go so smoothly, urged us to complete our tasks quickly because he wanted to leave Pultusk for Serock an hour before the Polaks did in order to avoid a clash with them on the road. But things happened differently: The Polaks, seeing that the driver with the *zhides* had run off, they began to chase them with their "*resarske britchkes*" ("knight's horse-drawn carriage," referring to a covered wagon that had more metal on it than wood, as a knight had "metal"), they harnessed up two horses to them, and chased Leibele's weak little horse to the village of Kluski, four kilometers before Serock. With wild cries of "Go to the Jews!" they began to jump off the wagon and with stones and sticks they headed towards us. We became very frightened. Only Leibele remained calm in his place near his horse and wagon, and quickly said: "Those of you who are weak, run away!" Some of us ran off, as much as we could. Not knowing what to do or where to run, I instinctively jumped down and ran in the direction of Serock and remained standing about 50 meters distance from the hooligans. It is impossible to describe the heroism that our wagon driver demonstrated - one against 50 or more. One after another, he dodged the stones and sticks, grabbed a stick from one of them and beat them right and left and threw one on top of another. The hooligans were upset and ran off, and I continued running in the direction of Serock. Ahead of me, there were also a few young boys running, but I remained the last one. After this episode, the bandits wanted to take revenge on anyone they could, so they began to chase me with their horses. But with superhuman strength, I ran another two kilometers, until they and their horses reached me. When I sensed three bandits about five meters behind me, and heard a cry of: "Jew face! I'm going to kill you!" I appeared, unbeknownst to them, to turn left into a field in the direction of the Narew, and the big miracle was that it was a mountainous area there, so that the bandits, who were running towards me with momentum, came out at the bottom of the mountain. In order to reach me, they had to climb back up the mountain. Meanwhile, I dragged myself to a cottage that belonged to a shoemaker, a Polak. I just went in, and the shoemaker, a fine man, quickly took in the scene. He immediately locked the door and glanced through the window. When he saw three ruffians with sticks in their hands looking in all directions, he quickly blocked the window and didn't even ask me what had happened. Anyway, I couldn't even utter a single word, so he held me for a moment and calmed me down.

[Page 164]

When I slowly came to myself, he put me to bed and several hours later, in the evening, he went to town to my parents to tell them to take me home.

[Page 165]

The Serock City Hall

## Our Former Hometown
### Elimelekh Hershfinger (Kibbutz Afek)
### Translated by Pamela Russ

Our little town of Serock did in general not lag behind the surrounding towns. There was a *shul*, a *beis hamedrash*, *steibelekh* (smaller places for prayers) - Ger, Alexander [names of different *khasidic* groups - a *Rav*, a *dayan* (religious judge who decides on issues of Jewish law and its applications to Jewish life), a Jewish community with caretakers of the *shul*, and a forward thinking youth. There were Zionist organizations from all groups - and also from the Leftists, a library, and a drama circle that would give performances several times during the year. The town had a mechanical mill that belonged to a Jew. Merchants - big ones and small ones, and market merchants. Workers: craftsmen, shoemakers, tailors - almost all of them earned their living from the town. All week, everyone was rushing, busy, and Friday afternoon they ran to the *mikve* (ritual bath) to wash and to shed the weekday burden, and become a different person.

In the home, by some more and by some less, things were ready for *Shabbos* - the house was cleaned, the workroom cleaned, and a white cover was tossed over the sewing machine. With one word - it's *Shabbos* in the world and by us in our town.

Friday nights, when the people would come home from *shul*, everything was changed over and scrubbed. The table was covered with *challah* and wine for *kiddush* (ceremonial blessing made over wine on Friday nights), and the whole family sat around the table not rushing as they would during the week. The youth left for their organizations to attend meetings, and some to the theatre shows, or the next day, on *Shabbos* afternoon, would just simply stroll around leisurely. During the summer they would go to the Narew River to the beach, or to the Napoleon mountains to relax.

The Jews of Serock tell that when Napoleon went to Russia with his army, Serock was an important point for him. He ordered that the mountains become embankments (defense posts). On *Shabbos* evening, young and old would go out strolling, girls dressed in modern clothing, young men in nice suits, on the main street May Third, from which one street leads to Warsaw and the other to the major city of Pultusk.

[Page 166]

In the evenings, some go out for entertainment, some go to community meetings at the Jewish People's Bank or to the charity meetings to decide how to distribute loans.

In my town, you were born, raised, grew up, got married, and brought in new generations. The entire town rejoiced when someone had a happy occasion. And the reverse, when someone had a tragedy, children and families, young and old, cried. There were peaceful times, and hard times passed. During the winter, around the warmth of the oven, the older people would tell of former times, and the *bubbeh* (grandmother), while plucking the feathers and blowing her nose in her apron, would sigh and say in agreement: "Yes, yes, children, it's true. That's how it was." During bad times, Jews recited Psalms (*tehilim*) and tried to revoke the decrees. There were good Jews who put forth worlds before God, sacrificed their lives, fasted each week on Mondays and Thursdays, so that times would be good again. There were times like that.

It was at the end of 1933. Mendel Bobek died at the beginning of the winter. Daily, he would go to prayers in *shul* to pray with the *minyan* (quorum of ten men) and to learn Talmud right away early in the morning. He did not live only for himself, but he kept in mind all the poor workers. When he died, the entire town showed their respect, escorting him until the cemetery, and they asked that he intercede for the whole nation of Israel because a new Haman had arisen, an enemy of the Jewish people, who had a plan to destroy all the Jews. They asked him [Bobek] to cry to the heavens but the gates were locked.

Bad times began for the Jews in Poland from 1936 until 1939, when WWII broke out. A Fascist might came to power. It began with an economic uprooting of the Polish Jews and then became pro-Nazi. The Polish government, with Skladkowski at the head, decreed to rip out business from

Jewish hands, and the *owszem*\* [literal translation: "of course," implying consent to economic boycott], was enough for the Polish anti-Semites. The Polish press wrote very frankly and openly the greatest abuses against the Jews. Also in our town Serock the Polish anti-Semites did not hold back. They set up pickets in front of Jewish stores.

\*The infamous *owszem* or economic boycott politics began in June 1936, after being suggested in the inaugural speech of the new Prime Minister of Poland, General F. Slawoy-Skladkowski. This policy encouraged Polish customers to boycott Jewish businessmen, shops, handicraftsmen, and factories. Actively implemented by the nationalist extremists, the policy consisted of more than propaganda. It involved picketing Jewish stores and threatening Poles who dared enter, smashing store windows, overturning stalls and pushcarts, destroying merchandise, and knifing and beating Jewish owners and did not allow the Polish people to buy anything from the Jews, but only from the newly arisen Polish merchants. That's how the crisis began for the Jews in Serock. (See http://davidhorodok.tripod.com/4a.html.)

[Page 167]

In Warsaw, Polish students were always permitted to fight with the Jews in the Jewish neighborhoods; also in the small towns, and Serock was included. We Jews in Poland became lost. We would bemoan our situation to the police, but the guards that maintained order just made fun of us. After that came the pogrom in Przytyk with the famous judgment against the Jewish youth that had the audacity to stand up in opposition. Also, in Brisk and Minsk-Mazowiecki and in other towns, Jewish goods and possessions were being lost. Jewish blood became cheap. To cut or tear out a Jewish beard until there was blood was a common occurrence, also to throw out a Jew from a train car while it was travelling was a form of entertainment for the Poles. The same Polish women entertained themselves by laughing at the Jew who was pleading and crying that he is a father of children: "*Tateleh, mameleh, kinderlekh* (children)." They laugh even harder. If a Jew went into the village, he returned beaten up and bloodied. We remained without protection, the earth burning under our feet. One is insecure on the street - travelling or even at home. Daily one hears bad news from Germany of the Jews there. Everything is locked away from the Jews. A black cloud is moving towards us.

The Poles take the Zaolzie territory from the Czechs, and important visitors come from the Third Reich to visit the Poles. External Minister Beck maintains the best relations with Nazi Germany. Before the end of 1939, the Poles became busy with themselves but nevertheless, they did not forget to torture the Jews. Even on our Jews of Serock, a heavy burden of fear is pressing down.

[Page 168]

## My Town (*Shtetl*)
### Yisroel Markewicz (Tel Aviv)
### Translated by Pamela Russ

The day began with the opening of the stores, the warehouses, and the bakeries. Still half asleep, we would run to buy baked goods, and to charm the woman baker for the tasty, black corn bread, and some to Zlate the baker for fresh *latkes* and a flat roll with onions. It began with a rush of people. Everyone was in a rush: some with the wagons to ride to the trains - and later with the buses - to Warsaw, and others rushed to work or to the villages. The young boys went to *kheder* (religious school) and some went to the public school. The small merchants and those who went to the villages searched for a means to earn a few *zlotys* for a day's wages.

Before noon, the few Jewish unemployed would wander around the streets. They would look for means to pass the time, some would gather to discuss politics at Meyer the barber, and some would gather by Berish Rosenfeld in a soda shop. In the evenings, they would assemble in the various organizations, where the majority of the Serock youth were organized to meet. There was the *Shomer Hatzair, Beitar*, and so on.

When I remember the small town of Serock, where our near and dear ones lived for generations, I see all kinds of figures and personalities from our Jewish life in our *shtetl*. Jews from all levels struggled with their daily lives, some with work, and some with business. There was great unemployment, there were no factories. There were two mills where ninety percent of the workers were Polish. City hall did not employ any Jewish workers. Jews worked only in certain vocations and there was not enough work for all. At daybreak, while it was still dark, the Jews would awaken and go to *shul* to pray. The first one was Avrohom Yankel Pnjiewski. He would open the *shul* and recite Psalms until more Jews would arrive and they would begin the prayers.

The largest part of the working youth assembled in the People's Education League that made a great contribution to the cultural evolution. The committee had a huge and wealthy library, and twice a week, they would exchange books. There was a lot of activity there for the advancement of culture, led by Yosel Feinboym, and there was a good drama circle led by Shlomo Ostrowski who presented the best of the Yiddish classics. There was an active speaker's circle, with lectures on political economics, socialism, literature; and there were recitations, *kestel oventen*, "*Kestel-oventn*" [evenings with a variety of speakers and writers presenting their ideas, designed for people with little education, with open debates and free discussion], and other cultural attractions.

[Page 169]

That's how the small town of Serock lived until the destruction.

**A House in Serock**

[Page 170]

# Figures from My Childhood
(Memories)
Kalman Kuligowski (Buenos Aires)

### Translated by Pamela Russ

As an orphan at three-and-a-half years old, I started saying *Kaddish* (Mourner's Prayer) for my young, deceased father, may he rest in peace, who was torn away from us at such a young age. I began to go to the *Beis Medrash* twice a day where they stood me on the bench near the *Bimah* (Torah stand; podium). The face of Reb Mendel Bobek shines before me, with his white beard, as he took care of me making sure I would recite *kaddish,* and also the wonderful big Jew, Reb Khaim Shlomo *Shokhet* (the ritual slaughterer) with his good heart, who even during prayers would smile at everyone. I started going to *kheder* (religious school for young boys): for some time to Reb Khaim Leyb, a teacher from the old times. After that, for a few weeks I went to Reb

Khaim Yoine, may he rest in peace, and also to Reb Efraim Sandler, of whom the children were very frightened. But he taught me in a more modern fashion. Also, Reb Yehuda Leyb Gutkowski planted in me a little Jewishness, even though sometimes he would give me a smear with a belt that had a button (buckle). Also, Reb Hersh-Efraim Bugoslowski was my teacher. But my beloved mother Rokhel Laya was my best teacher. She knocked into my head the first letters of the *Alef Bais* (Hebrew alphabet), not thinking about the constant worries of earning money for bread.

[Page 171]

Still as a young boy, I joined Beitar that was set up in the mill of Berl Izkowicz and Motl Melnik. From that time on I began to think about a Jewish state. That's how we grew up with many who today are living in Israel. Even in difficult times, we would gather and have discussions. One tried to outdo the other and show him how to build a better world, a better future, and most important, a Jewish state. They had already begun attacking the Jews, especially in the marketplaces and fairs. They would attack the Jewish storekeepers. Jewish life had become tense. The dark news from Germany worried us in Serock. It's a good place now to remember the Jewish heroes from that time. Two heroic Jews struggling against a huge mob supported by the Polish police gave significant blows to the thugs. I remember them respectfully: Motl Bornshtayn (the son of Shalke the shoemaker) and Herhshel Pnjewski - even with one hand (his other hand was not well at the time) he beat them over their heads with sticks.

Today there are no more Jews in Poland. There are no Jews of Torah and wisdom, no Yeshivas (religious schools), no little *shuls*, no *khasidim* (pious Jews), no merchants or craftsmen.

There remains an eternal wound.

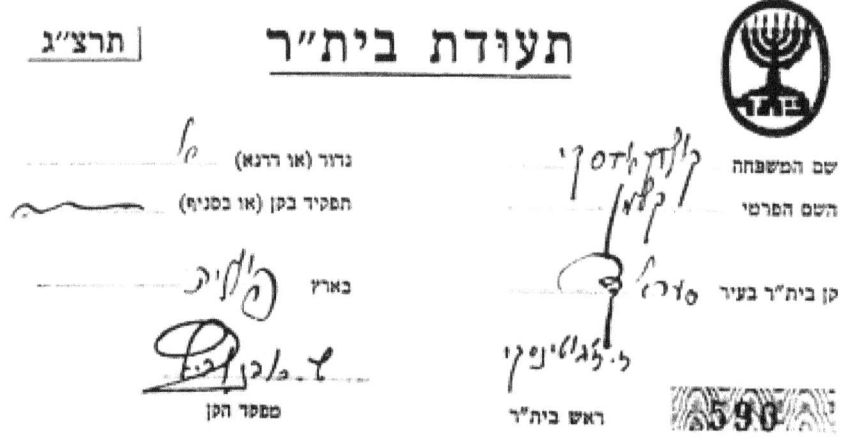

[Page 172]

# The Serock Self-Education League And Her Activities
### Shmuel Brukhanski (New York)

**Translated by Pamela Russ**

The Serock library under the name Self-Educational League had a great influence on the cultural evolution and intellectual design of the majority of the Serock youth.

A group of pioneers established the library at the beginning of the 1920s. The town was beginning to recover after the damage of the First World War and the Bolshevik invasion. Those youth were already more seasoned in culture understood and felt the need to establish a "culture corner" where the working youth could assemble and receive an intellectual, cultural education. The initiators were energetic young men, enthusiasts, and they threw themselves - body and soul - into this initiative. The founders of the library were: Khaim Kopetch (today in Argentina), Yekhiel Meyer Zakharek, Avrohom Gutkowski (Growski), Yosef Feinboym (today in America), Wolf Gerwer, Shloime Ostrowski, Hershel Mendzelewski, and Soro Sandler.

The first activity was organized and it was to raise a little money and to receive from the authorities a legal status for this type of organization. They met with the well-known Jewish writer and community activist Noakh Prilutzki, at that time the leader of the Jewish "People's Party," and the library received legitimate status under the name "Self-Education League." They managed to acquire a few books from a library that had existed earlier under the name "Progres" - founded by Shmerl Ashenmil (today in Argentina) and Shmuel Doner (today in New York). They collected a certain amount of money and bought more books, rented a location in the town's marketplace, and began to recruit members. With time, the number of members grew, and the activities were extended. Friends Khaim Kopetch, Yosef Feinboym, and others, began to manage a multi-faceted literary job.

[Page 173]

They organized several evenings during the week "*kestel oventn*" (evenings of free [open] debates), discussing actual questions of literary, social, and political topics. They discussed various party programs, local events, and so on. Also, many self-educational circles were established. They studied literature and history. There was also a speaker's circle, where they openly presented speakers. From time to time, we would bring as speakers, our lecturers: writers, editors, journalists, or literary critics. There was also a drama circle under the directorship of a very capable and gifted artist Shloime Ostrowski who was an actor in the youth theater for some time in Warsaw under the management of Yosef Rotboym.

Shloime Ostrowski threw himself into this work with all his soul, and the drama circle was our pride. The drama circle grew steadily with renewed energies - and among them, one of them was me. Many talented youth had an opportunity to display their talent. We presented the best pieces of the Jewish classics, for example: Peretz Hirshbayn's "*Der Iberiker Mench*" (The Extra Person), "*Der Inteligent*" (The Intellectual), "*Miryam*" (Miriam); Gordon's "*Di Shekhita*" (The Slaughter), "*Gott, Mench, un Teivel*", (God, Man, and the Devil); Sholom Aleichem's "*Dos Groyse Gevins*" (The Great Lottery), "*Menchen*" (People); Bergelson's "*Der Toyber*" (The Deaf Person); Leyvik's "*Hirsh Lekert*" (Hirsh Lekert), and many other pieces and one-act plays from the best of the Yiddish repertoire.

Our performances had great success, and the room was always crowded. There were both the intellectuals and the working class Jews and their families in attendance, and everyone greatly enjoyed the Yiddish shows. The town became vibrant. Also from the neighboring towns: Pultusk, Wyszkow, Nashelsk, Radzimyn, and Jablonna, the youth would come to our performances. On several occasions we were invited to the neighboring towns to perform, and we had great success. The profits went towards buying new books. After each performance we were able to buy several hundred new books. The library already owned several thousand books.

But the profits were not the main thing. The drama circle brought a lot of life to the organization. The rehearsals, the readings, and the managing of the works stirred up an interest in literature and art.

[Page 174]

I would like now to mention some of the participants in the drama circle: Shloime Ostrowski (stage manager), Avrohom Jazombek, Feivel Borow, Moishe Bresler, Feige Bresler, Hershel Zalcman, Shmuelke Brukhanski, Moishe Gutkowski, Moshke Wrubel, Maleh Mendzelewski, Yidel Mendzelewski, Feivel Gal, Dvoire Kreda, Soro Bayle Gzhebjeniazh, Moishe Yosel Ubagi, Yakov Brukhanski, Hershel Rosenfeld, Feivel Pshikorski, Itche Leyb Shteinski. The artwork was painted by my talented brother Shepsel Brukhanski. He also painted portraits from the Jewish classics that decorated the walls of the library. Fishel Sterdiner was the technical person. After Shloime Ostrowski left for Warsaw, we hired a stage committee consisting of Avrohom Jazhamberk, Moishe Yosel Ubagi, and a script writer.

The League was not only occupied with cultural and intellectual work for the youth, but also occupied with their physical development. We ran diverse sport activities, such as: ping pong, basketball, and later a football team made of several groups. A special paid instructor trained the members. We would organize matches with other teams. Our sportsmen were outstanding with their excellent playing. Every time when there was such a match, the town came alive. The Jewish band would march through the streets with two groups, and the crowd gathered at the sports place, to the competition. This brought some cheer to the gray lives of our town.

That's how the work of the Self-Education League went on until Hitler, may his name be erased, destroyed our town.

[Page 175]

# The Beginning of the Modern Cultural-Social Activity
## Yosef Feynboim (America)

### Translated by Pamela Russ

Serock, as one of the several towns during the Czarist rule, belonged to the typical Jewish settlements in their social and economic life - frozen and conserved in survival of life. The Jews in the small town of Serock had no outlook for a better future.

The small group of individuals with their various theories had no power and did not have the opportunity to change anything in the direction of stirring up the society to an intensive cultural-social life.

Only in 1915-1918, during the First World War, did the social and cultural life of the youth and the small Jewish settlements expand. The youth began to search for answers to the problems and the first modern culture institution was established in Serock - the library and culture club by the name of "Progress."

**A Youth Group at the Narew**
**From right to left:** Rokhel Izkowitz-Czesner (in Israel), Yosef Feinboym (in North America), Feivel Borow, Khana Broyde, Yisroel Wolinski, Rifke Kuperboym

[Page 176]

It is important to mention a list of people who did the following work with the deepest commitment: the Ashenmil brothers, the family Shtelang, Grosbard, Kopetch, Doner, Kleinman, Blumberg; and the younger ones: Ostrowski, Feinboym, Grosbard, Gerwer, Gal, Jurkowicz, Zakharek, Yekhiel Meyer Warsawski, Faskowicz, Tikulski, Friedman, Czesner, Rosenberg, and so on. The great movement to raise the level of culture began by the youth. This "Progres" institution developed many parts of the cultural-social work, such as: the library, evenings of debate, holiday entertainment, lectures, discussion evenings, literary trials, drama circles, choirs, etc., and to that end, there was a list of appropriate institutions. Also, individuals from the older generation were drawn into the new life. It was becoming lighter and brighter in the dark surroundings. There existed the organization *Hechalutz*, professional unions, educational leagues, *Hashomer Hatzair*, *Mizrachi*, and so on. There began long and earnest disagreements about national and social freedom, art, literature, sculpture, music. In this detail, all the Jewish differences were set aside among those involved in culture activities: literary evenings and discussion evenings were done in partnerships.

Our small town Serock baked itself deeply into our hearts, where we were raised, and the Bug-Narew rocked us with their waves, where that "steaming well" with the Napoleon mountains listened quietly to our songs, to our loves and our confusions, where our grandfathers and great-grandfathers lived for hundreds of years, gave life to and raised new generations. From all of that, nothing remains.

I was in Serock in September 1964, and went across the town in its length and width. I looked for traces and signs of our hundred-year life in Serock...

Tragically: empty and dark. I had the feeling that the entire nature there, together with the Bug-Narew, was orphaned. The entire beauty around her is saddened and troubled, because the most beautiful and the best of her fortune were cut off: the Jewish surroundings and her dream-laden youth from my town Serock.

[Page 177]

# Jewish Serock
## by Zwi Apelboim (Beit Shemesh)

**Translated by Pamela Russ**

Serock is a city that grew out of a town after many years of being on the dirt roads of Warsaw, Zegzhe, Pultusk, Makow. The town began building itself at the end of the 14th century on the shores of the rivers that ran together: the Bug and the Narew, and they called it "Serock on the Narew." With time, when the town started to grow, they began to build houses on the nearby mountains where the Warsaw-Pultusk highway ran.

It was built as all the other towns of that time: on both sides of the highway, single level houses were built on the ground. Across the highway, in the direction of the market, a large street was built, named Kosciuszko Street, with houses that were almost all single level, and there were many stores and a Jewish public school. Parallel to that street there was the so-called synagogue street where the large, tall city synagogue was built, along with a *bais medrash*, ordinary houses, and a grain mill that belonged to the Nowogrodski family. Higher up on the highway, a Jewish blacksmith shop was built belonging to Aba-Leyb Fridman.

There were other streets, sparse with houses, such as the *mikve* (ritualarium) street, where the Rav of the town lived, and where the Yakov Aryeh, the carpenter, had his workshop. Off the *mikve* street, there were a few little streets with a few built up paths, where there were several hardworking Jewish families living, up until the Catholic Church [on that road].

The market was a large square: from all sides were single level houses built on the ground. Near the main street, there was a well, and in the large area of the market, every Tuesday and Friday, the farmers from the nearby villages would come and sell their home grown produce.

When market day had ended, the farmers allowed the Jewish storeowners to buy whatever they needed.

[Page 178]

# Serock - A Long Time Ago
## by Refoel Fridman (Kholon)

### Translated by Pamela Russ

The Jewish settlement of Serock lasted about 250 years, until its end. Before the town was established, on the other side of the Narew, there was already the solid, longtime established village of Orczekhowa, where a few Jewish families lived. The Serocker elders would discuss among themselves that this happened because the Polish rule at that time declared that Jews were not allowed to settle in Serock, which at that time was a village of only non-Jewish residents. The town was in need of Jewish business. The elders also said that the village of Popowa, that was situated on the road to Wyszkow, was a settlement established earlier than Serock. When the Serock Jewish settlement was already a large one, they still buried their dead in the Jewish cemetery in Popowa. Years later, when the decree that Jews were not permitted to work in agriculture (or anything to do with the fields) was passed by the cruel Polish, the majority of Popowa Jews were also forced to leave their village and settle in Serock. In that way, the Jews of both villages combined to establish the town of Serock.

Even years ago, they used to call some of the Serock Jews by other names, for example, "the Popowa Jew." One such Jew was called "the Popowa baker." I also remember once, when I was with my grandfather Reb Khaim Shlomo the *Shokhet*, that we went to Popowa. The *Shokhet* went there to slaughter ducks. My grandfather told me that many Popowa Jews settled in the new town of Serock for the abovementioned reasons.

**A street in Serock**

[Page 179]

Until the outbreak of World War One, there were about 3,000 Jewish souls living in Serock. And because Jews there were a majority, the local non-Jews decided to add on a few neighboring villages so that for all those around a Christian mayor would be chosen.

The Serock Jews were occupied primarily with business and handwork. All the blacksmiths were Jewish. Other than my grandfather, there was one other *shokhet* - Reb Refoel. Because of arguments that lasted years, an additional two *shokhtim* (plural) were taken in from other parts - Reb Mendel from Popowa and Reb Eliyohu from Ostrow-Mazowieck.

The elderly Rav always had a quorum (*minyan* - ten men) in his home for prayers. The men of the *Khevra Kadisha* (burial society) and the regular people prayed there. While the Rav was still alive, the city took on another Rav - the son of the Wyszkow Rav.

In Serock, on the way to the cemetery, there was a well that was called "the boiling little well." The Jews of Serock would draw water from there and wash their sick eyes. Jews who were sick believed that water from this well would give them a full recovery.

There was one Jew with a black little beard who was called "Nokhum'ke." During the days of *slikhos* (days before Rosh Hashona), he would knock on people's closed shutters before daybreak and call out: "Get to *shul*!" On Fridays before candle lighting time, Nokhum'ke would blow his trumpet so that the shopkeepers would lock up their stores. I remember Avrohom Yankel, the smith, who ran into the *bais medrash* every day with a fiery intensity. Avrohom Yankel was always the first one to be with the first *minyan*.

[Page 180]

These were the Serock Jewish teachers: Khaim Yoine, Refoel Minkes, Dovid Itziks, Khaim Yehoshua, and Avrohom Leyb. The school aged children were not eager to go to all of these teachers. They did not want to go to Khaim Yoine, Refoel Minkes, and "*Palgei Nizka*" (the "streams of damages") because these teachers used to beat the children and the others didn't.

There was also a teacher in Serock that had come from Radzimyn in order to learn Talmud and commentaries (*Gemara* and *Tosefos*) with the older boys.

**Serock Jewish soldiers in the Czar's army**

[Page 181]

In the year 1922, near the old pharmacy, the *Kheder Yesoidei Hatorah* (name of boy's school) was established under the supervision of the *Agudas Yisroel* (Orthodox Rabbinic Council) directorship of Reb Itche Swarc and others. Other than Talmud and its commentaries, twice a week they also studied secular subjects such as mathematics, the Polish language, and history. These subjects were taught by the Jewish teacher Khaim Jurkewicz from Pultusk.

In order to learn more about worldly subjects than was taught in *Yesoidei Hatorah*, those who could afford it, would also study with the "enlightened" Jew from Serock, Eliyohu Aron Rosental. They also studied Hebrew with Khaim Hersh Klaynman, the son of the glazier.

At the time of the First World War, the German occupying rule prohibited food from being brought in from the villages. Because of that, there was a hunger in the town. Jews and Poles smuggled in food products for big amounts of money, but the majority of the Jews in the town did not have the money to buy any of these foods. The result of this was that there were outbreaks of typhus and cholera epidemics - and there were many victims.

In 1920, the Bolsheviks moved in to Serock. During a major shootout behind the town, a bomb was thrown and two Jews were killed - a grandfather and grandson. Shortly after that, a second bomb went off near the house of Khaim Shloime the *Shokhet*, and this one killed Minke the chicken dealer, also Khaim Dovid's wife, and two other Jews were wounded.

After that, when the Bolshevik army retreated from Serock, the "*Halertchikes*"[1] moved in and began to make trouble for the Jews. They began robbing from the Jews, beating them, and tearing out their beards. This went on for three days.

In the year 1922, there was a terrible economic crisis in Serock, and not having anything to do, there began an immigration to Argentina.

[Page 182]

At the beginning of the 1920s, Zionist parties began to form in Serock: *Algemeineh Zionisten*, and *Mizrakhi*. A short while later, *Hekhalutz* was established with the writer of the "Shuros Be'rosh."[2] After that, the communist *League* was started that did conspiratorial work under the mantle of Jewish cultural activities. By the end of the 1920s, the *Shomer Hatzair* was established by Yekhezkel Fridman who perished, of blessed memory, and Lianka Goldman (today is Israel), and also the group *Ha'oved Ha'Zioni* (the "working Zionist") under the directorship of my unforgettable brother Shakhne Fridman, of blessed memory.

The Zionist parties raised the youth with a Zionist spirit. Every week there were lectures of local and foreign Zionist speakers. Henokh Warsawski (today Khanokh Vardi) from the *Shomer Hatzair* was an exceptional lecturer. Also, Yosef Tikulski had a great influence on our Zionist youth.

**A Serock Jewish soldier in the Polish army**

[Page 183]

When the university opened in Jerusalem, there was a great celebration in Serock. Almost all the Jews in the entire city gathered in the city's *shul*. There was singing and dancing all night, and they collected money for Israel.

The youth began to prepare themselves for *Aliyah* (immigration to Israel). Some participated in what was called *Hakhshara* (training for *aliyah*) in Grokhow and in Szeczyn near Byalistok. Some of these people actually received certificates and did make *Aliyah*.

**Translator's Footnotes**

8. These were soldiers under the command of General Jozek Haller during and after the First World War.
9. Lit.: "Headlines." This may have been the name of a newspaper published by the *Hekhalutz* group in Serock.
10.

[Page 184]

# The first buds of Hebrew education in Serock
## Shlomo Rabinowicz/Rabinowitz (Haifa)

### Translated by Sara Mages

Serock was a town in Poland where many Jews lived. Most of the Jews gave their children a religious education. Hebrew schools didn't exist. The children studied in the *"Kheder"* (the name of the Jewish school at that time), the teachers were *"Melamdim,"* or as they were called "Rabbi." A child, who didn't listen to him, or refused to learn as the Rabbi demanded, received an unpleasant punishment in the form of whipping in front of all the children in the room. The hours of study were from eight in the morning to six in the evening. The children sat crowded on benches at a long table facing each other, and in that manner they studied. The study in the *"Kheder"* lasted up to the age of 14-15. Many continued to study in the Yeshiva and others went to work, some to their parents' shop, some to find a new craft, and all of this without the possibility to progress.

At the same time, many parents wanted to give their children a modern education. A number of parents gathered together and decided to establish a Hebrew School where the education will be modern.

**Chaim Jorckowicz, the state Elementary School teacher, with a group of students**

**Standing in the first row from right to left:** Shmuel Margolis, Sheindil Bernstein, Chava Barab, Shlomo Rabinowitz.
**Sitting:** Rivka Wolinski, Rivka Barab, Chaim Jorckowicz, Gitele Grinberg, unidentified female

[Page 185]

They traveled to Warsaw, found a well-educated Hebrew teacher by the name of Halperin, and brought him to our town. Thus, the first Hebrew School was opened in Serock under the direction of the teacher Halperin. The classroom seating arrangement was changed: the students didn't sit facing each other, but all sat facing the teacher. Another innovation that was introduced to the school is teaching boys and girls together. There were thirty boys and girls in the school. The students studied Hebrew, arithmetic and Polish. The students were very successful in their studies because the teacher was excellent.

**The first Elementary School in Serock**
In the center: the teacher-principal Halperin

*[Page 186]*

Also, great was their desire to learn and the parents had great satisfaction from their children. Then the troubles started: When it became known in the city that the students were studying the holy language and the Bible without a hat on their head, and boys and girls study together, the religious extremists boiled with anger - one night, they broke into the school, smashed the windows and damaged the furniture. The next day when the students came to school they were stunned at the sight of the frightening image. But the desire to learn was great: in a short time everything was repaired, the studies continued to operate as usual, but the bad impression remained. The matter became known to the city's rabbi, an 80 years old Jew, a wise scholar. He invited the teacher Halperin to see him, apologized for what happened, but at the same time asked our teacher not to teach Hebrew without a hat, and to separate the boys and the girls. After a two hour argument it was finally agreed that the boys will wear a hat during Hebrew and Bible studies, but the teacher didn't give up on the matter of schooling boys and girls together. The studies with the teacher Halperin lasted for around two years and everyone was satisfied, but to the great sorrow of the parents and the students, he emigrated to his family in the United States and the school was left without a teacher. The search for a new teacher lasted a long time, and with difficulties another one was found. Unfortunately, it turned out that the students knew Hebrew better than him. After the exam that the new teacher gave during his first class, he corrected spelling mistakes that weren't mistakes at all. Of course, the parents immediately dismissed this teacher. The search for another teacher came to nothing, and the school closed. Some of the students continued their education in the state's Elementary School, and in the afternoon they studied Hebrew with the teacher Zvi Kleinman, who was the only one able to teach the children, myself included.

One thing is certain: those who received the foundation of their education in the school where the teacher Halperin was teaching, will know, and will remember, the teacher who introduced us to the good atmosphere of the Hebrew language that inspired the youth who grew up in our city. Unfortunately, only a few of them were left after the last World War.

[Page 187]

# The Modern *Kheder* (Jewish School)
## by Melekh Mendzelewski (Bat Yam)

### Translated by Pamela Russ

Among all the Serock Jewish schools in the 1920s, the most respected was the *kheder* of Reb Elye Aron Rosental, of blessed memory. He prayed in the *Mizrachi minyan* (*shul*), and he partook in helping *Keren Kayemet* (Jewish National Fund). His school used two rooms with long benches for sitting, a blackboard where the teacher translated his lectures for his students, and even a bell to ring for break as in a *shkola*, or a modern school.

In *kheder*, they learned Hebrew, *Tanakh* (Torah, Prophets, Writings), religious studies, and worldly subjects such as: mathematics, Yiddish, history, Polish, and even geography.

Many of the survivors received their first bit of knowledge - history and love of Israel - here in this school. Who of them does not remember the first Hebrew song, *Al Hakhalon, al hakhalon amdah zipor yafa* (A beautiful bird is on the windowsill), *Shaon metakteik tak-tak* (The clock is ticking, tick-tock), *Kukurikoo, Koreh Ha'tarnegol* (cukoorikoo, says the rooster), or "*Di Sokhe*" (The Plow) sang in Yiddish, and many more such songs were sung by these students.

For younger children, a young, engaged woman was hired for the "*Frebluvka*"[1] or the "*Okhranka*"[1] girls. Each child had a small blackboard with a piece of chalk to write, and each received a cup of cocoa and a roll each day.

When the children went for a walk with their teacher, they were all dressed in blue and white aprons with white and blue braided hats made from crepe paper, since there was no money for material and there were no subsidies in those days for schools or for *Frebluvkas*. The school existed from tuition that was paid, and not all parents had the possibility to make uniforms for their children for the *Frebluvka*.

The *morah* - that's what the students called their teacher - learned with his students with a lot of patience and dedication, and tried to help his students understand the material with allegories from the Bible, and stories...... in order to learn and know, to raise their morals and love for their friends, and not to be overpowering at the cost of weaker ones. And when he discovered a student that was talented and wanted to learn, but didn't have any money, he would tactfully (so as not to embarrass him, God forbid) bring the child back into school or give him separate classes, even on the Sabbath. He never thought about himself, that he had to rest. He could not remain indifferent to talented children, but hoped that the fathers would pay when they would have the means. He already brought in an orphan, almost forcing him to learn. "Jewish children must study with anyone's help, it doesn't matter who, as long as they are learning. He who is intelligent will manage to develop himself later on." This is what the teacher always said.

[Page 188]

He didn't earn much as the teacher in the *kheder* anyway, and he lived in real poverty. There were parents who paid regularly for their children, but there were also those who didn't care that they had to pay, and the teacher did not have the heart to remind the child. In general, he felt it was beneath his dignity to beg for tuition payment because it had to be the parents' moral obligation and they had to know that this was how the teacher earned his living. And when his need became too great, he would give his wife a list of names of those who owed him money, but she would always come home embarrassed, without a cent, complaining about her fate and her children's fate.

Reb Elye Aron, of blessed memory, also had a group of students, older boys and girls, who had completed school. He gave them lectures in Hebrew and bookkeeping, and many of these worked later on as bookkeepers. For a certain period of time he also worked as a bookkeeper for Moishe Rosenberg in the mill, and gave lectures on the Sabbath for free to intelligent, poor children, because by that time, he already had some earnings. He also was involved with community activities such as *Mizrachi, Linat Hazedek* (charity for the sick), and generally helping others discreetly, in whichever way he could.

When the mill burned down, he went back to teaching children, which again became his main source of income. He was always a believer and hoped that things would get better.

Of course, because there was always *tsores* (problems) in Serock, the depressed and confused would always come to him for all kinds of help. Reb Elye "the master" would write letters for women to their husbands in America, and the letters were almost always successful. The men would respond from across the ocean and immediately send money and with time, brought over their wives and children to them. He would also write requests in Polish for unfortunate people who found themselves in difficult situations. He was always ready to make it easier for someone. His letters and requests were able to move even stone. And those who suffered felt relieved. He would celebrate with them as if he himself would have been helped.

[Page 189]

In the beginning of the 1930s, when it became impossible to earn a living from teaching, and the children had grown up, he left Serock and moved to Warsaw where he worked as a bookkeeper and taught Hebrew. He died in the year 1938 on *Shavuos*. His wife, Dvoire Rosental, died in the Warsaw ghetto. May their memories be blessed.

**Translator's Footnote**

11.   Both of these words are obsolete Polish terms for a kindergarten. One is "*okhronka*," which usually denoted a kindergarten ran by a religious institution, and the other is "*freblowka*," denoting a more modern and lay approach (after F. Frobl, a German pedagogue). [*Thank you to the many translators who assisted with these definitions.*]

*[Page 190]*

# Our Town ...
## by Yosel Grosbard, of blessed memory

### Translated by Pamela Russ

Quiet, calm, and modest, our town lies between wide, spread out fields and meadows, between mountains and waters, as if God had the intention of giving it all good things, as a father to its only child; it actually smiles to him who sees that the sun should not be stingy with her warm rays.

Our town lives as a world, modest unto herself; among God's big worlds, she calmly takes her place. Our waters, the Narew and the Bug flow by unnoticed in their shores, as if they do not want to disturb the calmness of the town.

And beautiful, as if childishly naïve, our town appears in her yellow gray spring dawn, when the morning is still wrapped in the dew, and transforms herself in the rays of dawn's light. Then, it appears, as if a loving, compassionate child and a mother's soft lap have awoken from a quiet, sweet dream. And in the evenings, when the sun's last, dark copper brown rays die off in the river, our town falls asleep, dreaming with the hopes of a fresh tomorrow...

**A Serock Landscape**

*[191]*

And thus, in a fluid calmness, we live in our town, day after day, summer after spring as if here time had no power, and so it never gets old - and the sky here is never cloudy - noisily, here the birds are always singing, and the fields are always green!

The water, the mountains, the fields have much to tell about young girls' dreams and young men's longings. So many, scattered all over you - how many songs, tender from girls' hearts, broken from unfulfilled longings, lie secretly within you!

Yes, my town! Yes, her waters, fields, mountains, and valleys, you are rich without bound.

Whole worlds of magic lie within you! And still, so not haughty; so calm and modest.

**By the Narew (River)**

*[192]*

My beloved town! You have to have partly grown up with you, part of you has bathed in your waters, warmed in your sunrays. It's a piece of magic that comes from you alone – to be able to recognize you, to be able to feel you! ... And because I am a child born in your lap, and raised in your arms, and my heart flamed like a rose because of you; and because, my most beautiful, youthfully spun dreams are sown over your meadows and waters; and in minutes, sweetly intoxicated, I have drunk until delirium (?) from your magical nectar juices; therefore, no matter what life will throw me, no matter what will knock at my door; my ideals will change, dreams will disappear and become forgotten, but my small beloved town – I will always, always remember you …

("*Unzer Vort*" [Our Word] 1, Pultusk, 1928)

[Page 197]

The Nazi murderers enjoy themselves by pulling off and burning the beards of Jews (the photo was taken from the Murshas{?} archive)

# Destruction
## The Destruction of Serock
### by Moishe Gudes/Godes (Tel Aviv)
### Translated by Pamela Russ

I arrived in Serock on Monday, 22 Kislev (Hebrew month), December 4, 1939, one day before the expulsion, and heard that in Nazielsk they had expelled the Jews that day. My brother Yankel was in Nazielsk for business and was expelled with the other Nazielsk people.

I was with my ailing father, Reb Yitzkhok Hersh, and my sister Khaitche Jonisz-Gudes that night. They started banging at the door at dawn. We already knew that they would force us to leave. My mother and my sister then took some clothing with them, and I took from my sister-in-law Yokheved a sack with bed linen and clothing. When we opened the door, the Germans came in and ordered us to go to the marketplace. When we said that we couldn't leave our sick father, they said that he would follow after us. We approached our father and kissed him good-bye. He could already hardly speak, but he said to us: "How can you leave me alone?" The Germans were standing by, but because of their orders we had to leave.

When we arrived in the marketplace, there was already a big crowd. Soon there was an order from the SS men that anyone with a horse and wagon should go home and hitch up their wagons to gather up the sick ones with their bed linens. I suffered terribly for having left my father alone, so I said that I had a horse and wagon. I went back home alone to see what was going on with my father. As I approached the house, two SS men came over to me, and one pointed his gun at me, ready to shoot. The second one stopped him. I had to go back to the marketplace without ever seeing my father again.

There was a young man in town, the son of Efraim Sendler, the *melamed* (teacher). While standing in the marketplace, two SS men went over to him with revolvers, put them to his head to shoot, and then began to laugh uproariously. They kept the revolvers at his head for a few minutes. The young man was sobbing and looked to the side. After that, they left him alone.

[Page 198]

When it was daylight, the marches began. Five in a row, we left Serock. The train was a very long one, and behind us were wagons carrying the sick: Mendel Markewicz the butcher, Rokhel Zlals, Faige Wenger, and others.

Yisroel Iser Hiler, a cloth merchant from Serock, who was held up several times before in order to squeeze money from him, was released at the time of these marches and he came bareheaded with us, directly out of prison and straight into the rows.

The German people warned us that whoever would be found having some money on him would be shot. The Jews were terrified and emptied their pockets, giving everything away.

All the elderly who stopped and didn't have the energy to continue on, were beaten to death. That's how the older teacher, Yitzkhok Blakhman, was beaten, wanting to see my father on the way and staying behind as one of the last. With all my energy, I pulled him deeper among us in the crowd, until we were lucky to seat him on a wagon. When we arrived in Nazielsk, it was already evening. They chased us with beatings to the Nazielsk *shul*.

In front of the *shul*, there were two rows of SS men and *Volksdeutchen*[1] and they were beating people over their heads. The entrance to the Nazielsk *shul* had several steps to go down. People didn't notice these steps out of fear, and one person fell on top of the other.

The horses and wagons and all the belongings were very quickly confiscated in Nazielsk. I did not remove my brother's sack with his linen from my back, even as we entered the *shul*. That's how I saved his bed linen.

There were many Jews among us from Pultusk, Popowa, Zator, Zegzhe, etc. When we entered the *shul*, we saw a swastika on the place of the Holy Ark (place where Torah scrolls are kept). Everything else had been removed from the *shul*.

Soon, the SS men came into the *shul*. We didn't know for what reason, and everyone pushed himself closer to the wall out of fear. In the end, they took ten men out to work. Among them were Laybish Shmerl Winogard, the kvass maker [kvass is a common fermented drink used in Russia, non-alcoholic and beer-like] (Mendel Hiler's uncle), and Yeshayohu Bobek (a cousin to Yehoshua Dovid Bobek). The work entailed digging a large ditch not far from the *shul*. They had to take down all the sick people from the wagons and lay them out in rows in the ditches.

[Page 199]

Yeshayohu Bobek (the shoemaker) heard talking between my sick father and Mendel Markewicz.

Mendel the butcher said to my father that he was cold. My father answered him that soon we will all be warm.... That means he understood that they were going to be shot. Furthermore, I was told that Mendel the butcher cursed and swore at the Germans, and assured them that they would have an ugly ending.

The shooters were young non-Jews boys (*shkotzim* – derogatory term) from the "*lakhe*" (A German neighborhood near Serock), and were under the command of an SS man.

They told these ten Jews to turn around during the shooting. After the shooting, they were ordered to throw in the dead and then say *kaddish* (prayer for the dead). They were then ordered to go into the *shul* where they told everyone what had happened.

This took place on the 24th of Kislev at night in the *shul*.

They rarely let anyone out to take care of personal needs, and so, not being able to help themselves, people relieved themselves in the *shul*. The following day, at daybreak, they chased us out with sticks and beatings for four kilometers to the train. They kept back many people to clean the *shul*. They were ordered to use their nails to quickly clean the walls and floors, all the while being beaten. Among these who were held back was my cousin Shloime

Zalkes. Afterwards, he told us everything. After all that, they had to run four kilometers to catch up to the crowd.

The border guards from the General Government[2] were already standing at the train. Serock and Nazielsk were now joined under the German Reich and the Jews were under a protectorate. The murderers performed the most sadistic acts against the Jews. They told the Rav's son, Shlomo Morgernstern, to put on his *tefilin*, and Yakov Leviner, to roll in the mud outside in the cold. He wanted to remove his outer clothing...... so that later he could put back on his dry clothing, but they didn't let him do that. The one who was tortured paid dearly with his health and with great humiliation. So, he didn't live long after that.

[Page 200]

In Nazielsk, while waiting for the train, the border guard searched everyone's packages and took many things away, and then beat the people over their heads, chasing them to the wagons. I, looking through my things, received a beating over my head with a stick. The train was locked. We had no idea where they were taking us. Three days and three nights we went from station to station. For that time of three days, we were without water. The little children's terrible cries for water and bread went directly up to God. They tried to save those children who were breastfed by spitting into the babies' mouths. In many places, the Polish people would try to bring us water for money, but the Germans didn't let them through. In one station, at night, we heard the wagons opening and then we heard shooting. It was dark and airplanes were roaring. After opening the wagons, they chased us into the open without escort to Biale-Podlaska. The Jews from Biale-Podlaska really deserve praise. Almost the entire town came out and brought us whatever we needed. The poor man brought water. In a short time, the Jews were satisfied and had their thirst quenched by the Jews from Biale-Podlaska.

Everyone took families home with them – as many as they could. As for me, a certain religious Jew, Yakov Kano, set me up with him. I told him that I also had a mother and sister, so he took them in as well.

Since I was in Biale-Podlaksa for two weeks, I saw the lot of the Serock Jews. Very quickly, a kitchen was organized by Menakhem Kronenberg and Yakov Dovid Wolman at the head, and whoever wasn't embarrassed would go there and have a meal.

Many Serock youths crossed over the Vistula River into Brisk on the Bug River, many through other means. Some died in Biale-Podlaska; some – I among these – went to Warsaw through Miedzyrzecz.

[Page 201]

There were two trains from the Nazielsk train station: one to Biale-Podlaska and another to Lukow.

## The Warsaw Ghetto

My in-laws crossed over with their button factory from Neustadt to Warsaw and worked with thread buttons. At that time, when I went to my father, may he rest in peace, in Serock, they took away my factory in Nowidwor. Because of the denunciation, my wife had to give the motor that I had hidden to the Germans within one day. Since I had nothing to do in Nowidwor, she left to her parents in Warsaw.

When I returned from Biale-Podlaska, my blood turned foul from fear. I lay sick at my in-laws' house on Karmelizka 8 for a few months, and couldn't do any work. After that, I went to work with thread buttons.

When there was discussion about a ghetto, they started to bring food products into Warsaw, and whoever had the good sense, strength, and money, prepared enough food for himself. I myself prepared three kilo potatoes, one kilo carrots, and a small grinder to grind barley cereal that was cooked together with the potatoes.

While the Germans locked up the ghetto, they looked for ways to close off any means of entering or leaving. Had they not forcefully chased the Jews out of the ghetto maybe we would have found some sort of solution about getting food that was smuggled in from the Polish side to the Jewish side. Kozhe Street was Jewish on one side and Polish on the other. The Germans closed the windows on the other side so that food wouldn't pass to the Jews. Nonetheless, food for the entire Jewish Warsaw passed through on wheels. Jewish carriers worked hard at this, risking their lives.

Each day, life in the ghetto became worse. People died in the streets from hunger. The *Khevra Kadisha* (Burial Society) had to take ten bodies at a time in their wagon. In every house, each day, you could find someone dead from starvation.

[Page 202]

Very soon, there was an epidemic of typhus and other diseases.

After each time that a yard with typhus was cleaned, there were still another two weeks after that where the people would be forced to the baths. Many died of starvation in those times. After that, they started to snatch young people for work, from which they didn't come back.


## In the Neustadt Ghetto

I myself changed my pass to make my age older, but when I saw that they are also taking older people, I began to hide. When I saw that the Jewish police came with their list at night to take Jews, I hid in the self-built bread oven. Many times I would go on the fourth level (floor) and hide there under the boards of an attic.

When I saw that I could no longer stay in the Warsaw ghetto, I left for Neustadt.

On Mjodowa Street, there were three guards. On the Jewish side, there were Jews, and on the Polish side, there were Poles and also a German. The Jewish policeman took five Marks and divided them among the three, and I went through just showing a piece of paper.

As I came to the Polish side wearing a long winter overcoat and carrying a bundle, soon two street boys on Mjodowa Street came to me and said point blank, without any pity, that soon I would be snatched up because I am dressed in a long coat and am carrying a bundle. They offered to take me over to Praga. I presented them with a price (5 zlotys) and they took us in and we went to Praga. Under a bridge, they robbed me of everything, even my *talis* and *tefillin*, and threatened that if I would say even one word, they would take me right to the Germans. They searched me and took away all my money, and so I was able to say "with my staff alone I crossed this Jordan...."[3] When I came to Pelcowizne, there were German guards, but they were preoccupied with a big smuggling deal going on with a Polish man, so we passed through peacefully to Legionowa.

We spent *Shabbos* in the Legionowa ghetto. I went to pray in a home and there I met many Serock Jews: Henokh Paskowicz with his children and grandchildren, Pesakh Kanjer, and others. I ate at Faivel Hiler's place.

[Page 203]

On Saturday night, after *Shabbos*, I joined a smuggler's group to go to Neustadt. I sold my last shirt and for that money I received one kilogram of bread that I and my wife ate on our way to Neustadt. We passed through forests en route, until we arrived at the Narew River. There, there was a border between the Reich and the General Government. Through signals with flashlights, the non-Jewish smugglers helped us cross in a small boat and took five Marks per head. At dawn, we entered the forest of Nazielsk. There, the head of the smuggler's group left us, and we made our way through the forest on our own until we reached the edge of Neustadt.

Behind the town, there were 100 young men working, that the *Judenaltester* (representative of the Jews, responsible for the Jewish prisoners) had to put up for work. The work consisted of taking out of the fields the huge rocks that interfered with the ploughing. We had to carry the heavy, huge rocks to one place and make meter-sized rocks to sell and to send over to the train. The German mayor took away all the money that was earned. The mayor was from Silesia, spoke Polish and German, and was a fiery anti-Semite. He did not move without his rubber truncheon. After work, the Jews would "organize" whatever was possible – trade something or buy something from the non-Jews and bring it into town to eat.

I joined up with these Jews and then after work went back with them to the town. The same way, I went with them to work, because I wanted to do some sort of business and make some money. Local Polish non-Jews kept guard over us.

Many times it happened that the mayor met us after we left work and searched us, but his attendant and escort was a Polish boy who was paid very well by the Jewish community. When the mayor told him to harness the horses, he did that for as long as it took him to warn the Jews not to take anything back on this trip.

[Page 204]

With time, the boys didn't want to let us get off from work anymore. Because of that, we couldn't do any more business on the way to work. I decided to go into the villages myself to do business there.

At 12 o'clock at night, I crawled through the fence that surrounded the ghetto, and I found myself on the Polish side. My wife, who escorted me until the Polish side, for sure could not sleep that night. Coming into the pharmacist's house on the Polish side, I looked around to see if I could see anyone, and then entered the churchyard.

Once, while crossing over onto the Polish side, they found me and shone a lamp right onto me, then started to chase me. I went to the organist's house in the court, and hid in a pile of chopped wood. I stayed there for a few hours listening to hear if anyone was walking around. When I saw that it was daylight and that if I was caught they would grab me for work on the Polish side, I decided to go further. I went on all fours, and went out of the court that way. I approached the fence of the church and in that manner, lying flat down, crawled quite a distance. Suddenly, someone jumped me. I thought I was now lost for sure. This turned out to be a Polish guard from the ghetto. I gave him something and also told him that I would be back the next day.

Through paths of cornfields, I walked for eight kilometers. As I was going through a forest, I lay down to sleep. This was my first restful sleep without any fear. Then I continued on until I came to a village. There I sold suits of clothing, plush blankets and tablecloths, and received eggs and chickens for them. I didn't go around in the village the entire day, but I stayed in a stable and slept there. When I learned that SS men were in the village, I went into a bathroom.

In the evening, when things calmed down in the village, I went out again to do business. It was dark when I was on my way home, and you couldn't see anyone in front of your eyes. I followed a star. Once, when there were no stars, I used my memory, and because of a crossroad in the path, I ended up in an unfamiliar village. In that area, there were many villages of German people.

[Page 205]

The only thing that is left for me to do is open a door somewhere and go into the home of a German person. So, without any other option, when it was already daylight, I decided to go ahead and go in. I opened a random door, and to my great fortune, I met familiar non-Jews. I apologized, said that I had gotten lost, and soon left with the intention of going home.

Once, it happened that I met a person at night that was standing at a distance and not moving. It was very dark and I remained fixed to my spot. Seems that the person thought that I was an SS man, and I was thinking the same of him. But after standing there for ten minutes, the man disappeared.

Once (this was before Pesach of 1941), I went to a village and was carrying a suit of clothing to sell, and a raincoat, a piece of material, and a plush blanket wrapped around myself. When I arrived in one house, I presented the things to sell. There was a Jewish boy who joined me, Plutnik from Neustadt, and together we bought 150 eggs. At a distance, a German property manager noticed us and started to shout: "Halt!" He was about 200 meters away from us. My friend said to me: "Let's run away." I said we shouldn't because the German certainly was armed and in this field there was no protection for us. We started to run and hid the 150 eggs in the yard. The evil man also went into the yard and caught us. He noticed the hidden eggs and asked what we were doing here. We replied that we worked in this area. He took us into the home of one of the non-Jews, made him responsible for us, and went to get a wagon to take us away. During this time, I hid away our things in the home of this non-Jew. When he came back with the wagon, I had only the suit and the raincoat on me. He told us to get onto the wagon, and we asked where we were going. He said, "to Szczecyn." We told him that we lived in Neustadt and that he should take us to our mayor. He didn't want to do that, we pleaded with him again, but he remained stubborn. So, giving us no choice, and with a gun in hand, he took us to the commando in Szczecyn, and we were convinced that there we would be killed. The police commandant searched us and found a package with eggs.

[Page 206]

He begins to scream: "Our soldiers in the hospitals and on the front need these and you are smuggling them!" They search us and also find a few German Marks and take them away. The German man opens up my coat and shows the commandant that I am wearing two suits and a coat. "He's a smuggler!" The commandant replies, "He's in my hands now, you can go." Then he says to us, "Take these eggs into the kitchen to the cook of the command center. It's a shame to waste all these eggs."

The commandant locks us up in a village "*koze,*" a temporary prison. My friend begins to cry and scream: "Mama, help me!" I tell him to recite some Psalms, pleading to God for salvation, saying: *Mi'maamakim, korosikho hashem* (from the depths I call to you, God). Soon, the door opened and the commandant came to us and said that if we were willing to chop up the logs that were in the yard, we could go free.

There was work there for two or three days. The commandant ordered us to bring tools for work.

We asked the messenger that brought the tools to tell the commandant that we were hungry and had not eaten in two days. The commandant ordered that whatever was left in the kitchen, the cook should give us to eat.

It had been three years since I had eaten such food – potatoes, soup, meat, white bread. After the three days of work, we were notified through the cook that our work was over. Then we asked her if there was any other work for us. She asked us to wash the floors, then she went in and said that we were asking to get our passes back so that we could go home in an untroubled manner. He assured us that if we would not leave immediately, he would kill us. We ran off right away and were reunited with our commando, then together left to Neustadt.

The praise and joy at home was great. I even managed to conduct the last *seder* on *Pesach* with the four cups of wine, using red borscht.

After the holiday of Sukkos 1941, they closed up the ghetto with SS guards and armed German citizens, and ordered us not to leave. During that time, I and a few other Jews continued to work in Pultusk and the surrounding areas until the end of the year 1941. There were no Jews left there, and all the shuls had been burned down. We worked as planters (turning over the soil).

[Page 207]

In the final days of the year 1941, when the order was given to liquidate the Neustadt ghetto, they sent us back to Neustadt.

The ghetto was closed down. We knew what was coming. I planned with the entire family to sneak out at night into a forest behind the town, and to take along shovels and dig ditches for us. We would live in there, and from time to time go out to the villages and find food. But when it was the last minute of completing this plan, my hands wouldn't work [I couldn't do it] and we did not go out.

For two weeks, we were captive under the uniformed German people. In the last few days, an order came to the senior Jews [those that took responsibility] that they should bring out all the handicapped and elderly. The old, religious families left for the assembly place. They also took the senior Jews.

All the elderly Jews and the handicapped were loaded into the farmers' wagons, and driven to the nearest train station, then with Jews from other cities, they were all taken to Auschwitz.

During that time, Jews from Drobnin, Sczeczyn, and some from Czekhanow were all forced into the Neustadt ghetto. The space in the ghetto was extremely small. Seven or eight families lived in one room. With me, they placed a few families – a hat maker from Drobnin and his five grown daughters. His entire fortune consisted of a bed – that was a few boards banged together – and a little bit of straw. The entire family slept on that with all the children. In another corner, there was another family – a woman, two children, and a niece.

Once, early in the morning, an order came that they were going to take us all out in the middle of the night. This was the last time that the baker baked bread. In the middle of the night, they gathered us all into the marketplace. The Jew hater, the mayor, ordered that in all the villages they should set out farmers' carts. We left on foot with the bed linen on the carts. On both sides of us we were guarded by armed German people and SS men, and they herded us towards Plonsk to the Jewish ghetto.

[Page 208]

We were quartered in Jewish homes, and there was no food in Plonsk. Suddenly there was an order that all Jews should assemble in the marketplace. There we received an order, under penalty of death, to hand over all German money. The German people went around with suitcases and everyone threw in whatever he had. After some time, they began physically searching people for money. They pulled out one Jew from his row, searched him, found some small change, then shot him on the spot.

Since my wife was dressed well, it seemed as if she was rich. They took her away into a room with other women and searched her for money in hidden places. I thought I had lost her, but she came back. After that whole scene, we were told to go back home.

A day or two later, they told all those from Neustadt to come forward and they told us that we would be taken to the train. We went to the loading place. There, on the boarding place, they gave us some bread. I took along two bottles of water because I had already been through this in the Serock herding nightmare and knew that thirst was worse than hunger.

Being chased on foot for four kilometers from the Jewish ghetto until the train station, they set us out in fives. The SS men moved us quickly, and no one wanted to be the last in line. In my row, there was a woman – a widow with a six-year-old child. It seems that her husband was no longer alive. When the SS men herded us and we had to run quickly, the small boy, weakened and hungry, had no energy to run. The screams from the child to his mother went directly to Heaven. The child asked his mother to pick him up, but the mother herself had no energy, and she dragged the child by the hand and screamed at him. I saw this whole thing, so I picked up the boy and quietened him down. When they warned me that I would stay behind and be beaten, I didn't answer. I carried the boy for some more time and wiped his tears.

[Page 209]

When we came to the train station, they chased us with beatings into the wagons. One bottle of water got broken in the process. I remained with one bottle, locked in the wagon for two days.

Slowly, after two long days of passing through many different stations, we were all drained, and arrived late at night to the tragic place of Auschwitz. This was in the first half of January in 1942.

**Auschwitz...**

[This moving paragraph is written in Hebrew]:

*"I am the man who saw the pained ones suffering by the wrath of the stick. If only my eyes could become a stream of water and a source of tears and I could cry day and night for the destruction of my nation. If only I could have wings of an eagle, I would be alone on the mountaintops and I could release the cries of my brothers and sisters who, with my own eyes, I saw how they burned and how they were strangled in the furnace of flames."*

After they chased us out of the wagons, when we arrived in Auschwitz, they put me together with my wife among older people who would go directly to the crematoria.

The SS men who worked with the trains, searched the people. When they liked a face, they sent this person over to be with those who would go to the labor camps. Even though at that time no one knew yet where they would be taken, I still noticed how many people wanted to run from one side of the rows to the other, how many had to go to the camps, but the SS men ran after them and beat them with their machine gun butts and dragged these people back to the right places. After looking through all the people, one SS man came over to me and told me to go to the other side with the workers. Then I said to my wife: "I'm not leaving you. Wherever you go, I will go." My wife answered: "Moishe, go to the other side. Maybe you'll remain alive and be able to take revenge for my blood." During that speech, an SS man ripped me away and I went to the row that was going to work.

Women were taken to another side; about 100 young women were put separately to go to the labor camp. I, the believer, saw a miracle happen right then.

The Jewish commandos, that were called "Canada,"[4] forcefully took the children away from their young mothers and gave them to the older women or grandmothers so that the young women could go to the working camps. Or, because of the young children, they also sent young mothers to the side of death. Heartrending scenes played out there. Of the 1800 Jews that came from Neustadt, 350 men and 100 women went to the camps – and among them were my wife and I. Of all of these, after the war, there were only a few men and twenty or so women. From a town of 1800 Jews, approximately three *minyanim* (quorums of 10) remained.

[Page 210]

Going from the train on foot in the middle of the night to the camps, they herded us into a Block. There was no talk of sleep. We were standing on our feet all night. From time to time, a *Kapo* (inmate in charge of work team) came running in with a long whip, and all of us would huddle against the wall.

Jewish prisoners would approach the windows to try and "organize" some food from the newly arrived. They told us: "Soon they'll take everything away from you, so you may as well give it all to us." That's how people began parting with whatever they had.

They following morning, they took us to the baths. They took away everything from us and we received camp clothing from material made of wood. We almost froze to death from the cold. We were kept locked in quarantine for two weeks just in case there was any typhus in the ghettos, but they didn't let us rest. When all the prisoners left in the mornings to go to work, we were set out on the yard in the Block, and that's how we had to stay for eight hours until all the commandos arrived in the evening back from work and did a roll call to make sure no one was missing.

When the numbers added up correctly for the entire camp, then everyone went into their Blocks. In the evening, we received a little of the bad food from lunch, and they began teaching us how we had to stand with our bowls by the boilers. The senior Block person poured in a little soup and we had to leave right away (that was in the Block). In a very few minutes, all the food had to be distributed. Our hands were trembling with fear. If someone didn't put his cup exactly in the right place for the food – on the rim of the boiler – the murderers used the spoon …… to pour the hot food over the person's head, and he did not get any more food. Some didn't want this bit of food so that they wouldn't have to get hit by these hooligans – the Block elders.

[Page 211]

In the two weeks of quarantine we did not have any information about our families because no one was allowed to come near us. After the two weeks, when we already had gotten the numbers on our forearms (the numbers were given by pricking the arm with a needle and using dye for the number formation), and when we were now dressed like all the other prisoners, we were now told that we should go work.

*Kapos* came from all kinds of terrible commandos, and people fell like flies because of them through beatings and hunger, from cold, and from the difficult work. They came to find new victims among those newly arrived.

The first day I fell into a commando whose job it was to drag sand out of water using a machine. For about six or seven kilometers, hungry, we had to carry hammers and all other types of iron tools to the job site and back. On the way back, we each held onto a friend, or a friend held onto us. Often, not going to work was even worse. Coming back to my Block 10 (Auschwitz 3, a duplicate camp), we had to stand for roll call for a long time until all the commandos had come back and had handed over all their accounts to the Nazi officer at the gate, and miraculously, everything tallied correctly.

In our Block of the newly arrived, I heard someone call out: "He who is a tailor should raise his hand!" They counted all those who raised their hands and told them to go out of their line after eating and to register in the administration room. Then they called out: "Whoever is a shoemaker, electrician, or has other skills should also raise their hands."

I thought: Dear God, if only my father would have taught me a trade, I would be able to survive, because to work the way I am now, it's impossible to survive.

A minute later, they called out: "Whoever can make baskets, raise your hands." I had forgotten that I once learned how to do this as a *khalutz* (pioneer) in *Hapoel Hamizrakhi*, preparing to go to Israel and work in agriculture. My parents had convinced me to learn a trade and I went to a Polack and paid 200 zlotys so that he could teach me to weave baskets. (Before that, my trade was oil-maker.) When they called out: "Whoever can weave baskets raise your hand," this came into my head, and after I raised my hand they told me to get out of line. They told me to go to the administration room right after lunch. When I came there, the writer, a Pole, said to me in Polish: "A Polish Jew is a basket maker?" But when I told him that I paid 200 zlotys for a Polack to teach me this trade, he believed me and he gave me a note and told me to go to the Block. The Block manager gave me a large portion of bread for the next day, and some soup to eat and told me to go from Block 10 to Block 4, among only Poles. Block 10 was made up of only newly-arrived Jews, under a Polish Block guard, a cruel man, worse than Haman. For no reason, he would use his truncheon. We would cower between the beds, terrified of taking a step forward, terrified of uttering a sound. The fear of death in the Block was unimaginable. For any little thing, we would get beaten: for eating, for making the bed badly, etc. For every little thing, he would taunt us with disgusting words. When they took me over to Block 4, it was as if I had left hell for freedom.

[Page 212]

In Block 4, there were only Poles and Ukraines. They played harmonicas, moved around freely, spoke freely and loudly. I – one Jew – got lost among them. The following morning, they took me away to work at a company called "*Kommando Gertnerai (Gardners of) Rajska*" (name of a Polish village). The basket makers were sent ten kilometers to the Vistula River to cut reeds (thin sticks). When we arrived at the shore of the Vistula, my strengths were not those of the non-Jews, so I got beaten by a Kapo, a terrible Jew-hater. After that, they tattled to the sergeant that the Jew didn't do any work.

The sergeant came over to me and began shouting: "Cursed Jew! You lied! I'll teach you. You'll get *shteibunker*!" (standing cell)[5]

The hooligans laughed at me. When lunchtime came (they didn't bring any lunch), there was an hour's rest. The workers made a fire, warmed themselves, and told many anti-Semitic stories against the Jews. The SS men did this: they said, "Soon we will chop you up and burn you on the fire." I am one Jew among so many wolves.

[Page 213]

In that time, I took a few reeds and began weaving the frame of a basket. The scoundrels came and grabbed away the cover (of the basket) and laughed at what "the Jew" had made. They took this over to the sergeant. When he sees the work, he came over to me and said, with these words: "Jew, you're lucky that you know how to work. Otherwise, I would finish you off." After lunch, they didn't bother me anymore. In the camp, they no longer gave me work of only carrying things.

The next morning, there was an order that the workers would no longer be going to the Vistula to collect reeds, but we would be going along to the garden market. They gave us a room there and built some work tables and we sat down and began weaving baskets. Of all the Polacks who passed themselves off as workers, there was only one young Polack who worked well, who had completed trade school. I was in second place. The other non-Jews had smuggled themselves in for work. Through using their "connections" there was a Polish professor and a Polish captain who also smuggled themselves in for work, and they knew nothing. It was warm in the room. In order that our hands do not slow down, it had to be warm.

When I started the work, I saw that I had already forgotten a lot, but by watching how the master worker did his work, I copied him. The others sat and pretended to work. The SS men came in every five minutes to see how the master worked, and I am weaving a basket and the others are sitting like dummies and are still at the beginning. He began to understand what was going on. From then on, they started treating me a little differently. The other scoundrels were very afraid that they would be thrown out of this commando. So, whom do they approach? In time of need, they go the Jew. They did a trade with me, for the bread that they got in their packages. That which I finished, they would take from me, and that which they made, I would complete. Meanwhile, I had bread and a warm room. I was very nervous about the lot of my dear ones and my acquaintances. My peace was ruined.

[Page 214]

Once, when I went out at night to find out how things were going for the residents in Block 10, they told me who was in the hospital. The Jewish doctors who worked there saved people's lives with whatever they could, but then the hospital filled up, and SS men came with buses and ordered the doctors and their aides to leave. The SS men brought thugs with them and they chased out the sick people into the cars and drove them off to Brzezinka (Birkenau -- a forest a few kilometers past Auschwitz). That's where the crematoria were. When the hospital was empty, people still kept coming there all the time until it would be emptied again. Meanwhile, some people had the good fortune of getting better and of coming back to the camp. When I would tell all the Jews: "Jews, don't go to the hospital. You'll all be taken from there to the crematoria." Many of them laughed me off and said: "You see, people are coming back." But in truth, only a small number came back. When the hospital filled up again, they were all taken again to the crematoria.

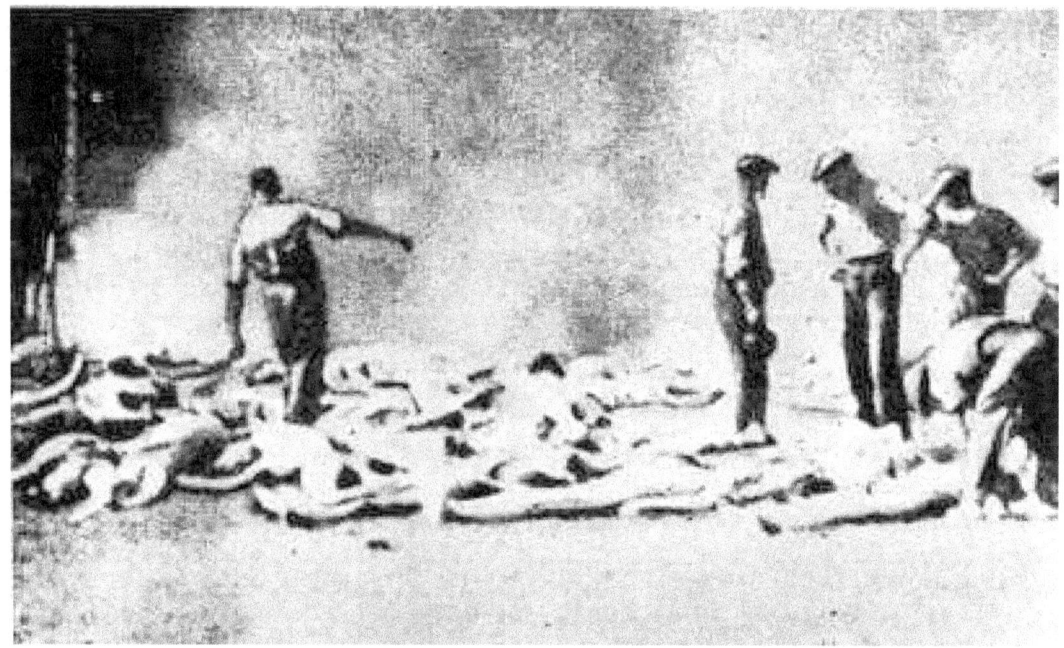

**The *Sonderkommando* (these were prisoner-laborers attached to a specific "special action" or task) dragging the gassed Jews to the crematoria**

[Page 215]

And so, in that way, of the 350 Jews, within about one month, there were not even 100 left. When we came back from work, I asked what had happened to the women. If they told a Jew that he no longer had a wife or children because they had all been burned, the Jew would spit into the other person's face. They had convinced themselves that the women were sent to another work camp and that the children, in groups of five, were being cared for by another woman.

During that time, I received a message from the men who went to work that they had seen a commando of women pass by as they were going to work, and that my wife was one of these women. When I discovered that my wife was alive, I began to look for ways to be able to see her. Through the men's commando that came to the women's camp – electricians, locksmiths, cabinetmakers, etc. – I sent a letter that I was still alive and I was in the gardener's unit, so she also put herself in the group that went to work there.

I "bought" a few potatoes for a portion of bread and put them into my belt. That's how I went to work and I gave my wife baked potatoes. Once, my wife told me she had no shoes. She came to work with rags bound on her feet, and she was afraid that she would be sent to the crematoria. I then organized a trade in my Block for a pair of shoes. The next morning, I squeezed the two shoes under my belt and brought them into the Rajsko gardens for my wife. This is what happened: I took a bucket, put the shoes in, and covered it. I went to get wood and coal to warm up the workroom. I went especially near the women's commando, turned over the bucket, and said not one word to her. My wife picked up the shoes. With time, she had a better commando and they told her to say that she had a husband in the "Canada" commando. Maybe the female *Kapo* would permit her to work there.

The first few months, I worked in the Rajsko gardens. I had a warm room, baked potatoes, and even from time to time received something from the "higher up" people.

[Page 216]

Once, when I was standing at roll call, there was an order to give in our caps to be washed and to go bareheaded. And that was in the middle of winter.

They put aside boxes, and everyone had to put in their caps. Here the non-Jews, the hooligans, began to have some fun – they didn't put their caps in, they threw them. For that we all got a punishment that everyone should lie down on the ground. The SS men were standing by with revolvers in their hands. We had to roll around outside for an hour's time, so much so that I was left breathless.

In order not to forget, I have to give over in a few words about a duplicate camp (a copy) that was not far from me, whose goal was to cynically fool the world – and particularly, to fool the Red Cross.

In these Blocks, there were beautiful, red-colored floors, beautiful waiting rooms with mirrors, the food was clean – and there were no crematoria. This is what they showed to the foreign visitors from the Red Cross as a sample of a labor camp.

I remember once there was supposed to be an important Nazi guest, and they mentioned the name of Eichmann, may his name be erased. They cleaned the camp for a few days. In these festive moments they let us bathe after work. We had to strip naked in the middle of the winter, leave our clothing near the bed, and run in the frost for a few streets to the baths. And all sweaty, come back to a sparkling barrack.

One day, an order was given that the gardening commando of Rajsko would be transferred to Birkenau, another camp near Auschwitz, because the Rajsko gardens were closer to Birkenau than to Auschwitz. As I came to Birkenau with my commando, I was once again among non-Jews, but the regime was a little easier. After work, I went out to see what was going on with the other commandos, and saw that the horrors were tremendous: people were sleeping in the holes in the walls. They were being beaten to death, and the worst was to stand for general roll call for 4 to 5 hours after work. There was never a shortage of "reasons" for this: an error in calculation, "deserters," and besides we were all superfluous in this world anyway. Standing in these rows with terrible stomach cramps and horrific pains, the only thing that churned around in my mind, back and forth, was: *Eli, Eli, Lama Azavtani? Me'ayin yavo ezri?* (God, why have You forsaken me? From where will come my salvation?)

[Page 217]

Before the victims went to the crematoria, they were first tortured by the Block supervisors. Even today, before my eyes, stand the naked, emaciated people (skeletons) like herring, sacks of bones without even a drop of meat on them, lying every morning in groups in front of the Blocks. The managers and cleaners had thrown them out. If a person had diarrhea and could not make his way to the bathroom, the supervisor and the cleaner would beat him with sticks and throw him out the door where he would freeze. In this camp, there was no sanitation system – in the entire region there was only one water pump.

After eight months of work in the garden commando of Rajsko, along with many Polish doctors, military personnel, teachers, and guards, the entire commando consisted of about 100 men.

Then, a senior SS leader (First Lieutenant) came and saw that people were wandering around idly, so he asked that the commando be reduced to 30 people. That small piece of bread that we had received in the evenings along with the soup and a small piece of margarine, I had to sell in order to get fifteen potatoes from the commando that did the peeling. Many of them died from the beatings they got for "organizing" potatoes from the kitchen. Despite this situation, people risked their lives. On the day that there was no inventory taken, they "organized" again. I took the fifteen potatoes under my belt in the morning to work, baked them in the ash from the oven, and ate this twice a day along with the margarine. There was a Polish captain with me. He could not make any baskets, so he would switch with me. I would give him the beginnings of a basket that I had made and for that he would give me part of his package that he had received from home. The Germans wanted to have a Polish allegiance, so they made concessions with the Polacks and permitted them to receive packages. I told my wife, who was in the women's camp in Auschwitz, to present herself to the women's overseer of the gardeners of Rajsko, and that's how we would be able to see each other. The contact was through the men who went with the men's commando to the women's camp to work as locksmiths, electrical mechanics, and carpenters. The best organizers were the water pipe cleaners when they cleaned the reservoir and the bathrooms in the women's camp. In the large reservoir, all the letters that husbands and wives and friends wrote to each other were hidden. They bought things of value and paid with food (this commando comprised only Jews). The exchange went through some civilized non-Jews who worked as laborers in the camp. Also, these non-Jews were searched at the gates and risked their lives with this.

[Page 218]

Once, at a meeting, my wife said to me that she won't be able to come to work because once again she had no shoes. Her feet were wrapped in rags. Just at that moment, a *Kontrol* went by the women's camp. They gathered together all the women that did not go to work, among whom was my wife. She pleaded with the women's *kapo*: "I can't go to work. Why are you sending me to be burned?" He replied because soon he would have to send them all to the crematoria. Then, the junior *kapo* walked by and saw my wife whom he did not know, and told her to run away. That's how she was saved from death at that time. She let me know right away that she was playing with her life because she didn't have shoes.

I told her to come to me quickly with the rags on her feet, because I managed to "organize" a pair of shoes. It happened when we exchanged shoes at night in the Block. I took a pair of new shoes and did not part with the old ones. In the morning, leaving for work, I carefully brought the shoes to the commando, and hid them under the reeds (we were not permitted to speak to the women). I took a bucket, put the shoes in, and pretended to go bring wood and coal. I went near the women and turned over the bucket and my wife grabbed the shoes. That's how she once again regained her wits.

[Page 219]

The Jewish women's commandos were from all kinds of places. There were women from Paris, but within a few days they all died from walking ten kilometers to work every day to the gardens without any food all day, and from dysentery as a result of the dirty water that they had.

The commandos again filled up with women from Greece, but within a few days they disappeared. In the Rajsko commando there was a terrible *Kapo*, a former thief and then camp prisoner. This murderer killed many Jews. He would beat them with a board at work and in the fields. Once he took me out into the snow and said: "You didn't wash yourself today." He pushed me into the snow and rubbed my face. I could hardly catch my breath. But he got his end as well. One fine day, he began to have stomach cramps. He was taken to the hospital and never seen again. It was said that the underground of Polacks who worked in the camps, had poisoned him. Once, a sergeant came to me and ordered that I make him a whip. When the whip was ready, he told me to bend over, and he began beating my behind with the whip. At first, I remained silent, but soon I began to scream. That's when he said: "Now I know that the whip is good."

## In the Potato Hall Commando

After they threw out the Jews from the gardening commando of Rajsko, it became very bad for me. I became part of a commando that built cellars for potatoes, and labored hard for a year. Meanwhile, my wife moved to a better commando for sorting packages that the newly transported brought with them. At the stations, these packs were loaded onto buses, driven to stores, then to Germany. When I worked with the potatoes, they selected a *Sonderkommando* for the crematoria because the former commando had already been alive for too long. The Germans didn't want the world later to be able to find out anything from those who did the burning. So, just about each half year they would burn the old *Sonderkommando* (about 200 men) and choose new ones from the camp.

[Page 220]

My wife found out about this and wrote me a letter with these words: "Moishe, I heard that they are going to select a *Sonderkommando*. If you get chosen as a *Sonderkommando*, go over to the electric wires that surround the camp and end your life. I don't want that my husband should be one of those who set fire to the Jewish nation. If I will hear that you've done that, then I will also go to the wires and do the same." I thought about it at that moment and decided that if I would be chosen, I would say: "Shoot me! I'm not going!"

On the day that they chose the *Sonderkommando*, an order was given that the Jews should not go out to work and have to assemble in the large yard.

I went to a different Block, went to hide under a bed, and stayed there deathly afraid until the Polacks came from work in the evening (forget about eating any food – since the fear was greater than the hunger). So I gave praise to God – and went back to my Block. The *Sonderkommando* had been chosen. I informed my wife that everything had passed in peace.

Work in the potato commando ended and those left were assigned the job of filling the cellars with potatoes. All day we had to carry heavy and long sacks and all the while we were beaten and chased by Polish *Kapos* and SS men.

Then my wife suggested to me that I go work in the Canada commando (called "Canada" because Canada is a rich country) at the train station receiving the transports.

I made it through three selections in Block 31 in Birkenau. The first time, of 300 Jews, half remained. After the second selection, a little over thirty remained, and the third time it was already too horrific – I didn't want to remain alive. I was completely scratched up and the Germans hated that. When Dr. Mengele noticed that a body was bloated and swollen or looked like a sack of bones without any meat – the person was ready for burning. A Polish writer went along with him. We ran naked across the Blocks, and whoever number the doctor asked to be written down, that person was already finished. At night, they called out all these numbers from the Blocks and these people were taken to the crematoria.

At the last selection, the Polish writer grabbed me by the hand and wanted to write my number. I pulled myself away from him, and the head bandit gestured with his hand that he should let me go. That's how we were the last sixteen Jews that remained from several hundred. It didn't take long, and soon the Block was filled again with newly-arrived Jews.

*[Page 221]*

## The "Canada" Commando

My sister Khaitche, Jonisz-Gudes, came from the camp Majdanek. When the Russian front was coming closer, they did another selection: the weak ones had to march in one row and the healthy ones in another row. My brother-in-law, Yekhiel Jonisz, fell in with the weaker ones and my sister with the stronger ones that were sent over from Majdanek to Birkenau. Some 20,000 weakened Jews, among whom was Yekhiel Jonis, were all shot to death.

*[Page 222]*

**A gas chamber**

My sister was in a good commando in Birkenau. Their job was to clean the bathrooms and toilets. She brought two American gold dollars with her. These gold dollars were given over through a middleman to the Block elder, a German *Volksdeutch* who later ordered that I be moved over to the Canada commando.

I started working in the warehouse with the packages. When I opened each package and saw pictures of families, my blood froze in my veins. I imagined each family alive and standing right before me. Because of that, I didn't want nor couldn't even taste any of the food that there was in these dead packages.

A long time passed and I didn't want to taste anything from these packages. Several of the religious Jews in the camp, after a serious legal debate (arguing the details of Jewish law), concluded that I was permitted to eat from these foods so that I could give away my portion of bread in the camp to another Jew and save his life. When I came home from work at night, my acquaintances were already standing and waiting for me, and asking, as if talking to their father: "Moishe, what did you bring for us?"

When I found sausages, I carefully placed them under my foot and would walk on my tip toes for one kilometer until I came out of the warehouse. In this commando, they searched you very carefully. At the doors, there were boxes, and they told us that if we found any valuable items in the packages, we should put everything into these boxes. Anyone found with anything on him, would be shot on the spot. Many Jews were shot in this fashion. I myself took food in the early times, because for that all you got were a few beatings. For the pieces of sausage that I took with me, I saved one Jew. If someone wanted to move to a better commando, he had to give something to the *Kapo*. You could buy him off with a sausage. Once I brought a few thousand pieces of stones for cigarette lighters (*rods made from iron-cerium were filed down and used for improvised cigarette lighters*), and with that saved some Jews. Lately, I started to "organize" valuable items and with that helped a cousin transfer to a better commando.

[Page 223]

This is how I had seven good months. I was calm and was able to look around and see what was going on in the camps. I didn't want to go to the trains and to the warehouse, but I couldn't get out of it, so after many beatings from the Canada *Kapo*, I was dragged to the trains. A train arrived from Latvia and among them were many cold wagons and more than half the people had perished during the transport. When they took out those who were still alive and put them together in one place, I talked with them. An elderly *khassidic* Jew asked me where they were being taken. I froze and didn't know what to say. I decided to reply, and told him that he is going to his forefathers Avrohom, Yitzkhok, and Yakov, and he should tell them that it is already enough suffering for us.

### The Jewish Uprising in Auschwitz

I lived next to the Block where the Jewish *Sondercommando* lived. Their task was to burn the gassed bodies in the crematoria and then to scatter the ashes so that there would be no memory of them. The *Sondercommando* were "changed" and shot every few weeks. Right after that, the murderers chose other healthy Jews in order to serve the Satan in hell down here on earth.

My eyes saw how the Jewish nation was being extinguished in flames and I was infused with a feeling to strengthen myself with all my energies so that I would be able to tell the world about this mass murder.

I did everything to get into the barracks of the *Sondercommando* at night. That's how we helped some Jews from Serock and Popowa that belonged to this tragic unit. I listened to their stories that confirmed everything that my eyes saw.

**The crematoria where the gassed Jews were transformed into ash**

The Jews from Bedzin and Sosnowiec were of the last to arrive in Auschwitz. They knew that they were being taken to their death. Right at the train station they protested and didn't want to go to Birkenau to the crematoria. The SS encircled the Jews and shot them all with their machine guns right in the train station.

[Page 224]

The Germans in Warsaw and in the surrounding areas, wanting to fool those Jews who were hiding in the area or in bunkers, sent out Polish instigators to spread a rumor that for a specific sum of dollars these Jews will be acknowledged as American citizens and will be sent abroad.

Thousands of Jews were fooled with this. They paid huge amounts of money, seated themselves in comfortable wagons along with uniformed Germans, and were taken "abroad" – to Auschwitz.

Once, a large transport of "American" Jews arrived. When all had disembarked from the wagons they were asked politely to undress and go wash up in order that they could be taken to a "different place."

[Page 225]

These Jews began to scream: "No! No!" Among them was a woman, an actress. When they asked her to undress, she refused. A higher ranked SS officer wanted to know the reason. Her answer was: "You will not see my naked body." She turned toward her husband so that he would react (support her). Then, the husband grabbed an iron object and threw it with force at the head of the SS man who became confused and fell over. Soon another SS murderer became involved, and pulled out his gun and shot the actress's husband. There was a big tumult, a large group of armed SS men ran over, and all the newly arrived were shot dead.

Once, a transport of Greek Jews arrived. Some of them were set up as *Sonderkommando*. In the crematoria of Birkenau, when a lot of burned bodies were gathered up, the ashes were taken out into cargo trucks and dumped into the Vistula River not far from Cracow.

In this kind of transport truck, two Greek and a few Polish Jews once went along. The driver and the escort were armed SS men. When they came to the Vistula to dump the human ash, the two Greek Jews attacked the two escorts, beat them up, took their weapons, jumped into the water, swam to the other side, and ran away. They were not caught. The Polish Jews, who didn't have the courage to do what their brothers from Greece had done, were taken back to the camp where they were murdered in a horrific way.

In mid-summer of 1944, they burned an entire Jewish *Sonderkommando*. On that same day, a new transport came, made up of Jews from Makow, Mlawa, Popowa, and Serock. Soon they did a strict selection and those who remained were taken as the new *Sonderkommando*. Among them was the *dayan* of Makow, Moishe Margulis from Serock, and the two Margulis

[Page 226]

Very often, I found myself with Moishe Margulis in the Block of the *Sonderkommando*. He said nothing, but raised his eyes to the heavens, nodded his head, and gave a profound sigh. Moishe Margulis, my relative and neighbor from Serock, was forced to become a servant in the hell of this earth.

On Rosh Hashana and Yom Kippur I prayed together with the *Sonderkommando* in their Block. They prayed fervently and everyone recited the *kaddish yosom* (prayer recited by one who is orphaned). The one who led the prayers was the *dayan* from Makow and his *kaddish yosom* unsettled me terribly. Until this very day, I hear his echoes. In middle of the prayers, one man, a terribly pained person, began to curse and blaspheme against Creator. We didn't say anything to this man; his pain was very deep: his pain – our pain.

In 1944, between Rosh Hashana and Sukos, Moishe Margulis said to me: "Yes, yes, this Simkhas Torah I will dance with my father at the Amshinower Rebbe's." I said to him: "Moishe, what are you saying? You'll survive the war!" Moishe placed his strong, blackened hands over his heart, lifted up his red-rimmed eyes to Heaven, and began to sing a khassidic melody: "*Eli, Eli, Lomo Azavtoni?*" (My God, why have You forsaken me?) I cried along with him.

**The Revolt of the *Sonderkommando***

One late morning, Sukos 1944, I was occupied with cleaning water pipes, not far from the crematoria. Suddenly, I see one of the crematoria burning. It soon became clear to me that the *Sonderkommando* had made a revolt. At dawn there had been a selection and the entire commando and everyone else was incited to rebel. First, they suffocated the guards and threw a few Germans alive into the burning ovens, the worst of the Jew haters. Then they set fire to the barracks, the camp, and the crematoria. When everything was already burning, they ran off into all four corners to get out of Birkenau. The fire spread, and dense smoke covered the sky, and there was mass confusion.

[Page 227]

The sirens soon started to blare and the entire huge military might was mobilized and set on alert. Hundreds of SS men on motorcycles began to chase us, shooting those on the run and searching for those in hiding.

Many of those who were running were shot and those who were captured and brought back were beaten and assembled together on an open place not far from the burned camp. Not one of those who ran off merited to live until they were free.

Everyone was forced to lie on the ground face down. Among those, was also Moishe Margulis, and the SS men shot them all with their machine guns.

Moishe Margulis's promise was fulfilled. This Simkhas Torah he was freed.

**I Leave Auschwitz**

At the end of the year 1944, the Russian and Polish armies moved closer, up to 60 kilometers before Cracow. From a distance we could already hear the shooting of cannons.

The murderers decided to evacuate all the healthy people from Auschwitz. The weaker ones, those who couldn't march any more, were put aside, taken to the forest, and murdered there.

One day, they chased us out of the barracks and told us to get into our rows. I went into the train that took me, along with hundreds of other Jews, to the very sad camp Stuthof, near Danzig. I was there for three months, worked at digging up potatoes, and did other hard work. We were given only enough food to sustain our souls.

After three months, we were taken over on foot to a miserable camp in the village of Rybno (?) near Danzig. We all agreed to work in Danzig in the factories that produced secret military materials. As an electronics technician, I worked by the underwater boats (submarines). They taught me how to weld, but after that they regretted doing so and later did not allow me do the welding for the secret materials.

[Page 228]

In those times, in the military factories in Danzig, there were tens of thousands of vocational workers from all the nations of Europe. These aforementioned had a large dining room where they were served well, but the Jews did strenuous work and were given a very meager diet. Our energies began to give out. Lunchtime, when the civilian workers finished eating, we snuck into the dining room and like cats licked all the plates and gathered up the garbage.

But even this pleasure the SS men would not allow us and with beatings they chased us out of this Garden of Eden. When the Russians began to bomb Danzig, our situation improved. From that time on, we ate together with everyone else in the large room.

We, the starved 1500 Jews, could not stand still in the rows for food. We simply went crazy from starvation. The SS men, with their manner, tried to quieten us and the civilian Germans begged us to calm down.

When Danzig was heavily bombed and the city stood in flames, the Germans evacuated us from the camp. In middle of the night, 1500 half dead Jews began a march, but it was already without organization – again, we received no food. Hundreds died en route from weakness. The SS escorts were confused – sometimes beating us, sometimes complimenting us. We spent nights in churches and also under the free sky and no one from the German village population brought us even a little bit of water. Not one camp wanted to take us in. Airplanes were constantly bombing.

A commandant from a large SS camp – not far from Konigsberg – had mercy on us. He gave one large barrack for all the Jews.

In the barrack there was a lot of pushing, a narrowness, and suffocating air – tens died each night. In the surrounding area of the barrack there were also no washrooms and no water. They didn't let us out of the camp because of the epidemic of typhus.

[Page 229]

We were like lepers.

The Germans were afraid to approach us and in the last two weeks we didn't even get our bread rations.

When the hunger became terrible, we pleaded with the Germans to release us and let us cook the carcasses of the horses that were lying in large numbers on all the roads. Sometimes the SS men allowed us to do this.

Even the carcasses of the horses began to disappear. Once I bought a bottle of horse blood from a Polack, warmed it up and drank it I searched the camp for all kinds of horses' bones and gnawed at them all night and by doing that ruined even my good teeth. When not even bones were left, I searched for grass, but in the winter it was all mouldy. I cooked this mouldy grass, added noxious bones, and said: "Master of the Universe, You can sustain me even with grass."

**Before the End**

We started to hear cannon shots. The Russian artillery had bombed the entire area. Our camp was in a valley, so miraculously we were saved. The mayor of a nearby town decided to dig a long, deep canal in order to stop the oncoming march of the Soviet tanks. He mobilized the civilian population and also asked us for a large portion of bread and meat to go along with it, because the majority of the Jews were in a situation of fighting off their own death.

I was also drained, my feet were swollen from the cold, I couldn't move, and was waiting for death.

One day, before dawn, I looked through the window of the barrack and saw that all the roads were black with people. All the village Germans had begun to run – some on foot and some in wagons. That's how we ran from Serock and from Nowy Dwor to Warsaw a few years ago. That same day – it was March or April 1944[6] – the commander of the SS came and told us that the Germans were leaving this place and anyone that wants to join them could do so.

[Page 230]

I and the majority of the Jews decided to stay, not looking at (caring about) the consequences.

In the middle of the night, a military patrol arrived and took the SS men and left quickly. The SS men who were supposed to shoot us, this time did not follow through, wanting to get an alibi for themselves. Only the Jews were left in the huge camp. Soon a Russian intelligence group arrived, and waiting for my death, I heard cries.

"Jews! *Gevalt*! Our friends are here!"

We told the Russians about the canals set for the Russian tanks, and they quickly went to investigate.

In the morning the Russian military entered the camp – we are now free people!

With our last energies, we stood up from our cots, went outside, and put out our hands for food. The Russians gave us marmalade, and cans of preserved meat and bread.

Everyone grabbed the food – but our intestines couldn't handle the food. Soon dysentery broke out from which 75% of those remaining alive, died.

After the Russians had arrived, they took us over to the hygienic homes of the SS and brought local Germans to take care of us. I was hardly alive, but in these final moments, I strengthened myself. I started by drinking only tea with sugar cubes until my stomach cleaned itself out. After a few weeks, I was able to stand on my own feet. All those who died in camp from dysentery were buried in a communal grave.

After I got better, around April 1944[6], I went to Poland to look for my brothers and sisters, but I never found anyone.

**Translator's Footnotes**

1. Referring to ethnic Germans rather than German citizens.
2. This was an area of the Second Republic of Poland under Nazi Germany during World War II, designated as a separate region of the Third Reich between 1939–1945
3. Book of Genesis, 32:11, "Now I have nothing and I need your help" as Jacob pleads to God for His help.
4. The workers in "Canada" sorted out the belongings of incoming prisoners, taking everything that could have been of value for the Third Reich.
5. Behind an opening in the wall, through which only a bowed man could go, there was a cupboard-like space of 80 x 80 centimetres, 2 meters high, so that you could stand freely. Four prisoners were pushed in there with the help of a stick, and, the door locked with bars. They remained there until morning. In the evening they were released and taken to work, but for the night they were again pushed in, like sardines, and locked with the use of iron bars until morning.
6. The author indicated 1944, but clearly it is the end of the war, so, the correct year should be 1945

*[Page 231]*

# In Years of Terror
## Chava Konkol-Kanarek (Tel-Aviv)

**Translated by Sara Mages**

It was Friday, 1 September 1939, when the war broke out. On that Sabbath eve German planes passed over my hometown Serock. They flew low and cast heavy shadows and great terror. The first four days of the war passed in great fear, and on the fifth day we tasted its first taste. On the same day the city was bombed and in this bombing we lost our oldest brother, Shmuel z"l. Our entire family quickly fled to the other side of the Narew River.

After the conquest of the city by the Germans all of us returned to Serock because the bombings ceased, the shots fell silent and silence prevailed. However, a few days later the Germans ordered all the Jewish men to gather in the Great Synagogue. Only the elderly returned to the families who waited for their loved ones. All the young men were taken from there and expelled to Germany. That day my older brother, Moshe Kanarek, didn't return to our home.

A short time later, all the Jews, including my five sisters, were expelled from Serock to Biala- Podlaska. My parents and I weren't among the deportees because at that time we were with my aunt in the village of Zatori across the Narew River. When the news of the expulsion reached us we headed to my aunt, my mother's sister, who lived in Wolomin.

My aunt received us well, but the concern for my sisters didn't leave us for a moment. My aunt, who felt sorry for us, traveled to Biala- Podlaska and brought all my sisters with her.

Again we were together at my aunt's house. It was good to be together, but we were forced to separate because my aunt couldn't support us all. Then we knew the hunger which began to plague us. Mother had another sister who lived in the village of Wieliszew near Zegrze. Therefore, my sister Chana and I traveled to this aunt. Her husband was a tailor and we helped him with his work. A short time later our mother came to Wieliszew, and then my sisters Masha and Leah. Since there wasn't enough room at my aunt's house, we rented a small narrow room in a Polish woman's hut and lived there. It wasn't long before the whole family joined us, and all of us huddled together in the small and narrow room - only to be together.

We lived in Wieliszew until 1940. In October of the same year we were expelled to Ludwisin Ghetto near Legionowa. In the ghetto we suffered from constant hunger and feared annihilation.

[Page 232]

Every day my mother and sisters tried to sneak into the nearby village to try to exchange the remainder of our shabby clothes for bread, potatoes or other food items. When they were lucky, we had something to eat and the great hunger ceased for a short time.

At that time I left the ghetto and went to my Polish woman who lived in the village. The Polish woman was kind to me and I stayed with her for about ten months. The police learned about it, came to arrest me and sentenced me to death. They let me go after I cried and pleaded, but under the condition that I would return to the ghetto. I returned to the ghetto.

A bitter cold prevailed in the winter of 1941. We didn't have wood or other materials for heating. In addition to hunger and fear we also suffered from the intense cold that penetrated the bones. Father couldn't see us tormented by the cold, and under mortal danger went to the nearby forest to collect firewood. Once he got caught and was beaten all over his body. He returned wounded and bleeding, fell ill and never recovered. Without food, medical help and medicines - my father died on 19 March 1941.

In one of the cold autumn days, in one of the Sabbath of 1942, large buses arrived to the ghetto at five o'clock in the morning - to expel and liquidate the ghetto. My family managed to escape from the ghetto to the nearby forest. Two hundred Jews were shot and killed on the spot. Only a few escaped and the rest were deported. I, and ten other people, hid in a cellar. We were in the cellar for the entire Sabbath. As evening fell we sneaked from the cellar and each one of us turned in a different direction.

I walked three kilometers to my Polish woman's house. I knocked on her door and she opened it for me. When she saw me she wrung her hands, crossed herself and called out - how did you manage to survive this hell? She gave me food and drink, and when I recovered she told me that my mother and my little sister Leah are in this village and they're looking for me. The Polish woman's son immediately went, under the order of his mother, to find them and a short time later brought them to me.

We stayed with this Polish woman only three days. In the middle of the night we had to leave because rumors have already started to spread that Jews are hiding at Jaworoska's house.

We fled to the forest. In broad daylight lay in various hideouts and at night we went out to look for food. We were in the forest for three weeks, in hunger, cold and fear. Another blow plagued us in the forest - lice. The tiny varmints didn't leave us for a moment.

After three weeks of wanderings, filled with sufferings and hardship, we had no other choice but to try and return to the Polish woman. When she saw us again before her, she got scared and horrified. She immediately locked the door and took us to the attic.

[Page 233]

She brought us food, water, clothes and a dense teeth comb.

We hid for three days and three nights in the attic. On the fourth day the Polish woman said that she's couldn't support us all, but she's willing to take one of the girls. Since I was in grave danger because of my prominent Jewish facial features and since I used to live with the Polish woman - I was chosen to stay.

My mother and my little sister Leah left and reached Warsaw. Mother's Polish friends, who lived in the suburb of Praga, hid them for several days but they couldn't stay there because they were afraid of the Germans and Polish informers. One day, as they wandered hungry in one of Praga's streets, they saw an elderly woman with a trustworthy appearance who held a package in her hand. My mother dared to ask her for a piece of bread for the girl. The woman didn't hesitate, opened the package, which contained her meal for work, gave it to my mother and said: "if you want, give me the girl and I'll bring her up at my home." My mother was very happy, gave my little sister to the Polish woman and received her address in exchange for her daughter. With stinging tears in her eyes she watched her little daughter walking away with the Polish woman. She stood for a long time in place - stood and couldn't move. The girl also turned every few steps to mother, and their gaze met through a double screen of flowing tears. It was the last time that they saw each other. Later, mother came back to the village and told me what had happened to her and my little sister. She gave me the address of the girl's guardian and I corresponded with my sister through my Polish woman.

The winter of 1943 has come. Mother was with me all the time but we had no food and we suffered greatly from hunger. Also the good Polish woman and her 12 year old son endured famine. Every evening, at sunset, mother went out to look for food. When she was lucky she returned with something hidden under her clothes, but most of the time she returned with nothing. After the spring thaw mother moved to the home of an acquaintance in the same village.

Sometime later, my mother met aunt Tova from Wieliszew. My aunt lived for some time with her two little children in the surrounding hills and groves. After she met my mother they were together, but it didn't last long. In May a manhunt was carried out in the area, my aunt's two little children were abducted, and probably shared the fate of all the Jewish children in Poland.

[Page 234]

My mother and my aunt managed to escape from the manhunt, but because of the circumstances they separated three weeks later - each to her own fate. My mother's fate was to fall victim to a Polish informer who handed her over to the Germans. She was arrested, and didn't return. My aunt, on the other hand, lives today in the United States.

I stayed with my Polish woman until the autumn of 1944. I didn't see sunlight since the end of the summer of 1942. I hid days and nights, without air and light, because all the villagers knew me. They weren't allowed to know that I was staying with the Polish woman for fear of denunciation.

When the Russian troops approached the environments of Warsaw the German authorities started to expel the Polish population from many locations. The Polish woman and her family were among the deportees, and I joined them. I covered my head and face with a scarf so, God forbid, no one will recognize me. The German policemen led us by foot, a distance of thirty kilometers, to the other side of Warsaw, to an industrial area.

It was already evening when we approached the destination of our difficult walk. A great fear fell upon me because of the danger that the Germans will find out that I was Jewish we get to the place. Also the Polish woman, who walked with me the whole way, contracted my fear. Therefore, three kilometers from the factories we escaped from the rows and hid.

The next day all the deportees were sent to work in Germany, and by miracle I was saved from this fate.

From there we walked to Pruszków because my Polish woman had acquaintances there. We were there only a short time and traveled to Częstochowa. From there we planned to travel back to Warsaw, but I never got there because a manhunt was carried out midway. All the young people were abducted to dig excavations. At that time I was already 21 - old enough to be abducted. All the pleas and tears of my Polish woman didn't help. I was among the many abductees. I was led under a heavy guard, together with other abductees, to the prison in Piotrków and from there to work in Sulejow.

I was abducted and led to work as a Christian Pole. When I was the village my Polish woman altered my appearance. My hair was bleached and also the color of my eyebrows and eyelashes was changed. I had a proper identification card. My name was Krisztina Leszczyński - I was born in Poznan and, according to the card, I was legally baptized as a Christian at the holy church of the "Virgin Mary." My last place of residence was 12 Stalowa Street, Praga. All of this was written and signed in my papers and well etched in my memory so, God forbid, I'll never forget or make a mistake in one of the details. I spoke fluent Polish and my Polish accent was flawless. This card stood for me at time of trouble and more than once saved me from extinction.

[Page 235]

When I was brought to Sulejow the work supervisors asked me all sorts of questions: about my education, knowledge and profession. When I stayed with the Polish woman I learned to type on a typewriter. I told them that I was a typist. Therefore, I was assigned to work at the office. I typed the lists of those who were abducted for work.

I worked at the office for two months in constant fear, and in the immediate vicinity of my supervisors. I couldn't stand the burden of this fear, and asked to be transferred to work in the kitchen which was outside the camp. I worked in this kitchen, together with five Polish women, until we were librated by the Russian Army in 16 January 1945.

Even after the liberation I wasn't able to reveal my Judaism and origin. As a Pole I slept at the home of the Polish woman Piechotowa and I had to pretend that I was a devout Christian. I said a prayer every evening and went to church every Sunday. I stayed with this Polish woman a month after the liberation, and also when I left her she didn't know that I was Jewish.

A month after my release I arrived to Lodz and only there I met other Jews. From an acquaintance I learned that my two young sisters, Masha and Feiga, are alive and live in Biala- Podlaska.

Soon after, I began to correspond with Tova and Chana who were in Germany. With the help of the Jewish committee in Praga I learned that my little sister lives at the home of the Polish woman who received her from my mother. One day, I also received the news that my second brother was in the army and that a letter arrived from him to Serock.

With joy I also received the news that my townsman Konkol, my future husband, was among the survivors.

Shortly after, all the survivors of our family, apart from our parent and older brother who perished in the great destruction, were found and gathered. Now, when I'm in Israel with my husband and my two sons, I wonder about the road of tribulations and the hell of the years of terror.

[Page 236]

# Help Under All Conditions
### by Itkah Miedownik (United States)

**Translated by Ruth Kilner**

Several years before the outbreak of the Second World War, I was living in Warsaw, the capital. With the increase in tension in 1939, I couldn't shake the feeling that war would break out soon, and I advised everyone to stockpile foodstuffs. I remember that then, I had a horrific nightmare about war and the atrocities suffered in wartime: the vision of this dream proved to be a cruel and freakish prophecy that would be fulfilled. I dreaded the upcoming horrors, but I hadn't estimated the extent of the terror.

War broke out. I worried and feared for my family, from whom I remained far.

Before travelling to Serock, Dr. Frieda Epstein told me that an explosion had hit Yaakov Rosenberg's house, and dozens of lives had been lost including Yaakov, Henya and Estusha Rosenberg (Avraham was at the front of the house), Chaya Schwartz and her husband and children, and many more.

I was relieved to see that all my family was alive and they still had something to eat. The Germans forced them to work, but at least they initially also fed them. No-one was sure what tomorrow would bring. I was very afraid for the fate of my relatives. As long as I controlled my worry, I knew that I would be able to adjust to any situation. I was very brave; I didn't fear the Gestapo or anyone else. I seemed to simply generate miracles: more than once I found myself in the lion's den.

The first time I traveled to Serock after the German occupation, there were widespread rumors that everyone will be deported. Fear gripped us all, but no-one had any advice. Rumor had it that some people had started to escape from Serock. I returned to Warsaw since I needed to support myself and my family. I was offered employment positions in several different German offices in Warsaw, including Brühl Palace, since I knew German. But I didn't want to work for the Germans, and I supported myself by selling personal clothing.

On December 5th, 1939, I prepared myself to travel once again to Serock to bring back several items. At that time, Serock had been annexed to East Prussia and acted as the border between the General Government and East Prussia. I travelled as far as Legionowo, and as I prepared to enter the train that went to Zegrze, I met Leibel Wellensky. He asked me, "Where are you headed?" I answered him, "To Serock," to which he told me, "There is no reason to go; no-one is left there. No-one. Everyone was deported at 4 o'clock this morning." Despite these bitter tidings, I wanted to go, but he held on tightly to me and used force to stop me from going. In the end, he convinced me, and didn't go. I started to run around frantically, asking if anyone knew to where they had been deported. I received different answers: some people said that in Rembertów, they heard the deportees shouting, and that they were deported to Nasielsk. I immediately got onto the train that went to Nowy Dwór, and on the way, I kept asking about the deportees until we arrived at Nasielsk. At that station, a German officer approached me and started talking to me. In all likelihood, he wanted to gain my attentions as a brave man, and he immediately started off by telling me that his job is very interesting. "Today, we got rid of the Jews," to which I responded, "How could you do that to those poor people?" He responded, "Are Jews really considered people?" What else could I have said to him? I diplomatically managed to extract from him the fact that the Jews of Nasielsk were rounded up together with Jews from other cities and deported beyond Ciechanow. At Nasielsk station, there were many signs of the tragedy strewn around: I saw pieces of clothing, prayer books, phylacteries, and the like. I immediately travelled to Ciechanow. There I asked, as though I had no personal agenda, about the deportees. I learned that they brought several people through Mlawa. Unfortunately, I had to sit for a full night at the Ciechanow train station since there were no connections. Several gendarmes, who were on night duty at the train station, took me to the hut where they sat and warmed themselves round a fire. Their faces were dreadful, and awoke fear deep within me, but they were kind to me, since I spoke to them in German. I knew how to mislead the biggest villains, and this helped me in the future through my life more than once in the years to come. From Ciechanow, I travelled to Mlawa, where they told me that the deported Jews had travelled through Mlawa and on to Działdowo. I travelled to Działdowo, but found no traces of them. I returned to Legionowo, where I learned from friends that information had arrived about the Jews of Serock; that they were in Lukow, Miedzyrzec, and Biala Podlaska. I immediately travelled to Lukow where I found my mother, my sister Leah Weitz and her children, my sister Gittel, and many friends. First and foremost, I gave them a few zloty before I travelled on to Biala Podlaska to search for the rest of my family. In Biala Podlaska, I found my father, my sister Pessel, and my brother with his wife and children – everyone. I can't begin to describe how that meeting with everyone felt, because of my sheer and utter excitement. However, the moment I spotted my sick father, lying down on some hay on the ground, my pain and grief felt no bounds. There were 20 people living in the dingy and dirty house. Even before they had arrived, there were evacuees from Suwalki and other villages had been living there. The tragedy that I watched unfolding before my eyes cannot be described. It made a terrible impression on me, seeing these masses of people with the yellow star upon their clothes. I heard firsthand all that had befallen them: I heard how they had been taken for three days in sealed carriages, without any food, without any water; how the children licked the dew from the windows to satisfy their thirst – but that was only the start of the tragedy. They also suffered from several beatings. Those who found themselves with a few zloty were beaten until they lost consciousness. Since the people of Serock had expected the deportation, they all tried according to their means and abilities to gather and hide some money. My sister Gittel took silver 5-zloty coins and turned them into buttons, which she sewed onto her dress. The Germans discovered this, and she was beaten according to the number of buttons she had. My nephew Yaakov Weitz only hid a single zloty in his pocket; the Germans took his zloty and punished him with a dreadful beating.

[Pages 237 and 238]

I couldn't waste any time; I had to do something. The first thing I did was to unite my family in Biala Podlaska so it was easier for me to help them all. Their living conditions were shocking. My heart had splintered into shards, but there was nothing that I could do then and there to help. Many deportees from Serock started leaving the place to which they had been deported. Some people managed to escape to Warsaw or elsewhere, but the vast majority remained in Biala Podlaska.

Things had gotten a little better for the Rosenberg family since Rivkale started to work as book-keeper in the flour mill. The flour mill belonged to a Polish family friend, Jan Korlevski. Old Rosenberg and his son Feivel earned some money by working at the mill. Faige also worked and earned some money. They helped others, but couldn't feed everyone. In the beginning, they had a nice apartment, but then they lost it. I travelled to visit family in Lódz, and I asked them for some clothes and bedding for my parents. I filled a large sack with all the items I got in Łódź and I brought it all to Biala Podlaska. I was happy that my elderly parents would now be able to sleep; to rest their heads on a pillow, and cover themselves with a blanket. I dressed them, gave them plenty of clothing and bedding and then I returned back to Warsaw.

The Jews were persecuted at every step. There were laws that Jews were to wear white ribbons with a blue star. I didn't wear one; I knew that as a Jewess, I wouldn't be able to support myself or my family. I looked for, and found, a room to board with an Aryan family, and registered under a false name with Łódź as my place of residence. At that point, identification cards were not yet mandatory. As an Aryan, I was accepted into the apartment. By now, Poles were not renting rooms to Jews. This was at the start of 1940. People I knew were trying to sell their jewelry (gold, diamonds, and so on), and I acted as the broker for large transactions. I traded with Henech Hochman. I did not earn too badly, but I had many obligations. I was in constant contact with my family. I sent them money and parcels. When my sister later came to Warsaw with her children, she found a temporary refuge with her sister-in-law Chaimovitz, who lived at 46 Novolipki Street. In Biala Podlaska, the lice simply ate the children, and she could no longer cope with the situation.

The entire burden of supporting my family lay upon my shoulders; I had to support the family in Biala Podlaska, and my sister and her children in Warsaw. I also had another two sisters in Warsaw. I went hungry more than once so the children could eat. The children appreciated it, and every time I visited, they said, "You are our most beloved aunt. Were it not for you, we would have starved long ago." And they were right.

*[Page 239]*

In the meantime, the remainder of my family moved from Łódź to Warsaw. The Germans would rob the Jews of their luggage along the way, so I took their possessions and expensive clothing on the train with me. Their furs, I wore.

One time, a pure-bred Polish woman travelled with me. They thought she was a Jewess, and made her strip, examined her, and took away all her possessions. All my Aryan friends suffered from the Germans' suspicion that there was a Jewess among them.

Once, a German gendarme suspected that I was a Jewess. It was in early 1940 and I was walking with my friend Dr. Malkovich along Marszałkowska Street. The gendarme's suspicions were arisen because Dr. Malkovich was wearing the white patch, but I wasn't. He stopped me with these words, "You are a Jewess. Show me your photo identity card." I kept my head, and I took an old insurance card from before the war out of my wallet, as that was the only identification paper I had. When I showed him the "identity card", I spoke to him in German, and said, "Here are my papers; do you really think that I am a Jewess? Please think. Does my walking with a Jew really mean that I must be one too?" The gendarme was confused, blessed me, and said, "Forgive me, Fräulein, I made a mistake." He didn't even look at my papers, although I thrust it right under his nose.

I am certain that the Germans would have been unable to catch me if it were not for a Polish informer who brought me to the Gestapo.

Although I must admit that there were Poles that helped to save Jews, there were many, many Poles who informed on Jews to the Gestapo.

My cousin, who was the manager at the Jewish bank in Łódź, lived in Warsaw and had to manage his businesses to support his family and keep them alive. He was unable to travel personally, because Jews were forbidden to travel on buses or trains, so I acted as his emissary, and was obviously compensated with a handsome salary.

I always walked about around the German mail buses between Warsaw and Tomaszow Mazowiecki, laden with cash. I took on all sorts of work simply to support my family. My mother, father, and sisters Pessel and Gittel had moved to Łomazy, 18 kilometers (11 miles) from Biala Podlaska. My sister Pessel managed to earn some pennies from sewing. During this period, people were still relatively happy and enjoying some freedom. Oh, alas for that freedom! It was pure heaven compared to the terrible days that came after.

[Page 240]

In early 1941, the Germans established the ghetto in Warsaw. To begin with, the ghetto was open and people could come and go freely.

Then, business slowly dwindled and I had to take a job in a private German office. My whole life was split between my work, rushing to and from the ghetto, and maintaining contact with Biala Podlaska and Łomazy: I was there every holiday.

The train only ran as far as Biala Podlaska. From there to Łomazy – 18 kilometers (11 miles) – I had to walk on foot, often in the frost and the freezing cold wind. I recall one dreadful journey around Christmastime 1941. When I returned from Łomazy to the train station in Biala Podlaska, a strong, freezing cold wind tossed me about like a ball. I caught a chill, and suffered from a high fever, but I somehow came out of it safely. I was terrified to fall ill, because if I got sick it would mean the end of my family.

The day they closed the Warsaw Ghetto was the hardest point of my life. It happened on the 15th of November, 1941. I could not bear the thought that I would no longer be able to see my sister and her children. Their meagre food rations quickly dwindled, and I did my best to provide whatever was missing. I kept in constant contact with Dr. Sonja Pilkenfeld, daughter of Yeshayahu

Rosenberg and cousin to Avraham Rosenberg, who lived at 1a Zielna Street. Although this house was within the ghetto, its rear windows, half of which were covered in bricks, faced the Aryan side. In the evenings, I stood below the window and Dr. Sonja lowered me down a basket on a long rope, I filled it with food items, and then it was pulled back up.

This went on for some time. I spoke to my family on the telephone, and we worked out a system of signs so we could arrange when to pass the food through the window that overlooked the Aryans. Using these signs, we worked out how and when it would be convenient to see one another.

To begin with, we arranged meetings by the ghetto wall at the junction of Smolna Street and the Mirovski Market. The fence there was made of wood, and there were holes between the boards. My sister's children always came there; they would thrust their hands through the slits, and I would fill them with whatever I could, and we would exchange a few hurried words. I had to be brave, and I could not cry, because my tears would arouse the attention of the Aryans.

All this happened right in front of the gendarmes. Sometimes, I would even manage to get their permission to go inside the ghetto. I concocted all sorts of excuses: for example, that I had taken a garment to be mended by one of the Jews, and I had to pick it up, otherwise I would lose it. I promised the gendarmes that I would return immediately, and I always kept my promise. I entered the ghetto, walked a few steps through, and went into one of the houses on Smolna Street, where I quickly passed my sister some bread and sugar, etc. We exchanged a few words, and I left again through the guard's gate.

[Page 241]

At those times, if it was necessary I could display a German work permit. I didn't have any other papers. In contrast to all those around me, at no point during the occupation did I have Aryan Papers. I never had the sums of money needed to pay for a set of papers that would testify that I was at least four or five generations pure. I did have a forged birth certificate, although I never used it. I knew to show nothing in preference to a certificate like that. At any rate, I had never needed to show Aryan papers.

Any time I started a new job, I was never asked to show papers testifying to my Aryan roots, because I was always recommended by Aryan women, and no doubts were ever aroused as to my racial legitimacy. I should mention that those who recommended me never knew the truth of my real roots.

I met with my sisters and my cousin from Lódz in the court building on Leszno Street. The Jews entered the building from Leszno Street, and the Aryans entered from Biala Street. This was a very dangerous meeting place, and spies lurked at every step in the corridors. I didn't think about this, and brought parcels, bread, and money. In these corridors, in front of German eyes, I passed these gifts to my family. It was not easy to take things from the court into the ghetto, because when the Jews left the court building, they were examined thoroughly. They had to hide everything well under the bricks, and to take out new things each time. These corridors were our main meeting place once telephone contact with the ghetto had been cut off completely.

Bad news arrived from time to time from Biala Podlaska and Lomazy, and I felt like I was living in purgatory. Hundreds of people passed by my office each day, and I was certain that one day an undesirable client would come in and expose me until finally the dreaded day arrived. A German-Polish client by the name of Jan Michaelik from Serock appeared in my office, after which the blackmail immediately started. His wife started blackmailing me over the telephone. As a result, I fell sick, with a fever of 40° Celsius (104° Fahrenheit). My family knew nothing about this blackmail otherwise they would have feared for my life.

The situation in the ghetto worsened every day. People died by the thousands from hunger. I advised my sister, Leah, to return to Biala Podlaska or Lomazy with her children.

The court building on Leszno Street was turned into a German hospital, and ceased to be a meeting place. Most of the ways to gain access into the ghetto were blocked up: I had to find a new way. I started to go via the roofs of the nearby houses. I penetrated the ghetto in the middle of the night via the roof of the house at 52 Złota Street. I came out on Sienna Street and I visited my whole family. I put on the special Jewish symbol, since it was dangerous for an Aryan to wander the streets of the Jewish ghetto. I had to smuggle my sister Leah's bedding and other belongings out of the ghetto, and take them to Lomazy. With a sack full of items, I walked back over the rooftops and was caught by some Polish informers. They let me go for a substantial sum of money.

*[Page 242]*

I took the items to Leah in Lomazy personally. My heart broke when I looked upon the white faces of my family. I had done all I could for them; I helped them even when it put my own life in danger. They all remembered how I gave them loaves of bread through the ghetto fence, right in front of the gendarmes. At first there had been fences, then walls sprung up in their place, and walls of terror around them. It was hard for me to live, my family's terror, the insecurity, hopeless lives – all of this crushed me and I worried that I wouldn't be able to hold out.

At Christmastime, 1941, I travelled to Biala Podlaska and Łomazy. The degenerate poverty in which my brother, sister-in-law and their children lived (they lived in the synagogue) is indescribable. Their faces were filthy, bloated and infected. My heart broke with the sight of them, although it wasn't only my relatives that lived in these conditions: there were many, many more people in the same position.

When I arrived in Lomazy on foot, I found my sister Gittel critically sick with typhus and everyone walking around in shock. I knew that everyone could be infected with this accursed disease, because they all slept together. Gittelle was dying, but occasionally she recovered consciousness and I would comfort her, and she begged of me, "Itke, get out of here. Otherwise you'll catch my sickness. You must stay alive!"

I brought the local doctor, Dr. Kaszminski, to see her and to bring her medicine for free, as she had no money. Dr. Kashminski was a kind man who helped others.

There was no ghetto in Lomazy until very late on, and the Jews were able to move around relatively freely.

With a broken heart, I returned to Warsaw. After some time, I received notice that my sister's situation in Łomazy had improved a little, but my second sister, Pessel, had fallen ill. Everyone was infected with typhus. I made sure to keep my connection to them strong.

From Biala Podlaska and Lomazy, I received letters to the address of my friend, Zophia Prunchek, 42 Zlota Street, who would from time to time go into the ghetto and take food to friends.

It was dangerous for me to receive letters from my parents to my own address. I sent

[Page 243]

them money and parcels to the address of Kowalski, the Polish owner of the flour mill in Łomazy. He would sometimes give them a little flour or some groats.

The news that came from Biala Podlaska and Łomazy was frightening, each and every time. Reginka Rosenberg also wrote to me.

Shortly before Passover, 1942, my father died. Two weeks later, so did my mother. My sisters didn't mention this in their letters. Then I stopped receiving letters from Biala Podlaska and Łomazy. In early summer 1942, I received my sisters' last letters, in which they told me not to send them anything, because they didn't know what any day would bring. I could sense what was coming, and that was when the mass slaughter of the Jews started. It was impossible for me to travel there to see them, because I couldn't leave my work. In August 1942 – or September 1942 – Kowalski, the miller from Łomazy (a Polish man, who once worked in Moshe Rosenberg's mill in Serock) came to Warsaw, and I met with him. At first, he wouldn't speak, but eventually he told me everything: On July 7th, 1942, all the Jews had been expelled from Łomazy: 1900-2000 people were herded into the Łomazy forest, and all were murdered. They were all buried in a mass grave, including many who were buried alive.

That same summer, the Jews in Biala Podlaska were massacred. I don't know the exact date, but I believe it was the same month of the same year: July 1942.

Until today, I can't describe what happened to me that day. I remember that on the night of July 6th, 1942 I had a dreadful nightmare. I woke up after hearing the calls and cries of my sisters and their children. "Irenka! Irenka! Save me!" I am certain that my dearly beloved relatives died with my name upon their lips.

I couldn't accept the idea that I was now alone in the world, and I hoped that I would yet find survivors from my family.

At the end of December, around Christmastime 1942, I visited the killing fields of Biala Podlaska and Lomazy. In Lomazy, I did not find a single live soul. I arrived in front of the small home in which my parents had lived, and I fell into a dead faint. To this day, I don't know for how long I laid in the snow unconscious. I awoke, and arrived back to Biala Podlaska with great difficulty. When I arrived, I learned that the Jews were deported in haste, with the Germans shooting at them like ducks. The Poles also played a part in this murder. The Pole Marian Wolenski, who served in the criminal police force and was originally from Czestochowa particularly excelled at this. He also informed on me to the Gestapo; told them that I was a Jewess, but a good friend vouched for me and told them I was her cousin. Kowalski told me that even after liquidation of the ghetto in Biala Podlaska, he received a letter from Faige Rosenberg-Cohen (daughter of Moshe Rosenberg) from Miedzyrzecz. I read the note myself, in which she requested the small sum of money that the miller from Miedzyrzecz who now lived in Biala Podlaska owed her. We had not yet managed to respond to her when all traces of her disappeared.

*[Page 244]*

The last news of Old Rosenberg (Moshe) and Feivel, his son, came from Terespol. We surmised that they had managed to escape, but they since had disappeared.

Indeed, the end had come for Biala Podlaska and Lomazy. The tragedy had left its mark on me. I had to be courageous, and I could not cry in the light of day. However, I wept through the night without respite and without constraint, and thoughts of the inhumane suffering tortured me.

I remained in contact with the Warsaw ghetto until the last moment. The news came that came from the ghetto worsened every time. About my sister in the Warsaw ghetto, I heard nothing.

I heard that the Stashalkovsky family (a large Polish family from Serock), who lived in Warsaw during the war, had sent food parcels to Leah Horowitz in Majdanek for a period of time. It was from them that I heard how the Kipperbaum family had been lost. The way I heard it, Old Kipperbaum (who owned the wine store in Serock) called out in an insane voice, "Let me take a bite to eat out of the cupboard." I met Sara (Sabina) and Regina (Rivka) Kipperbaum more than once on the Aryan side. They were selling candies. I think and assume that Sabina managed to survive. All my family in Warsaw and Łódź were killed.

I went through some tragic times in 1943; when the ghetto burned, who could have felt my pain?

I continued working. On March 2nd, 1944, a Polish detective by the name of Jak arrested me next to the tram stop and took me to the Gestapo on Szucha Boulevard. What I felt then can only be understood by people who were arrested then. In brief, none of the Gestapo agents could understand how Jak dared to arrest me on the street, because they were all convinced that I wasn't a Jewess. Sturmführer Brandt himself, head of the department called me to him and personally examined the build of my body, especially my head and nose; he spun me round to look from every side: was it straight, the correct angle, and a non-Semitic shape. I didn't appear to have a Semitic shape; it was a Mongolian type.

I also had to take a Roman Catholic test on religion. I didn't do very well on this test. Throughout the examination I remained quiet; brave; I smiled. The Gestapo agent asked me, "How can you smile in a situation like this? Do you not know what awaits you?" Throughout this ordeal, I heard compliments from the Gestapo agents, "Smart lady," "Intelligent woman."

The situation got worse, but at the last moment I was helped by a man who worked for the Gestapo: a Jewish man who went by the false name Lobo (I also knew his family name, although I forgot it). His name was Ignatz, Master of Law. He was asked by Brandt if my Polish accent was good and pure. Lobo confirmed that my accent was excellent and correct. The Gestapo agents admitted themselves that my German accent was very good.

[Page 245]

I spoke to them without an interpreter. Lobo advised me to admit to Brandt that I was of mixed race. "Mixed race class A." I listened to him, and I told this to Brandt. On this basis, I was freed, but ordered to report to him again after one month. I was mentally broken and devastated, but I continued to work. Friends advised me to run away as soon as I could. Lobo pleaded with me to report and to explain that I still didn't have my father's papers. I explained that my father was an Aryan, but my mother was a Jewess. People of mixed race were treated as Aryans, but I had to prove the Aryan ancestry of one parent.

I listened to Lobo, and on April 10th, I reported to the Gestapo offices on Szucha Boulevard. I showed them my certification and the official letters from

Łódź that included the request to send me my father's papers. All of this was very little.

My friends left me, as though forever, because they did not believe I would come out of there alive. I felt like I was walking straight into the lion's den. And indeed, they stood there ready to arrest me. Lobo ran to and fro between Brandt's room and that of his secretary; he was irritated, but tried to comfort me, and said to me, "Don't worry, you'll get out of here. I am responsible, and you will get out of here. You have so much courage, you need to be free."

I waited in the room in terror. I expected death. At one point, the secretary returned from Brandt and walked into the room, and said to me, "So, Fräulein, you're staying here?" I replied to him, "I am always happy to be around intelligent people." Then he asked me, "Are you not frightened? You are technically free, but you must report here every two days."

I never once reported. Lobo told me over the telephone that I had to disappear. I disappeared, and that's when my hell began. Usually, friendships diminish in times of disaster. I left Warsaw for a while, but I returned after about a month. I had nowhere to live; I couldn't wander round the streets of Warsaw, because so many people recognized me. My life was indeed bitter. I was told that the Gestapo was searching for me, and they were very angry with me. One of my friends introduced me to someone, who under normal circumstances I wouldn't have even looked at, but at this point, I was desperate for help.

I could probably have taken steps within a certain class of society and had false papers made. I had to change my papers, and register somewhere, but this hooligan, Henrik Gorzinski, extorted close to 3,000 zloty from me, for which he made me nothing. Instead of papers, he started to intimidate me. That was not his real name. He forged false papers for himself, each time under a different identity.

[Page 246]

One month, I lived with Zophia Pranchek, 42 Złota, without being registered until she found herself being put under pressure and threatened for helping Jews.

Jackals disguised as human beings started to turn a profit from the tragedies of their fellow man, and I was one of their victims. At this time, I was offered significant help by Mark Fischer, a friend from my study bench, the son of one of the professors at the political gymnasium. He procured papers for me, together with 500 zloty each month from the Jewish Committee. There, I appeared as Sara Goldmecher. I had no idea if he was alive or not; all traces of him had disappeared. I also got a few hundred zloty from my friend Heinz Stanislav Jadobon. I also have no information about him – he had simply disappeared.

My life had no value. In July, I left Warsaw and I stayed in one village with friends, but the ground burned beneath my feet and at the end of the month, I returned to Warsaw weak, nervous, and resigned to my fate.

On August 1st, 1944, rebellion broke out in Warsaw, which I encouraged with my whole being. I hoped that from this moment, I would no longer be hunted like an animal.

My hope was proved false. After suppressing the rebellion, the troubles increased. I wandered from place to place until January 1945, when Warsaw was conquered by the Polish army.

Page 247]

# The Inquisition in *Shul*
## Zwi Kleinman, of blessed memory

### Translated by Pamela Russ

Sunday, September 10, 1939, the day after a German soldier was shot by a Polish storekeeper for robbing his store, a mass of German soldiers prepared for fighting was released across the city – primarily on the Jewish streets. The assault was so tremendous that many people were convinced that the Polish military had again invaded the city and that both armies were meeting head on fully armed. But it wasn't the Polish army that the Germans had come to meet. They had come to "pacify" (calm down) the town that was preparing to put up a resistance against the military, preventing them from re-entering the city.

Very soon, in the first few minutes, were heard terrible screams from those who were being beaten and those who were beating, at the very same time. German soldiers spread out across the city to search the houses. Not one room was left unturned, destroyed beyond recognition. All mirrors were smashed, all the paned doors of the credenzas were broken up, all the linen was shredded and torn – so much so that it was impossible to recognize what once was. Not one door remained unopened; not one lock could withstand the power of the soldiers' fists and boots.

As they stormed into the houses, they did not distinguish between men and women, the young ones or the elderly, the healthy ones or the ailing. All, with an extraordinary atrocity and sadism, were hurled into the streets – some through the door, some through the window. The "lucky" ones tore themselves away, young and healthy people. After receiving the first beatings, they quickly found refuge somewhere outside of the house. The older and weaker people, who could not disappear so quickly, received murderous beatings. Even the children were not spared this sadism. All the streets were filled with these victims who no longer had any remaining resemblance to anything human and emitted eerie cries, because before coming to the market where all the Jews were forced to assemble, they all had to pass through the seven generations of hell from the various German guards that were in the corners of the streets, and take along "provisions" for the journey: smashed up heads, broken noses, beat up sides.

*[Page 248]*

Meanwhile, Jews did not forget that they were Jews. After surviving such a difficult trip, they set themselves aside to recite Psalms and Vidui (prayer of confession recited before death) with great passion in order to prepare themselves for the lengthy and final journey that awaited them. It was a sure thing for them, that all the people in the city would be shot out of revenge.

**The place where the Serock *shul* stood**

Herding the people into one place was done with such a storm, with such a rage, and with such foam on the soldiers' mouths, that no one doubted the end was near.

The entire marketplace was surrounded by a larger number of armed soldiers who with great fury chased the people from one corner to another.

The Psalms and reciting of *Vidui* were choked together with the cries of the elderly and the sick, along with the screams and convulsive cries of the women and sobs of the children.

At the very same time, there was a fight between the Polish army that was located two kilometers from the town, on the other side of the Narew River, and the German army that had just about walled in the missiles and machine guns in the city. Bullets from both sides flew over the city, over the heads of those stampeded together in the marketplace. Every shot and explosion from the grenades that fell nearby aggravated the chaos even more and evoked fresh cries and screams each time.

[Page 249]

Afterwards, a German officer came into the marketplace, and was informed about the terrible crime that the city had experienced – the murder of a German soldier, and that according to the law, all the people of the town had to be murdered like dogs, but that they – the Germans – were refined people and so would release all women and children from all punishments, but the men would have to be punished and therefore they will have to be imprisoned.

Now the real wailing began from the women – those who were forcefully torn away from their husbands. In the end, some policemen arrived and ordered the crowd to march, and finally we were herded into the *shul* that was transformed into a prison camp.

In the *shul*, the Jews saw the great massacre that had taken place there just a few minutes earlier. All the lecterns were broken, the Holy Ark was smashed up, the Torah scrolls were shredded and parts of them were thrown into a toilet, and the rest were stomped on with boots. They were spat on, and covered in garbage and excrement, and then finally burned. All the prayers that were etched into the walls were scribbled on or rubbed off.

Seeing this horrific desecration, the Jews dropped their heads in despair, and then this question was raised by not only one of them: "Wouldn't it be nicer and better for God if only the hands of the vandals would wither?"

An hour later the same Jews were forced to set fire to the Torah scrolls that were lost in the corners, and one Jew refused to set fire to them and for that he was severely beaten. He took a long time to set the fire, but it wouldn't light, so with his own hands he had to throw the scrolls into the toilet.

In the *shul*, they started to try to lie down on the broken benches.

[Page 250]

Some of the non-Jews, who lived among the Jews, were chased together with them into the *shul*. Among them were the pharmacist and the post office manager, both known anti-Semites.

The guard that was assigned to watch this group, approximately 300 persons, was very tough. If you went to the window to try to get some air, you got murderous beatings. It was very difficult to get permission to go to the washroom so you had to resign yourself and hold yourself back with all your strength. The majority of those gathered held themselves back from eating the food they had brought from home in order that they wouldn't have to come to the state of asking for permission to use the bathroom.

The front came closer, and each time there were fresh military units and their officers. Knowing about the Jews who were in the "prison camp," they came to look at them and then they would thunder against the "*Juden*" and then beat them.

On the second day, an officer came and sat at the entranceway that led from the *shul* to the *bais medrash* (place of study). Everyone had to pass his table as they went from the *shul* to the *bais medrash*. The Germans spread tables across the entire width of the *bais medrash*, which everyone had to jump over in order to get from there into a smaller room that used to be a classroom. The younger ones, who were able to get to the other side very quickly, got away with lesser beatings, in relative terms, whereas the older and weaker ones, experienced the taste of death. For them it was a real *gehenem* (hell), and their wails and cries went straight to heaven.

Every time after this sort of a test – that cost him dearly – the victim tried to turn over on his other side but lay faint on the ground. His tormentor exclaimed his joy and satisfaction and applauded.

After this control, all the people were crammed into a narrow room where it was very warm and humid. After four hours in this narrow, warm room, the guard allowed the group to go back into the *shul*.

[Page 251]

That same day, the Germans took out an old man, 75 years old, one of the great Torah scholars and enlightened Jews of the town, Reb Yitzkhok Blakhman, and accused him of preparing arms to confront the Germans when they would march into the city. The accusation came from the fact that when they had robbed his store that had kitchen products, they found a few dozen knives.

The response from this elderly man, whose age and frailty were evidence to the fact that he did not have the power to fight with soldiers, helped very little. He was severely tortured. The people who saw this, cried. It is incomprehensible how this weak man remained alive. After that, when he was relieved of this accusation, they found another opportunity to beat him: They told him to move about very quickly – with lightning speed. The elderly man, who normally would walk very slowly, after receiving these blows, could hardly even move at all. None of his pleas helped. The old man simply remained lying on the ground. The Germans pounded all over his body with their boots.

Under their terrible behavior and under a very rigid regime, the assembled group in the *shul* lived like this from Sunday to Thursday. On Thursday, another officer came, repeated Monday's speech, and in the end all the people between 18 and 45 years of age were divided into two groups, from which one was sent on foot to Pultusk. Children under 18 and those over 45 were let go.

**(From the archives of the Jewish History Institute in Warsaw)**

[Page 252]

# From Serock, Jablonna – Legionowo, Through the Warsaw Ghetto to Treblinka

### Shlomo Sterdiner (Ramat Gan, [Israel])

#### Translated by Pamela Russ

Soon after the Germans captured Serock, they took over all the bridges. The community of Jablonna Legionowo, 15 kilometers south of Serock, was comprised mainly of Serocker Jews who settled there primarily to be able to find financial opportunity in the last few years prior to the outbreak of World War II. Shortly after Serock, Legionowo also fell, and the Germans immediately demanded a large fee. Since it was not possible to raise such a large sum within the allotted time, the murderers arrested 21 Jews, among whom were Reb Moishe Wisniewicz and his son Jidel Jakov Leviner, and so on, may G-d avenge their blood, who even after the monies were paid, were murdered nonetheless.

A short while after the invasion, the Germans established a ghetto on Legionowo in the section of the city that was called Ludwiszyn in which they also amassed the Jews from the surrounding towns and villages, such as: Piekele, Dombrowa, Henrykow, and so on.

There were many Serocker Jews in the Legionowo ghetto, who had run away from Biala Podlask, Lejkowo and Lomza, where they were sent from Serock in December 1939.

Life in the ghetto was tough and bitter. We had to give away all the valuables, fur coats and gold to the murderers.

October 15, 1942 (Simkhas Torah [the last day of the Succot holiday and normally a day of great celebration with the Torah]), the Jablonna – Legionowo ghetto was liquidated in a horrific manner. (This town was called – and this is factual – the extended Serock.)

Some of the Jews were murdered on the spot, some of them tried to escape and hide in the surrounding forests, and the rest were transported out in simple railroad cars and taken to Radzymin – a distance of 40 kilometers – where together with the local and rest of the Jews, were all taken to Treblinka.

[Page 253]

## The Journey of Pain

On the 28th of April, 1943, at 4 o'clock in the afternoon, they led us through the burning streets of Warsaw until we arrived at that bloody place (called the *Umschlagplatz,* [German: reloading point – This was the place where the Jews were gathered and prepared for being shipped out.]) That is where I already began to see our tragedy. I began to look around, seeing how our sisters and brothers lay murdered by the hands of the Nazi murderers, who were even seen to dance in the Jewish blood. When they took us to the trains, I noticed that on the other side there were two rows of SS (*Schutzstaffel,* Nazi security officers) standing. Between the rows of these murderers, individuals passed, one at a time, both men and women. Some of the women carried children in their arms, tormented and exhausted from hunger. They had already been sitting in the buildings of the *Umschlagplatz* for a few days, and in that way, by the time the people walked between the rows until the trains, they were already downtrodden. For those who didn't go the way the murderers wanted, there stood a special band of murderers ready and waiting for Jewish blood, always with their pistols and machine guns ready and extended towards the unfortunates, who were already unsteady on their feet, and they immediately opened fire on the innocent victims. With a cry of "*Shema Yisroel*" (the final prayer recited before death, indicating the acceptance of G-d's Will), they fell to their death.

Right after that there was a command given to the workers of the *Khesed Shel Emes* (Jewish organization that prepares the dead for burial), to clean up the area. At the same time that the workers were cleaning the bodies away to the side, the murderers were going back to look for new victims. Two Jewish workers carried one Jewish victim. Noticing that the victim was heavy, one SS officer asked the worker: "Is this too heavy for you? Then I can make it easier for you." He takes both of these workers away from this place and directs them towards the mountain of our victims, and commands the two workers to lie down. One of the murderers takes out his bayonet and plunges it right into one worker's heart. The second worker, seeing the death of his friend, started to run. A volley of bullets was released, and he fell dead.

And still, back to the rows, the work goes on. People go and they fall. Blood is flowing as we get to the railroad cars. Now, in the cars, begins the real tragedy. One person begins to scream: "Where is my husband?" And one woman screams: "They've murdered my children! Let me out! Let them shoot me! I want to die the way my children have died!" One hears screams: "Where are my sister and brother? They've already been murdered." All you hear is lamenting cries. And the car is crowded. We can't breathe already. People are pleading: "Water! We're dying!" People scream so long for water, that eventually they die of hunger and thirst. People are piled on the sides, one on top of the other. By the time we left, 17 women and 8 men had already died.

The people stopped screaming. It became silent in the car. A deathly silence ruled over our heads. Then we hear about new victims. I squeeze myself close to the other side by the window and see that they are leading large groups of people. It seemed that they were removed from the bunkers. When these people neared the cars, we saw that their faces were black and they were in a faint.

[Page 254]

There was no more talking. Everyone was pleading: "Master of the Universe, just end it all for us. Don't let us be tortured for a long time in the cars." Soon we heard them open the doors to the car, and the beatings and shootings began. People are pushing very hard in order to get into the cars more quickly. From the wagons is again heard the lamenting cries: "Where are the children? I have lost the children!" And the murderers are strolling back and forth outside the cars. They are laughing and they call to us: "Do you want some water? Get out [of the railroad car] and give us your gold." When they receive no answer, they begin shooting at us and kill five people. The murderers open the doors of the car and point their extended machine guns at us. When we saw the wild looks directed at us, we became silent for a time. This enraged them so much that they took a 23-year-old woman off the train. The murderers led her away, and approximately ten minutes later a shot was heard. Everybody froze. We heard the footsteps of the murderers approaching. They are here! Our hearts beat in terror. Soon the doors to the cars open and the murderers yell: "Two men get out!" Opposite the door were sitting two men. They stood up, became very pale, and cried out to us: "All of you stay alive! We've had enough." And they went out of the car. As they were jumping down from the train, they called back: "Live and take revenge!"

[Page 255]

Soon others came and shut the doors to the railway cars. Near the small wired window, I stand and watch how the murderers lead our Jews along the same route in which the young woman fell to victim. It is quiet in the car for a while. I strain to look through the small window and see how those who were taken away are carrying the shot woman back to the cars. They open the door to another car and put the young woman in. Soon, a lamenting cry is heard from her mother who recognized her. On the side sits an elderly Jew who cries: "Beloved people, how good it is for the daughter of this mother. She [the daughter] had a merit from heaven because she did not have to continue in this way of hunger and thirst then be burned in the coal ovens." Soon everyone in the cars began to cry, and for a long time nothing was heard but the moaning.

Around six in the afternoon, we heard the locomotive's whistle. Everyone sits down, heads bent towards one another, and they say: "These are our last hours. We are going to be sacrificed [murdered]. Who will avenge our blood? Who will know what will happen to our bodies?" And we hear the second whistle. Our fear begins to take hold, and our hearts pound. The train leaves that bloody place. After a few minutes, it stops at the train station in Gdansk. There, two wild thugs take us over, running from one car to the next. They steal, beat, and murder. The Jews are screaming to our Polish neighbors: "Bring us some water! We are dying of thirst!" And they ask for 500 zlotys to bring the water. A woman who is fainting, pleads with them: "I'll give you my coat. Just give me a bottle of water." One of them replies: "Give me your coat and a bottle and I will give you some water." The woman pulls her coat off and gives it away. No one comes back. And there is no water. The people stand and watch as the wild Ukrainians snatch off our clothes and sell them. The crowding is huge. They are pushing and rushing to get our clothing as quickly as possible. How great was our shame. On the side, one Jew sat and moaned. "Jews, we have nothing to lose. We have to end our lives so that the wild beasts can no longer torture us." A woman, a doctor, replies: "We have to live and suffer until we get to that place." She doesn't realize that we are going to Treblinka, she thinks we are going to Lublin, Trawniki, or Poniatowa, there where all the Jews are working and where we will work too. We Jews know too well that we are born only to give away all our belongings to strangers.

[Page 256]

We were 120 people in the car. Every bit of time we looked out the window. Where are we? Are we going to Treblinka or to Lublin? Soon, another discussion begins in the car. One says that this is the route to Treblinka. Everyone becomes depressed. Everyone is sitting and moaning. Where will our bodies go? Who will know of us? One woman asks to be allowed near the window. "We are going to Lublin," she says. Everyone breathes more easily. Another scream is heard: "Water!" We were faint, but there was no water. There were screams: "Save us, people! You have a responsibility to save a person from death!" We ride into the night, and we have little air. We hear as two young men are sitting on the side, talking about nothing and working diligently. It's already nighttime; we think it is about eleven o'clock. It becomes quiet again. These two young men are still sitting and working their pocket knife, trying to cut through the floor. We hear a train whistle, implying that we are nearing a train station. The shooting does not stop. People are jumping from the cars and the murderers are shooting. Soon we hear a signal and the train stops at the station in Demlin.

It's already eight o'clock in the morning. Through the small wired window, there is some light. And the people are asking again and again, for water and water, because we are dying of thirst. The train does not stay for long, and we are off again. The doors always remain closed. Even if someone would have wanted something, he would not be able to get it. In the car were dead bodies, and on the sides were people in misery, waiting for the same end. The young men are still sitting with their pocket knife and are working very hard until they successfully cut through the thick boards of the car. Just before Lublin, one of the young men stands up and shouts: "We have cut through the floor! Everyone can save himself! The time is short. I am from Warsaw, and my name is Hershel Eisen. I lived on Niezke Street, number 12. If we don't give in, you will always remember this." Until we reached Lublin, approximately 20 people got out. Then we already heard a train signal, and the train stops. We arrived in Lublin. It is May 1, 1943. They open the doors to the cars, and the SS men go through all the cars and ask: "How many dead are there?" We say how many, and they go away laughing with extended guns. Then we notice how a train worker is taking a woman to the SS men. One SS man takes her near a car and asks her who she is. She immediately says: "I am a Jewish woman." He pulls out his pistol and commands her to lie down. The woman doesn't obey quickly enough, and gets hit on the head from the murderer's gun. She immediately falls to the ground. One man in the group says to shoot her. The murderer shoots her and they walk off, looking at all the wagons. At lunchtime, we noticed that some higher ranking officers had arrived, and one of the SS men gave him a report. They went through each of the cars.

[Page 257]

During my time in the Warsaw Ghetto, I met the following *landsleit* (people from the same town): Dovid Warsawski, Shia Zilbershteyn, Judah (Jidel) Kuligowski, Shloime Ostrowski, Rozenberg, Josef Fishman, my brother-in-law Skurnik with his wife and two children, and my brother Fishel Sterdiner.


**In Treblinka**

As we were waiting at the station in Lublin, the German murderers would not stop the killings. An order was given that half the trainload should go to Majdanek, and the other half to Treblinka. I remained in the train headed for Treblinka. Riding back, we already understood where we were going. Late at night we arrived at the station in Malkin. There Pollaks were walking around, and we asked for water. Their answer was: "It's already not worth your while to drink. The end of your life is already not too far. Throw down what you have and maybe your guards will let you have some water." Women took off their rings and threw them down. The murderous guards picked up everything that had been thrown down and began shooting directly into the train. The SS men heard the shooting and came out of their cars, and ordered that the doors of all the cars be opened, and that they begin smashing the people on their heads with the guns. In my car, there was a bloodbath. And that's how they took us right away from Maklin to Treblinka, a stretch of seven kilometers.


*[Page 258]*


We arrived at the iron gates of Treblinka that were opened with much whistling and signaling. We hear the whistle and the train stops. In a few minutes, they opened the cars with a murderous yell: "Get down!" Feeling the tragedy of our brothers and sisters, everyone jumped down screaming *Shema Yisroel*. I held on to my son who was fifteen years old. He said to me: "This is the end of our lives." They are shouting "right," "left," and my son and I went to the right. It was nighttime. By that time we were already separated from our dear ones. They began to take us between mounds and pits. Everyone understood that these pits were prepared for us. We were already so downtrodden from exhaustion and starvation, and from closer up we already smelled the odor of burning humans. No conversation was allowed, yet everyone was mumbling *Vidui* (the final confession before death) and *Shema Yisroel*. And that's how it went until we came out of the deepest valley.

Not far from us, we see a high barbed-wire fence. Soon we are near a tall wall where SS men were standing. They shouted: "Get in, you lousy Jews!" They led us to huge barracks. Immediately the order was given that we stand in threes so that they could count the crowd.

That was on a May night, it was really cold and there was a lot of fear. You could hear everyone's teeth chattering, but we were not permitted to talk. The murderous Ukrainians were speaking Russian and gestured across their throats [implying death]. "Tomorrow you are coming into the forest. You've lived enough." That is how the night went by, in pain and agony, until daylight arrived. Each person looked at the other and thought about the hardship of the end of our lives. Where did they bring us for more torture? My son looked at me and I at him, the pity was great, but no one could help. We can't even cry or scream. We can only choke back the tears. It is getting lighter outside, and we hear screaming: "Get up! Everyone out to the roll call!" From the barracks, Jewish victims are running out, everyone naked, with torn shreds of clothing. Whoever is not running, gets beaten. One falls over the other, they push a wagon full of dead bodies. Right after the roll call, they take some of our group to march to Maklin in order to work at the train station there. My son and I remained with the second group to work where we were. That's how the work day went, in deathly perspiration. The Ukrainian murderers shot some people in our group. We had to bring those who were shot into the camp's yard. There was a group of people there who were digging ditches, and that's how they buried the bodies.

[Page 259]

On the second day, a new work day, the same beatings and shootings began again. So much so, that we all envied those who were shot. We were working alongside those who had already been in Treblinka for a longer time, and they told us what went on here. Barrack #1 was called the "death barrack," and barrack #2, for now, was called the "living barrack." The skilled workmen labored in shops – shoemaker, tailor, carpenter, weaver, locksmith, and so on. One expert worker was a young man from the town of Sterdin, near Treblinka. When he heard them call me by my name Sterdiner, he came right over to me and asked me why they call me Sterdiner. He thought I was from his town and said to me, that if I am a skilled worker, he would take me out of death barrack #1 and get me into barrack #2.

I told him that I was a good carpenter, so he went to the SS man and told him that there was a good workman here. The SS man came over to me immediately and asked me all kinds of questions about what I was able to do, and I responded to it all.

On the third day, right away in the morning during roll call, the SS man came over to me and asked me if I could sort the barrack walls. I said 'yes,' and the SS man told the young man to give me work and to take all of us out to the place where the walls were laying. As soon as we began working, the Ukrainians began to take aim and shoot some of the workers.

[Page 260]

At noontime, the SS man came out to the work place to see how the work was going. Seems that the work pleased him. As we came home from work dead starved, and we got some bread with some warm water, the same young man came over to me, Yitzkhak Majdenberg, may he rest in peace, and told me that the murderers were satisfied [with the work]. I asked the young man to tell the SS man that we couldn't work because they were shooting at us. He went to the SS man and told him what I had said. The SS man came to the work place and ordered them not to shoot at us. Yet, we were beaten and punished, until living became too awful. We had no strength left; the end of our lives had come. Deathly hungry, we practically crawled to the "death barrack," lay down on the hard boards, one of us on top of the other, and we heard the wild, drunken cries of the SS men and the Ukrainians. They come right over to us and yell: "Jews! Get out!" And the murderers stand by the door with their clubs and pistols. They are shooting and beating. Jewish blood is spilling and there is no one to help. We fall one over the other. One is shot, the other is wounded, until the murderers became tired of this game and left. The night passed, and once again, in the morning, we are standing at the roll call. The murderers are looking for anyone who has a scar from the beatings. Anyone with these scars is told not to go to work. This was already a sign of death.

That's how the days passed. Groups of people came, and after losing their strength, through the *Selektzia* process ["selection" process of separating the healthier from the weaker, ultimately those who would live and those who would not] they would be sent to the crematoria. I and my son Avrohom, may he rest in peace, were working as glaziers for the barracks that we were building. Another "selection" – to the left, to the light. When it came to my turn, the SS man asked me what was my vocation, so I answered that I was a cabinet maker. I got the order to go to the right. Next was my son. When the SS man asked him what was his vocation, he said he was a barber. My son and I got together again. Those who went to the left were immediately taken to be burned, and we, those who went to the right, were taken to various places of work. They took me into a large workshop of carpentry where there were Jewish craftsmen and several other Jewish acquaintances from Warsaw. After the SS men left the workshop, the Jews told me that they had been in

Treblinka for over a year. One person wanted to know what was new outside of Treblinka. I had to tell him the truth – that they were liquidating the Jews from all the cities. Even Warsaw was already emptied from Jews. Everyone sighs; the agony is tremendous, and there is no help.

[Page 261]

I received an order from an SS man to build a file cabinet. With some help, the job got done. The next morning, when the murderers came into the workshop and began inspecting the cabinet – and fortunately they liked it – they immediately told the writer (Dr. Reisner) to send me and my son to the baths for disinfection, and to move us over to barrack #2. There, in barrack #2, the Jewish *kapo* [a prisoner in charge of other groups of prisoners] took care of us. He immediately helped me get a bed and set me up with a group that was receiving better food. Several times, the murderers asked that they put in some wheat pieces for us. For us, those days were like holidays. And this barrack was a little cleaner. Neither the Germans nor the Ukrainians came in too frequently. Again, we went to work without breakfast, and no bread. Everyone did his best to find whatever was possible – some grass or a plant. We separated one from the other. We Jews from barrack #2 were forbidden from meeting with others in order to prevent any bonding.

After two months and becoming acquainted with everyone, the prisoners shared a secret with me. One of the Jewish workers came over to me (his name was Pinkhas Weisman, may he rest in peace; he later died in Israel) and said to me: "Be informed that, all of us as one, have decided to make a revolt because our life is no life, watching day after day the torture of our brothers and sisters. We have to enact this as quickly as possible." He immediately explained to me how this revolt was to take place. Every morning, the murderers would go around and inspect the workshops. The organizers had already scheduled the days and what time these inspections would take place. Each one of us had received an order that when the murderers would show up in our workshop as in the other workshops, they would have to be murdered. Everywhere, there were sharp axes prepared.

[Page 262]

The day arrived and we were waiting for the set time. Suddenly, we see that we are being surrounded by SS men and Ukrainians, and the order was given: "Jews! Get out!" Then we understood. The end of our lives had come. Right away, we were told to stand in rows and put up our hands. They started to search us for weapons. The murderers knew everything, even what time the revolt was to be. They knew who had the weapons because a tattle [spy] had told them everything about us. Meanwhile we were standing, hands in the air, until the order came to drop our hands. With clubs, the murderers beat our bodies. Then began the investigation – who had brought the arms.

There was a young man with us; he was from Germany. They took him out of the rows so that he would tell them who had told him to bring the weapons.

When the young man wouldn't answer, they brought over a large barrel and filled it with water. They took him by his feet, and with head bowed, they put him into the water [and held him there], then took him out. They repeated this. He was almost punished to death, and yet they still asked the information of him, until the young man screamed: "The day of revenge will come!" Seems that they understood what he had said, and then they proceeded to cut off his ear. After this bloody ceremony, they took another 17 Jews out of the rows, amongst them the *kapo*. They called him Ignacz, a Jew from Warsaw. All he thought about was how to free himself and others, and how to take revenge on those murderers. Each one of us wished our own death. The order came to get back to work. Downtrodden and broken, we went back to the workshops.

Soon, the *unterscharfuhrer* (junior squad leader) Lantz, came to us and yelled: "Who else wants to be shot?" Some of the Jews stepped forward and said "Shoot!" and proceeded to tear their clothes. The SS man left right away. In the evening *they took two Jews out of the barracks. We didn't see them any more, but we noticed traces of their blood when we went to work.*

[Page 263]

This is how '43 and '44 went by, until the day came when Treblinka was to be liquidated along with the rest of the few remaining Jews. It was Sunday, July 23, 1944. There were still over 500 Jews in the camp. We saw how they turned over all the booths of the watch towers, we saw the end of life was near. Six o'clock that evening, all the SS men and Ukrainians came into the camp and began to scream: "Jews, come out and lie down!" When we, the few Jews of the carpenter workshop began to hide, the murderers came in and began to chase us out with sticks until we would lie down on top of the others. I fell down on top of a Czech who was a fifth generation convert. He had been a terrible tattle all along and he'd had better accommodations. Seeing that now he too was to be killed by these murderers, I felt better. After 20 minutes of lying there, the order was given for us to get up. They took us between the walls of the entrance gates, and in groups of 20, led us into the forest, not far from the camp, to a large ditch. Soon we heard a lot of shooting, then silence. The murderers had come for a fresh group of 20 victims to take to the ditch. But right near the gate, beside the Jews, there was a great bang, and there was great confusion amongst the murderers. There was only one pistol and one bullet. Nonetheless, in the riot, some of the Jews managed to run away.

The rest of us remaining Jews, they took into a bunker where we spent the night. In the morning, again we were taken into the camp and divided into groups of 20. Every group received the order to complete the work for the *Wehrmacht* [armed forces]. I was in carpentry with two other men, but because those killers had murdered my 16-year-old son, I was unable to do anything with my hands, and for that I was strongly beaten. The SS men strongly pushed me to complete the work. My friends calmed me down and we began to think of ways to free ourselves.

In approximately the next seven days, of the 20 men in our group nine remained. They killed people every day. October 1, 1944, 5 a.m., the SS men ordered us to be ready. A few days after we left Treblinka, we came to a place near Krakow and again we were separated for work under the watch of the Ukrainians. Again, we were murderously punished.

[Page 264]

Then we were again taken to another place, near Kazimierza Wielka, and we had to do dirty work. But in this time, the Russian army had been consistently moving forward. The SS again prepared to move us out to Wolbrom to the Gestapo, and there to tie us with wires and murder us. We arrived in Miechow at 11 o'clock at night. While the SS men were sleeping, the remaining nine of us began to run back.

We heard shooting, and as I was running, I fell into a ditch of snow. The cold refreshed me, and I began to run the same way back, following my footsteps in the snow. About one kilometer later, I arrived in a village.

Searching for the other eight hidden Jews, a German soldier stops me and asks me where I am going. I answered him in Polish, and since he did not understand what I said, he let me go. Going a little farther, I arrived in the town of Sandomierz. It was already daylight, and there I saw a lot of German military and also a lot of other murderers.

I went to a farmer and asked for something to eat, but he tells me to run away as quickly as possible because the Ukrainians were catching many people to take them to work in Germany. I try to explain to him that I see few Germans, but he explains to me that not far from here are the front lines and the German military is lying in the trenches.

After, I asked the farmer to have mercy on me because I was dying of hunger and exhaustion; he takes me to the gate and shows me at a distance a farmyard where he says I can find shelter. I start to go on that way, and hear shooting all around me. As I come to the yard, a Polish woman sees me and asks me where I am coming from. Once I told her that I was running away from the Germans, she quickly took me into a cellar where there were already many women and children. The nine remained. They killed people every day. October 1, 1944, 5 a.m., the SS men ordered us to be ready. A few days after we left Treblinka, we came to a place near Krakow and again we were separated for work under the watch of the Ukrainians. Again, we were murderously punished.

[Page 265]

Soon all the women and children that were hiding came out of the cellar, but I still remained there. The Christian woman takes me into the house and assures me again that everything will be all right. Already, there was Russian military everywhere, and they were talking to all the farmers in the villages.

In the house, again I was given food. Her husband asks me all kinds of questions and gives me advice that after such a hunger I should be careful with my eating until the doctor has had a chance to examine me. Meanwhile, again there was another change on the front, and the Germans came back.

I started to look for a road to a settlement, and decided to go to Pinczow, around 35 kilometers away. I went back to Sandomierz, and from there to Pinczow that had already been liberated. There I saw the first Jews. After sleeping on the floor that first night, I went to Radom, where there already was a Jewish committee, and I received help.

After a few days, on January 29, 1945, I left for Prague by train. On the Prague Jewish committee, where there were already Jews from the ghettos, camps, and Russia, everyone registered their name and current address in order to make it easier to find dear ones.

After great searching for family and friends, and after finding some people from my town, I went to Germany through Austria, then to Israel.

*The author of this testimony, Shlomo Sterdiner, on the 26th of November, 1966, came forward as a witness in Vienna (Austria) in a process against one of his torturers, the foreman Leopold Lantz, who one month later was sentenced to ten years in jail.*

[Page 266]

# The Destruction of Serock
### Hillel Friedman (Petakh Tikva, [Israel])

**Translated by Pamela Russ**

Two days before capturing Serock, the Germans began their bombing and scores of families were killed, and along with them was Yakov Rosenberg in whose cellar they were hiding. With great effort they removed the victims from there and buried them in a *brider kever*[1] in the cemetery.

On Sunday morning, we already felt the enemy's hand. It was a pogrom. They also killed four Polaks and took Jews to bury them the very same day. Then they took all the Jews, old and young, also the non-Jews, and assembled them in the large *shul* that had been cleaned out. On Wednesday they said that all those over 45 and under 17 can leave the *shul*, and the rest stayed in the *shul* until Thursday, 10AM. They were taken in pairs into the *bais medrash*. There, a line of SS men herded them into the women's *bais medrash* and there beat all the Jews. People passed out. At night they had to break open the windows for some air – and it was like that until Friday, the next day.

Friday morning, the second day of Rosh Hashana, year 5700, September 15, 1939, they allowed us to go into the small *bais medrash,* and by 10AM we had to be ready to march. Where to, we had no idea. It was said, to work.

At 10 o'clock, everyone was taken out, set up four in a row under the supervision of a pair of Polish *shkotzim* who understood a little German: Zygmunt Wzjesyn and Sobolowski, and a son-in-law of Itche Majer Wajngart from Sosnowiec (he also knew German well) and Shloime Borenstajn. They had to take us to Pultusk to the German Commander, with the order that for every one that escaped, ten others would be shot. Among us were also many young Polaks, so we believed that for sure they were sending us to work. The second day of Rosh Hashana, Friday evening, we arrived in Pultusk. We were soon separated from the Polaks and were herded onto the first floor of the building without windows or doors. (The Polaks were set up below us.) With great beatings and smashing, we were chased up. There were no steps, but there were two ladders that we had for climbing. I received a terrible blow from a German. We were kept on the roof the entire night.

[Page 267]

On *Shabbos*, first thing in the morning, they sent up civilian Polish hooligans, and among them were from Serock: Suski and Kopjec, superintendents from Rosenberg and Malawanczyk. These two pointed out the two Jewish wealthy men – Hurwic and Dovid Rosenberg, who were stripped naked and murderously beaten. And after them – all of us. The Polaks, who were chased out with us, helped with the assault.

On *Shabbos* at 10AM, there came an order from the German powers that we were to be sent on foot to Czekhanow to the train. We put up some resistance against the German might, and wouldn't come down from the roof. We were sitting naked and were searching for our clothes. After half an hour, an officer approached and ordered that we be given our clothes. The Polaks brought back a lot of the clothing and put them in the yard in a box, and everyone had to go and identify his own clothes. Since that was impossible, we put on what we had – much of it without underwear.

After that we were sent out towards Czekhanow, escorted by Germans on bicycles and carrying guns. They soon began with their beatings. The first one that was shot was Avrom Ostrowski, and he fell right near my feet, and that was because he had no energy to walk. That was before Golomyn. After that there were more victims: Yosef Borenshtajn and Avrom Spilke. A few kilometers later, Hersh Leyb Shnajder died, (son-in-law of Pesakh Shnajder); after him the son-in-law of Gutman Bobek – Leizer (from Pultusk; died from blows of a rifle butt). He begged to be shot, and the German answered that it would be a waste of a bullet. The heat was great. Jews from other cities who came with our transport died as well – Hershel Stajnski's son. Eliyahu

Pnjewski and others who had no energy to keep walking, we carried on our backs until Czekhanow even though this was a great danger. In the afternoon there was a downpour of rain and hail – this completely sapped our energies.

[Page 268]

We arrived in Czekhanow on *Shabbos* night. Some non-Jews came out with water, but the Germans began shooting them. The last victim of this journey was Pinje Sokol the watchmaker (Blinc, the barber's son-in-law). That's how the tragic journey from Pultusk to Czekhanow looked.

In Czekhanow, they took us to the military barracks and put the group in rows on the road until eleven at night. Whoever sat down got a bullet. During this time, the Germans prepared a demonic plan: Between the road and the entrance to the barracks, they ordered that a big ditch be dug out and filled with dirty water. They positioned a narrow wooden "bridge" across this ditch. At night in the dark, when everyone was exhausted, these thugs ordered us to run quickly across this narrow bridge into the horses' stalls. They chased us, one on top of the other, with blows and beatings, and whoever fell in there could not get out any more. That's how scores of people died.

In the stalls, the Germans searched to make sure there were no Jews among the Polaks, since they risked being shot. The first ones to come out of this type of group were two Pultusk Jews, and they were almost killed. I grabbed my cousin and the Stajnskis in order to run to the other side, and it worked. But later I climbed on a log and fell unconscious. All the Serockers were searching for one another and they found me in an unconscious state and saved me.

They kept us here until Sunday morning without food. Sunday morning they told us to go out and collect carrots, told us to get dressed – many of us were simply naked. Each of us received one quarter of a moldy, black bread from the Polish military, that they had thrown away. Those that had not left some of the carrots for later suffered terribly from hunger and thirst. They hurried us again to the train in Czekhanow until we arrived there at eleven in the morning and we waited there until five in the afternoon. Then they hurriedly crammed in about 80 men into a horse's wagon, and that's how they rode us around in the train for a full day.

[Page 269]

The next day, Monday during the day, they let us out at a station and within five minutes, we all had to have a drink and return to the wagons. We attacked the water with greed – many contracted dysentery from this. We returned to the wagons already with more beatings because there were no steps and it was difficult to climb into the wagons. Yehuda Leyb Stajnski received terrible beatings as he was climbing into the wagon, and a German helped him by stabbing his backside (to hoist him up) with a bayonet and wounding him terribly. That's how we were brought to Riesenberg (East Prussia) on Monday evening.

As we arrived in Riesenberg, they immediately separated the Jews from the non-Jews (they were sent to a different camp), the Jews were sent to a stall for horses, and all were ordered to grab a little bit of hay. They gave two bundles of shredded hay for 400 people. This was to be used for sleeping purposes. That's how we got "organized" and everyone went about arranging his own business. There were about 100 Jewish Serockers. The next day, Tuesday at noon, they opened faucets of water, and there was a great crush of people (trying to get some water), and everyone was beaten with sticks. On Tuesday around four o'clock, a German came in and ordered that we pick out the oldest in the group so that we could get food.

The leader of the group of the Serockers – Fishel Sterdiner, I, and Dovid from Orczikhowa (from the other side of the Narew), went to get food for all the Serockers. We got a few biscuits, a small piece of liverwurst, a quarter of a bread, and a small piece of margarine for each person. That was hardly enough for one meal. On Wednesday morning, they gave us a little coffee. Our job was to pick the leaves off the trees and dig field toilets. Several times we were beaten because we fought over a bit of straw before going to sleep.

[Page 270]

On Yom Kippur, we organized a quorum (*minyan*). On those days when we didn't work, we were closed up in a stall, and we had half an hour to take care of our natural needs. That's how we lived until *Chol Hamoed Sukos,* year 5700. We received lunch from a boiler (large pot). We ate in another camp. There were four camps: 1) a military one for Polish prisoners; 2) a military one for Jewish prisoners; 3) one for Polish civilians; 4) and one for Jewish civilians. Once, we were feeling sick, one person vomited, and there was a tumult. The Germans came in and quieted everything in their own fashion. Yakov Kaluski and Pinkhas Kaluski were also there.

The religious Jews ate hardly anything from the boiler. We gave them our bread and we took their soup. For the end of Yom Kippur we prepared bread and coffee for them. The last day of *Chol Hamoed Sukos,* the SS man came in asked who wanted to go to the Bolsheviks. The first second, this made a fearful impression, because everyone was afraid to answer. Maybe this was a provocation, but soon hands began to go up, so that soon almost everyone in our camp raised their hands to leave. That same day, he prepared a list of names on the condition that we had to clean out the carpenter's factory from dirt. With our last bit of strength, we cleaned everything out, so that there could be no excuse (for not being allowed to go).

The next day early morning, when it was still dark outside, everyone was taken out into the yard, set out in rows, and all the names that had been written down were called out. Each person received half a bread, and we were taken to the train near the camp.

They assured us that after today we would be with the Bolsehviks. They loaded us onto wagons that were in more humane conditions, and each person received an identity book saying that the person was in this camp and whatever he owned he had a right to keep. On the second day, in the morning, the train stopped in a place. At a distance we saw Polaks with lacquered caps – we started to shout to them, that they should open the wagons. As luck would have it, there were some Polaks with us who also shouted to those other Polaks outside. "Brothers, open!" There was one non-Jew that went over and opened a Polish wagon, and with our plea, also released us. We were in Grabowa near Ostrawenka. Some left to Ostrawenka, and among those were Alter Wisnjewicz, my brother, and several other Serockers. They went over to the Russian side.

[Page 271]

I and another group of Serockers went home through Ruzhyn. On the way, we were met by Germans on horseback. They detained us and took our apparent identity cards, and said that this was "*scheisse*" (shit).

We were told to lie down in the field and not to move. This lasted until evening, until they assembled all the people, including the Polaks that were in the camp, and then we continued on the road of Pultusk -Serock.

That evening they set us up in military rows and said that they are taking us through Ruzhyn with the excuse that before us there were Greeks that had attacked the stores, and that after they will have taken us through the city, we would be able to go wherever we pleased. This was all a lie because as we approached the road that goes to Krasnaselsk, the attitude of the Germans that were directing us was a better one than that of the Germans who had captured us. We asked them why we weren't going via Ruzhyn, and we were answered that we had not come out of camp with a fixed direction. On the way, they even allowed us to rest (it was eleven o'clock at night) and to go to the peasants in the village and drink some water. After that, we went until Krasnaselsk until five in the morning. There we were led into a church and were given bread to eat. In town they said there were no Jews left.

We had a few incidents with the non-Jews in the church. This lasted until five o'clock at night. Big trucks with armed SS men arrived, and again they asked us if we wanted to go to the Bolsheviks. We said yes, we already had resigned ourselves to everything, and saw that this was the devil's game. The process took an hour until they had separated the Jews and removed them from the church, and again they were set in rows. Each person received half a bread with two spoons of marmalade. They loaded us onto the trucks that closed automatically, and drove us back to Ostrawenka. There we were placed in the middle of the marketplace, and we saw Jews at a distance who mourned for us. No one was allowed near us. That's how we stood in the marketplace for an hour, then were driven with the trucks for another 20 minutes, stopped again in the middle of the road, and with a yell, we were ordered to get out. As soon as we got out, the trucks disappeared. We were left alone in the field and again didn't know what to do. Some began to go to Ostrawenka, and a new round of shooting from machine guns began, and we started to run on the road to Lomzhe. At night we spread out among the non-Jews. They told us that there was no one there – no Germans, no Russians.

[Page 272]

In the morning, we began to go in the area of Lomzhe, and we saw Jews going around in wagons. They said to us: "Go children, *Moshiach* is waiting for you." After a few kilometers, we met a farmer who was leading cattle.

It became easier for us – everyone already had swollen feet, and continued running in the area of Lomzhe.

Arriving in the evening two kilometers before Lomzhe, several Cossaks on horseback with guns aimed at us, came towards us. They detained us and asked who we are. None of us knew any Russian, only Polish. They took us into their group, and brought us to Lomzhe. Behind the city was the military headquarters. Those that had brought us here told them that they had brought people who don't understand what is being said to them. They sent us an officer, a Jew. He asked us if we were Jews. When he heard that we were, his eyes began to tear up. He consoled us saying he would take care of us and that he knew what was going on "there" with us. They gave us food right away from the military pots. After that, they took us into town and handed us over to the Jewish community. We arrived in Lomzhe on *Hoshana Raba*, year 5700.

[Page 273]

Lomzhe was destroyed. We spent the night in a small *shul,* and the next morning we went to the commissioner of the city to look for work. He told us that he didn't have anything yet, but meanwhile, he told us to go to Bialistok. We said that we have no money, so he gave us coupons for haircuts and three extra rubles for pocket money so that we would be able to buy food. That same day, we left for Bialistok.

In our group were: Fishel Strediner, Yehuda Leyb Shtajnski, Eli Pnjewski and his brother, the son of Dudek, Hershel Bernshtajn, the son of Shlomo Leser, and Yitzkhok Koifman. We spent the night in two villages – Gotch and Zawadi. There were a few Jewish families living there.

That's how we went out of the German hell and arrived in Bialystok.

**Translator's Footnote**

1. A Brider Kever, or Brother Grave was a temporary (public) grave for those who while alive did not belong to an organization that had a cemetery. After a few years, the remaining bones were burned. Not having a Jewish cemetery posed a serious problem (since burning the bones is against Jewish law) and caused great pain for the surviving family members.

[Page 274]

# Wandering

**Miriam Krikah-Kanarek (Ganei Tikva, [Israel])**
**Translated by Sarah Mages**

When the war broke out I lived in my birthplace Serock.

I was too small, actually a girl, to understand the concept of war but in its early days I felt, in a tangible way, that it carries within it death and sufferings.

On 1 September 1939, when I was getting ready to go to school, the radio announced the approach of German bombers and as a result we fled from our home to the other side of the Narew River, to the meadows of the German residents because it was quiet there.

We packed bedding and other necessities and lived for several days in a large barge, which was used for the transfer of cattle, near the shore of the Bug River.

A few days later we went back home and then we learned that the city was bombed and my older brother was killed in a cellar together with 42 people. It's impossible to describe my grief, especially the grief of my mother who lay on the grass next to the house and cried for days without a break. It was a tragedy for my mother because my big brother was to be married.

I got up at 3 o'clock in the morning to stand in line for an additional loaf of bread.

Many Poles Germanized, meaning, turned into "Volksdeutsche." They did it for a drink and boasted about their German origin. Several days later, the Germans collected all the Jewish men in the Great Synagogue. They released the elderly and the young were expelled to Germany. Among these young men was also my brother who managed to escape and spent the war years in the Soviet Union.

The hunger has grown, sadness and fear prevailed. My father and mother left in our boat for our aunt, who lived in a nearby village across the Bug River, to bring a little food for the winter. On the same day, meaning, 5 December 1939, the Germans woke us up with brutality and expelled us from the city. It was early morning and we didn't have sufficient time to take our clothes. My big sister was forced to leave the house in her sandals. We wanted to escape to the other side of the Bug River to evade the disaster, but a Pole informed on us and shouted: "Jews." At that time we were in the middle of the Narew River. The Germans shot at us and miraculously the bullets only hit the water. The man who transferred us to the other side had to return to the shore, and the Germans started to kick and beat us. We arrived to the market running and when we got there a frightful sight was revealed before my eyes. All the city's Jews, about three thousand people, were there. They loaded the sick on carts and then began the journey on foot to Nashelsk. Our neighbor came running and with tears gave us bread for the road. During this historic "pilgrimage" which lasted, if I'm not mistaken, an entire day, they beat, shot, murdered and chased us like animals. Many died on the way. My sister's sandals ripped and she had to run barefoot on the snow and on the ice.

[Page 275]

When we arrived to our destination, to Nashelsk, they put us in the municipal synagogue in terrible crowded conditions. We were beaten, and shots were heard throughout the night.

In the morning they led us to the train station where we went through a meticulous search. They were looking for gold and valuables, and when they found ritual articles like: *tallit, tefillin, siddurim,* etc. - they burst out laughing and desecrated them. To many they cut the beards with great cruelty and ordered them to wash in the mud. They undressed people, took my sister to the toilet and conducted a search as she was totally naked because they suspected that she had hidden valuables in a certain place. They pulled gold teeth from people's mouth.

To this day I don't know, and I think that I'd never know, why a German slapped me very hard. What for? When we were inside the cars the doors were locked and in this way they led us for three days without water and food. The worst part was the thirst. My younger sister begged, like out of a dream, that we'll look for something for her to drink in the bucket. My sister and I sat on the floor next to the toilet and when we were thirsty we licked the dew from the windowpanes.

Various rumors circulated in the cars: some said that we'll be concentrated in a concentration camp surrounded by barbed wire. Others said that the Germans will kill us or take us to Germany for forced labor. In fact, we were led through East Prussia to Biala- Podlaska.

From the train station in Biala- Podlaska we were led to the synagogue and on the way we were met by the local Jews who were crying. The Jews took us from the synagogue to their homes. I found very decent people. My legs were swollen and my toes froze. I rested. There wasn't enough food, but it was better than we had before, there was also a warm stove there.

A short time later our aunt, who lived in Wołomin, found out that we were Biala- Podlaska. She came and took us to her. The journey to Wołomin was in freight cars, and with blows the Germans ordered my aunt to open and close the door.

We found our parents and our sister at my aunt's house. They managed to evade the expulsion to Nashelsk because they were with my aunt in the village near the Bug River.

My uncle in Wołomin was a good man and an excellent tailor, but it was difficult for him to support sixteen people during the war (there were eight of us and eight of them).

[Page 276]

The hunger and cold bothered us because the winter of 1940 was very difficult. I taught the neighbor's children and in return I received some food.

Thanks to the fact that one of my sisters was a seamstress and started to work, we were able to overcome everything. We rented a room where the whole family lived. My sister was given bread, potatoes, etc. in exchange for her sewing work. My mother sold tomatoes and in return received sugar, bread, canned food, and other products.

Thus life continued until the end of 1940, the year in which rumors started to spread that the German authorities decided to concentrate the Jews in certain locations, and only there they would be able to move freely. In simple words - put us in a ghetto.

From here begins the second part of my life. I was in a ghetto in a place called Ludwisin near Warsaw. We were given a small room which also served as a kitchen. To this day it's difficult for me to understand how eight people were able to live in such a narrow space. My little brother was in Soviet Russia. At that time began the struggle for existence, the war against hunger. We used all the means in order not to die of starvation. Mother wandered around the nearby villages and sold soap. In return she received bread, potatoes, and some soup that revived our souls. Of course, my mother's wanderings were forbidden and any carelessness could have resulted in her death.

My sister and I helped our mother with her work. My two sisters knitted good sweaters. We obtained torn sweaters and they knitted new sweaters from them. Father brought wood from the forest, but he didn't have shoes. His feet were wrapped in rags and he always had a cold. Once the Germans caught him, beat him brutally and as a result he fell ill. He came down with pneumonia and without any medical help he died on 18 March 1941.

I will never forget one incident: once, when I crossed the ghetto's border with bars of soap, I was caught by a Gestapo man and a Polish policeman. To their question "what are you doing outside the ghetto," I answered that I wasn't Jewish. However, my excuses and proofs were of no avail and I was taken by force to jail. The favorite amusement of the S.S. men, who peeked into the jail cell, was to shoot into groups of Jews or individuals that they didn't like. I cried incessantly in prison. I separated from life and my parents. I didn't want to die and fought for my life despite my young age. "They" were strong, and the fate of the Jews was sealed - what was at that time the value of another Jewish child?

[Page 277]

The guard, who took pity on me, told me that the S.S. demands a ransom for me.

I was taken by a German into the ghetto, to the Judenrat, and there he demanded a considerable amount of money for me. The Judenrat's chairman didn't want to hear about it and explained - "there's no money, because the money must always be in my drawer in case the S.S. men demand large sums of money from me. Once, there wasn't money and fifty Jews were killed." In comparison to such reality, who and what am I? But my fate to live was sealed. The weeping and pleading of my mother, who knelt on her knees, helped. She promised the Judenrat's chairman that she would return the debt after she'll sell her old sweaters, and what else can she offer? The Judenrat's chairman felt sorry for me, the S.S. man agreed to a smaller sum- and I was released.

All this didn't scare me and I often crossed the ghetto's border. I traveled by train to many places to obtain food so I wouldn't die of starvation and diseases together with my family. My sister tried to dress me nice so I wouldn't get caught dressed like a "damned Jewess." And so, I wandered to feed my family. However, despite all my efforts, there were times when I only ate green grain and if there was none - I ate grass. I was especially afraid of the typhus which killed many in our ghetto. I lived under these conditions until they began to talk about the liquidation of the ghettos. Every day brought new news and no one understood the word "liquidation." I didn't know that the meaning of the word "liquidation" is: gas chambers and crematoriums for the Jews of Poland.

One day, everyone talked about the upcoming liquidation of our ghetto, and we waited all night like sheep who do not object to their slaughter. At 4 o'clock in the morning - I don't remember the date - it was in the autumn of 1942, I heard the sound of busses near our house. Without a moment of thinking I fled through fields and swamps to the nearby forest. From a distance I heard shots, screams and the barking of dogs. It was absurd to stay there because the Germans searched everywhere and also in the nearby streets. The unforgettable moment of separation from my parents and family came. We kissed and each one of us went to look for a place to hide from imminent death. I gave my mother a kiss, and it was the last kiss. I didn't see her again because she was shot by the Germans.

I left, together with my sister Feiga, by train to Zegrze where we found a shelter from death and hunger inside a deep granary. At the same time the Germans conducted a thorough search for Jews in the area. From there I traveled to Siedlce, to the sister of the Polish man who hid me in Zegrze. He told me that no one knows me there, but there's a danger of the evil eye. The sister of the Polish man didn't know that we're Jewish. I worked for her in the field in hard work. It was good, but it only lasted for a week because the good guardian couldn't keep a secret. The police arrived quickly, and we were expelled accompanied by insult.

[Page 278]

What next? I was sure that at that time there were still Jews in Biala-Podlaska Ghetto, and innocently went to the train station. There, I was warned that the Germans abduct young women to work in Germany. It was the autumn of 1942. It's true that youth hid, but for me there was no difference because I aspired for the moment that will bring me faster to the end of my wanderings and to this miserable life.

When I arrived to Biala I found that the ghetto was heavily guarded. I wandered in the streets, walked from house to house and asked if I could get a job as a maid, nanny etc. My sister found a job - I had no luck.

We fabricated a story that we are from Kobrin, our house was burnt and with it all of our papers, but no one believed our story. We were advised to tell the truth because it would be easier to obtain the necessary papers for me. My sister Feiga received the requested card and I got a job after three days of wanderings.

The person who gave me the job was an intelligent woman. I didn't reach prosperity because poverty was general, but a little food and a few rags to wear constituted a great treasure for me.

The abundance didn't last long because three weeks later the woman learned my true identity. With heartache she took me out of her house because I and her family were in danger of death. In addition, six Gestapo men lived behind the wall.

Where to go? Where to wander? I went to my sister Feiga but without any results. I went back to the street and found a job. The Pole that I worked for was a bad man - I got bread by weight and quantity, and I was barely full. I took care of a child, did all the housework and also cared for 60 rabbits, chickens and goats.

When I checked the chickens if they have eggs and one egg didn't come out, my employer hit me and said - where's the egg?

I stole bread and ate it at night in my bed. I was very scared to go to the city, which was a distance of several kilometers from the village, because once I couldn't find the way back. I was lost and cried bitterly. But it didn't last long and once again I went out to look for a new workplace.

I found a new job as a maid and farm worker in a certain village. I fed the pigs, chickens and cows, and learned all kinds of agricultural work. The owner of the place was a forester, a very good man. His wife was also young and I befriended her. She washed the laundry of the Russian partisans and in return received fat and money. I also enjoyed it. However, also this time my happiness didn't last long, because the farmers in the area started to whisper that I was Jewish and my employer received a lot of money and gold from me.

[Page 279]

One day, I traveled to the city by train and when the Gestapo inspected the documents I announced that I left them at home. Of course, the Gestapo man didn't believe this story, and since I was wearing a Russian-style jacket he thought that I belonged to the partisans and led me to the forest to kill me. At the same time the man, who stood next to us, protected me. He said that he knows me, I live in his village and also the "Voit," the village head, can confirm it. He was struck on his head, fell to the ground, the Gestapo men kicked him and their dogs had bitten him. Apparently I was designed to live longer. The frightened village head testified with chattering teeth that I work in the village and he knows me well.

However, the forester asked me to leave his home because a group of Gestapo men lived nearby. Some time later I learned that the forester was shot by them and was buried behind the pig pen.

During the Russian partisans' nightly visits I begged them to let me join them. They promised to take me, but an evening has passed, many days and nights have passed, and they didn't come. The partisans clashed with the Germans and transferred their bases to more distant forests.

However, the forester didn't leave me without a way out and asked his nephew, who lived in the city, to give me a job. His nephew had a little boy and a tiny farm. Of course, they didn't know my identity and that I was Jewish. I started to work for him. Over time this family moved to the former Jewish ghetto where they received a three bedroom apartment and also a room for me.

It was good for me there. The family was good and the woman was like a sister to me. The head of the family tried to get an identity card for me, but at the same time he was arrested and shot.

Once, when we left the city for the summer house, all the documents were inspected on the way but our cart managed to escape and I survived. I was also stopped when I walked with the little boy, but I managed to escape.

Hunger penetrated our home after the murder of the head of the family. I woke up before sunrise to stand in a long line for a loaf bread and a little low-fat milk. Then, the mother of the murdered man came to live with us and supported us with her money. This mother-in-law was a bad woman. She abused us and caused a lot of trouble.

[Page 280]

The wife of the murdered man always cried and our situation worsened. At the same time I received an identity card thanks to the efforts of the murdered man's friend. I played with the card for many hours and kissed it. I couldn't sleep at night because thanks to this card I became a different person and I was no longer Jewish, meaning, that I saved my life.

The landlady told me that now, when I have the documents in my hands, I should look for another job because I no longer need to suffer from hunger and her mother-in-law. I didn't want to leave her and her sick little boy, and shared the order of life with her. But life has its own rules and a short time later I left her. I got a job with three elderly people. The food was first rate, the salary was high, gifts, cinema, a day off on Sunday, etc. However, rumors started to circulate that the front was approaching, and my employers fled to another location. Then, I rented a room with a poor family and worked as a maid for the Germans, but they also packed their belongings and got ready to escape. I started to work as a janitor at the local slaughterhouse. I had no shortage of meat and fat. I also brought decent chunks of meat to my landlady and revived her soul.

Suddenly, the front got closer and again: war and bombings. I escaped to a village where I worked in the fields also during the bombing - it was July 1944. However, I didn't get enough food for this work and left to look for another job. When I didn't find another job I decided to return to the city by foot, a distance of 24 kilometers. On the way to the city, not far from a certain village, three soldiers on horseback that their uniform was different from the Germans' uniform, suddenly appeared behind a mound. They asked me about the distance to Warsaw and if the Germans are nearby. The farmers stated that they were Russians - and it was the first time in my life to see Russians. The Russian soldiers ordered us to return to the village, but a bombardment and an exchange of fire had started on the way. This war was for the occupation of the nearby town. I hid in the field, inside the standing wheat, and a short time later left for the road together with a young woman. The road was littered with bodies, horses and military equipment.

Biala- Podlaska looked dead, the streets were empty and the city was destroyed.

Thus, without expecting it, the time of my redemption has arrived. I didn't dream about it and didn't look forward to it, because I was convinced that the Germans will stay in Poland forever. Now, their time has come - the fascist beast, which carried with it only destruction, was gone and liberator Red Army and the Polish Army, which saved millions of people regardless of religion and nationality, penetrated Poland.

[Page 281]

There was no work, so, what next? My aspiration was to return to my people and be Jewish because that's how I was born. The problem was how and in what way to fulfill this aspiration. Fear and trembling flooded me, I was afraid to enter a Jewish home and get closer to a Jew. I looked behind me in the street to make sure that no one was following me, and after that I entered a Jewish home. At first they didn't believe that I was Jewish, asked me about my knowledge of the language, and only after many investigations believed me.

I saw how we are recovering slowly, and that human dignity is coming back to us. We didn't have enough food and all the Jews engaged in trade. This trade was pitiful, but it was enough for a little bread. The Russian soldiers helped us by giving us food and clothes.

I decided to set out and look for my family. I left for Warsaw in a military truck and in the Jewish committee in Praga I learned that one of my sisters was alive, and that one of my cousins was alive and living in Warsaw. Following these reports I learned that another sister survived and lives in Lodz.

I continued to wander from village to village. It was an intense winter and the snow reached the knees. I found an aunt and her three daughters - but I didn't find my mother.

Later, I traveled to Lodz. I brought my aunt to my cousin, and slowly slowly the family reunited. A short time later I found my brother in the Polish Army, and also learned that two of my sisters were in Germany. However, my happiness didn't last long. One of my sisters left Lodz and I, together with my sister Feiga, remained in a difficult situation, without an apartment and without food. Therefore, I decided, under Feiga's advice, to travel to Danzig. I was hoping to get one of the apartments that remained empty after the Germans left. My thought was verified. In Danzig I received a beautiful furnished apartment. I worked in a coffee house and Feiga in a hospital, and under the terms of that time we had enough food. I was there until I immigrated to Israel.

[Page 282]

# Experiences during the Second World War
### Avrohom Spilke, of blessed memory

**Translated by Pamela Russ**

### a) By the Germans

Four days before Rosh Hashono, year 5700 (1939), on Shabbos night, the German military entered our city, and very soon German soldiers were seen in the streets. Jews remained inside their homes, closed and locked up. No one went near any windows for fear of being noticed by the soldiers. All the curtains of the windows were let down until the floor. A dead silence reigned in the homes. The heavy stomping of the horses was heard along with the commotion of the soldiers in the streets. The sun was shining as usual, sending her rays to the earth. The monotonous silence did not last long. Before we had a chance to acknowledge or observe the uninvited guest, rumours reached our ears and we saw how the Germans smashed open doors and windows from stores and homes, and began to rampage, steal, and destroy whatever they found. That same day, they removed all the residents from their homes and hiding places, regardless of religion or origin, young and old, women and children, and took them all to the large marketplace. Soldiers with machine guns surrounded us. The cries and screams went until the seventh heaven. We thought we would be slaughtered like sheep. The danger was in front of our eyes. Parents and children, neighbors and acquaintances all embraced and kissed, saying goodbye to one another.

Suddenly, a commander got up and gave a signal that we should be quiet, and he began speaking to us: "A terrible (undignified) thing has happened in your city. One of our soldiers has died among you and because of that crime you are now all commanded to be shot, but I'll do you all a favor: women and children will be let go, but men and boys will be detained in a concentration camp for a few days."

[Page 283]

They turned the large *shul* into a camp. We went through terrible things there, and one cannot even relate some of it. They didn't allow us to take care of our basic needs. We stood in line for several hours, we were given a small piece of bread as food and a little water, we slept on the floor and our bones were crushed from lying on the earth for so long. Dampness was everywhere; our clothing tore and became dirty from the mud and dust. Hands and faces were not washed. The water that we received could not quench our thirst. Our lips were dried out. This former *shul* now became a hell for us. From time to time, a German jumped in with a whip and whipped us murderously until we fell into an unconscious state.

Once, some German "doctors" came in and ordered that whoever was sick or handicapped should allow himself to be examined, and whoever would be found to be sick would be immediately released. Understandably, there were those among us who were sick. The "doctors" ordered that they be examined in a separate room. We did not know that there were other murderers there with batons and bayonets who were beating everyone mercilessly. Whoever ran, they would beat because he was running too quickly. Whoever went slowly was beaten because he was too slow. When we heard the screams and cries of the victims, we didn't want to go have ourselves "examined." Then, they forced even those who were healthy to be "examined"; these were then beaten. They herded us into a small, narrow room where you couldn't even stand. We stood crushed and pressed together like one lump, sweat was pouring off our bodies. Our legs were trembling from standing so long, but no one dared open his mouth or move so that the same viciousness should not be repeated. That's how we stood for several hours, stuck to the ground in fear and trembling.

**The Nazis torture the captured Jews**

On the eve of Rosh Hashono, in the afternoon, the Germans took 50 men for work behind the town. When we arrived there, we were ordered to run around in a circle for two hours. Then we were told to dig up ditches with our hands and to fill them with rocks. This had to be done quickly and efficiently, and whoever did not rush when he worked was beaten without mercy. After that, we were ordered again to dig a deep ditch and to put some people inside and cover them with rocks and earth up to their necks. That's how these victims remained for over an hour and then we were told to drag them out by holding onto their hands. When this was not possible, they helped pull these men out with their bayonets, and that's how they wounded the victims. After all that work, we were ordered to sing. We sang the Rosh Hashono melodies. Then they took us back. When we arrived at the *shul*'s courtyard, they had us line up in a long row and cut off the beard and sidelocks from several young men. When we arrived at the camp, we collapsed to the ground in exhaustion and were completely depleted from the terrible work.

That's how one week passed. The elderly and the children were let go and the younger ones remained in the camp. They told us that we were going to work in their country. Before we were sent off, we were set up in two rows and several of us were elected as supervisors over the others, and if one person would try to run away while we were in the middle of the way, ten men would be shot to death. We understood what was waiting for us, but we couldn't help ourselves. With moaning and crying and an ocean of tears, on the second day of Rosh Hashono, 5700 (1939), we were taken on a distant, unfamiliar route.

On the way, my energies began to get weaker. The sun overhead burned, and it seemed that the sun, the earth, and the Germans were allies in having us killed. The gardens and fields were in full bloom.

Would we see our beloved ones alive ever again? This question accompanied us the entire way. On the way, an event happened: someone from our camp ran away. And before anything could happen, he jumped into the Narew River and swam to the other side. We brought him back because we were afraid of the consequences.

When we were just behind the town of Pultusk, a troop of Germans with batons came toward us. They chased us until the courtyard of a camp in Pultusk. We stayed there for an hour and had to listen to insults, then they told us to climb up into an attic. Whoever didn't climb up the ladder quickly, was murderously beaten. Many fell to the ground covered in blood in an unconscious state. At night we went to lie down in the attic that was not yet finished being built. There were limestone, cement, bricks, sand, and stones strewn everywhere.

In middle of the night there was a tumult. They brought us another group of barefoot, naked people who were crying and moaning, and we cried along with them. That's how the night passed. The following morning, the Germans came with soldiers that were prisoners, and they began to rip off our clothing and tear off our shoes. Whoever put up any resistance was horrifically beaten.

After a few days of hunger and torture, the Germans ordered us to begin to make our way to the city of Czekhanow – a distance of about 40 kilometers. From there – they promised us – we would go to Germany by train. That day was *Tzom Gedaliah* (the Fast of Gedaliah; a fast day on the day following Rosh Hashono), 5700 (1939) and was for me and the others a blazing hell. Until midday, the sun burned strongly, so that even the shirt on the body was too much. After that, there was a terrific rain and hail storm, and so we splashed in water up to our knees. That day, we were judged to overcome the "*arba misos bais din*" (four forms of death as decreed by the Jewish courts in Talmudic times mentioned in the Yom Kippur prayers: stoning, burning, beheading, strangulation) – depression and destruction. I will remember this day forever, because that day my eyes ran with blood. The Germans ordered us to run (to race) the entire 42 kilometers while they rode on bicycles. They didn't let us rest; we were not allowed to drink water; there was not even a discussion of any bread; and even the running they told us to do was sometimes in fields or through ditches and again on the highways, and so on, while all the time they were jabbing everyone with their bayonets. Whoever fell while running or resisted something was immediately shot and cleared off the road.

*[Page 286]*

I wanted to rest for one minute and tie up the laces of my shoes – at the same moment I heard shooting coming from my direction, and soon they pushed me into a ditch. Suddenly, I hear one German say to another: "He's still alive. Let's finish him off." Soon I hear another shot, but to my good fortune, I regained my senses, stretched out my legs, dropped my arms, shut my eyes, stopped breathing, and pretended to be dead. When they saw that I was "dead," they left me in the field. I was abandoned, beaten and wounded, in a pool of blood. I wanted to get up, but couldn't. I saw how young, non-Jewish children were trying to figure me out. When I asked them for a little water, they disappeared. And that's how I remained, lying there in pain for a half hour. Later, someone approached me with a bottle of water, looked around to see if anyone was watching. He gave me some water to drink and then hurried away. Nighttime was approaching. I was seized by terror. They would bury me here like a dead horse, and my name would be forgotten forever. That's when I got up, with my last energies, and crossed the highway to the other side where there was a little house. When I got there, I collapsed, having no strength. A peasant came over to me and told me to go into his house – he would go first, and I should follow. In order to save myself, I crawled on all fours. In front of his house, the man's wife was standing with tears in her eyes, and in a tearful voice, she said to me: "I would gladly take you into my house, and I have great pity on you. My children are crying, they know what happened to you. But what can we do? The Germans said that if they will find anyone hiding Jews in their homes, they will be dealt with exactly as with the Jews." She gave me a sweet tea with syrup and a small piece of cheese, and then told me to leave. Without having a choice, I dragged myself back to that first place. There were two empty rooms there, I was afraid to go into the first one. So, I went into the second room, but there it was full of water and mud all over the floor. Feeling faint, I stretched out on the ground to rest my broken bones. Now I started to feel my wounds. Blood was flowing and I didn't have anything with which to stop it. I groaned and cried, but who could help me at this time? That's how I lay all night, in great pain, and thought about my bitter fate. Before daybreak, I heard talking in the other room. One was saying to the other: "Go and see what happened there." The second person responded: "I'm scared. You go." Suddenly the door opened and someone appeared. A deathly fear grabbed me. Soon he asked me what happened. I told him of my terrible tragedies, and he shook his head to show that he felt sorry for me. I asked him how is it that he is here. He told me that he lives in a village near the city of Czekhanow, and because of the shootings, he and his family ran away to save themselves. And now he is going back home. You couldn't move around at night, so because of that, he and his family had come in here to spend the night. He heard my groaning and tossing all night, but because it was dark, he was afraid to come into the room to me. I begged him to take me with him until the city of Czekhanow, but he didn't want to and soon left.

[Page 287]

I was alone again, abandoned from all. My pains worsened, the blood that was running from my wounds congealed, and I became horribly cold. My strength began to completely give way. I could not figure out from where I would get any help. I hardly crawled to the door to have a quick look at what was going on outside. I suddenly saw how a few Germans on bicycles are standing in that place where I had fallen, and they were asking each other where I could have gone and who could have taken me. I was seized by a cold sweat. I was terrified that, God forbid, they would come back and look for me, so I crawled back to my place and hid crunched up in a corner, anything so that they shouldn't detect me. My lips quietly whispered a prayer to God that I should be saved again from their hands.

[Page 288]

These were my thoughts, when a door opened and someone came in with a bottle of tea mixed with honey and gave me some to drink, then asked me how I was feeling. Some other people came in after him, and they spoke quietly to one another about what they should do with me. There were children outside who were standing by the window and were thinking about me as well. One said to the other: "He won't live." I thought they were right, but I was very pained by their talk. How could I die in such a worthless place. My heart began to pound from fear of this very thought. Soon, one of these people approached me, and told me that I should go ahead to the nearby village and they will follow me. I got up and left. In the village, they brought me some warm water and soap. I washed off the blood. They poured a disinfectant over my wounds and wrapped them with rags. I received some milk and lay down on the straw against the warm sun. After a few minutes of lying like that, they told me to go back to the first place. I begged them to have some mercy on me, but the fact was that the Germans had said that no one was permitted to hide any Jews.

Without any hope of being able to stay here, I had to go back to the first place. As I was making my way across the field, deep in my thoughts, a peasant approaches me (one who was working in the fields with horses, and near him was his wife and a farmhand): "Foolish man," he says. Where are you going? There the Germans will pack you up and make an end to your years. If you've remained alive, now you'll be giving yourself over into their hands. Go hide yourself in the field, behind the wheat barn, and after that I'll see where to hide you." I went to hide there and then he came to me and gave me some milk to drink, and found me a better place to hide, and then I lay there and fell asleep for a few hours. When I awoke, I see two people standing in front of me and saying they are going to tell the Germans about me, that I am hiding here. They put the question to me as to why I had remained a Jew. I should have converted and put an end to my Jewishness, and that way I would not have these terrible difficulties. Their words burned into me and pierced through me. I wanted to respond to them, but I was frightened. All I asked what that they shouldn't tell anyone that I was hiding here. When they left, I watched them until they disappeared from my sight. I was terribly afraid that they would reveal the secret about my hiding there. With nightfall, two boys woke me up, gave me some milk to drink, poured the disinfectant on my wounds, rebandaged them, and told me to follow them. They were holding my hands and they led me to the field. In the middle of the way, they said: "We are going to hide you in a stable and we'll put out a rumor in the village that you ran away somehow, and whoever calls out to you, don't answer." They told me their names and said that when they will call their own names I should answer, and they will bring me food and drink. We came to a place, they opened the door, put up a ladder and I climbed up high. The ladder was removed and the door was shut.

[Page 289]

When I went to sleep, I suddenly heard footsteps approaching, and this happened often. I lived in tremendous fear. My brain almost exploded from so much thinking and worrying. At dawn, someone brought some food and a little honey. I told him where I came from and what terrible things had happened to me. His eyes had tears as he felt compassion for me, Then he took my hand and said: "Don't be afraid, don't worry. I will treat you as a father to a son I will give you food and drink, you will lack for nothing. When you will be feeling better, I will take you home." He told me that in the field there were many bodies of murdered people -- from those who had been with me. I couldn't tolerate this and began to cry terribly, for joy that I was saved, but on the other hand I cried for the young people who were still alive yesterday, young and fresh, and now they lay dead, strewn across the field.

[Page 290]

Three times a day, this peasant came to the stable to bring me food. He comforted me and spoke to me. Once, this peasant came to me during the day and said: "You need to know that it is terrible. The Germans are coming to this village and want to spend the night in the stables. They've already looked through some of them and even this one in which you are sleeping. It might be that they'll use this one for sleeping. What should I do with you? There is no place to hide you. This is a small village and the neighbors will soon find out that you are here in the village. It might even be that they'll give you up. So, what should we do?" He thought for a while, then smiled with joy. "I found a place," he said. "Behind the stable there is a lot of straw. I'll make a deep cellar for you there, let you in, and give you enough food for two days, then close you in very well so that no one will suspect anything. But be careful not to cough even once. You'll stay there until they leave." At dawn, he came and called out with joy: "Come out, don't be afraid. They just left." I returned to my resting place.

A day before Yom Kippur eve, lying there and thinking about my fate and whispering a prayer to God that He should not forget me and should send me some help, I suddenly hear a voice calling my name, telling me to come down. I don't answer. Once again, one of these people swears that "We are four Jews and we know you well. We are from the city of Pultusk. Don't be afraid." I was sure these were Germans. But I had no way out, and so I went down. In fact, there were actually four Jews and they said to me briefly that since tomorrow was Yom Kippur and they would be going home, they would wait for me here and I should prepare to go with them to Pultusk. They would give me a signal – if they will say "Moshiach" (Messiah) then I should go down immediately.

[Page 291]

They left and I returned back up to my place. Soon the peasant came to me and described what had happened: "These Jews have an orchard in another village, and there they found out that a Jew had been wounded on the road and that he was hiding in a village behind a wheat barn and that he disappeared in an unknown manner. This news did not let them rest and they began asking around until they came to this village. I was standing with some other farmers, when a few of these Jews came up to us and asked if we knew anything about a young Jew that was wounded here. I understood that they meant you. I gave them a signal that they should be quiet. That's how it was. Afterwards, I told them where you were."

The farmer left and I remained alone, thinking about the salvation that would come. I couldn't fall asleep. The night passed that way. I was in the same position as the prisoner who doesn't believe and is surprised by his release. At dawn, the farmer came to me, and with tears in his eyes and a choked voice, said to me: "I saved you from a certain death, protected you from terrible things, you had a safe place with me, and now you're going home to your parents. Will you remember me for good things? Will you write me a letter about how the trip went and what your parents say about me?" And with a laugh, "How much will you pay me for this?" I swore to him that I would not forget him my entire life. He thanked me for that and gave me his address. I ate and drank. Then we said goodbye to each other with great sincerity. He embraced me and kissed me and cried terribly. I thanked him greatly, and he quietly left. Later, his wife and son came and said goodbye to me as well and wished me a safe trip to my parents. They gave me milk for the way. After these goodbyes, the four arrived. I went up onto the wagon, and the farmer and his wife and children were standing at a distance and watched as I left.

As I was leaving the village, some of the farmers recognized me and asked how I came here. We were now on the way to Pultusk.

[Page 292]

On the way, there were troops of Germans, but they didn't pay any attention to me. I was still terrified. We knew their actions well and the wounds were still too fresh to be forgotten. One German, an infantryman, blocked the four men and told them to stop. The driver was just about to hold up the horses when that same minute a large truck went between the German and the wagon, so that the German was forced to move to the side of the highway. The driver used that minute to whip the horses and we quickly left that place. The German began to shout that we should not move, but the driver did his job and rode onwards. That's how I was saved from another tragedy that could have happened.

I arrived in Pultusk safely. It was Yom Kippur eve. Everyone wanted to know what had happened to me, and nothing else. One woman had pity on me and took me into her home. Later, after lunch, I went out into the street to find out what was new, and someone who once was in Serock recognized me and pleaded with me to come to his home. I didn't let him go on for too long, and soon I went with him. I ate the evening meal there and then went to *Kol Nidrei* (Yom Kippur eve prayer). The cantor sang with a broken heart and a hoarse voice, and everyone was taken with fear and with trembling because of the Germans who were roaming the streets. I imagined that I was hiding in secret cellars of the Marranos in old time Spain. We did not go pray the next day because were afraid of being caught and taken to work. I prayed at home with heartfelt, deep sincerity. I remembered the little *shul* from the last year. Before *Kol Nidrei*, my father and mother would wish me, my brothers, and my sisters everything good and now I have to be with strangers and eat at a stranger's table. I prayed that it be an end to the year of curses, and the beginning of a year with blessings. That's how the holy day passed, with intense prayers. On Sunday morning, a doctor checked me, gave me an injection, bandaged my wounds, and told me that I should stay in bed for three days.

As I was leaving the doctor, I meet a driver from our town. He wanted to take me home with him to Serock. I told him to give my parents regards and that my sister should come to see me. My sister did come and hardly recognized me. She asked me what happened and how it all happened. I told her everything and she wanted me to go home with her, but the doctor had told me to stay in bed for three days and on the third day to go see him again. I wrote a few words to my parents and gave the note to my sister. She promised that she would come back again the next day and take me back home with her. But to my great misfortune, something different happened. Instead of going home, I was chased out of each house in Pultusk and sent out of town, and now I had to find a different route.

[Page 293]

The evacuation happened on Tuesday, one day before Sukos eve, year 5700. After 12 o'clock noon, when I was preparing to go to the doctor, I see that everyone in the house is sobbing. I ask what happened, and they tell me that all the Jews from the city are being forcefully evacuated into one place, and soon I saw a few armed Germans had gathered in that same place where I was and they had asked all the residents to leave their homes and take nothing with them. I went along with all the other Jews to this place where the Germans had ordered everyone to go. On the way I saw different groups, young and old mixed, walking and crying. When I arrived at the designated place, I saw that it was not possible to live through the screams and crying that ripped through everyone. We stood like that for a few hours. After that there was a vicious interrogation. Some were interrogated three times, then whatever they found was taken away, and then they were told to go to Russia. One Jewish young man, from rage, shouted: "There have never been such barbarians!" For these words, the Germans threw him into the water. This young man was able to swim and he actually swam to another place. The Germans accompanied us with gunshots that fell like hail until a kilometer into the way.

I survived the first evacuation. For me, there was now no goal, I was escorted with pain, troubles, exhaustion, and hunger. I wandered from village to village, from city to city, spent nights in fields, ate raw beets, roasted potatoes, and sometimes I fasted four or five days and filled my stomach with water – anything, so at least my soul would survive. My strength became less and less, my feet could hardly move. I was afraid that on the way I would faint from hunger and thirst. In one place, I stayed for a few days, slept in a stable, and ate roasted potatoes and drank water. One evening, a peasant woman, in a place we used to rest, said to me that the Jews better leave this village because the Germans were coming here. The Jews pretended not to hear. Then this peasant woman began throwing all the Jews out of her house, so that we were forced to get back onto the road. I and a few other families then tried to settle in another village, but soon we heard how they had tortured many Jews in a nearby town. A troop of Germans had gone in there and taken all the men who were there and ordered them to do work labor under the lashes of a whip, and then the orders came to continue running, then to lie face down on the ground and dig face into the sand. To anyone who raised his head to catch some air, the Germans pushed their feet into this person's head and forced the face to go down into the sand. This "news" made us panic terribly, and out of fear we immediately left the village. I took hold of my staff (walking stick), and once again trudged forward with this group of Jews until we arrived in a little town, Dlugosizedlo, where there was a summer house. When I entered the town, I saw a tumult of people that were on the street. When I asked about this commotion, they answered that these were refugees who were chased out of a town and who wanted to rest up here. I hid in this town for a few days, and after that the Germans gathered up all the Jews into the marketplace and one of them said to those gathered there: "Be informed that those who just came here must leave this town immediately and the residents must leave within two hours and can take along some things, but only within those two hours. After that, no things!"

*[Page 294]*

There arose cries and moans, and people began to move from their places with bundles on their backs. The people where I had stayed were good friends of mine, and piled on my back a big bundle with blankets and clothing.

I continued going until the evening, when I reached the city of Ostrawenka. I stayed overnight in that city and the next day I crossed over the Russian border without any interference except for the fact that the German guard interrogated me. When I saw the first Russian soldier I wanted to recite a blessing over him (make a *bracha*), but when I went a little further on and the road was split into many directions, and to Zambrow as well, the patrol didn't permit me to use the highway and told me to go in the sand for about 20 kilometers and that would take me to a small town. All this time, there was no food.

*[Page 295]*

I arrived in this small town in the evening, but no one took me in to sleep. Everyone closed their door and I had to sleep in the *Bais Medrash*. The following day, I was examined by the city doctor. He rebandaged me and said that the wound was healing. After that, I continued moving on. I dragged myself until I arrived to the train. I spent the entire night at the train station. The following day the train arrived. I could barely climb up onto the train – a sea of people was pushing to get on. Everyone wanted to get to Bialystok as soon as possible. In the middle of the way, the train had to stop a few kilometers ahead of some water. Some rushed to get to the water to have space in a small boat that went back and forth between shores and then they would catch the other train that was a few kilometers on the other side of the water. Hardly alive any more, I barely managed to get onto the train. I was very thirsty but there was no way I could help myself. Someone sitting near me had a bottle of water and I asked for a drink but didn't receive one. I arrived in Bialystok in the evening.


**b) By the Russians**

I wandered the streets with the bundles that my friends from Dlugosedlo had given me. In the middle of the street, I was stopped and they asked me to get into a car. There were already many people in the car. I was very happy. The car went behind the city. The Russian soldiers showed us where to go and they said they would bring us food. We waited for an hour, then two, and more, but we saw no food nor heard anything about it. We were so disappointed, and each took a little hay, put it on the floor, and went to sleep. The following morning we went into the city to look for food. I left my bundles behind where I had slept and asked someone to keep an eye on them. The city was filled with many refugees, those who had been expelled from many different cities. At the community center, there were all kinds of lineups: one for food, one for housing, and one for medical attention. I lined up for the doctor and for food. I went into the community center and they told me that there were no more coupons for food, only some to see the doctor. Since I wanted to see the doctor, I said that I was sick, but that meanwhile I was very hungry. I had already been fasting for several days. I have no more energy to survive. They felt sorry for me and gave me a coupon for lunch in the community kitchen. I went to stand in line for lunch. I stood for four hours, just barely arriving at the small window for lunch. While receiving a small cup of soup and a small piece of bread, the narrow space and terrible pushing caused the soup to spill and I was left with an empty cup in hand. I ate the small piece of bread, and filled myself with cold water in order to quench my thirst.

[Page 296]

I went outside to see what was new and I met my friends that had come from the camps. We were overjoyed. They couldn't believe that I was alive. I asked them about my brother, but they didn't know anything about him. After that, we spent the night in a *bais medrash,* and there saw very sad scenes: people were searching for shirts, for clothing. One Jew was standing almost completely naked and was searching. I couldn't find a clean place. My friends from Serock found me another place – a different *bais medrash.* There I had as much tea as I wanted and a lot of bread – enough even for the next day. We pushed the benches together and went to sleep.

In the morning, I went back to the first place. The first snow had fallen. The streets were covered with a white blanket. I went with joy because I now had a comfortable place to rest myself. I took my bundles and went back into the city. That same day, I found my future brother-in-law who had also been evacuated from his city of Ruzhyn. He had come with materials that he had saved from there, so that next to me, he was a wealthy man. We could not stay together. There were tens of thousands of refugees that had come to Bialystok. That was everyone's fate. They too, as I, had to stay in the *batei midrashim* (plural of House of Study [*bais medrash*]) and sleep on the ground. My brother-in-law opened a little store and made a lot of money, such that I already was able to have a good breakfast, lunch, and supper, to my satisfaction. Many military personnel were customers, so that everyone was able to make nice money. The military personnel, and even the higher ranks, bought everything in the streets that they saw: manufactured goods, fancier goods, fruit, foods, and mostly watches. They bought everything without bargaining. For many, this was the first time seeing many of these things. The military personnel were generally polite. They greeted everyone sincerely, regardless of belief. They spoke to everyone about all kinds of things. Business grew and became very popular. Some people became wealthy. Many made good lives for themselves. One could go anywhere, in or out, without being afraid of anyone. One thought that the issue of neediness was resolved. Prices of everything rose. One had to line up for everything: from bread to a needle. There was no other way to get anything. That's how normal life went. People stopped thinking about their future – only one thought held everyone: trade, money, business, and nothing else.

[Page 297]

I thought differently about life and also about the setting I was in. My earlier dreams were spinning again. Sleeping on the floor of the *bais medrash* did not still my pains and sufferings. I did not stop missing my parents, brothers, and sisters. There was no thought of staying here. Many times I cried terribly, separated and locked away, barefoot and naked as I was. Everything was expensive and hard to get. The beddings that I had carried on my back someone had stolen from me on the road. Not knowing the fate of those dear ones I had left back home did not let me rest. One night, my thoughts began to rage within me, from early evening until late at night: to leave or to stay? yes or no? to go home or to stay in a strange place? Finally I decided that I had to go home. The border was very securely guarded but fear of it did not hold me back. So that very night, at 2AM, I took my walking stick and went on my way. En route, I met some Polish soldiers. I spoke with them, and they agreed to take me with them on their way. Like that, we went together until we arrived at a village. There, a peasant convinced the soldiers that they should not take me with them any further. So, I continued on my own. On the way, I met a young non-Jewish man who had a bundle on his back. I had a talk with him and he told me that he too was crossing the border and if I wanted to cross the border with him, I would have to pay. I agreed and went along with him. The same non-Jew told me that he lived close to the border on the other side, and that I would be able to spend the night there. Near the border, there was water that one had to cross. But when we got near the water, the patrol guard told us to stop. At that moment, the non-Jew jumped into the water and I was left alone. I tried to do the same, but I couldn't. Meanwhile, the patrol guard came closer and I became frightened and jumped halfway into the water. The non-Jew gave me a yank so that I came out safely on the other side of the water. The soldier began screaming that we should turn back, but we began to run with all our strength until we came close to the non-Jew's home.

*[Page 298]*

I entered the house hardly alive and hardly dead. I received food there and paid dearly for that as well, and also for sleeping on the ground that was covered in straw. I was afraid that someone would recognize that I was a Jew, so I went to another peasant and asked that he shave me and paid a lot of money for that because he threatened to tell the Germans that I was a Jew. The following day I paid the non-Jew who had crossed the border with me double what we had arranged because he also threatened me.

*[Page 299]*

I paid another peasant to take me further on the way, but after one kilometer he threw me off the wagon. I dragged myself on foot from village to village. In the evening (when it was dark, you weren't allowed to move around), I arrived in another village and asked each peasant to allow me to spend the night and said that I would pay for it, but no one would allow me to stay and they each said that soon I would arrive at a Jewish village. It was nighttime, and I was once again seized by fear of the Germans. I was warned that I should not show myself outside at night. I began to run with all my strength and decided to spend the night in a field in an abandoned stable that I had noticed. But because of the terrible cold and fierce winds I continued on my way. I was in a terrible situation, when just at that time, a wagon passed on the road. I quickly ran over and asked the peasant where he was going. The peasant answers me that he is going to the village where I want to go. It was not easy to convince him to let me go with him. On the way, he asked me for tobacco, and I just happened to have some. It was as if I had revived him from the dead, because you couldn't get tobacco even for money.

When we arrived at the village where I had wanted to go, it was already dark. When we entered a house, there were several people we recognized. They welcomed me warmly, brought me bread and tea, and asked me where I had come from and what was new "there." I described a small part of what had happened to me, and then they made a bed for me on the floor. In that house, some people I did not know were spending the night, and there really was no bed for me. I thought about how I would continue on my way in this terrible wind. At dawn I went on my way. When I came near the water that was near our city, I had to pay a lot of money to be taken across by boat and then I went into the city. Each house and tree was familiar to me. I had thought that

I would not see any of this during my lifetime, so now everything looked newborn. When I entered our terribly missed and much dreamed- about city, I began to sob terribly. I was not recognizable by anyone. When I went into my house, they thought I was a poor man coming for a piece of bread. At that moment, I cried out: "Don't you know who I am?" I was all ragged and torn up – so much so, that it was difficult to recognize me. My parents and my sister were kissing me and crying when they realized that they were looking at me before their eyes. I described to them my difficulties, and then went directly to sleep. The news of my return went through the town like lightning. All my friends and acquaintances came to see how I was. Everyone was interested to hear what was happening on the other side of the border where most of their dear ones were situated.

[Page 300]

I spent the entire day in the house with people I knew, but in the evening it was uncomfortable for me because until five o'clock one could go in the streets, but afterwards my friends were unable to come see me. No electricity was permitted to burn at night, so I went to sleep very early. My large and rich library, which I had compiled with great care, had been completely burned. In my library I had: *Shas* (Mishna) with Talmudic commentaries, a selection of old and new Hebrew literature, hundreds of Yiddish books, and books in Polish. In my small *bais hamikdosh* (temple), there was a special section of philosophy, psychology, and social sciences. Scores of youths drank from this well – and all this was burned in Hitler's bonfires.

In this depressed atmosphere, I spent several weeks. I thought that this house would be a place of refuge, of rest and contentment. But this didn't last long. One morning, a day before the eve of Channuka (1939), there was a banging at the door and everyone was told to leave the house. We were ordered to go to the marketplace. The Germans forbade us from taking anything along. When we arrived there, we saw all the residents from the city, young and old, women with tiny children in their arms, the sick and the frail, those crippled in the feet or hands, and people who needed to be supported. When the Germans appeared in this place with their wild murder, everyone began pushing to hide behind the other.

[Page 301]

People were looking for their children, parents, one for his mother, one for his father, a sister and a brother. The cries, wails, and screams went directly to heaven. It was dark outside, cold all around, we were standing naked and barefoot for a few hours until the Germans cleaned the Jews out from all the houses and hiding places and brought them to this place.

We were beaten, broken, and bloodied by these murderers, and stood like this until daylight. After that, we were ordered to turn around and move from this place. We moved and cried. Everyone looked back to catch a final glimpse of the city that he had to leave. All the goods and possessions that people had collected over generations, all that had to stay. The *shul,* the *bais medrash,* the holy books, and other things were left without ownership. On the way, the only thing that was heard were moans and groans that tore through people's hearts. Without food, without drink, we trudged all day. In the evening, when the sun was already setting, we arrived in the city of Nazielsk. There, the Germans that were directing us on the way searched us and took our money. After that, bands of armed Germans with sticks and truncheons came and beat us mercilessly and told us to run quickly. Whoever fell, they befell like wild animals. We ran like that until we arrived in the city near the *shul.* At the *shul,* the Germans set themselves into two long rows, and everyone was beaten that way. Blood ran. With split noses, broken bones, bloodshot eyes, broken hands and feet, cries and groans, the crowd was chased into the Nazielsk *shul.* That same evening, near the *shul,* many were buried alive. The people who buried them heard the others' cries for help and mercy. They cried continuously. After that, the Germans called out: "Whoever has cigarettes, gold rings, or suitcases, should give them here – those who resist will be shot." Out of fear, people gave away everything. After that, we lay down on the ground in the *shul,* one near the other, to pass the night. Everyone was drained from the whole day.

[Page 302]

The following morning, they ordered us to leave the *shul,* and again they put us three in a row and told us to move on. They kept back about forty men to clean the *shul* and also the streets. Then we had to do all kinds of exercises and rub our fingers on the walls for a few hours, and then we were told to run for a few minutes until the train – about six kilometers. When we arrived to the train, they set us out in one long row and searched everyone. Everyone was ordered to strip naked, and the women had to wash the men with the water from the puddles. Women were searched naked also in front of everyone's eyes. Girls and women were raped and beaten. Whatever they found was taken away, and the person who had the possession was murderously beaten. That was the last step of their barbarism. The Germans spared no one: men, women, boys, girls, and even small children. Here they had the opportunity to take the last few pennies and the last bit of blood that anyone had.

After these tortures, they ordered us to go into the wagons of the trains. They locked them, and took us for three days and three nights without water and without bread. Many times they stopped between deserts and we thought that they would push us out into the sand. We had no bathrooms. People suffered from this terribly. We had no bread to eat. The worst thing was that we had no water. We almost died of thirst. When it rained, we licked the drops and the dew from the windows to still the thirst, but this did not help. When the Germans caught us in this "thieving" act, they beat us murderously. We thought we would die on the way until we would get to Biale. We were locked in the train all night. We screamed for water until the non-Jews from nearby secretly brought us water, taking one zloty for a glass of water.

The following morning, at ten o'clock, the Germans took us into the city. There, the resident Jews brought us bread and water, and took each of us into their homes and gave us food and rest. They treated us with courtesy, and comforted us saying we would get back to our home. In the meantime, we had found a place of refuge. From there, many people spread out into the surrounding areas, some stayed in that place, some went to Warsaw. We also went to Warsaw. We went through a lot on the way. When the Germans found a Jew on the train, they beat him, threw him off the train, and took away everything. We fortunately found a car on the train that had only non-Jews and we hid behind them so that no one could identify us. Suddenly, some Germans came on board and immediately recognized the Jews (they thought I was a non-Jew), the Germans beat them terribly.

[Page 303]

After riding all night, we arrived in Warsaw and found other people from our town. During this time, there was an institution established that took care of these poor refugees and provided them with food and sleeping accommodations, and also some clothing. When I saw this, I thought: "God of Israel shall not deceive," and "Israel is never left as a widower." There will come a better tomorrow.

*From the archives of the Jewish Historical Institute of Warsaw*

[Page 304]

# War Experiences
### Rivka Mendzelewski (May), Cholon

**Translated by Pamela Russ**

### a) By the Germans

A few weeks before the war, I was in an orchard in Moskowice – between Serock and Wyszkow. Thursday, ten days before the war, my partner Zalman Khainewer received an order to present himself to the Polish army. We left the orchard with all the fruit, and seven days before the outbreak of the war, on Shabbos, we returned home to Serock.

There were groups gathered in the streets. On Tuesday, September 5, 1939, in the middle of the day, bombs began to fall. The first were by the trenches, the second by Yakov Granjewicz, and the third by Yakov Rosenberg in a bunker where 70 people were hiding; the fourth by Aron Leyb

Zilbershtayn, the butcher; the fifth by Kuzhnicki in the oil factory; and the sixth and seventh fell by Motel Mendzelewski.

After this bombing, everyone went to hide in their houses. When it quietened down, we went to dig up Yakov Rosenberg's cellar. Among the victims were: Yakov Rosenberg, Henya and Estusha, Moishe Pshikarski with his wife and two children, Esther Pjenicer with her son Pesakh, Shmuel Kanarek, Khaitche Swarc with her husband and two children, and a grandchild of Taperek, and many other Jews from the surrounding towns. On Tuesday evening, we gathered up all the bodies and buried them all, in a common grave, I think.

Wednesday and Thursday we hid among trees. On Shabbos at about four in the afternoon, we saw Germans ride by on motorcycles from the area of Warsaw going to Pultusk. At night, from Shabbos to Sunday, they entered Serock.

Sunday morning, September 10, 1939, the Germans began to destroy Jewish stores and throw the merchandise into the streets. My fruit, that was in the cellar of Yakov Arye the carpenter, was also thrown out by the Germans. When I went over to just have a look, a German accused me of having said that the Germans are worse than the gypsies so I immediately received a smack and then he added that if he would have a gun in his hand he would have shot me dead.

[Page 305]

That same Sunday, around ten or eleven in the morning, they herded all the Jews into the marketplace: men, women, children, and the elderly. Among us were also some Polaks. We were all gathered together, then someone came on a motorcar and ordered that the women and children be released and the men herded together into the small *shul*. (There were horses in the large *shul*.) They set up a large fence around the *shul*. The men received food that was prepared by the women. They remained there until the eve of Rosh Hashona.

Three days later, they released from the *shul* the men who were forty-five years and older and young boys age fifteen and under, and after that, on the second day of Rosh Hashona, year 5700, the detainees still in the *shul* were sent off to Pultusk. They were there for one day. On the way from Pultusk to Chekhanow, the Germans acted murderously. Whoever couldn't walk, they shot. Where the transport stopped, I don't know. My husband was freed in Pultusk because of a bad leg.

We remained in Serock until the last evacuation. During that time, we found some hard work cleaning the palace of Radziwill (Yitzkhok Konjer also worked there). Within two months payments were given only a few times. On the eve of Sukos, they herded the Jews out of Pultusk across the Narew River, and then allowed them to go wherever they wished.

The mayor was a *volksdeutch* (of German ethnicity rather than of citizenship). On Monday, December 4, 1939, Menakhem Kronenberg was summoned to the police station where he was told that no one should be afraid to open their stores and that they would have to have signs in German and Polish. That was on Monday. That same day, at 2am, they began the vicious expulsion. We were sleeping and we heard banging on the shutters, and a Jew was screaming: "Motel! (That was my father-in-law, where I was living.) Get dressed, they're chasing us out!" And soon we heard banging and yelling: "Jew dogs! Get out!"

I, my husband, and my daughter of several months, my father-in-law and mother-in-law and their children, all went out to the marketplace. Already the entire town was gathered there. The screams were heard until the Heavens, children lost parents and – the reverse. Everyone carried a bundle on their backs. When they were chasing the Jews out of their homes, the Germans and the *volksdeutchen* (while laughing) beat us murderously. They placed us four in a row and then we left to Nazielsk.

[Page 306]

On the Nazielsk highway, there was a Polak on his way to the mill of Moishe Rosenberg with a wagonload of grain to be ground. A German military man approached the Polak and threw the grain on the ground and told me and the child to get on the wagon with our bundle. Also, Esther, the daughter of Itche Meyer Soljazh, and her two children, boarded the wagon and we went to Nazielsk.

Those who couldn't walk were beaten. The *volksdeutchen* also beat those with whom they had dealt with before – Moishe Pjenik was beaten very badly.

An hour before we were forced out, my neighbor (Zlata – Motte Ber's grandchild) gave birth to a child. They chased her out regardless, and on the way she hemorrhaged.

We arrived in Nazielsk on Tuesday evening. The weather was fine. In Nazielsk they shot the old man Goodes, Mendel the butcher, and Zakharia the tailor's daughter-in-law (Feigele Wenger). They were buried in one grave.

When they were forced into the *shul*, they were beaten. The Germans put down a basket and everyone had to put their keys there.

In the Nazielsk *shul*, everyone also had to give away anything of value. Wednesday morning we were chased out of the *shul*, several tall men were selected: all the Zilbershtayn butcher brothers – Moishe, Shiya, Nekhemiah, and Hershel Mak. In the hallway of the *shul*, they had to scrape the walls with their nails and while they were doing so, they were being beaten over their heads until they were bloodied, and they had to sing Hatikva and other songs. The Germans themselves brought rags with cold water to put on the Jews' heads.

When we left the *shul* to go to the trains, I also went in a wagon and the men went on foot a distance of six kilometers. Before that, about 30 men were taken out of the rows. Among them were: my husband, Yakov Leyb Fefer (Khana Perl's husband), Feige Bresler's husband Yosef Doren. They were taken out to clean the *shul*. They beat Yosef Doren (Yosef the butcher) very badly, shot him through his head, then took him to the doctor. They cleaned the *shul* with their hands. After that, we went to the train. When I arrived there, there was already a full car and – they left.

[Page 307]

In front of the train there was a lot of mud. As we were going into the cars, we were searched and beaten terribly. Whenever they found money on someone, that person was beaten on that part of his body where it was found.

Yakov Leviner was forced to "bathe" in the mud. Khaim Hersh Kleinman (the Hebrew teacher and son of Yisroel Yitzkhok the glazier) was beaten very badly.

When we had to go into a car in a second train, the thirty men who were forced to clean the *shul* arrived, and we were not permitted to look at them nor were they permitted to look at us. Before we went into the wagon cars we again were searched and beaten. In this wagon car were also: Mottel Mendzelewski and his wife and two daughters, me and my own child, Pesakh Kanjer and his wife, Yitzkhok Kanjer's wife (Khantze Khmilirz') and their child, Eliyahu the ritual slaughterer (*shokhet)* with his wife and mother-in-law, Liftche Kuzhnicki and the son Shlomo Dovid Kuzhnicki and the daughter-in-law Feigel from Ostrolenka, and a couple from Pultusk with their four children. It was a regular passenger car. As soon as we went in, they covered the windows and locked the doors. This entire time I knew nothing about my parents. During the search, they beat Dvoira (a grandchild of the Kovaleks), so much that she lost her mind. They also mercilessly beat Itchele Pshikarski (the small Itchele).

Wednesday before noon, we left Nazielsk. One train went to the left, and one to the right. We arrived in Praga on Thursday night. At the station, Polaks threw bread to us and water. After that, we went to Siedlice, and also passed through Malkin. After going for a while, we stayed in one place until dawn. When it got light, we saw that on the other side there was the other train that had left before us, and we were positioned one opposite the other. We saw how families were torn apart. Pshikarski's daughter Soroh was in one wagon, and her child of six months was in the other.

[Page 308]

They brought her the child. This was in Biale-Podlask. On Friday, some Polaks brought us food to buy. The first train stayed in Biale-Podlask and my train went to Lukow. When we arrived there Friday late afternoon, the Jews in Lukow welcomed us warmly. There I met my husband and my parents and my sister Malka. They came over to me. Shabbos morning, I met Meyer Blekher's wife and children.

When we got off the train, my husband's brother Hershel Mendzelewski from Legionnowa, met us there with food. In Lukow heard that Khaim Shlomo the *shokhet* was close to death. On Shabbos night (Saturday night), I, my husband, his parents, and my parents left by train to Warsaw. On the way, we met Dovid Rosenberg and Borukh Yosef Melnik, the father. We arrived in Warsaw on Sunday afternoon. I stayed with my child in Warsaw, along with my father-in-law and mother-in-law. My parents left for Legionnowa to my sister Dina. I worked in Warsaw, and after a few weeks, Malya and her child Khana, and I and my child Rokhel left for Bialystok.

In order to travel free on the trains you needed a special permit that cost a lot of money.

I went to Wolomyn to my parents to say goodbye and thanks to their help, I was able to get for a nice sum of money the much coveted travel permit. On the way from Wolomyn to Warsaw, I witnessed horrific scenes: Jews were murderously beaten, they were thrown out of rushing trains, and so on.

After a short time of being in Warsaw, we – that is I, my husband Yakov and daughter Khana, my sister-in-law Malya and her child – decided to go to Bialysotk via Siedlice. This was at the end of the month of February, 1940, in a terrible frost. We left Warsaw by train and arrived in Siedlice. There in the train station Polish hooligans beat us up, and a Jewish woman had pity on us and took us all into her house.

In Siedlice, a Jewish woman gave us the address of a Polak who would take us across the river into the Soviet zone.

[Page 309]

In the evening, we left Siedlice and spent the night at this Polak's house, and the next morning we left for another village near the Bug River. At this Polak's house where we were, the border guard came in but didn't bother us. We crossed the Bug that night, in forty degree frost.

We continued to wander from one village to another, and we were also robbed on the way. An honest peasant drove us in a car. Finally, we arrived in Siemiatycze at a Jewish family, from where they took us to the train station that would take us to Bialystok. My brother-in-law, Yehuda Mendzelewski, was already in Bialystok earlier on. I lived there at the family Perlman on Kupiecka 19. I also met Golda Leviner, Yenta Spilke, the Nowogrodskis, Yisroel Wolinski, Fishel Sterdiner, Khaya'le Zakharek with her son and daughter, and Yitzkhok Wolinski. Once, when I was standing in my row, I heard that a woman from Serock was in the hospital and that they were planning to remove her leg. I left to go to the hospital and there I met Mindel Rosental (Labzhak's daughter). They actually had removed all the frostbitten toes from both legs.

This tragedy happened to her as she was going across the border the same night we were. There were other Serocker in Bialystok.

We were there from February until the end of June 1940. Then suddenly, they started to send all of us refugees off. For that they told us all to get Russian papers – we also registered to get Russian papers, but then we registered to go back to Poland and thankfully, because of that, we remained alive, since they sent us away from Bialystok on the echelons (trains) with all our bundles. We rode for several days with this train. The Russians gave us food. We bought food at each station, and quick help also accompanied us. Khava Barab and Eliezer Eikhenbaum were also with us.

The train brought us to a village where they sat us all on a type of boat and took us to another village near Wologda-Uz'le. Afterward we went to the village Wokoti where barracks were prepared – one house for a few families. There was a bakery there and a general kitchen (mess hall). All you saw were trees and sky, it was very cold, and we had stove heaters. My daughter very soon got the measles. The men soon began the work of chopping trees. Bread was given according to a normal amount – 800 grams a day. In the early times of work, they wore nets on their faces because of the flies.

*[Page 310]*

I worked cleaning private rooms, then I worked at sharpening the axes and saws, and finally – by cutting meter length wood. For the children they made a daycare and a school. There was also a laboratory. We were in this place for fourteen months – until September 1941.

We couldn't go around freely, only within the district of the camp. We received mail from Warsaw, Wolomyn, and Ukraine. Faige Khaynower sent me several packages with money and needles for sewing.

In September 1941, they told us we were free. We selected an area from the map – far from Moscow and Ukraine, and we went through the White Sea. (Thanks to Shikorski's arrangements, all the Polish citizens were freed.) We received food on the way, but the conditions were very difficult. We were taken to Kubisov, and from there to the Urals to the city Omsk. We worked there in a large electric station. There, were also: Yakov and Yehuda's family, and Yakov's sister, and Reb Eliyahu Aharon Rosental (the teacher) and the entire large family. The men organized themselves for work in the factory. Whatever one had, one sold. We suffered with hunger for three months – after that I settled myself into a very good place, in a mess hall kitchen (dining room) where there were 5,000 people (I started as a cleaner). I moved up to the highest position – to the key holder for the store, and portioned out the food. No one in my family was hungry any more. Yakov's sister worked in a bakery, Malya worked in a house, and so it wasn't so bad any more.

In 1943, I became very sick, and lay for half a year in the military hospital where they saved me. After I recovered I went back to work. Not far from our lodging, there was a center for all the Polaks, run by the Polish liberation committee, under the direction of Wanda Wasilewska. Our children studied in the Polish schools. There we also received products and clothing from America. We also got Polish newspapers such as: "New Horizons" and a Jewish newspaper "The Star" from Kubisov.

*[Page 311]*

Correspondence with Poland was practically completely cut off. Occasionally we received letters from Simkha Grinboim, Avrohom and Feivel Pshikorski. I wrote a letter at the end of the war – May 1945 – to the magistrate of Biale-Podlask, inquiring about my dear ones. They replied that those living were: Golda Belison, Yitzkhok Kanjar, and a few Serock Jews.

At the beginning of 1946, we were given an order to prepare ourselves to return to Poland within the new Polish repatriation. The Russians paid us for our work and we began to prepare for our travels. We bought clothing, baked cakes, etc.

At the beginning of the month of March, 1946, we boarded good wagons and travelled for a month to Poland. As we arrived in Przemysl, and the NKVD (the secret police for the Soviet Union) said goodbye to us, took away our working booklets, and exchanged our Russian money to Polish money. From Przemysl onward began a terrible and bitter route. We transferred over to another train that had wide rails and where there were many Polaks who were taken over from east Galicia to Lower Silesia in the new part of Poland. Civilian Polaks taunted us, cursed us, and shot at us. All the Jews grouped together into three special wagons that were headed only to Warsaw. In my wagon there was: me and my entire family, and also the families of my brother-in-law Yehuda and his sister-in-law Khaya.

Our train arrived in Warsaw at night at the end of the month of April, 1946, to the train station with the name "Towarowe" and we remained in the wagons for ten days. The day after we arrived, we received food from the Red Cross. We were actually of the first ones to return from Russia.

*[Page 312]*

My brother-in-law Yehuda and I left for Praga to the General Jewish Committee, to find out about our dear ones and friends. The Committee immediately sent us food, sweets for the children, and a nurse to examine us. Everyone was happy, most importantly, with our little children.

Right after that, the Jewish Committee got us a place to live in the barracks of the former *Hakhshara*-place of the *Hekhalutz* in Grokhow (near Warsaw). We left the wagons and went to our new place, and we were there for the month of July, 1946.

The news of the huge destruction shook up all of us – I was very depressed and cried terribly for all my dear ones.

Every day we went to Praga and at the Jewish Committee on Targowa Street we met the few remaining others. Once, my husband and I met Gitele Rosenberg (today in Silesia), who gave me the first greetings from my brother Yeshayohu Mai, who was in the hell of Auschwitz and who is today in Munich. This news (of my brother) brought a new life to my soul; I began to breathe more freely.

We were very encouraged (felt revived) when one day in the Jewish Committee we met the soldier from the Jewish brigade, Henikh Warshawski (Khanokh Werdi). We soon went to Grokhow and there he told us about those few remaining ones from our town who were now all over Poland, and also commiserated about our painful lives.

At the end of July, 1946, we left Poland via Czechoslovakia and came to a refugee camp Bad-Ebensee (Austria). There I gave birth to my son and received the first letter from my brother Yeshayohu.

In Ebensee the situation was terrible, and after three months we arrived at the DP camp Ansbakh, Germany (American zone), where we were for two years. At the beginning of 1949, we left Germany, and went to Israel via France on the ship "*Negba*" (southwards). Here began a new chapter of our lives.

[Page 313]

# At the Time of Destruction
### Arye Yagoda (Kfar Hasidim)

**Translated by Sara Mages**

I was born in Serock. I was 17 at the outbreak of the Second World War and a member of "*Hashomer Hatzair*." When the town was bombed we hid in a cellar. At the same time a bomb fell into the cellar and killed seventy people, most of them Jews.

My family escaped in a wagon in the direction of Miñsk-Mazowiecki, and after that to Warsaw. We stayed with my uncle who lived in 8 Tabrada Street, Warsaw. When the bombing of Warsaw began we moved to 22 Zapla Street. The entire city of Warsaw was burning and we didn't know where to run. My sister had a little boy and it confused us. I remember that after that we spent the night in a cellar in 66 Shenna Street.

When the Germans occupied Warsaw we returned to Serock. Our apartment was seized by the Germans and all the books - *Shas, Poskim* etc. were torn and desecrated.

One day all the Jews gathered in the Great Synagogue by the order of the Germans. The young people were sent to hard labor in Germany. Some of them were murdered on the way and a few managed to escape to Russia.

It was the eve of Chanukah when the Germans ordered all the Jews to gather in the market. They weren't allowed to take any luggage with them. Each took what he was able to grab in a hurry. My father didn't sleep at home that night because he missed the police hour (7 in the evening). The Germans led us to Nashelsk and locked us for the night in the synagogue. There were all kinds of abuse: they selected a group of people, ordered them to stand next to the synagogue's walls and scrape them with their nails.

The next morning they chased us to the train station accompanied by beatings and when we got there they robbed us. Those who didn't give their money voluntarily were stripped naked and thrown into puddles of cold water. In this manner they wanted to frighten us so that we would give them everything that we had.

They transported us to Lukow in locked cars. There wasn't a drop of water and people licked the dew from the windowpanes.

The community of Lukow couldn't accommodate all of us so some of us traveled to Biala, others to Mezrich, and we were transferred by carts to Kotzk. After a two week stay in Kotzk I traveled to Biala where I started to work for the *Schutzpolizei* [security police].

[Page 314]

I was sent to work there by the community and for the work I received half a kilogram of bread per day. At first I worked in the kitchen and later with the horses. I lived in 28 Grabnowski Street.

When Biala Ghetto was liquidated at the end of September 1942, we, 300 Jews, were transferred from the *Schutzpolizei* to the SD (Sicherheitsdienst [Security Service] the intelligence agency of the SS) supply camp which was located in the military barracks of Biala.

At that time I fell ill with typhus and for five days went to work with a high temperature of forty degrees because I was afraid that they would shoot me on the spot. After five days I was forced to lie in the barrack because I couldn't stand on my feet. A few days later we were ordered to gather in order to move to another camp. Those who were sick were told that they could remain in the camp. I felt the danger and despite my weakness I got up and dressed. Others tried to hide and those who were captured in their hiding place were shot on the spot. The 60 sick people, who remained in the barrack, were murdered. The Germans ordered us to line up in groups of seven.

An SD officer rode a horse at the head of the column and the soldiers of the "*Wehrmacht*" marched on the sides. To our question: "Where are we going" they answered that "they were leading us to a camp from which we wouldn't be able to escape." We looked back and saw a large number of wagons loaded with shovels and hoes. One of our townsmen, Yisrael Rozynek, started to flee. They shot after him, but they weren't able to hit him because he managed to enter the forest. The soldiers were only able to shoot from one side because if they shot from both sides they could have hurt each other. I don't know who cried "Horra" first, but all of a sudden everyone began to shout and flee. I was very sick but I also fled. The vast majority of the people who fled to the right were shot by the Germans. I fled to the left and reached the forest.

I met one of the escapees in the forest. He was completely naked so I gave him some of my clothes. We entered the home of a peasant woman and asked for a little water. "Run - she shouted - I'm afraid." In another house a peasant woman gave us a slice of bread and told us that there are stacks of hay in the field and we could hide there. We lay inside a stack of hay while two policemen searched for us in the immediate vicinity. They asked the farmers if they saw Jews, but luckily no one saw us and the farmers turned their heads as a sign of negativity. At night we went to look for food in the farmers' huts. One peasant woman ran from her house when she saw us, but a decent farmer lived in the next hut. When I opened the door he told us not to enter because strangers were staying with him. He allowed us to settle in his barn and later brought us potato soup. He led us to the road and showed us the way to Miêdzyrzecz. We arrived to Miêdzyrzecz at three in the morning and crept quietly to the ghetto. It was immediately after the liquidation and great fear overcame us to the sight of neglect.

[Page 315]

Broken doors and windows, feathers in the street, and it seemed that not a living soul remained there. It was in October 1942. We saw light in one house. We knocked on the door. Several people, who were sick with typhus, lay in a narrow room and despite the danger we stayed there till morning. The ghetto in Miêdzyrzecz was not fully liquidated and there was still a large number of Jews in it. We turned to the community and started to work in the furniture warehouse. The furniture were robbed from Jewish homes and concentrated by the Germans in the building of the Great Synagogue. I work there for half a kilogram of bread per day but it was possible to sneak out of the ghetto and buy bread from a Polish baker. We feared the final liquidation all the time and devised a plan on how to escape to the forest. Once, a group of us left the ghetto armed with axes and our slogan was "we wouldn't surrender to the Gentiles." Suddenly we heard "stop" and shots. We ran back to the ghetto. We slept in bunkers and decided that we would only go to work if we will be able to escape from there. On 1 May 1943, at 7 in the morning, when we gathered to go to work outside the ghetto we were attacked by the strong guard of the S.S. They led us to the train station and locked us inside freight cars.

Several thousand people traveled in the locked freight cars without water, bread etc. It was a terrible journey. I saw people who drank their urine. In one car they broke the door and jumped out. The Germans shot after them. In our car several people struggled to jump from an open window. Many died on the way. After we arrived to Majdanek I was assigned to a group of ten whose duty was to remove the bodies from the cars. There were about 70-80 bodies there. Gold and money were scattered on the ground and nobody paid attention to it. The bodies were covered with tar paper. After the selection I was given a note with a number. I hung it on the chest next to my right arm. I was in the third field in block number 3. It was very bad in Majdanek. A roll call was held at three at night. Out of fifty people, who left for work in the morning, three died before noon. We were always beaten. The Kapo, who was a German criminal, was cruel. He climbed with all of his weight on the necks of those who fell from weakness and strangled them to death. There wasn't a quiet place - they beat us everywhere. They brought us to a building site, gave us nails and ordered us to bend and straighten them - this was the work. At that time many transports arrived with Jews from Warsaw Ghetto.

On 6 July 1943 they transferred me to the camp in Skarzysko-Kamienna. There were about 10000 people, men and women, there. Those who were there for a while were dressed well because they were able to take something from home with them. We, who came from Majdanek, were torn and worn - a slice of bread was a treasure for us and we attacked all the food. There was an ammunition factory in Skarzysko-Kamienna with three departments A, B, C. I was accepted to department A which was the easiest one. There, we made satchels for guns. Department C was the worst one.

[Page 316]

Many died there of hepatitis. Everyone worked without a mask and without gloves and the fumes poisoned the people. The camp's commander, who was fat and hunchback, was called Kinmman. Many Jews were murdered by a Gentile named Vujicik. I got sick and couldn't walk. I knew that I would be shot if I couldn't work and for that reason I hid. A young doctor name Nickelberg, who was a good surgeon, saved me. He operated on me and I was able to work. I wanted to escape from this camp, but I wasn't able to. Several of us wanted to flee to the nearby forest, but after I carefully checked the guarding I realized that we wouldn't be able to do so.

One person escaped and when he was caught he was immediately executed in front of us. The Jewish police helped to guard us.

The work in the department was conducted in three shifts. Sunday was a day off from work. The food was very bad, 400 grams of bread and a liter of soup with "potato latkes" for lunch. Those who had a little money were able to buy additional food. The local Poles, who worked in the factory, smuggled lentils to the camp. The Jews bought the lentils, cooked and sold portions in boxes. Those who were able to buy such a portion weren't as hungry as others. The worst place to work was in the galvanization department which was supervised by the murderer Vujicik. It was a miracle when someone was able to survive for more than two months. Skarzysko-Kamienna was in fact a labor camp. The factory was called HASAG [Hugo Schneider Aktiengesellschaft].

On 1 August 1944, we were evacuated from Skarzysko-Kamienna. We traveled for several days in locked cars and arrived to Buchenwald. There, we were quarantined for eight days. Those who were fit to work were given injections. We were given other clothes and also bathed. In the camp we slept in tents. When we arrived to this place a skinny red-haired prisoner appeared and questioned us if there were any Jewish policemen or kapo among us. We pointed at several them and they immediately disappeared.

I met the aforementioned red-haired prisoner after the war, but I don't know his name. He did his best to help us: gave us bread to eat and clothes to wear.

After the quarantine we were led to Schlieben near Leipzig. It was a village and we lived in huts. I worked in a factory that manufactured anti-tank weapons. The work was conducted in two shifts of 10 hours each. I worked in the traffic department. Schlieben was a concentration camp. We were given stripped prisoner clothes (in Skarzysko-Kamienna we wore regular clothes). Roll calls were held morning and evening. We left for work at 6 in the morning. The young S.S. man, who led us to work, beat us all the time and for no reason. After work we rested on wooden bunks.

[Page 317]

There were dozens of people in each hall. We were always hungry. We got a little bread, a few potatoes and beets for lunch. In the evening we got a little butter, margarine or marmalade. We always complained about the food.

At the same time a transport arrived with Jews from Hungary who lived separately. At first they said that the food was sufficient for them, but a short time later they died and fell like flies - they didn't have Majdanek behind them. They weren't used to such suffering. There were many religious people among the Hungarian Jews and all of them spoke Hungarian. They didn't know Yiddish and we weren't able to talk to them.

The factory director was Pilz. He examined the work and often gave us severe beatings. The name of my supervisor was Fugel - he wasn't one of the worst. The head of the block was a decent Jew named Zinger.

My closest friends were: Mitek Artman from Warsaw, Yanek Anman from W³oc³awek, Fishel Klinger, and Feibel Szwarc from Byalah-Podalska who worked with me in Skarzysko-Kamienna.

A tremendous explosion occurred in the factory a short time before the evacuation of Schlieben Camp. The explosion was so strong that shrapnel hit our residential camp which was about two kilometers from the factory. Firefighters also arrived from Berlin because the warehouses and the cellars were full of ammunition and explosives. Many of those who worked the night shift were killed. The S.S. men took us to the open field because they were afraid that the camp will explode in the air. At that time it was told that the blast was the result of a sabotage operation that was organized by several prisoners.

We rebuilt the factory but didn't manufacture weapons as before. In April 1945 I got sick. We managed to obtain some grain and baked them in the camp after work. I went outside heated, caught a cold, and fell ill with severe bronchitis. In addition, I had an eye infection and erysipelas on the face. We had a doctor, a Hungarian Jew, who treated me.

On 12 April 1945, we were transferred from Schlieben Camp to Theresienstadt.

The journey in locked cars lasted eight days without water and without bread, and was accompanied by bombing. The Jews welcomed us nicely in Theresienstadt. Immediately after our arrival they gave each one of us a piece of sugar. There was an entire city there. Those who were there for a long time lived in apartments, we were given barracks.

We didn't work. We lay in the barracks and waited for those who will come to lead us to our death. We didn't think that we will survive.

In fact, I can't remember much from that period because I was weak and critically ill.

[Page 318]

The Jews who came to us only spoke German. In the camp I saw Jewish money with the image Moses and the Tablets of Covenant. The Germans printed this money so that the Jews wouldn't be able to buy anything out of the ghetto.

The Russians who captured the place liberated us.


**My road to Israel**

After the liberation I was taken to a hospital. A few days later I tried to leave it because there were rumors that it was possible to travel to Israel and later it would be difficult to leave the Russian zone. I left Theresienstadt on May 10, 1945.

The transport was organized by the Joint. I traveled to Landsberg where there were nearly ten thousand people. We lived in the Germans' barracks. We received food stamps that we were able to sell outside the camp. I was in Landsberg for several months. After that they transferred me to Bad-Nauheim and from there to Bergen-Belsen.

The Jewish Brigade transferred groups of Jews through the German-Dutch border. Two soldiers led us to a forest and busses were supposed to wait for us on the other side. There was an agreement with the Dutch border guard to let us pass. I don't know how we fell into the hands of the British. The soldiers of the Jewish Brigade managed to escape and the British took us to prison where we sat for three months.

For the first six days each one of us sat in a special cell. Later, we were in a camp together with Nazi criminals. Krupp and Hitler's secretary were there. The food was worse than the German's food. The Nazis received packages and we were isolated from the world. The people of the Brigade didn't know where we were for a long time. The British wanted to force us to admit that we were led by the people of the brigade, but we told them that we didn't know each other and each one of us was searching for his relatives. One Englishman threatened us with his dagger and shouted: "Tell the truth!" I lost 16 kilograms during those three months because we weren't able to warm our feet all that time. We lived in tin shacks with a cement floor.

The Red Cross took us later to Bergen-Belsen. I arrived to Israel in *Aliyah Bet* [the illegal immigration to Israel] in March 1947.

**(Translated from Polish by H.V)**

[Page 319]

# In the First Days…
### Alter Grinboim (Tel Aviv)
### Translated by Pamela Russ

When the war broke out, we were in Legionowo together with many Jewish families because in Serock there were no longer any opportunities for earning a living. Right away, on the first day, airplanes flew across the sky over the town. President Moscicki spoke at 7:30, saying that the Germans had invaded Poland. There was great panic. Everyone immediately stopped working and every night we went to guard the train lines and the military posts – the orders for this came from the police.

One day, when I went to guard the railway that surrounded Legionowo, a policeman with a weapon in his hand came to tell me that I must leave Legionowo on the nearest train. When I asked to go and see my parents, he said to me that he had orders to shoot if I would refuse him. I was forced to get on the train that was going in the eastern direction.

Because I felt responsible that I had left my parents without any notice, I decided to run away with three other people. When the train stopped in Praga, we jumped off the train hoping to reach my sister Esther who lived on Rabina Meiselsa Street in Warsaw (street named after the Chief Rabbi of Warsaw, Rabbi Meisels, who died in 1870) in order to gain contact with my parents and wife in Legionowo.

While wandering around Praga in the dark, we happened to come into a military zone. We were detained, and we discovered that they had mistaken us for German spies and had decided to shoot us. A Polish officer approached us and asked and confirmed all the details, and finally realized that we were all Jews, that we had been born in these towns, and that we were not spies. He decided to keep us until morning and then allow us to enter Warsaw. As we arrived to my sister's house on Rabina Meiselsa Street, we found my brother-in-law, sister, and their child in the house. I told them everything, and soon we heard city councilor Stazinski speaking on the radio saying that Warsaw would defend itself until its last drop of blood with the Pollaks and Jews. He called up all men to come forward and be part of this defense. Since I was all alone, I immediately stepped up to join the defense. My job was that after an airplane would fly overhead, I would climb onto the roof and throw down flares onto the street.

[Page 320]

Before Rosh Hashana, the Gerer Rebbe made a public statement that everyone should pray with great earnest that on Yom Kippur everyone would be able to pray in Gur [home town of the Gerer khassidim] and that the Germans should have their downfall. At that point, the Germans took over the city of Gur. The Germans, knowing about the Rebbe's public statement, intentionally bombed the Jewish quarter at the time of Rosh Hashana. The most intense attack came on Rosh Hashana morning at 7:30. Going out of the gate, I saw one of the most terrible sights ever. The entire entrance court of Nalewki 39 lay in destruction. Hundreds of Jews were standing near the ruins and, sobbing, were searching for their family members. At that moment, I saw one Jew who was standing there only in his night shirt holding a burnt up child in his arms, screaming in confusion: "G-d, look at my child!"

The screams continued the entire Rosh Hashana, until nighttime. The only food that I had for me, my sister, her husband, and child, came from a jar of sour pickles that we picked up from a blown up factory that had made preserves – this was on a nearby street where hundreds lay dead from German airplanes.

One early Wednesday morning, four weeks after that bombing, it became silent. I went out on Zamenhof Street, and I saw hundreds of people running in the street, shouting that the war had ended...

From time to time, a Red Cross plane flew overhead. Shortly after lunchtime, there were committee announcements that because Warsaw had no electricity, no water, and no food, they had to surrender to the German army.

[Page 321]

After reading these announcements, hundreds of Jews began to tear the hair from their heads.

I remained like that until the beginning of Sukkos, and afterwards, the Germans informed everyone through posters that those who were from outside of Warsaw had to go get permits on Marshalska Pilsudskiewo Place, and then they would be allowed to go home. Walking through Nalewki, I saw a horrifying thing: A German truck had stopped and tens of armed Germans had blocked off the street and had dragged every Jew with a beard onto the truck, by their beards. They didn't bother me because I was clean shaven.

When I came to Pilsudskiewo Place, where there were thousands of people, announcements were made on the loud speakers in Polish and German: "Attention Polish citizens! Please stay in your places. Soon the German power will come into Warsaw!" I happen to be standing near the twelve gates. Not far from me a truck drove by and I saw as they opened all four sides of the truck that were covered with canvas. They brought out an old German general for whom they performed all the German military marches. The parade went from 10 until three in the afternoon. After that, the announcement was made on the loud speaker that special permits were necessary only for those with cars, not those on foot.

Coming back to my sister on Rabina Meiselsa Street, I said good-bye to her, to my brother-in-law, and to the child, and started out to Legionowo on foot. My first encounter with the Germans came in Pelzowicszne. Near the old synagogue that stood by the highway (a wooden building), there was a military fenced in area. Hundreds of people were gathered there waiting to go through.

As we were waiting, a short German approached and called out: "Are you Jews?" Everyone was afraid to answer. A Pollak who was waiting with us, answered: "Yes!" The German announced that all the Jews would be beaten to death. I understood the bitter destiny that awaited us. At that moment, a German officer appeared and asked about everyone's personal documents. Everyone was processed and permitted to pass through the fence.

[Page 322]

I wandered along the highway until Legionowo. Hundreds of families were waiting there for their dear ones. Amongst them were my parents and my wife. They couldn't imagine that I was still alive. I remained in Legionowo for a few days. We couldn't go to work because we couldn't maneuver the streets. Every person was taken to work.

One day, I went to my father who lived on Szenkiewicza Street in a storefront. At that moment, two armed Germans entered. Seeing my father with a beard, one of them screamed; "Jew!" and right away, with a force, spit directly onto his face, and left. My father and mother cried bitterly. I was terribly moved, sensing what was waiting for us. A few days later, about one week after Sukkos, my brother Nekhemia arrived. He was mobilized in the Polish army for entire duration of the war. Because the future looked bad, we took the road east.

My parents, who were terribly broken, decided to stay where they were and let fate do with them as it would. Not being able to watch the pain of my parents, my sister Malka decided to stay with them.

I, my wife, my brother Nekhemia, and my sister Miriam, made small packages, and our elderly mother and our sister escorted us for several kilometers. The heart rending screams of my mother, sister, and father are impossible to forget for my entire life. And that's how we wandered: We traveled only at night, during the daytime we lay in the woods. On the way, we met hundreds of Jews, but all of them were in small groups, terrified of being shot by the Germans. We met Pollaks and German townspeople, from whom we had great problems. We went through Radzymin, then through the old Jewish town of Wyszkow that was completely in ruin. The only thing standing was the Catholic church. We also went through Jadowo and straggled until the tragic train station in Maklyn, a place that as gruelingly familiar with acts of hatred.

[Page 323]

As we approached the station in Maklyn, a Pollak met us and immediately informed us that we Jews should save ourselves and not go to the station because they were all being shot there. Soon we noticed as tens of Germans were approaching us with their dogs, and they were shouting: "Stay where you are! Put your hands in the air!" In this situation, the Pollak told us not to try to run away because they would catch us anyway. One person managed to sneak off into the woods. In a minute, we were surrounded by Germans who were screaming: "Jews! Move forward!" And we were marched to the station. There were Germans standing there who laughed at us. "Fresh Jews!" There were many Jews in a fenced off area with tall wooden fences. They announced that anyone who had any money or weapons should immediately hand them over or he would be beaten to death. Soon after that, men and women were separated, and all the men were told to get completely naked. All our clothing was filthy from the roads, anything else that had a reasonable appearance, they took away. As my brother Nekhemia took off his good coat, a German came to measure him, then disappeared with him.

After that, we were told to get back into the remaining things and we were led to work in the bombed out station, divided into all kinds of groups. I fell into a group that carried rails. While doing that, they told us to sing and be cheerful. Suddenly, they told us to drop the rails from our shoulders. Many were hurt that way. That's how we worked until three in the afternoon without any food, not knowing our destiny nor the fate of our wives.

A German officer lined us up in a row and said: "Know that you are wandering away from the dirty Russians, and any of you that will wish to go back will be killed." And then they started to beat us. The officer told us to start running ahead, and we began running in the indicated direction. Over our heads, bullets began to fly, and we fell to the ground.

We heard screams of "Shema Yisroel," and "Where are our brothers and our sisters?" and so on. But not looking at all that, we crawled slowly on all fours. When we came close to the border crossing, the shooting stopped. Some of us stood up, many remained lying on the ground, and I don't know what happened to them.

[Page 324]

Behind us, we noticed that a group of women was running and screaming: "Where is my husband?" and so on. I recognized my wife and my sister Miriam among the women. Soon, a German patrol officer approached us and told us that we could not remain there and that we had to move on. I went to look for my brother Nekhemia, but couldn't find him. We had to go with a group, and when we came to the border crossing they received us politely and told us to give them our money and weapons. After a brief search, the crossing bar was opened and we were told to move forward. We immediately saw a Russian military person. He said to us in Polish: "Don't cry, here we don't shoot." They immediately sat us down at a table where they registered the newcomers. They told us to go to the nearest train station and go to Bialystok, because we couldn't stay where we were. Not obeying what the Russian military person had told us, I, my wife, and my sister decided to go to the nearest house and spend the night there, hoping to find out what had happened to my brother Nekhemia. As it happened, we found a house with a Jewish family that allowed us to spend the night. To our great excitement, there was a knocking in the middle of the night, and there stood a group of young men, among them my brother Nekhemia. Everybody cried. The following morning we went to the train station and left for Bialystok.

We arrived in Bialystok at the beginning of November, 1939. There, a committee assigned us places to sleep and we were given ration cards. We wandered around like that for two weeks, and then registered at one of the registration locations to go to Russia to work. We left Bialystok by train in one car, and my brother and sister in another car. On the way they detached the cars so that I lost contact with my brother and sister. My wife and I were left off in White Russia [Belorussia] in a city called Orsa. Here, I and my wife started working together in a tailoring shop. At that time, we started writing to Legionowo and my parents through the Red Cross.

[Page 325]

After writing several letters, we received a reply from my father. He wrote that they took all the Jews out of their homes, and also from the surrounding towns, and set up a ghetto in the Ludvishiner fields. My father told me that they cut off his beard and that he was together with my mother and sister, and that a speedy outcome is waiting for them.

As I was reading the letter, I saw that through the Red Cross we were able to send packages to Germany. I left immediately, and after great effort, I was able to get papers and arranged to send every month up to 20 kilograms. I immediately made a package of provisions: rice, coffee, tea, etc., and sent it off to my parents.

To my great joy, in a few days I received a reply from my parents, that they had received everything, and that I had simply saved them from hunger and great need.

My wife's parents, who were also in the Legionowo ghetto, decided to go and live together with my parents, because they [my in-laws] had nothing to live on. And so, each month I sent them 20 kilograms from which two families were able to live until the German-Russian war broke out on June 21, 1941.

A month before the outbreak of the German- Russian war, I received a letter with a photograph of my family. They had risked their lives to do this (taking photographs in the ghetto was forbidden). This is the only memento I have of them.

As the German-Russian war broke out, the city of Orsa was bombed heavily, and we were forced to leave on the first flight. We had to leave everything behind, and went through Smolensk, Penza, and beyond. We continued like that until Kakant, near Tashkent. There, they took us out of the transport, and directed my wife and me into the village of Nursuk where we started to work in a wine factory. In a short time, I was mobilized into a working troop and sent to Omsk in Siberia to work in a factory of rubber tires. Knowing that I had left my wife in a difficult situation, I begged the administration of the factory and they allowed my wife to come to me. She came with malaria. That's how we lived in Omsk until the end of the war.

[Page 326]

Soon, when the war ended, we asked the NKVD [Russian acronym: the "People's Commissariat for Internal Affairs," the public and secret police in Russia] to be able to return to Poland with the hope that maybe we would find some remaining close ones because we knew that the Germans had killed Jews. With the first train that left Omsk in 1945, we came to Wroclaw, and from Wroclaw to Reikhenbakh. We started to search for contacts, and decided to go to Warsaw to look for our relatives. In Reikhenbakh we received notice that my brother Nekhemia and sister Miriam had arrived from Russia, and we met up with them right away. We received notices that all our dear and close ones had gone into the gas chambers of Treblinka and Majdanek, and we were advised not to go in the direction of Warsaw because the AK groups were tormenting the Jews. [AK: *Armia Krajowa*; trans: Home Army, was the dominant Polish resistance movement in World War II German-occupied Poland. AK members' attitudes towards Jews varied widely from unit to unit.]

Shortly after, we left Poland through Czechoslovakia and Austria, and we came to the Kassel camp (in the British zone). We were there until August 1948, then afterwards left for Israel.

[Page 327]

# In the Sway of Destruction
### Written by Feiga Kanarek–Magid
### Translated by Ruth Kilner

I remember well the little town in which I was born. To this day, I remember the noise and vitality of Serock: the din of the streets; the joyful laughter of the youth filling the courtyards.

How can I not remember our bustling home: my parents, my two brothers and us six girls? I close my eyes and I see my big brother, Shmulik, who taught dance in our house. I vividly recall the sounds of the dance music, and the feet that hesitated and tried to dance. Pairs of dancers failed and then succeeded. Many of my sisters' friends and boyfriends passed through our home. Festivals and holidays in our home were happy occasions, particularly the winter festivals – Hannukah and Purim. The games. The joy. The laughter. We would prepare our fancy dress costumes for Purim. I remember that Chana, Tova and I were unrecognizable when we dressed up as gypsies. They went into town to visit the houses of the rich folk to tell their fortunes, and in return they were given money to help the needy families. Their prophecies flowed like a cornucopia of blessings. On Hannukah, we had donuts and potato latkes. Even today, their smell in my nose arouses a wave of nostalgia, and their unique taste stimulates my palate. When one of the guests was caught in the act of biting into a doughnut filled with hot pepper and a generous helping of salt – Oh! How we roared with laughter.

And I remember how we fished for little fish in the river and the pond. How pleased we were when we managed to catch the tiny fish from the river beside the house! Our parents were fishermen, and we had several boats. We all knew how to row the paddle boats and how to sail.

I also recall the Christian festival that fell during June, St. John's Day. The Polish youth would celebrate and sing, gathering together on the river bank, decorate the big boats with torches lit up in a range of colors, and set sail with song and dance.

My childhood years in my hometown, Serock – how wonderful they were! In August 1939, I turned fifteen years old. At the end of my fifteenth year, September came. It was a bitter September that put a bitter end to my happy childhood years.

With the bombing of Serock, many victims fell, and our young, carefree life was destroyed. My eldest brother was killed in the bombing.

Five days after war had broken out, the Germans occupied the town. My brother's funeral was held at night, and I couldn't even accompany him to his final resting place. I quickly learned things I did not already know. I knew what an air raid was,

[Page 328]

I was introduced to the cruelty of the death that killed my brother, I had tasted the sudden departure of my brother, four years older than me, who left without any parting words, wrenched away from us suddenly, and deported to Germany.

Even in the early days of the occupation, our German occupiers displayed the hate they felt towards the Jewish population. Decree after decree was issued. One of the first orders imposed the contributions – a type of monetary penalty, allegedly for protection, which in reality was just the start of the ills and hate of the Jewish people. They demanded sums of twenty five thousand zloty. The money was collected from all the Jews, barring none, until they managed to scrape together and collect the sum of twenty five thousand zloty.

A few days went by, and a quieter atmosphere prevailed. The decrees and edicts seemed to be lessening. Stores and bakeries reopened. We would stand in long lines through the nights to receive our bread rations and in the morning there was always joy upon receiving the warm and steaming bread.

But the reduction of the Germans' cruelty didn't seem to last, it was just intended to mislead us and to lull us into a false sense of security – as was their way of the mass slaughter in their kingdom of murder.

It happened suddenly, and was as terrifying as thunder from the heavens. We lived a fair distance from the center of the terrible events that happened in our town. With the rising of the sun on that black and bitter day, our Polish neighbors scared us out of our beds with the shocking news that all the Jews were being deported out of town.

Only after we had jumped out of our beds, terrified and panicking, did the crying and wailing voices reach our ears from the town center – which was where the murderers had been gathering the unfortunate deportees since four o'clock that morning. My mother, father, and older sister Chava were not at home. They had gone away for a few days to our family in the village Zatory to try and bring back a little food for us over the winter. Consequently, we were only five sisters left in the house.

To this day, I remember the strangled whispers of my sister, Tova, when I was still drowsy and half asleep: "Get dressed, children. Get dressed quickly! We need to get away!"

And when we made the effort to put on our clothes with frenzied motions of fear and terror, questions about our fate came out our mouths in strangled tearful voices, eyes welling with tears, "Where to?"

We wanted our mother and father and in the blink of an eye, we all had an idea: "Let's go to them! To Zatory!" Our neighbor, the aristocratic Pole,

Vilkovski, agreed without hesitation to take us on the boat down the river. But we hadn't managed to cross the Narew and evil screams terrified us, *"Zurück Schnell!* Come back now!" Germans, accompanied by a mob of

[Page 329]

Polish youngsters threatened us with their weapons. Left with no choice, we returned the boat to the river bank. When we landed on the bank, we received a barrage of beatings and blows from rifle butts, which hit our heads and the rest of our bodies.

Little Tova was stood next to the wall, and the Germans screamed, "You wanted to escape? You like to take risks?" and they beat her without mercy. Our hearts were in our mouths with fear lest they tell them to kill the girls. Beaten and battered to a pulp, blood poured out of us, and they accompanied us with cursing and more beatings, to the area in the marketplace where they were gathering the Jews for deportation.

Every Jew in the city was gathered in the marketplace. From there, they marched us all to the train station at Nasielsk, accompanied by an armed escort. That was on the fifth of December, 1939.

We arrived at the train station in Nasielsk in the evening. We were all beaten, harried, exhausted, and hungry. There was no train; it hadn't arrived. An hour later, they rushed us with a torrent of beatings towards the Nasielsk synagogue. At the entrance to the synagogue, not a single one of us managed to escape the brutal beatings that rained down on our heads, faces and anywhere their hands could reach.

The following day, early in the morning, they rushed us back to the train station. There, they started searching us. They were looking for money, gold, and jewelry. They looked everywhere: in our clothes; in our belongings; and on our bodies. We were searched roughly and without boundaries. In the process, they cut beards, and sheared them with rusty knives. Then, they ordered us to bathe in the swampy water and to roll around in the mud. Dirty and dripping with water, they finally herded us into the train carriages that awaited us. In the train carriages, which were sealed, we travelled for two days in different directions without food, and without as much as a drop of water. Thirsty, and hungry, exhausted and short of air to breathe, crowded and choked, we were five sisters together with each of us in the sealed carriages. At the end of the journey, we arrived at Biala Podlaska. One family took us – the five of us – for a few weeks, and in January 1940, we were taken by our uncle to Wolomin, near Warsaw, where we were reunited with our parents and our sister, Chava. In Wolomin there was a heavy famine; we had to wander onwards, and we stayed with our aunt in Wieliszew (near Zegrze), where we lived in a small room. The mother sold old clothes; my sister, Chana, sewed a little – and we lived in great hardship. This is how we lived as free people for a year, until one bright day , I found myself – together with the Jews of the surrounding villages – to the closed ghetto in Ludwiszyn, next to Legionowo, in October 1940.

The ghetto was closed and sealed. Food was rationed. We started to starve, and this caused weakness and disease. We knew that if we were to do nothing to help ourselves, it would mean the end of us. Mother and I made a decision and snuck to the edge of the ghetto. We walked to the closest village to sell the few belongings that we had left. Our fear was great to cross the borders

[Page 330]

of the ghetto, but our hunger was greater than our fear. But our bravery only helped in the tiniest of ways. Our hunger increased and increased, amplifying and becoming intolerable. Under those dreadful conditions, my father fell ill and died on March 19th, 1941. October 1942 brought our ghetto's turn for extermination, and the residents were taken to Auschwitz and Treblinka – to a certain end.

The silence of the night was broken suddenly by a sudden frightful commotion with whistles, sirens, the clatter of cars, and screams. The dense dark of the ghetto was lit up by a terrible fire. All the prisoners in the ghetto were taken from their homes and gathered together, next to the *gmina* (municipality).

But we didn't go. When the sun came up and we saw well what had happened outside, Mother made a decision, "We're going to be taken to the unknown? No!"

Mother then watched and saw by our house that Jews were sneaking over the ghetto wall, and she said, "Jews from the ghetto are escaping to the Aryan side, to the nearby forest. We should go too."

And so we did. We slipped away and escaped into the forest. We hid there all that day. In the evening, the Poles told us that the Germans had surrounded and besieged the forest.

It was clear to us that we had to go, to escape, but how and where could we go? Where could we turn? Danger lurked at every turn, despite which we had to tempt our fate and look for a way out. With bitter regret, we realized that we could not endanger all of us together, and it would be best to split up in case – G–d forbid – fortune didn't smile on us. At least it would not then mean the end of all of us. My little sister Leah and my sister Chava went to some Polish people we knew that lived not far from the ghetto. My two eldest sisters headed towards Lublin, where they were caught as Polish women and taken to work in Germany, where they remained until the end of the war. Marisha and I headed towards Zegrze, and from there we went to Biala Podlaska for the second time.

I will never forget that tragic farewell, with the ghetto burning from afar in the background. It was dreadful!! Our mother's wails shook us to our very souls. Poor Mother feared for all our fates. She worried they would take us. Her final words ring in my ears until this very day. "Write to me, my darling girls..."

These were the last words I heard from my mother's lips, and I never saw her again. In Biala Podlaska, it was cold, and it snowed. We had intended to go to friends, Yechiel Wiernek and his family from Serock, whom we knew should be in the ghetto. We asked about Grabarska Street, and we were told that it was a street watched well by the German gendarmes, since September 26th, 1942, when the ghetto was destroyed and all the Jews were removed.

"Don't go there, they'll shoot you," they warned us. "Where will we go and what will we do?"

[Page 331]

we asked ourselves. Left without any other option, we took the only possibility: to go to the Poles.

The day was already approaching evening, and we couldn't find anyone willing to accommodate us without identity papers. On the way, a miracle happened to us, and a good man provided us with lodging for the night. All that day, no food had come near our mouths. Hungry and cold, we couldn't close our eyes, and we worried – what would we do come morning?

We decided to search for work as Polish housekeepers, obviously for families that wouldn't demand to see identity papers. After a lot of searching and inconvenience, we found what we wanted.

I found a job working for a family with three children. There was a lot of work, and it was hard, but I was happy because I had a roof over my head and something to eat. One time, it occurred to my employers to ask for my identity documents. I made up some lie, one that I had ready if it was ever necessary, and I somehow managed to assuage their minds. After a while, they began to suspect me; that I was a Jewess. Their fear grew and I was worried that my fervent denials were not lessening their suspicions. After working for eight months, they fired me and asked me to leave them, but they didn't make things worse, and gave me the address of another employer.

My new address was of a prosperous farmer and flour mill owner in Janów Podlaski. Again, I wasn't asked for identity papers, which was lucky as I didn't have any. This farmer had a large family: the husband, his wife and five children, his brother, and soon afterwards, a sixth child was born. There was even more work, and it was difficult, between the large farm, home, and mill, but I was compensated well with plenty to eat, and after years of hunger, I had also now tasted satiety.

Working here, I also scored identity documents. The family I worked for had a friend who worked in the municipality offices. She tried for me and managed to get me my long-awaited papers with photo, all according to law. According to my papers, I was Helena Barbara Dombrowska, a Catholic Christian, born in Serock on the banks of the River Narew.

My work in the house was, as I said, extensive, particularly on the farm, where they had 22 pigs, 65 rabbits, many chickens, and more. In addition to all this, there were five small children that needed looking after. The eldest was only seven years old. Consequently I worked incredibly hard.

Once, my sister Marisha visited me and saw how hard I worked. Her place of work was not as hard. She persuaded me to leave Janów and to return to Biala Podlaska. I was tempted.

I returned to Biala Podlaska for the third time, at the start of 1944. And once again

[Page 332]

I looked for work as a servant. This time I chanced upon a family of fewer means. They supported themselves with difficulty, and even so they wanted a servant. I couldn't hold onto this job, with this poor family for long, and I soon moved to work for a different family.

My new employers were not bad to me, because they did not suspect my true ancestry. Were they to have suspected me – G–d forbid – my fate would have been cruel and bitter, because they were anti–Semites.

Each day, they would come home from their work with "good news" on their lips. "Do you know, Helenka, what happened today in Lublin?"

I never answered, and waited in fear for what was to come, which never took long, "Listen to what's written in the newspaper: seven Jew boys were riding on the train, the Germans checked their papers, and eventually identified them as Jews."

My heart beat fiercely and I twisted my face into a smile. Meanwhile, he continued, "They didn't kill them then and there. They put them onto a transport which will take them and many more to their end."

A shiver suddenly shook my entire body, my contorted face continued smiling and I heard my lips saying, "Good for them. They shouldn't have been there."

As I said these words, my heart twisted with pain, my head burned, and I was filled with impotent rage. I was exhausted and flagging in this house too, I didn't have quite enough to eat, but I didn't leave them, because of how things worked out.

It was spring, 1944. With the end of the snow, the frozen Polish rivers trembled and thawed with a raging din, removed the sprinkling of ice that covered them through the days of the winter in their mighty flow. Spring winds brought the news that the front was coming and that the Russian army had freed the Eastern frontiers of Poland.

We could hear the noise of battle and echoes of explosions clearly in the silence of the night. The lady and the master of the house were afraid of what might happen. They considered running away, but were too afraid to leave their house, and their shop where they sold writing goods was far from their home. They feared that they would be blockaded by the Communist Russians, who were about to enter the town. Consequently they decided to stay put and to send their four children to relatives. The master moved into the shop and it was my job to take him his food. On my way to the shop, I had to cross the bridge over the river. I knew this way and this bridge well. On one of these trips, with food for the master, my toes froze during a gale and ice storm.

[Page 333]

I had to take the children in a cart, harnessed to a horse to their grandmother and their aunts, who lived in a small town close to Biala. We travelled for many hours.

The sounds of shooting and explosions got louder and louder. After several close and short battles, the Russian army liberated the village from the Germans; then the area; and then the whole of Poland.

The coveted liberation had arrived. The big dream had become reality. Our bold fantasy had been realized. This was now reality, and it was hard to believe that we were indeed free.

The entire last night before the liberation, we couldn't sleep. Sleep was impossible because of the shooting and the explosions. The retreating Germans plundered, pillaged, and robbed. Before escaping, they torched villages, towns and cities. The entire horizon was red with flames. It seemed that the whole country was alight.

The following morning, the streets were filled with large bearded soldiers. Tattered and ragged, but singing and dancing around the bonfires, roasting butchered pigs and calves on them, filling their mouths with hunks of meat.

"Helenka, what a pity, look at those poor soldiers!" and I explained to the children that these are the soldiers from the frontier, who defeated the Germans and drove them away. This is the victorious Russian army. They liberated us and brought us freedom and safety. Let's celebrate with them, because we are so happy!

That was in July 1944. Our area was freed from the German's cruel regime, but the war continued. All around us was the home front, close to the frontier. Many casualties were brought every day and every night – how much suffering, misery and misfortune? Volunteer nurses and doctors rushed to help, and their hands were full, administering first aid to the casualties.

It was then that I was told that I had also been orphaned from my dearest mother. She was murdered on 22nd May, 1943. I remembered that emotional farewell at the crossroads. My heart had known what would happen.

After the liberation, I continued to work for the same family. Life started to return to something resembling normal.

Once, my sister Marisha came to me with the most surprising news, "I just heard them speaking Yiddish on Brzeska Street! There are Jews!"

And indeed, there were still Jews alive. And the Jews that remained were no longer hiding away.

And Marisha continued and spoke to my heart,

[Page 334]

"Do we still need to conceal ourselves? Do we need to wear a mask over our faces and work as Polish women? We have also been liberated, this freedom is also ours, and it has given us back our rights to us to not only live as Poles. We shouldn't hide our ancestry and to what people we belong."

I had no doubt that my sister was correct.

The mistress was religious and I had to go with her to Church and imitate her: to murmur prayers, to cross myself no end, and to kneel. And I was a Jew! How my soul longed to be liberated from this forced conscience, from this depressing nightmare!

After I left my work as a servant to the Christian family, I found a job in a Jewish café.

At that time, they were urging us to go to Russia, but we refused all these suggestions, because we wanted to gather together and regroup all the shreds left of our family. Since our family had been split up, and the war spread us all over, we had not heard anything about anyone else.

First, we discovered our sister, Chava, who lived in Lodz. She came to Biala Podlaska and took Marisha and me with her to Lodz. We then found our brother, Moshe, who had been serving in the Polish national army since its establishment by Wanda Wasilewska.

Chava went to Israel, and Marisha and I remained, to wait for the remainder of our family, hoping to find them.

In Lodz, the State Office for Repatriation, PUR, actively called to the younger generation to rise up and rebuild the land of Poland. The youth were in particular demand to volunteer and sign up to repatriate and rebuild the western regions of the state.

Marisha and I travelled to Gdansk on the Baltic coast, where we received money, clothing, blankets, a tidy furnished room, beds and bedding. For the first time in years, we lived like human beings. As poor orphans, we were also entitled to healthy food and special treatment, and we returned to life. I worked in the municipal hospital.

About a year later, Marisha married and got a large and beautiful apartment. I moved with her, and lived together with her and my new brother-in-law: a deputy in the Polish army.

Once, this brother-in-law came with me to work, and told me that a relative had come, and he wanted to introduce her to me. Carefully, and not all at once, in order not to stun me, he revealed to me the happy news, that my sister Tova-Tussia had come from the land of the forever damned, from Germany. I was deliriously happy. I almost lost my mind when Tussia revealed to me the knowledge that our sister Chana was also still alive, and was married and living in Lodz. We also heard, in a roundabout way, that our little sister Zussiya was also alive.

[Page 335]

In summary: We were six sisters and one brother all still alive. Other than Zussiya, we all knew about each other. We didn't know where the little one was or how to find her.

All of us called Zussiya 'the little one.' And we had to find her.

We knew that the little one should be by the old woman in Praga, on the outskirts of Warsaw, who tool her in from our late mother in those ravaged days. We also remembered the name of the street where the old Christian woman lived – Targowa Street.

However, where to start looking for her now, after everything that had happened? I went, to the Jewish committee in Praga. I was incredibly tired. Wearing boots up to my calves, with no socks, I rushed from place to place on foot, because I had no money to travel. My feet ached terribly. When the committee gave me the address, I didn't walk: I ran with a sense of urgency, as long as there was breath in me.

With ragged breath, I arrived at the school in Wileska Street where my little sister studied. I knocked on the classroom door, and I asked about Zushka Kumaya. The teacher asked the girl with that name to please leave the classroom with me. I saw my sister, ten years old, stand up astounded, and it seemed that she didn't recognize me.

I didn't know my own soul after all the tragedy. My heart pounded hard, hammers beat my head from the inside, and I didn't have the strength to stop the stream of tears that flowed from my eyes. I covered my little sister's eyes and face with kisses. She looked more and more bewildered, and did not open her mouth. I asked her quietly and without emotion, "Do you not recognize me?"

Yes. Of course I recognize you; you're my sister. But... go away. I can't talk to you here. Go away and come later to my aunt's house. Here is the address."

She gave me the address. I gave her a final kiss, and left as I was told. I did not return to Gdansk that day with the wonderful news that I'd found our little sister. I chose to only go home with Zussiya herself.

I stayed, and met the aunt herself. I spoke with her at length. I also spoke to my sister who asked me to take her with me. This was not an easy thing. But despite the difficulties, she sat with me, my little sister, that same evening, on the train that took us together to Gdansk .

That was when I left my work at the hospital. Tova took me and our sister Zussiya to The Ichud's kibbutz.

[Page 336]

Aunt Kumaya did not agree to return the girl to us, and could not accept the fact that we had taken the girl from her and were not bringing her back. She claimed that the girl belonged to her, as she had brought her up, paid for her and looked after her through the four hardest years of the war, which would be equivalent to forty normal years.

"I am Zushka's mother!" The old woman claimed with emotion, "Because the woman who brings up and educates a child is considered her mother. I brought this child up and educated her."

In this situation, a trial had to take place. Zussiya had to declare in our presence and in that of her 'aunt' that she wished to stay with us.

And our little sister, who had spent several weeks with us, could not declare in front of the woman that she didn't want to be with her. So the ruling could not be set in law.

The Jewish committee was prepared to grant the old woman, who was lacking in means, a quantity of money and clothing in return for her giving up the child. But she was not interested.

Every weekend, the old woman would come from Praga to the kibbutz, to take Zussiya for an outing. I worried a lot about these outings, and I considered them dangerous, but we couldn't refuse the woman, who bitterly claimed, "Why are you so worried? I shan't eat her. I looked after her for many years, and now you want to prevent me from talking to her, once a week?"

And indeed, every weekend, when we weren't working, the Aunt would come and take Zussiya out.

I would chaperone these outings, since they worried me. I would walk a reasonable distance behind them, and follow their footsteps carefully. On these walks, the old woman would impart many things onto the little one's heart. And my ears caught snippets of the following.

"You are already too big, my Zushenka. You should know to answer fully, 'yes' or 'no'. Don't agree to stay with your sisters, they'll get married, and then you'll be a servant, to look after their children… things like this have happened before. Stay with me and be my daughter. Things will be good for you with me, you will be educated, and everything you want will be yours. How can you leave me, an old woman, alone? You are my closest soul, come with me and be with me together and you won't lack anything, and if you come with me, you won't need to live around all these Jews…"

One weekend, I was on duty in the kibbutz, and I couldn't chaperone the walkers. I sent Tova in my place, and I warned her to watch every step and that the old woman takes with the girl. And what I feared happened.

Aunt Kumiya was saved for one moment, and in the Sopot train station, not far from Gdandsk, she jumped with Zussiya onto a train passenger carriage, and the two of them disappeared from Tova's sight. When Tova realized what had happened, she ran, with all her strength, to Marisha and Leon, her husband, in Oliwa, a small town near Gdansk, and burst out in painful wails to them,

[Page 337]

"We lost the little one, save the child!"

Leon hurried immediately to the police station, and police officers and soldiers were sent to search for Zussiya on the train.

The search stopped passenger trains. People's papers were checked to find our sister, who should have been there with Mrs. Kumaya. I was almost driven crazy with pain and anger. I rushed to Marisha and the two of us sat and worried for our little sister who had either been tempted or kidnapped by her aunt.

We didn't have long to wait. That day, Zussiya herself burst into the house, nervous and short of breath. She answered our questions and told us: "The Aunt dragged me with force into the train carriage. She asked me to accompany her, and then again carried on pleading with me. 'Zushenka, you need to decide now. Escape from the life that awaits you; run away from the Jews and come with me!'"

When the train set off towards Warsaw, the little one had jumped out the carriage. The old woman tried to stop her flight, and caught her coat pocket, which ripped and remained in her hand.

Zussiya came back to us without her coat pocket, but also without the nightmare of the old woman. She returned to us so we could stay together.

That was in spring, 1946. In November 1946, we left Poland.

My path to Israel took me through Vienna, Austria, and Italy, where I stayed until early 1949.

My travels ended on March 13th, 1949 – the day I arrived at the coast of my homeland Israel, with my husband and children.

[Page 338]

# The Destruction of Serock
### Yehuda Mendzelewski (Bat-Yam)
### Translated by Pamela Russ

At the end of summer 1939, the bright sky of Serock became dark and suffocated with smoke. Like wild vultures, the Nazi murderous airplanes rushed in and sowed death, not sparing Serock. The first innocent victims, a group of fifty Jews, died in Yankel Rosenberg's cellar. The murderers revealed themselves very quickly. They lurk like thirsty animals, staring everyone in the eyes: "Jude?"

Serocker Jews felt the huge tragedy, people were beginning to hide in their houses. The next day brings the first order that each Jew aged fourteen and over must gather in the marketplace. From the marketplace, they push everyone into the *shul*. After a few days of torture, they release the very old, and the rest are chased wildly into the neighboring town of Pultusk. After several days of torture, they chase us again to Chekhanow. On the way to Chekhanow, the ones who couldn't keep up were shot on the spot. Among them were: Avrohom Ostrowski, Pinkhas Sokol, Faivel Rubenshtayn, Ginsberg, and others. The rest of the half-dead Jews are taken through Mlawa to the concentration camps. After a few weeks of agony, a few of these Jews come back to Serock. But they didn't allow the Jews to rest for long.

After squeezing out whatever monies they could, they put forth the gruesome order on the night before the eve of Khanuka, that the city of Serock must become *judenfrei* (cleansed of Jews). The massive destruction had begun. With fiery eyes, ready to strike for the most trivial disobedience, they drag together all the Jews, until the last one, to the marketplace. They don't keep them long and soon chase them off again. Some of them get the butt of the guns over their heads, and some get it with the boots, or others are simply shot. Also, there was a pit prepared, into which these people were thrown alive: Feigy Wenger, Mendel Markowicz, and Goodes, with the confused outcry: "Murderers! May your names be erased!" and "Shema Yisroel," their lips pained with these words. That is the first hell until Nazielsk. In the Nazielsk *shul*, no one is kept for more than one day. Yosef Doron is shot there. (After he is shot, they order that he be taken to the doctor.) The herding from Nazielsk to the train is horribly gruesome – a six-kilometer route. Barefoot and bloodied, Jews are dragging themselves to the wagon cars, leaving thirty Jews in Nazielsk – the strongest, specially selected by the bandits in order to clean the *shul*. They are ordered to scratch the walls with the tips of their fingers. When the flesh of the fingers gets ripped until the bone, the murderers order them to scratch harder and order them to sing *Hatikva* and other Hebrew songs.

[Page 339]

In this scene with these bandits, if this "entertainment" would take too long, the order came forth: "Within six minutes, everyone has to be at the train." They are wild with those Jews who are barely alive, mercilessly beating as they are climbing into the wagons. Confused, the women are crying, horrific is the crying and the wailing of the children. One person doesn't know of the other. There are two echelons, with the Serockers in the dark wagons, day and night, moving over the cursed German ground, without food and without water. Children are pleading with cries for water and they lick the steam off the barred windows. After four days of dragging themselves this way, our Serock Jews found themselves in the Lukow station in Biala-Podlaska. There they were freed.

The exhausted Jews from the difficult, agonizing, journey begin to revive themselves slowly thanks to the compassion of the Jews from Lukow and Biala-Podlaska, who welcomed the Serock Jews warmly. Our Serock Jews tried to get themselves settled in. A small group was forced to run further across the border into Russia, again experiencing the "seven levels of hell."

Evacuations begin in all the towns and cities. Jews are locked up in the ghettos where hunger reigns, cold, epidemics – and after that, death. Thousands, tens of thousands are taken daily to the gas chambers.

[Page 340]

## Escape from Death
**Nekhemiah Grinboim (Tel Aviv)**
**Translated by Pamela Russ**

In 1939, eight days before the outbreak of the war, I was drafted as a serviceman to the Polish army, and was sent to the Modlin fortress. There I and other Jewish soldiers fought a strong enemy that was armed with the newest war technology. What the Polish army looked like at that time was well known to everyone.

I was at the front for about six weeks and in the front lines. I was one of the luckiest ones and was not wounded.

At that time, at the beginning of the war, there were about 50,000 soldiers mobilized in the Modlin fortress, and when the Germans invaded there and took us as prisoners, about 2,000 remained from the 50,000. The rest were either killed or wounded, or taken prisoner. The prisoners were chased on foot by the Germans from Modlin to Mlawa. This march lasted five days because the Hitlerists [Nazis] did murderous experiments on us. They moved for three days and three nights without food and without drink. On the fourth day, they took us out on the field, brought over a bread machine, and threw small pieces of bread into the mass of people. Each one fought with the other over these, and they photographed these scenes. After that, they took us behind Mlawa, where a temporary camp was prepared.

We had to stay a few days in that camp, waiting to be sent to East Prussia to work in the mines. The Germans positioned themselves in two rows, about a hundred in a row, and we had to walk between them. As we were walking between them, they "honored" us with the butts of their munitions and smashed us on our hands and heads, and whoever tried to bend down [to avoid being hit] had to go back and walk through these rows three times, being beaten until death. There were many deaths as we went into the camp.

[Page 341]

In the camp, everyone was soon divided into separate barrack: Jews, Polaks, and *volskdeutchen*. The Germans informed the Jews that no one would ever go out of this camp alive.

As I watched each of these scenes that went on with the Jews, I promised myself that I would escape at any cost, even if I would have to pay with my life. I befriended several Jews from Warsaw. Together we decided to run away from the camp at 2am, knowing 99% that we would be killed, because there was an order that whoever approaches the wires at night would be shot on the spot.

We had decided to escape at 2am, so we found the moment when two German soldiers with machine guns fell asleep. We crawled over the fence and ran into the forest. We stayed there until morning. We had an acquaintance in Mlawa. This acquaintance went into the nearest village and brought us peasant clothes and we dressed as peasants and that's how we made it to Warsaw successfully. I left for Legionnowa where my parents lived at that time. When I arrived home, I couldn't show myself in the streets because the Germans would snatch me up for work. That's when the son of Khaim Rosenberg, Moishe, was killed. He didn't allow himself to be caught, and a German shot him on the spot. Since I already knew the murderous ways of the Germans, I decided to escape to Bialystok to the Russians, taking with me my brother Alter, and my sister Miriam, and my friends Yakov and Shmuel Burkhanski (the *khazan*'s son). In Bialystok we registered for work and that's how we spent the rest of the war.

[Page 342]

## Escape from the Nazi Hell
### Avrohom Khaim Pshikarski (Atlit)
### Translated by Pamela Russ

It's Tuesday, the fifth day of the Second World War. Several German planes flew over the town and have begun to bomb. The first bomb fell by Gershon Meir at the oil factory. Fortunately, no one was hurt there. There was a terrible uproar in the town, the cries were heard far away. As people held crying and frightened children by their hands, they went into the cellars of their houses.

The owner of my house, Yakov Rosenberg, had a large cellar, or as it was called a "*skhron*" (bunker) where the "*shomer hatzair*" organization used to meet. As soon as Yakov heard the planes flying overhead, he shouted to his daughters, and they all quickly went into the cellar. Just minutes later, the cellar was filled with people, and among them were also refugees from Nazielsk.

When they started to bomb the town, I was at the butcher shop with my son. My brother Moishe came running over to figure out where we should run and hide. I told him that we should run to Yakov Rosenberg's cellar, and that we should do this right away. My brother wanted my son and me to go with him. But as we stood close to his house to run into the "bunker," my son tore himself away and wanted to run home saying that if his mother wouldn't find us in the butcher shop she won't know where we would be and she would become terrified.

So my brother Moishe and his wife and children went into the cellar. As my son and I were going back to the butcher's, we saw airplanes stormily flying overhead and two bombs fell – one in Avrohom Shenker's house and the other in Yakov Rosenberg's "bunker." We stood still, very shaken. Later we found out that all the people in that "bunker," including my brother, his wife and his children, were killed. The total was 50.

[Page 343]

That same evening, all the people came out of the cellars and went out onto the streets, preparing to leave Serock. The following morning, some on foot and some by horse and wagon, left for Warsaw or other places. My family and I, and all my other relatives, had the idea of going to Kowal, especially because I had done business there for many years and knew the whole area well. I soon harnessed some horses and a wagon, put everything that we could onto the wagon, and went with my family to Kowal.

When we arrived in Zegrzhe, from where a highway leads to Struhe – the road to Kowal – the military was standing there and they didn't allow us to go onto the highway. We had no choice but to go to Warsaw.

When we entered Praga, it was already dawn. Suddenly we heard the terrible noise of airplanes flying overhead, and soon heard the horrific explosions. Miraculously, we were unhurt. In the middle of the day, we entered Warsaw. We stayed in Warsaw until the Germans came there. After that, my wife, children, and all the relatives, went back home to Serock by horse and wagon, leaving my mother and me. When they safely arrived at the Zegrzhe bridge, they were detained by German soldiers. The Germans ordered them all to get down from the wagon. Then they were searched. They took away a pocket-watch from my father-in-law, then amid wild screams, they cut off his beard along with a piece of flesh. A terrible outcry came forth from the women and children. The Germans became even wilder and began beating anyone they felt like beating. Later, after stealing whatever they wanted, they ordered the people to get back up into the wagon and they let them cross the bridge.

The following morning, I left Warsaw with my mother. We went on foot to Pelcowizna and wanted to keep going beyond that, but the Germans stopped us and didn't let us go, so we had to turn back and were separated from the family. We never made it into Warsaw. We sat down in a field near the highway and waited until the Germans would disappear from the road. That's how we waited for forty-eight hours – sitting there without food or drink, until other Germans permitted us to move on.

*[Page 344]*

Completely exhausted, when we came to the Zegrzhe bridge (eight kilometers from Serock), the Germans did not allow us Jews to cross the bridge. We entered Zegrzhe and went to the house of our acquaintance Dvoire Kohn, who had a food store. At night, as we were sleeping on her floor, a familiar Polak by the name of Khips came in, and told us how he himself saw how the Germans shot Moishe Pjenik and another Jew (I can't remember his name now) not far from here. This night was now a very painful one for me, and I couldn't sleep.

In the morning, when I went out into the street, I saw a non-Jewish woman riding in her carriage. I stopped her, and when I heard that she was going to the market in Serock, I begged her to take me along.

At that very moment, a wagon filled with Jews came by, so the German told my driver to go ahead and cross the bridge, and that's how I was home again.

A few days later, the Serock resident Khaim Futerman, who was among the Jews in the wagon on the Zegrzhe bridge, described to me how the Germans cut off the beards from the Jews and along with that took some flesh, ordered them to dance, ordered them to use their fingernails to rub off the blood from the wagon until it would be clean, and then these Jews were ordered to go back where they came from. Khaim Futerman himself came to Serock not using the bridge but came from another direction. In order to bring my mother home, I paid a non-Jew a fine price and he did bring her not via the bridge but from a side and distant route.

Before I even had a chance to look around and see what was going on in Serock, I already heard about the order that the butchers had to leave their butcher shops so that they could sell the meat for free. I immediately left to go to the non-Jews that I knew in the villages. When I arrived in the village of Avrem to the peasant Sawicki, whom I knew for many years, he did not even let me onto his doorstep – didn't even put out his hand in greeting as he had always done, saying he was not obligated to put his life in danger after he himself had heard the Germans in the Pultusk marketplace that any non-Jew that would hide a Jew, would be burned along with his "secret."

*[Page 345]*

Nonetheless, I didn't lose all hope, and I went to the rich man Ortokhowski. As it turned out, this rich man did let me in, saying: "Take whatever you want, Jew, because the German bandits will take everything from me in any case." I told him that I wanted two cows from him. On my way back home, I met another peasant that I had known from the Czepow area. This peasant told me the same things. When I arrived in my house, I immediately summoned my non-Jewish worker Stanislaw Bzhezhewski, and when he came, we went together to get the cows. We chased the cows into Noakh Ogrodower's barn that was in my mother's courtyard.

Just after I slaughtered the cows, someone outside gave a yell that a German was going by. I quickly locked the barn, leaving the *shokhet* there. My Polish worker and I went out into the street. When we reached the gate of my mother's courtyard, a German with a rubber club in his hand detained us and asked if we are Jews. The non-Jew shook his head saying no, he was not Jewish, and the German told us to move on. After leaving the German for some way, I looked back and saw how he went into the courtyard and whoever he saw he beat murderously with his rubber club.

There, about ten people were beaten. Among them were my brothers-in-law Yosef Hersh and Alter. As I was standing that same day, a preoccupied person in my butcher shop, I suddenly saw that same German near me with his club in hand. I became frightened and the German let out a wild scream that I should go out into the street. I immediately ran out and saw that all the Serock butchers were standing in a row. The German put me near Yosel Hilel's brother and then took all of us to the police. When we were already all there, I saw through an open window how many Polaks had gathered there, smiling as if they were taking great pleasure in our tragic situation.

*[Page 346]*

In a large room at the police department, there was an old German with a cross face. "Our" German proudly informed him that he had brought all seventeen "Jewish pig butchers." The old German replied to him: "Why did you bring these swines here? You should have shot them all on the road."

At that moment, the two Polish policemen entered, Postek and Dudowicz, who had put themselves at the service of the German government, and said that they needed workers. The old German said to them: "Take them away, these shits!" So, all of us seventeen butchers followed these two policemen. On the way, I pleaded with the policeman Dudowicz, with whom I was always friendly, that he should let me go, but he wouldn't hear of it, exactly as if he didn't know me.

The policemen took us to Moishe Rosenberg's mill, where we found several hundred Serock Jews working. Their job was to put heavy cases of munitions on the cargo trucks. Seeing what was happening to these few Jews, I dreaded what was coming. You could not recognize Dovid Rosenberg, he did not resemble a living human being. Yisroel Isser Hiler, Mendel Hiler's son, had his small beard torn off along with some flesh. Others were very depleted and broken.

We, the newcomers, were mixed in with the other Jews, and also began to work. At twelve o'clock noon, a woman brought food for the yellowed Moishe, Aron Leyb the butcher's son. The yellowed Moishe asked me to come eat with him. When we finished eating, a German with a gun in hand, said to us: "After *fressen* (eating like a pig), you have to rest." Just as the yellowed Moishe sat down on a rock, the same German came to him and with the butt of his gun gave him such terrible beatings that Moishe turned over several times. When I saw that, I went to mingle with the working people. I slid down my hat until my nose and went diligently to work. Suddenly I saw how the wild German was looking for me among the workers.

[Page 347]

I felt the danger and tried to find ways to prevent him from recognizing me. Who knows if he wouldn't have found me if Khaim Gimpel's horse and wagon hadn't passed by me just then. The wagon had two moving cows tied to the back. I quickly ran over to the cows and with a twig in hand, urged them on. The German didn't see my face, and that's how I was successfully able to go back to town.

In my house, when I recovered from this event, I said to my wife and children that we couldn't wait any longer and that we all have to go to Kowal that now belonged to Soviet Russia. Even though we couldn't all leave at the same time, it was decided that for now I should be the one to go, leaving food and money for my family. So I, along with another group of young men and women, was on my way with a wagon. We went in the direction of Malkin near the Bug River.

When we approached the Wierzbicz bridge, the armed Germans there told us to turn back warning us that if someone would try to get off the wagon, he would be shot. Since all of us had decided that we wouldn't go back home, we turned onto the road to Pultusk in order to get to the Russian side from a different route.

After going for a while near Kleczew, again we were detained by two Germans who by chance happened to be going by in their car. They got out of their car and ordered us to stop. Our wagon stopped, and we answered their question by saying that we were going from Warsaw to Makow. Then they told us to get down from the wagon and then they began to search for whatever they could find. When they find some kitchen dishes, one of them said: "Yes, these are probably those wanted thieves who robbed the store in Pultusk. We have to take them there and have them arrested."

[Page 348]

Having said that, they took our kitchen things and put them into their car, got back in, and left immediately. We were left confused and not knowing what to do – stay here or leave. We remained there like that for about two hours and then seeing that no one came for us, we left. That evening we arrived in Makow. We went to the *shul* from where heartrending cries were heard. The *shul* was filled with refugees. We found out that recently many men had been captured for work and no one ever saw them come back. Because of that, we decided not to stay and before daylight we left for Krasnosielc. That evening we arrived in a village near Ostrolenka. One Jew lived in that village. It was not far from the Soviet border. We spent the night at the place of that village Jew. In the middle of the night, we awoke suddenly, terrified by the loud knocking at the door. We heard someone speaking loudly in German saying that we should open the door. When the door opened, two Germans came in and began shooting with their guns until the bullets ran out, and then ordered that no one move from their spot. They tore up the whole house, and taking only a pair of boots, they left with many coarse, perverse words. To my good fortune, they did not notice my boots.

When it was daylight, I went out into the street, and soon I met a non-Jewish acquaintance and begged him to take me across the border. He agreed, but wanted fifty zlotys. Since my cousin Moishe Winegrad, the son of Itche Meir, Roiza's,[1] was with me, I had to pay another fifty zlotys for him, and the smuggler successfully got us across the border.

**Translator's Footnote**

1. Unsure what author meant by "*Roiza's*" in this context, or to whom he is referring, if that is the case.

[Page 349]

# The German Inquisition
### Brokhe Hadas Pzykorski (Atlit)
### Translated by Pamela Russ

For several months, my three children and I were in very difficult circumstances because of the Germans. Since we knew that they were chasing the Jews out of the cities, I was prepared for that. Once, at night, my neighbor Zalke Kuligowsky, touched me on my shoulder and said that we had better get up because they were chasing the Jews out of our city.

Because of the terrible chaos, I didn't know what to do, and leaving the children alone in the house, I ran to my father Berl Zukor. There I found my sister Etke and brother-in-law Avrohom. I begged them to come with me and help harness up the horses. On the way, we saw a great commotion in the town. The wild Germans were chasing Jews out of their houses and were beating them with rubber clubs. My father and my brother Noakh, very upset, ran back to their home, leaving me standing alone. I did not run after my father and brother, and with a pounding heart, barely dragged myself to my home. My three children were sobbing with fear. I composed myself and took the necessities from the house and went with the children to the marketplace.

The dark marketplace was filled with Jews and packages. The Germans were shouting wildly, didn't let anyone sit down, and ordered everyone to line up in a row. I saw how the Germans took some Jews to the market well and shot them. We were overtaken by a shudder, but we were terrified to scream or cry.

A bit further away, the city non-Jews were standing quite pleased, and watched our situation calmly.

Before daylight, the Jews were chased on foot to Nazielsk. On the way, 30 kilometers, many of us had to stop; whoever couldn't go on was shot.

In Nazielsk, we were all herded into the city *shul*. At the entrance, there were two armed German guards, standing there with rubber clubs in their hands. Everyone who passed by them was beaten over the head. The small Itchele Pshikorski was beaten so terribly over the head, that later, when someone dragged him into the *shul,* he was already dead.

[Page 350]

That same night, the Germans took men out of the *shul* and took them somewhere. When they came back, they told us that they had to dig a deep ditch in order to bury five Jews who were shot not far from the *shul*.

The following morning, we were all chased out of the *shul* and taken to the train. When we arrived to that place, we saw empty baskets set out. The Germans ordered everyone to strip naked so that they could search all the clothing. They took everything that anyone was hiding. My sister-in-law, Rokhele Pshikorski, did not allow herself to be stripped naked, so a German beat her wildly and murderously, and then tore her clothing off her. My good fortune was that they didn't find the money that was sewn into my son's clothing.

With my own eyes, I saw how the Germans stripped naked the son of the Serock *Rav* and ordered him to "bathe" in the mud that had collected after a heavy rain. When the *Rav*'s son was already lying naked in the mud, the smiling Germans called over Shiele Gerbel's wife and ordered her to scrape his body with a brick.

Then they ordered the *Rav*'s son to get up and put on his *tefilin* that he had with him. When he tied the straps of the *tefilin* around his left hand, the Germans broke into laughter. After that, one of them went over to him and tied a ringing alarm clock tightly to the straps and ordered him to run and dance with it. He had to dance like that for a long time, and the Germans did not stop to goad each other on with laughter.

Later, we were chased into wagons that had been prepared. During this time, we were escorted with wild curses and terrible beatings. In the wagons, we sat very cramped and felt faint – so much so that it was very difficult to recognize a human face.

[Page 351]

My sister-in-law, Sorotche, Meyer Blekher's daughter, was clutching a nursing baby. A German tore the baby away from her and threw it into another wagon. For three days, around the clock, this nursing baby was fed by depleted, exhausted women, who themselves had nothing in their mouths.

After moving for a few days, our echelon (train) stopped in the Biala-Podlask station. The locked wagons were opened and they told us to go where we wanted. We went into the city, and the local Jews came to greet us. They welcomed us warmly and took us into the city's *shul* that was already prepared with all kinds of food. Later they put us up in Jewish homes.

After a certain time, we heard rumors that the Germans were going to set up a ghetto in the city. Since my husband and grown daughter were already on the other side of the border, in Koval, I didn't want to stay here any longer and looked for means to run away. I didn't think for too long, so I and my children and brother and sister ran into the forest that leads to the border. Before we reached the forest, once again we fell into German hands. A German searched us all, but did not find what he was looking for. We survived with just beatings. We figured it was a miracle that the German, who searched everyone thoroughly, did not notice how my son Yosele, who had all the money sewn into his clothing, was hiding from him, and, in fact, this money enabled us, with the help of a non-Jew that we paid, to smuggle ourselves across the already well-armed Soviet border.

[Page 352]

## My Childhood Years
### Arieh Mendzelewski (Ramat Gan)
### Translated by Pamela Russ

In the year 1939, when the war between Poland and Germany broke out, I was seven years old and lived with my parents in Serock.

When the Germans entered Poland and took over Serock, they took all the Jews and Polaks and set them out in the marketplace that was filled with munitions. The Germans threatened that if we would not confess who had killed one of their soldiers, everyone would be shot. People were sobbing and screaming. I cuddled up to my mother and she would comfort me. In the last hours, an officer came in and announced that the person who had killed the German soldier was found. They released all the Polaks and kept all the Jews. They also released the elderly and the children, those between the ages 17 and 35 are the ones they took. Among them was also my older brother. After that, the Germans demanded payments, and said forcefully that if we would not pay the sums demanded, then all the Jews in the city would be chased out. The detained Jews were later chased for 70 kilometers on foot, and whoever fell down was immediately shot.

After two months, only half of these people came back – my brother among them. It became festive in the house, but not for long. A short while later, there was a commotion in the streets. Soon all the neighbors from the court gathered together and started to cry. All the Jews were then chased into the marketplace, and whoever tried to run away, was shot immediately. They chased us on foot to the Nazielsk train and at the same time there were beatings and threats that anyone who was found with more than one zloty would be shot. At that point, I was hardly able to walk. They herded us into the Nazielsk *shul*. At the *shul*, the Germans were standing set out in two rows with guns and chunks of rubber in their hands. They told us to run in a row and then they beat us wherever we were. They locked us in the *shul* all night, without food and without drink. Many people passed out.

[Page 353]

The next morning, they chased us to the train, and pushed us all in through lots of mud. If they found anything in anyone's possession, they killed and beat the person. We rode in a closed wagon for three days, without food or drink (I licked the dew off the shutters), until we reached Biala-Podlask – and there we were freed.

We lived in the *shul*. The situation was terrible. My oldest brother left immediately for Russia, and I and my parents went to Warsaw to my mother's sister. My father and brother worked together in a coal mine. Things were still going for us in 1940, but when the ghetto was set up in Warsaw, things became even more difficult. I would smuggle myself out of the ghetto on the Polish side to buy bread and other products for us. Once, when I was trying to sneak back into the ghetto, a Polish policeman saw me and began to chase me. When I saw that he was close by, I dropped to the ground. He kicked me, beat me, took away all the products, then let me go home.

From that time on, my father didn't let me go smuggling, even though there was a terrible hunger in the house. My brother managed to get out of the Warsaw ghetto and into the Legionowa ghetto, where the situation was better. My cousin, who smuggled all kinds of things from Warsaw to Legionowa, took me along with him. I jumped on the tramway that went through the Warsaw ghetto, along with him. A Polish policeman was standing at the door. My cousin immediately put money into his hand, and the policeman moved away from us. We arrived to the main station of Warsaw. Right away, there was a search by the SS. My cousin disappeared and I remained alone with the packages. When I saw that they were close to me, I grabbed the packages, and ran out from another side and found my cousin again. He and I went to another station, from which we went to Legionowa. That's how, slowly, my entire family ended up there. Because of great need I had to find a job and worked for a Polak. Every day, right in the morning, I stole my way out of the ghetto and went to him, then late at night I had to return to the ghetto. He was afraid to keep me overnight. I had to work very hard there to earn the food. After that, the Germans announced that any Polak that would be keeping a Jew, would be shot along with his entire family. Then the Polak fired me and I left to look for new work, but no one wanted to have me. For several non-Jewish families I would gather their goats and stay with them all day in the fields.

[Page 354]

One day, when I went to pasture the goats, I saw a German man. As I was running away, I fell on a fence and tore a vein in my leg. The blood began to spurt out. The non-Jews did not know what to do, so they began to pour on iodine, but that didn't stop the bleeding. They were afraid to take me to a Polish doctor. They put me in a pig sty and I stayed there for a day and a night. The wound kept bleeding, and I had no more energy to breathe. I felt that I would die any minute. After that, the non-Jews put me into a wheelbarrow and pushed back to the ghetto, and then they left. Some Jews recognized me and ran to inform my parents. My mother came and took me back into the ghetto. I lay there sick in the ghetto for more than half a year. The whole time I had the feeling that soon they would chase us out of the ghetto, and I would often grab my stick, which helped me walk, and would run out of the ghetto. I could also not take care of my wound because every minute I was sure that they would be taking us to Treblinka. And any time that a car would drive through the ghetto, I became so terrified that I was paralyzed on the spot, and even if I would have known that this would mean my death, I would not have been able to run away. Once, when I was on the Aryan side, I heard that they were going to chase the Jews out of the ghetto. I immediately ran into the ghetto to inform my parents of this news. They said, "It doesn't matter, we weren't going to live anyway. They don't want to go around among the Polaks. They're going to shoot us all anyway." And I so wanted to live. I begged my sister that she should go with me, so she replied that wherever her parents would go, she would go as well. It was very difficult for me to separate from her, but I wanted to live, and I felt that this was the end.

[Page 355]

It was very early, still dark outside, when I wanted to smuggle myself out of the ghetto. But by that time, the ghetto was already surrounded by gendarmes and policemen who shot any person that tried to run away. Not looking at that, I ran to the wires, crossed the border, and ran into the forest. (I was ten years old then.) In the forest, I met a woman that I knew, with a child half a year old, along with many other familiar Jews. The Jews gathered together in a group, because each one thought he could help the other. I went into another direction with this woman, although the Germans began to shoot at all of us regardless. We slept under a tree. From time to time, I would bring the woman some bread from non-Jewish acquaintances, as well as some milk and other things. This was already at the end of October, 1942, such that it was already impossible to sleep outside because of the cold. The woman went away to live with a non-Jew, and I was left alone. One night I slept in a bathroom, another night in a barn. That's how I tortured myself for three weeks. My Polish acquaintances used to smuggle from Legionowa to Malkin until the border. Wherever there were Russians, that's where things were cheap. I begged them to take me with them, but they were afraid to do that. Once I waited until they were about to leave, and I followed them. Wherever they went, I went, and it was that way until Malkin. Before leaving the station, there was a massive search, where they checked packages and documents. I waited and trembled, and got closer to the gendarmes. When they had finished checking a woman, I went with her and ran to catch up with the Polaks, but they told me to go away because they were now going to the border and were afraid to take me along. I roamed around for a long time and didn't know where to go. It was already late at night, so I just went into a house and begged them to let me stay the night. The first thing they asked was if I was a Jew. I showed them a medallion that I was wearing, and swore to them that I was Polak. The following morning, I asked the direction of the border, and I left. There were many shepherds there, and I asked them what to do. They said that during the day, because of all the guards, it was impossible to cross over. Later, I intentionally chased the cows across the border and ran to help look for them. I crossed over the wires and ran far into the village. After running quite a bit of distance, I saw a guard, and started to work the earth with a shovel that was lying near a tree. When the German approached me, I had already filled an entire sack with leaves. He asked me where I was from, and I pretended not to understand, and I left in the direction of a hut. When he saw that I was going in the direction of a house, he left. On the way, I met a farmer going with a wagon and I asked him the way to the village because I wanted to work as a farmhand. He started to laugh and said: "You're still too small and no one will hire you." I began pleading with him, so he started to ask me all kinds of questions, from where I was, and if I was Jew. In the end, he said that he would take me to his son, to play with a young child. I was overjoyed and waited impatiently to get to a warm house.

*[Page 356]*

I rode with this peasant for 30 kilometers, from the border to his son, and I was there the entire winter. By summertime, they started to suspect that I was Jewish. When they wanted to send me to the "farm," I ran away from them and went to the village-magistrate in the same village to tend to the cows. Every morning and every night I said the Christian prayers (the Rosary) that I learned from the last farmer, and I behaved like any other Christian and went to church. I would guard myself against the Germans that would always come to visit him. For one year, it was very good there with him, but when he found out that I was a Jew, he told his neighbors. I pretended to know nothing, and continued to stay with him. There was a Russian man who lived with and worked for the village magistrate. The magistrate shot him along with two of his friends, but on the second night, some partisans came in and looked for the magistrate. He was not in the house. Later, he thought that I had turned him in. While I was lying in bed in my clothes, just before going to sleep, I hear talking and see the magistrate and a friend of his who is holding a gun and is saying to the magistrate that he must be searched. The magistrate shows him that I might wake up. At that point I well knew for whom they were preparing themselves. When I got up from the bed, he asked me where I was going so late at night. I told him that I had to go out for a minute and I would be back right away. I went out of the house and ran to a village, looking back each minute to see if they were chasing me. I came to a non-Jewish acquaintance and asked her if I could stay there over night. She asked what had happened, that I came running so late at night. I told her that the magistrate wanted to beat me, and so she let me stay the night. The following morning, she tried to convince me to go back to him, assuring me that he wouldn't do anything. So, I went home that morning. When he asked me where I had been, I told him that I had slept in a barn. Two weeks passed like that, and he was good to me, but nonetheless, I guarded myself each night.

[Page 357]

Once, when I came back from the field, I saw two strange people in the house. As I entered the house, one of them signaled the magistrate, asking if this (pointing at me) is "him." I understood what he meant by that, and at night I left to another farmer and slept in the barn. The next morning, I returned, but they had already left. I stayed a little longer with him. And when it was lunchtime, I looked for a place to run to. Once, when I was lying on the bed dozing, I saw on the other side of the window a whole group of people, and the magistrate was among them. Before that, I had heard many different languages that they were speaking between themselves. They thought I didn't understand. One of them said to the magistrate that if the *stanyazhchuk*[1] (the first one, who came a few days ago to shoot me) did not betray you, so it was definitely your little farmhand (meaning me) who did it. I was very frightened and pale – my death was coming closer and closer.

The magistrate told him that yesterday, "he" [meaning me] didn't come back for the night, the devil only knows where he is, and the thought strengthened in his mind that "he" (meaning me) had told the partisans about the murdered Russians.

[Page 358]

A few times, the door to my room opened and a few farmers looked in to make sure that I was there. Instinctively, I got off the bed, jumped into another room, and wanted to jump through a window and run away. The last minute, I held myself back from doing this because I was afraid that I would be seen, and the game would be over. I went back into the corridor where I heard a voice saying: "Let's go, he's sleeping." I went into a neighbor's house. Everyone was lying in bed, but no one was sleeping. They probably also knew of the plan to shoot me. Quiet as a cat, I crawled under the stove, blocked myself up with rags, and shivered with fear.

A few minutes later, I heard the magistrate calling me and asking the neighbors if they had seen me. The neighbors and the magistrate lit up the house with batteries [small lights, like flashlights], and looked for me a long time under the beds. I remained under the stove this whole time, frozen in place, until dawn.

When I was sure that everyone was sound asleep and that everything around was still, I snuck out of the neighbor's house, went back into my room at the magistrate's, took my clothes out of cupboard, and like a flash I left for another village. There I worked for a farmer tending his cows. This new boss was actually a friend of the magistrate. The entire time that I was with this new boss, I was always terrified and always thinking that any minute they would shoot me. The Russian front came closer; the bullets from the artillery were already very close to us. I left the house because I was terrified that they would kill me and say that I was killed on the front. Now I was in the field all the time, among all kinds of crates. Russian planes had begun bombing very heavily. Many German soldiers would go through these fields. That's how I spent the time until the liberation.

[Page 359]

After the war, when I went back to Serock, I did not find my parents. I left for Legionowa, where I was in the ghetto, with the hope that I would find someone there, but found no one from my family. I was afraid to tell even the Jews that I was Jewish. When I met a Jewish doctor that had once cured me, he told me about everyone. He also gave me the address of a cousin of mine in Warsaw. I went there and stayed only a short time. Very soon, I went to join a group preparing to leave for Israel. The anti-Semitic attacks in Poland at that time did not allow us to stay there any longer. With that group, I left on the Exodus ship, and with the help of the English military, I was taken back to Germany to the rest of the surviving refugees.

**(Central Historical Commission in Bavaria, 1947)**

**Translator's Footnote**

1. A *stanyazhchuk* is likely a commissar of the rural police. (Unsure of this translation.)

[Page 360]

# From the Destruction and Wanderings – To Israel

**Pinkhas Kaluski (Kfar Monash)**
**Translated by Pamela Russ**

The second *Shabbos* after the outbreak of the war, German tanks and armed cars appeared in the streets of the town. On Friday night, German motorized military units filled the streets and alleys of Serock. I, my father, brother, sister, and grandfather Yidel Pjenik, may he rest in peace, left our home and Friday night we went to our relative Reb Gedaliah Leviner, and there, together with other neighbors, we hid in his cellar. Late at night, German soldiers wanted to invade our place, but thanks to the screams of the children and women who were with us, the Germans went away from the cellar. The following morning, we men went out of the cellar and I saw how the Jewish houses and stores were destroyed and robbed.

Right in the morning, the SS began to gather up all the men from the town and locked them up in the large Jewish *shul*. Once a day, they allowed children to bring us some food. The *shul* was very cramped. After that, they released all the elderly people. We were locked up in there until the second day of Rosh Hashona, 5700 (1939). After that, they sent us over to Pultusk to a prison. The next morning, they ordered us to get into rows and begin our march to Chekhanow. The Germans chased us all day, without food and without water. There were among us those who could not run any farther, and they dropped to the ground; the Germans shot them. That's how the first victims fell, on the way to Pultusk-Chekhanow – Avrohom Ostrowski was one of these victims on this road.

Everyone's energies were drained, and they were without strength. Once, when we stopped, we fell onto the puddles of water that had gathered on the ground after the strong rains and hail that fell then, and quenched our thirst a little with the dirty water. When we arrived in Chekhanow in the evening, they took us into the horses' stalls from the former Polish cavalry regiment. German soldiers with guns were standing at the gates and beating the people. Many of us were beaten very badly. After coming in there, we fell onto the bare ground, and lay there all night. In the morning, we received old, mouldy bread that was left over by the Polish military – and again we were told to stand in rows and to march in the direction of the train station.

[Page 361]

As we were marching through the streets, we were approached by women and children with food, but the Germans didn't allow them to give any to us and they shot them. One woman who risked giving bread to one of us was wounded in the shooting. When we arrived at the train station, they put 100 men into a wagon. The wagons were small, and the tightness was terrible, no food and no water, and no sanitation facilities. We were locked in the wagons from outside and were there for about two 24-hour days until we came near the German town of Reisenberg in East Prussia. There, once again, we were put into horses' stalls, and hungry, we stayed there for a few weeks.

Suddenly, there came some news that they were sending us back to Poland. We were back in the cargo trains, and taken back to Ostrolenka. The Germans allowed us to go back one time to our home Serock, but after a few kilometers they warned us not to go in the direction of Warsaw but to go in the direction of Lomze, which the Russians had taken. At night, they took us near to Lomze and ordered us to run, as they were shooting over our heads. That's how we ran for about two kilometers, and then as we saw that the Germans are not running after us, we roamed around all night until we came to a village. The residents told us that the Russians were in Lomze and that they got along well with the civilian population.

When we arrived in Lomze, we found some Jews there. They gave us some food and a place to sleep. We were without clothing and very worried about our relatives that were left at home. I and a few others decided to risk it and go back to Serock and then come back to Lomze. Our journey took a few days. We had plenty of scares from the Germans that were on the road. We would spend the night with the village farmers.

[Page 362]

When we arrived in Serock at night, it was with great difficulty that we managed to make our way across the Narew because the bridges were destroyed. In Serock, they were overjoyed to see us. Many came to ask us about their relatives. We told them everything we knew and suggested to them that they come back with us to the Russian side, but they didn't listen. Then it was still possible to save oneself from the German murderers' hands.

The three days that we were in Serock, we had to hide in the cellars because the Germans captured young men for all kinds of work and did terrible things to them.

After we prepared ourselves for the return trip, we left Serock at dawn, taking some clothing for us and some for the relatives. We went to the Narew River and asked for help from an acquaintance Fisher Wilkowski. He took us by boat to the other side of the river Narew. We started to go on the road to Wyszkow.

When we arrived back in Lomze, our friends and relatives were overjoyed. We brought them real greetings from their relatives who had remained in Serock. Some of the Jews of Serock had come with us. Among them was my sister Khaya (she came to our father in Lomze after I had already left there). After that, I went to Bialystok, whereas my father and a few others remained in Lomze waiting for news from the family.

There were many Jews then in Bialystok, having come from Warsaw and other cities. There were organized kitchens for the needy. I immediately registered to go to Russia to work. After, when a train for people to go to work was organized, they sent us by train to Russia. When we arrived in the city of Polotsk, all of us were taken to the baths to wash.

[Page 363]

Our clothes were disinfected and we were taken to the designated places, until everyone had set himself up with work.

I began working and earning money, saving some to buy some clothing and also to send my father and sister in Lomze some money for Passover 1940. Later, I received a letter from them saying that they had been sent far north in the district of Arkhangelsk at the White Sea. (The Russians at the time sent out the Jews who had wandered in – those who didn't want to get any Russian passes and who had registered to go back to the Germans.) I got the address of my grandfather Zishe K. from Wyszkow and his son Yekhiel and his daughters. I immediately tried to get them to release me from my work in Polotsk and went to Orsha to my relatives. While in Orsha, I had the opportunity to send packages with food products to my relatives in Arkhangelsk.

June 22, 1941, the Germans attacked Russia and began to bomb the cities. The city of Orsha was heavily bombed, and people began to run away – among them were also my relatives. I left Orsha and later, with an echelon (train) went to the Urals. I was there for about three years, got sick with malaria, and suffered terribly.

All the while in Russia, I missed my town of Serock very much. And in the year 1944, when the Russians began to march forward and liberate Ukraine and White Russia, I volunteered to go into the Polish army that had been organized in Tchokolow, using the name Wanda Washilewska, so that I would be able to get to Poland more quickly. Once we had set ourselves up in a unit, we were sent past Kharkow, to Sumi, in Ukraine. There we received military training. After a few weeks, they sent us into Polish territory. For a short time, we were in Lublin. There we met Jewish partisans and others hiding in the forests. They told us the horrifying descriptions of the crematoria in Majdanek, Auschwitz, Treblinka, and other murdering camps where in this way the majority of Polish Jewry was tragically killed. In Lublin we also found remaining mountains of shoes and clothing from these martyrs. Then we were sent into the direction of Warsaw, Palenicz, Praga, and other places on the eastern side of the Vistula. In Praga, we were able to see the burning houses of Warsaw. That's when there was the uprising of the Polish people, and the Germans burned entire streets and houses, and threw hand grenades many times on the Targowa Street in Praga where our unit was stationed. There were victims from our side as well.

*[Page 364]*

In the year 1945, the great offensive began by the Russian and Polish military. We forced our way across the Vistula and chased the German military until German territory. There, the Germans put up an opposition, but after some struggle, we broke their opposition and continued with our march. That's how we moved forward, and in March 1945, we came to the Elba River, where the American military arrived on the other side of the river.

In a few weeks' time, they sent our unit back to Warsaw. The city was completely destroyed. A few streets remained complete, which the Germans seemed not to have destroyed as they were leaving the city. Many times I roamed around the burned down streets of the Warsaw ghetto.

Then I asked permission from the military and I went to see our town of Serock. I took along a Polish soldier and fully armed, we went on the road. The roads then were unsafe, with gangs of Polish thieves wandering around, from the A.K. (Polish Home Army), along with others who did terrible things to the Jews. When we came to Serock, we found the city dead as a cemetery. The majority of Jewish homes were ruined, or in fact, were completely wiped out. One could only see the cellars of the houses. This picture made a horrific impression, as I remembered the former Jewish population with the romantic youth, with all the parties, libraries, Jewish stores and craftsmen – the shoemakers, tailors, carpenters, blacksmiths, tinsmiths, porters, wagon-drivers, teachers slaughterers [*shokhtim*], burial society, Jewish schools, religious schools, the big *shul*, and the smaller *shuls*. The Germans also destroyed the Jewish cemetery, the tombstones and the graves. Anything that was connected to Jewry was destroyed.

*[Page 365]*

I wanted to get a way from there as quickly as possible so that I wouldn't see the destruction. When I came back to Warsaw, I found out that a few surviving Jews were gathering in Praga. Also, some Polish Jews were coming back from Russia. On Targowa Street in Praga, I met Arke Gerwer (who was also in the Polish army), Rivkele Rosenberg, and also with two sisters Rivka and Rokhel (our neighbor Shaike Meyer's daughters). They were in the camps. A few times we searched through the Warsaw ghetto and walked through the destruction and looked through the cemetery on Ganshe Street, on whatever remained whole, even the tombstones.

When I found out about those who had returned from Russia, that my father and sister had also come back, and that they were sent to Sosnowiec, I went there right away to find them. Our meeting was very emotional. We cried for joy.

After I came back to Warsaw, I asked my head commander to be discharged from the army, and after a few months I was released and I went to my relatives in Sosnowiec.

Then communes were formed for all kinds of groups. The goal was to organize the survivors and send them over to Austria, Germany, Italy, and France, and from there to go on to Israel. Along with them were those members of the *Bricha*[1] and soldiers from the Jewish brigade. One of them was our close neighbor and friend Khanoch Warshawski (Werdi). We were very happy and went with him to Lodz, to meet more Jews from Serock.

After that, they sent us through Czechoslovakia, Austria, and then Germany, to the UNRA camps (United Nations Relief and Rehabilitation Administration), and from there in September 1948, we went on *aliyah* to Israel.

**Translator's Footnote**

1. The first organized immigration movement of Jews from Eastern Europe across the occupied zones and into Israel.

[Page 366]

# From Nazielsk to Biala-Podlask
### by Tzvi Kleinman
### Translated by Pamela Russ

After the Serock refugees were released from the Nazielsk shul, an event that took place on December 6, 1939, all the Jews were moved into the street that goes to the train station, a distance of about eight kilometers. They were set in a row, according to German orderliness. As the Jews were being chased out of the shul, they were beaten terribly, and the crowd ran in all directions. Parents lost their children and children lost their parents. All those who were lost tried to find their dear ones, and for that they received new beatings.

Polish merchants brought bread and milk to the starved people, but only for a price. However, the German guards did not permit them to get close. In the end, the row was completed and everyone made ready to leave. The day was dismal, the roads wet and muddy. The Serock Jews had a very difficult journey. They were starved, exhausted, and broken from the horrific night in the Nazielsk shul. They were hardly able to drag their feet and carry the tired, fainting children in their arms. The guards pushed the people intentionally into the muddiest pools, taking great pleasure in doing this. The Germans did not permit the Jews to move slowly, so they used rubber hoses to chase these Jewish tired bodies forward. From a distance, the building at the train station was now visible, and soon also the cargo train that was standing nearby. A first glance at the cargo train gave the people a fright, as they were hoping they would not be crammed into these open wagons. The cargo train actually left, and a passenger train arrived to take its place.

As they got closer to the train, the guards began to try to make order in the crowd. The chaos was terrible because there was no way they could figure out what the Germans wanted. One minute they were chased to the right and another minute to the left. The line slithered like a snake, but they did not want to break it so that they would not give the guards the opportunity to beat them. But it didn't help. The line tore and crumbled. They simply could not withstand the murderous beatings in the deep muds that seemed to have been especially prepared for the Serock and Nazielsk Jews.

[Page 367]

Eventually, following the guards' orders, the Jews positioned themselves opposite the passenger train that was ready to take in the harassed Jews. The "escorts" were, as it seems, not yet ready for this task. They had set out baskets and suitcases in various places along the length of the train and prepared to do a search among the Jews to see if they had any money with them. The search was very severe. They stripped people naked, tore off their clothes, cut off buttons, and opened the trunks.

The search among the women was conducted sadistically and murderously. Women were not searched outside, but were searched in the wagons. The screams that were heard through the windows of the wagons were horrific -- not screams of pain, which one was already used to, but screams of humiliation because of the search that was going on.

During the search, there were terrible beatings for those where they had found money or jewelry, and also for those who they noticed were throwing money or other valuables into the mud. Many people were forced to lie in the mud and smear themselves on all sides, while others were tortured in other sadistic ways.

After this torture, only then were the Jews allowed to enter the wagons under a barrage of more beatings. The Jews took off their shoes in the wagons, emptied them of mud, dressed themselves as best as they could, and then seated themselves on the benches. Those who had not yet suffered through the search procedure that began with beatings as you were getting undressed and as each part of your clothing was being searched, and ended with you rolling in the mud, envied those who had gone through this and were already in the wagons.

[Page 368]

Finally, the searches ended. The wagons were locked and sealed shut.

There were all kinds of rumors circulating among the Jews about where they were being transported. Everyone hoped that the best place would be to go to the other side of the border, to Russia. Everyone waited very impatiently for the minute that the train would move from its spot. Soon, a long and shrill whistle was heard and that meant the Serock Jews were saying goodbye to their homes and to their possessions. You cannot take more than your memories along with you on this journey in exile, which could last for an unknown length of time. A second whistle. A third whistle. The train began to move, heading west.

Where are we going? What will they do with us? Everyone asked these questions with great fear - Where to?

At first, we thought that we would change trains, but when we saw that we were travelling for too long, we figured that the station in Nazielsk was too small and we would change trains in Chekhanow. When the train passed through Chekhanow and kept going in the direction of the German-Polish border, the Jews decided that the Chekhanow station was also too small and the real place would be Mlawa. But when the train did not stop in Mlawa either and continued going west, the Jews dropped their heads in confusion and put all their musings aside. Everyone became like paralyzed. What are the Germans thinking of doing with such a crowd of people among whom there are so many elderly, sick, and tiny children? All kinds of conjectures, one more horrific than the next, were expressed: They would take this crowd of people to a faraway place and shoot them all or blow them up with mines; or they would all be abandoned in a faraway place in a forest and let die from cold and hunger; the Jews would be taken to the French front and be sent out in the greatest hail of gunfire.

*Caption*: **Harassing the Serock Jews**

[Page 369]

The train continued to go very quickly and did not stop in any station until Willenberg (East Prussia). The voices of the Jews became more confused by the minute. One minute, you jumped out of your seat and paced for a few steps in the sealed wagon, then in another instant you jumped wildly to the window and searched blindly into the darkness that was wrapped around everything.

Many people openly stated that if they would have any poison they would immediately put an end to their lives and not wait for more pain and anguish. Everyone was certain that nothing good was waiting for them.

The train stopped in Willenberg and remained there for a long time, then turned around to go back in an eastern direction.

Ha! What happened? Everyone was asking. That elderly man who had continuously said that they would not take Jews to Germany now looked victoriously at his stubborn opponent. The Jews revived a little, became comforted, and remembered that this was the first night of Khannuka, remembered the bravery of the Hasmoneans and the great miracles that had taken place at that time, and they sought comfort for their frightful situation. The train began to rush at top speed. Jewish hearts raced at each station. During the middle of the night, the train began to go in another direction. They stopped trying to figure it out.

A great desperation overtook them.

[Page 370]

In the morning, the Jews sensed that they were on Polish soil. Sure enough, soon they saw the Rembartow station and an hour later the train reversed and went back to Warsaw, stopping in the eastern station.

The train was standing there, and there was no sign of letting the Jews out of the wagons. The commotion at the eastern depot was huge. Suddenly, terrible screams were heard from the Jews being beaten as they were standing near the depot and were waiting for the train that was to go east: some to Siedlice, some to Miedzyrzecz, some to Biale, and so on. All the Jewish passengers who had purchased tickets to go to these places were herded by a whole unit of civilian Germans who were murderously beating the Jews and grabbing the bundles and valises that the Jews had with them. The chaos was terrible. They were chasing the harassed Jews from one place to another until they dropped without any strength left. Through the windows of the sealed wagons they could see how some *Volksdeutsche*[1] (literally, Folk-Germans, "people whose language and culture had German origins but who did not hold German citizenship") chased the Jews and then used their feet to kick down some of the Jews who by that point hardly resembled anything human. Their faces were bloodied and they were hardly able to remain standing. The scene was horrible. When the Jews on the train witnessed what was going on with the Jews outside, they began to cry loudly. In the end, the captured Jews in the depot were shoved into the wagons of the "Jew train" and experienced the journey of exile along with the Serock Jews.

The hunger began to be more and more torturous. Because of the cramped space, it became very hot and damp, and the thirst was so terrible that people licked the moisture off the window panes. This, however, helped very little to quench anyone's thirst, and particularly the thirst of the little children who could not be comforted by anyone and who cried with all their might: Water! Water! The mothers, hearing their children's cries, became like wild and ran to the windows, banged on them, and screamed: Water! Water! But the guards did not allow anyone to come close to the train to give the children some water.

[Page 371]

In the afternoon, the train began to move and at around six in the evening it arrived in a station in Biala-Podlask. A half an hour before arriving in the station a conductor went into the wagons and informed the Jews that there was going to be a search and that anyone that had money or jewelry should give it to him to hide and that after the search he would return the belongings for some compensation. Many people who still had something with them, and especially the newly captured passengers, allowed themselves to be taken in, and gave away their last pennies. There was no other search after that.

After midday, they opened the wagons and herded out all the people onto the road that led to Biala - two or three kilometers. There were more beatings, but a little less than before. In the town, the "escorts" freed the group of harassed Jews and delivered them into the hands of the Biala Jews who did much for them.

**(From the archives of the Jewish Historical Institute in Warsaw):**
This report was only qualified later as a continuation by the same author on page 247.

**Translator's Footnote**

1. http://en.wikipedia.org/wiki/Volksdeutsche

[Page 372]

# The Road of Pain
### by Yehoshua Bobek/Babek Tel Aviv
### Translated by Pamela Russ

When the war broke out in Poland and the Germans came to Serock, they chased all the young people into the *shul*. On the second day of Rosh Hashanah, they moved us all on foot to Pultusk, and from there to Chekhanow to the train for Germany and the camp at Riesenberg. We were there for more than four weeks, and then we were sent to the Russian border to Lomzhe. From Lomzhe I went to Bialystok and worked with my own skills and had a good income. Since I was worried about the fate of my wife and children, I decided to stay in Bialystok for five weeks. I went until the train station Ostralenka. There was no one in the train and I went until Wolomyn and spent the night at Khava Calkes' home. The next morning I went to Radzimyn and then back to Serock. When I arrived in Serock, the people had already made their fourth contribution (*had gone through the fourth search*). I saw right away that this was a "death contribution," and that's how it was.

At one in the morning, everyone was chased out of their houses and into the streets. The Germans took everything away from us, put the children into the wagons, and moved us to Nazielsk. Those who couldn't walk were shot. The entire road was lined with murdered Jews.

When I arrived in Nazielsk and came into the *shul*, I saw the walls of the *shul* splashed with Jewish blood. People lay down on the ground to rest from the bloody journey, and everyone fell asleep. Four SS officers came in and said that all the young people should voluntarily go to work, and those who wouldn't cooperate would be made *kaput* (would be killed). We gathered all the young people for work. They took thirty-one people behind the *shul* near the bathroom, and they were ordered to dig a ditch eight meters long, four meters wide, and two meters deep. This had to be completed in about a half hour. They finished digging the ditch on time. The Germans came and ordered Tuvia, the *shamash*'s son-in-law, to go into the ditch and come right out of it.

[Page 373]

At the same time, the SS men in the *shul* said that the sick people would be sent to a hospital.

At the site of the pit, the people were stripped naked and shot immediately. The last one was Mendel Katzav. He took several bullets before he died, and we had to stand ten meters away from the pit. When the people were already lying spread out across the pit, they called us over and told us to fill in the pit that had dead eyes. After filling the pit, there remained a lot of earth. We had to dance on the top of the pit until all the earth became flat. After that we had to go bring greenery to put on top of the pit so that it would not be recognized.

When we finished the task and came back into the *shul*, it was soon daybreak. At seven in the morning, we were all herded out of the *shul* and taken to the train. There, all the people who had money or gold were told to give it away. A person who was found with dollars, was stripped naked and beaten. I myself saw how they found $50 in Moishe Sosinak's sister's corset, and they beat her mercilessly for that until she fell dead under the wagon.

After that, we were moved from Nazielsk. We were without water for two days. The children licked the moisture from the window panes. We arrived in Biala-Podlask and were taken to the *shul*. I decided that I had to go live privately. I was working with tin and bought and sold for the people in the ghetto. When I saw that they were forcing all the people into the ghetto, I took my wife and children and left Biala-Podlask and went to Warsaw, then from Warsaw to Ostralenka, crossed over the border, then came to Bialystok. I worked there until they sent us to Arkhangelsk for hard labor - to chop trees in a forest. I worked there until the war between Germany and Russia broke out. In 1941, we were freed from this work and sent to Arkhangelsk. My wife, children, and I travelled for five weeks in forty-five degrees freezing weather. My wife became sick on the way and we had to stop in the city of Gorky and take her to a hospital where she remained for a few months and then died. I was left with three small children. I looked for a Polish orphanage for the children.

[Page 374]

After that, I worked for two orphanages until the end of the war, and then I went with all the children to Poland.

When I came to Krakow, Polaks were standing around and shouting: "The onions are stinking again!" From Krakow they sent us to Latvia, Lower Silesia, two kilometers from the Czechoslovakian border. I was there for three weeks and then went to Czechoslovakia and from there to Austria to the Wegsheidt camp. After a few weeks I went to Germany to the American zone. I was in the DP camp Eshwegen for three months and then went to Israel on the ship Exodus. The British had us on the ocean for three months until they brought us back to Hamburg (Germany), and then to Ferindorf, and there the British liberated us. In 1948 I arrived in Israel legally.

[Page 375]

# The Evacuation of Serock
### Translated by Pamela Russ

The town of Serock lies on the right shore of the Narew River and before the outbreak of the war, boasted 650 Jewish families, which accounted for forty-five percent of the population. On the second day of the war, the first refugees from Makow and Chekhanow arrived in Serock. A day later, refugees arrived from Pultusk, Nazielsk, and Wyszkow. On the fifth day after the outbreak of the war, September 5, 1939, the government institutions began to prepare to leave. That same day at around 11 am, German planes appeared, and they dropped thirteen bombs onto the city. One of these bombs landed on a Jewish home and buried thirty-nine bodies, all Jews, under the rubble. These Jews were hiding in a cellar. This tragedy threw a terrible fear over the town. In this cellar there were a large number of young people and from several families there was not even one survivor. That same day, about one quarter of the Jews left the town, looking for protection - some went to the neighboring town of Legionowa and some went to Warsaw. The conflict near the Narew lasted about a week, and the first German soldiers entered the city on September 29. That same evening, in a non-Jewish store, a German soldier was killed. The owner of the building and the two neighbors were shot immediately. The following morning, the Germans took three Jews, among them a father and a son, and ordered them to dig a pit. These Jews were under the impression all along that this pit was for them, because that's the message they were given. In the end, the three murdered non-Jews were put into this grave. That same day, the entire population was herded out to the marketplace, not leaving a single living soul in any house. An officer announced the death of the German soldier that, according to wartime laws, required that the most important people in the city be shot. Still, he felt bad for the people, and he let the women and children go. But the men ages eighteen to forty-five were detained and sent to concentration camps. It's understood that the Torah scrolls were first ripped then burned. Life in the camps was very difficult and cost the lives of ten Jews, fathers and children. All the Jewish stores in the city were blown up and looted by the local Polish population that helped destroy the Jewish goods and possessions. Jewish society, for all intents and purposes, came to a halt. The city was filled with military, and Jews - both men and women - were taken away for all kinds of labor. The troubles among the Jews increased daily. There was no trade and no work. On the eve of Sukos, some Christians told about the evacuation of the Jews in Pultusk. It was impossible to verify this information, because communication between the Jews of the two towns was not possible. A short while later this information was confirmed and the Serock Jews prepared for an evacuation as well. Meanwhile, winter was approaching, it became cold, and the first frost and snow appeared. The Jews comforted themselves thinking that in the winter surely they wouldn't be chased out. That's also what the *Volksdeutche* (see note p. 370), Folk-Germans, thought. They had been on good terms with the Jews until the outbreak of the war.

[Page 376]

At the beginning of November 1939, the mayor of Pultusk called together the Jewish representatives of Serock and informed them that they would have to pay 15,000 zlotys within twenty-four hours. Pleas went unheard. Six days later, they added a payment of 10,000 zlotys. Collecting this sum of money was extremely difficult. And two weeks later they again added another 5,000 zlotys. That money too was collected. Everyone gave the last bit that he had earned, hoping that this would save the Jews from evacuation. On December 3, a security committee from the German government levied a monthly tax on all the Jewish storeowners and workmen. The tax was paid the following day, almost willingly, hoping that this would prevent the evacuation from happening. Sunday, December 5, 1939, at 5 am, the entire Jewish population in the town, regardless of age, and without sparing even the very sick, was alerted by German gendarmes and policemen and all were chased out of their houses and herded to the marketplace where everyone huddled together like sheep. This situation did not last long, and the evacuation began. They had to stand in a row. Only very few people had some of their clothing or bedding with them. But even this was lost on the way. One autumn morning, the entire Serock Jewish community, after losing all their possessions for which generations had worked, began marching to Nazielsk, a distance of more than twenty kilometers. Only the sick and the very young children were permitted to ride. The crowd arrived in Nazielsk that evening and spent the night in the Nazielsk *shul*, a very beautiful building that had been emptied of every single item that had any connection to a *shul*. In the place of where the ark used to stand, there was a swastika. The group was moved into the *shul* almost like a parade. Each person walked through a cordon of gendarmes in full uniform. Only three sick people, two men and one woman, didn't live to do have this great honor, the guards shot them in the *shul*'s courtyard. The night seemed eternal and there was not enough room for the entire crowd who for obvious reasons huddled against the walls. No one sat, no one stood, and of course, no one lay down. They sort of floated in the air.

[Page 377]

The second day, that is December 6, 1939, the people were moved out of the Nazielsk *shul*, again with great ceremony. The security was tightened so that no one would be able to buy food or run away. The Germans told everyone that they were being taken to the station that was about five or six kilometers from the city. The road ran through a very muddy area and many shoes remained stuck there. Everyone was taken directly to the wagon cars, but getting into the cars was not so simple. Many Jews were forced to bathe in the mud, naked, because an intensive search took place to make sure the Jews weren't smuggling any foreign currency. Only after "cleansing" everyone from every bit of dirty money, gold, and other worldly things, were they permitted entry into the wagons. The goal of the trip was according to everyone, to be taken east - to the Lublin area. How amazed everyone was when they felt the train going back west, that is to East Prussia In fact, they were travelling to East Prussia until Willenberg. They arrived there at six in the evening. It is not possible to describe the feelings of the people who broke their heads all this time trying to figure out where they were being taken and what was going to be done with them. One thing is for certain - if they would have had poison with them at that time, there would have been plenty of victims. At the Willenberg station, the train turned and went back. That's how the Jews went all night, and then again no one knew where they were going.

Only the following morning, December 7, 1939, the Jews saw that they were on Polish soil, and the train stood in Warsaw in the eastern depot. There were many Jews on the platform waiting for trains going to many different places. All the waiting Jews were forcefully crammed into two wagon cars that contained the harassed people from Serock. Horrific scenes played out here. Finally the train moved in a western direction, and at the beginning of the evening, the train arrived in Biala-Podlask. The train remained here all night. During this ride, all this time, no one was permitted to buy any food. Some tore the hair from their heads as they heard the cries of the young children. Thirst drove everyone to the point of wildness. Finally, Polish women and youths appeared, who sold water for a good price. When such a bottle came into the wagon, there was a terrible uproar, and one person tore it out of the other's mouth. But the little water could hardly quench anyone's thirst and the need for water was intensified, and then everyone looked for a way to get some sleep for a little time. That's how the night passed. The following day began with the worry of what will be. What will they do with this crowd of Jews?

[Pages 378 and 379]

Finally, around midday, they opened the wagons and with ordinary sticks and other similar items, the Jews were chased out of the wagons and ordered to stand in a row, then herded towards the middle of the city. The Jews were left in Biala-Podlask, and the authorities felt relieved of their responsibility over these harassed people, and left them without guards. The Biala Jews already had experienced this sort of thing, and they undertook to prepare coffee, bread, tea, and boxes of food for this new group. That's how they made these Serock Jews understand that they were among other Jews. Biala community workers and other ordinary Jews also joined in trying to provide the refugees with food and drink. For some they got places to live. The Biala Jews fulfilled the *mitzva* of *hakhnosas orkhim* (providing hospitality to guest) to the highest degree, and not only for the first few minutes. There were also landlords who took entire families into their homes and shared all their belongings with them. One has to remember that in Biala there were already about 3,000 Suwalk refugees from before that the city was caring for. Right after *Shabbos* a complete list of all the arrivals was compiled. Brotherhoods (*landsmanschaften*) of Serock and Suwalk refugees, who were also set up in the general city's committee, occupied themselves with action help for the benefit of the people. The help was such that each person received one quarter of a kilo of bread and a bowl of soup, daily. The Serock people were set up in the city committees through Hersh Kleinman and Menakhem Kronenberg, former elected members of the Serock community.

**(From the archives of the Jewish Historical Institute in Warsaw. The author's name is unknown.)**

[Page 380 - Hebrew] [Page 391 - Yiddish]

# From Auschwitz Prisoner # 24667
### by Rokhel Brandt (Nahariya)
### Translated by Pamela Russ

Winter 1942, terrible cold. Wherever I go, the sanitation facilities are horrific, without any plumbing and without any water to drink. We hadn't washed ourselves for months and worms were eating away at us. On Sundays, when we didn't work, our great pleasure was to clean our clothes from lice – those tiny murderers.

The terrible cries from the sick and the frail was "Water! Water! Only to wet my lips!" One gave away one's entire portion of bread just for a few drops of water.

How did I, as well as others, organize to have water for drinking and for selling?

In the entire camp, there was only one washroom with only one faucet for the German guards. If you went in there without permission, you could pay with your life. Nonetheless, we risked our lives and looked away from the possible consequences. In the middle of the night, when everyone was deeply asleep, I went down from my cot, and quietly stole into the bathroom. I didn't want to think about the life threatening consequences, and more than one of us really did pay with his life. With a pounding heart and trembling hands, I filled a few bottles with water and – ran! I returned to my block, tired and scared. More than once I was beaten over the head with a stick.

[Page 392]

The water that I had worked so hard to get, I sold for a few pieces of bread. I was satisfied with my "prize" and with the bread that I prepared to eat the following day, so I wrapped the treasured bread in a rag, put it under my "pillow," and fell asleep.

Just as I awoke in the morning, I immediately noticed that the rag with the bread was missing. I cried, pleaded, begged from those close by, but it didn't help. I didn't even get a small piece back.

For nothing. The dream disappeared. And hunger was gnawing and gnawing.

Our Block was a big one, filled with many girls. Fifteen girls slept on each bunk bed. The bunk beds were many leveled and made of wood. The girls were covered with one dirty blanket. Each person pulled at the blanket towards her side. They are screaming, moaning, and crying. No one wants to sleep at the edge of the bed.

At four in the morning, a group is awoken to bring the black coffee from the kitchen. It's still dark in the Block and we can't find our clothes. It's hard to get up. We are all tired from the forced labor and from sleep deprivation, but there's no choice because we – and I among them – have our turn today to bring the warm, black drink. I wake up and move my neighbors. They wake up. We're all weak. We are hunched over as we carry the heavy iron pots. But we have to go; they are chasing us with sticks. A guard was escorting us, and for the slightest thing he rewarded us with a rap. Because of this strict guard, we couldn't even steal a few sips of the coffee. The coffee was divided among the important ones, and the rest was given to the supervisors.

When we had completed the coffee business, the morning roll call (*appel*) begins. It takes three to four hours to complete. We stand there frozen in our miserable clothing and wooden, Dutch clogs. All the hundreds of girls are shivering, and to keep warm, the girls huddle close to one another.

[Page 393]

The German overseers can never finish counting. They always think that the count is higher or lower than it shows on the list. They beat and kick during the count. There is no end.

Finally, there is a long whistle that signals the end of the *appel*. Everyone gets into their row to go to work. The sick and weak girls begin to run off, hide in the bathrooms, barracks, and under the beds. But it doesn't help. The overseers quickly assemble them, beating and kicking them without mercy.

All kinds of diseases found their way into our camp.

The disease that was most widespread and most terrible among the girls was called the "death disease of Auschwitz." The symptoms for this were swollen feet.

The secondary most prevalent diseases among the girls were dysentery, malaria, and finally, stomach typhus.

It was a winter day in 1942. A deep snow covered the ground, and there was a terrible frost. My hands and feet are almost frozen and I feel that my energies were dropping away. At dawn, when they awoke us for the morning roll call, I felt terrible pains in my head, my lips were dry, and my feet like cement. With superhuman efforts, I got down from my bed. My face was burning, I drag myself out of the Block, and I get into the rows for the *appel*. My friend Irke holds me under the arms so that I shouldn't fall over.

I tell her categorically: "Iritchke, today there is no way that I will be able to go out to work."

Irke explains the huge danger of staying in the camp. She convinces me to gather all my strength and go with everyone to work.

However, all my efforts were to no avail. I fell without energy, and after that couldn't get up.

Tens of rows of girls go out to work and I am lying behind a wall, all curled up, my eyes red with fever – the death disease of Auschwitz befell me too.

My friend Irke bends over to me and says: "Listen to me, Rokhel I won't leave you behind. We'll go into the gas chamber together because I won't be able to survive everything."

[Page 394]

So I say to Irke: "Listen to me. Go out to work. You are young and healthy, and maybe you'll survive it all. The war won't last much longer. You won't help me with this, if you die together with me."

My pleas and tears made no difference. And dear Irke stayed with me.

## In The Death Block # 25

There were about 200 girls remaining with us in the Block. Suddenly, we heard whistling: All those who stayed were called to an additional *appel*. Not all those who remained behind were sick; many of them were barefoot and naked.

After this extra *appel*, all of us were chased out of the barracks, and like animals we were all herded into Block #25, the "Death Block." An SS man opened a heavy and tall steel gate and locked us in the yard of the Death Block. The yard was surrounded by tall walls.

Nothing bothered me anymore, let things be what they will be. I only desired to lie quietly on the floor or on the plain ground. A terrible panic overcame me as I looked at the barred windows. The Death Block is filled with dead and sick people. It's dark all around, and a suffocating stench fills the whole Block. Dead people are lying here already for more than a week. Those who are still alive are screaming: "Kill us! Don't torture us!" Irke and I were sent to a bunk bed where there were eighteen half dead women.

Those who stayed in Block #25 were not obligated to be at the *appel*, because they were all headed for their death.

Irke is sitting next to me and moaning.

Five days I lay like that almost unconscious, only now and then calling out: "Water, water, Mama..."

[Page 395]

Irke fed me all this time with small pieces of frozen snow.

On the sixth day, I regained consciousness, sat up, and looked around. A terrible moaning came out of me: "Where am I? I am going to my death!"

I felt bad for Irke. I have to save her life at any cost.

Today, an SS doctor is supposed to come to see us. All those on duty were sweeping, cleaning, dragging – they were preparing for something. There's a doctor coming and we're not too happy about that.

"Girls," I say. "We have to ask the doctor that he allow those of us that are healthy to leave this Block."

The girls laugh at me. "She's dreaming while awake – in the time of near death. There's no hope for us. We have to die."

Suddenly, I hear an order being shouted: "Attention!"

In the doorway there appears a tall figure wearing glasses. It's the SS doctor. There's a sadistic smile on his lips, and in his hand there is a truncheon.

I don't know from where I gathered my strength. I quickly jumped down from my bunk, and now I am standing close to the doctor. I quickly began to speak, and scores of girls surrounded us, all of them shouting: "I am healthy! Let us live! Let us out of this Block!" There was a great tumult, one out-shouting the other.

The doctor didn't say a word, remained still with folded arms, then shouted out: "Block commandant! What do they want?"

She explained to him that there are scores of girls in this Block that are healthy and who did not go out to work because they do not have shoes, and in the meantime there had been a selection, and these girls were taken over to Block #25.

The doctor screamed: "So then what do you want?" The girls answered: "We want to live and work!"

The doctor ordered the Block commandant to call this Block to an *appel*. There was great chaos, pushing, running, and crying.

[Page 396]

The *appel* takes place outside in front of the Block. The healthy ones quickly set themselves out in rows. Each is trembling, thinking: "Maybe he won't select me!"

One slight finger gesture determines life or death. Left means death, right means life.

And maybe the opposite? Who can read the thoughts of a murderer. Slowly, the half dead girls get down from their bunk beds. They move like shadows, their eyes dim, their faces yellow and swollen. All of them want to live, each wants to save herself. Only the dead bodies lay still and calm in the yard. For a moment, I envied them.

We are standing in fives. The doctor, followed by the Block commandants, walked past, looked, judged, and selected.

Only ten girls out of the hundreds were deemed well enough to leave the Death Block. Among those who were "lucky," were me and my friend Irke. The rest were quickly and brutally sent back to the Block. I could not turn my face to watch the entire camp of women and their terrible fear. Through the walls, I could hear horrific screams, crying, and quiet death moans.

I don't know how to express my feelings of that moment when the heavy, tall, steel gates of Death Block #25 opened. No one ever came out of that Block alive.

I ran through the death gates with hysterical speed. This was, as they said, the first and only time that ten Jewish girls came out alive from Death Block #25.

**In The Hospital**

An SS man took me and the other nine girls over to the hospital (*reveer*). The hospital looked like any other regular Block, but the roll calls there were short.

There were not many sick people there. Dr. Rose, a French inmate, gave us our beddings and explained the hospital's regulations.

[Page 397]

Tired and confused, I went to lie down. But is it possible to rest here? From the other side of the Block, I hear ringing of hysterical laughter and a cry. One unfortunate is "calling" her children – she has lost her mind – wrings her hands and cries to those who are close by. Suddenly, she spreads out her hands as if she is hugging and stroking someone. Tired, she sits down on her bed and sings a sad lullaby.

The crying stops and it becomes quiet in the Block for a while.

Late at night, loud screams wake me up. I raised up my head and through a small window I see large cargo trucks have driven into Block #25. Under a hail of beatings, the women are chased onto the trucks. The sick and weak ones are tossed aside like sacks, one on top of another. The majority die on the spot.

The trucks drive in the direction of the crematoria – a bit longer and they'll go up in flames.

What a miracle happened to me and Irke. We had saved ourselves. I couldn't believe this myself.

Broken, I moved away from the window and didn't know whether to be happy that death had passed me by. I am scared and have no energy to think of death. I so badly wanted to live.

It's already one week that I am in the hospital. From all sides, one hears: "Dr. Rose, I want to live, help me!"

Dr. Rose, a 45-year-old French woman, with a nice and gentle face, moves around among the cots. She has a nice word for everyone. In the pocket of her white coat she always has useful and good things such as aspirin, drops, and even a candy. She strokes, appeases, and quietly encourages: "Girls, a bit longer, a bit longer. The time is coming closer, strengthen yourselves, a little patience."

Yes, but how is one to survive?

At night, after so many heartfelt and humane words from Dr. Rose the murderers brutally tore the majority of women out of the hospital and send them directly to the crematoria.

*[Page 398]*

Irke and I were saved once again. How to call this? Blind luck or just good fortune? The fact is that once again, death passed me by.

I am confused. My head is spinning. Just a minute ago, one of those who was tortured was sitting next to me telling me about her distant Greece, and was singing sentimental songs. She talked about her mother with reverence, with love; her eyes glistened and she was completely aglow.

On the nearest cot was Janet who dreamed about her three-year-old daughter Paulette, who was left in a village with strangers. Would Paulette recognize her? Would she run towards her and embrace her? Would her "parents" give her back?

Janet talks about her Paris, the Eiffel Tower, and so on. She shows off with her France.

At that moment, when she was dragged down from her cot, she screamed, bit with her teeth, and put up a strong resistance. But it didn't make any difference. The murderers were stronger. She was exhausted, but shouted: "Let me live! I left behind a small, beautiful daughter, my daughter..."

As she was near the door, she turned to us and said: "Say hello to my Paulette ..." In a weakened voice, she muttered the child's address. I couldn't understand her anymore, and she disappeared. And suddenly, everything disappeared and it became quiet. The chaos disappeared along with the lives of scores of young girls.

A deathly silence was all around. I don't have the energy to leave Irke even for one minute. It's dark, the lights are out. Irke gets up and searches for my hand.

"Rokhel, are you sleeping? It's a miracle again, a higher power!"

"A regular occurrence. Do you believe in God? I think there must be a higher power that decides everything."

[Page 399]

"Rokhel, we have to run away from this hospital because there won't be a third miracle at the next selection."

So, we ran away from the hospital.

Two skeletons, two ghosts, helpless against the merest wind, lost themselves among the Blocks in search of shelter.

Irke and I found a new Block and quartered ourselves there. All the girls were afraid for us and asked with astonished eyes: "How did you get back here? No one has ever come out alive from Block #25! We mourned for you, thinking you were among the murdered."

The next morning, I went with everyone else to work to dig ditches.

All of us are sunken in, weak, and we are all cold in these tattered clothes and in the wooden Dutch clogs.

My friends and I put in all our efforts to stay alive.

I acquired the reputation of being a capable worker and won the trust of the German overseers. This allowed me from time to time to organize a little food for survival and to give some to friends close by.

The distance to work was eight kilometers. I did the trek without feeling my feet. From time to time, my friends actually almost carried me, holding me under my arms.

We went to work via the train ramp of Auschwitz. The road to the women's camp in Brzezinki (Birkenau) passes through the railway on the western side of the Auschwitz station. On the left side of the railway we see a big station that is called the "Jewish line," which is designated to carry Jewish transports. Later a special side line was built that went from the main gates of Auschwitz directly to the crematoria.

In the area of Birkenau, there were four active crematoria where in one 24-hour period they gassed 40,000 people and burned 12,000 people in the ovens. The rest of the corpses were burned in nearby forests in bonfires.

[Page 400]

Each gas chamber poisoned 2,000 people in about 20 minutes. In order to trick all those who were brought "for work," they were told that they were going to the showers after a long trip, and so they were given soap and towels.

The gassed corpses were hauled over to three crematoria to be burned by the *Sonnderkommando*[1] that were made up of young, strong, Jewish prisoners.

From time to time, the Germans killed off all the *Sonnderkommandos* in order that the world not become aware of all these murders.

Moishe Margulis, my neighbor from Serock, belonged to this horrific group. He was part of and died in the resistance of the *Sonnderkommandos* at the end of the war in 1944.

Every day, long transports with Jews came from the camps, prisons, and ghettos.

One day, transports with Jews from Belgium and France arrived. All of them were dressed nicely and had many valises, and carried children in their arms.

These Jews were calm and understood that they were brought here for temporary work.

Their first shock was when the Germans separated the families. Children, women, and the elderly were loaded onto trucks and all the men went on foot. This alone did not yet open their eyes to what was waiting for them.

When they passed by close to us, many times we called out to them in different languages: "Jews! You are going to your death like sheep! Put up resistance! Scream, fight, it's already the end! Because in a few hours you won't be alive!"

They didn't believe us and they all died.

One particular transport is etched in my mind. The boys of the *Sonnderkommando* told us the following facts with an extraordinary passion: In the transport of the day before, there was an energetic Jewish woman who understood as soon as they arrived in the station that they would all be taken to their deaths. In an unexpected manner, when the SS man turned around, she deftly and quickly grabbed his gun out of his pocket and shot him on the spot. That SS man was a well-known gangster and sadist. To avenge what she had done, the Germans immediately shot everyone right then and there. After that incident, the Germans increased the security over the future transports.

[Page 401]

**The Large, General Selection by Dr. Mengele and His Bandits**

Autumn 1942. Our camp is packed with women. Fresh transports come every day, there are 20 women sleeping on each bunk bed. Typhus is raging, and all the infirmaries are full.

One sunny day, our camp was overtaken by an exceptional fear. We found out that in this camp are the greatest murderers: Camp Commanders Kremer, Uberke, Mandel; the SS man Mahl, Dr. Mengele, Rudolph Hoess, and there was also a strict guard all around.

SS men and overseers with huge, wild dogs stood by each barrack.

"What will be?" one asks the other. Suddenly we hear the whistle for an *appel*. This was a roll call in the middle of a bright day; that was always an omen of terrible things.

Many sick and weakened women are hiding in every hole – under the covers, in the bathrooms, in canals – but the dogs, both human and animal, find them all. They beat them murderously, blood is flowing, and the dogs rip the last shreds of filthy clothing off their bodies.

Also the patients in the hospitals were ordered to come to the *appel*. Hundreds of women are standing and waiting: Commandant Kremer, Hoess, Uberke, Mandel, Dexler, Tauber, Mahl, and more, all according to their rank. Dr. Mengele and his assistants – in the second row.

[Page 402]

And once again, chaos. Pushing and violence. What's going on? Now we know for sure: Soon there will be a general selection. Everyone will go between the two lines and they will "check" each person.

Every person, very tense, is standing at the *appel*.

The march begins. Single file, with hands stretched out in front, each woman walks down the pathway between the sadists. The murderers look on, and Dr. Mengele indicates with his finger to the right or to the left. To the right means that the girl will go to Block #25 (death), to the left means that she will go behind the fence of the hospital (life).

I know what is waiting for us. Everyone wants to be the last one, and goes to stand at the end of the line. Everyone is afraid, I am afraid of the hell. Everyone is smoothing down her hair and is washing her dry lips, eyes, and face with saliva. I have a tiny mirror, and it goes from one hand to another – everyone wants to see herself.

And the march goes on.

I say to my friend Irke: "Now we can say goodbye to each other forever. Look at my feet. On one foot there is a shoe, on the other is a rag." Irke doesn't answer. I rub my cheeks to look better.

Will I pass this time? Will I be lucky again this time? In such a short time, I have wrestled with death three times.

Will I outlive the others?

There's no time to think – my turn is coming closer...

Just a bit more and I stand in front of the court of law: death or life!

My heart is racing, my legs shake from weakness. But I strengthen myself, and in a voice under my breath, I say: "Life! You must live!"

"Life! Life!" the voice rings in my ears, and a final kiss to Irke. I get closer and I am between the lines of the gangsters. I smile. My face is shining with fear. Life or death, life or death – I am going around in circles as if in a carousel.

Dr. Mengele's finger indicates for me to go left...

I go, I waver. I go behind the fence of the hospital. My friends fall on me with warm kisses. They are so happy. "You are saved!"

[Page 403]

I stand near the wire fence and look towards Irke. I wonder what will be her fate.

And... Irke also passes through! She approaches me and says in astonishment: "Did this happen again by chance?"

Those girls that were sentenced to death by Mengele try to run away from the walled-in area of Block #25. They climb up the walls, call out, cry, beg for help – but no one can do anything. The SS men are beating murderously, and their hands are ripping off clothing along with pieces of flesh.

The infamous general selection – the Germans called it the "general cleaning" – lasted for several hours.

From the large women's camp in Birkenau there was only a little group of young girls left, and I was among them.

The selection was over – the SS men left the camp.

A small group of saved girls is standing and trembling, no one has the energy to say anything. I am alive, but is my life certain?

At the gate of Block #25 there is a long row of trucks. German soldiers open the heavy, steel gate, and angrily they push themselves inside. With whips and truncheons they beat the remaining, terrified women. They are loading up one truck after another. From a distance, we hear the screams: Take revenge for us and for our deaths! Maybe you'll survive! Revenge!"

The last truck disappeared onto yet another page of the history of Auschwitz.

The crematoria are burning – flames of people's former lives are rushing through the chimneys.

All night after this selection, a group of girls was standing – and I among them – one pushed close to the other. What was I thinking then?

Yes, I looked into the eyes of the tormented, beaten up girls, and in that minute of human contact, a spark of hope awoke in me.

With the appearance of our brokenness, with the appearance of our encased dead bodies, we promised that if we would remain alive, we would tell everything.

[Page 404]

And on that night, we trembled and screamed to the whole world: "Where are you?"

And we trembled even more when we thought that Hitler had conquered and ruled the entire world, and Auschwitzes and Birkenaus were being built everywhere.

We tossed away those thoughts and said to ourselves: "No! No! That's not possible!"

And if Hitler does not rule over the entire world, then why are you all so quiet?

How can you sleep peacefully, eat, and play with your children at a time when it is hell here?

And what if only evil people will remain alive?

## The Final Attack of Our Camp

In the middle of the night of January 18, 1945, the Germans began their final attack of my camp – the women's camp in Birkenau (Auschwitz).

The lights were turned out, there was confusion among the inmates. Everyone is whispering. One tells the other that the front is coming closer to us, and in these last minutes they want to kill us.

In my knapsack there is a piece of bread and a cat. We are worried, and wait for further orders.

And what will be next? What will happen to us? Where will they take us?

The sick and frail remained in their confusion and pain. They stretch their dried out hands to us and beg for help and salvation. We could do nothing for them – we had to go.

There are long rows, they are counting us. They are beating and kicking us.

My friends and I are crying and moaning. Finally, we wipe our tears, one comforts the other.

I march, we march in the darkness of the night a cold night, and walk through the accursed gate of Auschwitz.

[Page 405]

We have left Auschwitz. Is that possible?

The morning star is shining. I turn around and see at a distance the piercing wires of the cursed camp.

I and the complete mass of people move away from there and the entire abyss of the last few years stands alive in front of me, with all its details.

We march on foot, far away from Auschwitz.

Where to?

**Translated and edited from the Polish [into Yiddish] by Khanokh Werdi**

**Translator's Footnote**

1. "Special commando" was a euphemism for the prisoner-laborers forced to do jobs like stoking the crematoria, shaving newcomers' hair, processing seized belongings, helping unload trains, removing corpses from gas chambers, etc. Such laborers were told they could live in exchange for their hard effort, but there were regularly killed off and replaced.

*[Page 406]*

# Wartime Experiences
### By Laya Kamelgorn-Blumberg (Kiryat Ono)
### Translated by Pamela Russ

In May 1939, I and my entire family left to go to Ciekhocinek to our summer house. My father had orchards from the landowner Trojanowski in that place. Our partner was Yosef Sterdiner (now living in Israel). When the war broke out, we were still in Aleksandrow Kujawski. Not far from the train line, about 500 meters from our house, the first bomb fell. The train traffic was immediately disrupted and we were separated from all other parts of Poland. After the outbreak of the war my father said to us that he wanted to be buried near his own father – and not here. We decided to go back to Serock. We packed everything onto two bicycles and left to Brisk Kujawski.

It's worth noting that the landowner Trojanowksi, who hid the fruit in the cellars, told us: "Don't go to your deaths – if you have to go, then go east." We spent the night in a village in Brisk Kujawski.

The following morning, we were on the way again, when suddenly we were attacked by Germans on motorcycles with guns aimed at us. My father became frightened, the bicycle was dropped to the side, and he fell faint on the ground. A German told us that we shouldn't be afraid but that we should go back. We actually did go back 60 kilometers, to the landowner. He gave us two rooms and brought us food. We stayed there for seven weeks. After that we rented a wagon and began our journey to Serock.

We travelled until Kutno and waited there for one week for a train to Warsaw, and after that finally arrived to Warsaw. In Warsaw we rented a wagon and went to Serock. At each security stop, we had to show our travel papers and then we were searched.

[Page 407]

We arrived in Serock at dawn at the beginning of November 1939, and our house was locked up. We stayed with Hershel Borenshteyn (Sumtak) on Kosciuszko Street 20, together with Moishe Fogelman. There were no young people in the city.

My brother Nakhman ran away to Ostrow-Mazowiecki and from there we received a letter from him saying that he had been saved by an old non-Jewish man on the day that the terrible slaughter occurred. From Ostrow he went back to Serock until he came to the other side of the Narew. The Germans did not allow him to enter, but after my mother's plea, that with luck was heard by an older guard, they let him back in. My parents and my family did not want to leave Serock under any circumstances. My mother scolded us and pleaded with us children to leave the German hell as soon as possible.

In total, we stayed in Serock for two or three weeks. Shmayohu Zeidman, a friend from Wielisowo, who was blond and looked like blond Aryan and circulated freely from one border to another, guaranteed to get us across the Russian border.

At the end of November 1939, we – I, my brother Nakhman, and the blond one, left in a wagon to Zegzhe, and the next day we went by train to Ponjatow (before Warsaw). From Ponjatow we went through fields until the Vilna station in Praga. My young brother Benjek stayed with our parents in Serock.

We arrived in Malkin in the evening. There were thousands of people there, and we heard screaming and shooting. From Malkin, I went alone following the instructions of my overseer, then following the train line for a half a kilometer, and then turning left where the top of a church marked the road to the Russian zone.

The Germans detained me several times, and at those times my blood ran cold.

I moved forward with great momentum and arrived late at night to Zaremba Koscielnie on Russian ground. All the trains were overly filled and it took three days until I arrived in Bialystok.

[Page 408]

In Bialystok I again met up with my brother Nakhman who had gotten lost on the road. I could hardly recognize him. When he arrived in Malkin, the Germans caught him and beat him mercilessly. After that, he managed to disappear amidst the masses of people that were found around and in the station. Bialystok was crowded everywhere. There I also met Khaim Eliezer Gzhebieniazh and from him I found out about the evacuation in Nazielsk and in Biale-Podliask.

In Bialystok I lived with an uncle. Then I left with my husband to Brisk. And after two months we went back to Bialystok. That night there was an investigation and all those who had not taken on Russian citizenship were put in a freight wagon and they travelled for about eight days in terrible conditions.

In July 1940, we arrived in Orkhangelsk. In the middle of a huge forest there was an open space with three barracks. We then went by train 100 kilometers to the "camp." The women went by truck and the men walked for 100 kilometers through the forest where there were white bears. That was during the time of the White Nights.

We stayed in that camp for 14 months, until September 1941. The climate was cold, about 60 degrees. The men worked in the forest chopping wood, and the women directed the logs to the water. That was the normal job. We received a little bit of soup from the kitchen. All day, we existed from a bit of bread, 400 grams a day, and a woman that had a child also received some sugar. People simply starved and suffered from dizziness and loss of teeth.

At that time, I bore a child in the hospital, but the child got the measles. In Ulianowsk they told me very forcefully to take the child to the hospital. I carried the child through the winds, and as I arrived in the hospital, the sweet little girl died in my arms, and my anguish was tremendous. My husband came to me with great difficulty. I was very upset.

[Page 409]

In November 1941, I decided to go to Tashkent to the warmer areas.

We went by train from Ulianowsk, and at night we were attacked by bandits and thieves. I became ill on the train. On the way, when we stopped to transfer, we stayed over in a *kolkhoz* (collective farm) in Bukhara, where our acquaintances from Praga were also staying. After great difficulties, I went into a hospital and was there for two weeks. When I got better, I left to the *kolkhoz*. There were two groups of Polish Jews there. We worked hard and got a half a kilogram of dried plums and some flour. Those women who were weak or who had received notices from their doctors received an extra half kilo of bread. My husband was also very sick and after that he also left to go work in a *kolkhoz*.

I learned to speak Uzbek and worked in a children's institution. I took care of the children and then took them to their mothers in the fields. We remained in the *kolkhoz* for one year.

Later they sent us to a lime factory in Kagan, and we lived near an Uzbek cemetery. The end of 1942 was the most difficult time, a time of real hunger. If I didn't work, I received no food. Those who did hard labor received 600 grams of bread a day.

We stayed in Kagan until the end of the war. In April 1945, I gave birth to a boy in the hospital.

My neighbor Khaim Gudes was at the *bris*. When I was in Orkhangelsk, I wrote a letter to the Rav of Biale-Podliask to see if he could find my parents – I received a very sad reply.

Until the end of the war, I didn't know about the enormity of the destruction of the Polish Jews.

In April 1945, I found out from Khaim Gudes about all of this, and that all our close ones were no longer alive.

At the end of April 1946, we left Poland, and we travelled for a few weeks until we arrived to Szeczyn. I stayed there for three weeks and had a nice home. There I met Pesakh Pienik and Shloime Paskowycz. My husband went to Praga and lived there with a cousin. We remained in Poland for a few months and later went to Austria and there we found my brother Nakhman. We were there – in Ebensee – for 14 months. With us were Yehuda Menzelewski, Yakov Menzelewski, and their families, and the daughter of Yakov Stelang (now in America). I left Austria for Germany. There I found my family and the Fogelman brothers, and I gave birth to my second son (1948) in Aswega, Kassel.

[Page 410]

In January 1949, we arrived in Israel.

[Page 411]

## Yekhiel Rosenberg, may his blood be avenged
**By Shlomo Sterdyner**
**Translated by Pamela Russ**

Yekhiel Rosenberg, a Jewish merchant, owned a large store of wood and was recognized in all the Jewish institutions. He was also president of the Jewish communities in Nowydwor and Legionowa. When the Germans invaded Legionowa, they forced Yekhiel Rosenberg to be the representative of the Jews in Legionowa, and that's when his tragic fate began.

Every day, he had to bring a few hundred workers to do all kinds of work in the barracks where the German military and railroad workers were stationed. But he still did very much to help the Jewish forced laborers: He risked his own life and won over the German officer, making it a bit easier for the Jews. Each day, about 250 Jews were forced to go to work. When the officer returned the Jews, Yekhiel Rosenberg was waiting for them and asked each one how their day had passed – when he heard that it was very difficult, he immediately began thinking of ways to make things easier.

That's how ghetto life went. There was fresh news every day. Once, there was an order to bring forward a certain number of healthy Jews to send them out to the camp. Other cities complied, but Yekhiel Rosenberg listened and did not let one Jew leave the ghetto.

In the ghetto, there was talk that from certain cities they were starving the Jews to death in the Panikhow forts where cholera had broken out. The Germans, afraid for themselves, began to chase the swollen and broken Jews across the border of the German Reich into the province (that was three kilometers from our ghetto). On the way, and at the border, many Jews died. Then the order came to burn all those who had died. The rest of the Jews came to us in the ghetto half dead, and from them about half died during the day. Yekhiel Rosenberg went to the mayor, and got out of him a little bit of food and organized to cook something for these people. Because there was no room by us, he convinced the mayor to transfer these Jews to the Warsaw ghetto. He connected to the Jewish community in Warsaw who sent representatives to help bring these Jews over.

*[Page 412]*

During this time, and wanting to help, Yekhiel Rosenberg wrote a plea to the governor of Krakow. Because of that, Rosenberg was summoned to the Polish police commandant. SS men were already waiting for him there. He was locked in a cellar and then he was beaten until he was unconscious. When the Polish commandant went down to the cellar and revived him somewhat, a non-Jewish acquaintance brought him back to the ghetto. I was Yekhiel's neighbor. Soon, Dr. Finkelshtayn came, our ghetto doctor, and he sat with him for a few days.

Every day there were new orders, and Yekhiel again began his activities, and with an even greater fear, had to follow very carefully each order from the Germans. Later, because of one denunciation, one Jew was sentenced to death, and Yekhiel, with all kinds of objects from his house, saved this Jew from the hands of the murderers. Very often, Yekhiel risked his life to save the lives of Jews in the ghetto.

When they liquidated the ghetto, they took the people by horse and wagon to Radzymin. At the *Aktzia* ("action" of gathering and murdering the Jews), they selected 13 men to bury those who had been shot. Yekhiel Rosenberg was among these men who helped bury the others. Other Jews remained to clean up the ghetto from all the victims. That's how we worked for two days in the Legionowa ghetto. On the third day, we were taken to Warsaw to Zhelasna Street, to a place the Jews called "the slaughter house." From there, under the watch of SS men, we were taken to the ghetto prison where the Jewish police took over charge of us. All 13 of us were in one room. The Jewish police commissioner came to visit the ghetto prison and told us that he would help get us out and to work in the Warsaw ghetto.

The following morning, a certain Jew (Vogel) came with an SS officer and took everyone to 16 Nizke Street. The next day an SS man led us to a large group and all of us together went out to work. They took us to Fransciscan (Franciszkańska) Street, where there were large platforms. We were ordered to clean houses and stores of all types of goods. All of us were taken to different kinds of storehouses: separate for furniture, separate for[1] clothing, separate for machines, and so on.

[Page 413]

Again, Yekhiel was our representative, and around us there were groups of Jews from Legionowa (from the ghetto and of those who had run away). There was now a larger family.

It was this last day when the flames of the real fire began. The final *Aktzia* was beginning. There was shooting on all sides. Some of the Jews resisted. On the *Umschlagsplatz* (gathering point where Jews were assembled then put on death trains), they did a selection again – to the left, to the right... and then we were separated. Part of our group was taken to Treblinka, and some became workers at the train station.

Within a few months, they had taken the entire transport to Treblinka. In this transport, there were many people from our town. Then, again we succeeded to take some of the Jews out to work: Yekhiel Rosenberg and his son Moishe, Yosef Fishman and his 12-year-old son, Avrohom Kronenberg, and Leibish Bzhansi. This last one died of dysentery. His final words were: "Take revenge for our blood!"

[Page 414]

Yekhiel Rosenberg, who had the misfortune of being in a group of unqualified workers, later died along with them.

**Shloime Sterdiner**
**Ramat Gan**

**Translator's Footnote**

1. The Yiddish word "" as it appears here may have a typographical error and may actually be "*vesh*," translated as "clothing.".

[Page 417]

# Serock After The Holocaust

[Page 417 - Hebrew] [Page 449 - Yiddish]

## I Am Looking for My Brothers and Sisters
### by Khanokh Werdi
### Translated by Pamela Russ

In the summer months of the year 1945, after the downfall of Hitler's Germany, I joined up with the Jewish Brigade in northern Italy, in the town of Treviso, on the Italian-Austrian-Yugoslavian border.

Every opportunity and every moment was used to search for surviving Jews in all parts of Europe that were under Hitler's occupation.

The Brigade was converted into a "magic-watch" and into a hopeful place for the refugees - and they began streaming there in masses, from all places.

In Treviso, the Brigade established a large and well organized house of immigrants that served as the first resting place for all the new arrivals and as a bridge to Israel for those who were saved from the European death toll.

In this "cemetery," many moving events took place: men found their wives, and parents found their children. The Brigade's soldiers, occupying themselves with the new arrivals, recognized their friends from home and from school - heartfelt embraces and hot tears flowed freely.

After a few days of rest, the "rested ones" were taken to various points in northern, central, and southern Italy, and several times I called out through the loudspeaker: "All those from Serock and from the surrounding places are asked to present themselves to me right away!"

A young girl came towards me with sure steps, and I recognized her immediately - Golde Belinson.

[Page 450]

The joy and excitement was great. I was now conversing with the first survivor of my town! Golde told me briefly of the destruction of our community, about relatives, friends, and acquaintances, and about her life for a few years as a Christian in a village with a fine Polish family. We exchanged information and addresses.

Golde left soon afterward for southern Italy on her way to Israel, and I planned my travels on the dirt roads of the refugees. That means that I decided to gather together all the survivors from my town and take them all to Poland.

Winter of 1946: I went to Poland via Belgium, Germany, and Czechoslovakia. My first stop in Poland was in the county-town of Katowice, where I arrived on a dark, frosty night by express train from Prague.

I settled in the large hotel, the Monopol, near the train station that was reserved only for officers. My arrival to this hotel at this hour was such a phenomenon that it evoked a great interest among Polish and Russian officers who were seated at the hotel bar.

The hotel manager spoke to me in English and when he took me to show me to my room, I felt as if someone else was escorting me with an interesting look

The very next morning, the hotel manager presented himself to my room and requested, in a soft and fine voice, that I not leave the hotel because I had been invited to the Katowice Central Police Inspector's, and in about a half hour, a special messenger policeman would escort me to the Inspector's main quarters.

I felt that the invitation did not bode well for me at all, and thought carefully about how to react.

*[Page 451]*

At that moment, my escort appeared, in a beautiful private car, and I was asked very politely to accompany him.

The Central Police Inspector welcomed me very politely - he spoke to me in English - and offered me a delicious *schnapps*. After we became comfortable with one another, he asked me what sort of activities I was undertaking in Poland.

And here, my reply caused unexpected excitement: I responded quietly and calmly in Polish that I was Jewish, born in Poland, and that I had sworn after the war's destruction that I would find my parents, relatives, and friends. In the end, I asked him to give me the maximum help that he could.

The Inspector became very excited, and when he began speaking in Polish, I recognized from his speech that he was a Russian in a Polish uniform.

Our conversation, in which I was asked hundreds of questions with a worldly scope, lasted a few hours and ended when I mentioned a few familiar names, members of the Central Committee of Polish Jews, who could confirm my identity and my beliefs.

After this lengthy conversation, I was invited to lunch in the officer's club.

Before I left back to my hotel, the Inspector "begged" me not to leave the city of Katowice until after our second meeting three days later.

We said goodbye warmly.

Of course, I fulfilled his request, and I did not leave the city.

During these days, I allowed myself to walk around the city streets for a little while, and visited the Jewish Committee on Marjocka Street 21.

[Page 452]

There I met surviving Jews and listened to their statements. I began to absorb some of the atmosphere of the Jewish Polish valley of death. For hours I leafed through the lists of survivors - maybe I would come across a familiar name.

From my conversations with the survivors, I discovered that there were Jews in the *Hachshara Kibbutzim* (training farms) in the nearby surrounding areas such as Bitom, Sosnowice, Bendin, and so on.

They were spying on me, my steps were being watched, and I returned to the hotel as the sun was setting.

After three days, I met with the Inspector of the Katowice Central Police for the second time. This time he was not alone - near him was seated a high ranking Chief Officer who had a Semitic appearance and who spoke a first-class Polish.

In the beginning, both were asking me about the life of the Jews in the refugee camps in Germany and Austria, and in the end there was a discussion between us about global political problems and the general objectives of the super powers after World War II.

This time, I had lunch with them in the officer's club and when we returned to the office, the high-ranking Chief Officer said: "I and my friend the Inspector ask for your forgiveness in detaining you in our city. We agreed that your information was accurate and so decided to help you with your difficult task."

I noticed a tear in his eye when he uttered these words.

Before we parted, he gave me a printed letter of recommendation in Polish and Russian in which all military and police official powers were asked to help me with all their facilities.

This document enabled me to move around freely with or without a uniform in many areas of Poland.

I shook their hands warmly, and immediately went into the nearby areas.

## Bitom

In the *Hachshara Kibbutzim* of *Hashomer Hatzair* and *Ha'oved* on Grinwalska Street 6, I met many friends and spent time with them until late into the night. I listened to their stories about the camps, the forests, the pain, the wanderings, and the partisans' struggles. Then I answered their questions about the war of immigrating to Israel and the *Haganah* (the underground paramilitary group in Israel), about our strengths and their future.

[Page 453]

In the orphan house of "Dror" on Wilszika Street 43, I found out for the first time about some others from Serock who were in the region of Krakow.

I spent time with the children, taught them Hebrew songs and games, and told them stories about life in Israel.

Their eyes were shining. I became attached to them, and they to me. They stroked my uniform with such love.

Our fates became intertwined - we sang quietly together, and when they fell sweetly asleep, I went into a corner, and my lips uttered: "These are lambs. What sins have they committed?"

I left for Krakow, and my first stop led me to the Jewish Committee, Dluga Street 33. The courts were alive with refugees from the area. I was quickly surrounded, and hundreds of hands were stretched out to me. "*Sholom Aleikhem*, Brigadier!" I clutched the martyrs' hands to my heart and their eyes told all their secrets. There was a tumult, an excitement. All were asking about their relatives, about the Brigade, and about Israel. Everyone is remembering addresses, dates, places, events - and I am drowning in an ocean of pain.

The excitement subsided, and everyone sat down on the ground on a cobblestone, and I spoke words of hope and comfort.

The sun set. Some asked the gnawing, deep question: Why did help come so late? Why were we so isolated?

The street lights were lit. Everyone got up. I held private discussions.

[Page 454]

I took down addresses and wrote descriptions of events in my notebook, discussing and counseling about issues of the future.

That evening I found out that two women of Serock, Gitele and Soro Izkowicz, were alive and living in Jelena Gora, Lower Silesia.

I left right away to Bitom, and from there sent a special trusted messenger to Jelena Gora to confirm that these two sisters were really living there, and if so, to set up times to meet with them.

The information turned out to be correct, and with agreed conditions, I set out by train from Krakow towards Jelena Gora.

I sat at the window, nervous, thinking about the upcoming meeting with the two sisters, and suddenly - the train stopped in the middle of the way at a small green forest.

I didn't understand what was happening. I looked out and saw that we were surrounded by Polish soldiers.

The door opened. An officer came into the car, and he called out in a clear voice: "All Jews and Communists get off the train!"

A shiver went through me. I understood that these soldiers belonged to the "*Armia Krajowa*" ("Home Army"), an illegal reactionary, anti-Semitic, military organization that warred against the new Communist regime in Poland, and who, after the liberation, had already murdered hundreds of Jews that were fortunate enough to survive the Nazi hell.

[Page 455]

No one moved from his place.

After a few minutes, the officer stood near me, saluted, and asked me quietly in Polish to go outside with him and identify myself.

My eyes stared at him, and then when he pretended to think that I didn't understand any Polish, he repeated his polite request in French, and finally in a fine English.

I answered him in English that I was a representative of UNRRA and that in Jelena Gora there were representatives from the Polish government and from the British embassy waiting for me so that I could officially give over a large transport of condensed milk to the Polish children.

[Page 456]

The officer went out to his friends and told them what I had responded. This evoked a great discussion among them.

The officer returned to the car and categorically told me to go with him "because they want to hear this explanation directly from your mouth."

Not really having a choice, I went out of the car with him. The soldiers immediately surrounded me and measured me up from all sides. I repeated the aforementioned response to the officer that now took on the role of interpreter.

Khanokh Werdi (Warsawski) near a bunker in the Warsaw ghetto, where his father, Reb Dovid Warsawski, the ghetto-fighter, and his mother Freidel, both died. May their blood be avenged

The band of people began to shout: "He looks like a Jew. We have to finish with him!" And so on.

I mustered all my physical and mental energies in order to appear quiet and calm, and from afar they were discussing me. Who knows, maybe these were to be the final few minutes of my life.

Before my eyes, all of the events of my life were passing by. Was this the last event?

Quickly I chased away these terrible thoughts. I lifted my head and looked around with open eyes - slowly smoking my English pipe.

They completed their discussion and the officer asked that I show him my documents.

I reasoned - that the above demand is not appropriate to the conventional international behaviors and requests of high-ranking military people that are in foreign countries, and that in England everyone had the greatest respect for the Polish soldiers, and in exceptional cases, such a military person can get his information only in a military or civilian police station - but under no circumstance can he get his information in the middle of a road. But all these thoughts were of no help to me.

After a calm back-and-forth, I gave the officer my UNRRA document.

He quickly assembled the entire band of men, and declared that they were not permitted to detain me because this issue was tied to international organizations with which they wanted to maintain good relations.

[Page 457]

I thought the issue was closed, but suddenly one rogue stood up, and speaking in a good English, demanded that he, along with the officer, should also examine my British military documents.

When I heard this, a shudder went through me: In that document it was indicated that I was of the Jewish faith.

And so, both were standing near me. The officer asked me again to show him my British military documents. I began to discuss this with him, but when I realized that I would not be able to change anything, I put forth the requested documents and both of them examined the papers.

The officer was ready to return the documents to me, but then the second one began to shout: "He's a Jew! He's a liar! We have to finish him off!" And with that he looked with disgust directly into my eyes to see how his yells affected me.

I continued smoking my English pipe, but what was going on inside of me, only I alone knew - and still feel until today.

Once again, I was surrounded by these bandits. I answered the officer's additional questions saying that I was a Jew, born in Israel, a British citizen that had been serving in the army for many years, and that I was recently sent out for UNRRA to carry out humanitarian missions for the benefit of the hungry Polish children.

After these explanations, new discussions took place among the bandits. Some of them were pointing their guns in my direction, others were calling me offensive names, and so on.

I took out my watch: This party had already taken over an hour, which to me seemed like an eternity. The Polaks that had remained in the cars were looking out of the windows and laughing.

I was leaning on a tree, filling my pipe with tobacco, and spread around a wonderful aroma and calmness. A few steps away, I was being judged for life or death.

*[Page 458]*

One of the bandits put his verdict out openly and stuck out his tongue to me. Everyone was laughing and shouting: "Hang him!"

The officer was screaming and swore to them that he would not fulfill their wishes, not because he had pity on me but because hanging me would be an act against the British and against international organizations. Everyone became quiet and after rethinking the issue, they bought into the officer's explanation.

After a few minutes, the officer approached me, returned both documents, excused himself, and explained that in times of war many unfortunate situations happen.

He asked me to forget this "painful" occurrence and not to tell the government in Jelena Gora about this. He squeezed my hands, saluted, and escorted me into the car.

The Polish passengers looked at me with admiring eyes and I sat down in my previous place.

Night fell, I looked out, and the train began to move.

At the Jelena Gora station, the sisters Soro and Gitel Itzkowicz were waiting for me impatiently. We recognized each other immediately.

A profound experience, tears, and silence.

They seated me in a private car, and we arrived to their house.

Twelve years earlier, I left them as young girls and now before me sat grown people, filled with life's pain and wisdom. I was in their house for two complete days. They quietly and calmly told me of their life story from the beginning of the war until the last days. Not having any other choice, they lived as Christians in all kinds of places in Poland, and were supported by two kind Polaks.

*[Page 459]*

For hours we sat and remembered people from our town and their painful journeys until their end.

Sorole and Gitele spoke - each word a flame, each word an accusation.

We talked about their future plans, and I asked that they not forget their people.

Soro and Gitele were tired of their suffering, wanderings, and fear. I also spoke about the problems with the Polaks where they had been, and they assured me that each decision Soro and Gitel would make separately, they would agree to follow through together.

We set up a second meeting and I left Jelena Gora.

I went quickly back to Krakow because in the last few days, in the process of repatriation, the first transport of Polish Jews arrived there from Russia, and among them was a group from the Warsaw area.

The courtyard of the Jewish Committee was filled with the newly-arrived. I spoke to many of them, listening to all their stories. I scanned the lists of the repatriated but unfortunately did not find even one acquaintance.

For the next few days, I visited the temporary homes of the newly-arrived, and a Jew from Wyszkow told me that according to his information, there were a few Jews from Serock in Czestokhowa in the area of Bendin. That same person gave me the relevant addresses.

I left immediately to Czestokhowa with rented transportation and came to the designated address - the *Hakhshara Kibbutz* of Dror that was located in the region of the Jewish ghetto that had been completely destroyed during the time of the final resistance against the German murderers.

The *kibbutz* supervisor, after hearing my presentation, delivered me into the hands of his friend who was my guide during that entire visit.

I visited all the surviving Jews in their residences (from a large community that numbered in the tens of thousands, there remained only a few hundred souls) asked around for acquaintances, checked addresses, and still found no one.

*[Page 460]*

Here too, as happened before, I participated in an open meeting of all surviving Jews in the large hall of the *kibbutz*, spoke about Jewish strength, about the Haganah, the Jewish Brigade, and also showed them potential direction for their future. There evolved a long side-tracked dialogue and we parted with the first morning-star.

I decided to search through the entire area of Zaglembie Dombrowskie (the area of Bendin).

I went to Sosnowicz and my first visit was to the Jewish Committee, Modzhejewska Street 5. There I went through the additional lists of the survivors, asked for information from the Serock Committee, and then went into the courtyard to meet the survivors and talk to them. In the middle of these talks, someone placed his hand on my shoulder, and as I turned my head I saw that near me stood Reb Yakov Kaluski, my neighbor, the son-in-law of Reb Yehuda Pjienek, may his blood be avenged. We kissed and embraced. I don't know how long we remained in that position.

He took me to his room, and right away his son and my friend Pinkhas appeared, along with Pinkhas' daughter Laya and her *khatan* (groom) Reb Yakov Leyb Manelo. There was great joy.

I spent a few days with them. Each one of us told of our life's experiences in the first few days of the war right through to the community's destruction, our wanderings in Soviet Russia, the repatriation, and everything else up until these final moments. Yakov was teaching *Torah* to the surviving children and Pinkhas was still serving in the Polish army.

I tried to comfort them with hopes for a better tomorrow.

We planned all kinds of things and set a time for a second meeting. While we were saying our good-byes, Yakov told me that in one of the local *kibbutzim*, there were some Jews from Serock. Finally, we took a photo of all of us.

*[Page 461]*

After a few hours of intensive searching, I found the following people from Serock in the *kibbutz* of the leftist *Poalei Zedek* organization on Targowa Street: Khayale Zakharek (Wolinski), her daughter Laya and her *khasan* (groom) Moishe Zilbershtayn.

Here too the joy was mixed with bitter memories and a deep excitement.

Khayale, the daughter of Reb Yitzkhok Wolinski, may his blood be avenged, in a contained voice, told over of the destruction of the many branches of her family and of the death of her husband Moishe Leyb Zakharek, may his blood be avenged, who simply died of hunger in Russia when there was no help for him. She told of the superhuman challenges of feeding and raising her young daughter Laya in the horrific conditions of the never-ending wanderings. She remained silent about her own sufferings. I comforted her.

I left after some time in that region and visited Catholic churches and private Christian families with the goal of finding and saving Jewish children and returning them into the lap of their own people.

After completing all that, I left for Zebzhedowice, a border town between Poland and Czechoslovakia, and one that served as crossing point from Poland to the refugee camps in Germany and Austria, in order to find traces of other Jewish survivors from Serock.

Here, in this town, there was activity as in a beehive. I collected information, put rumor to rumor, and was convinced that I was to find more Serock Jews in the new assembly points - established in the time of the repatriation: Lodz, Warsaw, and Wroclow.

On Passover of 1946, I celebrated the first *seder* in Krakow in one of the *Hakhshara Kibbutzim*, not far from the historical place Wawel, and the second *seder* was in Katowice with surviving Jews from other European places.

[Page 462]

# May 1946

I go from Katowice with the express train to Warsaw. It's a long, strenuous trip. In the cars it is very cramped and damp. Even though this train is an express train, it stops at every station and masses of passengers loaded up with large baskets filled with food, shove their way into the cars with original Polish curses.

One sees clearly that masses of people are smuggling illegally, a consequence of a poor economic system.

In the cars, Polish children are singing about the greatness of Warsaw and the heroism of the Polaks during the German occupation.

The passengers converse loudly with each other, and when they touch on a Jewish topic, one sees and feels how their understanding becomes dulled - the atmosphere becomes filled with hatred and poison.

Night falls. We are approaching Warsaw - formerly the largest Jewish community in Europe.

My heart is pounding. Through the windows you can see mountains of destruction. While they were checking the train tickets, a pushing and shouting began. People are running from one car to another and the ticketers are whistling and arguing. My car was emptied. Two military men approached me, asked for my documents and when I showed them the letter of recommendation from the Katowice local Inspector, they saluted, begged pardon, and left.

Ten o'clock in the evening. I stepped on Warsaw ground after a lapse of twelve years. The area of the train station was desolate. There is a silence outside, a darkness.

I straightened out my uniform, checked my weapons, and went forward cautiously until I arrived at Poznjanska Street 38, where the *Hachshara Kibbutz* of the *Shomer Hatzair* was located.

[Page 463]

I knocked at the door. Silence. After a minute, the door slowly opened. I imagined that I would be welcomed with joy.

Young men and women appeared, survivors of partisan groups, death camps, and repatriates from Russia. After a cup of tea, we got into a deep discussion until late into the night.

Just before going to sleep, we heard a loud knocking at the door, and there stood several Polish soldiers, and among them, a tall officer.

At first sight, I began to tremble and patted my gun, but soon I calmed down and became very excited: The tall officer was my former counsellor in *Hashomer Hatzair*, Pinkhas Stern (today in Israel) from Jablona.

We greeted each other warmly and then silence. Afterwards, he described to me his journey of pain up until these last minutes and then asked me to describe the Jewish military power in Israel. Everybody woke up, jumped down from their cots, sat down on the bare floor - a tight camp of friends.

I felt and sensed that my descriptions about the physical Jewish powers in Israel were healing their wounds and strengthening their desire for a new, free life.

Pinkhas told me that in these last few days a transport had arrived to Praga-Warsaw from Russia - during the story of the repatriation - and in this transport of Polish Jews were a few people from Serock who were being quartered by the Jewish Committee in different places in Warsaw and the surrounding areas.

I didn't close my eyes all night. The following day, early in the morning, I left the *kibbutz* and went in the direction of Praga.

The whole region was one mountain of destruction.

[Page 464]

The bridges across the Vistula were ripped up and one could only cross with a long, narrow, military pontoon.

At 10 AM I arrived in Praga and went directly to the Jewish Committee, Targowa Street 44.

Hundreds of Jews, some in uniform and some not, old, young, pale and frightened, are besieging the Committee and the surrounding areas.

I went directly into the information room, spent a few hours searching through the lists of survivors, of those who had returned, and the orphanages, but did not find any names from Serock.

I was sad and embittered, I tore myself away from the lists and went down to the court.

News that a soldier from the Jewish Brigade was there spread quickly among the Jews, and soon I was surrounded by them in the yard, and they greeted me with: "*Sholom Aleichem*, Brigadier!"

I spoke to everyone all at once. I was asked about relatives in Israel and in other countries, shown addresses, and listened to requests. After that I comforted everyone. Tears flooded from their eyes and I was filled with the pain of my nation.

And in the middle of this group gathered here, there suddenly was a movement: One woman comes out of the rows of people, approaches me, and in a tearful voice, cries out: "Henokh!" I turned and looked at her but didn't recognize her.

In front of me I saw an anguished face showing infinite pain the woman strains herself and in a whimpering voice, says quietly to me: "I am Itka Mjadownik, a friend of your sister Laya," and she fell down in a faint.

She immediately received medical help and was taken away to the closest first-aid room. After reviving, she told me about her pain-filled journey up until that moment.

[Page 465]

My neighbor Itka Mjadownik, the flower of the town! How tortured you are by the German and Polish beasts!

Itka told me that just today, a few hours ago, after years of solitude and fear, she removed the mask from her face and saw living Jews as if for the first time, mingled with them, and spoke their language. On the lists of survivors she did not find one single name of a relative or friend - and so her excitement was tremendous when she saw me, let alone in the uniform of a Jewish Brigadier!

Itka spoke and wept quietly. I heard the cries of the entire nation. I walked with her to her friend's place in Praga and on the way she told me that our fellow resident, Khava Greenberg (Swarcberg), the sister-in-law of Jidel Birnbaum, is still alive and living on Jagelonska Street 27.

We set another meeting very soon at the Jidel Birnbaum's house, in a few days' time.

I was invited by the principal administrators of *Hashomer Hatzair* to join on May 8 in a march to the burial place of Mordekhai Anjelewicz, may his blood be avenged, Commandant of the Jewish resistance in the Warsaw ghetto on Mila Street 18.

The transport train used by all the *kibbutzim* from Warsaw and the surrounding areas, professional groups and delegations from the Jewish and Polish political parties - went for a few kilometers and stopped at the bunker where the Commandant and the entire group was killed.

With a holy shudder, I stepped through the gates of the blood-soaked Warsaw ghetto where hundreds of thousands of Jewish lives were lost and also where the tall flag of the ghetto resistance was raised - the flag that saved our national, human pride.

[Page 466]

I didn't listen to the speeches and stood slightly apart, absorbing the madness of the surrounding destruction. I shut my eyes and saw in my vision the former golden Jewish life in Warsaw in all her colors.

Voices came over me, I opened my eyes and - empty and destroyed, everything gone up to its source. Winds blow remnants of old names, faded *seforim* (religious books), dishes, children's carriages.

I stood pensive like that, when I hear a shout: "Henokh!" I turn around and see that in front of me is Khaitche Jonisz-Gudes (the wife of Yekhiel Jonisz, may his blood be avenged). Embraces, greetings, and contained tears.

Khaitche tells me about her sufferings and wanderings. Her husband, my friend Yekhiel Jonisz, was murdered in Treblinka. Her parents and Yekhiel's parents died in the death marches. By good fortune, Khaitche remained alive.

She told me that her brother Moishe and his entire family, as well as her youngest brother were alive and had gone to a camp in Germany on their way to Israel.

We moved away from the crowd and Khaitche led me through the snaking roads of the ghetto where she lived for a short time until she and her husband were transported to Treblinka.

We stopped at a place that once was famous in the Jewish Warsaw courtyard -- Nalewki 39 until Kupjecka Street.

After many weavings in and out, Khaitche showed me a battered bunker, in which, according to her memory, my parents, Reb Dovid and Fraidel Warsawski, my sister Layale, her husband Aharon, and their little daughter Malkele, may their blood be avenged, all were hidden and then killed.

I bent down, gathered stones from around, and build a tombstone. I stood there for hours and secluded myself with their memory.

[Page 467]

Khanoch Werdi (Warsawski), first on right, with two other fighters at the bunker site, where his father, Reb Dovid Warsawski and his mother Fraidel were killed, may their blood be avenged

Before leaving that place, for the first time I said the orphan's *kaddish* (prayer for deceased parents).

With pride I listened to Khaitche's words, that my father, may his blood be avenged, was one of the heroic fighters during the times of the resistance in the Warsaw ghetto in April 1943.

The day passed. I took Khaitche back to her *kibbutz* and there I was greeted warmly by all the members.

After supper, I discussed the disputes between Israel and the British government, about the current wanderings of the Jews who remained in Europe, and about the *Aliyah* possibilities. The general discussion went until morning.

*[Page 468]*

In the last days, during the times of the repatriation, many Polish Jews returned to Soviet Russia.

From time to time, I waited for the trains in the eastern stations in Praga. These trains were bringing Jews from many different countries.

There I learned that several surviving Serocker families were in the Warsaw area. In the central organization for the Polish Jews (Praga, Seroka 5) I was informed that some of those who had returned had been given quarters in the former *Hechalutz* colony in Grakhow near Warsaw.

Early one morning, I left for Grachow and there I found: my friend Jidel Mendzelewski and his wife Mala (formerly Rozental), their brother Yakov Mendzelewski and his wife Rivkale and a young daughter.

There was tremendous joy.

Their stories are without end: experiences until they left Poland, wanderings in the huge and expansive Russia, struggles with hunger, and then about the present hopes for a better future.

We shared the meal for the poor, and then prepared to leave.

For a few days, we searched for Serockers as we walked through the streets of Praga.

Rivkale Mendzelewski-Maj told me that her brother Yeshayohu was still alive and was staying in a refugee camp in Germany.

I received an express letter from my esteemed friend in Israel - Malkele Rozenberg-Bernshtayn, who begged me to find her young sister Shaindel-Sabina, who supposedly, according to her information, was in Warsaw (living as a Christian).

*[Page 469]*

For this task, I joined up with a Polak, a trustworthy and honest person, who also helped Jews during the time of German occupation, without any compensation, and he was familiar with all the residents of the Polish neighborhoods in Warsaw that had not been completely destroyed - and I asked for his help.

After many searches, that lasted several days, I got Sabina's exact address: Warsaw, Tamki Street 13, at the house of an old Christian family.

With a special messenger, I sent Sabina a letter in which I tell her who I am and then I ask her to set a time for us to meet so that I could give her a personal greeting from her three sisters in Israel.

I received her answer that same day, in which she asks that I come to see her right away.

The following morning, I went to see her - we went along with two other boys - and were welcomed by Sabina and the Christian innkeeper (who had taken in Sabina). Sabina-Shaindele (the daughter of Moishe Peretz Bernshtayn, owner of the bicycle workshop), twelve years ago still a young girl, is now filled with pain and without dreams.

Briefly, these are her experiences:

"At the outbreak of World War II, I happened to be at my sister's house in Legionowo.

During the time of the liquidation of the Ludwiszyn ghetto at the end of 1942, I was lucky enough to be able to escape to Warsaw, and after lengthy exertions, was also able to buy Aryan papers. After more lengthy searches and wanderings, I found a room at this innkeeper's place. She's a gentle and good woman. I live in constant fear and am afraid to leave this Christian area and go back to my own brothers."

She told me all this in Polish in the presence of the innkeeper who was the only one who knew the secret that Sabina was Jewish; the woman would never reveal Sabina's secret.

Her story ended. Her tears are falling and she asks me for advice.

[Page 470]

I told her about those who were saved that I had met, about their plans, and then gave her a personal greeting from all her three sisters in Israel.

I comforted her and advised her about what to do. I invited her to the meeting of all the Serockers in Praga. The meeting would be held in a few days.

After much deliberation, she agreed to come.

I visited the orphanage in Otwock where I was invited by the directors, the women Y. Blum and Winowar.

The orphanage was in the middle of a forest. The rooms - clean and spacious. The children are treated well here and some of them have even begun to laugh.

In this "home," under the supervision of the Jewish Committee for the Polish Jews, there are children who are orphans, and even some who as nursing infants were given over by their parents, who had no other choice, to Christian families and Catholic churches and some of them were even taken off the streets.

Most of the children have no idea who their parents are, and their daily language is exclusively Polish.

Their ages were from four to sixteen.

The older children attend the general, government public school. Back "home," there were courses in Yiddish, literature, and Jewish history. Here there is also an active course in Hebrew.

I spent the entire day with the children, and they asked me to tell stories and teach them songs.

Everyone sat in a row and began to sing. I told them about Masada, Bar Kochba, about the Jewish Brigade, and sang "*Al Khalon, Al Khalon*" (On the Window, On the Window), "*Mal'u Asomeinu Bar*," etc.

The directors were leaning against the walls of the room and were glowing with joy. Even the children forgot everything and were very happy.

[Page 471]

I searched the lists of children's names in the orphanages and found not even a hint of any from Serock.

Late at night, I returned to my lodgings in one of the Warsaw *kibbutzim*.

With the hope of finding survivors, I visited Legionowa where tens of Serock families had settled a few years before the war in order to try to earn a living.

This place was familiar to me from before the war, but now was a wasteland and only a few people moved through the streets as ghosts. There were only a few Jews in this place, and one of them, Bacz Shmuel, told me that the majority of the survivors from Serock were in the refugee camps in Germany, and no one came back to Legionowa.

He told me the following about the bitter end of those few from Serock:

Yosef Fishman was transported from the Warsaw ghetto to Treblinka, and his wife Khava Fishman-Melnik died in the ghetto of hunger.

Aron Paskowicz, may his blood be avenged, was shot in the ghetto. His wife Khana Paskowicz-Fajnboim and Khaim Wajnkrancz died in Treblinka.

Khaim Wajnkrancz's young son, may his blood be avenged, was close to the fence around the ghetto, and he had no way out so he jumped into the Vistula and drowned.

Mashke Paskowicz and Nomi Wajnkrancz, may their blood be avenged, were shot by the Polak where they were hiding.

Rabbi Henokh Pakowicz, of blessed memory, came to his children in the Legionowa ghetto in Biale-Podlask, as he was expelled with all the other Serock Jews at the end of 1939.

[Page 472]

Hershel Finkelshtajn, may his blood be avenged, was shot in the place where he was hiding.

Khana Rozenberg, the wife of Yekhiel Rozenberg, may their blood be avenged, was shot during the liquidation of the ghetto by Polaks who found out about her hiding place.

Reb Khaim Rozenberg, may his blood be avenged, died in Treblinka, and his wife and daughter Sala were shot while they were hiding after the liquidation of the ghetto.

I left Legionowa very depressed and went back to Warsaw. I went directly to the Central Jewish Committee to look through the revised lists of those who had just arrived from Soviet Russia. I bathe in a sea of papers, search, compare - all without results.

As I was leaving the office, a nice young man approached me, embraced me, and said: "Hey, my instructor! Don't you recognize me? I am your Khenokh Simkha Wenger!" I recognized him immediately. When I left Serock he was still a child and now, in front of me, a man stood as tall as a tree. He walked with me to my lodgings, not saying one word all the way. I was puzzled by his behavior, and when I asked him about the reason for his silence, he answered me not with any words, but with a broad smile. I invited him to join the upcoming meeting of the Serock survivors. He agreed to come, but after that moment, there was no trace of him.

That same evening, I participated in a special coordinated meeting of the Warsaw-Praga *kibbutzim*.

I was asked to look through a number of Catholic churches in the northern part of Warsaw with the goal of finding Jewish children who were hidden there and to bring them to Jewish institutions.

I flew to Danzig for a few days, then visited Szczecin, then came back to Warsaw.

*[Page 473]*

In the second half of the month of May, in 1946, all the Serockers met in the house of Khava Grinberg (Swarcberg), Praga, Yagewonska 27.

At this meeting were: Itka Mjadownik, Yehuda Mendzelewski, Male Mendzelewski-Rozental, Shaindele-Sabina Bernshtayn, Khaitche Gudes-Jonisz, Manja Swalberg from Wyszkow, Reb Yakov Kaluski's sister, and myself.

We stayed together very closely and were seeped in reconstructing events, dates, places, happenings, and so on.

Some of those from the lively group found themselves together for the first time - and the whole story became revealed to them.

Slowly, we ate, drank, and quietly sang songs of youth -- of hope and change.

The night slipped away, and suddenly there was an excitement: The door opened, and into the room with joy and tears came our dear friend Hillel Freedman, the son of Abba Leyb the blacksmith, may his blood be avenged. We all got up, surrounded him, and then Hillel told us of his experiences, beginning with his first evacuation to Pultusk, then his stealing across the border, and then his war years in Russia - until these last moments.

He finished, remained silent, and was overjoyed that after all these years of suffering and wandering, he found himself together with friends from his youth.

A little later, the door opened again and another survivor appeared on the threshold - Bunim Ogrodower - who was welcomed with shouts of joy and warm kisses. Bunim was silent and couldn't even utter a single word because of this great excitement.

I set up meetings with everyone in many different places. Everyone's goal was to leave Poland and to begin a new life in our historical fatherland.

[Page 474]

At these meetings I was informed of other surviving Serockers who were living in Lodz.

We were all encouraged and parted with the morning light.

A few days after these abovementioned meetings, I went to Lodz.

At that time, there were a few thousand Jews concentrated in Lodz from all types of camps, from the forests, and former residents of whom there were now more than were in the capital of Warsaw that was destroyed.

I went right away to the place of the city's Jewish Committee that was on Srodmieska Street 32. Masses of Jews are crowding around the house and its surroundings. Without hesitation, I went to the information room and began to look through the general and state lists. I was luckier here than in Warsaw and I found some reliable addresses and familiar names from our town and its surrounding areas.

I learned some important information from a dependable employee of the education department of the Jewish Committee. This information was very useful in my search for survivors - and also for children in the Catholic churches - in all parts of Poland.

Here also, news spread very quickly that a soldier from the Jewish Brigade was present, and when I went into the court, I was surrounded by my tormented brothers with warmth and joy. After a wonderful welcome, embraces, and tears of joy, I asked everyone to tell me of their requests.

They brought a table and bench and for hours I wrote down addresses of relatives in Israel and in other countries, whom I would have to inform about the related survivors.

After this registration, they asked me many questions and in my related answers, I told them about the Jewish powers and their struggles against the British government in Israel, about the ways of the refugees and their future.

*[Page 475]*

They listened intently. Teardrops glistened in their eyes and together with them, my heart beat with a deep-seeded yearning for freedom.

A dear thing, the dearest gift of all, I carry with me - and will always carry - from this gathering: As I finished my words, an older, thin, gray-haired woman, dressed in black, approached me, placed her two hands on my head, and with a clear, ringing voice, said - in Hebrew and Yiddish - "God should protect you from difficulties and pain, because you have become enmeshed in our hurt and tears."

And the entire crowd responded: "Amen!"

A Jew from Wyszkow, who walked with me to my lodgings, told me that my friend Khonon Rozenberg is alive and is in one of the local *kibbutzim*.

In the evening, I was invited to the *Shomer Hatzair* kibbutz for a speech on Kilinski Street 49, and the minute I walked through the doorway, my friend Khonon Rozenberg appeared. We embraced each other and for a few minutes we couldn't - from being overwhelmed - say one word.

We went to sit down in a nearby room and Khonon told me about the death of his family: his father Moishe and mother Miriam, his sisters Rivka and Faigele, his older brother Faivel - uncles, aunts, male and female cousins, may their blood be avenged.

The Rozenberg family in Serock was the largest and most extended, and comprised about 150 souls.

Khonon described the story of his wanderings in Soviet Russia and his return to Poland until these last minutes. He also told me that his cousin Neshka, the daughter of Shmuelke Rozenberg, of blessed memory, was alive and still living in Poland.

*[Page 476]*

In the morning, we both went out to look for townsmen in the places where the Jews lived.

We found Vita Zbik-Ribalski and her husband and two children on Kilinski Street 7.

From her we got additional addresses and right after that we found Faivel Zukor, the grandson of Reb Dovid Rozenberg and Yitzkhok Meier Zukor, the town's *mohel* (one who performs circumcisions), may their blood be avenged. The abovementioned told me about their experiences and clarified the extent of the destruction.

We set up a second meeting.

The majority of the survivors were thinking of not staying in Poland, and leaving the country was a permanent goal.

Addresses become invalid (useless) and it was very important to be at the arrival and departure points.

The majority of the youth, who decided to make *Aliyah* directly to Israel, organized themselves into *kibbutzim* from all types and from all directions.

One day, I visited the *Hekhalutz Hamizrakhi kibbutz* on Poludnjawa Street 20, and had a remarkable experience - here I found the four brothers Nowogrodski (children of Reb Menakhem Nowogrodski, of blessed memory, the kasha maker): Yosef, Yeshayohu, Shmuel, and Yisroel - healthy, beautiful, and whole!

The combined deep experiences are hard to describe. We held each other and sank in talks for hours. They told me that their sister Bina was also still alive and was in Germany.

I spent a full day and night with them. During mealtime, together with the entire *kibbutz*, I sang and taught them this song: "*Halu, galu, even gal, meheirim khatzbonuha...*" (round, round, the stone goes round, let's chisel it quickly...)

[Page 477]

When we finished saying the blessings after the meal, I offered some words of comfort and also showed them different roads to achieve their dreams of freedom.

The brothers and I agreed to a second meeting in a few days at the home of Faivel Zukor.

Our group was slowly growing.

I was invited to visit the Jewish school under the management of the director Mendel Mann.

I was described in detail and introduced to the children by the director. They welcomed me warmly, and greeted me with the words: "*Borukh Habo!* (welcome) to the shade of our refuge."

The majority of the children had been living in churches or with Christian families for a long time. Some of these children were even taken off the streets by some compassionate hands.

A few of the children were born in Soviet Russia and returned from there with their parents just a few weeks ago.

According to their age, they truly were all children, but really they quickly grew up because of their difficult life experiences.

I sang Israeli songs for them and told them children's stories. The children sang these songs: "*Al khalon, al khalon, amda zipor yafa*" (on the window, on the window, sits a pretty bird...), then "*Oifen pripetchik*," (In the fireplace...), and so on. Then we had a lengthy, open discussion. They asked about the Brigade and the struggles they faced, about children's lives and relatives in Israel, and looked in wonder at my uniform.

The older children made a bigger fuss, with their colorful, sharp, life wisdom.

We said good-bye with a final, lively *Hora* and my promise to remember them.

*[Page 478]*

The school director, Mendel Mann, asked me to visit the orphanage in Helenuwek near Lodz, where there were children from the Warsaw-Pultusk area.

I visited the orphanage in Helenuwek that was under the jurisdiction of the Central Committee for the Polish Jews, and was warmly received by the directress Frau Feingold.

I searched through the children's list and found three children from Serock, children from Laya, daughter of Reb Yosef Gzhebjeniazh (the tailor from Nasielsk), may his blood be avenged.

I spoke for a long time with the three sweet children, but they had nothing enlightening to tell, because during the wartime they were still very young.

I assured them that I would visit Serock and give their mother Laya their warm regards.

There were 100 children in this orphanage, ages 3 to 17. The older ones, starting at 8 or 9, attended the government public school in the city, the younger ones remained here.

Here there were groups (circles) for Yiddish, Yiddish literature, and Hebrew and Yiddish history. All the education was conducted in Polish.

I was invited to a discussion with the older children. I talked about the surviving Jews in Europe, about the struggles of the Jewish Brigade, about Jewish settlement in Israel, and about life for children and youth in Israel.

I was asked many difficult questions, and some of them I was not able to answer.

"Why do they hate us?" "Why did the entire world allow Hitler, may his name be erased, to murder so many Jews?"

Because of the strained atmosphere - in a children's and youth home! - we were not able to end the discussion with song and dance. We quietly separated.

*[Page 479]*

I met two children there whose history reflected the deep abyss of the destruction:

1. The girl. Pretty and slender. She was raised for a few years in a Catholic church and when they brought her to Helenuwek, she kept screaming: "I don't want to be with Jews! They killed Christ!" Today she is a different person.

2. The 18-year-old was in Mathausen and worked at burning dead bodies in the crematoria. One day, into his hands fell the cold, dead body of his own father who because of his height did not fit into the oven. The sadistic *Kapo* wanted to cut the body into a few pieces but the small child, the son, spread himself across the body and did not allow the *Kapo* to touch his father.

This time, the *Kapo* relented and the body was burned whole.

The children loved their teacher Lanja, and they call her Mama. She had lived in ghettos and death camps, and was miraculously saved. Before the war she worked with Dr. Janus Korczak and Stefanja Wilczinski in the well-known orphanage in Warsaw on Krokhmalna Street. She put forth her holy work and sacrificed her life for these victimized children.

After hearing the chapters of these humbled children's lives, I left this place, in a depressed mood.

In the abovementioned institution, I received information and addresses about places where there were other children from Serock.

I left Lodz in a few days, and began travelling in the wide and large surrounding areas - and once again: churches, Christian families, religious discussions, and negotiations with priests, Nazarites, nuns, and I met some children as well.

*[Page 480]*

The task was not for nothing. I found some children - not from Serock - and delivered them over to the appropriate institutions.

When I came back to Lodz, I met friends and colleagues from the *kibbutz Dror* on Narutowicz Street and there received additional addresses of Serockers who were in that place.

I met Rivka Kuligowska (today Wisocka), the widow of Avrohom'tche Wisnjewicz, may his blood be avenged, in her house on Zakhodnje Street 34, together with her husband and young son, and heard about her wanderings and horrors up until this day. Another drop in the cup filled with poison.

In June 1946, there was a gathering of the Serockers in Lodz at the home of Faivel Zukor. The attendees were: Khana Rozenberg, Vita Zbik, the four Nowogrodski brothers, Hillel Friedman (who came from Warsaw especially for this gathering), Rivka Kuligowska, and I.

The joy was tremendous. Questions and answers without end. We sang and for a short time, we forgot what had taken place in our lives these last few years.

In the middle of the singing, the door opens and we see: On the doorstep stands Mala Rozenberg-Joskowicz, the daughter of Yekhiel Rozenberg, may his blood be avenged. She is standing there with her husband.

We immediately absorbed them into our group. Embraces, kisses, questions and answers - and tears of joy in our eyes.

We continued until late into the night. We exchanged information and promised one another to stay in contact because in the coming days some of these people will begin to make their way to the borders.

[Page 481]

I visited the Jewish Historical Committee on Narutowicz Street 32, and met with the scholarly secretary N. Blumental.

I asked if there were any documents there that were relevant to the Serock community, such as diaries, community ledgers, pictures, etc. The polite secretary informed me that all the material they were given was not yet completely sorted, and he assured me that every relevant document that he would find from now on and in the future would be at my disposal to copy.

And that's how it was. A year after finding the Ringelblum archives, we found authentic writings of articles about Serock written by Tzwi Klajnman and Avrom Spilke, may their blood be avenged.

The editor of the Jewish newspaper "*Dos Naye Leben*" (The New Life) that was published in Lodz four times a week, permitted me to search through the file of Jews from Poland and from elsewhere who came with all kinds of situations, with the goal of finding out names of people in the cities with whom until now they'd had no communication.

Thanks to the file, I was able to communicate with many people who had left Poland, and also with those in general who had not come back to Poland, and I found myself in the refugee camps in Germany and in Austria.

A few times, I placed notices in this newspaper to all the Serockers, and asked them to contact me or, depending on their address, my brother Yekhiel Meier in Israel.

I went to Warsaw for a few days to meet those newly arrived from Russia.

This time, my friend Hillel Friedman accompanied me, and after long searches on the first day we found Leizer Kohn in Praga, from our town, and on the second day - A. Borenshtayn who lived in the community barracks on Panska Street 20. In that same place, there was also the only surviving *Bais Medrash* that remained.

*[Page 482]*

In these very poor and old barracks that were left from all the great property of the large Jewish community in Europe, tens of families from all parts of Europe were quartered here by the Jewish Committee, and among them were the sick and frail.

Our townsman was very excited to see us and we awakened some hope for life in him.

We went to be part of the *minyan* (quorum) for *mincha* and *maariv* (evening prayers) and at the end of the prayers they all said the special *kaddish* for orphans.

My uncles Benyomin and Yakov Kristal and their families from Serock, may their blood be avenged, at the time of the war, lived in the nearby house on Panska Street 18.

I stood in front of that house, looked for their traces, and only crumbling, destroyed walls remained witness to the lives that were torn away.

I found out that a certain number of Jews - and among them some from Serock (and they mentioned the name of Yitzkhok Kanjer, today in Israel) - had returned to Baile Podlusk and the surrounding areas, disregarding the fact that they were told not to go there because in those areas the Home Army (AK, *Armia Krajowa*) had murdered some surviving Jews who had gone there to visit their home towns.

I decided, ignoring the danger, to visit these abovementioned places. So, the next morning I left for Biale with a rented car, accompanied by two armed Jewish soldiers who were serving in the Polish army.

(The majority of Serockers were brought to Biale Podlusk toward the end of the expulsion of Serock, at the end of 1939. Tens of families were also quartered in the surrounding towns of Lukow and Lomazi [Lomzay].)

*[Page 483]*

We came to Biale Podlusk and went around in the streets and alleys to find Jews, but unfortunately, without results. We went to see the mayor of the city who expressed his "deep anguish" that only a few Jews had returned, but in a short time, for "incomprehensible reasons," had left the place as well.

Before we left, we went to visit the "pig market," the concentration place and place of pain for the Jews during their final torture on September 26, 1942.

In this place, there was a horrible torture of a young boy of Serock, Zishe Goldberg, may his blood be avenged, the son of Yakov Goldberg who had a manufacturing store in Serock at the head of Kosciuszka Street, above the cellar of the baker Reb Yitzkhok Weinkrantz, may his blood be avenged. After the sadists had jabbed out his eyes, he was beaten terribly with sticks and bayonets. Zishe, may his blood be avenged, did not ask those murderers for mercy. He held himself heroically, and during the actual time of the torture, he said to his murderers these severe words: "You are strong men in relation to the helpless Jews, but you will pay dearly for this. You will be defeated in this war and the Jewish nation of the entire world will take revenge on our blood."

These words gave impetus to the wild rage of the murderers and they tortured him more intensely until, with great anguish, he exhaled his final breath.

We left Biale Podlusk as mourners and arrived in Lukow. Here too we did not find one single Jew. The Polaks approached us with suspicion and from the local government organizations we received evasive answers.

*[Page 484]*

We arrived in Lomazi (Lomzay) at around noon. The town was *Judenrein* (cleansed of Jews). The Polish mayor brought us to the place where the Jews of Lomazi were murdered. Among them had been several families from Serock, such as: Reb Yakov Yehoshua Mjadownik and his entire family, may their blood be avenged, and more, who were murdered on the night of Elul 4, 5702 - August 17, 1942, in the grove behind the city, and were buried there in a communal grave.

We united with their memory. We said *Kaddish* and *Keil Moleh Rakhamim* (prayers for the dead) with them - and then we parted.

From one of my Polish friends, I found out that some children from Serock and from other places were living with Christian families and Catholic churches in the area of the city Dzialdowo, near Mlawa.

I boarded a train in Warsaw and when I arrived in the station in Nazielsk, I disembarked. In this place, Serockers that were expelled were tortured and beaten at the end of the year 1939. They were viciously herded into two trains and after a journey of a few days they were brought, completely depleted, to Biale Podlusk, Lukow, and Lomazi.

An old train worker showed me the torture place in the area of the "mud" where our finest and most gentle were forced to "bathe" themselves before they were forced into the wagon cars. I was filled with pain. I then continued with my journey and boarded the second train to Mlawa where some survivors were waiting for me. These survivors were living in a hotel on Dzheromski Street 2.

Of a community that consisted of tens of thousands of Jews, there were now in this place just some tens of Jews. These survivors gave me a lot of material and pictures of the destruction of the Mlawa ghetto.

About the family of my brother Yekhiel Meier, I discovered that his wife Ester'el and their young daughter Khana, may their blood be avenged, were transported from the Mlawa ghetto to Auschwitz on January 2, 1943, and were murdered there with all the other tortured people.

[Page 485]

The Mlawa Jews provided me with additional information about places and surroundings where there were Jewish children and one of these Jews accompanied me on my visits to the Catholic churches and the private homes of Christian families.

Within a few days, we had searched through a large area and were fortunate enough to free tens of Jewish children and take them over to the appropriate places. There were no children from Serock among these.

## The Visit to Serock

At the end of June 1946, I went to visit Serock. For safety reasons, I went with a rented car from Warsaw to Zegzhe, seven kilometres before Serock. From the Zegzhe train station, military fortresses and barracks in the area were destroyed.

There I met some Polish acquaintances from the village Wjelisow. They warned me about the Home Army (AK) bandits, and they didn't understand my desire to visit a place that had been completely destroyed.

In order to get to Serock, you have to cross the Narew River, and because the bridges to cross the river had been destroyed, I was taken across by fishing boat for a large fee. On the other side of the river, on the main road, a passenger wagon with two horses was waiting. I recognized the wagon driver immediately - my friend the Polak Ceslaw Sokolowski, the former partner of our townsman Reb Yitzkhok Ickowicz who was fortunate enough to get to Israel before World War II.

[Page 486]

The foreman told me about the period of the German occupation, remembered names of his Jewish friends and acquaintances, and kept silent about many of his experiences. He also warned me about the groups of bandits, then he invited me to spend the night.

The wagon moved from its place. The surrounding landscape - familiar. More than once did I go on foot this distance of seven kilometers - from Zegzhe to Serock and back.

Now we are passing the small forest of Zegzhe, where the famous palace of Prince Radziwill was once located.

In the area of this very forest, we - the *Shomer Hatzair* and others - organized our excursions and bathed our feet in foot baths, in the clear waters of the river. The forest is green and beautiful. In this forest, Jews from Serock and the surrounding areas were tortured. Will the trees ever tell what went on near them? The leaves rustle, the birds are singing - in my ears, I hear a cry and a moan.

We are getting closer. On the right is the Narew River and the hills, where during the summer months all sorts of summer activities of the youth organizations took place. A little farther is the village Bankowce that was the crossover point of the bridge, from the right to the left bank of the Narew. From there, were roads that wound through the German villages to Radzymin and the large huts that belonged to the surrounding farmers.

The width of the river at this point is a few hundred meters. For many years, the "ferryman" Reb Yehoshua held this job, and we called him Shia Pshewaznik (the ferryman boss) - who was outstanding in his physical capacity, his fine character, and was respected and loved by all.

When we came to the borders of the town, I got down off the wagon. On the left I see the Christian cemetery with its tall, white fence, upon which one cannot find any sign of war.

Opposite there, left of the main road, is the flour mill of Berl Ickowicz and Motel Melnik, may their blood be avenged. I approach the mill and hear the sound of machines. The yard is full of farmers, wagons.

The Polish miller answers my questions, saying that he had leased the mill from the government, because the previous owners were herded out of the city by the Germans, and no one knows about their fate until today. He began to defend himself, declared that his hands were "clean," and "assured" me that if the previous owners were to return, he would leave the mill immediately.

*[Page 487]*

I find myself at the top of Warsaw or May Third Street. All the houses on the right side - the houses from Graniewicz to Tuvia Freedman, and on the left side - at the front from Finkelshtayn, Shmulke Rozenberg, Moishe Rozenberg and the houses in their large yards - were erased from the earth, without even a trace. The entire area is almost completely cleaned and plowed. In that area, the only thing that is left is the one new house of Reb Yeshaye Hofman, may his blood be avenged. I approached the building with a shudder, and immediately realized that the magistrate and the post office were located there.

There I met the familiar Polak Stefanczik, the former and current postal director and former anti-Semitic manager.

He recognized me right away, and began to tell me about his great friendship with my father, may his blood be avenged, and with all the many branches of the family Rozenberg of which, to his "great regret," no one survived. From him I also heard a "declaration" about his father's good deeds toward the Jews during the occupation.

There is a silence all around. No one is seen outside.

He introduced me to the new mayor, Latallo, a blacksmith from Zegzhe, an old Communist who asked me to be careful and then invited me to spend the night at his home. Latallo did not know the Serock Jews. According to him, there were a certain number of Jewish children with Christian families in this area and he assured me of his help if I was ever having difficulties getting into those or any other places.

After drinking tea, the mayor accompanied me for several hours while I went around the rest of the town. The entire nearby street - starting with Dr. Bak until the residence of Aba-Leyb Pniewski, the houses of the barber/surgeon Tik, the basket maker, Reb Gedalia the shoemaker, and Yosef Yagoda - were completely burned down. The rest of the street, on both sides, until the house of Reb Yakov Rozenberg, may his blood be avenged - destroyed and had falling walls.

*[Page 488]*

Near the former store of Reb Dovid Milshtayn, may his blood be avenged, at the end of Warsaw Street, on the Nazielsk main road, a monument that is swimming in red flowers has been put up in honor of the Polish and Russian liberators of the city.

I set down the left side of the street, pass the houses of Henokh Paskewicz, Eliezer Orel, Gedaliah Tukulski, Yizkhok Meier Kuperboim, the shoe store of Shmuel Frenkel, the teahouse of Khinke, may their blood be avenged, and I go into the yard of the house of Rivkale Malawanczik, #22, where I lived with my parents for several years. The yard is neglected, the houses in the front and in the yard are destroyed. Our former family house has turned into a granary. The house of my former neighbor, Reb Yishaye Melnik, both Dena and Shimon Katz and Khaitche, the daughter of Reb Yitzkhok Swarc, may their blood be avenged - wasted and empty. The former barbershop of Meier Ubagi, may his blood be avenged - a teahouse for passersby.

I stood in my destroyed yard, where I had spent some of my most beautiful years, remembered all those lives that were cut off - and dropped my head.

My companion, a simple peasant, crossed himself. I placed myself in the doorway of my former house, I silently whispered: "My dear parents, my dear neighbors, where are you?"

I silently left the house of my young years. I passed by the house of Reb Itche Meier Tik, may his blood be avenged, and went into the yard of Dembowski, house #18, where I spent my childhood years.

The long yard is wasted and half burned.

As I was standing in the destruction in the center of the yard, I remembered these neighbors from my youth: Reb Shmuel-Eliyahu Sterdiner, the glazier, his son Reb Avrohom the carpenter and their families - very devout, charitable and sincere, hard-working people; Reb Moishe ben Peretz Bernshtayn, the mechanic, who tried to understand every screw and wheel - smiling and good hearted; Reb Hershel the tinsmith - a refined and quiet man; Reb Yitzkhok Meier Bernshtayn, the teacher - there were several times that I was glued to the window of his *cheder,* listening to the stories that he told his students; Reb Berl Pokorski, the barber - a kind and honest man; Reb Yidel Pienik, the storekeeper - the one who regularly read the Torah studies and recited Tehillim; Reb Yeshiye Miara, the storekeeper - a quick-tempered nature with an open hand for every needy person; R. Y. Gurman, the hardware store owner - a straight, and quiet man, may their memories be blessed.

[Page 489]

I closed my eyes. All of you, my dear neighbors, seem so alive - I embrace and gently touch you all.

I left the yard of my youth and went to the other side. I arrived to the destroyed house of Reb Yakov Rozenberg, may his blood be avenged, and at the end of Warsaw and Kosciuszko Streets, I placed myself at the entrance to the ruined cellar that was a shelter, in which 70 Jews were murdered by German bombs in the first days of World War II. I knew all of those 70 people. My pain is tremendous. The sky is overcast; it's thundering and raining and it seemed as if the sky itself was releasing tears upon those who died.

As I went down Kosciuszko Street, I met a Polish man that I knew, Wiezhbinski Jan, an active Communist, who was very happy to see me. He said that he would be at my disposal all the time that I would be in Serock and would, for security reasons, accompany me on my travels. At this point, the mayor left us.

After a few steps into this street, I met the only surviving Jewish soul that was left from the entire community after the expulsion - Laya, the daughter of Reb Yosef Gzhebieniazh, may his blood be avenged, -- the tailor from Nazielsk. (Her residence was located in the house of Baila Ostrowski.)

[Page 490]

Tears of joy and emotion ran from her eyes and without stop, she repeated: "And so, I was not forgotten, and so someone remembered me!"

I gave her regards from her children, whom I had met in the orphanage in Helenuwek near Lodz, and her eyes lit up with joy. For hours she told me about her painfully difficult experiences at the time of the great devastation, and about her husband who was murdered in a horrific manner by the German sadists because he generously helped the many persecuted Jews.

Her recounting flowed without end, for hours, as if from a bubbling well.

Night fell. It is pitch black outside. There is no one in the area - only one Jewish soul lives here - on a street, a cemetery.

Wiezhbinski accompanied me to the house of the mayor Latallo. I lay down on the bed and fell into a deep sleep, tired and satiated with pain.

The following day, I planned my travels.

## Kosciuszko Street

All the houses on the right side of the street, starting at Pesakh Lewiner's store until the house in which lived Reb Menakhem Mendel Frenkel, the *shokhet* (ritual slaughterer) from Pupa, are destroyed and no one lives in them. Some houses remained but only on the left side.

I walk around in the street's destruction. The sky is cloudy, winds are blowing. Some Polaks walk by quickly, throwing me glances. Over some of the destroyed stores, signs remain, and I read: Selling oil - Yakov Gudes Barber- Zishe Welner.

[Page 491]

Butcher shop - M. Zilbershtayn Grocer - Moishe Margulis... and no more.

I went into the destroyed yard of Kuzhnicki, and stopped near the place where the *cheder* of Reb Khaim Yona the teacher, may his blood be avenged, used to be, and where I used to study for a few years. I noticed a broken chair and a familiar long bench - maybe I once sat on it at the time when I lived in the imaginary world of my teacher, the master of dreams, with whom I would stroll as a regular house guest in places such as Nardo'ah, Sura, Pompedisa, Mata Mekhasya (cities mentioned in the Talmud), and others, and I was friendly with - close friends - Shmuel Yerkhinai, with Abai and Rabba, with Rav Huna and Rav Ashi - who knows? (These are names of great Rabbinic teachers and scholars noted in the Talmud.)

Not far from this place was the *cheder* of Reb Yakov Yehoshua Merlo, of blessed memory, to whom the children were attached, and they loved him dearly. I look for whatever has left a trace - and find nothing.

I leave my childhood circle, cross the street and remain standing in front of a destruction that once was the house of Reb Menakhem Mendel Bobek, of blessed memory, the shoemaker - a wonderful man for the people, from whom bubbled goodness and compassion. An honest, hard worker and a truthful man - a *mentch*.

The small street of the old Rav, may his memory be blessed, was burned down. There was no trace of the ritual bath (*mikva*). The lodgings of the beautiful shoemaker family Bukhenek, on the hill right across the Polak Sokolowski's yard, was half burned and turned into a chicken coop.

[Page 492]

# The Four Cornered Marketplace

There, all the houses are broken down. The only things that remained whole are the city's spring in the center and the large bridge rocks. I stand on this place, where on December 5, 1939, it was the last time that the remaining Jews of the community were herded together by the German sadists. The Jews were beaten and tortured, and finally expelled to Nazielsk.

These huge rocks on the bridge were silent then, and silent now as well - will they ever tell over the truth?

I went into the destroyed houses where once lived the hardworking Jews, where the porter Simkha Krawiecki, the animal trader Welner, Hillel the butcher, may their blood be avenged - people of the fold, who worked hard for their earnings all week, but Sabbath eve they threw off this yoke and became free people.

People with a compassionate heart and a giving hand for every fallen and embittered person. All of that was torn down by an evil hand. Have they taken revenge of all this yet?

As I passed the former grain mill of Reb Menakhem Nowogrodski, may his blood be avenged, at the end of Market Street, I thought I heard the noise of the millstones and see the mill owner as he stands bent over: with one hand he fills up the sacks, and in his other hand he holds his Book of Psalms (*Tehilim*) and his mouth is singing the verses.

I stopped at the house of Sojnok, the firemen's bandleader. I went up to the devastated first floor, and went into the house where my dear, unforgettable grandmother Jore Krystal, of blessed memory, lived. My grandmother was an *eishes khayil* (woman of valor). She was widowed at a very young age, and was left with eight young children. She maintained and supported her home, raised and married off her children, and also found time for community activities such as: help for poor children and for bedridden pregnant women, giving charity discreetly, and so on.

She was my protection and my guardian, when I ran away from my father's, of blessed memory, punishment, for my mischief, I went to hide at her house. Her image is etched deep in my heart. I dropped a hot tear and quietly moved away from this beloved spring.

[Page 494]

The majority of the Jews of this town would immerse themselves there for purification on Fridays before the Sabbath day.

An old fisherman tells me: "A sadness has befallen us, a punishment from heaven."

When I asked him: "Where are the Jews?" he answered: "The waters have covered them over." The spring has long forgotten Jewish laughter and the Yiddish language.

I left my childhood circle, and I go up - striding through the market, and I arrive at the small street that leads to the large *shul*.

I walk with measured steps, then stand still, and see: the large, city *shul*, the community building, the large shteibel of the Gerer *khassidim*, and their house in which the family Zukor lived, honest, hard-working people, were erased from this earth and left no trace.

Nature on the right side is teasing me. Gutecki's garden is blooming, growing as it once did.

My head is spinning, something is humming in my ears: I hear hammering on the anvil, and I find myself standing at the blacksmith, Reb Abba Leyb Fridman, the blacksmith, a man of honesty and truth, a man of great heart who leads the prayers (a *baal tefila*), who does the Torah readings, and is the beadle in the House of Study (*bais medrash*).

The smithy is destroyed, the house dilapidated, and to his memory, I whispered: "Happy are those whose way is perfect" (*ashrei temimei derekh*, from Psalms).

With a shiver I prepared to visit the cemetery of our community.

In the bright morning, I walk on the road that leads to Pultusk and 25 kilometers before the village of Bierzwice, I turn right and walk about 200 meters and arrive at the large sawmill; to the left, a distance of about 10 meters - there should be our cemetery.

[Page 495]

I look to the left and don't see a fence or any tombstones, so I ask my companions (my companions then were my acquaintance Wiezbinski and an armed policeman) if we had gotten lost. They were quiet.

Then, a small built Polak (I recognized him immediately) approaches me. This is Kendzherski, the long-time caretaker of the Jewish cemetery.

He removed his hat, shook my hand, and said: "They, the Germans, destroyed the cemeteries - the old one and the new one, tore down the tombstones, turned over and plowed the earth, planted seeds, and look at this field in front of you - rich, thick food for our cows."

For a few minutes I was frozen.

Opposite me, the Narew River is shining with all its splendour, but here - opposite this entire cosmos - the crime was covered with greenery over the rest of our dearest and most beloved from generations long ago. The cows chew slowly - there is no crying, no protest.

My throat is choking with tears - how low we have become!

I united with their memory, went to stand on a tall hill in the middle of the field, and loud and clear began to say *Kaddish*, and at the end I said the *El Moleh Rakhamim* (prayers for the dead).

My companions crossed themselves and answered "amen."

I said goodbye to those hidden in the field - maybe I am the last one to visit the community of his parents.

Very sadly I returned to the city, and the police commissioner comforted me.

I glance again at the market, the streets, the lanes. It's as if the town has caved in. With one look you can see to the other end of the city. The distance decreased with the lives that were cut off.

[Page 496]

I separate from my former community - the end of the thousand-year blood novel with Poland.

In the last minute, in the middle of the road that leads to Nazielsk, I shook the hand of the only surviving Jewish soul in the city. This is also the road upon which, during the time of the destruction of the community, the final march of the expelled Jews took place - I left Serock.

After leaving Serock, once again I visited all the meeting points of the Serockers, such as Warsaw, Lodz, Sosnowicz, Krakow, Katowice, Sczeczyn, and Wraclaw. I completed the lists of the survivors that were found in Poland, and those in the refugee camps in Germany and in Austria set future visits with me in Europe and in Israel.

I felt a holy responsibility for the Poland I left behind, to visit the death camps of Auschwitz and Birkenau.

I left Katowice with the accompaniment of my friend G. Eibeshicz and a rented car to go to Auschwitz, and we stopped at the famous gate on which these words are hanging: "*Arbeit Macht Frei.*"

I am inside - in hell. I walk through the empty, vast barracks, among scores of tall, twisted fences.

Here, in a precise and cold method, and with ferocity, a million people were systematically murdered, the majority of them were Jews. I saw mountains of shoes, forks, spoons.

I stood by the broken down crematoria and froze with those who were burned, stoned, and hanged.

Quietly, I left this hell.

The ground is burning under my feet: the Polish security agents limited my going around freely, and systematically watched me.

[Page 497]

"*Yetzias Polon*" (the exiles from Poland), in all its energy, and in its center of gravity, they are all in the refugee camps in Germany, Austria, and Italy.

I hurriedly parted from all my friends, left Poland, and went to Czechoslovakia through the Zebzhidowice border crossing.

At the Marowska Ostrawa train station in Czechoslovakia, I was arrested by the military Czech police, and was placed in a clean, orderly room, and I sat there for seven days, not knowing the reason.

My verbal and written protests remained unanswered. I have to mention that I was treated well: I received newspapers, good food and drink, and also cigarettes.

On the eighth day, a tall, sympathetic officer appeared, to whom I was drawn with confidence. He explained to me that the reason for my arrest was a request received from the Polish government to send me back to Poland who was accusing me of hiding children who were raised in institutions and with private families. He informed me that the abovementioned request was sent through him to the central Czechoslovakian agency in Prague for a decision, but he, from his side, recommended that they release me.

To this gentle person, I described the destruction of the Jews in Poland and explained the problem with the surviving children who were, without choice, given over to churches and to private Christian families.

The officer broke down in sobs like a small child, gave me a kiss, and left the room.

I was drained and exhausted, I threw myself down on the bed and soon fell asleep.

The following morning, as I woke from sleep, I found a beautiful bouquet of flowers on the small table, and at the door, all my baggage that was taken away from me at the time of the arrest.

The officer appeared again at lunchtime, told me that I was free, and placed a free train ticket to Prague in my hand, and accompanied me to the station where we parted warmly.

*[Page 498]*

I flew from Hanover (Germany) to Prague and there met with a woman from our city, Soro, the daughter of Reb Berish Soljarzh, may his blood be avenged. There was great joy. Twelve years ago, I left her a small child, and now in front of me sits a pain-laden woman. I comforted her and advised her about the future.

From Hanover, I flew for a few days to Paris. There I met with the following Serockers: my uncle Yekhiel Krystel (who died in Israel), Moishe Yosel Krawiecki, Simkha Esterowicz, Moishe Lewiner, and Yidel Birnboim. This last person told me that he was in the death camp of Auschwitz, and just by chance he was saved, and also that our city's Moishe Margulis, may his blood be avenged, died there as a hero, participating in the well-known uprising of the *Sonderkommando* against their torturers.

From Paris I went for a special visit to the refugee camps in Germany and Austria - and in each place I looked for traces of our townspeople.

From Israel there is news about a bitter struggle with the British mandate powers: sieges, weapon searches in the Jewish settlements, and internment of the illegal immigrant into camps on the island of Cyprus, and so on.

I returned to Israel.

I found a pack of letters at my brother's house from survivors in Germany, Austria, Cyprus, about whom until now I had no idea.

*[Page 499]*

Our camp was growing.

In January 1947, I openly placed a notice in the newspaper "*Lekarov ve'lerakhok*" ("Near and Far"), issue #63, (17 Shevat, 5707 - 1947), printed in the section for searching for relatives through the Jewish Agency in Israel, a list titled "*Seridei Kehilas Serock*" ("survivors of the community of Serock"). At that time, there were 160 names, and also a brief commentary on the destruction of the community.

The majority of the survivors made Aliyah to Israel and became wrapped up in their lives. Scores of them immigrated to North and South America, and to France.

A Jewish State was established that takes in her homeless children.

Despite the devastation, life weaves itself to a better, more just, and beautiful future.

[Page 500]

# The Jewish Serock
# (A visit after the destruction)
### By Sh. L. Shnayderman, New York
### Translated by Pamela Russ

A feeling of great sadness befell me when I arrived at the empty marketplace in Serock. Over the half caved-in, wooden houses with the leaking roofs full of holes, overgrown, the tower of the Gothic church stretched to the sky, [the church] that was built at the end of the fifteenth century by German crusaders. Here and there were individual passersby in worn out clothes. In an empty gray shop, which I entered, situated at the end of the market, I received the grim news that in this town, where about one century ago there was a deeply rooted Jewish life, now there wasn't even one Jew.

The only thing that the Nazi swastikas have left from the old Serock community is a hard-covered book, bound in yellowed parchment. The pages, to the very edges, are dense with the writing of the names of the newborns in the town. The book is found at the local historian [chronicler], Irena Zakzhewska, a long suffering, elderly, well-established woman, who was commissioned by the city council to write a monograph of Serock, that is now preparing to celebrate its 900th year anniversary of the town.

I leafed through the book, in which the majority of the names were Jewish, and had the feeling that I was holding the souls of the Jews in my hands – the Jews for which there weren't even any tombstones left. The historian explained to me that already in the fourteenth century there existed a Jewish community in Serock and a walled *shul,* and thanks to the influx of Jewish merchants, Serock – even at the early date of 1425 – was granted the status of a city and with that set itself up as an important business center on the road between Poland and Russia.

The rivers Narew and Bug that merge at the entrance-way to the city, provided a most important communication means for merchants that the Jewish merchants brought here and spread across the settlements of Mazowie.

[Page 501]

Because of her strategic location, Serock was often the victim during wars and invasions. During the time of the Napoleon march to Moscow, there were terrible battles in Serock, and the church and the *shul* – the tallest buildings in the town – were damaged in the artillery duels between the two warring armies. Later, these two buildings were reconstructed. From the Napoleonic wars, the name "Napoleon's mountains" is truly derived well from the mountains that were behind the town and that were the place of strolling and romantic rendezvous for the Jewish youth of Serock.

At the time of the Hitler invasion of Serock, of a general population of 6000, only about 100 people remained alive. The majority of the Serock Jews that were saved, about 60 in total, are now living in Israel. The rest are spread over the world. A larger group of surviving Serock Jews are today in America.

Those Serock Jews that remained alive remember with special reverence, the victim Leibel Blumberg, who in the bitterest moments, in the hours of devastation, comforted the depressed, resigned Serock Jews. A talented fiddler and musician, Leibel Blumberg sang and played his fiddle in the Biale ghetto, and playing so, was how he went to the gas chambers.

Serock was a poor town, but with deep foundations of religious and worldly institutions, with a public bank, and a community charity fund (*gemillas khesed* fund) that was a vital support for the hundreds of poor Jewish merchants and workers. A report from the community fund in Serock, that was printed in the Jewish weekly "*Unzer Vort*" ("Our Word") from the neighboring city of Pultusk, gives us an idea about the bitter economic situation for the Serock Jews of that time – a situation that is representative of the hundreds of similar Jewish towns in Poland.

*[Page 502]*

The report says that the *gemillas khesed* fund in Serock distributed loans of 50 to 150 zlotys to Jewish store owners and handworkers. In approximately one year, the fund had a total of 43,000 zlotys. That means more than 400 families to support – more than half the Jewish population on Serock had to be supported by this *gemillas khesed* fund.

As in all the other towns, in Serock there were numerous parties and organizations that had bitter disputes among themselves, not always ideological, but in these struggles the Jews from the towns were able to express their vitality

That's how, for example, in this same Pultusk weekly, a report was printed about the annual stormy meeting of the cooperative public bank in Serock, during which time the management of the Agudah was put aside and the management now went to the hands of the workers: Yosef Orol, Aron Gzhebieniazh, and the merchant Moyshe Margolis.

The disagreements between the Agudah and the workers were so ugly, that the head people came to the meetings from Warsaw, the headquarters of the Jewish Cooperative Public Bank in Poland. They were: A. Berkenheym and Avrohom Shmoysh. The latter is now in New York.

The Jews in Serock, for whom a loan of 15 or 25 zlotys was really a question of survival, saved up this little bit from their own mouths and gave their few poor pennies (*groshen*) to the Jewish institutions in town.

Serock had a public elementary school, a library, and a drama circle, a public university, and a choir. There was a lively, evolving Jewish youth, that belonged to the various groups. The *Khalutz* movement (Zionist youth movement) was particularly strong in Serock, and a significant number of youth actually did move away to Israel.

[Page 503]

Serock also produced a talented young writer and painter, Yosel Grosbard, who shortly after the outbreak of the war took upon himself the responsibility of Yiddish literature and art circles in Warsaw. In his deeply moving songs about the *shtetl*, there was an expression of the mood in the lyrics and the eye in the painting.

In the year 1939, practically on the eve of the catastrophe, Yosel Grosbard wrote a song in which the confusion that ruled in his home town of Serock is described. It was almost an omen for the huge, oncoming, destruction:

*The summer has already flown away with the last bird.*

*The days are filled with grayness,*

*The settlement has wrapped itself together,*

*Embracing as children with a mother.*

*The muddy fall is now here,*

*The sky is a patchwork – gray on gray,*

*The roads mirror themselves naked and pure*

*In puddles, mud, and rains.*

--------------------------------

*There are more poor men than before, Fear and lurkers – wait at every door, Not only at Reb Gedalya's are the shutters locked, It seems that in the morning, the night comes in to stay.*

Today, Serock is empty. It's a dead town with hardly 2000 residents, where it becomes night right in the morning. There are not only no Jews left in the town, but after the liberation no Jew even tried to resettle there.

I visited City Hall in Serock, that administers from a wooden little house in which there used to be the cooperative bank and the *gemillas khesed* fund. The chairman of City Hall, Stanislaw Sowa, complained to me about the sad situation in the town that had lost all of its reason for existence. The people are moving away to the larger cities and to the new industrial centers.

[Page 504]

"From time to time," the chairman of City Hall said, "I receive a letter from the Serock Jews in Israel or America, who ask about their close ones, or about the graves of family members. But I have nothing to report to them. In the year 1941, the Nazis ordered both cemeteries be ploughed over – the old cemetery and the new one – and since the liberation I have not seen a living Jew in Serock."

As if escorted by the shadows of the vanished Jews, I made my way slowly through the empty, many little streets of Serock, walked up the steps of the little wooden houses, and listened to the vague drone of the guide that the chairman of City Hall had provided for me.

This was the pre-war teacher of the Polish public school in Serock, Antony Ribnicki, who mentioned the names of the former landlords of these houses that were still standing in the marketplace and on Kosciuszko Street – the main street of the town.

The gray-haired, middle-aged Ribnicki spoke about his former Jewish students in awe. He told me that they were exceptional in all studies, even in the study of the Polish language. This evoked jealousy among their Polish friends, and not only once did this incite anti-Semitic incidents.

"Because I was so committed to my Jewish students," said the public school teacher of Serock, "some of the darker elements called me *pokholek zhidowski* (Jewish servant)."

This former teacher showed me a wooden house on a side street, and said to me that that was where the union of professional Jewish workers was located – tailors, shoemakers, and carpenters.

*[Page 505]*

"If they would be here," he said, "the town would look different. But they were all killed in Auschwitz. Only a few were saved – a certain Feynboim, who is now in Warsaw. The others are in Israel or in America."

This Polish man, who was telling me that even before the war he belonged to the radical teacher's union, and therefore he was discharged from his position, spoke with great reverence about the old Rav of Serock, whose name he no longer could remember. But he described him to me as having a rich face and a snow white beard, and as a great scholar for whom "even the worst hooligans in the town had respect."

My guide also knew to tell me that in the 1920s, there was a tumult with a rabbi in Serock, a man of miracles. (He used this expression: "*Cadik Cudatworca*," a miracle man.) Nearby, he showed me a house with a steel balcony, where the Rebbe lived.

This former teacher, as such, brought to life many colorful episodes from the not so distant Jewish past of Serock, of which there was no trace left. Only from the spirit of the tragic remainder of the Serock Jews, who are spread all over the entire world, do the vanished faces live from this poor but wonderful town at the shore of the river Narew.

Around the turn of the century, Serock had a reputation as an important community among the smaller Jewish towns around Warsaw. The glory of Serock is exceptional in the Jewish world, and came about in the second half of the past century when the star rose in the genius of Rav Yosef Levenshtayn.

He was born in the year 1837 in Lublin, into a family of great rabbinic ancestry, and the young genius was caught up by the liberal tide that ruled in Poland in the era of the uprising in the year 1863.

*[Page 506]*

In the year 1874, Rav Yosef Levenshtayn was invited to assume the rabbinic leadership of Serock, a role that he held for a full half century, until his death in the year 1924.

The Serock Jews, among whom there were many learned people, surrounded their spiritual leader with a rare love – the leader that at so many different times received requests to assume rabbinic leadership in many important communities in Poland and even outside of Poland. Rav Levenshtayn, however, declined all of these glowing requests and remained with his poor community.

In this quiet town, where the train never stopped, Rav Levenshtayn led a rich life and even left a large inheritance of religious books that hold a prominent place in rabbinic literature of the new times. Other than spiritually rich commentaries on the Torah and Talmud, the Serock Rav also created a monumental work, a sort of rabbinic lexicon. This is "*Dor ve'Dor ve'Dorshov*" (Generation and Generation and his Generation) that contains 6600 biographies of rabbis and rabbinic dynasties.

The son of the Serock Rav, Berish Levenshtayn, had a printing company in Warsaw. He occupied himself primarily with printing rabbinic books, and first printed his father's books. Other than that, all his years, Berish Levenshtayn worked on a fixed calendar that he completed and printed shortly before the outbreak of World War II. It's not known whether there are any surviving examples of this calendar. The son of Berish Levenshtayn, a grandson of the Rav of Serock, became the son-in-law of the well known Rav of Warsaw, Rav Zwi Yekhezkel Mikhelson.

Another grandson of Rav Levenshtayn, Shmuel Donner, who is now in New York, told me that his grandfather was an enthusiastic reader of modern Jewish literature. He actually sent him, the grandson, for these books to the town library, that, in fact, Shmuel Donner helped build.

"When we in the library received the Yiddish translation of Darwin's *Origin of Species*, that was published in New York Shmuel Donner told me, "my grandfather was one of the first in the town to read the work. That was practically in the last few months of his life."

*[Page 507]*

A third grandson of Rav Yosef Levenshtayn, a brother of Shmuel Donner, is one of the most popular, modern painters in America. That is Efraim Donner, who is particularly familiar with the landscape of the aristocratic Newport, Rhode Island. It's an unusual situation, that a rabbinic grandson of a poor, scattered Jewish town in Poland should become a recognized artist in historic Newport, the summer residence of the American industry magnates.

*[Page 508]*

The father of Efraim and Shmuel Donner, Rav Yakov Donner, a son-in-law of Rav Yosef Levenshtayn, is well known in the scholarly circles in New York. A large crowd comes every *Shabbos* to the Brooklyn Jewish Center to hear his lecture of a page in Talmud that Rav Yakov Donner studies there already for the last twenty years.

The Serock Jews in America, the old and established as well as the newcomers, keep themselves as one family and belong to the old Serock Society that is run by Hyman Dresner as president, and Louis Sosniak, secretary.

In the homes of all former Serock residents, the picture of the great sage Rav Levenshtayn hangs. This, the grandson Shmuel Donner, a true master of dreams, printed especially from the original picture of his esteemed grandfather.

What is relevant about this miracle worker from Serock, about whom the Polish teacher was telling me in a tone as if this was a face from the distant past, was about the young rabbi, Rav Aharon Katzenelenbogen, of blessed memory, who came from prestigious rabbinic ancestry, and came to Serock at the end of World War I from a town in Russia. The poor in Serock were drawn to this young rabbi – the butchers, the wagon drivers, the village merchants, and the porters, all who struggled for their daily living.

In this time of frightful need that ruled in the Jewish towns in Poland, it was no wonder that the struggling and confused Jews were easily drawn to one that – even for a moment – would tear them away from the weekly gray, hopelessness.

The Rebbe, about whom his followers said that day and night he occupied himself with *Kabbala* (mystical studies), made no external impression of being a Kabbalist. He was always well dressed in a satin long coat, suede [or chamois] boots, an expensive *shtreimel* (round fur hat), and his light blond little beard nicely combed. Also, the Rebbetzen (his wife) had a reputation in the town as a beauty and was always elegantly dressed.

*[Page 509]*

Once, on *shvi'i shel pesach* (the second to last day of Passover), after prayers, the Rebbe with his entire congregation, went singing and dancing in the streets, and went in the direction of the market. The Rebbe went onto the balcony of his house. The Rebbe's followers assembled all the sick people in the town, among them a young man, the baker's son-in-law, who for many years had suffered from a difficult sleep disorder.

Shmuel Brukhanski, one of the surviving Serock Jews, who as a very young boy was witness to this extraordinary scene, told me that after the Rebbe gave a scream, "Stand up and walk!" the sick young man, to everyone's shock, got up and walked. Shmuel Brukhanski was a close observer of these events that occurred with this young Rebbe. Shmuel Brukhanski is now in New York, together with his brother Yakov. Their father, Menakhem Brukhanski, was the cantor in the city of Serock, and a brother to the famous Wyszkow cantor, Malkhiel Brukhanski.

The news about the miracle with the sick young man spread quickly in the surrounding towns, and Jews came from all around asking for help from the Rav of Serock.

The Serock Rebbe left two sons that were then still young boys – one ten years old, and the other fourteen. These two boys settled in Warsaw on Zamenhof Street and quickly became known as the "young rabbis."

Every year, they would travel to Serock and there have a community event (*a tisch*) and also lead the congregation in prayers in the big *shul*. These two inheritors of the Serock *Maggid*, actually belong to the small court of the surviving Jews of Serock. One son is in London, and the other in Israel.

My guide in Serock, the elderly Polish teacher, took me to the Warsaw highway to show me where the Serock cemetery was located and where was the grave of the Serock Rav. He told me about the original tombstone of the young chairman of the professional union of Jewish tailors, shoemakers, and carpenters in Serock, Yankel Kuzhnicki, who was tortured during a strike by the Serock police and then died in the prime of life. Among the traditional half-rounded Jewish tombstones, there was an original monument on the grave of a young martyr, that was in the presentation of a broken down tree.

*[Page 510]*

From all this, there is no memory left. On the place where there was the Jewish cemetery in Serock, on that early fall, sunny afternoon, freshly ploughed fields were spread out, and in the silence one could hear the rush of the Narew River.

I left Serock with the bitter feeling that every trace of the 500-year-old Jewish history had been wiped out.

**("Forward" – abridged)**

[Page 511]
# Characters and Images from the town

[Page 512]    Blank

[Page 513]

**Reb Yaakov Khenokh Cymerman/Tzymerman**

# Reb Yaakov Khenokh Cymerman/Tzymerman,

# Of Blessed Memory (Z"L)
## Translated by Pamela Russ

Reb Yaakov Khenokh Cymerman/Tzymerman, of blessed memory (Z"L), was born somewhere in the year 1883 in Serock. Also his father, Reb Yitzkhok Meyer (called Itche Meyer the Khasid), and his mother Brayna, and even his grandfather were all Serockers.

Reb Cymerman was a student of the Serocker Rav, Rabbi Yosef Levenshtayn, of blessed memory, and he was married in Ostrolenka. After the days of being supported by his father-in-law Reb Yitzkhok Mordekhai, he returned to Serock and occupied himself with business. He was a tremendous student of religious studies and a very wise man.

When he was in his twenties, Reb Cymerman settled in Danzig, and was very active in the Jewish community and in organizing the Orthodox Jewish life.

In his thirties, Reb Cymerman arrived in London, where he has elected as the chairman of the *Vaad Harabbonim* (established Rabbinic Committee). Later he took the position of Chief Rabbi for the United Orthodox Communities (Federation).

[Page 514]

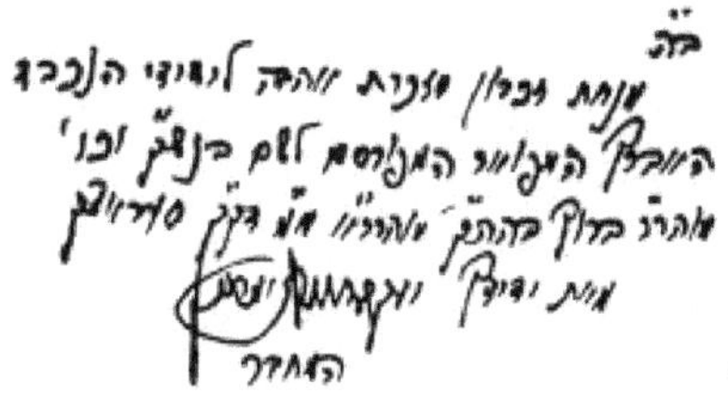

ספר

# אמרי יעקב

מבאר מקראי קודש ומאמרי רז"ל בטוב טעם ודעת
בלשון צח ונקי על פי משל ומליצה בעזרת חונן לאדם
דעת. המעיין ימצא בו דבר בעתו לכל עת בשנה,
חומר גדול לדרוש. לרבנים ומטיפים, אשר הכנותי
בעזרת האל מפרי עמלי

מאת הרב המחבר

יעקב הענך בן לאאמו"ר ר' יצחק מאיר זצ"ל,
צ י מ ר מ ן

לונדון     ת ש ״ ד     לפ״ק.

בדפוסו של י. נרודיצקי, 131־129, רחוב קאוועל, מזרח־לונדון.

**Cover of Reb Cymerman's book (*sefer*) titled *Imrei Yakov*, "The Sayings of Yakov." Published in London, 1943**

[Page 515]

Reb Cymerman soon became well known as a community minded businessman among the Jewish population, and among the youth as well, in the entire England.

After World War Two, Rav Cymerman was very involved with getting help for the Jewish refugees from Europe and became known as a great philanthropist and was well being loved in all of England, even among the assimilated Jews within the youth. He was also regularly invited as mediator in many problematic situations.

Rav Cymerman died in 1964 in London. Thousands of Jews escorted him to his final resting place. He left three sons and a daughter: The oldest son, Yosef Eliezer, is a well-known businessman and the director of the Jewish Federation. The second son, Borukh Moyshe, is a leader in the *Agudah,* and writer for the weekly *Agudah* paper, in English and Yiddish. The third son, Yitzkhok Meyer, is a merchant; and the grandson, Binyomin Cymerman, is a professor in London.

Rav Cymerman was the author of the book "*Imrei Yakov*" (The Sayings of Yakov), in two volumes, and also left much correspondence that has not yet been printed.

**Rav Yosef Katzenelenbogen**
**(Serock – London – Tel-Aviv)**

[Page 516]

# Reb Menakhem Brukhanski
# The Serocker Cantor
### by Shmuel B.

## Translated by Pamela Russ

Menakhem *Khazzan* (the cantor), as he was called, when he was about 61 years old, was destined to struggle with difficult situations for his very existence. But still, he did not become broken, and until the very end of his days, he remained a great believer who carried the challenging situation on his shoulders with strength.

He was born in Lomze to religious parents of aristocratic descent. His father, the cantor and ritual slaughterer (*khazen* and *shokhet*) in Lomze, was Reb Eliyohu Brukhanski. His mother, Fruma Gita-Raizel, was a great-granddaughter of the first Lomzer Rav, Reb Zalman Khosid, of blessed memory. He was raised with the true, Jewish, religious spirit. His father died while he was still young, and he had to support not only himself but also his entire family. He and his two brothers – the elder, Malkiel, who was already then a great musician, and the younger one, Yakov-Kopel – would leave home and travel around from town to town to *daven* on *Shabbos* and to give concerts in order to give his mother and the children some livelihood. They had a huge success with their concerts. They enriched everyone with their wonderful singing. More so, the older one, Malkiel, began to write his own compositions that many cantors used. They were presented with the best marriage proposals, and that is how Malkiel became a son-in-law in Pultusk and the cantor and ritual slaughterer in Serock. My father and this younger brother spent much time with Malkiel and sang in his choir. My father married Shepsel Farber's daughter, Bina Khaya, of blessed memory. He studied how to be a ritual slaughterer. When Malkiel left later on to be the cantor in Nadvorna, my father took over his position in Serock. He hoped with time also to become the ritual slaughter. He was loved by all. He was a strong baritone, and had a clear diction with a Lithuanian dialect. Every word was clear as pearls. He instituted a good choir (with the best voices) of upper class boys who wanted to be in the choir. I remember some of it as if it were today:

Yekhezkel the glazier's son; Yisroel Issur Blumberg; Yekhiel Meyer, the son of Elya Khaim; Zishe Vayngrad, Butche Kristel; the sons of Dovid Varshavski, Yekhiel and Khanokh (and Khanokh was the initiator of the Serocker Memorial Book). Also singing were: Khaim Eliezer Gzhebyenyazh, Yisroel Dovid Markevich, Borukh Gurman, and my two brothers Shepsel and Yakov. I also sang in the choir and enjoyed it immensely. Before the holidays, my father would practice with all the choirboys all the holiday prayers, and the heartfelt melodies were carried from the open windows into the streets, and many people would stand nearby and listen.

*[Page 517]*

Later, a shocking event happened in our house. Before the end of World War One, my beloved mother, Bina Khaya, left this world at a young age, leaving four children – one daughter Leah and three sons. My father, just as the rest of us, was broken and depressed from this tragedy. The house began to fall apart because my father did not have the wherewithal to raise the children so he married a second time. The family grew and the income lessened. It was impossible to support the family from a cantor's income. At the same time, he was offered a wonderful cantorial position in Sopot, near Danzig. The previous cantor had left for four years, and he was supposed to come back after that. These four years are the best ones, one can say, that we had. Materially, we revived a little.

*[Page 518]*

My father died of starvation in the Jablonner ghetto in 1942. May their blood be avenged.

*In honor of his memory*
**Shmuel B.**

[Page 519]

# Our Neighbor Reb Mendel Frenkel,
## *may he rest in peace*
### by Yakov Brukhanski, New York

## Translated by Pamela Russ

The ritual slaughterer *(shokhet)* from Popowo, Reb Mendel Frenkel, was a neighbor of ours, right next door, for many years. His windows from one side looked out on the street corner of the market, and from the other side onto Koshtchushka Street. He was also revered by all the other neighbors of the houses. His household consisted of two sons and three daughters, and he built a respected, aristocratic family. Reb Mendel created a good name around him.

As he greeted everyone he met with a staunch "good morning" using the hard consonant sound of the "R" (of the "*raish*" in "*gut morgen*"), inwardly, he was soft and gentle. He never told anyone what was permitted and not permitted on Shabbos (meaning he never reprimanded nor patronized anyone). Since I was then a young boy, one particular scene is etched in my memory

It was early one morning in the 1920's. Over Poland there raged all types of military groups and their generals, and all kinds of murderers such as Petlura and his gang, General Haller and his gang, the *poznanchikes* [1] that controlled Central Poland, and our town came under their rule. The first thing they did was to implement tough anti-Jewish laws. The generations of Polish-German hatred that had been soaked up was poured out onto Jewish heads. One of their decrees was to grab Jews off the streets and from their homes for forced labor and for punishment. We were shocked and as if hit by thunder, when in the middle of one day three *poznanchikes* with their scarred noses and twisted mustaches stormed into our house and went straight to the disguised door that was hidden by a cabinet, and without even a question, they moved the cabinet and broke open the door to the last hiding place.

1. Poznanczyk in Polish - a native of Poznań, a city in historical Great Poland; in Prussia 1815-1919; now in Poznań province, W. Poland. (Extract from Encyclopaedia Judaica). Poznanczyk was also the nickname given to soldiers and officers of the Polish military units (Armia Wielkopolska) during the Uprising of 1918-1919 - a military insurrection of Poles in the region called the Grand Duchy of Poznań against the German/Prussian forces [from Wikipedia]).

*[Page 520]*

And from there they dragged out three Jews and a grown son. They sadistically beat my father and the others, and Reb Mendel Frenkel and his oldest son Shmelke Frenkel, may they rest in peace, began to scream. When they sadistically beat my father and the others, I screamed wildly and couldn't watch. Soon they began ripping out pieces of Reb Mendel's beautifully kept beard. Fists full of hair were ripped out, and the blood ran like water. Reb Mendel moaned, never screamed. The murderers celebrated after that and cut off only one side of the beards from every one of the men, then chased everyone into the streets with their whips. There were already other groups of Jews there, waiting to be sent away for hard labor outside of the city, to dig trenches. Reb Mendel the *shokhet* went with his beard bandaged up for a long time after that. With time, the murderers disappeared like a bad dream.

Under the rule of Marshal Pilsudski, the Jews were able to catch their breath, and a restraint [of the violence] came to our city Serock. The children grew up and replaced the elderly, and some were later caught up in the progress of things, attaching themselves to the Zionist and culture organizations. Every *Sukkos* holiday, my father and I would go the Reb Mendel Frenkel's *sukkah* just for *kiddush*, even when I was already all grown up. I especially enjoyed Reb Mendel's leading the morning services (*davening shakharis*) for the holidays. The best *davening* was when his son-in-law whom he supported, Reb Moyshe Mendel Litman Razenowicz, would help him. His baritone was heard clearly, and I was accustomed to hearing beautiful music from my father, Menakhem *Khazen*, may he rest in peace, whom I would also help with the services and with the large choir. Nonetheless, I loved Reb Mendel's moving and spiritual *shakharis*, much of which I remembered for a long time, as well as his glow as a dignified aristocrat. Once the glow and pride suddenly disappeared, and a difficult change took place in the house of the Popover *shokhet*. This was in the mid-thirties, that was also the beginning of his end.

*[Page 521]*

Reb Mendel was one of four *shokhtim* (ritual slaughterers) who, while he was still a young man, was granted his position by the Rav and Elder Reb Yosef Levenshtayn, of blessed memory. So, he was then secure with his livelihood. As the other *shokhtim*, he was first responsible to G-d, then to the Rav, then to the community. It happened, though, that Reb Mendel was forbidden to practice by the new Rav, Rev Yizkhok Morgenstern. I don't know the real reason to this very day. Maybe, because of the arguments of the butchers and the Rav, in which sometimes the *shokhtim* happened to take the wrong side, or maybe it was because of Jewish law, and maybe once he didn't slaughter according to the law. For Reb Mendel this was too hard of a nut to crack. He was of the sort that went into an argument and couldn't put up an opposition. But it was even more difficult for him to swallow this from embarrassment and confusion. Because he didn't know if he would ever be able to support his family after this, he took this very much to heart, and G-d should protect us, he lost his mind. He stopped talking to people, confused everything, and stopped eating and drinking. It was useless to try and convince him of anything, even if his family or neighbors pleaded with him, and he even wouldn't listen to the doctor who tried to encourage him to bring some food to his lips – not in a nice way, not in an angry way. He began to flicker like a light. His thin body shrank more and more every day, and from his stately beard there remained only a thin bunch of hair because he did to himself what the "*poznantchikes*" once did to him – pulled out his beard one hair at a time.

*[Page 522]*

In a short time, Reb Mendel exhaled his last breath, and his soul departed at the age of 58. His wife couldn't survive this, and the following year, she joined him in his eternal rest. The rest of the children, two sons and two daughters, along with their families, were destroyed by the Germans, along with all their townspeople – their sisters and brothers of Serock. Only one daughter remained alive – the oldest, Golde Leah (today – Trebrin). She left for America at the beginning of the thirties and lives in Brooklyn today with her children and grandchildren.

**Yakov Brukhanski, New York**

[Page 523]

# Mendel Bobek / Babek
*May his memory be blessed*
## by Melekh Hershfinger

### Translated by Pamela Russ

In 1933, he died in a Jewish hospital in Warsaw after an operation. He requested that he be buried in a cemetery in Serock near the grave of the elderly Rav, where he had purchased a plot when he was still alive. When the Warsaw burial committee (*khevra kadisha*) brought Reb Mendel to town, there was a large crowd waiting on the Warsaw highway to give him their last respects, and they escorted him to his home. The following morning, when the *khevra kadisha* had done their rituals, the entire town assembled.

How does Mendel *jekeles* (the simple one), an ordinary Jew, a shoemaker for generations, come to deserve such respect?

It seems that even those in his home – sons, daughters, daughters-in-law, and sons-in-law – didn't know what kind of father they actually had. Shoemakers, tailors, and other townspeople recounted the type of person he was. A dedicated father to his children and devoted father to us. Who will now come to us on Friday to see if the kitchen is warm and if we are preparing for *Shabbos*? If he would see that the kitchen is cold and that the rooms are even colder and that no one is saying a word to the others, Reb Mendel would take out 10 zlotys from his pocket, and he would say: "Here, I'm lending this to you, and, woman of the house, hurry go get food and don't forget a bottle of wine for *kiddush* on *Shabbos*." And if we held back, he comforted us saying G-d would help us pay it all back.

That's how he would go around to a few families. He sensed who had meager earnings that week. He didn't think about who had old debts that were not paid back. Reb Mendel was the son of Yankel the shoemaker, who had no means to have his son go to school, but only sent him to *cheder* so that he would know how to pray *(daven)*. That was it. Soon after that, he went to work, becoming a shoemaker, helping his father earn a livelihood for the family and then becoming an honest Jew. That's how he was raised. But in his heart, he earned a holiness through his compassion,. He felt sympathy for anyone who had pain, who had bad fortune, or if he found out that someone was hungry, he was committed to them all. When he was taken as a soldier to "Fonya"[2] (meaning to Russia – see footnote), he served dutifully, came home, married, and had a family.

# Translator's notes:

2. Taken from The Jewish Daily Forward *Stealing Fanny:On Language*. By Philologos, published July 15, 2009, issue of July 24, 2009.) Fonye almost certainly comes from Vanya, an affectionate form of Ivan, as in Chekhov's play "Uncle Vanya." "Fonya the thief" as a Yiddish epithet for the czar originally may have referred to the czarist practice of forcibly shanghaiing and impressing Jewish youngsters, sometimes barely in their teens, into the Russian army for terms of service of up to 25 years; the men entrusted with the task were known in Yiddish as *khapers* or "snatchers," and the Jewish community lived in great fear of them. Although this practice reached its height in the first half of the 19th century under czars Alexander I and Nicholas I, its origins go back to the 17th century, which did have one Czar Ivan, Ivan V. It is thus possible that he was the original "Fonya *ganef*," the czar who stole Jewish children. But it is also possible that, practically all the czars having had a reputation among Jews for rapacity and anti-Semitism, the original Fonya *ganef* was a different Ivan, such as Ivan IV, known as "the Terrible," who ruled for 50 years in the 16th century. "Fonya *ganef*"was not an epithet reserved by Jews for the czar alone. It also was sometimes used by them to refer to Russia or to Russians in general, or at least to Russians regarded as unscrupulous goyim. (The fact that most Russians thought of Jews as cheats and thieves just as most Jews thought of Russians that way is ironic but hardly noteworthy; prejudiced majorities and minorities have often projected the same negative images onto one another.) Remarks like, "Fonya *ganef* has gone to war against Japan," or, "One should never do business with Fonya *ganef*," could be heard often among the Jews of Russia prior to World War I.

*[Page 524]*

But one thing he didn't understand – that was the *davening* (praying), the Torah reading, and the few chapters in *Tehilim* (Psalms) that were recited daily. He prayed to G-d and didn't really know the meaning of what he was saying. So, he found a solution: He had a teacher (rebbe) come to his home night after night, for a few years, until Mendel understood what he was asking of G-d in the holy language of *lashon kodesh* (Hebrew). Let the women pray in the *mameh loshon*, Yiddish. And from then on he understood the sunshine in life. In the mornings, he was amongst the first ones to arrive in the *beis medrash* (House of Study), and even in the evenings he would learn in the *beis medrash* between *minkha* and *maariv* (evening prayers) with the *khevra mishnayos* (a regular evening group that studies the Talmud on a daily basis), and was also devoted to the burial society (*khevra kadisha*) and the *khevra tehilim* (the group that recited Psalms daily).

Purim time, money would arrive to his name – a few hundred dollars from the American Serocker Society – for help for the Serocker Jews for Passover, to help them bring in the holidays. In the town, they also collected monies for this cause. From Purim until *Pesach* (Passover) Reb Mendel didn't work in the evenings. The committee for distributing money for the needy was very busy. *Erev Pesach* (the evening of the beginning of Passover), he managed to finally catch his breath and was satisfied that all the Serocker Jews would have some taste of *Yom Tov*. The children sent a report to America stating how much money was given and to whom.

Reb Mendel had a *sefer Torah* (Torah) written, and led it into the *shul* (synagogue) under a *khuppa* (canopy) with music and dance and with a festive meal in the *shul* for all the Serocker Jews. He had broad shoulders and a round face with a nicely kempt beard, and his eyes looked at everyone with goodness. When he was happy, he would go into his house and sing and dance with his grandchildren, so lively that the house shook.

Friday afternoons, when he had stopped working and was preparing for *Shabbos,* he looked like another Jew – a *Shabbos* Jew. When he was escorting his *sefer Torah* into the *shul* under the *khuppa*, his face was all flushed, just as when he would distribute the monies amongst the poor. He left a large family: grown sons, a daughter, and grandchildren. We would all come to his gravesite every year in order to unite ourselves with his figure of light.

Note: The latter part of the last paragraph appears on page 525 of the original Sefer Serock.

**Melekh Hershfinger**

[Page 525]

[Page 526]

# My Brother
# The Poet – Yosel Grosbard
## by Yehoshua Grosbard, Haifa

### Translated by Pamela Russ

All of us in the house knew that Yosel would grow up to be a writer. Already in 1927, at age 22, he debuted in a journal that appeared in Pultusk. He published a poem titled "My Town" (Mein Shtetele), that drew the attention of a literary critic.

Yosel was born in the year 1905 in the small town of Serock, where the rivers Bug and Narew meet. He would always tell that as a young boy he would swim in the Narew and almost drowned there, and this bound him with love to the town. As a child he and his parents left to Ciekhanow where he completed public school and later helped his father as house painter.

In 1918, Yosel and his parents came to Warsaw. There he worked in a metal factory where he was worked very hard by his boss. At the same time, he was very active in the metalworkers' union and in the youth movement of the *Bund Tzukunft* (Future) and later in the *Komtzukunft*, and after that in the Communist youth parties. He studied hard in his evening courses and worked for a time with artwork, with the artist Moishe Appleboim.

*[Page 527]*

Later, Yosel and his family came to Ciekhanow once again. He was active in the Anski Library, read papers in philosophy, and in social and cultural themes. He wrote and published poetry in various periodicals in Poland and other countries, such as in the newspapers *Ferois* (Forward), *Literarishe Bleter* (Literary Pages), and *Unzer Veg* (Our Way). In his poems one can feel his strong ties to everyday life.

In "*Tzu Mein Lied*" (To My Song), published in Argentina's *Der Spiegel* (The Mirror), he wrote:

*Come down from your high places*

*Take off your dress of blue,*

*I'll furnish you with simple boots*

*And you'll walk beside me.*

In the song "Nem Tzunoif Ale Vartzlen" (Gather All Your Roots), published in Ferois:

*Let the joy of the dream fill you*

*From the smallest blade of grass and from each tree,*

*Oh, try your best to understand*

*The secret of -- wanting to grow and of being...*

*The restless sweetness in the air*

*Accept together with the nightingale's sweet song*

*See how the bird delights*

*As it faithfully builds its nest.*

Yosel's devotion to the concrete realities of his life becomes even more boldly expressed in his cycle of poetry, titled "Here" in the periodical *Ferois* in 1938:

*It's not only the vanished body of my zaide*

*Dust, beneath the moss-covered stone,*

[Page 528]

*Not only the lingering fear*

*Of my Mother's -- Father's present plagued days,*

*But also my proud bright dream*

*That springs up like a freshly blossoming tree --*

*My dream of the week to come*

*Is interwoven and tied to the earth -- here.*

In the second poem in the same cycle, he wrote:

*Here! – From the same mother's lap*

*As the pine tree, poplar tree, and the rose,*

*So it is that I am also from here.*

The theme of the cycle of the poems is interesting to note: "*A Grus Dir Bergelson Fun Shtetl*" (Greetings to Bergelson from the Town), published in the *Spiegel*, Buenos Aires, 1945. The editor added the following comments:

This poem was sent to us by the poet Y. Grosbard in the year 1938. Already at that time he sensed the huge destruction that was pushing its way into the Jewish cities and towns in Poland.

At that time, Grosbard wrote to us that "this song is the beginning of a cycle of poems titled

*Greetings to Bergelson from the Town*, that I am sending out to you shortly." We waited for the next poems, but meanwhile the war broke out and not only did we not receive any poems but there was no information, no sign of his life. Where is that beloved, sad poet Grosbard who believed in the year 1939 that "miracles would yet happen?"

In general, Yosel had a determined nature, loved to polemicize over all kinds of questions, and especially loved discussions in literature, poetry, art, and music. He sang and played music with heart. He disliked lofty language, as he wrote in his poem "*Aibigkeitz Dibrus*" (Everlasting Speech), published in *Yalkut Hamoadim* (2), Buenos Aires.

[Page 529]

*There are all kinds of words, hard as granite,*

*Crude, raw, that flow with blood.*

*Words, that strike like lightning and remain cold –*

*Bengali fire that quickly burns out.*

Yosel hated this cold, artificial fire, so he would experience life's events deeply. The war was difficult for him. When the eastern Jews were chased out of Germany, he wrote in his poem "*Pleitim*" (Refugees), published in the "*Folks Zeitung*" in June 1939:

*These days –*

*That flow past you*

*Are flames*

*Of a burning stream.*

*In the poem "Doh" (Here) from the cycle, the poet wrote:*

*And against today's dark waves*

*And against the enemy –*

*I will wrestle with raging force,*

*And I will fight with my teeth,*

*With my hand and feet,*

*Until –*

*From my land will rise*

*The brotherly hand…*

*In another of Yosel's poems, we read:*

*My doubting heart that never was*

*Believes – that miracles will yet happen.*

Unfortunately, he never lived to see the day of this wonder. These last years, I received from various friends cut out articles of newspapers and journals of the events around Yosel. Also, from his list of friends I received a cut out article in the Forwards, from January 23, 1960. There, the writer Sh. L. Shnayderman wrote the following about a visit to Yosel's hometown Serock:

[Page 530]

"Serock also produced a talented young poet and painter, Yosel Grosbard, who shortly before the outbreak of the war attracted the attention of the Yiddish literary and art circles in Warsaw. And his deeply emotional poems about the town were expressed in the spirit of the lyricist and the eye of the painter.

"In the year 1939, right at the beginning of the catastrophe, Yosel Grosbard wrote a cycle of poems in which he described the deep worries that were spread in his hometown Serock, it was a premonition for the great destruction to come."

[Page 531]

# "A Grus Dir Bergelson fun Shtetl" Greetings to You Bergelson, from Our Town
## by Yosel Grosbard,

### may his blood be avenged

### Translated by Pamela Russ

*With words from my gray mood,*

*I am writing a letter and a poem to you.*

*Oh, winds! Carry my greetings far away – About my town, tell all.*

*Summer has flown away with the last bird*

*The days – have filled themselves with grayness,*

*The settlement wrapped itself together Embraced, as children with a mother.*

*Gloomy fall is here now –*

*The sky is patched – gray on gray:*

*All the roads are bare and empty*

*Full of puddles and mud, after the rain.*

*Angry winds are storming*

*And neighing just like the horses*

*And wish to tear up hundred-year-old trees from here,*

*Deeply rooted in the earth.*

*The despair covers the narrow streets*

*And remains still at the end of the alleys*

*And wandering, he steps back,*

*Where else does he have to go?*

*The marketplace, old and withered with cold,*

*Once bustling – now a played out hero.*

*At a table, a woman with a basket freezes, a Jew,*
*And behind them the stones often shine red.*
*[Page 532]*

*The train station – an indifferent locale,*
*Its walls sinking and dreaming in permanent sorrow.*
*Trains come and leave quickly,*
*And soot and smoke quietly rock the way*
*In wealthy houses the radio is loudly playing concerts*
*And present-day joyful music as well.*
*And green parrots still draw out from envelopes*
*By katarinkes --- the blue good fortune.*
*There are more losers now than before,*
*Fear and angst await at every door,*
*Not only at Reb Gedalya's are the shutters banged shut,*
*It happens that in the morning, night lurks here…*
*Oh you great poet from afar*
*Forgive my depressed words.*
*My suffering heart that never did exist*
*Believes – miracles will yet happen!*

[Page 533]

# My Brother Shepsel Brukhanski, may his blood be avenged
by Yakov Brukhanski (Jack Bruks)

## Translated by Pamela Russ

As a young school boy, Shepsel already showed a talent for painting and carving. Not once did his Rebbe in school twist his ears for this. Later, though, his pictures decorated the walls in some of the classes of the Powszechner school in Serock.

At ten years old, Shepsel already had the taste of being an orphan, along with his older sister and two younger brothers. Hardship forced him to give up learning and painting, and he apprenticed for three years with a wood carver.

These new responsibilities and the disappointment of not being able to pursue his artistic talent, moved him early towards the ranks of the socialist movement. He read many books in the library of the Education League, where his portraits still hang of the classic writers of Yiddish literature and theoreticians of socialism.

*[Page 534]*

The local police, after visiting the Education League, looked for all traces of the painter. Shepsel left Serock and went to Warsaw. In his new home, he didn't look at his difficult economic situation; he helped his newly-arrived friends from Serock find work, and so on.

At the outbreak of World War Two, he lived in Legionowa (near Warsaw). The Nazis sent him with his wife and young daughter, along with all the Jews there, to their final destruction.

**Yakov Brukhanski
(Jack Bruks)**

[Page 535]

# Yakov (Yantche) Kuzhinksi, of blessed memory
### by Yosef Fajnboim

## Translated by Pamela Russ

He was born into a Khassidic family in 1902 (or 1903). From his youngest years, he helps his parents with their work. Their work in the oil factory is very difficult. This is a very primitive oil workshop. Farmers from the surrounding areas used to bring the rapeseed and for a certain price the Kuzhinski family would squeeze out the oil. The young Yakov (Yantche) with his young and feeble strength helps provide oil to the farmers.

When Yantche is 12 years old, he takes on the apprenticeship of a spats maker. After a few years of hard work, he becomes a self-sufficient wage earner, an associate of the boss (a journeyman) for a pitiful wage. (In those times, they would work 12 or 14 hours a day.) The young associate Yantche begins to feel the taste of a proletariat on his own shoulders, and becomes interested in literature – especially socialist literature. Very soon, he becomes politically and culturally educated, and throws himself with great enthusiasm into political activity. Yantche becomes one of the most idealistic young men of that time.

Soon, illegal revolutionary organizations begin to form, and Yantche is very active and dedicated to them. He has no fear, nothing is impossible – he becomes the real fighter in Serock.

In the year 1923, there are political arrests in Serock, and a line of socialists from the movement are arrested, including Hershel Mendzelewski. Other activists try to avoid the arrest by running away from the town or by hiding from the police. Yantche, being the technical person behind all the written literature, does not leave. He is responsible for the literary magazine, which is for him a holy cause. He doesn't want to leave his corner of his father's workshop where the literature is hidden, and when the police come to do a search and find – after a lengthy search – the illegal magazines and literature, Yantche is arrested. The sentence is severe: the methods that the Polish police used at that time with Jewish political arrests were very brutal and murderous. For five days they tortured him and tried to force him to give over the names of the rest of his colleagues in the organization. They knew that Yantche was the key to the illegal movement and they demanded information from him about his contacts and connections to the District Center, with the higher ups.

[Page 536]

**Yakov (Yantche) Kuzhinski, of blessed memory, in Otwock**

But Yantche, with his honest and determined character, did not release even one word. Beaten and bloodied, he was silent and with that showed his strength and his belief in what he thought was the right thing.

[Page 537]

Yantche was brought before a judge and was sentenced to a few years in prison. They couldn't break his spirit, but they broke him physically. Yantche became very sick in his lungs, and in general, the beatings took their toll on his health. After he completed his sentence, Yantche was a physically broken man, but remained with his spirit intact. His activities remained exactly as before, and his belief did not yield: He sustained the typical Jewish "sacrifice for the holy cause" that is so characteristic for many Jewish heroes in the history of martyrdom of the Jewish people.

After suffering for three years, Yantche died at the age of 26 (or 27). We organized a funeral as he deserved, and placed a memorial tombstone on his grave with writing in Yiddish. In those times, in Serock, these were called revolutionary acts.

Yantche's life and his death remained for the entire youth in Serock as a variety of colors and perspectives in their memories of a heroic figure.

May his memory be blessed!

**Yosef Fajnboim**

[Page 538]

# Neta Grabiya
## by Hanna Brauda

### Translated by Ruth Kilner

Neta Grabiya was born in 1913 in Ostroleka, as the firstborn son to Rav Menachem: Rabbi and Av Beth Din (head of the Jewish court) of the community in Sniadowo, near Lomza. He studied in the cheders (Hebrew elementary school) and Yeshivas (Hebrew high school) in Lomza and Grodno Lida.

He was orphaned by his father as a very young child.

In his youth, he and his widowed mother – who was remarried to the esteemed Rav Eliyahu Shub, of blessed memory – moved to Serock where he continued his studies in the Tachkamoni Beth Midrash for Rabbis in Warsaw.

During that period, he started working as a journalist. His first article – "The Sins of my Youth" (Yiddish: "*Zind Fun Mein Yugend*") in which he wrote about the life story and the troubles of the Serockan revolutionary, the late Yaakov (Yaantshe) Kuznicki, who was tortured by the Polish secret police – was featured in the daily religious newspaper, The Yiddish Daily (Yiddish: *Der Yiddishe Togblat*).

A vibrant life and new ideas led Neta towards the daily Zionist journal "Today" [Yiddish: *Haynt*,] and over time he became a member of the "Today's News" [Yiddish: *Hayntike Nayes*,] team.

My brother was very perceptive about our fate, and his articles about the troubles in the towns and villages of Poland, particularly in the famous town of Przytyk, were published on Page One of the newspaper, and caused strong repercussions within Jewish public affairs.

[Page 539]

Via a postcard I received from him via the Red Cross, I heard that his first child had been born during the bombing of Warsaw, in September, 1939.

My brother never realized his dream to write a book about Polish Judaism. He also never managed to publish our late father's writings – "Episodes from the Middle Ages" – or his translation of the Polish classics into Hebrew.

I do not have a copy of his articles published in *Haynt*, *Hayntike Nayes* and *Der Yiddishe Togblat*. The national library's collection in Jerusalem includes almanacs from the early twentieth century alone, which is most unfortunate.

Neta, of blessed memory, remained there, and perished together with the other martyrs.

My late brother excelled in kindness, and it was thanks to him that I was able to immigrate to Israel as a student. Before travelling to Israel, he gave me an article about our late father, saying that it would surely be safer with me.

His honesty, his modesty, his kindness, and his warm heartedness were cherished not only by his own family, but on all who knew him – friends and family.

He was one of Poland Jewry's most beautiful and delicate flowers.

**His sister,**
**Hanna Brauda**
**(Neve Oz, Israel)**

[Page 540]

# Captions translated by Ruth Kilner

R' Yossle "Alwanik"

R' Avraham Leiv *Melamed Daridakei* [lit: child teacher] and his wife, Tshortel

[Page 541]

***Der Orkester***
[Yiddish: The Orchestra]

[Page 542]   [Page 543]

**Football team**

**Young athletes**

[Page 544]

**Farewell ball for comrade Eliezer Haasman before his *Aliya* (immigration) to Israel**

[Page 544]

*[Page 545]*

**Aaron Novack the day before his journey to the United States of America**

*HaShomer Ha Tzair* (Young guardians) group

[Page 546]

**Group of young women from the public school**

**Group of youth from Serock**

[Page 547]

"Beitar" youth group

Football team

[Page 548]

**Group of "*Hechalutz HaMizrachi*" (Heb: Eastern Pioneer) young men and women**

**Farewell party for comrade Aaron Disner
before his Aliya (immigration) to Israel in 5695 (1935)**

[Page 549]

Group of young men and women from
"*Hechalutz HaMizrachi*" (Eastern pioneer) and "*Beitar*"

The "*Histadrut Tsionit*" (Zionist Union) – Farewell ball for teacher Chaim Yorkovitz before his emigration to America.

[Page 550]

**Group of school children at the public school**

**Group of young "*Hechalutz HaMizrachi*" (Eastern Pioneer) men**

[Page 551]

**Group of school children from the public school**

**Group of young women in the snow**

[Page 552]

"*Hashomer Hatzair*" (Young guardian) "*Lag Baomer*" voyage

At the "*Histadrut Tsionit*" (Zionist union) ball

[Page 553]

**Holy ark of Serock synagogue.
Drawn by Yehoshua Grossberg, Haifa**

[Page 554]

# Khannuka in the Big Shul
## by Yakov Mendzelewski (Kholon)

### Translated by Pamela Russ

As soon as the fall rains ceased, a frost froze over the soaked earth, and the first snow decorated the town in honor of Khannuka.

As evening fell, the shul street came alive. From all sides, Jews began to stream to the large shul and *Bais Medrash* to light the first Khannuka candle. Despite the weekday dress, a holiday spirit shone from the faces. The small Khannuka candles related that we have to have hope. It was mainly the children who enjoyed Khannuka, the beautiful young ones who went home from *kheder* in the cold autumn evenings, often hungry, with torn shoes – but on Khannuka night these children shone from joy at the time they would help their fathers light the candles and put them into the Khannuka "*menoras*" made from dug out potatoes with cotton wicks dipped into oil.

The children's eyes would sparkle as the *dreidels* fell onto the tables. The *dreidels* were made from spools. Since no one went to kheder on Khannnuka night, all the boys would come into the *Bais Medrash,* young and old – from those who were learning the *alef-bais*, to those who were learning *khumash* and *Rashi*, and *Gemara* and commentaries. These were students of the more prestigious teachers, such as Khaim Yoine, of blessed memory, his son Shimon Sep, of blessed memory, and Dovid Itzik Rubenshtayn, of blessed memory.

A great calm would embrace everyone when the *Baal Tefila* (the one who led the prayers) began his singing as he lit the main candle in the Khannuka *menorah* and recited the blessings. A resounding "Amen!" came from the shul. The spirited children tapped with their toes. Their great excitement affected the older people. One could see how the embittered workers with their faces wrinkled from great difficulties, smiled and laughed with tears. The young pranksters discreetly put out the main candle (*shamash*) during the prayers, in order to have to repeat the entire performance. Even the most prominent businessmen who prayed at the Eastern Wall of the shul ... with the Rav at the head, smiled happily into their white beards and didn't disturb the children's excitement with Khannuka.

*[Page 555]*

The Khannuka nights were stellar. The snow shimmered, lighting up God's little world. The trees were covered as if with white blossoms. And the river Narew, flowed quickly, as if rushing before it would freeze. Crowds went sliding down the mountains, and young couples would walk together closely, dreaming about their future good fortune. For the workers, with their books under their arms, their loads were evident, and they were deep in thought about difficult problems. Life dished out joy for them only on the tip of a knife. On this sort of a night, the moods improved, and they would throw snowballs with energy and fire, until pale cheeks turned rosy.

The Khannuka nights were filled with joy. The delicious aroma of potato latkes was smelled until late into the night. And from all the windows, the flames of the candles would dance slowly. Maybe the town already sensed the impending destruction that eliminated Jewish life from Poland, including our town Serock, together with the small Khannuka candles, forever.

[Page 559]

# Serocker Landsmanschafts in Israel and in the World

*[Page 559 - Hebrew] [Page 566 - Yiddish]*

## Aliyah from Serock to Israel

## Organization of the Emigrants from Serock in the State of Israel

### Introduction

#### by Khanokh Werdi (Ramat Gan)

#### Translated by Pamela Russ

The Aliyah from our town to Israel until the end of the 1920s was very slow.

At the beginning of the century only a few elderly made Aliyah to Israel, those whose highest ambition was to live out their years in the Holy Land, then to be buried on the Mount of Olives, and then merit the final resurrection of the dead (*Tekhiyas Hameisim*) without any "underground" travels.

In the revolution year 1905, a few revolutionaries ran off to Israel – those whom the Czarist agents were hunting – but there is no trace of them.

After World War I, and in the period of the fourth Aliyah in the 1920s, several families moved to Israel and went to live in the city and agricultural settlements.

A reception in honor of Mendel Kuligowski from Argentina, at the home of Shlomo Merla, z"l, in Tel Aviv

## A. At the end of the 1920s, until the outbreak of World War II, 1939

Thanks to the organizations of the Zionist movement and the youth *Khalutz* organizations, and the strategically increasing economic and political discrimination of the Polish organizations towards the Jews, there was a motivation for a larger Aliyah, particularly among the youth.

At the end of the 1920s until the outbreak in Israel of the events of 1936, scores of boys and girls and several families made Aliyah to Israel with the *Khalutz* and middle-class Aliyah.

Some of these new immigrants went to *Kibbutzim*, and the rest went to Tel Aviv, Haifa, and the surrounding areas.

[Page 567]

From the events in the year 1936 – and the Aliyah prohibitions by the British mandate powers – until the outbreak of World War II in 1939, some daring youth came to Israel after long travels and great dangers.

During that period we had no official *Irgun* (organization). The townspeople would meet at various opportunities at the homes of Kalman Wajnkrancz (Tel Aviv), Borukh Gurman (Haifa), and Aharon Czesner (Haifa).

## B. From the outbreak of World War II until 1950

With the outbreak of World War II, all ties with our close ones in our Polish town were cut off and we found ourselves in constant fear for their fate.

The first terrible news of the destruction of our community was brought by the brothers HaRav Yosef and Borukh Katzenelbogen and their sister Zipora, who were miraculously saved from Nazi hands and fortunately arrived here in Israel in the beginning of the 1940s after long travels and many dangers.

At the same time, a certain number of young men arrived who had run from the Polish army and General Anders.

During this time, some of our townspeople voluntarily enlisted in various defense units, as well as in the Jewish Brigade that fought against the German enemy on the Italian front.

The writer of these lines, who was in Poland in the year 1946, was fortunate to meet many of our survivors after the devastation and give them appropriate information and advice for their Aliyah to Israel.

The Aliyah for the rest of the survivors began in the year 1946. Our survivors shared the fate of the large crowds in the refugee ships, with which the British floats struggled mightily. Some of them were interned on the Island of Cyprus, and some of them were returned to Germany by the British.

*[Page 568]*

## The major Aliyah of our survivors began at the end of the War of Independence in the year 1949

Scores of families landed in our liberated ports and were quartered in emptied and abandoned houses.

The experience was huge and profound. Every day there were new arrivals – Oh! One searches for the other.

During this period, each long-time settler tried to help the newly-arrived in any way possible, without any type of general (formal) organization.

We have to mention separately that during that period our old friend, Shlomo Merle, of blessed memory, who died several years ago, displayed his bigheartedness and helped all those who needed, with his extended hand and warm heart.

## C. 1950 - The Activities of the *Irgun*

Scores of people we were taken to a camp of a few hundred, may God help that they increase. The majority of new immigrants needed advice, encouragement, financial help, and a social connection.

The needs showed that times were very ready for an organization for the camp – some sort of address where one could go for any issue. The first meeting of new immigrants and veterans came about in the carpentry workshop of Rephoel Friedman (Tel Aviv) – and subsequent meetings were at the place of Kalman Wajnkrancz (Tel Aviv). They called him "the Serocker Consul in Israel" – and they decided:

12. To call a country-wide gathering of all the townspeople who would set up the *Irgun* and elect a committee.

13. To set the 17th of Kislev as the annual Memorial Day in agreement with the decision that the Holocaust survivors had unanimously set when they had a special gathering during the time they were in refugee camps in all parts of Germany in the years 1946-1949.

[Page 569]

The majority of the new immigrants were concentrated in the southern part of the country, so that Tel Aviv became the center of all our activities.

On 17 Kislev, 5710 – 1950, there was the first countrywide gathering of our townspeople in the large hall of the Herzliah gymnasium in Tel Aviv, Akhad Ha'am Street.

Here, friends and relatives met for the first time. These were people whom the war and destruction had separated. The general conversation flowed without stop: screams of joy and sadness, laughter and tears, youth's memories and destruction – the first meeting of the leftover remnants.

That same evening was the first memorial gathering for our deceased ones.

At the time of this first gathering, it was decided to establish an *Irgun* (organization) for the Serockers in Israel, and there was an election held to set up a committee.

At the first meeting of the committee – the meeting was held in the house of Borukh Katzenelbogen (Tel Aviv) – it was decided to establish a fund for mutual aid that would be distribute loans without interest, to those needy friends (*khaveirim* or comrades).

The foundation capital was at first based on private contributions. The first contributions were made by the friends Shloime Merle, of blessed memory, and Refoel Friedman, may he have long life. The friends Markewicz Yisroel,

Mendzelewski Yakov, and Pniewski Yosef visited and received contributions from many friends in their private homes – in all corners of the country. Thanks to them and their loyalty, the fund was able to function very soon after its establishment.

During its existence, the fund distributed monies to many friends.

The unions of our townspeople in Argentina and North America soon responded warmly and sent significant sums to maintain the fund.

[Page 570]

The rise of our *Irgun* strengthened mutual rapprochement and mutual aid, and also created important social connections.

## D. The activities of the *Irgun*

Funding, management, distributing loans, taking care of the details of paying back, and managing the stability of the basic capital.

Taking care of needs in emergency situations with special subsidies.

## The annual meeting and memorial

Once a year, on the 17th of Kislev (December), we organize an annual country-wide gathering and memorial for our holy ones (victims). Many of our townspeople are involved in organizing this event. After the memorial service at this event, an accounting is given of the funding, general questions are addressed, and at the end a new committee is elected.

The committee inspires more social gatherings and personal connections.

We also meet at family events such as at a *bris,* wedding, bar mitzvah, birthday, and so on. Even in moments of tragedy.

## The Memorial Calendar

We set up a tombstone in memory of the destroyed Serock community in the wall of the Chamber of the Holocaust (*Martef Hashoah*) on Mount Zion in Jerusalem.

The unveiling of the tombstone in Jerusalem took place in May 1963 with almost all the adult townspeople from Serock in the country attending.

A representative of the Serock townspeople in London participated in this event – HaRav Henokh Zymerman, of blessed memory, and later, for the Yizkor book, he sent over the writings of his memories of religious life in Serock at the beginning of the century. He fulfilled his promise of doing so.

[Page 571]

# Sefer Serock

In order to eternalize the memory of our holy townspeople of the destroyed community, it was decided years ago to publish a memorial book titled: "Sefer Serock." All the townspeople were urged to participate by recording their memories of the distant and recent past and of the period of the destruction, and also to include all kinds of pictures of the town.

The writer of these lines spent years collecting all kinds of material about the town, and in 1958, during the annual gathering and memorial, distributed to all those present a questionnaire that was also given to our brotherhood organizations in Argentina and North America.

The preparations for this took very long and we had to overcome many unforeseen difficulties. The committee hired an editing team with full legal power, consisting of our friends Borukh Katzenelbogen, Shloime Sterdiner, and the author of these lines.

# Connecting to the Serocker townspeople in North America and Argentina

The committee is in regular contact with the brotherhood organizations in Argentina and North America.

In the last few years, our friends Shloime Ashenmil, Kalman Kuligowski, and Mendel Kuligowski visited us as representatives from the Argentina union, and friends Yakov Brukhanski, Yeshaye Maj and recently, the family Koperman and Shmuel Dunar visited as representatives from the North American society.

From the abovementioned unions we received contributions for our fund for mutual aid.

The Argentinian representative proposed that we build a "Serock House" – but because of the immediate shortage of monies, the project was not realized at that time.

## The last *Olim* (those who made Aliyah) to Israel

The large Aliyah of our survivors ended in the year 1952, and after that, within a few years, only few survivors came from Poland.

*[Page 572]*

By the end of 1956 (at the time of the Sinai War), several families came from Poland.

Recently, a few Serockers came from Poland that after the Six Day War in 1967 changed into an openly anti-Semitic country.

The following friends held office in the committee of our *Irgun,* from its establishment until today, and exchanged with each other:

Gurman Borukh (Haifa);

Grosbard Yehoshua (Haifa);

Werdiman-Warshawski Yekhiel Meyer (Kfar Witkin);

Werdi-Warshawski Khanokh (Ramat Gan);

Jaskowicz Malja (Tel Aviv);

Mendzelewski Yehuda (Bat Yam);

Mendzelewski Yakov and Rivka'le (Kholon);

Markowicz Yisroel (Tel Aviv);

Marle Shloime, of blessed memory;

Fogelman Bunim and Khava (Kholon);

Friedman Refoel and Zipora (Kholon);

Pniewski Yosef (Tel Aviv);

Pshikorski Avrohom, of blessed memory;

Rozenberg-Bernshtayn Malke'le (Tel Aviv).

The committee is also the same people for managing the fund for mutual aid.

## In closing

The committee, that was elected at the last annual meeting that took place on Sunday, 20th of Kislev – December 30, 1969, in the hall at Bais Wyskow, on 45 Bugersow, Tel Aviv, comprised of the following friends: Borukh Katzenelbogen (Tel Aviv) – chairman and secretary; Shloime Sterdiner (Ramat Gan) – treasurer; Khanokh Werdi (Ramat Gan); Yehuda Mendzelewski (Bat Yam); Rivka and Yakov Mendzelewski (Kholon); Markowicz Yisroel (Tel Aviv); Khava and Bunim Fogelman (Kholon); Yosef Pniewski (Tel Aviv); Malja Jaskowicz-Rozenberg (Tel Aviv); and Yekhiel Werdiman-Warshawski (Kfar Witkin).

The activities of the committee for years took place in the home of our dear Shloime Merle, of blessed memory, in Tel Aviv, and after his death, all the work concentrates in the house of our friend, may he live long years, Shloime Sterdiner (Ramat Gan, 31 Khivat Tzion Street).

With a tremor of love and pain, we remember our townspeople who died in recent years in Israel:

[Page 573]

Members of the committee: Shloime Merle and Avrohom Pshikorski, Tema Kalina, Zisel Iczkowicz, Golde Lajnwand-Belison, Priwa Lewinson-Perl, Khaya'le Zakharek, and Zilbershtayn-Rotman Zirel.

**May their memories be remembered forever.**

We bow our heads in memory of our sons who died on the altar in their most blossoming years as they were defending their country:

### Yehuda son of Zev, may his memory be blessed

Son of Khaya Wajnkrancz and Z. son of Zev (Kibbutz Ein Hakarmel)

Who fell in the Six Day War in 1967 during the liberation of Jerusalem;

### Tzvika Rozenberg, may his memory be blessed

Son of Elkhonon and Raja Rozenberg (Kfar Witkin)

Who fell on the eve of Yom Ha'atzmaut 5729 (April 1969) While defending the positions in Emek Hayarden

### May their memories be respected!

[Page 573]

**Reciting the memorial prayers (Keil Moleh Rakhamim) at the memorial service.**

[Page 574]

**The presidium of the annual memorial gathering in memory of the holy victims of Serock, in Tel Aviv. Opening the meeting, Chairman Borukh Katzenelbogen**

**Fragment of the audience during a memorial reciting the memorial prayers (*Keil Moleh Rakhamim*) at the memorial service**

[Page 575]

**The group honors the holy victims during the memorial service**

[Page 576]

**Serock Jews in the DP camps in Germany**

[Page 577]

# Serocker Countrymen in America
## (1905-1939 period)

### An Actual Report from Nakhman Feinboim

### Translated by Pamela Russ

According to what is known, Jews began coming to America from Serock after 1905.

They settled in the East Side, in New York, which was at that time the center of Jewish immigrants from Russia and Poland. The Jews that arrived from Serock lived, as did the other Jewish immigrants, in heavily poor conditions and unsanitary housing, suffering frequently from unemployment, particular difficulties in integrating into the new land, no language, and being totally unprepared for the enormous changes.

Because of all this, they searched for a sort of "place" for themselves. They began to get together to talk to each other and share the issues that pressed on their hearts. They would read letters from home. And, so, in 1913, the first organization of Serocker Jews in New York was established under the name "Khevra (group) Rav Yosef Levinshtayn, ob"m (of blessed memory)," named after the former Serocker rabbinic leader.

The organizers were: Moishe Finkelshtayn, of blessed memory, Harry Goldflam, Aharon Kronenberg, of blessed memory, Hershel Krimkowich, of blessed memory, Harry Bailinson, of blessed memory, Henokh Mai, of blessed memory, Yitzkhok Shikore, of blessed memory, Moshe Drezner, of blessed memory, Shaja Kuperman, of blessed memory, and Yosef Fishbayn, of blessed memory.

The responsibilities of the first group were: to meet frequently, to provide material and moral support to the newly arrived fellow countrymen, to send financial support to the poor countrymen and families in Serock, and the most important thing, to feel a little warmth from back home by just getting together.

The group under this name existed until 1918. During this time period, almost all the work described was undertaken by the above mentioned names, with great sacrifice.

By the end of 1918, more Serocker Jews began arriving in New York and began settling in other states, and because of various reasons they came to the center where it would be easier to get organized. The Khevra grew, gained new members, and at that point, changed its name to: "Khevra Tiferes Achim Anshei Serock" (trans: the "Society of the Pride of Brotherhood of the People of Serock").

*[Page 578]*

Because of gaps in the minute-book of this time period, exact details of the daily activities of that time are unknown. Nonetheless, it was known that this was the address for the newly arrived Serocker Jews in New York, where they received a warm welcome, some advice from those people who were already somewhat familiar with some of the life, and some material assistance. All this had tremendous value for the newcomer who was without a language in the new land.

Aside from the gatherings and the helping activities, somehow, despite incredible material difficulties, the society managed to purchase a plot of land for a cemetery. This [finding and purchasing the land] was a serious problem in America.

The society had approximately 80 members. In this time period, the work was done by the president, Reb [the title "Reb" is commonly used in Yiddish to address a male] Shlomo Meyer Orenshtayn, of blessed memory, and the secretary, Reb Yosef Fishbayn, of blessed memory.

For various and unknown reasons, in 1922, the society split, with approximately half the members leaving the group, and a second group was organized under the name: "Serocker Young Men."

In the management of the new group at the time of the founding, were: the president, Reb Harry Goldflam, of blessed memory; vice-president, Reb Harry Greenberg, of blessed memory; secretary, Reb Moshe Finkelshtayn, of blessed memory; minutes-secretary, Reb Layb Sosniak, of blessed memory.

In those years, new immigrants began arriving, Jews from Serock who survived the First World War, along with all of its events. These Jews had primarily other outlooks with regards to social and worldly problems that, understandably, affected the interaction of the Society.

Among the newcomers was Sam Dunner, who immediately became active. He became president in 1926, and later undertook other official positions.

The group of newcomers, with their sacrifices for the work of the organization, successfully united the two individual groups in 1937 under one name, the "United Serocker Young Men." The organization exists to this day.

[Page 579]

**A group of activists in the Serocker Landsmanschaft (Society) in America – arrived after World War II**

[Page 580]

A constitution was created that described to all the members the obligations of the organization and the rights of each member. The following are some of the most important rights:

Whatever assistance is given to a member in times of illness, for a funeral, or for a burial, is to the cost of the Society, and [burials] are to be in our own cemetery.

These were very important accomplishments under those conditions. During that time period, a second plot of land was purchased as a cemetery, which they visited every year before Passover; there were projects for fundraising for food for Passover ["*ma'os khittin*"] for the needy fellow Serocker in America and in Serock.

The new active group, with Sam Dunner at the head, understood that the future of the Society depended on the young children born in America who would find a place and take an interest in the Society. They started active projects in those years, and they successfully pulled in a group of second generation Serockers already born in America. Thanks to that, they received information about their ancestors, and with that ensured a part of the establishment of the Society to which their parents gave so much of their strength and heart.

## The Period of 1922-1931

The president and others who were active in various other positions during this period:

Reb Harry Goldflam, Yosef Fishman, of blessed memory, Moishe Finkelshtayn, of blessed memory, Harry Greenberg, of blessed memory, Layb Sosniak, of blessed memory, Sam Dunner, Dovid Mann, Avrohom Drezner, of blessed memory, Khaim Blakhman, of blessed memory, Ben-Zion Rozental, of blessed memory, Shaja Kuperman, of blessed memory, Moishe Drezner, and Ber Kulok, of blessed memory.

## Period of 1939-1968

The Serocker organization in America conducted regular activities until the outbreak of World War II – the terrible tragedy for the world in general, and for us Jews in particular. Information began to arrive about the liquidation of thousands of Jewish settlements – among those, was our beloved old home and its residents. There was no one to write to, no one to help. A town was erased with all our dear ones that remained there. The Serocker Society, just as the other Jewish Societies in America, believed that even after all that, someone would remain alive and need help.

*[Page 581]*

A special committee was established at that time, headed by Sam Dunner and Layb Sosniak, and in a short time, through extraordinary efforts, established a fund of $10,000. This was the source from which money was sent to each Serocker townsman who requested it after the war.

In 1949, survivors began coming to America from the German DP [Displaced Persons] camps and from other places.

Every Serocker that came found himself greeted warmly by the Serocker Society, and particularly from the Serockers Layb Sosniak and Sam Dunner.

The majority of the newcomers settled in New York, and mostly registered in the Society right way.

Those who survived the war in many different ways, brought with them fresh memories of our liquidated home, and special ties with the remaining Serockers everywhere. Understandably, this affected the morale of those in the society, and evoked more understanding [compassion] for the old home town.

The establishment of the country of Israel, with the huge change that came about for the Jewish nation in the entire world, and particularly here in America, also affected the Serocker Society.

Israel became an important issue in the life of the Serocker Society. Every year, Yom ha'Atzmaut (Israel's Independence Day) was celebrated. In those days, the Society purchased Israel bonds for $10,000. Simultaneously, the Society contributes annually to the "United Fund" and collects money from her members for Israel.

The society maintains the tradition of collecting money for food for Passover [ma'os khitin], and every year great sums of money are sent to each Serocker that requests assistance for Passover.

[Page 582]

Nowadays, regular meetings are held with all the members and with a report about the financial activities of the Society that have to be affirmed during the meeting. After that, other issues on the agenda are addressed.

All the people who hold positions are elected once a year at a special meeting.

The Society today counts approximately 150 members; most attend the meetings. The work is managed by the officers and the executive.

Aside from the regular meetings, every year there are Purim and Khannuka parties, where the members attend with their children, and we celebrate together.

Thankfully, a large number of activists from the old group and from the new post-war group in our Society were able to successfully work through all types of crises which other societies experienced as well, particularly between the older members and the newcomers. Many societies dissolved because of this. Our Society established good relations among the members, and maintained itself as a family.

We hope the situation will continue on for the memory of our holy ones and our old home. [The term "holy ones" has come to refer to those who died during the Holocaust.]

## The Special Activists during the Period 1939-1967

Reb Layb Sosniak, of blessed memory, finance secretary and minutes secretary, from 1922-1961 (when he died). He was the heart and intellect behind our Society.

Hymie Drezner, 1953-1964 – president. He gave so much of his time and energy, and moved the Society to a healthy financial state.

Sam Dunner, head of the executive committee, gave much effort and heart. Thanks go to him for the relations within the Society.

Yakov Brooks (Brukhanaski), was the minutes secretary after Sosniak's death. He organized a regular and good minutes-book, which will remain as a recorded document of the activities of the Society.

*[Page 583]*

The current president, Joe Kuperman, with his activities and understanding, in a short time established good relations in the Society.

Dovid Mann, of blessed memory, conducted honest work in the financial issues.

Vice-president Philip Roth. He is not a Serocker, but his wife is. Any time a task or favor had to be done for a Serocker, Philip Roth was there immediately [to get things done].

Mrs. Sosniak, the widow of Reb Layb Sosniak, of blessed memory, takes care of all the social problems.

Esther Dunner, Sam Dunner's wife, and Tzila Kuperman, president Kuperman's wife, takes charge of all the parties and all the evening events that the Society organizes.

A special place was allotted to the new group members that came after the war. Thanks to them, closer ties to the Serockers in Israel were formed, in terms of producing the Yizkor Book, and other things.

The administration of the Serocker Societies in 1970 was taken over from Dovid Mann, of blessed memory, by Irving and Walt Greenberg – the second generation of Serocker in America.

## The Administration of the Serocker Societies in 1968

President: Joe Kuperman. Vice-president: Philip Roth. Financial Controller: Harry Drezner. Financial Secretary: Dovid Mann, of blessed memory. Minutes Secretary: Yakov Brooks.

## Executive Committee

Chairman – Sam Dunner
Yosef Fineboim
Shmuel Brooks (Brukhanski)
Yehuda-Layb Shteinski
Shaja Mai

Irvin Birm
Nakhman Fineboim
Khaim Itzkowicz
Philip Kurski (Pshikurski)

The position of D. Mann, of blessed memory, was taken over by Irving [and Walt] Greenberg.

[Page 584]

פאראייניגטע סעראצקער יאנג מען, אינק.

**United Serotzker Young Men, Inc.**

CENTRAL PLAZA     111 Second Avenue, New York     ATLAS ROOM

שמחת בית השואבה און פעראייניגונגס פארטי

## Unity Celebration
### and Simchas Beis Hashoava Party

Dear Brother and Sister,

You are cordially invited to attend this historic

## Unity Meeting

SATURDAY evening, SEPTEMBER 25, 1937 at 8 o'clock at CENTRAL PLAZA, 111 2nd Ave, New York, in the beautiful ATLAS ROOM.

The long hoped for unity is here and every one must attend this important meeting.

1. Important Society matters of which you will be informed at the meeting will be taken up. It is essential that every member know these matters.

2. ELECTION OF NEW OFFICERS who can command your confidence.

3. NATHAN RITHOLTZ and his RADIO BAND will provide a gala musical program. Other forms of entertainment have been arranged.

4. A grand FEAST worthy of the occassion will be served.

Fraternally yours,

The Arrangement Committee of the
UNITED SEROTZKER YOUNG MEN, Inc.

LOUIS SOSNIAK, Sec'y     1735 Sterling Pl, Brooklyn
Tel. PResident 3-0397

Dr. MILTON BERGER, 51 Fifth Avenue, New York
GRamercy 5-3111

ווערטהער ברודער און שװעסטער !

איהר זײם העפליכסט אײנגעלאדען צו דיזען וויכטיגען און היסטארישען פעראייניגונגס מיטינג

וואס וועט אבגעהאלטען ווערען דיזען **שבת** אינער, דעם **25** סטען **סעפטעמבער**, 1937, אום 8 אידר שארף, אין **סענטראל פלאזא**, 111 צוײטע עוועניו, ניו יארק, אין דעם סענדזשעס **אטלאס רום**.

ברידער און שוועסטער, עם איז נעקומען דער לאנג ערװארטעטער מאמענט און עם איז נעוואלרען א פאקט או אלע לאנדסלייט וועלען באלאנגען אין **איז גרויסער קערפערשאפט** און עם איז אונבאדיננט וויכטיג אז יעדער איינצינער מעמבער זאל קומען צו דיזען וויכטיגען מיטיננ

1. עם איז דא פילע וויכטיגע סאסייעטי ענינים וואס וועלען אײך בעקאנט ווערען בײ דיזען מיטינג און וואס יעדער סעמבער וועט דארוסען הייסען

2. בי דיזען מיטיננ װעט פארקומען **עלעקשאן פאר נייע בעאמטע** וואס וואלן האבען אייער צוסדריען

3. עם איז אונז נעלוננען צו קריגעז אוניער לאנדסמאן **ניטען ריטהאלץ** מיט זיין **ראדיא בענד** ער וועט אונז פין אסמוירען און שאפען א יום טוב'דיגע שטימונג, מיר װעלען אױך האבען נאך ענטערטיינמענט.

4. ואחרון אחרון הכיב דאם לעצטע איז דאס בעסטע.

**א גרויסארטיגע פארטי** וועט סערוױרט ווערעי

האפענדיג אייך צו זעהן צו דיזעז וויכטיגעו מיטינג און אלע צוזאמען וועלען מיר פארברעננען אן אנגענעם און פארגעניגען וואס מיר וועלען לאנג גערענקעו

מיט ברידערליכען גרוס

די אריינדזשסענט קאסיטע פין די

פאראייניגטע סעראצקער יאנג מען, אינק.

לואים סאשניאק, סעק.

## Note about Simchas Bais Hashoeva:
## Translation: A Happiness of "Oneness"

*During the time of the Temple, a unique form of sacrificial offering was brought on the altar during the holiday of Sukkos. Each morning of Sukkos, water was poured on the altar when the daily morning sacrifice was brought. The pouring of this water was celebrated with much fanfare. The celebration was known as Simchas Bais HaShoeva, the Rejoicing of the House of the Drawing. ("Shoev" means to draw water.)*

In terms of the invitation in this text, it is quite auspicious to have a "Unity Meeting" on the night of Simchas Bais Hashoeva, a time that symbolizes unity, since it provides the Society's members with even more reason to celebrate.

[Page 585]

**A gathering of the survivors in America**

[Page 586]

# Serocker Countrymen in Argentina
## Shlomo Ashenmill (Buenos Aires)
## Translated by Pamela Russ

In the year 1923, when it became uncomfortable for the youth to continue living in Poland for all kinds of reasons, including anti-Semitism, political persecutions, and difficult economic situations, a large movement evolved of those that wanted to travel the wide world, wherever the gates were open. One of these places was Argentina, where a large wave of youth found its place with the great help of ICA [Jewish Colonization Association (philanthropic association assisting Jews with resettlement and finding productive employment)] that helped people settle into agricultural work.

Of the first pioneers from our home town Serock, were: Fishel Gutkovski, may he rest in peace, and his wife Ruda Leibgott, of those brave ones, Yitzkhok Perl, may he rest in peace, Khana Berenshtayn, may she rest in peace, Moishe Hokhman, may he rest in peace, and, may they live long, Mendel Kuligovski, Yekhiel Meyer Slomianski, and others.

Being in a strange land, in a strange environment, we got together every Sunday because that was the only day we were free from work. The gathering was held in the home of Fishel Gutkovski.

After some time, at one of these meetings, it was decided to set up a united group for all the Serocker because new countrymen were continually arriving, and those who were there earlier were no longer "green" [new immigrants], so they were able to help the new arrivals.

**A group of Serocker fellow countrymen in Argentina.**

A meeting was held and a provisional election was held. The first active participants were: Shmerl Ashenmill, may he rest in peace – chairman; Yitzkhok Perl, may he rest in peace – secretary. Announcements were sent out to all fellow countrymen in the city and in the province, saying that everyone should register in the Union.

The response was very good. And everyone was pleased with the notion of a united group for all the fellow countrymen.

At the time of the first meeting, there were approximately 15 members, and it was decided to immediately establish an assistance fund in order to help out the newly arrived with a large sum of money, for renting a home, and so on.

*[Page 588]*

Meanwhile, the number of immigrants from Serock continued to grow, and the Union grew with many more members. Everyone paid a monthly fee to cover the various expenses of the Union.

It happened once that the countryman Moishe Horowicz (his parents sold hats; I think they used to call him Aharon Leibes) became ill, and the doctor said that because of the climate, this person would have to return to Poland. If he stays here, he would soon die. We needed a large sum of money, and the situation was difficult. We were a total of 25 friends (members), and with great effort we saved our fellow countryman and sent him back to Serock. This was, I think, in the year 1925. Unfortunately, we have no documents of those times, and even a list of all the members does not remain. Therefore, many names of the countrymen are missing. Then there were Eliezer Merker, may he rest in peace, Alter Platze, may he rest in peace, Avrom Kahn, may he rest in peace, and others whose family names I have forgotten.

In the year 1928, Shlomo Ashenmill arrived from the Palestine, as it was called then, to Buenos Aires. He registered in the Union, and took over the position of secretary.

There were meetings every two weeks, and all kinds of issues were dealt with, particularly for distributing loans to the needy.

Once (I don't remember the year), we received a letter from Serock saying that Yakov Kuzhnitzki had died. The Youth Committee asked us to send some money to help set up a gravestone, which we did immediately.

When World War II broke out, our contact with Serock was severed because of Hitler's (may his name be erased) uprooting activities of the Jewish population in the occupied territories with the help of his ally, Stalin. We had no possibility of helping.

[Page 589]

In the year 1940, we decided to unite with the Pultusker countrymen into one union. A new provisional executive was elected which comprised: Moishe Monchazh, Aharon Yurkevicz – all from Pultusk; Shlomo Ashenmill, Kalman Kuligowski, Yekhiel Meyer Slomianski, and Shimon Shpilke – all Serocker. It was decided to promote the activity of increasing the number of members, and to call a general meeting to elect an executive, meanwhile, for one year.

The executive elected: Moishe Monchazh, may he rest in peace – president; Moishe Yakubovicz – vice president; Aharon Markevicz, may he rest in peace – secretary; Shlomo Ashenmill – vice secretary; Mendel Goldberg – treasurer; Leibel Forminski – vice treasurer; and friends: Mendel Kuligowski, Duvid Melnik, Nakhum Melman, Kalman Kuligowski, Yosef Karmel, Herzke Geluda.

When the jobs were distributed, it was decided that a mandate for the Union be worked out, to legalize and register the Union with the Argentinean government so that it be recognized as a social service institution in order to be able to distribute help to the needy and the sick, and so on.

In order to increase the funds of the Union, in addition to our other service activities, we presented theater performances and other events.

In 1941, a general meeting was held, to elect a new executive for the following year. The elected were: Mendel Kuligowski – president; Zalman Gurman – vice president; and Shlomo Ashenmill – secretary; Leon Kopelowicz – vice secretary; Moishe Monchazh – treasurer; Yoel Gutkowsi – vice treasurer; Miguel Vetshtayn – Spanish secretary. Executive members: Shlomo Wrubel, Kalman Kuligowski, Moishe Yakubowicz, Yosef Karmel, Duvid Melnik. And in the revisions committee: Yitzkhok Perl and Aharon Jurkowicz.

And in 1944, a new executive was elected: president – Yosef Karmel; vice president – Yoel Gutkowski; secretary – Shlomo Ashenmill; vice secretary – Kalman Kuligowski; secretary of the loans accounts – Miguel Vetshtayn (Mendel Kuligowski's brother-in-law); treasurer – Mendel Kuligowski; vice treasurer – Shlomo Wrubel; elected members – Simkha Goldmakher, Duvid Melnik, Aryeh Izenberg, Herzke Galuda; revisions committee: Mottel Kronzhek and Leon Kopelowicz.

[Page 590]

After assembling the executive, our entire work was concentrated on establishing a fund for the Serocker and Pultusker countrymen who saved themselves from the terrible tragedies. Every opportunity, festive occasions or other events, money was collected for the needy fund. In the beginning of 1945, letters began to arrive from the survivors for immediate help such as clothing, linen, and even medication for their health. With the help of the Joint [American Jewish Joint Distribution Committee – *a worldwide Jewish relief organization*] the first help was being sent out to our countrymen in Poland. Also, 15 boxes of tools were sent out, to be distributed to our countrymen wherever they were.

We received letters from all different places: from Paris, Belgium, Poland, Israel, and we establish written contact with them to send individual help.

December 11, 1945, we received a letter from Rav Yosef Katzenellenbogen, from Israel, where he writes the tragic news that on December 5, 1939, all the Jews from our town of Serock were forced to leave and many of them died and that we should maintain that day as the memorial day of their death (*yahrzeit*). From that day on, we keep this same date for the annual memorial day.

With the establishment of the State of Israel, almost all of our funds are transferred to help the State of Israel and for the survivors from our community. We received many letters with requests of all kinds. For every letter that we received, we sent out $25, in addition to food packages. We also sent to the few in Belgium and the few that remained in Poland.

Also, for the State of Israel, we contributed a significant amount of money, and collected for Israel at every opportunity.

In 1949, we received a letter from Lodz, Poland, from a woman survivor originally from Serock. She wrote that she is alone with a sick child, and the only help is penicillin, but she doesn't have the means to buy it. At that time, a special allowance was established by our government, and with great effort, we received it [the allowance].

After sending out the help, we received many letters of thanks, and this gave us satisfaction, knowing that our help had reached its goal.

[Page 591]

**Memorial for Serocker Countrymen in Argentina**

[Page 592]

In March 1947, the first 47 survivors from Europe arrived on the ship Compana. Among them were our fellow citizens from Pultusk, along with a small child. The father was from Biale. The Union immediately set them up with an apartment and everything else that a family needs – linen, dishes, furniture. We visited them often so that they wouldn't feel foreign at the beginning.

In 1953, we applied for a unification in Tel Aviv of the two groups – Serock and Pultusk, to raise a significant sum for the Gemillas Khesed (*community charities*) fund so that our work should be more concentrated and effective. As soon as we received a letter that the merging had taken place, we sent out the first $1,000 and 30 packages as gifts for Rosh Hashana. Within a period of a few years, we sent out money for the Gemillas Khesed fund. In 1959 we sent out $1,000, and in 1960, once more the same sum.

In 1960, we established our own loan fund that existed in our establishment now for many years, a credit co-operative, under the name "Sangeles" (*the Angels*). We also have our own building and from there we conduct our daily activities.

Our executive today consists of the following members:

President – Kalman Kuligowski; vice president – Herzke Galuda; secretary – Shloime Ashenmill; treasurer – Yosef Karmel; vice treasurer – Duvid Melnik; elected members – Nakhman Kershenbaum, Hersh Leib Shteifman, and Moishe Perl.

In the Union, there was also a women's committee, which comprised the following participants: Baltshe Fisherman, Frederica Karmel, Rifka Galuda, Ruda Gutkovski, Dora Kuligovski, Raizel Shpak, Khaya Shteifman, and Faige Perl.

The Union has 110 members – a combination of Serocker and Pultusker.

[Page 593]

**SOCIEDAD RESIDENTES ISRAELITAS de PULTUSK, SEROCK Y ALREDEDORES**
FUNDADA EN EL AÑO 1924 - 3 DE MAYO DE 1964

לזכר הנפטרים

| Nombre | Año |
|---|---|
| SZMERIL OSZENMIL | 1931 |
| MOISES GOLOMOCHER | 1933 |
| IACOW ARIE PIETRUCH | 1936 |
| LUSER MERKER | 1937 |
| ALTER PLUDA | 1939 |
| DAVID FURMAINSKI | 1939 |
| SIMCHO SZTAJFMAN | 1943 |
| IOEL MENDZELEWSKI | 1943 |
| MOISES VINOGURA | 1943 |
| IOLKE CUKER | 1946 |
| ELIAS MONCARZ | 1947 |
| SALOMON KOSAK | 1947 |
| SOLOMON IOSEF ZAIDENBERG | 1947 |
| ABRAHM LEIB BURSZTEIN | 1949 |
| MOISES IAKOBOWICH | 1949 |
| MOISES ADONAKLO | 1950 |
| ABRAHM MATES KNORPEL | 1951 |
| SZMIL BACHER | 1951 |
| JUNO BORENSZTEIN | 1953 |
| FISZEL GUTKOWSKI | 1953 |
| ARON MERKER | 1954 |
| LEON KOPLOVICH | 1955 |
| MOISES IOSEF HOCHMAN | 1956 |
| ISAAC PEREL | 1956 |
| IOCHMAN PIEKARSZ | 1957 |
| MAIER WAITZMAN | 1958 |
| FERNANDO DOBROVISKI | 1958 |
| BURECH MIOD | 1958 |
| GUSTABO ROTSZTEIN | 1958 |
| ZALMEN GURMAN | 1959 |
| IAKEW LIBER PINIEWSKI | 1960 |
| LUSER ZELMANOVITZ | 1960 |
| MOISES AZEPKO | 1960 |
| ABRAHM KON | 1961 |
| ISAAC BORENSZTEIN | 1962 |
| WELWIL TZAPNICKI | 1963 |
| SALOMON IOGODA | 1963 |
| MELKE K. DE SZLESINGER | 1939 |
| | 1941 |
| BASZE IAGODA | 1943 |
| CHAJA GITEL G. DE ASZENMIL | 1944 |
| RACHEL LEA S. DE GUCHENEK | 1946 |
| MINDA BEILA R. DE MERKER | 1952 |
| CHAJA BORENSZTEIN | 1952 |
| MALKE W. DE FURMAINSKI | 1956 |
| RIWKA RUCHEL FAIN | 1957 |
| RACHEL LEIA D. DE KULIGOWSKI | 1957 |
| GITEL IURKEWITZ | 1957 |
| TZIREL BLUMBERG | 1957 |
| CHAIA MALKO WOLER | 1958 |
| CHANA TZIVIE K. DE ZAIDENBERG | 1958 |
| RUCHEL SLOMIANSKY | 1958 |
| REVECA ROSA L. DE ENGER | 1960 |
| RIWCO V. DE KULIGOVSKI | 1962 |
| EVA R. DE LIPSKER | 1962 |
| LEA B. DE LIPOWICH | 1963 |
| ESTER S. DE BLUSZTEIN | 1963 |
| IDES M. DE IAKOBOWICH | 1963 |

[Page 597]

# Liberated by fire
## Yehuda Ben Ze'ev

**Translated by Ruth Kilner**

Son of Chaya (Vinkrantz) and Ze'ev Ben Ze'ev Kibbutz Ein HaCarmel Born on December 9th, 1935 in Kibbutz Ramat Rachel, Jerusalem. Fell in the six-day war, June 8th, 1967, in Jerusalem.

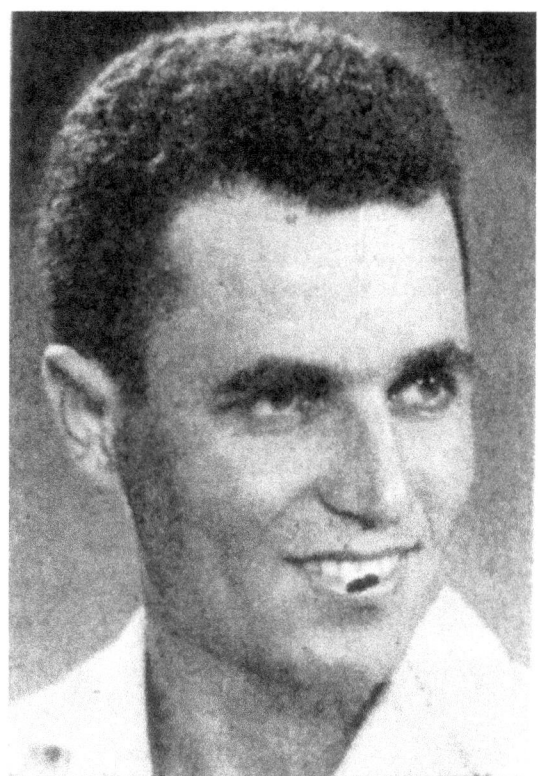

In my childhood days, I carried him on my hand,

His beauty and his grace imbued calmness all around him.

In his adolescence, I listened to his words that sprang from a clear and pure font.

In his bravery/valor, buds blossomed offering many fortunes,

When the enemy came upon us, he soared to a place where his booth stood

And he remains alive, forever alive, in Jerusalem of Gold.

**Kiryat Borochov**                                                **Hanoch Vardi**

## Heart's Desire

We visited Yehuda's grave, carved into the mountainside, and this is now part of the vista of Jerusalem. Jerusalem – where Yehuda was born, and where he spent his early childhood. The vista of Jerusalem and its appearance were entrenched into his blood, and each time he met the city he was excited anew, finding it inspiring and thrilling. Every time felt like a sacred pilgrimage.

[Page 598]

And his yearning and longing for the stones of Jerusalem matured. His heart's desire was fulfilled. Yehuda returned to Jerusalem, to rest there forever.

### That He Bought his House

Yehuda did not merit sitting around at home through his youth. His path was a wandering path: continuing education classes away from home, IDF, Oranim College, studies in Jerusalem. It may be that these wanderings fuelled his strong will, his yearning for his Home, for mankind's Home.

There were never any doubts about the value of home and its contents to Yehuda. He wondered about everyone who needed ideal justification of their lives in the kibbutz home. He did not recognize people's attachment to an intellectual way of life, but rather he understood people's attachment to living practically. The kibbutz was his home, the place he grew up. It was natural, simple, and perfectly self-explanatory.

He built his home, and it was a home furnished with love, filled with enjoyment, purity and beauty, where laughter echoed from the heart of his little one. He conveyed a boundless love to his loved one and daughter. And from here, threads of warmth and light were embroidered and lasted until the old age home.

The circle of life closed. The home was orphaned. And the bereavement process started.

**Ein Carmel**  **Yaakov Gordon**

## With This Jerusalem

You fell, Yehuda, in Jerusalem, the eternal Judean city. A son of Ramat Rachel, you freed the city of your birth. You loved Jerusalem so much: the stones, the roads, the dream within, the centers of wisdom – all this attracted you, and held you spellbound. Several times, you described Jerusalem as a magnet for you. And behold, Jerusalem took you, entirely, from us.

Today you remain there, you will never return. And with this Jerusalem, Peace within her name, you will be forever remembered.

**Ein Carmel**　　　　　　　　　　　　　　　　**Yael Refaeli**

*[Page 599]*

## Such Wide Skies Spread Over Jerusalem

Yehuda won't return to us.

Therefore we return to him.

We return to him from our everyday business, full of suspense,

From the smiling eyes of our children, from the depths of pain.

We try to press this knowledge to the depths of our consciousness. To trap it in the cellars of forgetfulness, to open a sliver of hope that is the blessing of the little ones...

And it tricks us ,and returns to us with a thunderbolt of pain.

It returns to us the beloved views of youth, to the rolling peals of laughter.

Returns to us the body's joy and strength.

Returns to us the pats on the shoulder, and the classroom bench,

Returns to us the dreams that were not fulfilled...

Pictures, pictures.

They return to us clear, floating and veiled. Which of them are new, and which are old?

But Yehuda – he will not return to us...

We know he fell. That he is buried with many of his friends, with the best of them.

We know.

We know how fierce the battle was, how mighty the fortress in the presence of your warm, young heart.

We know, but we are human. Only human. We want to believe, to find rest in a sweet illusion. To believe a little longer.

The stones on that hill, they are silent once more. Silent too are the tight-lipped wounded. Silent are the fallen lads.

But there the story has come, with a wild and terrible reputation, shouting from the soil and the rock. And the bulldozer at the end. Turns one hill into another hill, her stubborn and demanding trenches and weapons removed.

Today's Jerusalem shatters its partitions. It removes its battle scars, its armor, its arrow slits.

The heavens are spread so wide over Jerusalem, over its turrets, walls and buildings – Arab and Jewish.

Sky over all, and a fierce brightness that brings you to tears.

Jerusalem is tearful and turbulent.

*Page 600]*

The people stream by, stunned, to here and to there. The sounds of their lips, that mutter again here in the squares and there in the alleyways – vanishing like doves, that say: Maybe, finally, peace!?

And on Har Herzl, a breeze meanders, and the pines whisper a prayer.

**Kibbutz Ein Carmel** **Gali**

## The Summer
### By Yehuda Ben Ze'ev, of blessed memory

Let us talk a little about the not-so-hot subject of summer.

Fact: "He" is here, with us, within us. It – it is the great, broad, open summer.

"He": An Israeli with all 248 verses and little moments, a son of this land, the young and firstborn son, the glory and splendor of this place.

Not the paltry winter, the heatwaves where there are hot days between the rainy days.

Our ancient literature and the words of our sages date back to the days of the Mishnah and Talmud. All these years we have been a people settling on its land – and we have known only the summer and winter, and nothing in between them. Winter – the days of rain and cold; and summer– the days of heat and light. These are two, stitched together into the year, like all other contrasts integrated together: "seed time and harvest, and cold and heat, and summer and winter, and day and night," (Genesis, 8:22), and also "Summer and winter: you fashioned them" (Psalms 74:17).

Too short, and never considered are the interim periods between the two. The grumpy fall, which hastily slips away like a maiden at a street corner, and the unruly spring, furious like a madman who is dying, and who is concerned with releasing all his might before his days are over, and then only the great summer remains, the firstborn and the generation between the two of this land.

Why summer – rooted, the end (*ketz*)? – It seems to me that the end of the ripening of the fruit and its full maturation – happens in the season known as *kayitz* (summer). And indeed, it is not simply ferociously burning hot days; these days are not the season of yearning. This is the time of great fruitfulness. Summer, parallel to the fruit, represents plenty; it symbolizes blessing.

Winter is the time to plant seeds; spring is the season to breed and plant – it symbolizes awakening and intoxication, as the plants grow and flourish. And the summer – summer is the season of fruit and fruitfulness, the season of gathered blessings, the delight of the harvester. "Gather wine and summer and oil" (Jeremiah 3). Summer is the fruit, the blessing of the crop, it is like the vintage and the gathering: "the spoiler is fallen on your summer fruits and your vintage" (Jeremiah 48). The plenty and the heaps of grain, the bounty, the plentitude, the abundance, the blessing of plenty –these are all the soul's summer landscapes.

[Page 601]

We said, of all the children of the land, he is the most faithful and beloved of his parents. As he grew, there was no room for narrow passages, for small glimmering moments, for comings and goings. Shouting, and not moaning. A chasm. When we saw him close to us, many will cover their eyes with dark glasses.

Maybe like the great deeds of the sons of this land,

Like the great truths that were born here, so is the summer great, and great in its deeds.

The children of this place know of the great power and the many actions.

The days are long, and tired from the abundance. Thousands of channels, through which the blessing continues, brim with crops. Also the wind that blows as it comes brings with it activity and renewal, a type of harvest of long anticipation days;

Particularly in the hot days of summer – good, stimulating produce brings satisfaction to those who frequently seek her shade. And it seems to me that a great many of those in this camp were partners in this spiritual and cultural abundance.

We will yet remember the loveable intoxication of these nights, the summer nights. When you go out into these summer nights, they conquer you from the inside, and they strengthen you intently, with a strength equivalent to the strength of childhood memories, of the best story you ever heard.

**(From his Ein Carmel diary)**　　　　　　　　　　　　　　　**Yehuda Ben Zeev**

◇

[Page 602]

## Jerusalem
### For the soul of Yehuda Ben Ze'ev, a son of Kibbutz Ramat Rachel, and a man of Ein Hacarmel, who fell in Jerusalem
### by Egdar Eldan

Between you and her there was a cry.
Your mother wrapped your body in hers in the birthing room.
And then your bare feet
Wrote your years on her stones. A second cry on your knees
Opposite her skies, you cried to your father
And you went a distance to return to her. A third cry you did not cry
In vain you tried to rise
Toward Jerusalem, that lay dying in your childhood Above your darkening eyes
The nights glow.
*******************
You were the firstborn of death
And on you, Jerusalem rests.
Your mother, to her you were taken
She descends incessantly.
You will not rise to her
Because on you Jerusalem rests
And you on the nights of your mother.
Go in them, go and cry.
In her dream, she extends her hand
Crying out from stone to stone, on her back she supports
To hold Jerusalem, so it doesn't fall on you
Full of stone.
In order to not crush your body completely.

*******************
To your children, you are not.
To your mother, you died as you sleep.
Return to be a babe
Playing in the muddy puddles
Her eyes turning red.

*******************
Around you, the dark surrounds like a wall
Whose stones are ever cracking.
On her soles are stuck the lament
And death written before and behind.
Darkness surrounds your body as a wall.
You are surrounded by reversing movement.

The thread of distance twists and twists
Fastening your body around and back
Thought after thought
Dropping prayer to its knees
Opposite the blue, rising up like a wall. Now with forehead to the stone, turning purple,
On your lips, the stem that is revealed
On which glimmering moments are scratched
Without sunrise.

*[Page 603]*

Suddenly your body is dark, dark; darkness surrounds
And closes like a wall.
Listen, Yehuda – You are one.
*******************
A powerful tremor
Sun scattered by a gate
Sun veiled by sackcloth.
Before this night
Braids tinged with light.
An infant moon of blood
For tonight.
The star cools the star
The star drops against the star.
Like a wrinkled old fig in the powerful tremor
The name of this night.
The heavens that shattered
Landwards and wander
On the earth they search
For the one verse
And they find it.

*******************
All the time that they stop suddenly,
All the time that stands turning white
The weeping bones pass
No silence can quiet
The teeth that clamp as hill after hill
For a whole night the moon lends its voice
And the sun takes its place in the morning.
A boy was here. Here is love. Now
he is born in diapers of dust

The earth closes him in its vaults
From the cold floor rise the voices of his limbs
He will not come to us
Who call from the depths
We too are only
Toys of heaven
Crying out.

[Page 604]

## Tzvika Rosenberg, of blessed memory
### by Hanoch Vardi
### Translated by Ruth Kilner

Corporal **Tzvika Rosenberg**, of blessed memory, son of Elhanan and Raaya Rosenberg, Kfar Vatikin, born on Kibbutz Nir David on June 11th, 1949, fell in the Jordan Valley battle, 3 Iyar 5729 – April 21st, 1969.

Who spoke and who decided that we need to stand here and eulogize you, cut down in your prime?

Israel, the gazelle (Heb: *tzvi*),

A vacuum from your death

Why do heroes fall?

Our dear Tzvika, you were so delightful. Light and joy always radiated around you, You helped others with your kindness – You were so vibrant, so lively.

Elchanan, my dear childhood friend, the bereft Raaya, and dearest Mira – how can I comfort you? Or maybe I should ask, how can we all be comforted? The sacrifice was not only yours – he was ours: he was bone of our bones, and flesh of our flesh! Darling Tzvika, we are proud of you: you fell as a hero in the battlefield defending our renewed homeland.

[Page 605]

An elevation offering, the fire elevates completely.

With complete pride, value, and thanksgiving, we are surrounded by a deep sorrow and pain. And how can we be comforted? If your sacrifice was necessary, then everything on the earth, immersed in such precious blood, will be forever holy to us. We can now live safely and freely in our land.

And the solution, though maybe temporary, is as written in the book of Psalms:

Woe to me, that I sojourn in Meshech,

that I dwell among the tents of Kedar!

Too long have I had my dwelling

among those who hate peace.

I am for peace,

but when I speak, they are for war!

My dearest Tzvi,

You had the merit of being buried in the earth of your homeland, which you so loved.

You were one with everything around you. You loved each plant, each seed, each sprout – everything above us, to one side and the other – and now you will rest everlasting in their bosom.

Magnificent Tzvi,

The earth of your homeland will look after you, and your pure, bright, innocent, endearing, untainted soul should be bound with us in the bond of life and creation.

**Hanoch Vardi**
(Words offered at the gravesite on the 30th day after burial: 4 Sivan, 5729 – May 21st, 1969, Kfar Vitikin cemetery)

## Tzvi Rosenberg, of blessed memory

Corporal Tzvi Rosenberg of blessed memory, a son of Kfar Vatikin, fell in the Jordan Valley battle.

Tzvi, son of Elchanan and Raaya, was 19 when he fell. He was a child of tender age when his parents settled in Kfar Vitikin, 15 years ago. His father was the manager of the Moshav's water institute, and his mother worked in the kindergarten.

[Page 606]

After finishing the local school, he studied mechanics in the ORT vocational school in Netanya for four years. Immediately after finishing his studies, he was recruited into the army. Tzvi was a good-natured and friendly boy with many friends, and he was due to come home on Yom Ha'atzmut (Israeli Independence Day). His death put the village into deep mourning.

## Tzvika

With bowed heads, we stand beside your fresh grave. Your years pass before my eyes. I remember you as a small boy, pleasant and happy at kindergarten and in the local school. And behold, I remember the day of your accident, when by some miracle were you were spared. You fought between life and death; your will to live prevailed; and you were saved.

The years passed, and you grew up into a young man. You finished the local school and went to the high school in *Emek Hefer* (Hefer valley). A year later, you switched schools to Ort in Netanya. Time continued to pass, and your had to report to the army: tests; checks; questions about which corps; decisions.

Time continued passing, and your enlistment day arrived. The last night before your enlistment, you bade farewell to the neighbors and we all accompanied you to Hadera, and hoped you'd come home safely.

Your basic training weeks went by, and you were considered for the commander training course. Really? You could cope with the efforts required by this course after all that you went through following your accident? Although you told me more than once that it was not easy for you, your will to continue and finish gave you strength. You gritted your teeth, bit your lips, stifled the pain and finished the course.

Every vacation, even if it only lasted several hours, you came to us; always with a smile on your lips hoping that things would be better, quieter, and that we wouldn't worry. And this is how it was on your last vacation. After seven weeks, you had a vacation that only lasted a few precious hours. You came to us in the evening, tired after a long journey, and after the incident in which you were involved, and by a miracle were you saved. You told how in the next few days you would be having a longer vacation. You were happy, you smiled as always when you bade me goodbye...

And a week later, on *Yom Hazikaron* (Remembrance day), the terrible news arrived... Tzvika has fallen! This time, no miracle saved you, and death embraced you.

We are still in shock, and cannot yet believe it. Will you really no longer return?

**May his soul be bound up in the bond of everlasting life.**

**Shoshana**

[Page 607]

# In Memory
### by A. Turban, Kfar Vatikin
### Translated by Ruth Kilner

He came home from the trenches for the evening. "I'll be back for the holiday", he said. He returned home from the heights for an everlasting night.

Tzvika was born twenty years ago in Kibbutz Nir David. He and his parents lived on the kibbutz for two and a half years, where the partisans and ghetto fighters had gathered. They then spent six months in Netanya, after which they arrived at Kfar Vatikin.

As a child in kindergarten, Tzvika fell in love with flowers. He would sit in the neighbors' gardens and pick flower after flower, as his pleasure grew and grew. At times, he would empty all the ornamental gardens with his zeal for flowers. At school, he did not stand out; rather he always liked to conform. He was quiet, neat, and never raised his voice.

At eight and a half, a terrible accident happened to Tzvika. A wild horse hit him in his belly with a wagon shaft, and he sustained internal injuries. For two months, he lay in his sickbed, hovering between life and death. His doctors noted how unusual it was that he remained alive, with his pancreas torn and damaged so badly. Those were hard days, his family full of fear, as they stood by helplessly watching the wondrous fight their eight and a half year old child put up. His tremendous will and his love of life eventually won. He gradually recovered from his sickness, and after many months, he returned to us. At times, he felt strong pains, but he could hide it from most people, most of the time.

Having been off school for such a long period of time, Tzvika had to take private lessons to catch up with the rest of his class, but the gap was hard for him to close. He recognized this weakness, and consoled his parents, "Never mind, we don't all need to be academics. The country also needs good workers and tradesmen. The most important thing is to be a good person."

Within a short period of time, Tzvika had established a warm friendly connection with his teacher and her household. He quickly became like one of their family members. He would play with the children; tell them stories and include his teacher in his and his family's experiences. This was how he was with all his friends and acquaintances of which there were many. He would sit in the neighbors' houses and talk to them. He would tell them things and ask them questions, consult with them and show interest in what they were doing. And he was always available to help. He entertained many friends in his home.

[Page 608]

On Fridays after Youth Group, the children would meet up at Tzvika's, where he would host them and feed them, he would put in the effort and serve them the best at his table. And they would sit and chat, spending time together until late into the night. The habit of providing hospitality was deep seated in Tzvika's veins: it was his parents' house that planted this seed. And he cheerfully welcomed every person who came into the house with caring and warmth. He was always happy to serve guests in his house.

He started at the local high school, but after a year he felt a preference for the technical over the academic, and switched to the ORT school. He found his place in the agri-mechanics course, and he was decisively amongst the best and most diligent students.

When the six-day war broke out, and the village emptied of its high-school graduates, Tzvika and his friends started to organize themselves to help the farms that had been left without any work hands. The following day, the neighbor's son was called up to the army, and Tzvika took upon himself the milking, which he did perfectly and proficiently. This was not enough for him, and he went from neighbor to neighbor, offering his help to everyone. He collected eggs here... fed animals there... travelled to the field and brought back a wagon full of beets... ran to the orchard and moved the lines... and it was all done with zeal, and Tzvika was always ready to do more. When one of the neighbors offered to pay him for his help, Tzvika was offended and said, "If I hear anything more about money, I'm leaving this work."

When the time came for Tzvika to be tested and checked before his recruitment into the army, Tzvika started to worry. His fear grew daily, until he became miserable. He fell behind in his studies, and he was very depressed. He worried that he would not be accepted into the army due to his accident, and this ate away at him.

"It can't happen. Everyone will go to the army, but I won't. All my friends: Danny, Tully, Natan and David. They'll all volunteer for the combat units. And what will I do? Best case scenario, I'll be given an inadequate fitness rating, and I'll be a paper pusher. What a disgrace. I must go with them! I want to be like everyone else."

And Tzvika went to the army with his friends. He left ORT a year before finishing so he could go together with them. To everyone's surprise, he passed all his medical tests and was declared fit enough for combat.

Tzvika enlisted, and was sent to a squad officers' course. No-one could have been happier than he was, particularly after all the difficulties he'd had to overcome. He advanced thanks to the strength of his will, and he started to gain self-confidence. However, his pains then started to return. His friends convinced him to see the medical committee. It took a lot for him to agree, but he eventually complied. He managed to convince the committee that it was a childhood ailment that he suffered, and they eventually only dropped his health rating by a couple of points.

He remained a combat soldier, continued his course, and completed it.

Throughout the difficult time of his officers' course, Tzvika completed all his tasks and duties that he was given. He was a very good soldier: He didn't stand out; he didn't try to draw attention to himself; he always did his duty faithfully, and he never once complained to his friends that he found it hard.

[Page 609]

After his officer training course finished, he was sent to an artillery course. He studied the workings of Russian artillery seized during the six–day war, and upon completing his studies, he was sent to serve in the artillery corps.

Tzvika served in the artillery corps for close to a year. He and his team passed all borders, and they participated in many operations. Firstly, they partook in operations in the Golan Heights, in the cold and the mud, then in the Jordan Valley with its never–ending gunfire, and then by the Suez Canal, with its heat and dust, and finally at Al–Hama.

Tzvika had vacations very rarely. When he came home, he would soothe his parents, assuring they had nothing to worry about. Only one time, after a particularly long stretch of operations, he told his father, "We have a serious band, there".

In the heat of battle, he was excellent at keeping a cool and calm head. These characteristics afforded him considerable accuracy during operations, and his team quickly became the most exceptional squad. Every target hit made Tzvika roar with joy. His reaction served as an example to the rest of his team, who followed his orders wholeheartedly. Tzvika did not shout at his soldiers, rather, he led by personal example, and acted as a model. with dedication and responsibility, he and his quietness conquered the hearts of all his men. His honesty and his loyalty helped him become a truly beloved commander and friend. He would chat to the soldiers, show interest in their lives and tell them about his family, his village, and his plans; his sister, who was a better student than himself and of whom he was very proud; his parents, who worried about him and helped him realize his goals; his book that he loved, but mainly about his plans for the future.

Tzvika dreamed about farming. At first, he considered going to live on a kibbutz, but he decided that he would prefer to be a *moshavnik* . He hoped to buy a farm in the moshav, a goal fully supported by his parents, who had set aside all their savings for this purpose. Later, he came to the conclusion that a farm in an established village was not challenging enough, and so he aspired to go to a new moshav, and build something out of nothing.

When he received packages from home, he would gather his team together, and divide the parcel between everyone. This is also how he celebrated his nineteenth birthday.

Shy Tzvika, who loved everything to do with music, would break out in song, and his friends would join in. During one operation, the truck that stored all their equipment was hit, and it was destroyed. When he realized this, Tzvika burst out laughing. Everyone looked at him. "All my equipment is gone: my kitbag, my clothes, and my transistor. Never mind, my father will buy me new things. The important thing is that no one was hurt, and we're all fit and well."

Seven weeks in the Suez Canal. He went through many operations, and participated in all the battles. Finally, it was time for his longed-for vacation. Tzvika came home for one day. Tomorrow, he had to return to the squadron. His good friend promised him to save a bed in his neighborhood. The following day, he was supposed to have a regular vacation: a long vacation.

[Page 610]

The last battle was particularly fierce. The team, some of whose men had been wounded in the previous operation, fought long hours. The battery worked at breakneck speed. Their hits were accurate. In the end, the enemy's artillery had their battery in range. The command was given to enter the bunker. Tzvika ensured all his men were inside. He remained the last one. A direct hit – and Tzvika fell.

**"Mother! Understand that we are at war. Battles are taking place, and in battle, anything can happen. If something happens to me, don't break; don't let your spirits fall. Be strong. Life must continue!"** (From Tzvika's last letter)

(Emek Hefer Area News
Number 26–27
Tamuz 5729 – July 1969)


## To the Driver
### In memory of Tzvika, of blessed memory

If you travel in the North, certainly you know
He sits behind you, silently.
"Stop here at the junction," – as if you are rushing,
He says, "Thank you" – and disappears. And you wonder for a moment –
where was he from?
With his machine gun, and his black beret on his head,
He slept last night with his sights and bullets –
The fate of all who were the black beret. And you heard the news – maybe you recall –
The Canal, the Valley, and the Heights,

And the home, where nostalgia sings
All who wear the beret in silence... And once to holiday everyone went
New to her, so eagerly watched –


*[Page 611]*

Just one is not on the road
And you – oh, the anxiety – do you not feel!
Where did the proud and warm smiling one go?
Whose heart fills with mercy for him?
The morning breeze reveals the secret:
To the bosom of his beautiful land he returned If you travel in the North, certainly you know
He sits behind you, silently.
"Stop here at the junction," – as if you are rushing,
He says, "Thank you" – and disappears.

**Sergeant Flesher**
**Battery 130 Platoon commander**

## The Grey Day

1. Really, just a normal morning
Total silence, peace, tranquility.
Just birdsong,
Just normal flapping of wings.
 2. Suddenly, the familiar cry
Of the battery target.
 3. Immediately, we fastened our belts, We kissed the signs on our shoulders
Steel helmets on our heads
And immediately took our positions.
 4. Some seconds passed
and "Fire!" was heard from all sides.
Not much time went by
and we started firing too
spread all around.
 5. We silenced several stations
We silenced several batteries,
Here and there, hither and thither
 6. But he continued calmly,
"Fire!" he called stalwartly
And his hand pulled the rope.

7. A shell went over our post,
A shell came up short of our post,
But our team did not abandon our place.

8. Ordered to lay in place
And the team immediately
Listened to his instruction.

9. And suddenly… suddenly,
Always the same wayward shell
Landed on our position – And he is no more.

[Page 612]

10. Not so very long ago
We caught together on the hillside.
Not so very long ago
We called together, "Fire, Fire!"

11. We finished the course,
And started another,
And then another
And then time ended.
But who knew what
The artillery course
Could cause to occur?

12. Only yesterday I spoke to you,
Only yesterday I laughed with you,
We divided up our food and snacks,
And swapped shifts.

13. I heard your voice this morning
Your usual galloping laugh,
You were not scared – "Fire" you called,
And your hand pulled the rope with confidence.
But see, what happened.

14. My sleep is not sleep,
You are always before my eyes,
All the time I see you
And your laugh my ears always hear.
May his memory be forever blessed.

**David Malia**
**Member of Battery 130 Platoon**

Kibbutz Maaleh Hachamisha, 26 April, 1969

**Warmest greetings to you, Elchanan Rosenberg and family,**

You do not know me, but I felt compelled to write a few words to you about your son, Tzvika, of blessed memory, who was one of my soldiers.

Tzvika came to me to my unit after being a cadet in the army for a long time. In my unit, Tzvika transformed from a cadet into a soldier, and later into a commander, responsible for his own unit of soldiers.

The transformation from cadet to soldier is a process where all that has been learned must be implemented into action – the character, the self-initiative of the operator stands out. Tzvika proved himself completely in this important process.

He was a quiet lad, who preferred to hide his abilities – but he was very disciplined and was blessed with a strong will to do everything in the best possible way.

I could trust him with anything.

[Page 613]

At first, he was deputy commander of the team, working with new and unfamiliar artillery, but he worked dependably. Later, when the older soldiers in the team were released from the army, it was obvious and natural that Tzvika would take one of the most responsible positions.

I initially worried a little about Tzvika being so quiet, that he wouldn't be capable of raising his voice to the group when needed; that he wouldn't be firm enough – but his calmness and quietness managed to work with the team that he was given.

I have tried to paint you a picture of Tzvika's character as I knew him in the months he was my soldier, and as I remember him at the start of his steps as an IDF officer.

Never in my life did I think I would need to write these words about my soldier, I always felt confident that no one could hurt us, and we would never be overcome – but we are only made of flesh and blood.

I could not believe initially that Tzvika, of blessed memory, had fallen, but when I saw his photo in the newspaper, a shiver passed over my body and I suddenly felt as if he was standing there in front of me.

I am with you in your mourning.

I would like to say how important it is for Tzvika and the many others who have fallen, that we must live our lives in this country to their fullest – in joy, and sadness; through smiles and tears – because their deaths have given us our lives.

Be comforted amongst the mourners of Zion and Jerusalem. Yours,

**Kibbutz Ma'aleh Hachamisha**                                                           **Yosi Ya'ari**

[Pages 617-641]

# List of Martyrs

**For their souls and memories**

**This is a list of martyrs of the Serock community who were killed during the Holocaust period by the German Nazi oppressor**
**Transliterated by Ann Harris**
**Edited by Yocheved Klausner**

*Please note that at the right side, "Page" is listed; this is the page in the Original Yizkor Book, not the page number in this book, the translation.*

| Family name(s) | First name(s) | Maiden name | Sex | Remarks | Page |
|---|---|---|---|---|---|
| א Alef | | | | | |
| OGRODOWER | Shmuel Chaim | | M | | 617 |
| OGRODOWER | Beile Rachel | | F | | 617 |
| OGRODOWER | Alter | | M | | 617 |
| OGRODOWER | Breindl | | F | | 617 |
| OGRODOWER | Bunim | | M | | 617 |
| OGRODOWER | Golda | | F | | 617 |
| OGRODOWER | Frumet | | F | | 617 |
| OGRODOWER | Avraham | | M | | 617 |
| OGRODOWER | Noach | | M | | 617 |
| OGRODOWER | Dvora Zissel | | F | | 617 |
| OGRODOWER | Breindl | | F | | 617 |
| OGRODOWER | Chana | | M | | 617 |
| OGRODOWER | Josef | | M | | 617 |
| OGRODOWER | Rachel | | F | | 617 |
| OGRODOWER | Frumet | | F | | 617 |
| UBOGI | Meir | | M | | 617 |
| UBOGI | Basza | | F | | 617 |
| UBOGI | Matel | | M | | 617 |
| UBOGI | Chana | | F | | 617 |
| UBOGI | Israel | | M | | 617 |
| UBOGI | Necha Lea | | F | | 617 |
| UBOGI | Ester | | F | | 617 |
| UBOGI | Shmuel Yossel | | M | | 617 |
| UBOGI | Israel | | M | | 617 |
| URMAN | Bunim | | M | | 617 |
| URMAN | Feiga | BRESLER | F | | 617 |
| ITZCOWITCH | Berel | | M | | 617 |
| ITZCOWITCH | Baltcha | | F | | 617 |
| ITZCOWITCH | Meir | | M | | 617 |
| EIZENBERG | Chaim Shlomo | | M | Ritual slaughterer | 617 |
| EIZENBERG | Feiga | | F | | 617 |
| EICHENBAUM | Dov | | M | | 617 |
| EICHENBAUM | Golda | | F | | 617 |
| EICHENBAUM | Avraham | | M | | 617 |
| EICHENBAUM | Rozja | | F | | 617 |
| EICHENBAUM | David | | M | | 617 |

| | | | | | |
|---|---|---|---|---|---|
| EICHENBAUM | Yidel | | F | | 617 |
| EICHENBAUM | Sheina Rachel | | F | | 617 |
| EICHENBAUM | Hershel | | M | | 617 |
| EICHENBAUM | Sheindel | | F | | 617 |
| EICHENBAUM | Chaia | | F | | 617 |
| EICHENBAUM | Sheva | | F | | 617 |
| EICHENBAUM | Ester | | F | | 617 |
| INWENTARSCH | Chaim | | M | Dr. | 617 |
| OLDAK | Reizel | JASKOWICZ | F | | 617 |
| OSTROWSKI | Leib | | M | | 617 |
| OSTROWSKI | Beile | | F | | 617 |
| OSTROWSKI | Avraham | | M | | 617 |
| OSTROWSKI | Joel | | M | | 617 |
| OSTROWSKI | Shlomo | | M | | 617 |
| OSTROWSKI | Tema | | F | | 617 |
| OSTROWSKI | Ester | | F | | 617 |
| OSTROWSKI | Miszka | | M | | 618 |
| OSTROWSKI | Roza | | F | | 618 |
| APELBAUM | Yitzhak Meir | | M | | 618 |
| ORYL* | Josek | M | His occupation was "tailor" | | 618 |
| ORYL | Etka | WJELKABRODA | F | | 618 |
| ORYL | Israel | | M | | 618 |
| ORYL | Leizer | | M | | 618 |
| ORYL | Beile | | F | | 618 |
| ORYL | Israelik | | M | | 618 |
| ORYL | Lea | | F | | 618 |
| ORYL | Shepsl [Shabtai] | | M | | 618 |

## ב Bet

| | | | | | |
|---|---|---|---|---|---|
| BABEK | Menachem Mendel | | M | | 618 |
| BABEK | Jenta Gitl | | F | | 618 |
| BABEK | Gutman | | M | | 618 |
| BABEK | Chava | | F | | 618 |
| BABEK | Chana | | F | | 618 |
| BABEK | Yehoshua David | | M | | 618 |
| BABEK | Beile | | F | | 618 |
| BALDIGER | Tobe | | F | | 618 |
| BALDIGER | Antchel | | M | | 618 |
| BARAB | Josef | | M | | 618 |
| BARAB | Necha | | F | | 618 |
| BARAB | Fejwel | | M | | 618 |
| BARAB | Chava | SZTELANG | F | | 618 |
| BARAB | Manja | | F | | 618 |

| | | | | |
|---|---|---|---|---|
| BARAB | Rivka | | F | 618 |
| BARAB | Shulim | | M | 618 |
| BARAB | Ora | | F | 618 |
| BOGUSLAWSKI | Hersch Efraim | | M | 618 |
| BOGUSLAWSKI | Rachel | | F | 618 |
| BOGUSLAWSKI | Yeshayahu | | M | 618 |
| BOGUSLAWSKI | Chava | | F | 618 |
| BOGUSLAWSKI | Moshe | | M | 618 |
| BOGUSLAWSKI | Tziwja | | F | 618 |
| BOGUSLAWSKI | Moshe | | M | 618 |
| BOGUSLAWSKI | Rachel Lea | | F | 618 |
| BOGUSLAWSKI | Rivka | | F | 618 |
| BOGUSLAWSKI | Josef | | M | 618 |
| BERNSTEIN | Shmuel | | M | 618 |
| BERNSTEIN | Yakov | | M | 618 |
| BERNSTEIN | Matel | | M | 618 |
| BERNSTEIN | Chaia | LESER | F | 618 |
| BERNSTEIN | Hershel | | M | 618 |
| BERNSTEIN | Ester | | F | 618 |
| BERNSTEIN | Berel | | M | 618 |
| BERNSTEIN | Sara | | F | 618 |
| BERNSTEIN | Israel | | M | 618 |
| BERNSTEIN | Rivka | | F | 618 |
| BERNSTEIN | Josef | | M | 618 |
| BERNSTEIN | Golda | | F | 618 |
| BERNSTEIN | Shlomo | | M | 618 |
| BERNSTEIN | Sara | | F | 618 |
| BERNSTEIN | Israel | | M | 618 |
| BERNSTEIN | Beile Lea | | F | 618 |
| BERNSTEIN | Rivka | | F | 618 |
| BERNSTEIN | Tuvia | | M | 618 |
| BERNSTEIN | Bluma | | F | 618 |
| BERNSTEIN | Chaia | | F | 618 |
| BERNSTEIN | Perel | | F | 618 |
| BERNSTEIN | Avraham | | M | 618 |
| BERNSTEIN | Freida | | F | 618 |
| BERNSTEIN | Yehuda | | M | 618 |
| BERNSTEIN | Nechama | | F | 618 |
| BERNSTEIN | Yehoshua | | M | 618 |
| BERNSTEIN | Lea | | F | 618 |
| BERNSTEIN | Moshe | | M | 619 |
| BERNSTEIN | Chaim | | M | 619 |

| | | | | |
|---|---|---|---|---|
| BERNSTEIN | Jochewed | | F | 619 |
| BOCHENEK | Moshe | | M | 619 |
| BOCHENEK | Breindel | OGRODOWER | F | 619 |
| BOCHENEK | Arie | | M | 619 |
| BOCHENEK | Shmuel Noach | | M | 619 |
| BOCHENEK | Rivka | | F | 619 |
| BOCHENEK | Feiga | | F | 619 |
| BOCHENEK | Rachel | | F | 619 |
| BOCHENEK | Hinda | | F | 619 |
| BRUCHANSKI | Menachem | | M | 619 |
| BRUCHANSKI | Ester | | F | 619 |
| BRUCHANSKI | Shepsl [Shabtai] | | M | 619 |
| BRUCHANSKI | Lea | | F | 619 |
| BSJAZA | Chana | | F | 619 |
| BSJAZA | Baruch | | M | 619 |
| BSJAZA | Necha | | F | 619 |
| BSJAZA | Shlomo | | M | 619 |
| BSJAZA | Feiga | | F | 619 |
| BSJAZA | Leibisz | | M | 619 |
| BSJAZA | Shlomo | | M | 619 |
| BSJAZA | Necha | | F | 619 |
| BSJAZA | Malka'le | | F | 619 |
| BRINBAUM | Hershel | | M | 619 |
| BRINBAUM | Roda | | F | 619 |
| BRINBAUM | Feiga | | F | 619 |
| BRINBAUM | Estuscha | | F | 619 |
| BRINBAUM | Hersh Meir | | M | 619 |
| BLOCHMAN | Yitzhak | | M | 619 |
| BLOCHMAN | Sheindel | | F | 619 |
| BLOCHMAN | Yakov | | M | 619 |
| BLUMBERG | Alter | | M | 619 |
| BLUMBERG | Chana | | F | 619 |
| BLUMBERG | Israel | | M | 619 |
| BLUMBERG | Baruch | | M | 619 |
| BLUMBERG | Henne | ZACHAREK | F | 619 |
| BLUMBERG | Chava | | F | 619 |
| BLUMBERG | Shlomo | | M | 619 |
| BLUMBERG | Matityahu | | M | 619 |
| BLUMBERG | Berish | | M | 619 |
| BLUMBERG | Leibel | | M | 619 |
| BLUMBERG | Rivka | | F | 619 |
| BLUSZTEJN | Avraham Moshe | | M | 619 |

| | | | | |
|---|---|---|---|---|
| BLINDT | Hershel | | M | 619 |
| BLINDT | Chaia | | F | 619 |
| BLINDT | Shmuel | | M | 619 |
| BLINDT | Baltsha | | F | 619 |
| BELINSOHN | Zelig | | M | 619 |
| BELINSOHN | Rivka | | F | 619 |
| BELINSOHN | Itta | | F | 619 |
| BELINSOHN | Josef | | M | 619 |
| BERMAN | Perel | | F | 619 |
| BERMAN | Zlata | | M | 619 |
| BERMAN | Freidl | | F | 619 |
| BERMAN | Vitel | | F | 619 |
| BERNSTEIN | Moshe Peretz | | M | 619 |
| BERNSTEIN | Lea | | F | 619 |
| BERNSTEIN | Gitla | | F | 619 |
| BERNSTEIN | Chaim | | M | 619 |
| BERNSTEIN | Zlata | | M | 619 |
| BERNSTEIN | Herschel | | M | 619 |
| BRODZKI | Chaim | | M | 619 |
| BRODZKI | Chana | | F | 619 |
| BRAUN | Avraham | | M | 619 |
| BRAUN | Rivka | | F | 619 |
| BRUSMAN | Yidel | | M | 620 |
| BRUSMAN | Chava | | F | 620 |
| BRESSLER | Rachel | | F | 620 |
| BRESSLER | Moshe | | M | 620 |
| BRESSLER | Perel | | F | 620 |
| ג **Gimmel** | | | | |
| GAL | Moshe | | M | 620 |
| GAL | Bina | | F | 620 |
| GAL | Gawriel | | M | 620 |
| GOLDBERG | Moshe | | M | 620 |
| GOLDBERG | Rachel | | F | 620 |
| GOLDBERG | Yakov | | M | 620 |
| GOLDBERG | Lea | | F | 620 |
| GOLDBERG | Goltshe | | F | 620 |
| GOLDBERG | Mechl | | M | 620 |
| GOLDBERG | Zischa | | M | 620 |
| GUTKOWSKI | Szeina Rachel | | F | 620 |
| GUTKOWSKI | Yehuda Leib | | M | 620 |
| GUTKOWSKI | Chaia | | F | 620 |
| GUTKOWSKI | Frumet | | F | 620 |

| | | | | |
|---|---|---|---|---|
| GUTKOWSKI | Schepsl [Shabtai] | | M | 620 |
| GUTKOWSKI | Schepsl [Shabtai] | | M | 620 |
| GUTKOWSKI | Sure'tche | | F | 620 |
| GUTKOWSKI | Avraham | | M | 620 |
| GUTKOWSKI | Moshe | | M | 620 |
| GUTKOWSKI | Miriam | | F | 620 |
| GUTKOWSKI | Mendel | | M | 620 |
| GUTKOWSKI | Pesza | | F | 620 |
| GUTKOWSKI | Chana | | F | 620 |
| GUTKOWSKI | Henja | | F | 620 |
| GUTKOWSKI | Josef | | M | 620 |
| GUTKOWSKI | Chaim | | M | 620 |
| GUTKOWSKI | Shalom | | M | 620 |
| GUTKOWSKI | Feivel | | M | 620 |
| GUTKOWSKI | Chaim | | M | 620 |
| GODEM | Yakov | | M | 620 |
| GODEM | Jocheved | KRIMKIEWICZ | F | 620 |
| GODES | Yitzhak Hersh | | M | 620 |
| GODES | Rivka Beile | | F | 620 |
| GURMAN | Yitzhak Meir | | M | 620 |
| GURMAN | Chava | | F | 620 |
| GURMAN | Sara | | F | 620 |
| GURMAN | Lea | | F | 620 |
| GURMAN | Nechama | | F | 620 |
| GURMAN | Sheindel | | F | 620 |
| GURMAN | Tzipora | | F | 620 |
| GURMAN | Ester | | F | 620 |
| GURMAN | Feiga Hinda | | F | 620 |
| GURMAN | Tzvia | | F | 620 |
| GURMAN | Sara | | F | 620 |
| GURMAN | Menachem Mendel | | M | 620 |
| GURMAN | Moshe | | M | 620 |
| GURMAN | Leibel | | M | 620 |
| GIDZEWIERNIARZ | Josef | | M | 620 |
| GIDZEWIERNIARZ | Gitla | | F | 620 |
| GIDZEWIERNIARZ | Chaim Eliezer | | M | 620 |
| GIDZEWIERNIARZ | Sure'tche | | F | 620 |
| GIDZEWIERNIARZ | Lea | | F | 620 |
| GIDZEWIERNIARZ | Avrahamtsche | | M | 620 |
| GIDZEWIERNIARZ | Lyba | PIENIK | F | 620 |
| GLODEK | Chaim | | M | 620 |
| GLODEK | Hodes | | F | 620 |

| | | | | | |
|---|---|---|---|---|---|
| GLODEK | Feiga | | F | | 620 |
| GLODEK | Avraham | | M | | 620 |
| GLODEK | Rela | | F | | 620 |
| GLODEK | Sewek | | M | | 620 |
| GLODEK | Sender | | M | | 620 |
| GERWER | Rachel Lea | | F | | 621 |
| GERWER | Moshe | | M | | 621 |
| GERWER | Rivka | ROSENBERG | F | | 621 |
| GERWER | Chaim | | M | | 621 |
| GERWER | Shmuel | | M | | 621 |
| GERWER | Feiga | | F | | 621 |
| GERWER | Wolf | | M | | 621 |
| GERSTENSANG | Fishel | | M | | 621 |
| GERSTENSANG | Basha | | M | | 621 |
| GERSTENSANG | Herschel | | M | | 621 |
| GROBSZMID | Rachel | | F | | 621 |
| GROBSZMID | Moshe | | M | | 621 |
| GROBSZMID | Yakov | | M | | 621 |
| GROBSZMID | Dvora | | F | | 621 |
| GRABIE | Nute | | M | | 621 |
| GRANIEWICZ | Moshe | | M | | 621 |
| GRANIEWICZ | Yakov | | M | | 621 |
| GRANIEWICZ | Sara | WOLINSKI | F | | 621 |
| GROSBARD | Eliezer | | M | | 621 |
| GROSBARD | Miriam Feiga | | F | | 621 |
| GROSBARD | Chaim Hersh | | M | | 621 |
| GROSBARD | Yossel | | M | | 621 |
| GROSBARD | Lyba | | F | | 621 |
| GROSBARD | Henna | | F | | 621 |
| GROSBARD | Chaie'tche | | F | | 621 |
| GROSBARD | Mirel | | F | | 621 |
| GROSBARD | Perel | | F | | 621 |
| GROSMAN | Herschel | | M | | 621 |
| GROSMAN | Sheindel | | F | | 621 |
| GROSMAN | Chana | | F | | 621 |
| GROSMAN | Lea | | F | | 621 |
| GROSMAN | Rivkale | | F | | 621 |
| GRINBAUM | Aron Leib | | M | | 621 |
| GRINBAUM | Golda | | F | | 621 |
| GRINBAUM | Avraham | | M | | 621 |
| GRINBAUM | Mordechai | | M | | 621 |
| GRINBAUM | Rivka | | F | | 621 |

| | | | | |
|---|---|---|---|---|
| GRINBAUM | Shlomo | | M | 621 |
| GRINBAUM | Shmuel | | M | 621 |
| GRINBAUM | Sara | | F | 621 |
| GRINBAUM | Ester | | F | 621 |
| GRINBAUM | Malka | | F | 621 |
| GRINBAUM | Herschel | | M | 621 |
| GRINBAUM | Sara Rivka | | F | 621 |
| GRINBAUM | Ester Lea | | F | 621 |
| GRINBAUM | Heidl | | F | 621 |
| GRINBAUM | Zalman | | M | 621 |
| GRINBAUM | Gitla | | F | 621 |
| GRINBERG | Naftali | | M | 621 |
| GRINBERG | Chana | | F | 621 |
| GRINBERG | Moshe | | M | 621 |
| GRINBERG | Yenta | | F | 621 |
| GRINBERG | Zalman | | M | 621 |
| GRINBERG | Gitla | | F | 621 |

**ד Dalet**

| | | | | |
|---|---|---|---|---|
| DOMBAK | Avraham | | M | 621 |
| DOMBAK | Mirel | | F | 621 |
| DOMBAK | Sara Beile | | F | 621 |
| DOMBAK | Necha | | F | 621 |
| DORN | Hillel | | M | 621 |
| DORN | Chava | | F | 621 |
| DORN | Josef | | M | 621 |
| DORN | Rachel | | F | 621 |
| DORN | Ester | | F | 621 |
| DORN | Itshe | | M | 621 |
| DOBNER | Wolf Leib | | M | 621 |
| DODJY | Chaia | | F | 621 |
| DODJY | Shmuel | | M | 622 |
| DODJY | Hersch Chaim | | M | 622 |
| DODJY | Moshe | | M | 622 |
| DODJY | Sara Mindel | | F | 622 |
| DREZNER | Bezalel | | M | 622 |
| DREZNER | Yitzhak | | M | 622 |
| DREZNER | Rachel | | F | 622 |
| DREZNER | David | | M | 622 |
| DREZNER | Aron | | M | 622 |

**ה Hey**

| | | | | |
|---|---|---|---|---|
| HOCHBERG | Benjamin | | M | 622 |

| | | | | |
|---|---|---|---|---|
| HOCHBERG | Ettel | | F | 622 |
| HOCHBERG | Rivka | | F | 622 |
| HOCHBERG | Chaia | | F | 622 |
| HASSMAN | Herschel | | M | 622 |
| HASSMAN | Miriam | | F | 622 |
| HASSMAN | Rivka | | F | 622 |
| HASSMAN | Yehuda | | M | 622 |
| HASSMAN | Henna | KLEINMAN | F | 622 |
| HASSMAN | Itta | | F | 622 |
| HASSMAN | Reizel | MAK | F | 622 |
| HASSMAN | Chaia | | F | 622 |
| HASSMAN | Yeshajahu | | M | 622 |
| HOFMAN | Beile Lea | | F | 622 |
| HOFMAN | Yehoshua | | M | 622 |
| HOFMAN | Sarale | ITZKOVITZ | F | 622 |
| HOFMAN | Chana | ROSENBERG | F | 622 |
| HOFMAN | Reizl | | F | 622 |
| HOROWICZ | Yakov Mordechai | | M | 622 |
| HOROWICZ | Rachel | | F | 622 |
| HOROWICZ | Feiga | | F | 622 |
| HOROWICZ | Berel | | M | 622 |
| HOROWICZ | Lea'tche | | F | 622 |
| HOROWICZ | Aron | | M | 622 |
| ORENSTEIN | Yitzhak Aron | | M | 622 |
| ORENSTEIN | Pessa | | F | 622 |
| ORENSTEIN | Malka | | F | 622 |
| ORENSTEIN | Chaim | | M | 622 |
| ORENSTEIN | Perel | | F | 622 |
| ORENSTEIN | Malka | | F | 622 |
| HILER | Mendel | | M | 622 |
| HILER | Sheindel | | F | 622 |
| HILER | Feivel | | M | 622 |
| HILER | Benjamin | | M | 622 |
| HILER | Hinda | | F | 622 |
| HILER | Feiga | | F | 622 |
| HILER | Fruma | | F | 622 |
| HILER | Ester | | F | 622 |
| HILER | Rivka | | F | 622 |
| HILER | Rachel | | F | 622 |
| HILER | Israel Isser | | M | 622 |
| HILER | Fajtcha | MIELNIK | F | 622 |
| HILER | Rivka | | F | 622 |

| HILER | Rachel | | F | 622 |
|---|---|---|---|---|
| HILER | Chaia | | F | 622 |
| HECHT | Malija | ITZKOVITZ | F | 622 |
| HECHT | Arie | | M | 622 |
| ו Vav | | | | |
| WOLINSKI | Yitzhak | | M | 622 |
| WOLINSKI | Zlata | | M | 622 |
| WOLINSKI | Leibel | | M | 622 |
| WOLINSKI | Rachel | GRANIEWICZ | F | 622 |
| WOLINSKI | Leja | | F | 622 |
| WOLINSKI | Israel | | M | 622 |
| WOHLMAN | Yakov David | | M | 622 |
| WOHLMAN | Koppel | | M | 622 |
| WOHLMAN | Zelig | | M | 622 |
| WOHLMAN | Blima | ROSENFELD | F | 622 |
| WOHLMAN | Frywa | | M | 623 |
| WOHLMAN | Rozia | | F | 623 |
| WOHLMAN | Dobe | | F | 623 |
| WOHLMAN | Ester Malka | | F | 623 |
| WOHLMAN | Avraham Yitzhak | | M | 623 |
| WALER | Moshe | | M | 623 |
| WALER | Chava | | F | 623 |
| WALERSTEIN | Yechezkel | | M | 623 |
| WALERSTEIN | Malka | | F | 623 |
| WALERSTEIN | Reizl | | F | 623 |
| WALERSTEIN | Aron | | M | 623 |
| WALERSTEIN | Lea | WARSZAWSKI | F | 623 |
| WALERSTEIN | Malka | | F | 623 |
| WARSZAWSKI | David | | M | 623 |
| WARSZAWSKI | Freidl | | F | 623 |
| WARSZAWSKI | Lea | | M | 623 |
| WARSZAWSKI | Ester | SCHAPIRA | F | 623 |
| WARSZAWSKI | Chana'le | | F | 623 |
| WINAGORA | Matel | | M | 623 |
| WINAGORA | Doba | | F | 623 |
| WINAGORA | Itche Meir | | M | 623 |
| WINAGORA | Yidel | | M | 623 |
| WINAGORA | Chaim Yehuda | | M | 623 |
| WINAGORA | Herschel | | M | 623 |
| WINAGORA | Beile | | F | 623 |
| WINAGORA | Chaim | | M | 623 |
| WINAGORA | Shlomo | | M | 623 |

| | | | | |
|---|---|---|---|---|
| WINAGORA | Yakov | | M | 623 |
| WINAGORA | Avraham | | M | 623 |
| WINAGORA | Moshe | | M | 623 |
| WINAGORA | Shmuel | | M | 623 |
| WINAGORA | Chaia | EICHENBAUM | F | 623 |
| WINOGRAD | Itche Meir | | M | 623 |
| WINOGRAD | Beile | | F | 623 |
| WINOGRAD | Sheine | | F | 623 |
| WINOGRAD | Ester | | F | 623 |
| WINOGRAD | Jocheved | | F | 623 |
| WINOGRAD | Rivka | | F | 623 |
| WINOGRAD | Rachtche | | F | 623 |
| WINOGRAD | Lyba | | F | 623 |
| WINOGRAD | Moshe | | M | 623 |
| WINOGRAD | Feivel | | M | 623 |
| WINOGRAD | Isrulik | | M | 623 |
| WINOGRAD | Zisza | | F | 623 |
| WINOGRAD | Leibisz Shmerl | | M | 623 |
| WINOGRAD | Pesja | | F | 623 |
| WINOGRAD | Zisha | | M | 623 |
| WINOGRAD | Jocheved | | F | 623 |
| WINKRANTZ | Kalman | | M | 623 |
| WINKRANTZ | Shifra | | F | 623 |
| WINKRANTZ | Malia | | F | 623 |
| WINKRANTZ | Itchele | | M | 623 |
| WINKRANTZ | Ester | | F | 623 |
| WINKRANTZ | Chaim | | M | 623 |
| WINKRANTZ | Moshke | PASKOWICZ | F | 623 |
| WINKRANTZ | Beiltche | | F | 623 |
| WINKRANTZ | Tova | | F | 623 |
| WINKRANTZ | Nute | | M | 623 |
| WINKRANTZ | Libe | | F | 623 |
| WINKRANTZ | Yechiel | | M | 623 |
| WINKRANTZ | Rachel | | F | 623 |
| WINKRANTZ | Bunim | | M | 623 |
| WINKRANTZ | Tova | | F | 623 |
| WINKRANTZ | Chava | | F | 623 |
| WEINSTOCK | David Leib | | M | 623 |
| WEINSTOCK | Sara | | F | 623 |
| WEINSTOCK | Tova | | F | 624 |
| WEINSTOCK | Malka | | F | 624 |
| WEINSTOCK | Dvora | | F | 624 |

| WEINSTOCK | Simcha | | M | 624 |
| WEINSTOCK | Josef | | M | 624 |
| WEINSTOCK | Avraham | | M | 624 |
| WEINSTOCK | Shlomo | | M | 624 |
| WEINSTOCK | Chaim Eliezer | | M | 624 |
| WEINSTOCK | Chaia | | F | 624 |
| WEINSTOCK | Sheina Tamar | | F | 624 |
| WEINSTOCK | Arie | | M | 624 |
| WEITZ | Avraham | | M | 624 |
| WEITZ | Lea | MIODOWNIK | F | 624 |
| WEITZ | Rachel | | F | 624 |
| WEITZ | Malka | | F | 624 |
| WIERNIK | Menachem Mendel | | M | 624 |
| WIERNIK | Yechiel | | M | 624 |
| WIERNIK | Riekel | | F | 624 |
| WIERNIK | Chana | | F | 624 |
| WIERNIK | Tova | | F | 624 |
| WISNIEWICZ | Moshe | | M | 624 |
| WISNIEWICZ | Feiga | | F | 624 |
| WISNIEWICZ | Malka | | F | 624 |
| WISNIEWICZ | Avrahamtche | | M | 624 |
| WISNIEWICZ | Yidel | | F | 624 |
| WISNIEWICZ | Shlomo | | M | 624 |
| WISNIEWICZ | Israel | | M | 624 |
| WISNIEWICZ | Pessa | | F | 624 |
| WISNIEWICZ | Josef | | M | 624 |
| WISNIEWICZ | Necha | | F | 624 |
| WELNER | Mordechai Ber | | M | 624 |
| WELNER | Rachel | | F | 624 |
| WELNER | Avraham | | M | 624 |
| WELNER | Sara | | F | 624 |
| WELNER | Zisza | | F | 624 |
| WELNER | Michael | | M | 624 |
| WELNER | Lieber | | M | 624 |
| WENGER | Herschel | | M | 624 |
| WENGER | Feiga | | F | 624 |
| WENGER | Berel | | M | 624 |
| WENGER | Zacharia | | M | 624 |
| WROBEL | Herschel | | M | 624 |
| WROBEL | Rachel Lea | | F | 624 |
| WROBEL | Feiga | | F | 624 |
| WROBEL | Roize | | F | 624 |

| ז Zayin | | | | |
|---|---|---|---|---|
| ZACHAREK | Leizer Wolf | | M | 624 |
| ZACHAREK | Gele | | M | 624 |
| ZACHAREK | Henia | | F | 624 |
| ZACHAREK | Nute | | M | 624 |
| ZACHAREK | Moshe Leib | | M | 624 |
| ZACHAREK | Chaia'le | WOLINSKI | F | 624 |
| ZACHAREK | Monyek | | M | 624 |
| ZACHAREK | Chaim Yakov | | M | 624 |
| ZACHAREK | Gryna | | F | 624 |
| ZACHAREK | Meir | | M | 624 |
| ZACHAREK | Alter | | M | 624 |
| SALZMAN | Chava | | F | 624 |
| SALZMAN | Moshe | | M | 624 |
| SALZMAN | Chana | | F | 624 |
| SALZMAN | Manes | | M | 624 |
| SALZMAN | Matel | | M | 624 |
| SALZMAN | Zelda | | M | 624 |
| SALZMAN | Antchel | | M | 624 |
| SALZMAN | Zissel | | F | 624 |
| SALZMAN | Hersch | | M | 624 |
| SALZMAN | Lea | | F | 624 |
| SALZMAN | Antchele | | M | 625 |
| SALZMAN | Feiga | | F | 625 |
| SILBERBERG | Herschel | | M | 625 |
| SILBERBERG | Chana | | F | 625 |
| SILBERBERG | Shmerl | | M | 625 |
| SILBERBERG | Sara'ke | | F | 625 |
| SILBERSTEIN | Moshe | | M | 625 |
| SILBERSTEIN | Shifra | | F | 625 |
| SILBERSTEIN | Alta'le | | F | 625 |
| SILBERSTEIN | Moshe | | M | 625 |
| SILBERSTEIN | Feigale | | F | 625 |
| SILBERSTEIN | Geltche | | F | 625 |
| SILBERSTEIN | Gimpel | | M | 625 |
| SILBERSTEIN | Necha | | F | 625 |
| SILBERSTEIN | Aron Leib | | M | 625 |
| SILBERSTEIN | Chana | | F | 625 |
| SILBERSTEIN | Nechemia | | M | 625 |
| SILBERSTEIN | Mendel | | M | 625 |
| SILBERSTEIN | Mindel | | F | 625 |
| SILBERSTEIN | Yehoshua | | M | 625 |

| | | | | |
|---|---|---|---|---|
| SILBERSTEIN | Chaim | | M | 625 |
| SILBERSTEIN | Chana | | F | 625 |
| SILBERSTEIN | Rivka | | F | 625 |
| SILBERSTEIN | Rachel | | F | 625 |
| SILBERSTEIN | Moshe | | M | 625 |
| SILBERSTEIN | Nechemia | | M | 625 |
| SILBERSTEIN | Rivka | | F | 625 |
| SILBERSTEIN | Mindel | | M | 625 |
| ZLOTOGORSKI | Yakov Moshe | | M | 625 |
| ZLOTOGORSKI | Rivka Lea | | F | 625 |
| ZLOTOGORSKI | Zlatka | | F | 625 |
| ZELIKOWICZ | Leibel | | M | 625 |
| ZELIKOWICZ | Sara | | F | 625 |
| ZELIKOWICZ | Rachel | | F | 625 |
| ZELIKOWICZ | Rivka | | F | 625 |
| ZELIKOWICZ | Herschel | | M | 625 |
| ZELIKOWICZ | Avraham | | M | 625 |
| ZELIKOWICZ | Majtel | | F | 625 |

ח **Chet**

| | | | | |
|---|---|---|---|---|
| CHEINOWER | Moshe | | M | 625 |
| CHEINOWER | Necha Lea | | F | 625 |
| CHEINOWER | Ester | | M | 625 |
| CHEINOWER | Avraham | | M | 625 |
| CHEINOWER | Yossel | | M | 625 |
| CHEINOWER | Yeshayahu | | M | 625 |
| CHEINOWER | Pola | | F | 625 |
| CHEINOWER | Szprintza | | F | 625 |
| CHEINOWER | Feiga | | F | 625 |
| CHEINOWER | Chana | | M | 625 |
| CHEINOWER | Yeshayahu | | M | 625 |
| CHEINOWER | Hinda | | F | 625 |
| CHEINOWER | Breina | | F | 625 |
| CHEINOWER | Zalman | | M | 625 |
| CHEINOWER | Yakov | | M | 625 |
| CHEINOWER | Herschel | | M | 625 |
| CHAIMOWICZ | Meir | | M | 625 |
| CHAIMOWICZ | Lyba | | M | 625 |
| CHAIMOWICZ | Arie | | M | 625 |
| CHAIMOWICZ | Meir | | M | 625 |
| CHAIMOWICZ | Feivel | | F | 625 |

ט **Tet**

| | | | | |
|---|---|---|---|---|
| TOPEREK | Avraham | | M | 625 |
| TOPEREK | Majta | | F | 625 |
| TOPEREK | Hillel | | M | 625 |
| TOPEREK | Frida | | F | 625 |
| TOPEREK | Chana | | F | 625 |
| TOPEREK | Shlomo | | M | 625 |
| TOPEREK | Chaim | | M | 625 |
| TOPEREK | Josef | | M | 626 |
| TOPEREK | Elchanan | | M | 626 |
| TOPEREK | Pesach | | M | 626 |
| TOPEREK | Rivka | | F | 626 |
| TOPEREK | Yakov | | M | 626 |
| TOPEREK | Nachman | | M | 626 |
| TYK | Yitzhak Meir | | M | 626 |
| TYK | Chana | | F | 626 |
| TYK | Josef | | M | 626 |
| TYK | Simcha | | M | 626 |
| TYK | Tova | | F | 626 |
| TYK | Chaia | | F | 626 |
| TYK | Tanchum | | M | 626 |
| TYK | Maltsche | | F | 626 |
| TYK | Sabina | | F | 626 |
| TYK Genja | | F | Father was a *felczer* (surgeon) | 626 |
| TYKOLSKI | Moshe | | M | 626 |
| TYKOLSKI | Fride | | F | 626 |
| TYKOLSKI | Beile | | F | 626 |
| TYKOLSKI | Yossel | | M | 626 |
| CZAPINITZKI | Aizik | | M | 626 |
| CZAPINITZKI | Itka | | F | 626 |
| CIECHANOWITZKI | Rajtza | | F | 626 |
| CIECHANOWITZKI | Matityahu | | M | 626 |
| CIECHANOWITZKI | Jocheved | JAGODA | F | 626 |
| CIECHANOWITZKI | Tzirel | | F | 626 |
| CZAPINITZKI | Leibel | | M | 626 |
| CZAPINITZKI | Meir | | M | 626 |
| CZAPINITZKI | Malka | | F | 626 |
| CZAPINITZKI | Rachel | | F | 626 |
| CZAPINITZKI | Yehudit | | F | 626 |
| CIECHANOWITZKI | Yitzhak Meir | | M | 626 |
| CIECHANOWITZKI | Dina | MAIMON | F | 626 |
| CIECHANOWITZKI | Hillel | | M | 626 |
| CIECHANOWITZKI | Rivka | | F | 626 |

## Yod

| | | | | | |
|---|---|---|---|---|---|
| JAGODA | Gershon | | M | | 626 |
| JAGODA | Batia | | F | | 626 |
| JAGODA | Michael | | F | | 626 |
| JAGODA | Josef | | M | | 626 |
| JAGODA | Tema | | F | | 626 |
| JAGODA | Sima | | F | | 626 |
| JAGODA | Ester | | F | | 626 |
| JAGODA | Batia | | F | | 626 |
| JAGODA | Mirel | | F | | 626 |
| JAGODA | Itka | | F | | 626 |
| JAGODA | Sima | | F | | 626 |
| JAGODA | Henna | KALUSKI | F | | 626 |
| JAGODA | Shlomo | | M | | 626 |
| JAGODA | Dvora | SPILKA | F | | 626 |
| JAGODA | Chaim | | M | | 626 |
| JAGODA | Josef | | M | | 626 |
| JAGODA | Moshe | | M | | 626 |
| JAGODA | Frumet | | F | | 626 |
| JAGODA | Rekel | | F | | 626 |
| JASZOMBEK | Avraham | | M | | 626 |
| JASZOMBEK | Aizik | | M | | 626 |
| JASZOMBEK | Rivka | | F | | 626 |
| JANISZ | Beile Feiga | | F | | 626 |
| JANISZ | Yechiel | | M | | 626 |
| JANISZ | Frive | | F | | 626 |
| JANISZ | Chava | | F | | 626 |
| JANISZ | Yakov | | M | | 626 |
| JANISZ | Rivka | | F | | 626 |
| JANISZ | Itzel | | M | | 626 |
| JANISZ | Tzerka | | F | | 626 |
| JANISZ | Batia | | F | | 626 |
| JANISZ | Nechemia | | F | | 627 |
| JAGIELOWICZ | Welwel | | M | | 627 |
| JAGIELOWICZ | Tzvia | | F | | 627 |
| JAGIELOWICZ | Gitla | | F | | 627 |
| JAGIELOWICZ | Yehuda | | M | | 627 |
| JAGIELOWICZ | Matel | | F | | 627 |
| JAGIELOWICZ | Yakov | | M | | 627 |
| JAGIELOWICZ | Asher | | M | | 627 |
| JELEN | Herschel | | M | | 627 |

| | | | | | |
|---|---|---|---|---|---|
| JELEN | Zlatka | | F | | 627 |
| JELEN | Genendel | | F | | 627 |
| JELEN | Rivka | | F | | 627 |
| JERUSALEMSKI | Rafael Ber | | M | | 627 |
| JERUSALEMSKI | Matel | | F | | 627 |
| JERUSALEMSKI | Malia | | F | | 627 |
| כ **Kaf** | | | | | |
| KOHEN | Chana | | F | | 627 |
| KOHEN | Leibel | | M | | 627 |
| KOHEN | Josef | | M | | 627 |
| KOHEN | Arie | | M | | 627 |
| KOHEN | David | | M | | 627 |
| KOHEN | Dvora | | F | | 627 |
| KOHEN | Tuvia | | M | | 627 |
| KOHEN | Berel | | M | | 627 |
| KOHEN | Moshe | | M | | 627 |
| KOHEN | Shmuel | | M | | 627 |
| KOHEN | Golda | | F | | 627 |
| KOHEN | Rivka | | F | | 627 |
| KOHEN | Josef | | M | | 627 |
| KOHEN | Chana Feiga | | F | | 627 |
| KOHEN | Perel | | F | | 627 |
| KOHEN | Sheva | | F | | 627 |
| KOHEN | Asher | | M | | 627 |
| KOHEN | Feiga | | F | | 627 |
| KOHEN | Chana | | F | | 627 |
| KAMELHARZ | Shmuel | | M | | 627 |
| KAMELHARZ | Golda | | F | | 627 |
| KAMELHARZ | Chantche | KANIER | F | | 627 |
| KAMELHARZ | Sara | | F | | 627 |
| KAMELHARZ | Lea | | F | | 627 |
| KAMELHARZ | Herschel | | M | | 627 |
| KAMELHARZ | Elisheva | | F | | 627 |
| KAMELHARZ | Asher | | M | | 627 |
| KATZ | Shimon | | M | | 627 |
| KATZ | Beile Dina | | F | | 627 |
| KATZ | Chana | | F | | 627 |
| KATZ | Nechemia | | F | | 627 |
| KATZ | Moshe | BOTCHAN | M | | 627 |

\*Notes by Mrs. Ester GLAZER (nee ORYL) from Australia, originally from Serock
- Her sister Szajndla (Saba) ORYL (not on list) went to Treblinka in August 1942 at the age of fourteen- Her

mother, Etka, had a sister called Itka (not on list) - There was also a cousin called Julek ORYL who was in the Legionowo ghetto along with other members of his family and was probably fourteen or younger in 1942 - Not on list. Sala HOROWICZ, Mrs Glazer's best friend and the sister of Aron HOROWICZ - Mrs. GLAZER's grandmother lived in Serock all the time Mrs. GLAZER was a child and long before that, although we don't know where she was born. First she was DWOJRA ORYL and then DWOJRA RUBISZTAJN, though we can't be sure of the spelling of this last name. - Grandmother Dwojra brought up a cousin of Mrs GLAZER's called Gitla KOHN, (not on list) who was born in Serock and certainly lived there all her life until she was deported in December 1939

| Family name(s) | First name(s) | Maiden name | Sex | Remarks | Page |
|---|---|---|---|---|---|
| ל Lamed | | | | | http://www.jewishgen.org/Yizkor/serock/ser617.html - Index |
| LASKI | Herschel | | M | | 627 |
| LASKI | Lea | WOLINSKI | F | | 627 |
| LASKI | Rivka | | F | | 627 |
| LASKI | Miriam | | F | | 627 |
| LASKI | Beiltche | | F | | 627 |
| LITMAN | Mendel | | M | | 627 |
| LITMAN | Beile | | F | | 627 |
| LINKER | Golda Lea | | F | | 627 |
| LIS | Rachel | MAIMON | F | | 627 |
| LIS | Yakov | | M | | 627 |
| LIS | Rachel | | F | | 627 |
| LIS | Hadas | | F | | 627 |
| LIS | Tzippa | | F | | 627 |
| LIS | Rivka | | F | | 627 |
| LIS | Leibel | | M | | 627 |
| LIS | Rochtche | | F | | 627 |
| LIS | Hadassa | | F | | 627 |
| LIS | Chana | | F | | 627 |
| LIS | Jemima | | F | | 627 |
| LIS | Tzipka | | F | | 628 |
| LIS | Rivka'le | | F | | 628 |
| LIS | Chaim | | M | | 628 |
| LIS | Surete [Sara] | MERKER | F | | 628 |
| LIS | Shlomo | | M | | 628 |
| LIS | Josef | | M | | 628 |
| LIS | Beilke | | F | | 628 |
| LIS | Yehoshua | | M | | 628 |
| LIS | Brantcha | | F | | 628 |
| LIS | Yechezkel | | M | | 628 |

| | | | | | |
|---|---|---|---|---|---|
| LEBGOT | Mendel | | M | | 628 |
| LEWINSON | Avraham | | M | | 628 |
| LEWINSON | Ettel | | F | | 628 |
| LEWINSON | Josef Baruch | | M | | 628 |
| LEWINSON | Sabina | TYK | F | | 628 |
| LEWINSON | Meir | | M | | 628 |
| LEWINSON | Rafael | | M | Ritual slaughterer | 628 |
| LEWINSON | Lyba | | F | | 628 |
| LEWINSON | Arie | | M | | 628 |
| LEWINSON | Chava | HILER | F | | 628 |
| LEWINSON | Shalom | | M | | 628 |
| LEWINSON | Yitzhak Mordechai | | M | | 628 |
| LEWINSON | Jocheved | | F | | 628 |
| LEWINER | Yakov | | M | | 628 |
| LEWINER | Sheindel | | F | | 628 |
| LEWINER | Vitell | | F | | 628 |
| LEWINER | Sara | | F | | 628 |
| LEWINER | Hinda | | F | | 628 |
| LEWINER | Gedalja | | M | | 628 |
| LEWINER | Fride | | F | | 628 |
| LEWINER | Moshe | | M | | 628 |
| LEWINER | Pesach | | M | | 628 |
| LEWINER | Chava | | F | | 628 |
| LEWINER | Feiga | | F | | 628 |
| LEWINER | Leibel | | M | | 628 |
| LEWINER | Dvora | | F | | 628 |
| מ Mem | | | | | http://www.jewishgen.org/Yizkor/serock/ser617.html - Index |
| MAJ | Itche Meir | | M | | 628 |
| MAJ | Lea | | F | | 628 |
| MAJ | Dina | CIECHANOWITZKI | F | | 628 |
| MAJ | Yehudit | | F | | 628 |
| MAJ | Malka | | F | | 628 |
| MAJ | Moshe | | F | | 628 |
| MAJ | Sima | | F | | 628 |
| MAK | Herschel | | M | | 628 |
| MAK | Yehoshua | | M | | 628 |

| | | | | | |
|---|---|---|---|---|---|
| MAK | Chaia Sara | | F | | 628 |
| MAK | Antchel | | M | | 628 |
| MAK | Reizl | HASSMAN | F | | 628 |
| MALEWANCZYK | Rivka | | F | | 628 |
| MALEWANCZYK | Tova | | F | | 628 |
| MALEWIAK | Israel | | M | | 628 |
| MALEWIAK | Malia | INVENTAUSCH | F | | 628 |
| MALEWIAK | Josef | | M | | 628 |
| MALEWIAK | Shimon | | M | | 628 |
| MARGOLIS | Moshe | | M | | 628 |
| MARGOLIS | Sara | | F | | 628 |
| MARGOLIS | Josef | | M | | 628 |
| MARGOLIS | Chana | | F | | 628 |
| MARGOLIS | Shmuelik | | M | | 628 |
| MARGOLIS | Melech | | M | | 628 |
| MORGENSTERN | Yitzhak | | M | Rabbi of the city | 628 |
| MORGENSTERN | Avraham | | M | | 628 |
| MORGENSTERN | Henna Riwa | | F | | 628 |
| MORGENSTERN | Eliezer | | M | | 628 |
| MARKUS | Simcha | | M | | 628 |
| MARKUS | Chaia Beile | | F | | 629 |
| MARKUS | Shlomo | | M | | 629 |
| MARKUS | Bluma | ROSENBERG | F | | 629 |
| MARKUS | Chana'le | | F | | 629 |
| MARKUS | Herschel | | M | | 629 |
| MARKOWICZ | Mendel | | M | | 629 |
| MARKOWICZ | Mordechai | | M | | 629 |
| MARKOWICZ | Tema | | F | | 629 |
| MARKOWICZ | Roza | | F | | 629 |
| MARKOWICZ | Tova | | F | | 629 |
| MARKOWICZ | Sara | | F | | 629 |
| MARKOWICZ | Breindel | | F | | 629 |
| MARKOWICZ | Chava | | F | | 629 |
| MUSZKATENBLIT | Simcha | | M | | 629 |
| MUSZKATEN | Meir | | M | | 629 |

| | | | | | |
|---|---|---|---|---|---|
| BLIT | | | | | |
| MIODOWNIK | Yehoshua | | M | | 629 |
| MIODOWNIK | Pesja | | F | | 629 |
| MIODOWNIK | Gitla | | F | | 629 |
| MIARA | Yeshayahu | | M | | 629 |
| MIARA | Chana | | F | | 629 |
| MIARA | Rivka | | F | | 629 |
| MIARA | Fiszel | | M | | 629 |
| MIDE | Zalel | | M | | 629 |
| MIDE | Fruma Rojza | | F | | 629 |
| MIDE | Yechezkel | | M | | 629 |
| MIDE | Nachman | | M | | 629 |
| MIDE | Moshe | | M | | 629 |
| MIDE | Yakov | | M | | 629 |
| MAJMON | Reuven | | M | | 629 |
| MAJMON | Yitzhak | | M | | 629 |
| MAJMON | Yakov | | M | | 629 |
| MINTZ | Chaim | | M | | 629 |
| MINTZ | Reizl | ZACHAREK | F | | 629 |
| MINTZ | Rachel | | F | | 629 |
| MILLSTEIN | Yakov David | | M | | 629 |
| MILLSTEIN | Sara | | F | | 629 |
| MILLSTEIN | Shmuel | | M | | 629 |
| MILLSTEIN | Rachel | | F | | 629 |
| MEHLMAN | Beile Rivka | | F | | 629 |
| MIELNIK | Yeshayahu | | M | | 629 |
| MIELNIK | Hynka | | F | | 629 |
| MIELNIK | Hinda | | F | | 629 |
| MIELNIK | Sheindel | RUBINSTEIN | F | | 629 |
| MIELNIK | Bina | | F | | 629 |
| MIELNIK | Chava | FISCHMAN | F | | 629 |
| MIELNIK | Chaim | | M | | 629 |
| MIELNIK | Mendel | | M | | 629 |
| MIELNIK | Doba | | F | | 629 |
| MIELNIK | Baruch Josef | | M | | 629 |
| MIELNIK | Tova | | F | | 629 |
| MIELNIK | Chaim | | M | | 629 |
| MIELNIK | Chava | ZUCKERMAN | F | | 629 |
| MIELNIK | Sara | | F | | 629 |
| MIELNIK | Feiga | | F | | 629 |
| MIELNIK | Sima | | F | | 629 |
| MIELNIK | Chava | | F | | 629 |

| | | | | | |
|---|---|---|---|---|---|
| MIELNIK | Rivka | | F | | 629 |
| MIELNIK | Rachel | | F | | 629 |
| MIELNIK | Matel | | M | | 629 |
| MIELNIK | Gerszon | | M | | 629 |
| MENDZELEWSKI | Matel | | M | | 629 |
| MENDZELEWSKI | Gitla | | F | | 629 |
| MENDZELEWSKI | Feiga | | F | | 629 |
| MENDZELEWSKI | Herschel | | M | | 629 |
| MENDZELEWSKI | Chaia | | F | | 629 |
| MENDZELEWSKI | Rivka | | F | | 629 |
| MENDZELEWSKI | Bunim | | M | | 630 |
| MENDZELEWSKI | Ester Miriam | | F | | 630 |
| MENDZELEWSKI | Yehuda | | M | | 630 |
| MENDZELEWSKI | Yehuda | | M | | 630 |
| MENDZELEWSKI | Frajda | | F | | 630 |
| MENDZELEWSKI | Shimon | | M | | 630 |
| MENDZELEWSKI | Sara | | F | | 630 |
| MENDZELEWSKI | Yitzhak | | M | | 630 |
| MENDZELEWSKI | Herschel | | M | | 630 |
| MENDZELEWSKI | Tziwja | ZACHAREK | F | | 630 |
| MENDZELEWSKI | Frajda | | F | | 630 |
| MENDZELEWSKI | Yechezkel | | M | | 630 |
| MENDZELEWSKI | Miriam | | F | | 630 |
| MENDZELEWSKI | Yeshayahu | | M | | 630 |
| MENDZELEWSKI | Meir | | M | | 630 |
| MENDZELEWSKI | Dvora | | F | | 630 |
| MENDZELEWSKI | Shimon | | M | | 630 |
| MENDZELEWSKI | Sara | | F | | 630 |
| MERLA | Yakov Yehoshua | | M | | 630 |
| MERLA | Chaia Basha | | F | | 630 |
| נ Nun | | | | | http://www.jewishgen.org/Yizkor/serock/ser617.html - Index |
| NOWOGRODSKI | Menachem | | M | | 630 |
| NOWOGRODSKI | Chaia | | F | | 630 |
| NOWOGRODS | Rivka | | F | | 630 |

| | | | | | |
|---|---|---|---|---|---|
| KI | | | | | |
| NOWOGRODSKI | Golda | | F | | 630 |
| NOWOGRODSKI | Gitla | | F | | 630 |
| NEUMAN | Hersch Ber | | M | | 630 |
| NEUMAN | Feiga Gitla | | F | | 630 |
| NEUMAN | Yakov Arie | | M | | 630 |
| NEUMAN | Keile | | F | | 630 |
| NEUMAN | Chetzkel | | M | | 630 |
| NEUMAN | Zalman Yehuda | | M | | 630 |
| NEUMAN | Rivka | | F | | 630 |
| NEUMAN | Yakov | | M | | 630 |
| NEUMAN | Sara | | F | | 630 |
| NEUMAN | David | | M | | 630 |
| NEUMAN | Chaia Sara | | F | | 630 |
| NEUMAN | Mendel | | M | | 630 |
| NEUMAN | Yeshayahu | | M | | 630 |
| NEUMARK | Shlomo Meir | | M | | 630 |
| NEUMARK | Avraham | | M | | 630 |
| ס Samech | | | | | http://www.jewishgen.org/Yizkor/serock/ser617.html - Index |
| SOLOMON | Zalman | DZIEMAK | M | | 630 |
| SOLARZS | Yitzhak Meir | | M | | 630 |
| SOLARZS | Rachel Lea | | F | | 630 |
| SOLARZS | Golda | | F | | 630 |
| SOLARZS | Ester | | F | | 630 |
| SOLARZS | Yosef Shmaye's | | M | | 630 |
| SOLARZS | Naomi | | F | | 630 |
| SOLARZS | David | | M | | 630 |
| SOLARZS | Sara | | F | | 630 |
| SOLARZS | Sima | | F | | 630 |
| SOLARZS | Golda | | F | | 630 |
| SOLARZS | Berish | | M | | 630 |
| SOLARZS | Rachel | | F | | 630 |
| SOLARZS | Yehuda | | M | | 630 |
| SOLARZS | Zlata | ZLATOGORSKI | F | | 630 |
| SOLARZS | Meir Eliahu | | M | | 630 |

| | | | | | |
|---|---|---|---|---|---|
| SOLARZS | Tova | FRENKEL | F | | 630 |
| SANDLER | Efraim | | M | | 630 |
| SANDLER | Batia | | F | | 630 |
| SANDLER | Sara Rivka | | F | | 630 |
| SANDLER | Yakov | | M | | 630 |
| SAKAL | Israel Yakov | | M | | 630 |
| SAKAL | Sheindel | | F | | 630 |
| SAKAL | Beile | | F | | 630 |
| SAKAL | Nechemia | | M | | 630 |
| SAKAL | Fenja | | F | | 630 |
| SAKAL | Maltche | BLINDT | F | | 631 |
| SOSCHNIAK | Moshe Chaim | | M | | 631 |
| SOSCHNIAK | Rivka | | F | | 631 |
| SOSCHNIAK | Malka | | F | | 631 |
| SOSCHNIAK | Sara | | F | | 631 |
| SOSCHNIAK | Sheina Rojza | | F | | 631 |
| STERDIENER | Shmuel Eliahu | | M | | 631 |
| STERDIENER | Ester | | F | | 631 |
| STERDIENER | Yeshayahu | | M | | 631 |
| STERDIENER | Hinda | | F | | 631 |
| STERDIENER | Fishel | | M | | 631 |
| STERDIENER | Ester Lea | GRUNBAUM | F | | 631 |
| STERDIENER | Avraham | | M | | 631 |
| STERDIENER | Yechezkel | | M | | 631 |
| STERDIENER | Chaia'tche | | F | | 631 |
| STERDIENER | Moshe | | M | | 631 |
| STERDIENER | Vitell | | F | | 631 |
| STERDIENER | Chana | | F | | 631 |
| STERDIENER | Chaim | | M | | 631 |
| STERDIENER | Motl | | M | | 631 |
| STERDIENER | Litman | | M | | 631 |
| STERDIENER | Chana | | F | | 631 |
| STERDIENER | Byna | | F | | 631 |
| STERDIENER | Meshukam | | M | | 631 |
| SEMPF | Chaim Jona | | M | | 631 |
| SEMPF | Sheina Ribl | | F | | 631 |
| SEMPF | Yitzhak | | M | | 631 |
| SEMPF | Dina | | F | | 631 |
| SEMPF | Lea | | F | | 631 |
| SEMPF | Sara | | F | | 631 |
| SEMPF | Chana | | F | | 631 |
| SEMPF | Shimon | | M | | 631 |

| | | | | | |
|---|---|---|---|---|---|
| SEMPF | Vitell | | F | | 631 |
| SKORNIK | Shmuel | | M | | 631 |
| SKORNIK | Bluma | STERDYNER | F | | 631 |
| SKORNIK | Hinda Rivka | | F | | 631 |
| SKORNIK | Avraham Yeshayahu | | M | | 631 |
| SREBERNIK | Fenja | | F | | 631 |
| SREBERNIK | Tova | | F | | 631 |
| SREBERNIK | Chaia | | F | | 631 |
| SREBERNIK | Gedalja | | M | | 631 |
| SREBERNIK | Hersch David | | M | | 631 |
| SREBERO | Moshe Hersch | | M | | 631 |
| SREBERO | Beile | | F | | 631 |
| SREBERO | Zlata Perel | | F | | 631 |
| SREBERO | Lea | | F | | 631 |
| SREBERO | Shlomo Pesach | | M | | 631 |
| SREBERO | Tova | | F | | 631 |
| SREBERO | Tzipa | | F | | 631 |
| ע Ayin | | | | | http://www.jewishgen.org/Yizkor/serock/ser617.html - Index |
| ESTEROWICZ | Chaim | | M | | 631 |
| ESTEROWICZ | Rivka Lea | | F | | 631 |
| ESTEROWICZ | Fenja | | F | | 631 |
| פ Peh | | | | | http://www.jewishgen.org/Yizkor/serock/ser617.html - Index |
| FOGELMAN | Moshe | | M | | 631 |
| FOGELMAN | Chaia | | F | | 631 |
| FOGELMAN | Tuvia | | M | | 631 |
| FOGELMAN | Sender | | M | | 631 |
| PASSMAN | Leibl | | M | | 631 |
| PASSMAN | Gitla | | F | | 631 |
| PASSMAN | Simcha | | M | | 631 |
| POMOTCHNY | Herschel | | M | | 631 |
| PASKOWICZ | Henoch | | M | | 631 |
| PASKOWICZ | Reintche | | F | | 631 |
| PASKOWICZ | Miriam | KALINA | F | | 631 |
| PASKOWICZ | Arie | | M | | 631 |
| PASKOWICZ | Aron | | M | | 631 |

| | | | | | |
|---|---|---|---|---|---|
| PASKOWICZ | Pirel | | F | | 631 |
| PASKOWICZ | Chana | FEINBAUM | F | | 631 |
| PASKOWICZ | Yeshayahu Yomtov | | M | | 632 |
| PASKOWICZ | Chana | | F | | 632 |
| PASKOWICZ | Dvora | | F | | 632 |
| POKORSKI | Berel | | M | | 632 |
| POKORSKI | Dvora | | F | | 632 |
| POKORSKI | Shmuel | | M | | 632 |
| FUTERMAN | Chaim | | M | | 632 |
| FUTERMAN | Lea'tche | | F | | 632 |
| FUTERMAN | Chaim | | M | | 632 |
| FUTERMAN | Malia | | F | | 632 |
| FURMANSKI | Avraham | | M | | 632 |
| FEINBAUM | Moshe David | | M | | 632 |
| FEINBAUM | Bracha Malka | | F | | 632 |
| FEINBAUM | Chana | | F | | 632 |
| FINKELSTEIN | Mendel | | M | | 632 |
| FINKELSTEIN | Rivka | ROKITA | F | | 632 |
| FINKELSTEIN | Pesach | | M | | 632 |
| FINKELSTEIN | ItcheBerel | | M | | 632 |
| FINKELSTEIN | Henoch | | M | | 632 |
| FINKELSTEIN | Yossel | | F | | 632 |
| FINKELSTEIN | Bracha | | F | | 632 |
| FINKELSTEIN | Moshe | | M | | 632 |
| FINKELSTEIN | Mendel | | M | | 632 |
| FINKELSTEIN | Herschel | | M | | 632 |
| FINKELSTEIN | Regina | | F | | 632 |
| FINKELSTEIN | Sheina Ester | | F | | 632 |
| FINKELSTEIN | Bunim Leib | | M | | 632 |
| FINKELSTEIN | Manja | | F | | 632 |
| PINKERT | Tauba | | F | | 632 |
| PINKERT | Itche | | M | | 632 |
| PIENITZA | Shmuel | | M | | 632 |
| PIENITZA | Ester | | F | | 632 |
| PIENITZA | Pesach | | M | | 632 |
| PIENITZA | Shalom | | M | | 632 |
| PIENIK | David | | M | | 632 |
| PIENIK | Hinda | | F | | 632 |
| PIENIK | Chantche | | F | | 632 |
| PIENIK | Bracha | | F | | 632 |
| PIENIK | Melech | | M | | 632 |

| | | | | | |
|---|---|---|---|---|---|
| PIENIK | Lea | | F | | 632 |
| PIENIK | Moshe | | M | | 632 |
| PIENIK | David | | M | | 632 |
| PIENIK | Hinda | | F | | 632 |
| PIENIK | Melech | | M | | 632 |
| PIENIK | Miriam Reizl | | F | | 632 |
| PIENIK | Eidel | | F | | 632 |
| PIENIK | Reintche | | F | | 632 |
| PIENIK | Ester | | F | | 632 |
| PIENIK | Zlata | | F | | 632 |
| PIENIK | Naomi | | F | | 632 |
| PIENIK | Sara | | F | | 632 |
| PIENIK | Moshe | | M | | 632 |
| PIEKARZ | Yakov | | M | | 632 |
| PIEKARZ | Chana | | F | | 632 |
| PIEKARZ | Yeshayahu | | M | | 632 |
| PIEKARZ | Itka | | F | | 632 |
| PIEKARZ | Aizik | | M | | 632 |
| PIEKARZ | Sara Ita | | F | | 632 |
| PIEKARZ | Lea | | F | | 632 |
| PIEKARZ | Matel | | F | | 632 |
| PIEKARZ | Herschel | | M | | 632 |
| FISCHBEIN | Bezalel | | M | | 632 |
| FISCHBEIN | Rachel | | F | | 632 |
| FISCHBEIN | Sara | | F | | 632 |
| FISCHBEIN | Rivka | | F | | 632 |
| FISCHBEIN | Moshe | | M | | 632 |
| FISCHBEIN | Chana | | F | | 633 |
| FISCHBEIN | Israel | | M | | 633 |
| FISCHBEIN | Chantche | CIECHANOW ITZKI | F | | 633 |
| FISCHBEIN | Yehoshua | | M | | 633 |
| FISCHMAN | Moshe | | M | | 633 |
| FISCHMAN | Bracha | | F | | 633 |
| FISCHMAN | Feiga | | F | | 633 |
| FISCHMAN | Chaia | | F | | 633 |
| FISCHMAN | Josef | | M | | 633 |
| FISCHMAN | Chava | MIELNIK | F | | 633 |
| FISCHMAN | Feivel | | M | | 633 |
| FISCHMAN | Sheindel | | F | | 633 |
| PLUDA | Wolf Leib | | M | | 633 |
| PLUDA | Rachel Lea | | F | | 633 |

| | | | | | |
|---|---|---|---|---|---|
| PLUDA | Ester | | M | | 633 |
| PLUDA | Avraham | | M | | 633 |
| PLUDA | Sheina | | F | | 633 |
| PLUDA | Ejdel | | F | | 633 |
| PANIEWSKI | Avraham Yitzhak | | M | Known as "the old man" | 633 |
| PANIEWSKI | Yitzhak Aron | | M | | 633 |
| PANIEWSKI | Golda | | F | | 633 |
| PANIEWSKI | Masha | | F | | 633 |
| PANIEWSKI | Ester | | F | | 633 |
| PANIEWSKI | Shlomo Pesach | | M | | 633 |
| PANIEWSKI | Reuven Moshe | | M | | 633 |
| PANIEWSKI | Shlomo | | M | | 633 |
| PANIEWSKI | Beile | | F | | 633 |
| PANIEWSKI | Doba | | F | | 633 |
| PANIEWSKI | Ester | | F | | 633 |
| PANIEWSKI | Yeshayahu | | M | | 633 |
| PANIEWSKI | Hinda Rivka | | F | | 633 |
| PANIEWSKI | Ester | | F | | 633 |
| PANIEWSKI | Zalman | | M | | 633 |
| PANIEWSKI | Zissel | | F | | 633 |
| PANIEWSKI | Masha | | F | | 633 |
| PANIEWSKI | Chaia | | F | | 633 |
| PANIEWSKI | Sara | | F | | 633 |
| PANIEWSKI | Mendel | | M | | 633 |
| PANIEWSKI | Necha | | F | | 633 |
| PANIEWSKI | Masha | | F | | 633 |
| PANIEWSKI | Eliahu | | M | | 633 |
| PANIEWSKI | Herschel | | M | | 633 |
| PANIEWSKI | Herschel | | M | | 633 |
| PANIEWSKI | Chana | | F | | 633 |
| PANIEWSKI | Nechama | | F | | 633 |
| PANIEWSKI | Zelig | | M | | 633 |
| PANIEWSKI | Jenta Gitla | | F | | 633 |
| PANIEWSKI | Ester | | F | | 633 |
| PANIEWSKI | Yehudit | KRAWIETSKI | F | | 633 |
| PFEFER | Leibl | | M | | 633 |
| PFEFER | Chana | PEREL | F | | 633 |
| PFEFERBLUM | Yitzhak | | M | | 633 |
| PFEFERBLUM | Miriam | | F | | 633 |
| PFEFERBLUM | Avraham | | M | | 633 |
| PFEFERBLUM | Moshe | | M | | 633 |

| | | | | | |
|---|---|---|---|---|---|
| PEREL | Nachman | | M | | 633 |
| PEREL | Ester | | F | | 633 |
| PEREL | Sara | | M | | 633 |
| PEREL | Zlata | | F | | 633 |
| PEREL | Yakov | | M | | 633 |
| PEREL | Israel | | M | | 633 |
| PEREL | Aron | | M | | 633 |
| PEREL | Herschel | | M | | 633 |
| PEREL | Miriam | | F | | 633 |
| PEREL | Nechama | | F | | 633 |
| PEREL | Nachman | | M | | 633 |
| FRIEDMAN | Tuvia | | M | | 634 |
| FRIEDMAN | Feigale | | F | | 634 |
| FRIEDMAN | Roize | | F | | 634 |
| FRIEDMAN | Yechezkel | | M | | 634 |
| FRIEDMAN | Rivka | BIALOPOLSKI | F | | 634 |
| FRIEDMAN | Golda | | F | | 634 |
| FRIEDMAN | Sara | | F | | 634 |
| FRIEDMAN | Tova | | F | | 634 |
| FRIEDMAN | Berish | | M | | 634 |
| FRIEDMAN | Chaia | | F | | 634 |
| FRIEDMAN | Shechna | | F | | 634 |
| FRIEDMAN | Tzvia | | F | | 634 |
| FRIEDMAN | Hinda | | F | | 634 |
| FRIEDMAN | Zlata | | F | | 634 |
| FRIEDMAN | Simcha | | M | | 634 |
| FRIEDMAN | Berisz | | M | | 634 |
| FRIEDMAN | Rafael | | M | | 634 |
| FRIEDMAN | Mordechaj | | M | | 634 |
| FRIEDMAN | Moshe | | M | | 634 |
| FRIEDMAN | David | | M | | 634 |
| FRIEDMAN | Chana | | F | | 634 |
| FRIEDMAN | Simcha | | M | | 634 |
| FRIEDMAN | Rachel | | F | | 634 |
| FRIEDMAN | Rivka | | F | | 634 |
| FRIEDMAN | Abba Leib | | M | | 634 |
| FRIEDMAN | Chaia | | F | | 634 |
| FRIEDMAN | Rafael | | M | | 634 |
| FRIEDMAN | Rojza | | F | | 634 |
| FRIEDMAN | Dina | | F | | 634 |
| FRIEDMAN | Masha | | F | | 634 |

| | | | | | |
|---|---|---|---|---|---|
| FRIEDMAN | Eliahu | | M | | 634 |
| FRIEDMAN | Hendtche | | F | | 634 |
| FRIEDMAN | Tzvia | | F | | 634 |
| FRENKIEL | Menachem Mendel | | M | | 634 |
| FRENKIEL | Avraham Josef | | M | | 634 |
| FRENKIEL | Shmuel | | M | | 634 |
| FRENKIEL | Henna | | F | | 634 |
| FRENKIEL | Pinchas | | M | | 634 |
| FRENKIEL | Tova | | F | | 634 |
| FRENKIEL | Gitla | | F | | 634 |
| PSHIKARSKI | Meir | | M | | 634 |
| PSHIKARSKI | Pesza | | F | | 634 |
| PSHIKARSKI | Moshe | | M | | 634 |
| PSHIKARSKI | Neszka | JAGODA | F | | 634 |
| PSHIKARSKI | Ester Malka | | F | | 634 |
| PSHIKARSKI | Avraham'ale | | M | | 634 |
| PSHIKARSKI | Tzalel | | M | | 634 |
| PSHIKARSKI | Lea | BRODSKI | F | | 634 |
| PSHIKARSKI | Josef | | M | | 634 |
| PSHIKARSKI | Lebish | | M | | 634 |
| PSHIKARSKI | Zundel | | M | | 634 |
| PSHIKARSKI | Rachel | | F | | 634 |
| PSHIKARSKI | Sara | ZUCKER | F | | 634 |
| PSHIKARSKI | Itsza'le | | M | | 634 |
| PSHIKARSKI | Beile | | F | | 634 |
| PSHIKARSKI | Matityahu | | M | | 634 |
| PSHIKARSKI | Sara'tche | | F | | 634 |
| PSHIKARSKI | Baruch | | M | | 634 |
| PSHIKARSKI | Jocheved | WINOGRAD | F | | 634 |
| PSHIKARSKI | Chaia | | F | | 634 |
| PSHIKARSKI | Tova | | F | | 634 |
| PSHIKARSKI | Yakov | | M | | 634 |
| PSHEVOZJNIK | Yeshayahu | | M | | 634 |
| PSHEVOZJNIK | Gitla | | F | | 634 |
| **Tzadik** | | | | | http://www.jewishgen.org/Yizkor/serock/ser617.html - Index |
| ZWEIGAFT | Yitzhak | | M | | 634 |
| ZWEIGAFT | Necha | | F | | 634 |
| ZWEIGAFT | Alter | | M | | 635 |

| | | | | | |
|---|---|---|---|---|---|
| ZWEIGAFT | Ben-Zion | | M | | 635 |
| ZWEIGAFT | Chana | | F | | 635 |
| ZUCKER | Yitzhak Meir | | M | Ritual circumciser | 635 |
| ZUCKER | Beile | | F | | 635 |
| ZUCKER | Herschel | | M | | 635 |
| ZUCKER | Rivka | | F | | 635 |
| ZUCKER | Breindel | | F | | 635 |
| ZUCKER | Jocheved | | F | | 635 |
| ZUCKER | Yehuda | | M | | 635 |
| ZUCKER | Avraham | | M | | 635 |
| ZUCKER | Israel | | M | | 635 |
| ZUCKER | Josef | | M | | 635 |
| ZUCKER | Feiga | ROSENBERG | F | | 635 |
| ZUCKER | Herschel | | M | | 635 |
| ZUCKER | Chana | | F | | 635 |
| ZUCKER | Yehuda | | M | | 635 |
| ZUCKER | Moshe | | M | | 635 |
| ZUCKER | Sara | | F | | 635 |
| ZUCKER | Alter | | M | | 635 |
| ZUCKER | Sara | PSZIKARSKI | F | | 635 |
| ZUCKER | Josef | | M | | 635 |
| ZUCKER | Chantche | PSZIKARSKI | F | | 635 |
| ZUCKER | Zysza | | F | | 635 |
| ZUCKER | Jankel | | M | | 635 |
| ZUCKER | Joel | | M | | 635 |
| ZUCKER | Leibel'e | | F | | 635 |
| ZUCKER | Yitzhak | | M | | 635 |
| ZUCKER | Shlomo | | M | | 635 |
| ZUCKER | Chava | | F | | 635 |
| ZUCKER | Masha | | F | | 635 |
| ZUCKER | Moshe | | M | | 635 |
| ZUCKER | Beile Pessa | | F | | 635 |
| ZUCKER | Yitzhak | | M | | 635 |
| ZUCKER | Matel | | F | | 635 |
| ZUCKER | Israel | | M | | 635 |
| ZUCKER | Mordechai | | M | | 635 |
| ZUCKER | Sara | | F | | 635 |
| ZUCKER | Masha | | F | | 635 |
| ZUCKER | Chava | WINOGRAD | F | | 635 |
| ZUCKER | Moshe | | M | | 635 |
| ZUCKER | Berel | | M | | 635 |

| ZUCKER | Krasza | | F | | 635 |
|---|---|---|---|---|---|
| ZUCKER | Rajtcha | | F | | 635 |
| ZUCKER | Noach | | M | | 635 |
| ZUCKER | Avraham | | M | | 635 |
| ZUCKER | Itka | | F | | 635 |
| ZUCKER | Chana | | F | | 635 |
| ZUCKER | Chaia'tche | | F | | 635 |
| ZUCKER | Feiga | | F | | 635 |
| ZUCKER | Moshe | | M | | 635 |
| ZUCKER | Peretz | | M | | 635 |
| ZUCKER | Chaia | | F | | 635 |
| ZUCKER | Mindel | | F | | 635 |
| ZUCKER | Elka | | F | | 635 |
| ZUCKER | Shabsil [Shabtai] | | M | | 635 |
| ZUCKER | Elka | | F | | 635 |
| ZUCKER | Feiga | | F | | 635 |
| ZUCKER | Mindel | | M | | 635 |
| ZUCKER | Chaia'tche | | F | | 635 |
| ZUCKER | Pinchas | | M | | 635 |
| ZUCKER | Sara | | F | | 635 |
| ZUCKER | Moshe | | M | | 635 |
| ZUCKER | Sara | | F | | 635 |
| ZUCKERMAN | Matel | | F | | 635 |
| ZUCKERMAN | Tzvia | | F | | 635 |
| ZUCKERMAN | Leibel | | M | | 636 |
| ZUCKERMAN | Breina | | F | | 636 |
| ZUCKERMAN | Yehuda | | M | | 636 |
| ZUCKERMAN | Rachel | HOROWICZ | F | | 636 |
| TZIKORIA | Yakov | | M | | 636 |
| TZIKORIA | Dvora | | F | | 636 |
| TZIKORIA | Bejla | | F | | 636 |
| TZIKORIA | Alter | | M | | 636 |
| TZIKORIA | Chaia Sara | | F | | 636 |
| ZENTNER | Moshe | | M | | 636 |
| ZENTNER | Rivka | | F | | 636 |
| ZENTNER | Zlata | | F | | 636 |
| ZENTNER | Chana | | F | | 636 |
| ק Kof | | | | | http://www.jewishgen.org/Yizkor/serock/ser617.html - Index |

| | | | | | |
|---|---|---|---|---|---|
| KAZAK | Feivel | | M | | 636 |
| KAZAK | Hadas Lea | | F | | 636 |
| KAZAK | Chana | | F | | 636 |
| KAZAK | Avraham | | M | | 636 |
| KAZAK | Reizl | | F | | 636 |
| KAZAK | Yitzhak | | M | | 636 |
| KAZAK | Dvora | | F | | 636 |
| KOTSCHELIK? | Leibel | | M | | 636 |
| KOTSCHELIK? | Beile | | F | | 636 |
| KOTSCHELIK? | Necha | | F | | 636 |
| KOTSCHELIK? | Shmuel | | M | | 636 |
| KOTSCHELIK? | Shimon | | M | | 636 |
| KOTSCHELIK | Josef | | M | | 636 |
| KALECKER | Matel | | F | | 636 |
| KALECKER | Sara Rivka | | F | | 636 |
| KALECKER | Doba | | F | | 636 |
| KAVELSKI | Ester | | F | | 636 |
| KAVELSKI | Sara | | F | | 636 |
| KAVELSKI | Naomi | | F | | 636 |
| KAVELSKI | Josef | | M | | 636 |
| KAVELSKI | Moshe | | M | | 636 |
| KAVELSKI | Rivka | | F | | 636 |
| KALINA | Rivka | | F | | 636 |
| KALINA | Yakov | | M | | 636 |
| KALINA | Hertzka | | F | | 636 |
| KALINA | Yeshayahu | | M | | 636 |
| KALINA | Miriam | PASKIEWICZ | F | | 636 |
| KALINA | Chava | | F | | 636 |
| KALINA | Itche | | M | | 636 |
| KALINA | Gutman | | M | | 636 |
| KANAREK | Chaim Akiva | | M | | 636 |
| KANAREK | Ester Rachel | | F | | 636 |
| KANAREK | Avraham | | M | | 636 |
| KANAREK | Shmuel | | M | | 636 |
| KANAREK | Leibel | | M | | 636 |
| KANAREK | Gitla | | F | | 636 |
| KANAREK | Tova | | F | | 636 |
| KANAREK | Shmuel Eliahu | | M | | 636 |
| KANIER | Berel | | M | | 636 |
| KANIER | Roszka | | F | | 636 |
| KANIER | Pesach | | M | | 636 |
| KANIER | Chana | | F | | 636 |

| | | | | | |
|---|---|---|---|---|---|
| KANIER | Shmuel | | M | | 636 |
| KANIER | Rivka | SILBERSTEIN | F | | 636 |
| KANIER | Israel Zelig | | M | | 636 |
| KANIER | Beile | | F | | 636 |
| KANIER | Yechezkijahu | | M | | 636 |
| KANIER | Fruma Reizl | | F | | 636 |
| KONKOL | Yakov | | M | | 636 |
| KONKOL | Leibel | | M | | 636 |
| KONKOL | Zalman | | M | | 636 |
| KONKOL | Chana | | F | | 636 |
| KONKOL | Avraham | | M | | 636 |
| KONKOL | Michael | | M | | 637 |
| KONKOL | Rivka | | F | | 637 |
| KONKOL | Simcha | | M | | 637 |
| KONKOL | Sara | | F | | 637 |
| KONKOL | Chava | | F | | 637 |
| KOPATCH | Roiza | | F | | 637 |
| KARTOFFEL | Yitzhak Meir | | M | | 637 |
| KARTOFFEL | Sara Gitla | | F | | 637 |
| KATZENELLENBOGEN | Aron | | M | Rabbi. Known as "the Magid [preacher] of Serock" | 637 |
| KATZENELLENBOGEN | Sara | | F | | 637 |
| KATZENELLENBOGEN | Feiga Ester | | F | | 637 |
| KATZENELLENBOGEN | Mordechai | | M | | 637 |
| KATZENELLENBOGEN | Efraim Fishel | | M | | 637 |
| KATZENELLENBOGEN | Aron | | M | | 637 |
| KASCHITCHARZJ | Lipa | | M | | 637 |
| KASCHITCHARZJ | Hela | | F | | 637 |
| KWARTOWICZ | Zalman | | M | | 637 |
| KASCHITCHARZJ | Hela | | F | | 637 |
| KUZSNITZKI | Gerszon Meir | | M | | 637 |
| KUZSNITZKI | Liftcha | | F | | 637 |

| | | | | | |
|---|---|---|---|---|---|
| KUZSNITZKI | Shaye David | | M | | 637 |
| KUZSNITZKI | Feigale | | F | | 637 |
| KUZSNITZKI | Yentche | | F | | 637 |
| KUZSNITZKI | Mordechai Hersch | | M | | 637 |
| KUZSNITZKI | Yenta | BEHAGEN | F | | 637 |
| KULIGOWSKI | Yosef Shalom | | M | | 637 |
| KULIGOWSKI | Lyba | | F | | 637 |
| KULIGOWSKI | Abba | | M | | 637 |
| KULIGOWSKI | David | | M | | 637 |
| KULIGOWSKI | Tzalel | | M | | 637 |
| KULIGOWSKI | Chaia'tche | | F | | 637 |
| KULIGOWSKI | Avraham | | M | | 637 |
| KULIGOWSKI | Israel | | M | | 637 |
| KULIGOWSKI | Bunim | | M | | 637 |
| KULIGOWSKI | Josef | | M | | 637 |
| KULIGOWSKI | Kalman | | M | | 637 |
| KAUFMAN | Herschel | | M | | 637 |
| KAUFMAN | Rivka | | F | | 637 |
| KAUFMAN | Mordechai Hersch | | M | | 637 |
| KAUFMAN | Tova | KANEREK | F | | 637 |
| KAUFMAN | Yossel | | F | | 637 |
| KAUFMAN | Chana | GUTKOWSKI | F | | 637 |
| KAUFMAN | Yakov Yehuda | | M | | 637 |
| KAUFMAN | Yitzhak Aron | | M | | 637 |
| KAUFMAN | Israel Shimon | | M | | 637 |
| KAUFMAN | Yehuda | | M | | 637 |
| KAUFMAN | Chava | | F | | 637 |
| KAUFMAN | Sheidel | | F | | 637 |
| KAUFMAN | Menashe | | M | | 637 |
| KAUFMAN | Leizer | | M | | 637 |
| KAUFMAN | Zecharia | | M | | 637 |
| KAUFMAN | Ezra | | M | | 637 |
| KAUFMAN | Gedaliahu | | M | | 637 |
| KAUFMAN | Sheina Dvora | | F | | 637 |
| KAUFMAN | Nute | | M | | 637 |
| KUPERBAUM | Moshe | | M | | 637 |
| KUPERBAUM | Alta | | F | | 637 |
| KUPERBAUM | Rivka | | F | | 637 |
| KUPERBAUM | Ester | | M | | 637 |
| KUPERBAUM | Sara'tche | | F | | 637 |

| | | | | | |
|---|---|---|---|---|---|
| KUPERBAUM | Golda | | F | | 637 |
| KUPERBAUM | Golda | | F | | 637 |
| KUPERBAUM | Josef | | M | | 637 |
| KIRSCHENBAUM | Golda | | F | | 637 |
| KIRSCHENBAUM | Avraham | | M | | 637 |
| KIESELSTEIN | Golda | | F | | 638 |
| KIESELSTEIN | Elimelech | | M | | 638 |
| KIESELSTEIN | Rachel | | F | | 638 |
| KIESELSTEIN | Byna | | F | | 638 |
| KLEINMAN | Avraham Yitzhak | | M | | 638 |
| KLEINMAN | Chaim Tzwi | | M | | 638 |
| KLEINMAN | Regina | | F | | 638 |
| KLEINMAN | David | | M | | 638 |
| KLEINMAN | Yechezkel | | M | | 638 |
| KLEINMAN | Tema'le | | F | | 638 |
| KLEINMAN | Feiga | | F | | 638 |
| KLEINMAN | Israel Yitzhak | | M | | 638 |
| KLEINMAN | Sara | | F | | 638 |
| KLEINMAN | Asher | | M | | 638 |
| KLEINMAN | Rachel | | F | | 638 |
| KLEINMAN | Sheindel | | F | | 638 |
| KLEINMAN | Eliahu | | M | | 638 |
| KLEINMAN | Matel | | F | | 638 |
| KLEINMAN | Sara Rivka | | F | | 638 |
| KLEINMAN | Chaia | | F | | 638 |
| KLEINMAN | Doba | | F | | 638 |
| KLEINMAN | Josef | | M | | 638 |
| KRAWIETZKI? | Simcha | | M | | 638 |
| KRAWIETZKI | Yechezkel | | M | | 638 |
| KRAWIETZKI | Sara | | F | | 638 |
| KRAWIETZKI | Basza | | F | | 638 |
| KRONGOLD | Avraham | | M | | 638 |
| KRONGOLD | Sheindel | | F | | 638 |
| KRONGOLD | Chaia'tcha | | F | | 638 |
| KRONGOLD | Goltcha | MERKER | F | | 638 |
| KRONGOLD | Aron | | M | | 638 |
| KRONGOLD | Dvora | GRANIEWICZ | F | | 638 |
| KRONGOLD | Yakov | | M | | 638 |
| KRONENBERG | Menachem | | M | | 638 |

| | | | | | |
|---|---|---|---|---|---|
| KRONENBERG | Beile Gitla | | F | | 638 |
| KRONENBERG | Avraham | | M | | 638 |
| KRONENBERG | Herschel | | M | | 638 |
| KRONENBERG | Tova | | F | | 638 |
| KRONENBERG | Moshe Josef | | M | | 638 |
| KRONENBERG | Yakov | | M | | 638 |
| KREMKIEWICZ | Meir | | M | | 638 |
| KREMKIEWICZ | Chana | | F | | 638 |
| KREMKIEWICZ | Jocheved | GODES | F | | 638 |
| KREMKIEWICZ | Feiga | | F | | 638 |
| KREMKIEWICZ | Sara | | F | | 638 |
| KRYSTAL | Urie | | F | | 638 |
| KRYSTAL | Jenta | | F | | 638 |
| KRYSTAL | Ajzjk | | M | | 638 |
| KRYSTAL | Yakov | | M | | 638 |
| KRYSTAL | Sheindel | MAS | F | | 638 |
| KRYSTAL | Firka | | F | | 638 |
| KRYSTAL | Benjamin | | M | | 638 |
| KRYSTAL | Carla | | F | | 638 |
| KRYSTAL | Chana'le | | F | | 638 |
| KRYSTAL | Baruch | | M | | 638 |
| KRYSTAL | Itka | | F | | 638 |
| ר **Resh** | | | | | http://www.jewishgen.org/Yizkor/serock/ser617.html - Index |
| RABINOWICZ | Sara | | F | | 638 |
| RABINOWICZ | Eliezer | | M | | 638 |
| RABINOWICZ | Dozenewicz Mendel | | M | | 638 |
| RABINOWICZ | Moshe | | M | | 638 |
| RABINOWICZ | Reizl | | F | | 638 |
| RABINOWICZ | Mendel | | M | | 638 |
| RABINOWICZ | Moshe | | M | | 638 |
| RABINOWICZ | Reizl | | F | | 638 |
| ROSENBERG | David | | M | | 638 |
| ROSENBERG | Tova | | F | | 638 |

| ROSENBERG | Yechiel | | M | | 639 |
|---|---|---|---|---|---|
| ROSENBERG | Chava | EISENBERG | F | | 639 |
| ROSENBERG | Rafael | | M | | 639 |
| ROSENBERG | Chana | | F | | 639 |
| ROSENBERG | Feivel | | M | | 639 |
| ROSENBERG | Ettel | | F | | 639 |
| ROSENBERG | Chana | | F | | 639 |
| ROSENBERG | Herschel | | M | | 639 |
| ROSENBERG | Rivka | HILER | F | | 639 |
| ROSENBERG | Shraga Feivel | | M | | 639 |
| ROSENBERG | Chana | HOFMAN | F | | 639 |
| ROSENBERG | Rivka | | F | | 639 |
| ROSENBERG | Rachel | | F | | 639 |
| ROSENBERG | Chaim | | M | | 639 |
| ROSENBERG | Chava | | F | | 639 |
| ROSENBERG | Moshe | | M | | 639 |
| ROSENBERG | Chana | | F | | 639 |
| ROSENBERG | Goltcha | | F | | 639 |
| ROSENBERG | Sara | | F | | 639 |
| ROSENBERG | Yechiel | | M | | 639 |
| ROSENBERG | Chana | | F | | 639 |
| ROSENBERG | Moshe | | M | | 639 |
| ROSENBERG | Yitzhak | | M | | 639 |
| ROSENBERG | Rachel | | F | | 639 |
| ROSENBERG | Rachel | | F | | 639 |
| ROSENBERG | Avraham | FEINKIND | M | | 639 |
| ROSENBERG | Bluma'le | MARKUS | F | | 639 |
| ROSENBERG | Yakov | | M | | 639 |
| ROSENBERG | Hinda | | F | | 639 |
| ROSENBERG | Estushe | | F | | 639 |
| ROSENBERG | Avraham | | M | | 639 |
| ROSENBERG | Yeshayahu | | M | | 639 |
| ROSENBERG | Keila | | F | | 639 |
| ROSENBERG | Leib | | M | | 639 |
| ROSENBERG | Baruch | | M | | 639 |
| ROSENBERG | Shmuelka | | M | | 639 |
| ROSENBERG | Malka Ester | | F | | 639 |
| ROSENBERG | Yakov | | M | | 639 |
| ROSENBERG | Avraham | | M | | 639 |
| ROSENBERG | Meir | | M | | 639 |
| ROSENBERG | Feivel | | M | | 639 |
| ROSENBERG | Israel | | M | | 639 |

| ROSENBERG | Nachman | | M | | 639 |
|---|---|---|---|---|---|
| ROSENBERG | Moshe | | F | | 639 |
| ROSENBERG | Miriam | | F | | 639 |
| ROSENBERG | Feivel | | M | | 639 |
| ROSENBERG | Yakov | | M | | 639 |
| ROSENBERG | Feiga | KOHEN | F | | 639 |
| ROSENBERG | Rivka'le | | F | | 639 |
| ROSENBERG | Chana'le | KOHEN | F | | 639 |
| ROSENBERG | Aron | | M | | 639 |
| ROSENBERG | Ejdel | | F | | 639 |
| ROSENBERG | Roszka | | F | | 639 |
| ROSENBERG | Moshe | | M | | 639 |
| ROSENBERG | Alter | | M | | 639 |
| ROSENBERG | Itka | | F | | 639 |
| ROSENBERG | Benjamin | | M | | 639 |
| ROSENBERG | Miriam | | F | | 639 |
| ROSENBERG | Neszka | | F | | 639 |
| ROSENBERG | Israel Chaim | | M | | 639 |
| ROSENBERG | David Berel | | M | | 639 |
| ROSENBERG | Miriam | | F | | 639 |
| ROSENBERG | Shabsil [Shabtai] | | M | | 639 |
| ROSENBERG | Shmuel | | M | | 639 |
| ROSENBERG | Itta | | F | | 639 |
| ROSENBERG | Chaiake | | F | | 639 |
| ROSENBERG | Gitla | | F | | 639 |
| ROSENBERG | Rivka | | F | | 639 |
| ROSENBERG | Dvora | | F | | 639 |
| ROSENBERG | Tuvia | | M | | 640 |
| ROSENBERG | Yehudit | TCHAPINSKI | F | | 640 |
| ROSENBERG | Tzalel David | | M | | 640 |
| ROSENBERG | Pesza | | F | | 640 |
| ROSENBERG | Shamai | | M | | 640 |
| ROSENBERG | Yakov | | M | | 640 |
| ROSENBERG | Pessa | | F | | 640 |
| ROSENBERG | Josef | | M | | 640 |
| ROSENBERG | Neszka | | F | | 640 |
| ROSENBERG | Mindel | | F | | 640 |
| ROSENBERG | Chaim | | M | | 640 |
| ROSENBERG | Yakov | | M | | 640 |
| ROSENBERG | Sara | | F | | 640 |
| ROSENBERG | Lajbel | | M | | 640 |

| | | | | | |
|---|---|---|---|---|---|
| ROSENFELD | Berisz | | M | | 640 |
| ROSENFELD | Rochtche | | F | | 640 |
| ROSENFELD | Bluma | WOLMAN | F | | 640 |
| ROSENFELD | Henoch | | M | | 640 |
| ROSENFELD | Itka | | F | | 640 |
| ROSENFELD | Herschel | | M | | 640 |
| ROSENFELD | Beile | | F | | 640 |
| ROTMAN | Josef | | M | | 640 |
| ROTMAN | Henoch | | M | | 640 |
| ROTMAN | Itche | | M | | 640 |
| ROSZYNSKI | Jona | | M | | 640 |
| ROSZYNSKI | Chava | | M | | 640 |
| ROSZYNSKI | Yakov | | F | | 640 |
| ROSZYNSKI | Shimon | | M | | 640 |
| ROSZYNSKI | Shmuel | | M | | 640 |
| ROSZYNSKI | Chaim | | M | | 640 |
| ROSZYNSKI | Reizl | | F | | 640 |
| RUBINSTEIN | David | | M | | 640 |
| RUBINSTEIN | Rivka'le | | F | | 640 |
| RUBINSTEIN | Zlata | | F | | 640 |
| RUBINSTEIN | Benjamin | | M | | 640 |
| RUBINSTEIN | Sheindel | MIELNIK | F | | 640 |
| RUBINSTEIN | Sara | | F | | 640 |
| RUBINSTEIN | Feivel | | M | | 640 |
| RUBINSTEIN | Chana | | F | | 640 |
| RUBINSTEIN | Chava | YANISH | F | | 640 |
| RUBINSTEIN | Yitzhak | | M | | 640 |
| RUBINSTEIN | Yakov | | M | | 640 |
| RUBINSTEIN | Dvora | | F | | 640 |
| RUTA | Zlata | | F | | 640 |
| RUTA | Leibel | | M | | 640 |
| RUTA | Efrajm | | M | | 640 |
| RUTA | Hinda | | F | | 640 |
| ROKITA | Pesach | | M | | 640 |
| ROKITA | Sara | | F | | 640 |
| ROKITA | Chaim | | M | | 640 |
| ROKITA | Roize | | F | | 640 |
| ROKITA | Dvora | | F | | 640 |
| ROKITA | Rivka | FINKELSTEIN | F | | 640 |
| ROKITA | Avraham | | M | | 640 |
| ROKITA | Rivka | | F | | 640 |
| ROKITA | Malka | | F | | 640 |

| ש Shin | | | | | http://www.jewishgen.org/Yizkor/serock/ser617.html - Index |
|---|---|---|---|---|---|
| SCHAFRAN | Herschel | | M | | 640 |
| SCHAFRAN | Sheindel | | F | | 640 |
| SCHAFRAN | Beile | | F | | 640 |
| SCHWARTZ | Yitzhak | | M | | 640 |
| SCHWARTZ | Zlata | | F | | 640 |
| SCHWARTZ | Josef | | M | | 640 |
| SCHWARTZ | Nachman | | M | | 640 |
| SCHWARTZ | Chaia'tche | | F | | 640 |
| SCHWARTZ | Tova | | F | | 640 |
| SCHWARTZ | Tzirel | | F | | 640 |
| SCHWARTZ | Faja | | F | | 641 |
| SCHWARTZ | Herschel | | M | | 641 |
| STADTSINGER | Chaim Baruch | | M | | 641 |
| STADTSINGER | Moshe | | M | | 641 |
| STEINSKI | Gerszon | | M | | 641 |
| STEINSKI | Beile | | F | | 641 |
| STEINSKI | Israel | | M | | 641 |
| STEINSKI | Lara | | F | | 641 |
| STEINSKI | Shepsel | | M | | 641 |
| STEINSKI | Gerszon | | M | | 641 |
| STEINSKI | Jocheved | | F | | 641 |
| STEINSKI | Beile | | F | | 641 |
| STEINSKI | Tema | | F | | 641 |
| STEINSKI | Menashe | | M | | 641 |
| STEINSKI | Zecharia | | M | | 641 |
| STELANG | Eliahu | | M | Ritual slaughterer | 641 |
| STELANG | Rachel | | F | | 641 |
| STELANG | Chava | BARAB | F | | 641 |
| STELANG | Tema | ESTEROWISKI | F | | 641 |
| STELANG | Nechama | | F | | 641 |
| STELANG | Yakov | | M | | 641 |
| STELANG | Tzirel | | F | | 641 |
| STELANG | Rivka | | F | | 641 |
| STELANG | Yitzhak | | M | | 641 |
| SCHNEIDERMAN | Zalman | | M | | 641 |

| | | | | | |
|---|---|---|---|---|---|
| SCHNEIDERMAN | Tobtche | | F | | 641 |
| SCHNEIDERMAN | Ester | | M | | 641 |
| SCHNEIDERMAN | Chaia Sara | | F | | 641 |
| SCHNEIDERMAN | Yitzhak | | M | | 641 |
| SCHNEIDERMAN | Frive | Yanisch | F | | 641 |
| SCHENITZER | Eliezer | | M | | 641 |
| SCHENITZER | Rivka | | F | | 641 |
| SZPILKA | Benjamin | | M | | 641 |
| SZPILKA | Chaia Miriam | | F | | 641 |
| SZPILKA | Avraham | | M | | 641 |
| SZPILKA | Fajtche | | F | | 641 |
| SZPILKA | Mendel | | M | | 641 |
| SZPILKA | Sara | | F | | 641 |
| SZPILKA | Chaia | | F | | 641 |
| SCHAPIRA | Yossel'e | | M | | 641 |
| SCHAPIRA | Rivka'le | | F | | 641 |
| SCHAPIRA | Hadas | | F | | 641 |
| SCHAPIRA | Chaim Isser | | M | | 641 |
| SCHAPIRA | Avraham'ale | | M | | 641 |

Page 642]   blank.

[Page 643}

## In Memory of the Missing

[Page 644]   blank

[Pages 645-723]

# Memorials

# For Eternal Memory

**Mrs. Kuligowski Rivkah z"l**

A lovely type, a kind Jewish mother and a dedicated company-cultural leader. A witty and tasteful member, founder of schools for Jewish children and a range of institutions for social assistance.

In grief:
Former residents of Serock (in Israel)

Our dear Rivkah Wrubel-Kuligowski z"l
Died the 15th of May, 1962 in Argentina

In grief:
Her husband Mendel Kuligowski, son
Asher; daughters Hinde and Sarah;
Sister Chava, Brother-in-law, Sister-in-law
And the entire family.

Page 646

### Shlomo Merla z"l

Born in Serock in 1905
Died in Tel-Aviv (Israel) in 1965

In the prime of his life ...
In the prime of his years, the flame of his life was extinguished. He was one of our first pioneers [*chalutzim*], a hardworking person from his fresh young years until the final moments of his life. He was a co-founder of our organization and treasurer for many years. His home was always open to all those he met and all those in need. He was like a father to all the newly-arrived immigrants after the Holocaust [*churban*] -- he welcomed all with his simple and heartwarming popularity. He grew from his own difficulties and hard work, and when he finally was able to settle himself a little,
he died.

His family, and all his friends and acquaintances remember Shlomo, may his memory be blessed, with a holy tremor.

**May his soul be bound up in the bonds of life**

Page 647

**Shlomo Merla z"l**

Page 648

### Abraham Pshikorski z"l

Born in Serock--- in Year --- 1889
Died in Atlit (Israel)  24.September.1968

A modest, honest person with an open heart and a will to help anyone who needed assistance. All these good things he inherited from his beloved father Reb Meir z"l.

Abraham z"l experienced--together with his family---all the upheavals, troubles and pains from the era of destruction in Poland and in the great, wide Russia; and then succeeded to land and settle in the State of Israel.

His company was very pleasant. His smile warmed others, his hand comforted and gave life to others.

He was a member of the Vaad ha'Irgun for many years, always was ready for every demand and request. He was a working man his entire life, and it was at work that he raised up his pure soul.

With honor, we remember his name.

Page 649

**Abraham Pshikorski z"l**

### Alter Shlomo Wrubel z"l

Born in Serock in the year 1917.

He died at the airport in Rome, Italy --- mid-flight from Argentina to Israel on the eve of Israeli Independence Da --- (Jewish year) 5729 --- April 22, 1969.

Shlomo, of blessed memory, synonymous with Jewish destiny, lived in far-off Argentina at the end of the thirties to build his life and future.
Shlomo suffered all the upheavals and hardships of being a stranger in a foreign land: worked hard, raised a family, and much time, he started to establish himself and become settled.
He was the child of a family of laborers: the very symbol of simplicity, decency and all that is good.
As the years passed, so did wars, destruction and the rise of the State of Israel. The connection with him was renewed. At the threshold of the land of his dreams, his heart ceased beating. We were unable to embrace him, to hold his hand, to show him what he had yearned to see.
By the gates of the land...
His name is recalled by his family, all his friends and acquaintances with respect and reverence.

**May his soul be bound in the bonds of life.**

### Zahava - Golda Linonad (Beilinson) z"l

Born in 1917 - and passed away in Ramat Gan on 15 Elul, 5727, corresponding to October 2nd, 1967.

She was the child of a working class, honest and modest family. I remember the days of her youth, her laughter, her energy, her enthusiasm, her strong-mindedness, her warm-heartedness, and her loyalty.

From her childhood and her involvement in the Zionist youth movements, she dreamed a dream of the land of Israel, and only the certificate decree prevented this opportunity.

During the holocaust, she escaped the enemy, by managing to hide her identity, and live as a Christian in a village with an aristocratic Polish family.

Her life as a Christian was mingled with a period of worry, suspicion of the neighbors, and unexpected visits by German detectives. More than once - so she told me - her patience almost shattered from the overabundance of tension, but her vitality and fierce will to live and to win and see the downfall of her enemy gave her strength, her kept her emotionally and morally balanced.

After the holocaust, at the end of 1945, I met her out of the blue in a Jewish Brigade immigrant camp in Treviso, Italy.

She was like the first dove - she was the first living soul from my town after the destruction. This meeting gave me hope and encouraged me to search for other shards remaining in the vastness of Europe.

She headed south, and after a lot of wandering, she and her family arrived in Israel.

\*  \*  \*

I followed her absorption into the land of Israel. Here too, her energy, enthusiasm and faith proved to be a huge advantage. And when she arrived a little to her resting place and her birthright, it came to her as death robbed us of her. She amazed everyone, the hearts of her family and loved ones, her friends and acquaintances were overcome with mourning and deep sorrow.

\*  \*  \*

Zahava, of blessed memory, was a victim of the holocaust: During the period that she feared for her double life as a Christian, tiny seeds of destruction were sown in her body, which weakened her strength and positivity.

During Zahava's (z"l) life, all the upheavals of the stubborn, wandering, and bitter generation were although it set again far too quickly. One can only be proud of such a noble soul.

**Condolences to her family: To Shalom and Riva, her husband and daughter.**

**Shlomo Meir Kronenberg z"l –**

The story of his life, and an outline of his character

Shlomo Meir z"l, was born on the 9th of Av, 5668 (July 6th, 1908) in the village of Serock, near Warsaw. His father, Rav Menachem, of blessed memory, devoted most of his time for the greater good in his role as he community leader, the first manager of the burial society, the representative of the Jewish community at the town hall, and so on. At the age of fourteen years old, Shlomo Meir z"l was harnessed with the burden of earning a living, whereupon he started working in different factories around Warsaw, and his wage supported his family.

Shortly after he married, World War Two broke out. The village of Serock was one of the first where Hitler's thugs (may his memory be blotted out) came, and along with the rest of the Jews of the village, Meir z"l and his family started wandering, and after many troubles and hardships, they arrived in Bialystock, where many Jewish refugees had ended up. Some time after their arrival, the special police closed the area where the war refugees were living, removed many from their houses, including Meir and his family, put them into closed carriages, and took them into Russia, to the labor camps of the Komi SSR .

[Page 653]

During this difficult period - in the virgin forest of the Komi SSR and in their ramshackle hut in Kazakhstan - guests passing by always found a place to stay under their roof, and a portion of bread to eat.

At the end of the war, Meir and his family managed to leave Russia. After a stay at a refugee camp in Germany, they immigrated to Israel three months after the establishment of the state, where they settled in Afula.

Meir arrived in Israel naked and with nothing. The only possession he had was his burning love for our country. Because of this fierce love of Israel, he refused a tempting offer from a rich relative to settle in America. Meir, of blessed memory, started working at the post office in Afula. As was his way, he worked with dedication, with all his heart and soul. He was elected to the postal employees' committee, and then to the post of chairperson of the committee. He proved his dedication to the role and activity, always fighting admirably for others, less so for his own interests. He was also a member of the city's chessed (lovingkindness) committee, and a member of the Israel labor party (religious sector). He was chosen as the employees' committee representative to the religious committee by the local authority, in which he served as vice chairperson. He was also a member of the Great Synagogue committee, and here he proved himself as an organizer and a guardian of public funds. He initiated a renovation and beautification of the synagogue. He came up with a plan to establish a Yeshiva in Afula, where the Israeli children would be taught the blessings of the Torah and Jewish tradition, and he worked tirelessly to make sure it happened, because Meir z'l was a G-d fearing and commandment keeping Jew.

On Shabbat, 14th Tammuz, 5730, Meir, z"l suddenly passed away in his home in Afula.

At his funeral, in which many from within and outside his town
participated, the eulogies that were offered at his graveside made it clear what sort of a man Meir was.

**May his memory be a blessing!**

**Giso Shlomo Freiman (Afula)**

Page 654

**Kalman Weinkrantz z"l**

With bitter news, we have reached the end of the book - our
chosen and esteemed Kalman of the Weinkrantz family passed away in far-off
Canada.

There was a man, and he is no more…

He did what was right, and walked in innocence. He dreamed and fought since the dawn of his childhood for the rise of a national homeland. He was amongst the first immigrants and builders - and his destiny moved him, after working and creating here for many years - far from the birthplace he loved so much and to which he was connected with every thread of his soul and his being.

Kalman z"l was skilled in two generous and admirable traits: humility and hospitality. His home was always wide open - as in the tales of Abraham, our forefather - to receive guests blown to him by the four winds. Not only was his home open, but also his heart, his mind, and his whole existence - everyone was received with a pleasant countenance, with blessing, with warm-heartedness, and he was always willing to put himself out for other people.

Kalman 's z"l home was used as a contact point, as a place for anyone in need to meet and find relief. He fed the hungry in the manner of the verse, "The will be sated from the abundance of your house, and from the stream of your delights they will drink" (Psalms 36:9). He clothed the naked, and the weary found respite and a restful, tranquil place.

We loved him, we appreciated him, and with an embrace, we called him 'the Serock consul'.

Our condolences go to his family: To his wife and children. A foundation stone has been uprooted from within us.

May his soul be bound in the bonds of life and creation.

In sorrow,

The Organization for the Former Residents of Serock

Page 655

# Necrology

Page 656

---

**To remember our Venerable Father**

Our master and teacher righteous rabbi, Rabbi Aharon Katzenellenbogen, zt"l, [Maggid Serock] who loved Israel and salvation wholeheartedly, that his heart stopped prematurely and did not live to see the sparks of redemption

---

To remember our dear mother

Rebbetzin Sarah HY"D (may her blood be avenged)

Long-suffering and bereaved, who perished in the Holocaust of the Jews in Poland before she knew comfort

To remember our dear brothers
Mordechai, Ephraim, Fishel and Aharon HY"D (may his blood be avenged)

**Remembered forever:**

Rabbi Yaakov Josef Katzenellenbogen
Baruch Katzenellenbogen
Tziporah Arfa Levis Katzenellenbogen

Page 657

**Rabbi Mr. Aharon zt"l Katzenellenbogen**

**Rebbetzin Sarah and brothers Mordechai, Ephraim, Fishel and Aharon Katznellenbogen hy"d**

Page 658

## To remember forever

We honor and remember our dear parents
David and Fridl Warshawski
Our sisters: Leah-Esther Warshawski-Wellerstein
Our brothers-in-law: Aharon Wellerstein and their children Malka-Leah Wellerstein
Who died in the Uprising of the Warsaw Ghetto, Nissan tsh"g= April, 1943
Our grandmother: Yareh Kristal
Our uncles: Aizik Kristal, Yaakov Kristal, Binyamin Kristal, Boruch Kristal
Our aunts: Yenta Kristal, Sheindla Kristal, daughters Pira Kristal, Krola Kristal, Zlatka Kristal

Wife and sister-in-law Esther Warshawski (Shapiro)
Blessed is their memory
Who died in Concentration Camps of Majdanek, Treblinka and Auschwitz---the Period of the Holocaust

In perpetuity:
Yechiel Meir Warshawski---Vardimon
Henoch Warshawski---Vardi and his family
State of Israel, Kfar Vitkin—Ramat'Gan

Page 659

## Warshawski Family David and Fridl HY"D

Right to left (seated): David and Fridl. Standing, daughter Leah

## For eternal memory
Bruchanski Family

Our Mother: Buneh Chava z"l   Our Father: Menchem z"l

Our brothers: Avraham hy"d   Our sister: Leah HY"D

Page 661

Our brother: Shepsl hy"d

Our father: Menahem Bruchanski z"l Died Jablonna Ghetto 1942

Our mother: Binah Chanah z"l died in Serock 1918
(Second wife Esther, HY"D, killed by the Nazis)

Our sister: Leah with her husband Hershel Mendzelewski

And their children: Avraham, Sarah, Rivkah, Zisl and Raizl HY"D

Our brother: Avraham HY"D and our sister Sheindl HY"D

Page 662

## For eternal memory

To everlasting memory for our close relatives, killed in sanctity of Hashem by Hitler's murderers in the second World War

Father: Moshe David Feinbaum
Mother: Bracha Malka Feinbaum
Sister: Chanah Foskowitz (from Chaim Feinbaum)
Brother-in-law: Aharon Foskowitz
Their son: Beryl Foskowitz

Uncle: Hershl Grasman, his wife Shaindl and their 3 daughters: Chanah, Rivka and Leah; Alter Blumberg, his wife Chanah and their children: Mattis and Chavah; Leibl Blumberg with his wife and 2 daughters; Yaakov Baruch Blumberg with his wife and children; Yechiel Feinbaum with his wife and children; Baruch Novodvarski with his wife Sprintze (from the Feinbaum home) with 2 sons; Chaim Hirsh Grosbard with his wife Henne Miry (from the Blumberg home) and children: Jossel, Chaitshe, Liba and Perl.

Cousin: Leibl Blumberg, his wife Rivkah and son Beniek Baruch Blumberg with his wife and children; Israel-Issar Blumberg with his wife and 5 daughters; Rabbi BenZion Blumberg, (Rabbi in Lifne?), with his wife and children.

In sadness:
The surviving brothers Josef, Hershl and Nachman Feinbaum (New York)

Page 663

# For eternal memory

Bracha, Malka Feinbaum, Roza Foskowitz and children

In sadness:
Josef, Nachman and Hershl Feinbaum
New York (America)

## To Remember Forever

Our dear Parents: Yitzhak (Itsche) and Zlata Schwartz

Our brothers: Josef, Nachman and Hershl

Our sisters: Chaitshe, Tovah; Tzirl and Feya

Killed in the Great Destruction--- We will always remember them with a reverent shiver

In sadness:
 The survivors children Chavah Fogelman (Schwartz) and family of Leahtshe Schwartz

## To remember forever

Our dear family

Father-Mother: Moshe and Chaja Fogelman
Brothers: Toviah and Sender

Who were killed by the German-Nazi murderers

Sorrowful survivors:
Son and brothers sons Fogelman
Hershl Fogelman and his families
State of Israel, Holon

# For eternal memory

Our dear parents Hershl and Rodeh Birnbaum, Our
Dear sisters: Feyge, Esther
Our dear brothers: Hersh Meier and Josef

Who were tragically killed in the Great Destruction by Nazi murderers

In sadness:
Their daughter Rivka Prager and family
(Israel)
Their son Idel Birnbaum, and family
(Paris)
Their daughter Tauba Wrubel and family
(Argentina)

Page 667

## For eternal memory

My dear wife Rachel and my dear 2 little sons HY"D
Killed in Auschwitz

                In sadness:
                Father and Husband Idel Birnbaum (Paris)

---

## Eternal memory

Our dear uncle Leibl Kotszolek, the aunt Beila and her son Nachum, Shmuel, Shimon and Josef

Who the German murderers had killed

                In sadness:
                The Family in Israel

## For Eternal Memory

My dear sister, brother-in-law and children Shmuel Skornik, Blimeh Hinde, Rivka and Avraham hy"d of such a tragic killing by the Nazi murderer

                In sadness
                The brother Shlomo Sterdiner
                And family     Ramat-Gan, Israel

---

## For Eternal Memory

My dear brother Fishel, his wife Esther-Leah and child HY"D
My dear brother Moshe, wife and child

Who were killed by the first bomb that fell in the cellar
                of Yaakov Rozenberg z"l

                In sadness
                The brother Shlomo Sterdiner
                And family     Ramat Gan

Page 669

## Enduring memory

My dear parents Yehezkel and Miriam Mendzelewski
My brothers Yehoshua and Meier
My sisters Chaja and Devorah
My cousin Esther

Killed by the Nazi murderers

In sadness:
Aryeh Mendzelewski and his family

Ramat Gan

## To remember forever

Our dear mother Chanya Myrl Grinberg z"l (died in Israel), and grandson Tzvi Musberg, (who fell in the defense of his homeland)

With sorrow:
Their children in Israel, Chava Shalom Musberg
and her brother Pesiah

---

## To remember forever

Our dear uncle Leibl Kotsholek, the Aunt Beila and their sons
Nachum, Shmuel, Shimon and Josef

Whom the German murderers have killed

In sadness

The family in Israel

## To remember forever

Our dear parents Moshe and Feyge Wisniewicz
Our dear sister Malkaleh with her children
Our dear brothers Avramtshe, Shlomo and Idel HY"D
Our dear uncle Shlomo Wisniewicz, aunt Neche and children
Killed by the Nazis during the great destruction

        In sorrow:
Son and sister Khume and husband
Alter Wisniewicz           (Israel)

---

## For eternal Memory

Our dear Sarah Wisniewicz HY"D

In Sorrow:
The family in Israel

Page 672

## To remember for eternity

My loving and dear who were killed in the sanctity of Hashem by Hitler his name should be obliterated:

Father:
Sender Gerwer
Mother: Chanah-Leah Gerwer
Brother: Shmuel, and sister: Feyge

Your holy memory remains forever.  Let these lines serve
all as monument to your Holy Souls

In sadness:
Arkeh Gerwer with the family---
Toledo (America)

---

## To remember for eternity

Our loving and dear ones who were killed in the sanctity of Hashem
By Hitler his name be obliterated:

Our father: Yeshayhu Miara
Our mother: Chana Miara
Our brother: Fishel Miara with his wife and children
And also our loving sisters and brothers

Their holy memory will remain forever.
Let these lines serve as monument to your Holy Souls

In sadness:
Rachel Miara-Gerwer
Chavah Miara-Mitz'nik

Toledo, Ohio (America)

## For eternal memory

Let this be a monument for my unforgettable brother: Moshe Gerwer, his wife and children. He was killed as a hero.

In honor of his memory
Arkeh Gerwer (America)

## For eternal memory

My dear parents Litman and Chanah Sterdiner
My dear sister Bina with her husband Baruch
And their children Gershin and Meshulem HY"D
All died by the Nazi murderers

In sadness:
Son Josef Sterdiner (Israel)

## For eternal memory

Our dear father Eliyahu Aharon Rozental, guide to the Serocker youth, a mentsh with knowledge and good qualities, died in Warsaw from typhus illness on the second day of Shavuos 1938 at the age of 49 years.

Our dear mother Devorah, who is not coming to her grave in Israel. Her last words before she was killed by the Nazi murderers in 1940 were: Children go away and rescue yourselves! She was killed in the Warsaw Ghetto.

To honor her memory:

In sadness:
Their children: Mala, Bina,
Shepsl, Chayke, Rachel and Akiva.

## For eternal memory

Our dear brothers Yudel hy"d (died in the battle of the Warsaw Ghetto), Sister-in-law Feyge Kuligowski and her only son HY"D

In sorrow:

Megdal Kuligowski (Argentina)
Rachel and her husband Simcha Woller (America)
And the entire family

Page 676

## For eternal memory

We mourn the deaths of our dear parents: Berish and Chaja Friedman; for our sister: Tzviyah and Hinde Fridman; for our brother: Shaine Friedman; for our grandfather: Mr. Chaim-Shlomo Eizenberg; the old Shochet of Serock; for our grandmother: Mrs. Feygele, the old (wife of )the Shochet, who were murdered by the big enemies whose names be obliterated--- HY"D

The grieving
In sadness the surviving sons, daughter brothers and sisters:
Rafel Friedman and family, Israel
Chanah Golan (Friedman) and family Ramat-Hashavim, Israel
Megdal Friedman and family, Kfar Hasidim, Israel

Page 677

# Friedman Family

Bubbe Feygel

Reb Chaim Shlomo so"v(?)

Our sisters: Tzviya and Hinde

Our father: Berish

## For Eternal memory

My dear mothers Rachel Leah Kuligowski, (nee Drezner), z"l
Died in Argentina
The 5th of November 1955

In sadness:
Son Kalman Kuligowski (Buenos Aires)

Page 679

## To remember forever

Our dear mother Royze Wrubel

Our dear sister Feyge Wrubel

Who tragically perished in the great destruction

In sadness:
Daughter and sister Chava and the
entire family          (Argentina)

## For eternal memory

My father Dawid Cohen, mother, brothers, sisters and family HY"D

In sadness:
Daughter Sarah --- in Bnei-Brak

## To remember forever

In memory of my dear uncles --- Yitzhak and Chaim Rozenberg hy"d

In sadness:
Maleh Yoskowitz-Rozenberg and family (Israel)

## For eternal memory

I remember with anxiety my dear family
Father and mother: Moshe and Miriam Rozenberg HY"D
And brothers: Feivel, Yaakov
Sisters: Feygeleh and Rivkaleh
Feygeleh's children: Chanah, Aharon Cohen

Who perished by the hands of the Nazi satan

In grief:
Son Elchanan Rozenberg
And his family        (Israel)

## For eternal memory

In sadness and aching I am mindful of our dear parents
Itshe Meir and Leah May, our good and faithful sister Malka, our dear sister Dinatshe with her husband Yitzhak-Meir Czechanowski and their dear children Hillel and Rivka-Rachel

In remorse for the remaining children, sister and brother

Yeshayahu May and family (Brooklyn, America)
Rivkah Mendzelewski (May) and Family          (Holon, Israel)

# For eternal memory

With pain in my heart bewailing our dear parents Motl and Gitl, our dear brothers Hershl and his wife Leah and children Chaya and Rivkah, our dear sister Feyge Mendzelewski

In sadness the survivors:
Sons: Yehuda Mendzelewski and family
Yaakov Mendzelewski and family
Daughter: Chaya Wosk (Mendzelewski) and family

# For eternal memory

I bewail our dear and best
Parents: Hershl and Rachel-Leah Wrubel

Brothers: Chaim Eliezer and Asher with their wives
and children

Who were killed by the murdering Nazis' hand.
I will never forget them.

In sadness:

Mashe Wrubel-Pshikorski (United States)
Yisroel Wrubel (Montevideo)

# For eternal memory

My brother Asher Wrubel and family HY"D

In sadness:
Brother Yisroel (Montevideo)

Page 686

## To remember forever

I strongly lament my dear sisters Mashe and Esther Pniewski HY"D who died in the great Holocaust at the hands of our foes.

In sadness:

Brother Yosef Pniewski and the family
(Israel)

Our dear parents: Avraham Yitzhak and Sarah Kleinman
Our dear brother: Chaim Tzvi with his wife Reginah and their four small children: Dawid, Yehezkel, Temele and Feyge
Our sister: Shayndl
Our uncle: Avraham-Yehezkel Sterdiner, his wife and their children: Josef and Chaim-Hersh

In sadness:

Nicha Zilbersteyn and Gitl (Israel)

## For eternal memory

My dear parents Meir and Peshe Pshikorski
My dear brother Moshe, his wife Neshke and children
My dear brother Betzalel, his wife Leah and the children
My dear sister Sarah, her husband Alter Cuker and children
My dear sister Rachel
My dear brothers Zindl and Josef

Who died by the Nazis.

In sadness:
Feivl Pshikorski and wife Mashe

## Pshikorski Family

## For eternal memory

We bewail our dear family

Father and mother: Yitzhak-Meir and Chaya Gurman

Sisters: Sarah, Leah, Nechama, Shayndl, Tziporah, Esther Feyge Hinde

Who were killed in the Great Destruction by the Nazis their name be obliterated

In sadness:
Brothers: Baruch Gurman and his family (Haifa)
Betzalel Gurman and his family (Ness Ziona)

# For eternal memory

I bewail and remember with a holy shiver

My dear parents: Tzalel and Chayatshe Kuligowski
My dear brothers: Avraham, Yisroel, Bunem, Josef-Kalman

Who were tragically killed in the Great Destruction by the Nazi beast

In sadness:

The only surviving daughter Beila`
New York United States

## For eternal memory

Our dear parents Beiltshe and Berel Itskowitz HY"D
Killed in the Great Destructions by the Nazi Satan

In sadness:
Chaim Itzkowitz (United States)
Rachel and Aharon Czesner (Israel)
Sarah and Geniya Itzkowitz (Paris)

---

## For eternal memory

I bewail the death of our dear father Mr. Menahem-Mendel Markowitz and his family HY"D
Who were so tragically taken from us during
the Great Destruction by the German-Nazi murderers
I bewail their memory!

They in sadness survive
Son and brother: Israel
Markowitz    (Tel-Aviv)
Daughter and sisters: Rachel
And Leah and their families

## For eternal memory

Our sisters: Sarah and Maliye Itzkowitz HY"D.

Our dear grandfather: Reb Rafel-Ber Yeruzalimski z"l

In sadness

Perl and Shlomo Rabinowitz (Haifa)

Page 694

## For eternal memory

I bewail the death of my dear and close

Father-Mother: Aba-Leib and Chaya-Bracha Friedman

Sister: Rivkah-Roize Bernstein (Freidman), her husband and 2 children Etke and Itshe

Sister: Blume (Freidman), her husband and 2 children

Sister: Dinah Friedman

Sister: Mashe Friedman

Brother: Eliyahu Freidman and wife and children

Brother: Rafel Friedman

Hy"d

Who were killed in the Sanctity of Hashem by our great enemies,
The German murderers

In sadness:
The only surviving son and
Brother Hillel Friedman and his family
Petach-Tikvah, Israel

Page 695

## Friedman-Bernstein Family

Page 696

## To remember forever

Our dear parents: Menahem and Baile-Gitl Kronenberg; our dear brothers: Hershl-Tzvi, Moshe Josef and Yaakov Kronenberg, who died in Biala-Podlaski in 1940; our dear sister and brother-in-law Avraham and Rivkah (Lioski)

Who died in the extermination camp of Treblinka in 1944

In perpetual sadness:

Yehuda Kronenberg and his family---`
Afula, Israel

---

## To remember forever

My father: Avraham Tzvi Asman
My mother: Miriam Asman
My sisters: Hinde Belah, Chaniya and her husband, Chaya, her husband and child, Raizl and child, Ita Gitl
My brothers: Yehuda Aryeh (Idel)

Who died from the Nazi oppressors HY"D

In sadness:
The son: Eliezer Asman and his family

Page 697

## Kronenberg Family

## For eternal memory

I bewail the death of our dear unforgettable family

Father-Mother: Gershon and Sarah Steinski
Brothers: Zechariah, Moshe, Gitman and Menashe Steinski
Sister and brother-in-law: Temme and Feivel Wenger
Cousin: Leah Gibber

I will never forget they were united in the sanctity of Hashem
by the German-Nazis murderers

In sadness:

Son and brother Yehuda-Leib Steinski
Hershl Steinski          New York

## To remember forever

I bewail the death of our aunt Rivka Kalina with her two sons Yeshayahu and Gutman with his wife Miriam and their not yet born child, who were killed during the Great Destruction in Stolpz(??), Ukraine

I bewail my cousin Temme Kalina, who made it through the entire destruction and died in Israel

In sadness the remaining cousins
Yeshayahu May, (Brooklyn, America)
Rivkah Mendzelewski,(May), Holon
And their families.

Page 700

## For eternal memory

My father: Leibush Shmerl Winegrad and his wife
My brother Zushe and sister

In sadness:
Dora Rot (Brooklyn)

## For eternal memory

My sister Rivkah and her husband Mechl Hersh Elman

In sadness:

Leibl Rashinski     (America)

## For eternal memory

Dear grandfather Reb Laybl Lewiner HY"D

In sadness:
Golde Lewiner-Maliniak and her family

## For eternal memory

My dear Brother Berl Konier HY"D

In sadness:
Yitzkah Konier (Israel)

## To remember forever

My dear mother Zisl Salzman
My brother Hersh
And my sister Feyge
My aunt Golde Kirshbaum and her son Avraham

Matis Blumberg

Shlomo

Honor their memory:
In sadness:

Chaim Salzman and family
Brother Fogelman and family
And family Komelgorn

## To remember forever

I bewail our father and brother Yoel Cuker, who died while in battle with the German murderers

In sadness:

Son Mendl Cuker and family
(New-York)
Brother Chaim Cuker    (Israel)

## For eternal memory

My dear parents Hersh-Efrayim and Rachshe Boguslowski

My brother Moshe with his wife Rachel-Leah (from Chaim Wrubel) and
Four children: Chavah, Shayndl, Rivkele and Hersh-Yosef

My brother: Yeshayahu, his wife and four children

My sister: Rivkah with her husband Aizik (Joszambeck)

My sister: Tzviah with her husband and child

My sister: Chavah with her husband Yonah (Rashinski) with child

In sadness:

Daughter Liba and Ides Yosef
Goldstein (Paris)

Page 705

### For eternal memory

To remember my dear family. They were killed by the Nazi enemy.

Our parents Golde and Hershl Blindet sister and brother-in-law: Maltshe and Pinchas Kolaker HY"D; Brother: Shmuel Blindet hy"d

In sadness:

Daughter and sister

Regine Meier-Blindet, Ramat-Gan, Israel

## To remember forever

My dear parents Reb Yitzhak-Meir, Talmud Torah Teacher, and Sarah-Ite Kartofel
    Who were cut off by the German—Nazi enemies

In sadness:
Daughter---    In Argentina

---

My dear mother Rochel Stelung HY"D (wife from R' Eliyahu Shochet z"l)

In sadness:

Daughter Chana Broda    (Israel)

## For eternal memory

Sarah and Yehoshue Hoffman HY"D

In sadness:

Brother and sister Itzkowitz
United States and Israel

---

## To remember forever

My father: Avraham Tzvi Asman
My mother: Miriam Asman
My sister: Indeh Beilah
My sister: Inde Baileh, Chaniya and husband, Chaya, husband and child, Raizl and child
My brother: Yehuda Aryeh (Idel)

Killed by the Nazi murderers, hy"d

In sadness:
Son Eliezer Asman and his family
Haifa, Israel

## To remember forever

Esther Pienik HY"D

Raintshe Pienik HY"D

In sadness:
Pinchas Kaluski and family (Israel)

## For eternal memory

| My dear parents, brothers and sisters | My dear parents |
|---|---|
| Moshe Fishman | Yosef and Dvorah Jagoda |
| Bracha Fishman | Sister Sime and brother-in-law |
| Yosef and Feiga Niskah | Moshe Blustein and children |
| Baruch and Chaya Fokin | Sister Bashe, brother-in-law |
| Chava Shayndl Fishman | Elazer Solarz and child |

In sadness:
Yaakov Fishman           Haifa

In sadness:
Aryeh Jagoda   (Kfar-Hasidim)

Page 709

# To remember forever

Our dear parents Shmuel and Sarah Grinbaum

Our sisters Esther and Malka

Who were cut off by the Nazi enemy

In sadness son and daughter:

Nechemiah Grinbaum and family
Avraham Grinbaum and family
Miriam Baum and family
Alter Grinbaum and family

Israel

## For eternal memory

To our dear parents Reb Moshe Peretz and Leah Bernstein, and Gitl our dear sister

HY"D

In sadness:

Malka Rozenberg
Heleh Birnbaum and family
Frume Rabinowitz and family
Daughter and family in the United States

Page 711

## For eternal memory

Brother David, wife and children and sister-in-law Rachel-Leah and child
In sadness:
Brother Mendl Kuligowski
And family   (Argentina)

## To remember forever

My dear uncle

Zelig Beilenson with his family HY"D
In sadness:
Yitzhak Konier        (Israel)

## To remember forever

Our dear parents
Leibl and Dvorah Lewiner HY"D

Who died in the Great Shoah

In sadness:
Daughter: Miriam Lieber and her family
(Bat-Yam)
Daughter: Rivkah Lewiner-Pienik (Holon)
Sons: Yaakov Lewiner and his family
Zev Lewiner and his family

## To remember forever

Our sister and brother-in-law Beile Kleinman HY"D

In sadness:
Malka Grinberg and Fishel Sterdiner (Israel)

Page 713

## To remember forever

I remember with a holy shiver our dear parents Reb Yitzhak
Meir and Rochel Leah Solarz, Golde Soliarz-Lis HY"D
And young daughter Miriam hy"d

Who died by the hand of the Nazi murderers

In sadness:
Sisters: Sarah Gurman
Hinde Rubinstein and their families
State of Israel, Haifa

## For eternal memory

Avraham Cuker hy"d

I bewail with a shiver the memory of my dear family who were killed

Grandfather and grandmother: Yitzhak Meir Mohel and Beila Cuker hy"d
Parents: Yosef and Feyge Cuker HY"D
Aunts: Rivkah, Breindl and Yocheved
Uncles: Hershl, Yisroel and Avraham

                    In sorrow:
                 The only survivors:
            Feivel Cuker and family, Toronto
                           (Canada)

## To remember forever

My dears: Zelig and Blime Wolman HY"D

In sorrow:
Fishel Sterdiner (Israel)

---

To remember forever
I bewail the memory of my close and dear ones

Father-Mother: Gedaliah and Shayne-Dvorah Kaufman
Brother: Noach Kaufman with his wife and 3 little children HY"D
Brother: Nuta Kaufman HY"D

Who were killed by the hand of the Nazi enemies

In sadness:

The only surviving som and brother
Yosef Kaufman and family ---
Ness-Ziona, (Israel)

## To remember forever

In memory of my loving parents

Father and Mother: Feivel and Haddas-Leah Kozak
My brothers and sisters: Avraham, Itzik, Chana, Raizl and Dvorah Kozak

Who were killed by the Nazi murderers

In sadness:
The only surviving daughter
And daughter Tauba Kaufman (Kazak)
And family---- Ness Ziona (Israel)

## For eternal memory

Aryeh Weinstock
And Chaim and Chaya Weinstock and their children: Aryeh and Shayne Tamar z"l

In sorrow:
Family and Organization of Former Residents of Serock

---

### Yitzchok Meyer Apelboim, hy"d (may his blood be avenged)

Yitzchok Meyer Apelboim was one of the old time Gerer *chassidim*, and then afterward became an "enlightened" individual [*maskil*]. Other than studying in the *cheder* [religious school], his children also studied in the government public school, where they taught the Polish language, and they also studied privately.

Yitzchok Meyer Apelboim had a reputation as a scholar of Torah and Talmud studies. For several years he ran a *cheder* with tens of students. He was also a genius in medicine, would heal children with pneumonia for free, and in difficult situations, he would sit for entire nights with sick children and take care of them until they got better. He and his son, the journalist Yisroel Moshe, perished.
May their blood be avenged.

With sadness:
The family and organization of the émigrés of Serock

## To remember forever

I bewail the death of our dear parents Yisroel and Beila Leah Borenstein, our dear sister Rivkah (Cohen) with her husband, and children, whose lives were cut off by the German Nazi murderers

In sadness survivors
Chanah Diamant (Borenstein) and family
Yad-Eliyahu, Israel

Alter Borenstein and family
Petach-Tikvah, Israel

Page 719

### For eternal memory

I do not forget our close relatives

Uncle and aunt Bunem and Esther-Miriam Mendzelewski

Cousins Shimon and Hershl with their families

Cousin Frayde

Aunt Tovah with her husband Dawid Rozenberg with their children and their Families

Aunt Rochel Bresler with her children Tovah, Feige and Moshe Bresler with their families

Uncle Moshe Moak with his wife Sima and children Hershl, Shia, Antshl and daughters Chaya-Sarah

Aunt Rivkele with her husband Yosele Shpira with their children
Chaim-Issar and Hodes

                                              In sorrow their surviving
                                              Sisters-children:

                                              Yidl, Yankl and Chaya Mendzelewski
                                              With their families          (Israel)

## To remember forever

I bewail the death of our dear parents, sisters and brother-in-law

Father: Reb Menahem Ben-Tzion Nowogrodski

Mother: Chaya

Sisters: Gitl, Rivka and Golda

Brother-in-law: Avraham Kandel

Who died in the great Shoah at the hands of the Nazi enemy

Forever we will remember them

In constant sorrow:

Bracha, Yisroel-Yitzhak, Yeshayahu, Shmuel-Yaakov and Aryeh Nowogrodski
And their families---All in the State of Israel

Page 721

### For eternal memory'

Our aunt Golde Kizelstein (daughter of Rafel Ber) and
uncle Meir Noach; cousin Bina (who died in the Warsaw Ghetto).

Cousin Melech with his wife and daughter Rochel---killed in Russia,
Our aunt Tovia Baldiger (daughter of Rafel Ber, living
in Bialystok) with her children Maliye and Antshl--- died
on the way to Russia

Our uncle Dawid Berl Rozental (son of Shepsl Farber);
Aunt Miriam and her children: Itele, Shepsl, Roytshe,
Shmulik, Chaykele and Beltshe

All who died in the Warsaw Ghetto

Our aunt Shayne Rochel (daughet of Shepsl Farber);
Uncle
Yehudah Leib Gutkowski, and their children: Chaya, Frima
And Shepsl--- died in the Lukow Ghetto

In sorrow:

Children of Dvorah and Eliyahu-Aharon
Rozental          (Israel)

### My Mother's Candle Lighting

I remember the candle lighting of my mother Chaya Miriam, when she would light the Shabbath candles. A golden glow would fall across her pale, refined face. Dressed in Shabbath finery, we all sit around the table – and our father recites the *Kiddush* [blessing over the wine, welcoming the Shabbath]. I remember the last Shabbath, when Hitler took away my pious mother.

In sadness:

Irke Zhepko – Sznilko (?),Cleveland
(USA)

Page 722

## For eternal memory

I bewail the killing of my dear parents Binyamin and Chava-Miriam Szpilka HY"D

My brother s and sisters: Avraham, Mendk, Feytshe Hinde and Sorhele

Who were cut off along with all the saints by the
German-Nazi enemy in the Great Destruction in the 2nd World War

In sadness survivors:

Daughter and sister: Irka
Rszepka-Szpilka with her family
Cleveland (America)

To remember forever

My grandmother Soreh Rozenberg
My dear parents Berish and Dinah Blumberg
Brother-in-law Alter Rozenberg, sister and child
Brother Moshe Blumberg
and sister Chanah

In sorrow:
Shlomo Blumberg

Page 723

## To remember forever

Honor their memory:

In sorrow:

Brother Yehuda-Leib Steinski, and
Brother Yehoshua, and Moshe Wenger

{Page 725}

# Calendar of Events

**Translated by Esther Synder**

| | | 1939 | |
|---|---|---|---|
| 1 | September | 17 Elul 5699 | Outbreak of War |
| 5 | " | | Bombing of the city by German artillery and airforce |
| 6 | " | | Continuation of bombing and a direct hit on the large basement in the home of R' Yaakov Rosenberg z"l, that killed 72 Jews |
| 7 | " | | Funerals of those killed |
| 9 | " | | The city taken over by the Germans |
| | | 25 Elul 5699, After the Sabbath - Motzei Shabbat | |
| 10 | " | | Gathering of all the Jews in the market place Imprisonment of all the men - other than small children - in the Great Synagogue |
| | | | Stores are broken into and Jewish property robbed. |
| 13 | " | | Release of males under the age 15 and over 45 |
| | | | Brutality and torture of men remaining in the synagogue |
| 15 | " | | The first expulsion of all the men in the synagogue aged 16 - 45 - almost 500 people. Forced to walk to Poltosk. Many murdered on the way. |
| | | Friday, second day of Rosh Hashana, 5700 | |
| 16 | " | | Continuation of expulsion on foot from Poltosk toward Tzichnov. Murders on the way. |
| 17 | " | | Running all day toward train station in Tzichnov and a full day traveling in closed freight cars to an unknown destination. |
| 18 | " | | Depressed, hungry, wounded and tortured the exiles reached Risenberg, East |
| | " | | Prussia. Housed in abandoned army camp. |
| 19 - 30 | " | | In Risenberg camp. Hard work and brutality. At the end of the month a sudden release : some return somehow to Serock, the majority go to Bialystock, occupied Russian territory. Jewish property stolen and imposition of a collective monetary punishment. |

[Page 726]

| | | | |
|---|---|---|---|
| | October | | Some of those expelled return from the Russian side, some try to sneak across the borders and reach Bialystock. A few families manage to enter Warsaw in secret. |
| | November | Kislev - 5700 | Hunger, children dying, destruction of life, burning of the synagogue and desecration of the cemetery |
| | | | Daring escapes |
| | December | Kislev - 5700 | A second collective monetary punishment. Forced labor. Brutality. |
| 3 | | " | Third collective monetary punishment. Rumors of expulsion. Liquidation of the community and the second and final expulsion of all the Jews to Nashelsk, a distance of 21 km from Serock, arriving in the evening. Murders on route. |
| 5 | | 23 Kislev - 5700 | Imprisonment of the Jews - more than 1000 persons - in the Great Synagogue of the community of Nashelsk. Brutality. Murder nearby. |
| 6 - 7 | | " | "Walk of Blood" to the train station in Nashelsk, a distance of several kilometers, confinement in freight cars of two trains. |
| | | | Confusing travel of the train back and forth. |
| 8 | | Second day of Hanukkah, 5700 | End of train trip. The Jews dispersed among the communities of Biale Podlesek (the majority), Lukov and Lomaz. A few settled in Mazritz, Radzin and Shdaltz. |
| | | **1940 - 5700** | |
| | | | The last of the deported are dispersed in the Jewish communities of Biale Podlesek, Lukov and Lomaz. |
| | | | Hunger, forced labor and persecution |
| | | | Tens of the families secretly leave these communities in order to reach Bialystock, in captured Russian territory. |
| | | | Some men from Serock sent to forced labor in Beltz. |

[Page 727]

| | | | |
|---|---|---|---|
| | | **1941 - 5701** | |
| **In the beginning of the year** | | | Transfer of the elderly and unemployed to Opola, a village near Rusos. |
| | | | Prohibition to leave residences and to use private or public transportation. |
| **At the end of the year** | | | An order to hand over all furs to the Germans. A few Jews found hiding places with Polish families in the villages and began living as Christians. |
| | | | A number of babies were given by their parents to Polish families in order to save their lives. |
| | | **1942 - 5702** | |

|  |  |  | |
|---|---|---|---|
|  | March |  | Prohibition of Jews living in Biale to work in stores or factories dealing with food |
|  |  | After Passover 1942 | Execution of tens of Jews including some from our city |
| 10 - 11 | June |  | The first transfer of Jews from Biale to Moritch, and setting up the ghetto |
| 17 | August | 4 Elul | Execution of all the Jews of Lomaz in the forest near the city |
|  |  |  | The second transfer of Jews from Biale to Moritch |
| 26 | August |  | Heroic death of Zisha Goldberg z"l in the central square of Biale Podlask, due to his resistance to the terrible Nazis |
| 5 | October |  | The first transfer of Jews from Lukov and concentrating them in Moritch. |

### 1943 - 5703

|  |  |  | |
|---|---|---|---|
| 2 | May |  | The last transfer of Jews from Lukov and concentrating them in Moritch. |
| 17 - 18 | July | 14-15 Tammuz | The annihilation of the Jews in Moritch, where in the past year were concentrated all the survivors of the communities: Biale Podlask, Lukov, etc. |
|  |  |  | The survivors of our city were dispersed over the whole area of occupied Poland. |
|  |  |  | Some took part in the Warsaw Ghetto uprising. Some connected with the partisans and tens of others live as Aryans. |

[Page 728]

### 1944 - 5704

| | |
|---|---|
| The first part of the year | Annihilation |
|  | In the forests, camps and various hiding places. We move from one place to another waiting for the waiting for the fall of the enemy |
| End of the year | Defeat of the Nazi enemy on the Eastern front and the beginning of hope |

### 1945 - 5705

| | |
|---|---|
| The first part of the year | Defeat of the Nazi enemy and their full surrender in the month of May. |
|  | The few survivors gather together in the city of Lodz |
| The second half of the year | Beginning of the repatriation from Russia to Poland |
|  | Return of several families from Serock. The beginning of a small group in Warsaw. |
|  | Flow of Jewish refugees toward the refugee camps of the Jewish Brigade in Italy and among them the first remnants from Serock. |

### 1946 - 5706

| | | |
|---|---|---|
| **The first part of the year** | | Large repatriation from Russia |
| | | Groups of Serockites in Warsaw, Lodz, and Lower Silesia |
| **The second half of the year** | | Pogroms against the Jews in Kielcz |
| | | The survivors from Poland flee to refugee camps all over occupied Germany and strive to go to Eretz Yisrael. |
| | | Contact is established with the survivors in Poland and in the camps in Germany, Austria and Italy. |

[Page 729]

| | | |
|---|---|---|
| | **1947-1948 - 5707-5708** | |
| | | Almost all of our survivors left Poland and the refugee camps in Germany and Austria. |
| | | Embark on the ships of the "Ma'apilim" (illegal immigration to Palestine under British Mandate) |
| | | Arrested and put in detention camps in Cyprus |
| | | Some emigrate to the United States, France and Argentina. |
| | | The great majority of our survivors find refuge in the State of Israel. |

**(This list was prepared by Hanoch Vardi)**

[Page 730]

# I am Leaving You, Serock, my Town
### Translated by Ruth Kilner

Thirty five years have passed since I left my town, the domain of my childhood and my youth. On the day I left, on my way to Israel, I was accompanied by my family, and the adolescents that I was near and far from in opinion – everyone.

In my heart, I harbored a fear for their fortunes, and at the last minute, I turned to them and cried my fearful warning, "Come with me! Follow me!"

In my mind's eye, I can still see the town – and I will remember it forever – and all its forms: gloomy from the outside, but full of life and vibrancy from within.

And here it is: my parents, my family, and my friends; the anxious traders and storekeepers; our diligent mothers; the chorus of the *Beit Rabban* babes in the *kheders*, the schools, in the streets and in the houses; the weary and sweaty tradesmen ; the street porters and the village salesmen; the vibrant youngsters tortured with a yearning for perfection and liberation; the politicians who were silent about their status quo and the activists wanting change ; the Jewish imprint of the city's hill and valley with the river Narew, from within the echoing of whose waves Yiddish could be heard; the hidden places in the surrounding meadows and the hills.

A full world, whole worlds.

And my heart is languishing, and my entire being cries out from the ruin, the destruction, the devastation, the doom.

I hear the moan of the tortured, which accompanies me with every step and every stride. From the few who stood and fell at the hands of the accursed German Nazis before the whole world. The leaders of the free world knew of the annihilation of my people, and felt it, but did not help to the full extent of their aid.

Darkness covers the land.

Still and secretly floats the question:

Am I – are we innocent of all sin and transgression?

Did I do – did we do everything here for them there?

Here, life flows as normal, there, time flows silently to the land! ...

Is there to be no atonement for this sin?

The violin of wonders shatters and stops.

[Page 731]

I walk amongst your ruins, my town, I look for life yet there is none.

For you, my town, for the burned and plundered Serock, I weep, and ask about the fate of your remnants.

I part from you in awe and love – goodbye to your dust, a curse on your plunderers, and good hope to your descendants in the homeland and at all ends of the world.

**Yisgadal v'yiskadash (May he be exalted and glorified) ...**


**Your son,
Yechiel Meir Vardimon
Son of Friedel and David Varshevski (may their blood be avenged)**

# INDEX

## A

Abai, 326
Abish, 54
Abramowicz, 18, 19
Ahad Ha'am, 92
Ahare'le The Revolutionary, 26
Ailmakher, 35
Alexander I, 349
Alter, 253
Alter The Fisherman, 91
Anjelewicz, 307
Anman, 229
Anshmill, 31
Apelboim, 1, 4, 41, 119
Apelboym, 11
Appleboim, 351
Areh'le The Revolutionary, 74
Aron, 66
Artman, 229
Arzikhover, 66
Aschenmill, 74, 75, 78, 80
Ashenmil, 115, 118, 385
Ashenmill, 3, 6, 400, 401, 402, 403, 405
Ashi, 326
Ashkenazi, 54, 72
Aunt Miriam, 98
Avremel, 66
Avrohom Leib, 39, 71
Avrohom Leyb, 121
Avrohom Leyb The Teacher, 96
Avrohom The Carpenter, 324
Avrohom Yankel, The Smith, 121

## B

Babek, 2, 5, 28, 34, 36, 44
Babek, 427
Bacz, 312
Bailinson, 392
Bak, 324
Bakunin, 101
Baldiger, 427
Barab, 79, 94, 125, 223
Barab, 427, 428, 466
Barnshtayn (Barnstein), 90
Beck, 111
Behagen, 460
Beker, 65
Belinsohn, 430
Belinson, 295
Belison, 224
Ben Zeev, 411
Ben Ze'ev, 407, 410, 412
Ben Zev, 6
Berenshtayn, 400
Bergelson, 116, 353, 355
Berkenheym, 333
Berl, 68
Berliner, 30, 41
Berman, 430
Bernshtajn, 194
Bernshtayn, 311, 313, 325
Bernstein, 125
Bernstein, 428, 429, 430
Bialik, 92
Bialopolski, 454
Birkenheim, 33
Birm, 397
Birnbaum, 307
Birnboim, 331
Blakhman, 38, 133, 178, 395
Blekher, 222, 257
Blinc, 191
Blindt, 430, 449
Blochman, 429
Blum, 311
Blumberg, 2, 5, 80, 105, 118, 333, 344
Blumberg, 429
Blusztejn, 429
Bobek, 2, 5, 70, 93, 110, 113, 134, 190, 326
Bobek / Babek, 348
Bobek/Babek, 272
Bochenek, 429
Boguslawski, 41
Boguslawski, 428
Borenshtajn, 190
Borenshtayn, 32, 44, 74, 319
Borenshtayn (Shustak), 83
Borenshteyn (Sumtak), 289
Borenstajn, 190
Borenstein, 95
Bornshtayn, 114
Borob, 99
Borow, 105, 116, 117
Borukh Moyshe, 342
Botchan, 442
Botshan, 43
Brandt, 2, 5, 172, 173, 277
Brauda, 2, 5, 362, 364
Braun, 430
Brenner, 92

Bresler, 105, 116, 221
Bresler, 426
Bressler, 430
Brinbaum, 429
Brodski, 455
Brodzki, 430
Broin, 35
Brooks, 397
Brooks (Brukhanaski),, 397
Broyde, 117
Bruchanski, 429
Brukhanski, 1, 2, 4, 5, 102, 105, 115, 116, 338, 342, 343, 345, 347, 357, 358, 385, 397
Brusman, 430
Bsjaza, 429
Buber, 93
Bugoslowski, 114
Bukhenek, 11, 326
Burkhanski, 250
Bzhansi, 293
Bzhezhewski, 253

## C

Calkes, 272
Chaim Shloime The Ritual Slaughterer, 55
Chaimovitz, 166
Chaimowicz, 439
Charmilaz, 95
Cheinower, 439
Chesner, 29
Ciechanowitzki, 440, 444, 452
Cohen, 23
Cybulski, 11
Cymerman, 1, 2, 4, 5, 35, 54, 340, 342
Cymerman/Tzymerman, 339, 340
Czapinitzki, 440
Czesner, 1, 4, 90, 91, 118, 381
Czesner/Tz'esner, 1, 4, 91

## D

Dan, 84
Darwin, 336
Dexler, 285
Didak, 68, 99
Dmokhovski, 21
Dobner, 433
Dodjy, 433
Dombak, 433
Dombrowska, 241
Doner, 115, 118
Donner, 336, 337
Doren, 221

Dorn, 43, 44
Dorn, 433
Doron, 248
Dovid Berl, 98
Dovid From Orczikhowa, 192
Dovid Itzik, 40
Dovid Itziks, 71, 121
Dresner, 337
Drezner, 392, 395, 396, 397
Drezner, 433
Dube'le, 96
Dudowicz, 253
Dunar, 385
Dunner, 28, 393, 394, 395, 396, 397
Dziemak, 448

## E

Eibeshicz, 329
Eichenbaum, 426, 427, 436
Eikhenbaum, 223
Eisen, 182
Eizenberg, 426
Eldan, 412
Eliyahu Shokhet, 61
Eliyahu The Ritual Slaughterer, 221
Eliyahu The Shokhet, 55
Eliyohu Shokhet, 60
Elye Aron, Teacher, 129
Epstein, 164
Erenbaum, 95
Esterowicz, 31, 83, 331
Esterowicz, 450
Esterowiski, 466

## F

Fajnboim, 2, 5, 99, 359, 361
Farber, 343
Faskovitzes (Faskowiczs), 91
Faskowicz, 29, 68, 118
Faynboim, 79
Fefer, 221
Feinbaum, 451
Feinbaum-Paskoricz, 93
Feinboim, 3, 6, 32, 392
Feinboym, 112, 115, 117, 118
Feingold, 317
Feinkind, 463
Feivel, 65
Feivel Moishe, 68
Ferryman" Reb Yehoshua, 323
Feynboim, 1, 4, 84, 117, 335
Fineboim, 397

Finkelshtajn, 312
Finkelshtayn, 85, 292, 323, 392, 393, 395
Finkelstein, 451, 465
Fischbein, 452
Fischer, 173
Fischman, 446, 452
Fishbayn, 392, 393
Fisherman, 22, 405
Fishman, 65, 183, 293, 312, 395
Fishman-Melnik, 312
Flesher, 422
Fogelman, 9, 29, 32, 36, 289, 291, 386, 387
Fogelman, 450
Forminski, 402
Freedman, 29, 314, 323
Freidman, 11
Freiman, 478
Frenkel, 38, 324, 326, 345, 346
Frenkel, 449
Frenkiel, 455
Fridman, 1, 4, 100, 119, 120, 123, 328
Friedman, 2, 5, 9, 29, 94, 95, 118, 189, 318, 319, 383, 386
Friedman, 454, 455
Fugel, 229
Furmanski, 451
Futerman, 252
Futerman, 451

## G

Gal, 79, 116, 118
Gal, 430
Gali, 410
Galuda, 403, 405
Gavriel, 40
Gedalia The Shoemaker, 324
*Gedalya*, 334, 356
Gelbert, 7, 9
Geluda, 402
Gerbel, 256
Gershon Meir At The Oil Factory, 250
Gerstensang, 432
Gerwer, 79, 85, 99, 105, 115, 118, 266
Gerwer, 432
Gidzewierniarz, 431
Gimpel, 38, 254
Ginsberg, 92, 248
Gladek, 105
Glazer, 442
Glodek, 431, 432
Godem, 431
Godes, 431, 462
Goldberg, 1, 4, 16, 23, 320, 402, 552

Goldberg, 430
Goldflam, 392, 393, 395
Goldmakher, 403
Goldman, 29, 84, 123
Goldmecher, 173
Goodes, 220, 248
Gordon, 116, 408
Gorman, 9
Gorzinski, 173
Grabie, 432
Grabiya, 2, 5, 362
Graniewicz, 323
Graniewicz, 432, 435, 461
Granjewicz, 28, 43, 218
Granyevitzes (Graniewiczs), 91
Granyewicz, 76
Greenberg, 307, 393, 395, 397
Greenberg (Swarcberg), 307
Grinbaum, 432, 433
Grinberg, 105, 125, 313
Grinberg, 433
Grinboim, 2, 5, 29, 32, 34, 43, 44, 224, 231, 249
Grobszmid, 432
Grosbard, 1, 2, 4, 5, 118, 130, 334, 350, 353, 354, 355, 386
Grosbard, 432
Grosman, 432
Grossbard, 9
Grossman, 90, 98
Grunbaum, 449
Gudes, 2, 5, 132, 291, 313, 326
Gudes/Godes, 2, 5, 132
Gudes-Jonisz, 313
Gurman, 30, 325, 344, 381, 386, 402
Gurman, 431
Gutecki, 328
Gutkovski, 400, 405
Gutkowsi, 402
Gutkowski, 29, 32, 41, 105, 114, 115, 116, 403
Gutkowski, 430, 431, 460
Gzhebieniazh, 289, 325, 333
Gzhebjeniazh, 116, 317
Gzhebyenyazh, 344

## H

Hadas Pzykorski, 2, 5, 255
Haller, 27, 124, 346
Halperin, 47, 49, 126, 127
Hasman, 94
Hassman, 434, 445
Hecht, 435
Heftman, 76
Hendzhe, 101

Hersh, 21, 23
Hershel The Carpenter, 100
Hershel The Fisherman, 91
Hershel The Tailor, 55
Hershel The Tinsmith, 325
Hershfinger, 1, 2, 4, 5, 109, 348, 350
Herzl, 92
Hilel, 41, 253
Hiler, 133, 134, 137, 254
Hiler, 434, 435, 444, 463
Hillel The Butcher, 327
Hiller, 43
Hirsh, 71
Hirshbayn, 116
Hochberg, 433, 434
Hochman, 166
Hoess, 284, 285
Hoffman, 91
Hofman, 29, 33, 34, 98, 100, 323
Hofman, 434, 463
Hokhman, 400
Horowicz, 401
Horowicz, 434, 442, 457
Horowitz, 171
Huna, 326
Hurwic, 190

## I

Ickowicz, 322, 323
Iczkowicz, 387
Igelberg, 22
Ignatz, Master Of Law, 172
Innkeeper Yisroel, 18
Inventausch, 445
Inwentarsch, 427
Inwentarz, 29, 93
Irke, 278, 279, 281, 282, 283, 285, 286
Itche Meier, 69
Itche Meir The Mohel, 90
Itshkovitsh, 11
Itzcowicz, 92, 94, 96
Itzcowitch, 426
Itzkovitz, 434, 435
Itzkowicz, 23, 29, 302, 397
Ivan Iv, 349
Izenberg, 403
Izkowicz, 114, 298
Izkowitz-Czesner, 117

## J

Jagiello, 26, 53
Jagielowicz, 441

Jagoda, 2, 5, 43, 44
Jagoda, 440, 441, 455
Jak, 172
Janet, 282
Janishe, 66
Janisz, 441
Jaskowicz, 386
Jaskowicz, 427
Jaskowicz-Rozenberg, 387
Jaszombek, 32
Jaszombek, 441
Jaworoska, 160
Jazhamberk, 116
Jazombek, 105, 116
Jekel, 66
Jelen, 441, 442
Jerel, 70
Jerusalemski, 442
Jonisz, 93, 151, 308
Jonisz-Godes, 93
Jonisz-Gudes, 133, 151, 308
Jorckowicz, 125
Jores, 66
Jurkewicz, 46, 77, 122
Jurkowicz, 40, 118, 402
Juskowicz, 36

## K

Kalecker, 458
Kalina, 91, 105, 387
Kalina, 450, 458
Kaluski, 2, 5, 91, 192, 263, 303, 313
Kaluski, 441
Kamelgorn-Blumberg, 288
Kamelharz, 442
Kanarek, 2, 5, 86, 159, 219
Kanarek, 458
Kanarek–Magid, 5, 237
Kanareks, 91
Kanerek, 460
Kanier, 442, 458, 459
Kanjar, 224
Kanjer, 137, 221, 320
Kanarek, 1
Kapecz, 99, 101
Kapetch, 74
*Kapo,* Ignacz, 187
Karmel, 402, 403, 405
Kartoffel, 459
Kaschitcharzj, 459
Kaszminski, 170
Katsev, 11
Katz, 94, 324

Katz, 442
Katzav, 41, 90, 272
Katzenelbogen, 382, 383, 385, 387, 389
Katzenelenbogen, 1, 2, 4, 5, 55, 59, 337, 342
Katzenellenbogen, 7, 9, 14, 403
Katzenellenbogen, 459
Kaufman, 460
Kavelski, 458
Kazak, 458
Kendzherski, 328
Kershenbaum, 405
Khaim Ber, 44
Khaim Dovid', 123
Khaim Hersh, The Painter, 98
Khaim Leyb, A Teacher, 113
Khaim Shloime, 38
Khaim Shloime The *Shokhet*, 123
Khaim Shlomo *Shokhet*, 113
Khaim Shlomo The *Shokhet*, 222
Khaim Shlomo The *Shokhet*,, 120
Khaim Shlomo, The Shokhet, 68
Khaim The Fisherman, 91
Khaim Yehoshua, 121
Khaim Yoine, 39, 71, 114, 121, 378
Khaim Yona The Teacher, 326
Khaim-Isser, 27
Khaimowicz, 105
Khainewer, 218
Khanokh, 344
Khaynower, 223
Khinke, 324
Kieselstein, 461
Kinmman, 228
Kipperbaum, 171
Kirschenbaum, 461
Kiva, 91
Klajnman, 319
Klaynman, 122
Kleinman, 2, 5, 28, 44, 76, 81, 118, 127, 175, 221, 267, 276
Kleinman, 434, 461
Klinger, 229
Kohen, 442, 464
Kohn, 80, 252, 319
Kohn, 442
Koifman, 194
Konjer, 219
Konkol, 91, 163
Konkol, 459
Kopatch, 459
Kopelowicz, 402, 403
Koperman, 385
Kopetch, 1, 4, 32, 73, 105, 115, 118
Kopjec, 190

Korczak, 318
Korlevski, 165
Korngold, 75
Koshemacher, 11
Kotschelik, 458
Koval, 55, 69, 88, 257
Kovalek, 221
Kowalski, 170, 171
Krawiecki, 327, 331
Krawietski, 453
Krawietzki, 461
Kreda, 105, 116
Kremer, 284, 285
Krikah-Kanarek, 195
Krimkiewicz, 431
Krimkowich, 392
Krimkowicz, 35
Kristal, 66, 320
Kronenberg, 29, 42, 43, 44, 91, 95, 135, 220, 276, 293, 392, 477
Kronenberg, 461, 462
Krongold, 28, 31, 76
Krongold, 461
Kronzhek, 403
Krupp, 231
Krystal, 28, 327
Krystal, 462
Krystel, 331
Kucharzewski, 26, 53
Kuligovski, 400, 405
Kuligowska, 318
Kuligowski, 1, 4, 95, 113, 183, 381, 385, 402, 403, 405, 471
Kuligowski, 460
Kuligowsky, 255
Kulok, 395
Kumaya, 245, 246, 247
Kupchik, 23
Kuperbaum, 94
Kuperbaum, 460, 461
Kuperboim, 30, 34, 35, 91, 324
Kuperboym, 117
Kuperman, 392, 395, 397
Kuzhinksi, 2, 5, 359
Kuzhinski, 74, 359, 360
Kuzhnicki, 39, 83, 85, 219, 221, 326, 338
Kuzhnitzki, 402
Kuznicki, 99, 101, 105, 362
Kuzsnitzki, 459, 460
Kwartowicz, 459

## L

Lajnwand-Belison, 387

*Lantz*, 189
Laski, 443
Latallo, 324, 326
Lazar The Beadle, 89
Lebgot, 444
Leibgott, 400
Leser, 428
Leszczyński, 162
Levenshtayn, 336, 337, 340, 347
Levi Yitzkhok The Butcher, 55
Levin, 20, 23
Leviner, 65, 66, 91, 135, 179, 221, 222, 263
Levinshtayn, 54, 58, 76, 392
Levinson, 30, 55
Lewiner, 94, 326, 331
Lewiner, 444
Lewinshtayn, 37, 38, 39
Lewinson, 38, 387
Lewinson, 444
Leyvik, 116
Linker, 91
Linker, 443
Linonad (Beilinson), 476
Lipman, 84, 93
Lis, 443
Liss, 91
Litman, 62
Litman, 443
Litman Razenowicz, 347

## M

Mahl, 284, 285
Mai, 225, 392, 397
Maimon, 33, 34, 35
Maimon, 440, 443
Maj, 385
Maj, 444
Majdenberg, 185
Majmon, 446
Mak, 434, 444, 445
Makhlewski, 81
Mala Baila, 91
Malawanczik, 324
Malawanczyk, 190
Malewiak, 445
Malia, 423
Malka, 90
Malkiel, 343
Malkovich, 166
Mandel, 284, 285
Manelo, 303
Mann, 316, 317, 395, 397
Marcus, 30

Margolias, 68
Margolis, 91, 125, 333
Margolis, 445
Margulis, 154, 155, 284, 326, 331
Markevicz, 402
Markewicz, 1, 4, 112, 133, 134, 383
Markovitz, 9
Markowicz, 38, 248, 386, 387
Markowicz, 445
Markus, 445, 463
Marle, 386
Mas, 462
Mehlman, 446
Meier Moishe, 66
Meisels, 231
Melman, 402
Melnik, 29, 44, 65, 91, 114, 222, 323, 324, 402, 403, 405
Mendel The Butcher, 220
Mendels, 71
Mendolevsky, 9
Mendzelevski, 88, 90, 91
Mendzelevski (Mendzelewski), 88
Mendzelewski, 1, 2, 4, 5, 31, 83, 85, 88, 104, 105, 107, 115, 116, 128, 218, 219, 221, 222, 248, 257, 310, 313, 359, 378, 384, 386, 387
Mendzelewski, 447
Mendzelewski-Maj, 310
Mendzelewski-Rozental, 313
Mengele, 150, 284, 285, 286
Menzelewski, 291
Merker, 31, 65, 81, 402
Merker, 443, 461
Merla, 15, 381, 472
Merla, 447
Merle, 71, 382, 383, 387
Merlo, 326
Meyer, 21, 266, 344
Meyer The Barber, 112
Miara, 325
Miara, 446
Michaelik, 169
Mide, 446
Miedownik, 2, 5, 163
Mielnik, 434, 446, 447, 452, 465
Mikhelson, 336
Millshtayn (Millstein), 91
Millstein, 446
Milshtayn, 35, 66, 324
Milshtein, 11
Minke The Chicken Dealer, 123
Minkes, 121
Mintz, 80, 91
Mintz, 446

Mintz -, 80
Miodownik, 437, 446
Mjadownik, 307, 313, 321
Mjodovnik, 22
Moishe Avrohom, 66, 67
Moishe Yosel, 66
Moishe, A Scholar, 69
Monchazh, 402
Morgenshtern, 11, 38
Morgenshtern (Morgenstern), 91
Morgenstern, 91, 347
Morgenstern, 445
Moscicki, 231
Motel The *Shamash*, 96
Motele, 69
Motl The Butcher, 91
Muszkatenblit, 94

# N

Nakhman Shokhet, 68
Napoleon, 20, 110, 332
Neuman, 448
Nicholas I, 349
Nickelberg, 228
Nissels, 54
Nokhum'ke, 121
Novogrodski, 34, 90
Nowogrodski, 36, 119, 222, 316, 318, 327
Nowogrodski, 447, 448

# O

Ogrodower, 253, 314
Ogrodower, 426, 429
Oldak, 427
Orel, 324
Orenshtayn, 393
Orenstein, 434
Orol, 333
Ortokhowski, 253
Oryl, 34, 36, 43
Oryl, 427, 442
Ostrovski, 79
Ostrowski, 32, 99, 104, 105, 112, 115, 116, 118, 183, 190, 248, 263, 325
Ostrowski, 427

# P

Pakowicz, 312
Paniewski, 453
Paskewicz, 324
Paskiewicz, 458

Paskowicz, 11, 93, 94, 137, 312
Paskowicz, 436, 450, 451
Paskowicz-Fajnboim, 312
Paskowycz, 291
Passman, 450
Paulette, 282
Penivsky, 9
Perel, 453, 454
Peretz, 99, 100
Perl, 221, 387, 400, 401, 402, 405
Perlman, 222
Petlura, 346
Pfefer, 453
Pfeferblum, 453
Piechotowa, 163
Piekarz, 452
Pienik, 66, 95, 291, 325
Pienik, 431, 451, 452
Pilkenfeld, 167
Pilsudski, 80, 346
Pilz, 229
Pinkert, 451
Pinkhas, 303
Pinsker, 92
Pinyevski (Pniewski), 91
Pjenicer, 219
Pjenik, 36, 220, 252, 263
Pjienek, 303
Platze, 402
Pluda, 452, 453
Plutnik, 139
Pniewski, 91, 324, 384, 386, 387
Pniyevsky, 11
Pnjewski, 29, 37, 39, 114, 191, 194
Pnjiewski, 112
Podlaski, 241
Pokorski, 325
Pokorski, 451
Polakowicz, 23
Pomotchny, 450
Popover *Shokhet*, 347
Postek, 253
Prag, 30, 35
Pranchek, 173
Prilutcki, 83
Prilutski, 32
Prilutzki, 115
Prunchek, 170
Przeworznik, 11
Pshevozjnik, 455
Pshewaznik, 323
Pshikarski, 219, 221, 250
Pshikarski, 455

Pshikorski, 2, 5, 32, 34, 35, 38, 39, 91, 116, 224, 256, 386, 387, 473, 474
Pszikarski, 456
Pyenik, 79, 80, 81

# R

Rabba, 326
Rabbi Pinkhas Of Koretz, 57
Rabinowicz, 462
Rabinowicz/Rabinowitz, 1, 4, 125
Rabinowitz, 125
Radziwill, 219, 322
*Rashi*, 39, 71, 378
Rebbetzen Tchortel, 97
Refaeli, 409
Refoel The Shokhet, 68, 70
Refoel, Shokhet, 121
Reisner, 186
Ribnicki, 335
Ring, 48
Ringelblum, 319
Roiza The Laundress, 91
Rokita, 451, 465
Rose, 281, 282
Rosenberg, 2, 3, 5, 6, 9, 28, 29, 30, 34, 36, 38, 41, 43, 63, 65, 81, 90, 91, 92, 93, 94, 95, 118, 129, 164, 165, 168, 170, 171, 189, 190, 218, 219, 220, 222, 225, 248, 250, 251, 253, 266, 291, 292, 293, 294, 415, 416, 423, 550
Rosenberg, 432, 434, 445, 456, 462, 463, 464
Rosenberg-Cohen, 171
Rosenberg-Markus, 93
Rosenbergs, 63
Rosenfeld, 105, 112, 116
Rosenfeld, 435, 465
Rosental, 22, 42, 122, 128, 129, 222, 223
Roszynski, 465
Rotboym, 115
Roth, 397
Rotman, 465
Rozenberg, 11, 97, 98, 100, 183, 310, 313, 315, 318, 319, 323, 324, 325, 387
Rozenberg-Bernshtayn, 310, 386
Rozenberg-Joskowicz, 319
Rozental, 1, 4, 96, 310, 395
Rozynek, 227
Rubenshtayn, 248, 378
Rubinstein, 446, 465
Rubisztajn, 442
Ruta, 465

# S

Sakal, 449
Salyarzh, 30
Salzman, 438
Sandler, 40, 71, 114, 115
Sandler, 449
Sawicki, 252
Schafran, 466
Schapira, 435, 467
Schenitzer, 467
Schlyakhtus, 75, 76
Schneiderman, 466, 467
Schwartz, 91, 164
Schwartz, 466
Segal, 63
Sempf, 39, 46
Sempf, 449, 450
Sep, 378
Shamash, 77, 78
Shayer, 58
Shazar, 15
Shenker, 251
Shifman, 91
Shikore, 392
Shikorski, 223
Shljakhtus, 28
Shlomo Pesakh Melamed, 70
Shlyakhtus, 31
Shmeunz, 91
Shmijes, 71
Shmoish, 33
Shmoysh, 333
Shmuel B, 2, 5
Shmuel B., 342
Shmulewicz, 18
Shnajder, 190
Shnayderman, 2, 5, 332, 354
Shneider, 69, 91
Shoshana, 417
Shoshkes, 33
Shpak, 405
Shpilke, 29, 91, 402
Shpilke (Spilka), 90
Shtajnski, 99, 194
Shteifman, 405
Shteinski, 116, 397
Shtelang, 79, 118
Shub,, 362
Shulem Yakov, 55
Shvartz (Schwartz), 91
Silberberg, 438
Silberstein, 96
Silberstein, 438, 439, 459

Skladkowski, 110, 111
Skornik, 450
Skurnik, 183
Slomianski, 400, 402
Sobolowski, 190
Sojnok, 327
Sokalnicki, 47
Sokol, 191, 248
Sokolovsky, 11
Sokolowski, 322, 326
Solarzs, 448, 449
Soljarzh, 39, 331
Soljazh, 220
Solomon, 448
Solyarzh, 35, 38, 91
Soschniak, 449
Sosinak, 273
Sosniak, 337, 393, 395, 396, 397
Sowa, 334
Spilka, 441
Spilke, 190, 203, 222, 319
Srebernik, 450
Srebero, 450
Srebro, 62
Stadtsinger, 466
Stajnski, 190, 191
Stalin, 402
Stanislav Jadobon, 173
Stardiner, 7, 9
Stashalkovsky, 171
Stazinski, 232
Stefanczik, 323
Steinski, 466
Stelang, 38, 105, 291
Stelang, 466
Stelmakh, 91
Sterdiener, 449
Sterdiner, 2, 5, 95, 116, 179, 183, 184, 189, 192, 222, 288, 294, 324, 385, 387
Sterdyner, 2, 5, 291
Sterdyner, 450
Stern, 306
Stoler, 70
Stolyer, 77
Strediner, 194
Suski, 190
Swalberg, 313
Swarc, 30, 34, 41, 66, 122, 219, 324
Szpilka, 95
Szpilka, 467
Sztelang, 427
Szwarc, 229

## T

Taperek, 219
Tauber, 285
Tchapinski, 464
Tchernichovsky, 92
Teacher Lanja, 318
Temess, 90
Tik, 90, 324
Tikulski, 118, 123
Toperek, 440
Trebrin, 347
Trojanowksi,, 288
Trojanowski, 288
Tukulski, 324
Turban, 3, 6, 418
Tuvia, The *Shamash*'s Son-In-Law, 272
Tyk, 11
Tyk, 440, 444
Tykolski, 95
Tykolski, 440
Tzalke The Waiter, 98
Tz'esner (Czesner), 90
Tzikoria, 457
Tzukerman, 75

## U

Ubagi, 116, 324
Uberke, 284, 285
Ubogi, 27
Ubogi, 426
Uldak, 36
*Unterscharfuhrer* (Junior Squad Leader) Lantz, 187
Urman, 426

## V

Vardi, 1, 2, 3, 4, 5, 6, 7, 9, 25, 94, 123, 407, 415, 416, 553
Vardiman Werschevsky, 9
Vardimon, 3, 6, 94, 555
Varshavski, 91, 344
Varshavski (Warszawski), 91
Varshevski, 555
Vayngrad, 344
Vaynkrantz, 74
Veinshtok (Weinstock), 91
Vellner, 90
Vetshtayn, 402, 403
Viernik, 11
Vilkovski, 239
Vinkrantz, 407
Vishnyevitz (Wisniewcz), 91

Vogel, 293
Vujicik, 228
Vyernik, 80

# W

Wajngart, 190
Wajnkrancz, 312, 381, 383, 387
Waler, 435
Walerstein, 435
Warker Rebbe, Rebbe Yizkhok, 54
Warsawski, 66, 101, 118, 123, 183, 300, 308, 309
Warshawski, 30, 34, 35, 36, 41, 225
Warshawski (Werdi), 267
Warszawska, 94
Warszawski, 93, 94
Warszawski, 435
Warszawski-Vardimon, 95
Warszawski-Weridman, 93
Washilewska, 265
Wasilewska, 224, 244
Weinkrantz, 15, 320
Weinstock, 436, 437
Weisman, 186
Weitz, 165
Weitz, 437
Wellensky, 164
Welner, 326, 327
Welner, 437
Wenger, 133, 220, 248, 313
Wenger, 437
Werdi, 29, 225, 267, 288, 295, 300, 309, 380, 387
Werdi (Warshawski), 29
Werdiman (Warshawski), 29
Werdiman-Warshawski, 386, 387
Werdi-Warshawski, 386
Wiernek, 241
Wiernik, 66
Wiernik, 437
Wierniky, 93
Wiezbinski, 328
Wiezhbinski, 325, 326
Wilczinski, 318
Wilkowski, 264
Winagora, 435, 436
Wineberg, 69, 70
Winegrad, 255
Winekrantz, 41, 43
Winkrantz, 436
Winograd, 436, 455, 456
Winogura, 38
Winowar, 311
Wisniewicz, 179
Wisniewicz, 437

Wisnjewicz, 193, 318
Wisocka, 318
Wjelkabroda, 427
Wohlman, 435
Wolenski, 171
Wolinski, 93, 117, 125, 222, 304
Wolinski, 432, 435, 438, 443
Wolman, 465
Wrobel, 437
Wrubel, 116, 402, 403, 471, 475
Wzjesyn, 190

# Y

Yaakov Aryeh The Cabinetmaker, 91
Ya'ari, 424
Yagoda, 2, 5, 225, 324
Yakov Arye The Carpenter, 219
Yakov Aryeh, The Carpenter, 119
Yakov-Kopel, 343
Yakubovicz, 402
Yakubowicz, 402
Yanisch, 467
Yanish, 465
Yekele, 68
Yekhezkel The Glazier's Son, 344
Yekhiel, 344
Yekhiel The Fisherman, 91
Yellowed Moishe, 254
Yerkhinai, 326
Yezumbeck, 90
Yisroel Shmue A Shoemaker, 98
Yisroel Yitzkhok The Glazier, 221
Yisroel Zelig, 39, 71
Yisroel Zelig Melamed, 70
Yitzkhok Meier, 69
Yitzkhok Meyer, 41, 340, 342
Yitzkhok Mordekhai, 340
Yonish, 91
Yosef Eliezer, 66, 67, 342
Yosef Eliezer Shokhet, 66
Yosef Hersh, 253
Yoskovitz Rosenberg, 9
Yosl The Cabinetmaker, 91
Yotshenko, 11
Yurkevicz, 402
Yurkewicz, 81

# Z

Zacharek, 429, 438, 446, 447
Zadik, 101
Zakharek, 36, 115, 118, 222, 304, 387
Zakharia The Tailor, 220

Zakzhewska, 332
Zalcman, 105, 116
Zalman Khosid, 343
Zaltsman, 32
Zbik, 315, 318
Zbik-Ribalski, 315
Zeidman, 289
Zeitlin, 76
Zelikowicz, 439
Zentner, 457
Zilbershtayn, 38, 219, 220, 304, 326
Zilbershtayn-Rotman, 387
Zilbershteyn, 183
Zimerman, 34
Zinger, 229
Zlata – Motte Ber's Grandchild, 220
Zlate The Baker, 112
Zlatogorski, 448
Zlotogorski, 91
Zlotogorski, 439
Zlotogurski, 41, 43, 44
Zucker, 455, 456, 457
Zuckerman, 446, 457
Zuker, 107
Zukor, 100, 255, 315, 316, 318, 328
Zweigaft, 455, 456
Zymerman, 385

Cross reference (manual)

Khaim Yoine – see Stempf
Yosef Eliezer – Yosef Eliezer the shokhet
Yisroel Zelig – Yisroel Zelig melamed
Eliyahu the shokhet – Eliyahoo Shokhet
Ahad Ha'Aam - see Ginseberg

Names on Objects that could not be indexed using index utility

Waslutyanski – page 50
Eisenbach – page 50
Segal – page 50
Weinkrantz - 479
Katzenellenbogen – 481, 482
Levis Katzenellenbogen – 481
Warshawski – 483, 484
Warshawski-Wellerstein – 483
Wellerstein – 483
Kristal – 483
Warshawski---Vardimon – 483
Vardi – 483
Bruchanski – 485
Mendzelewski – 486, 544
Feinbaum – 487, 488
Foskowitz – 487, 488
Grasman – 487
Blumberg – 487, 527, 547
Novodvarski – 487
Schwartz – 489
Fogelman (Schwartz) – 489, 490
Birnbaum – 491, 492, 535
Prager – 491
Wrubel – 491, 504, 509, 510, 529
Kotszolek – 492
Skornik – 493
Sterdiner – 493, 498, 511, 537
Rozenberg, 493, 505, 506, 535, 544, 547
Mendzelewski – 494
Grinberg – 495, 537
Musberg – 495
Kotshole – 495
Wisniewicz – 496
Gerwer – 497, 498
Miara – 497
Miara-Gerwer – 497
Miara-Mitz'nik 497
Rozental – 499, 546
Kuligowski – 500, 503, 516, 536
Woller – 500
Friedman – 501, 502, 519
Eizenberg – 501
Golan (Friedman) – 501

Kuligowski, (nee Drezner) – 503
Cohen- 505, 506, 543
Yoskowitz-Rozenberg - 505
Czechanowsk – 507
May – 507, 524
Mendzelewski (May) – 507, 508, 524
Wosk (Mendzelewski) – 508
Wrubel-Pshikorski – 509
Pniewski 511
Kleinman -512, 537
Zilbersteyn – 512
Pshikorski – 513, 514
Cuker -513, 528, 539
Gurman – 515, 538
Itskowitz – 517, 518
Czesner – 517
Markowitz – 517
Yeruzalimski – 518
Rabinowitz – 518, 535
Bernstein (Freidman) – 519
Friedman-Bernstein – 520
Kronenberg – 521, 522
Asman – 521, 532
Steinski – 522, 548
Wenger – 522, 548
Gibber – 522
Kalina – 523
Winegrad – 525
Rot – 525
Elman – 525
Rashinski – 525, 529
Lewiner – 526, 537
Lewiner-Maliniak – 526
Konier – 526, 536
Salzman – 527
Kirshbaum – 527
Fogelman – 527
Komelgorn – 527
Boguslowski – 529
Joszambeck – 529
Goldstein – 529
Blindet – 530
Kolaker – 530
Meier-Blindet – 530
Kartofel – 531
Stelung – 531
Eliyahu Shochet – 531
Broda – 531
Hoffman – 532
Itzkowitz – 532
Pienik – 533
Kaluski – 533
Fishman – 533
Niskah – 533

Fokin – 533
Jagoda – 533
Blustein – 533
Solarz – 533, 538
Grinbaum – 534
Baum – 534
Bernstein – 535
Beilenson – 536
Lieber - 537
Lewiner-Pienik – 537
Rubinstein – 538
Wolman – 540
Kaufman – 540
Kozak – 541
Kaufman (Kazak) – 541
Weinstock – 542
Apelboim – 542
Borenstein – 543
Diamant (Borenstein) – 543
Bresler – 544
Moak - 544
Shpira – 544
Nowogrodski – 545
Kandel 545
Kizelstein - 546
Baldiger – 546
Gutkowski – 546
Zhepko – Sznilko – 546
Szpilka – 547
Rszepka-Szpilka – 547

www.ingramcontent.com/pod-product-compliance
Lightning Source LLC
Chambersburg PA
CBHW082008150426
42814CB00005BA/260